THE ESSENTIAL POPE BENEDICT XVI

THE
ESSENTIAL
POPE BENEDICT XVI

His Central Writings and Speeches

EDITED BY
John F. Thornton *and* Susan B. Varenne

INTRODUCTION BY
D. Vincent Twomey, SVD
Professor of Moral Theology, St. Patrick's College, Ireland

HarperOne
An Imprint of HarperCollinsPublishers

HarperOne

HarperCollins books may be purchased for educational, business, or sales promotional use. For information please write: Special Markets Department, HarperCollins Publishers, 10 East 53rd Street, New York, NY 10022.

HarperCollins Web site: http://www.harpercollins.com
HarperCollins®, ® , and HarperOne™ are
trademarks of HarperCollins Publishers.

FIRST HARPERCOLLINS PAPERBACK EDITION PUBLISHED IN 2008
Designed by Joseph Rutt

Library of Congress Cataloging-in-Publication Data is available.

ISBN: 978–0–06–112884–4

08 09 10 11 12 RRD(H) 10 9 8 7 6 5 4 3 2

"I who chose you and appointed you to go and bear fruit that will remain."
—John 15:16

We have received the faith to give it to others. We are priests meant to serve others. And we must bring a fruit that will remain. All people want to leave a mark which lasts. But what remains? Money does not. Buildings do not, nor books. After a certain amount of time, whether long or short, all these things disappear. The only thing which remains forever is the human soul, the human person created by God for eternity. The fruit which remains then is that which we have sowed in human souls: love, knowledge, a gesture capable of touching the heart, words which open the soul to joy in the Lord. Let us then go to the Lord and pray to Him, so that He may help us bear fruit which remains.

Only in this way will the earth be changed from a valley of tears to a garden of God.

—Joseph Cardinal Ratzinger,
from his homily at the Mass for
the Election of the Roman Pontiff,
April 18, 2005

The first rams of the flock, the blessed apostles, saw the Lord Jesus himself hanging on the cross; they grieved at his death, were astounded at his resurrection, loved him in his power, and shed their own blood for what they had seen. Just think, brothers and sisters, what it meant for men to be sent throughout the wide world, to preach that a dead man had risen again and ascended into heaven; and for preaching this to suffer everything a raving, raging world could inflict: loss of goods, exile, chains, tortures, flames, wild beasts, crosses, painful deaths. All this for heaven knows what!

I mean, really, my brothers and sisters, was Peter dying for his own glory, or proclaiming himself? One man was dying that another might be honored, one being slain that another might be worshiped. Would he have done this, if he hadn't been on fire with love, and utterly convinced of the truth?

—St. Augustine,
from Sermon 311, 2,
"Preaching that a dead man had risen!"

Contents

PART TWO

THE CHURCH

PART THREE

THE LITURGY

PART FOUR
THEOLOGY

PART FIVE
SCRIPTURE

PART SIX
THE PRIESTHOOD

PART SEVEN
CHRISTIAN MORALITY

Preface

When Joseph Cardinal Ratzinger was elevated to the office of pope as Benedict XVI, he became the twenty-first-century successor to Peter, the apostle whom Jesus himself established as the one who would safeguard his teachings. In his homily at the Mass for the election of the Roman pontiff on April 18, 2005, then cardinal Ratzinger described two essential qualifications for this office in service of the divine ministry: obedience and fruitfulness.

Quoting from John 15:14, "You are my friends if you do what I command you," he extolled the authentic freedom Jesus conferred on us by his own submission to his Father. "Not my will but Thine be done" (Lk 22:42) was the prayer wrung from Jesus during his agony in the Garden of Gethsemani before his arrest. Earlier he had taught his disciples to pray with the words, "Thy will be done, on earth as it is in heaven" (Mt 6:10). Knowing that we have been relieved of the burden of our autonomy, like the Prodigal Son returning home, we experience the joy of overcoming the rebelliousness that alienates us from God, who is the very source of our being, when we seek to do his will.

Cardinal Ratzinger reminded us that this redemption from sin that estranges us from God is promised to every single person, for it is God's will that no one shall be lost to him, but that all will be gathered into his kingdom. Cardinal Ratzinger then charged that we must be inspired by a "holy restlessness," which impels us to show to everyone we meet the gift of faith that confers friendship with Christ. Quoting John 15:16, "I who chose you and appointed you to go and bear fruit that will remain," he reminded us that all the material things we value will ultimately disappear in time. But the human person, "created by God for eternity," will live forever. So, then, what endures is love. The fruit that remains is the love we have for one another. Through obedience we are united to the will of God, who is Father to us all. And through faith in Christ and friendship with him, we are united to one another in the service of love, the fruits of which will endure for all eternity.

In his first encyclical, *Deus Caritas Est* (December 25, 2005; see p. 395), Cardinal Ratzinger, now Pope Benedict XVI, has declared that living as a Christian is not simply a matter of choosing a set of high ideals or a carefully considered personal ethical system. It is, rather, an experience of love that has been divinized by being purified of selfishness and lust. Our natural impulsion to love (*eros*) is met by God's transforming love (*agape*), which draws us beyond ourselves, healing our hearts and minds of the blindness of self-interest and enabling us to begin to see the world and one another with the eyes of Christ. Participating in God's own love this way, we can then turn toward others and "give them the look of love they crave" (p. 408). In this way we all become friends in Christ.

On April 20, 2005, Benedict XVI gave his first homily at the Mass following his election. He recalled the words Peter spoke to Jesus in his confession of faith: "You are Christ, the Son of the living God" (Mt 16:16). Jesus, in response, conferred on Peter the solemn office of leader: "You are Peter and on this rock I will build my church.... I will give you the keys of the kingdom of heaven" (Mt 16:18–19). In assuming the heavy mantle of Holy Father, Successor of Peter, Benedict XVI promised to make present in the world the voice of Christ, who declared, "I am the light of the world; he who follows me will not walk in darkness but will have the light of life" (p. 29). Offering his unconditional promise of faithfulness, the new pope prayed, "*Mane nobiscum, Domine!*" ("Stay with us, Lord!") (p. 29). And at his inaugural Mass on April 25, 2005, he pledged himself to the work of a good shepherd who loves and serves the people entrusted to him, feeding them on "the nourishment of God's truth" (p. 34). In another image from the gospel, that of the fisherman, he committed himself to the rescue of those living in alienation, "in the salt waters of suffering and death, in a sea of darkness without light" (p. 35). To show forth the light of Christ's message of salvation, to nourish the people of God with his truth, and to fight the many contemporary forms of alienation that keep people from living in hope and confidence—these are the pledges of Benedict XVI to all of us.

The pope has stated with utter clarity that the purpose of our lives as Christians is to make God visible in the world. It is by way of our own lives of obedience and love that men and women will come to see God. How important is this to Benedict XVI? In answer, he has said: "And only where God is seen does life truly begin" (p. 35). Only when we personally meet the living God in Christ do we begin to know what life is. "We are not some casual and meaningless product of evolution. Each of us is the result of a thought of God. Each of us is willed, each of us is loved, each of us is necessary" (p. 35). This is Benedict XVI's call to faith, to hope, to love, to trust, to confidence.

Fundamentally, only prayer can make it possible for Christ to be made visible to the world. In an address given at the Eucharistic Congress of the Archdiocese of Benevento, Italy, on June 2, 2002, then cardinal Ratzinger stated that "Christ teaches how God is glorified, (and) the world made just." He quoted from Luke 2:14: "Glory to God in the highest, and peace on earth, goodwill toward men" (p. 70). The very essence of prayer is praise. In the liturgy we come together to give glory to God through his Son, Jesus Christ, Our Lord. In this communion of praise, the many are united in partaking of the one bread of the Eucharist: "To communicate with Christ is essentially also to communicate with one another.... [E]ach of those who receive communion is 'bone of my bone and flesh of my flesh' (Gn 2:23)" (p. 76). Christ risen and glorified gathers us together, purifies us and transforms us in the liturgical sacrifice of the Eucharist, where we meet him and one another, united in his very body and blood.

This has been but a brief introduction to the mind and heart of Benedict XVI, successor of Peter and Holy Father to us all. In the readings gathered for this book, one will find again and again the same pulse of obedience, the same commitment to bear fruit that have marked the character and spirit of this remarkable man who dedicated himself to God at an early age. He survived the horrors of Nazi Germany and the turbulence of the Marxist revolution of the sixties, always serving the church he loves with unwavering will, profound intelligence, and great heart and soul, in a life marked by joy and gratitude. Through Benedict's life of service to the church, the light of Christ will shine more certainly and more clearly in the world today.

A few words are in order about the rationale for assembling a comprehensive book of selections from the writings of Benedict XVI. Prior to his elevation, Joseph Ratzinger devoted a career of several decades to teaching, writing, and church administration, and the written output he produced is enormous. Books, essays, documents, sermons, talks, speeches, interviews—practically every form of nonfiction has been ground from his mill.

In order to make sensible choices for *The Essential Pope Benedict XVI*, it was important, as our reading and research proceeded, to discern recurrent themes and preoccupations. The results can be pored over in our table of contents, organized under the rubrics "Sermons and Addresses," "The Church," "The Liturgy," "Theology," "Scripture," "The Priesthood," and "Christian Morality." The final choices for even this substantial volume seem to us modest when compared with the large amount of materials available to draw on. Thus the reader, after using the book, is strongly encouraged to look into its bibliography, selective though it is, too, and seek out his or her own favorite writings by Benedict for further reading.

We decided against opening every selection with an account of the item's original context or with a surmise of Benedict's intentions in composing it.

Our goal was to include as many of his own edifying words as we could within the confines of a commercial project. We assume it is Benedict, not his editors, the reader has come for.

Planning the book, we had in mind a novice reader in matters of theology, metaphysics, church history, Catholic dogma, or Vatican organization and politics. Nonetheless, we felt that we could assume a modest degree of previous interest in Ratzinger-Benedict; we also assumed that, if a technical theological or other esoteric term were encountered, the reader would readily find it explained in a desk dictionary or encyclopedia or, increasingly, on the Internet. As a practical matter, these selections are in fact so shot through with such ideas, terms, and allusions that it is not clear where to begin or end with notes or sidebars or explanations. Scripture citations have been reproduced from the original sources, but since some of the original annotation is inappropriate for a book of this sort, it has not been retained.

In resetting these texts, it becomes apparent that some of the originals were more hastily translated than others, so here and there the editors made silent emendations—not just to spare the reader inconsistent style choices but to spare him or her unnecessary infelicities where the sense of the writer had clearly gone askew in the translating.

Our primary goal was to produce in broad strokes, through his own words, a portrait of the man who is now leading a billion Roman Catholics worldwide into the new century and who is *ex officio* as well as personally of considerable interest to his constituents. Clearly he is also of interest to people of other faiths and indeed to those who have no formal affiliation but look to the pope as a source of moral strength and a force for positive change in matters of world justice, human rights, and the spread of peace in these troubling times. It is our hope that from this small effort readers will obtain not only a measured and comprehensive picture of Benedict, but one that might serve as a corrective to past assumptions about him, as well as a guide to his papacy now unfolding. If German theology has often provided the cutting-edge tools for interpreting Christianity over the past two hundred years, then having this original, stimulating, and authentic German theologian occupying the Chair of Peter is surely going to usher in an exciting era for the church.

So, to paraphrase a notion from Montaigne, we offer herewith a bunch of another man's flowers, providing of ourselves only the string to tie them together.

John F. Thornton
and Susan B. Varenne
New York City

Introduction

Joseph Ratzinger is, to the best of my knowledge, the first academic theologian in two centuries to fill the Shoes of the Fisherman, just as his immediate predecessor was the first professional philosopher ever to do so. However, he is also one of the least known of the great German and French theologians who helped shape the Second Vatican Council. This has much to do with the way theology developed after the council and the fact that, while still a professor, Ratzinger cast an increasingly cold eye on much that was to become theologically fashionable. Students of theology who quoted him were punished by their liberal professors, and those professors who did quote him—he is eminently quotable—would not reveal their source, lest the quote be rejected. When he took on pastoral responsibilities as archbishop of Munich and saw the devastating effect of some schools of theology on ordinary people's lives, he became more trenchantly critical. Finally, despite his best efforts to avoid higher appointment, he found himself eventually in the unenviable position of being made prefect of the Congregation for the Doctrine of the Faith (CDF). His task for the next twenty-four years was to help re-identify what had become the somewhat porous boundaries that define our faith, and to help define the church's teaching in the face of new developments in science, philosophy, and politics. Understandably, he soon earned a reputation as the Grand Inquisitor, *Panzerkardinal*, or "enforcer of the faith"—and was presented by the media as practically the enemy of humanity, again not surprisingly, seeing how the teaching of the church on issues that affect us all in the depths of our being has contradicted much that was fashionable.

Then, thanks to the media, came a turning point. Beginning with the way he presided at the requiem Mass for Pope John Paul II and conducted his first appearances after his election as pope, people encountered a personality other than the one they thought they knew. This time they were seeing an image unfiltered by any editor—a shy, humble, but courageous man, whose spontaneous smile exuded warmth and joy and hope. But it was also a man who was no longer the customs officer who had to decide what was allowed entrance to the church and what was not. He was now Christ's vicar on earth, the representative of him who is Love.

As pope, he has surprised many people, even professional theologians who had dismissed him without ever reading his writings. Even many theologians had assumed that his theology was limited to the (sometimes poorly written) documents he signed as prefect for the Congregation for the Doctrine of the Faith. Perhaps the most controversial document was *Dominus Iesus,* on the uniqueness and salvific universality of Jesus Christ and his church, which unequivocally reiterated the doctrine that the one church "subsists in" the Catholic Church, refused to use the term *church* for Protestant denominations, and described all other religions as "objectively gravely deficient." No doubt the content of such documents did betray his inspiration. But they are not simply his theology; they are the church's authoritative statements on matters of faith and morals—the source of and the parameters within which theology operates. Theology is itself, however, an attempt to discover the inner logic of that faith, to situate the Faith within the questioning of the world's great thinkers and the existential situation of today, to discover (insofar as limited mortals can) what is *God's view* of reality and the human condition. Few professional theologians were even aware that he had continued to write and publish as a private theologian while archbishop and later as prefect. But it is in those writings (together with his earlier, more scholarly works) that we find his own theology, his faltering but nonetheless stimulating insights into God's Word as a response to the crucial questions affecting humanity individually and collectively.

RATZINGER'S THEOLOGICAL METHODOLOGY

To appreciate Ratzinger's writings, one has to remember that all of his published material, official or private—and it covers a breathtaking scope of topics—is written from an explicit theological perspective. In other words, it is argued in the light of reason *and* revelation, revelation as found in scripture and tradition being the ultimate criterion. His theology is marked, first of all, by attention to the whole history of human questioning (philosophy) up to and including those questions articulated or implied by the situation in which we find ourselves today. Second, this theology is characterized by attention to the answers—often partial and inadequate ones—given in the course of history by the great thinkers of humanity, theologians and otherwise. Third, and most important, his theology is given its definitive form by listening to and trying to interpret God's revelation of himself in Jesus Christ, namely his design for humanity entrusted to the church and testified to by scripture read in the light of the history of dogma.[1]

I just used the word *history* three times. This is no accident. It is one of Ratzinger's basic methodological principles—following the examples of Plato, Aristotle, Augustine, and Aquinas—that no serious philosophical or theological question can ever be adequately posed or answered, however tentatively, if the philosopher or theologian does not listen to the objections to it; and this implies being at least to some degree aware of the history of the question (and of the prior attempts made to answer it). Even more significant for Ratzinger is the need for every Christian—and a fortiori, the theologian—to face facts squarely and not avoid what appears to be most unpalatable, even to be at variance with one's assumptions as to the content of the faith.[2] Those assumptions might, in fact, have to be revised, which is one of the tasks of the systematic theologian. All of Ratzinger's writings betray the courage to face any question or objection because of the confidence he has in the Truth revealed in Jesus Christ and handed on by the church's apostolic tradition.

The characteristics of all of Ratzinger's writing are his originality, creativity, and independence as a thinker. His more recent forays into moral theology and political science, though rooted in his early research in the history of dogma, are those of an original thinker conscious that his contribution to contemporary discourse is precisely that of a theologian. What I propose to do in the rest of this introduction is to provide an overview of his more important writings, beginning with his early publications.[3] Before doing so, I would like to draw the reader's attention to some of the major hallmarks of his writings and discuss the foundational research he carried out for his doctoral and postdoctoral dissertations, on which the entire edifice of his later writings is based.

SOME MAJOR CHARACTERISTICS[4]

Truth and Tolerance[5] is Cardinal Ratzinger's 284-page answer to the worldwide outrage at the publication of *Dominus Iesus* (August 6, 2000), the document issued by the Congregation for the Doctrine of the Faith, of which he was prefect at the time (the book was published in German 2003, American 2004). The document affirmed the absolute claims of Christianity and the Catholic Church vis-à-vis other religions. In the preface, he wrote: "As I looked through my lectures on [Christian belief and world religions] over the past decade, it emerged that these approaches amounted to something like a single whole—quite fragmentary and unfinished, of course, but, as a contribution to a major theme that affects us all, perhaps not entirely unhelpful." These sentiments highlight not only the dominant characteristic of the man   his humility and courage—but also the nature of most of his writings. They are fragmentary and mostly unfinished, but nonetheless accumulate to something like a single whole.

He is conscious of the fragmentary nature of all he has written, but he makes a virtue of this supposed weakness, caused by the simple fact that he was called to sacrifice the preferred life of an academic in order to serve the church, first as archbishop of Munich, then as prefect of the CDF, and now as pope. As he says in a recent publication, *Values in a Time of Upheaval: How to Survive the Challenges of the Future* (German 2005), "Perhaps the unfinished character of these attempts can help to advance thinking about them." Like his university lectures, all of his writings are contributions to an ongoing debate, first the scholarly debate within his own discipline—theology—and later, as he became more a pastor than a scholar, the public debate about the future of society and, above all, the church's role in it.

Despite their fragmentary nature, his writings do have an inner consistency; they do "amount to something like a single whole," as he himself puts it. And this is because he is not simply an outstanding scholar but also an original thinker. The result is an inner consistency that marks all his writings, while each individual piece stands on its own and nonetheless never fails to surprise his readers with its freshness, originality, and depth.

Ratzinger has been described as the consummate listener, and that is what he is, attentive to the voices of others, be they great or small, the famous thinkers of the past or his serious critics of the present. He listens to anyone who has anything to say, including his students. But most of all, he has given ear to the contributions made by great thinkers down through the ages. This capacity to listen with discernment, combined with his phenomenal erudition, makes him a superb partner in dialogue. One such dialogue took place in the Catholic Academy of Munich on January 19, 2004, with the neo-Marxist Jürgen Habermas of the Frankfurt School as his interlocutor. The main topic of the debate concerned the possibility of establishing those (objective) moral values needed for society to function justly, which Ratzinger called the "prepolitical moral foundations for a free state."[6] Habermas, donning the mantle of the Enlightenment, claimed that reason alone would be sufficient to the task, while Ratzinger disagreed. Reason alone had, in fact, failed in the past (a reference to twentieth-century ideologies). Reason needs religion, the crucible of human experience and source of human wisdom, to complete the task. In his paper, Ratzinger drew attention to the way the universalist claims of both the Enlightenment and Christianity, which have become universal in fact, are today questioned by other religious traditions that cannot be ignored but must also be brought into the debate aimed at establishing a moral consensus. The debate ended with the reciprocal recognition of the need for a "double process of apprenticeship" in which reason and religion would again learn to become dependent on each other (cf. *Le Monde*, April 27, 2005). Habermas was reported to have been quite overwhelmed by the quality of the debate.

Even when he was professor of Dogmatic Theology with a large doctoral colloquium—on average some thirty doctoral and postdoctoral students at a time during his tenure at the University of Regensburg—one heard the reproach that he had failed to form a "school of theology" comparable, for example, to those propounded by the other two great modern German-speaking theologians, Karl Rahner and Hans Urs von Balthasar. Certainly the subject matter of the doctoral and postdoctoral theses he supervised covered the whole range of the history of dogma and systematic theology. This range of subjects reflects the comparably vast range of subjects he covered in his own œuvre. Though at home in systematic theology, he never set out to create a system or "school of thought."[7] In that sense, he is a postmodern, but in fact he is more in tune with the original Christian thinkers, the fathers of the church. His theology is seminal, in a way I would like to develop in the next few paragraphs.

LIBERAL OR CONSERVATIVE?

In an interview after Benedict's election, Rodrigo Caviero of the *Correiro Braziliense* asked me to account for what is generally assumed to be the transformation of the liberal theologian before the Second Vatican Council into Ratzinger the conservative of more recent times. It is a question that many pose and one that I have dealt with in detail in another context.[8] My personal opinion is that placing great thinkers in pigeonholes often simply reflects unexamined prejudices. First as a professor and then as cardinal, Joseph Ratzinger, in the course of his life as a theologian, developed a rich, mature body of writings, as we will see. His writings are incredibly dense, in need of unfolding and development. They are in fact "seminal," seeds of originality and creativity, which future generations will bring to completion. I find his insights into Christian faith and modern life personally enriching and intellectually stimulating (as do my students, lay and cleric, male and female). They are invariably fresh and original. He is an exciting theologian, an original thinker awaiting discovery.

I can illustrate this through an experience I had teaching in the Regional Seminary of Papua New Guinea and the Solomon Islands, where I had to cover the theology of the Christian sacraments. Following the methodology of Ratzinger, my *Doktorvater*, I sought a starting point in the local culture, which is (broadly speaking) aboriginal and accordingly the happy hunting ground for anthropologists of all kinds. Botched attempts at the "inculturation" of the liturgy had created much theological confusion. An anthropologist confrere, Father Jim Knight, SVD, introduced me to the world of primitive rites—in particular the pioneering anthropological studies of Victor Turner and Mary Douglas, whose anthropology of natural symbols has thrown much light on contemporary developments in church and society. I was also introduced to the world of comparative religion (in particular Mircea Eliade). In my search for a theological framework with which to evaluate all that I had studied, it was Ratzinger who provided the hermeneutical key. I had brought with me to Papua New Guinea two thin pamphlets he had published on the notion of sacrament.[9] They not only provided me with the theological framework to evaluate contemporary primitive rites of initiation[10] and to situate them within the history of humanity that culminated in Christ. His insights also enabled me to appreciate the lasting significance of these rites and relate them to the Old and New Testament rites that culminated in the sacraments as we know them today. The ideas he had developed in the two pamphlets were seminal.

According to Ratzinger, the Christian sacraments are rooted in primordial human experiences that arise at crucial moments in life, namely fertility, birth, the transition to manhood, marriage, the assumption of leadership, and, finally death, the transition to the Beyond. Rites of passage were devised to deal with these liminal experiences, when man is most open to the Beyond. These rites all share a basic pattern, that of dying and rising to new life, such as to a new status in the community. These rites underwent a radical transformation during the history of salvation, when they were associated with defining moments in that history, such as the Exodus. This transformation followed a dual process: a moment of demythologizing and an interpretative moment, central to which was the prophetic word (which became scripture). It culminated in the central event of salvation history: the life, death, and resurrection of God become man, Jesus Christ. In time, the church developed rites around seven central passages from death to sin to new life in Christ, the seven sacraments. But the basic human experience first articulated in the primitive rituals remains the same. Ratzinger's insights, when implanted, as it were, in the humus of anthropology and comparative religion, helped me produce a rich crop of lectures, which, on my return to Europe, I delivered to an appreciative audience at the University of Freibourg (Switzerland) during the summer semester of 1984, when I was a visiting professor there.

From my own acquaintance with Professor Joseph Ratzinger, I can only attribute his perceived change from young liberal to old conservative to the fact that he is not simply a respected scholar and academic of international fame;

he is an original thinker. It is undeniable that before the Vatican Council he was, compared with the established theology of the day, liberal and progressive, not to say revolutionary. He himself said that his basic impulse "precisely during the Council, was always to free up the authentic kernel of the faith from encrustations and to give this kernel strength and dynamism. This impulse is the constant of my life."[11] In that sense, he is a critical thinker. Like every profound thinker who has engaged with the great thinkers of most cultural traditions past and present (his erudition is astonishing), he is not only an astute observer of society and culture, but he has always maintained a critical distance. This inner distance—born of his passion for the truth, his life-long search for the truth, and his capacity for self-criticism—enables him to appreciate and enter into dialogue with contemporary intellectual currents of thought, especially theological thought, which touches on the most profound of all human questions. While many theologians remained, it could be said, stuck in the heady liberalism of the late 1960s, Ratzinger moved on—and so began to appear conservative or traditionalist, neither of which labels do justice to the man or his writings. He soon turned his critical mind to the new theological establishment, thinkers who are still in power in most faculties, though their day is now more or less over. His independent thinking brought him into conflict with those who were caught up in what used to be called "the spirit of Vatican II," which in subsequent years turned into unthinking conformity with prevailing fashions.[12] To keep his independence as a thinker called for enormous character and courage (and wit)—helped by self-control in the face of his increasingly negative public image. That new image seemed hardly to bother him, convinced as he has always been of the long-term power of truth, this confidence accounting for his own self-effacement.

Ratzinger never took himself too seriously. He always retained his humor. This attitude, fostered by a consciousness that the truth is not created but discovered, and so stands on its own, regardless of the person of the theologian, also helped to keep him in constant dialogue with those who disagreed with him, trying to see their point of view, engaging in self-criticism (thereby remaining open to correction), and finding new ways to appeal to them. He seeks dialogue and understanding. He is concerned with the truth, which alone can make us free (as individuals and as a society), with the freedom of a love that engenders hope and joy.

FOUNDATIONAL RESEARCH

From the beginning of his own studies, he and many contemporaries in Munich sought an alternative to what had been the dominant system of

Catholic theology up to then, neo-Scholasticism. The latter was an attempt in the nineteenth and early twentieth centuries to re-create the medieval philosophical and theological system of St. Thomas Aquinas. It was, we can say in hindsight, an effort marred by the very rationalism it tried to overcome. Instead, Ratzinger turned to the great thinkers of the early church. For his doctoral thesis, he studied *the* father of the Western church—and of Western civilization—St. Augustine of Hippo in North Africa. Though he recognized the greatness of Scholasticism and its inner dialectic, which, properly understood, preserves the tension of that intratheological debate, which arises from a communal search for the truth, Ratzinger found this system of thought too impersonal. "With Augustine, however, the passionate, suffering, questioning man is always right there, and you can identify with him."[13]

His topic was Augustine's understanding of the church—and thus, by implication, his understanding of the state and the political significance of Christianity. His dissertation, *People of God and God's House in Augustine's Doctrine of the Church* (German 1954) is a classic. (Unfortunately, it has not yet been translated into English.) It is also the root of much of his later theology. It inspired his contributions to the documents of the Second Vatican Council and provided the inspiration he later needed to combat various misunderstandings of the council, not least the mistaken attempt to conceive the church as the People of God in more or less empirical or sociological, not to say political, terms.

His postdoctoral dissertation was devoted to St. Thomas Aquinas's contemporary, St. Bonaventure, who was also very much in the Augustinian tradition. Entitled *The Theology of History in St. Bonaventure* (German 1955, American 1971),[14] it is an analysis of the attempt by the great Franciscan theologian to come to terms with the then-new understanding of history conceived by the abbot Joachim of Fiore (ca. 1135–1202). The latter's essentially Gnostic speculations were taken up by some of the followers of St. Francis, known as the Spirituals, whose radical interpretation of Franciscan poverty combined with a Joachimite apocalyptic interpretation of history made them the first revolutionary movement of the second millennium. Their goal was to usher in a new age marked by a spiritual brotherhood of all men. They split the early Franciscans in two and forced Bonaventure, the master general of the young Franciscan congregation, to address Joachim's theories.

As Eric Voegelin has shown,[15] the speculations of Joachim of Fiore are in large part the source of modernity. They effectively helped replace the Augustinian concept of history that had informed Western Christendom up to then, namely that history was something *transitory*, the rise and fall of empires. Empires pass away, only the eternal *Civitas Dei* (the "citizenry of God," as Ratzinger translates it) lasts forever. Its sacramental expression is the church, understood as humanity in the process of redemption. Joachim proposed an exciting new conception of all of world history as a divine *progression* within three distinct eras, that of the Father (the Old Testament, or the period of the laity or patriarchs), that of the Son (the church since the New Testament, or the period of the clerics), and a third era, that of the Holy Spirit, the period of the ascetic monks, or Spirituals, which was about to begin. In the third period, all structures (church and state) would give way to the perfect society of autonomous men moved only from within by the Spirit. This understanding of history is based on what Voegelin calls "the immanentization of the eschaton," in other words, the assumption that the end of history is immanent to itself, an inner-worldly manifestation, the product of its own inner movement toward ever greater perfection, the Kingdom of God *on earth* within history. It is at the root of what we mean today by "progress." It underpins, albeit in different ways, both radical socialism and liberal capitalism. And it has had a profound effect on political life, giving rise to both revolution and secularism.

Bonaventure, according to Ratzinger, failed in his critique; it was not radical enough. But what is significant for Ratzinger's future engagement with political thought is that his sensitivity to the philosophical and theological issues underlying contemporary political life had been fine-tuned by his study of Bonaventure. This is seen in particular in his later treatment of the radical forms of liberation theology based on a Marxist notion of history that has its deepest roots in the speculations of Joachim of Fiore.

THE EARLY PERIOD

As a professional German academic first in Freising and then in Bonn, Ratzinger's early writings were devoted to fundamental theology, namely systematic reflection on the basic principles and presuppositions of theology. The subjects covered include the nature of theology as *Wissenschaft* (science or scholarship), the meaning of Christian revelation and so of tradition, as well as the nature of the church (ecclesiology). Related subjects he treated include ecumenism and the broader question of the relationship between the church and the world religions, with particular attention in his later writings to the relationship between Christianity and Judaism. Ratzinger stresses the affinity between reason and revelation (and so the church's appreciation of philosophy as an ally in its enlightened critique of myth both in antiquity and today). For Ratzinger, "reason" is our capacity for truth (and so for God). Like language, reason is both personal and communal by nature. Indeed so is revelation, the social dimension of which is found in the human-divine complex of tradition/church. Ratzinger's entire theological opus is rooted in scripture, the ultimate norm of all theology, judiciously interpreted using the findings of modern exegesis.[16] However, his scriptural interpretation goes beyond modern critical scholarship in the spirit of the church fathers, whose interpretation of scripture is based on the unity of the Old and New Testaments (the latter seen as the fulfillment of the former) and the unfolding of tradition under the direction of the Holy Spirit down to our own day.[17]

Ratzinger's early period was greatly influenced by the Second Vatican Council and its aftermath. He published several commentaries on texts issued by the council, as well as personal reflections on the four sessions of the council and its aftermath. He dealt with the vexed question of the universal nature of salvation and the particular nature of the church, which the council had posed with renewed sharpness, and which was often expressed in terms of Karl Rahner's catchphrase "anonymous Christianity."[18] Ratzinger developed his understanding of salvation in terms of *Stellvertretung* (representation/substitution), according to which, if I understand him correctly, the church continues to make effective in each generation the salvific action of Christ on the cross by which he redeemed the world. Just as the incarnate Word of God gave his life "for the many," so, too, individual Christians must live not for themselves but for others, while the church exists not for itself but for the rest of humanity and so enables Christ's grace to transform all those outside the visible church who follow the deepest stirrings of their conscience. His major writings in this area include *Revelation and Tradition* (with Karl Rahner, German & English 1965), *The New People of God* (German 1969), and the *Principles of Catholic Theology* (German 1982, American 1987), perhaps his most important academic writing.

THE MIDDLE PERIOD

Before looking at what might be called Ratzinger's middle period, I want to acknowledge that such divisions are somewhat artificial. There is also a danger that they might distract from an appreciation of the fundamental consistency in all of Ratzinger's writings. Thus, for example, in his final period he returned to his earlier interest in fundamental theology, in such books as *The Nature and Mission of Theology* (German 1993, American 1995) and *Called to Communion* (German and American 1991), which is a short course on ecclesiology, the fruit of his mature thinking. These works were greatly influenced by the specific dogmatic concerns that occupied his attention during his middle period, when he taught dogmatic theology and the history of dogma, as well as by later pastoral challenges he encountered as archbishop and cardinal. The numerous doctoral theses he supervised also influenced his thought.[19]

In all his writings, the church is seen as a divine/human reality that constitutes a *communio*—that is, humanity in the process of becoming one. The source of that unity is the Eucharist, the sacrament of the paschal mystery by which God in Christ reunited sinful humanity with himself. Communion in and with the one body and one blood of Christ in the Eucharist transforms the faithful interiorly or spiritually into the one body of Christ that is the church, "body of Christ" being the most distinctive New Testament and patristic description of the new People of God. But the church is not just a spiritual reality. It is a visible entity, at once local and universal, a communion of communities, whose visible unity is manifested and guaranteed by the apostolic succession in union with the Petrine ministry of the Bishop of Rome. The goal of the church, her basic mission, is "the incorporation of humanity into the life-rhythm of the Trinitarian God."

In this middle period (as professor of Dogma and History of Dogma at the universities of Münster, Tübingen, and Regensburg), Ratzinger produced his most famous book of all, *Introduction to Christianity* (German 1968, revised 2000; English 1969), which has since been translated into some nineteen languages, including Arabic and Chinese. His creative thinking on the nature of sacrament, developed in small but significant essays like *The Sacramental Basis of Christian Existence* (German 1966), already mentioned above, has yet to be absorbed into mainstream sacramental theology, as far as I can see. It has not even been translated into English. His thinking on the nature of the church was enriched by his reflections on the specifically dogmatic themes of Creation, Christology, Trinity, and Eschatology, as well his early reflections on the Eucharist and the nature of the liturgy, such as *The Feast of Faith: Essays in the Theology of Worship* (German 1981).

Most of his writings on the church's dogmas are occasional contributions to an ongoing debate and are thus of an increasingly fragmentary nature. Some of the principal works are to be found in the collection entitled *Dogma and Proclamation* (German 1973, American 1985). Also of note are his short books *The God of Jesus Christ: Reflections on the Trinitarian God* (German 1976, American 1978), *"In the beginning…": A Catholic Understanding of the Story of Creation and the Fall* (four sermons first published in German 1986, revised 1996; American 1990, revised 1995), and *Daughter Zion* (German 1977, American 1983), his major (but not his only) contribution to Mariology.

The most significant book of this period is perhaps his *Eschatology—Death and Eternal Life* (German 1977, American [enl. edn.] 1988), which is a well worked out, systematic textbook. This period is also marked by his growing concern with developments in catechesis, the handing on of the faith in schools and colleges, as reflected in the talk *Mediating Faith and Sources of Faith* (German 1983), which caused quite a storm when he gave it in France. These critical reflections on the contemporary situation of catechesis and its basic principles prepared him for his work as chairman of the commission set up by Pope John Paul II to oversee the composition of the *Catechism of the Catholic Church*, perhaps the most significant achievement of that pontificate.

THE LATER PERIOD

As already mentioned, Ratzinger, now cardinal prefect of the Congregation for the Doctrine of the Faith, continued to research and publish in academic journals. Though these writings must be regarded as distinct from the official documents that carried his signature, these two categories of writing were often related. His scholarly writings sometimes contributed to his preparation for the official documents or were reflections on those documents, in particular on their reception by the larger public, such as the extensive article that appeared in the *Frankfurter Allegemeine Zeitung* (September 22, 2000) responding to the controversy sparked by the publication of *Dominus Iesus,* which had stressed the absolute claims of Christ and the unity of his church. His publications during this later period include sermons, reflections, and spiritual exercises he gave as a bishop and pastor. All are marked by deep spirituality, simplicity of language, and beauty of expression, such as *To Look on Christ: Exercises in Faith, Hope and Love* (German 1989, American 1991). His pastoral concern also produced some of his finest writings on the Eucharist, such as the article "Eucharist and Mission" (*Irish Theological Quarterly* 65 [2000]: 245–64) and the essays and sermons collected by Stephan Otto Horn and Vinzenz Pfnür in *God Is Near Us* (German 2001, American 2003).

Ever since the council, Ratzinger was concerned with the way theological debate had moved dramatically out of the university seminar into the media, which, to put it mildly, has never been an ideal forum for theological debate. Theological ideas that had not yet matured were suddenly front-page news. Unused to any questioning of traditional doctrine, the public was suddenly confronted with interpretations that seemed to contradict their traditional understanding of doctrine. Unversed in academic theology, most of the faithful simply had to choose between the authority of the experts and the authority of what they had learned at school and from the pulpit. Many of these new theses have not stood the test of time, such as the "theology of compromise" in moral theology, and yet they have affected the lives of many, discouraging them, for example, from the often heroic effort needed to adhere to Catholic moral principles.

Debate among scholars is essential, but the most they can achieve is a temporary consensus to be replaced by a more compelling argument. Eventually what is of value in theological debate is incorporated into church teaching by the authentic magisterium, the church's teaching authority. At that stage, theologians have a different task, namely to communicate these insights into the church's doctrine to the public at large, to find a language and suitable images for truths that illuminate the human condition, and to enable us to engage in a critique of the dominant culture. But if the tentative theses of the theologians are presented to the public as "the last word" with full media coverage, then the result can only be confusing. This is what happened in the wake of the council, when some theologians were calling for their consensus at the time to be regarded as a kind of magisterium parallel to that of the pope and the bishops.

The resulting confusion among ordinary faithful, whose practice and devotion had already been shaken by the (necessary) reforms of Vatican II, was a real concern to Ratzinger—and, I think, remains so. Theology should inspire and give hope, not cause confusion and despair. His sermons from this period as cardinal archbishop of Munich show a theologian capable of touching the hearts and minds of the faithful (something the world at large unexpectedly experienced for the first time when he preached at the obsequies for Pope John Paul II and, again, after his election as pope, *q.v.* in this collection [pp. 17 and 25]). His own theology at this later stage was marked by his new pastoral concerns in responding to the growing secularism he observed around him and a related weakening of confidence in Christian, Catholic values. He responded as well to certain developments in the reform of the liturgy that alarmed him, such as a growing arbitrariness vis-à-vis church ritual. At this stage he turned his attention to the role of Christianity in modern pluralist democracy and the breakdown of society in Europe, as it collapses into the black hole created by the denial of the Absolute in public life. His podium was the pulpit, and his sermons and spiritual reflections from this period onward are in the tradition of the great fathers of the church, who forged their theology in answer to the needs of their flocks. His theological concerns were often dictated by current developments in politics and society in general, but in particular the pervasive moral relativism that undermines human well-being and erodes human communities.

As prefect of the Congregation for the Doctrine of the Faith, his task was quite different. There he had to defend the parameters within which theology (including ethics) and church life need to be conducted if they are to remain true to the Catholic and apostolic tradition. He had to do this in a rapidly changing world of high technology and political turmoil, and in the context of a church still reeling from the radical changes introduced by the Second Vatican Council. Developments in society and biotechnology threw up new social and moral dilemmas, which called for a refinement of traditional moral principles at a time when moral theology was in the process of renewing itself, a process that is only beginning to find some kind of closure. Put simply, the council called for a reform of moral theology, which up to then had been too legalistic (indeed rigoristic) and preoccupied with sin.

The initial attempts at reform produced two schools of thought. In the first school, morality was effectively reduced to one principle: calculating the consequences of an action and opting for the greater proportion of good in any human action. All actions were understood to be essentially determined by their circumstances or particular situation and were assumed to be by nature ambiguous; none was seen to be intrinsically either good or bad. What mattered was that the proportion of foreseeable good effects should outweigh the evil effects. The other school recognized a multiplicity of principles governing any action, while maintaining that some actions (adultery, perjury, murder) were always to be avoided because they were intrinsically wrong, irrespective of the circumstances. Both of these schools, it is now more and more recognized, were still operating from within a legalist mental framework, one tending to laxity, the other to rigorism, one dissenting from traditional Catholic teaching, the other defending it. Both have, under the influence of the contemporary recovery of Aristotelian ethics and the moral theology of Thomas Aquinas, given way to a recovery of *virtue* as the context for moral discourse. Virtue is ultimately concerned with happiness and holiness as the goal of human life. It reintegrates both the human passions and divine grace into morality. The new *Catechism of the Catholic Church* (1992), for which Ratzinger was finally responsible, has given official sanction, as it were, to the recovery of Thomist virtue ethics, while the encyclical *Veritatis Splendor* of Pope John Paul II (1993), to which it is presumed Ratzinger contributed, has brought to the debate between these two schools a kind of closure. It defends, among other things, the affirmation that certain actions *are* intrinsically wrong, and shows the significance of objective morality to stable political life.

Developments in inter-religious dialogue raised new questions and the need for further clarification. This called for an authoritative response from the church, which the Congregation, under Ratzinger's direction, provided, though it was understandably not always welcomed. And yet, Cardinal Ratzinger continued to lecture and publish articles and books in his capacity as a private theologian, entering into the debate and offering his opinions for critical assessment. This side of him was appreciated only by those who were not discouraged by his reputation as conservative or his position as prefect of the CDF. There is treasure here waiting to be discovered by younger theologians.

Many of his more recent theological writings were occasioned by his responsibility for overseeing the congregation's response to pressing issues, such as liberation theology and bioethics. The threat posed by liberation theology in Latin America provoked two documents from the congregation, *Libertatis Nuntius* (1984), *Instruction on Certain Aspects of the Theology of Liberation*, which criticized the revolutionary, neo-Marxist roots of this theology, and *Libertatis Conscientia* (1986), *Instruction on Christian Freedom and Liberation*, which outlined the basis for an authentic theology of liberation true to Catholic tradition. In bioethics, the Congregation published *Donum vitae* (Gift of Life) in 1987 to answer questions raised by developments in biotechnology, in particular experimentation on human embryos and in vitro fertilization. Other documents were inspired by Ratzinger's preparation for meetings of the Biblical Commission and the International Theological Commission, which he chaired and which produced important documents on the interpretation of scripture, the attitude of the church toward the Jews in the New Testament, and the renewal of moral theology. His reflections on these topics were published in theological journals and particularly reveal his mind.[20] For example, his article on the philosophical and cultural roots of contemporary biotechnology with respect to creating humans in laboratories[21] far exceeds the limited scope of *Donum vitae*, the church's response to artificial human reproduction and perhaps one of the most important documents issued by the CDF. His articles illuminate theologically that magisterial document.

From the center of the universal church, Cardinal Ratzinger had a unique view of world events, which affected his personal theology and found expression in his many writings of this period on what I call his theology of politics, in particular the political developments in Europe before and after the fall of the Berlin Wall, developments he commented on fearlessly and, indeed, prophetically. In this later period, pastoral concerns dominate his theological writing, very often sparked by crises affecting the worldwide church that called for an authoritative response from the Congregation for the Doctrine of the Faith. These concerns include liberation theology, dramatic developments in biotechnology, and, most recently, the relationship between Christianity and the world religions, a topic he also dealt with in his early formative period as an academic theologian. His mature reflections on this subject are to be found in *Truth and Tolerance* (German 2003, American 2004).

Space does not permit us to outline Ratzinger's theological evaluation of the world religions and their relationship to Christianity. What follows is but the tip of the iceberg. It is central to his thought that religions are not static entities but, like the culture they shape and express, are dynamic, ever-changing phenomena. According to Ratzinger, a shared cult is at the core of every ancient culture. This communal cult is rooted in a primordial experience of the ground of all being, which in turn defines the inner character of the culture. But cultures also exist in history, and so are subject to change (both enrichment and decay), depending on whether they are open or closed to the universality of truth. Furthermore, cultures interact. "Each particular culture not only lives out its own experience of God, the world, and man, but on its path it necessarily encounters other cultural agencies and has to react to their quite different experiences. This results, depending always on the degree to which the cultural agent may be closed or open, inwardly narrow or broad in outlook, in that culture's own perceptions and values being deepened and purified.... A process of this kind can in fact lead to a breaking open of the silent alienation of man from the truth and from himself that exists within that culture"[22]—when his conscience is stirred by encounter with the truth of human existence.

Christian faith results from God's communication of himself to humanity in Christ, who is the Way, the Truth, and the Life (Jn 14:6). When the revealed truth of Christianity encounters the search for truth in other religions and cultures, the result can be mutual enrichment, in which partial or still obscure truths in the other religions, in particular their own (self-critical) wisdom traditions, find their fulfillment in Christ. This is possible because of a conviction central to all wisdom traditions that has been denied in the modern world: "The conviction that man's being contains an imperative, the conviction that he does not himself *invent* morality on the basis of expediency, but rather *finds* it already present in things."[23] As a result, the great religious and wisdom traditions of humanity have flowed like tributaries into the great Christian vision of reality, since the dawn of salvation history. "The ethical vision of the Christian faith is not in fact something specific to Christianity but is the synthesis of the great ethical intuitions of mankind from a new center that holds them together."[24]

MAJOR INTERVIEWS

During his time as prefect of the CDF, Cardinal Ratzinger gave three important interviews to journalists, introducing the public to his theology—though they also involved him in controversy. The interviews were given over a short period of time; the second and third took place over two weekends when the cardinal and the journalist repaired to a Benedictine monastery outside Rome and spent the whole weekend in conversation. The first interview was with Italian journalist Vittorio Messori. It was held in the seminary in Brixen, South Tyrol, and was published as *The Ratzinger Report: An Exclusive Interview on the State of the Church.* This interview dealt primarily with internal church issues.[25] For younger Catholics, who were increasingly dissatisfied with the theology they were getting in the seminaries and (in particular) at the university level, it was an eye-opener that led to their liberation as believers.

The second interview was given to Peter Seewald, at the time a lapsed Catholic and a highly respected journalist with the left-wing German daily, *Die Süddeutsche Zeitung.* Published as *Salt of the Earth: The Church at the End of the Millennium,* it covers a much broader range of issues, including his own biography and the state of the world on the threshold of the twenty-first century.[26] It has inspired many, giving particular encouragement to the older generation, who remained faithful despite the candy-coated theology they were being offered at the time, which they knew in their heart of hearts could not answer the deeper questions of the human spirit. I refer here to the tendency of theologians to interpret the faith in the light of contemporary trends rather than interpreting contemporary trends in the light of the faith. The at times demanding nature of Christian faith and morals is often watered down to make it more palatable to a permissive generation. It is sweet-tasting but lacks real substance. Ratzinger, by contrast, has held firm to the intellectually and morally challenging truths of faith, throwing new light on them within the contemporary cultural context such that old truths made new sense. For example, when dealing with Creation, Ratzinger stresses the truth that at the origin of all reality is loving intelligence (the Word), not irrational blind chance. The effect of reading his theology has been truly liberating for many.

The same journalist, who in the meantime had returned to the church, conducted a third interview, which was more strictly theological. The result was a popular *summa* (systematic treatment) of Ratzinger's theology entitled *God and the World.* It is, in effect, a commentary on the content of our faith.[27] Also of note are two books he wrote toward the end of his time as prefect: his autobiography, *Milestones, Memoirs 1927–77*[28], and, three years later, *The Spirit of the Liturgy: An Introduction,* perhaps his most important work of this later period. It was written during a vacation in Regensburg, and Ratzinger hoped that his theology of the liturgy would give rise to a renewal similar to the important liturgical-renewal movement sparked by a book with a similar title published by Romano Guardini in 1918.

MORAL THEOLOGY AND THE THEOLOGY OF POLITICAL LIFE

Ratzinger's reflections on morality belong primarily to his middle period (see, e.g., *Principles of Moral Theology* [German 1975, American 1986]), while his theology of politics[29] can be traced back to his earliest research—his doctoral and postdoctoral theses—and to his first books, especially *Christian Brotherhood* (German 1960, English and American 1966) and *The Unity of the Nations: A Vision of the Fathers of the Church* (German 1971), both of which are developments of insights first found in his doctoral dissertation. The latter is fascinating, particularly for its insights into the potential evil of nationalism and its threat to the church as first perceived by Origen of Alexandria, the third-century founder of speculative theology. During his tenure as archbishop of Munich, pastoral concerns arising from developments in European politics have produced a mature theology of politics, early intimations of which can be found in the twelve sermons in *Christian Faith and Europe* (German 1981).

A representative selection of his writing on the theology of politics (including an important essay on liberation theology) is included in *Church, Ecumenism, and Politics* (German 1987; the English translation, 1988, is poor). He describes this collection as "essays in ecclesiology," politics and ecumenism being but two aspects of his theology of the church. His theology of politics combines a critique of modernity (understood as the attempt to create a perfect society by social engineering justified by one political ideology or another) with an attempt to delineate the contribution of Christianity to a humane society and to modern democracy. Here, conscience—understood as personal moral responsibility—plays a key role, as we will see below. Equally significant is the insight that, according to the New Testament vision, there is no place for a "political theology" (such as liberation theology) and, related to this, there is no template there for politics (and accordingly no justification for political ideologies in the strict sense of the term). Politics is the "art of the possible," the arena of practical reason (involving the virtues of prudence and justice), and so of compromise—albeit within moral parameters that are, in principle, non-negotiable, though today the latter are no longer recognized as such because of the dominance of rationalism and utilitarianism. Also significant for an appreciation of his political thought are the talks published under the titles *Turning Point for Europe?* (German 1991, American 1994) and, above all, *Truth, Values, Power: Litmus Tests for a Pluralist Society* (German 1993), which also contains, among other topics, his most important contribution to moral theology, namely, his understanding of conscience.[30]

To illustrate both Ratzinger's theological method and his understanding of politics, I would like to outline the content of one of his most important essays on democracy entitled "A Christian Orientation in a Pluralist Democracy?" (in *Church, Ecumenism, and Politics,* pp. 204–20).

The central question, as Ratzinger sees it, is: "How can Christianity become a positive force for the political world without being turned into a political instrument and without on the other hand grabbing the political world for itself?" His answer is threefold.

First, from its origins in the life of Christ, Christianity on the whole has refused to see itself as a political entity. One of the three temptations faced by Christ at the beginning of his public ministry was that of transforming the Kingdom of God into a political program. "My kingdom is not of this world," Jesus affirmed. "Give to Caesar what is Caesar's and to God what is God's." Caesar represents the state, the realm of political life, of practical reason and human responsibility. According to Ratzinger, the New Testament recognizes an *ethos,* or sphere, of political responsibility but rejects a *political theology,* that is, a political program to change the world on the basis of revelation. Thus all attempts to establish the perfect society (the Kingdom of God on earth) are rejected by the New Testament. The New Testament rejection of justification by one's own effort is likewise a rejection of political theology, which claims that a perfect society based on justice could be established by human effort alone. Perfect justice is, rather, the work of God in the hearts of those who respond to his love (grace). Justice cannot be achieved in society simply by changing the structures of society. It is, rather, the temporary result of continued imperfect efforts by society's members. To accept this is to acknowledge the imperfection that characterizes our human condition and to accept the need to persevere in one's moral effort. Such endurance in trying to do what is right, searching for the right solution to the practical difficulties that arise from daily life in common, is made possible by grace and the promise of everlasting life and ultimate victory in Christ. "The courage to be reasonable, which is the courage to be imperfect, needs the Christian promise [i.e., the theological virtue of hope] to hold its own ground, to persevere."

Second, Christian faith awakens conscience and thus provides the necessary foundation for the ethos of society. Faith gives practical content and direction to practical reason. It provides the necessary coordinates for practical decision-making. The core of the crisis of modern civilization is the implosion of the profound moral consensus that once marked all the great traditions of humanity, despite their superficial differences. If nothing is intrinsically right or wrong, conscience must be relegated to the private sphere, and law can no longer be regulated by morality. Accordingly, the most urgent task for modern society is to recover morality's meaning and its centrality for society, which is constantly in need of inner renewal. A state can survive and flourish only to the extent that most of its citizens are trying to do what is right and avoid what is wrong—insofar as they are truly trying to act in accordance with their conscience and striving to become virtuous. Thus genuine moral formation, by which one learns how to exercise one's freedom, is essential to establish justice, peace, and order in society. Moreover, it is important to remember that the basic morals of modern Western society are those of Christianity, with its roots in Judaism and classical Greek thought. The residue of these three traditions, filtered through the Enlightenment, gives modern democracy its internal ethical framework. When the Christian foundations are removed entirely, nothing holds together. Reason needs revelation if it is to remain reasonable—if it is to recognize the limits that define us as human beings.

The final point touches on a most sensitive aspect of the interconnection between Christianity and modern pluralist democracy. Today few will deny Christianity the right to develop its values and way of life alongside other social groups. But this would confine Christianity to the private sphere, just one value system among many equally valid ones. Not only does this contradict the Christian claim to truth and universal validity, but it robs Christianity of its real value to the state, which is that it represents the truth that transcends the state and for that very reason enables the state to function as a human society guided by the conscience of its members.

Thus we have a dilemma. If the church gives up its claim to universal truth and transcendence, it is unable to give to the state what it needs: the strength to persevere in the search for what is good and just—and a source of ultimate values. On the other hand, if the state embraces the Christian claim to truth, it can no longer remain pluralist, with the danger that the state loses its specific identity and autonomy. Achieving a balance between the two sides of this dilemma is a prerequisite for the freedom of the church and the freedom of the state. When the balance is upset and one side dominates, both church and state suffer the consequences. Christianity is the soil from which the modern state cannot be uprooted without decomposing. The state, Ratzinger insists, must accept that there is a stock of truth that is not subject to a consensus but rather precedes every consensus and makes it possible for society to govern itself.

The state ought to show its indebtedness in various ways, including the recognition of the public symbols of Christianity—public feast days, church buildings and public processions, the Crucifix in schools, and so on. Yet such public recognition can only be expected, adds Ratzinger, when Christians are convinced of their faith's indispensability because they are convinced of its ultimate truth.

In *Values in a Time of Upheaval: Meeting the Challenges of the Future* (German 2005), then cardinal Ratzinger discusses ways of recovering a moral consensus that is both objective and universal in a world marked by globalization and multiculturalism. In it, he returns again and again to the relationship between faith and reason, which was the subject of his inaugural lecture in Bonn in 1959 as a fledgling theologian. Now the topic emerges as an aspect of a wider and more complex picture of the challenges facing a society marked by modern terrorism, developments in biotechnology, globalization, and the undermining of traditional means of orientation within societies affected by the aftermath of the Enlightenment and the existence of highly influential mass media. Ratzinger argues that faith and reason, revelation and enlightenment, need each other to liberate the potential in each to confront, and help overcome, the dangers that threaten humanity today and in the immediate future. In this, as in all his writings, Ratzinger combines scholarship with originality. His analysis of current trends results in prognostications for the future, and all is expressed in a language that never fails to stimulate the reader and with a clarity that belies the depth of his singularly original theological reflections rooted in reason and revelation.

THE FIRST ENCYCLICAL

Pope Benedict's first encyclical, *Deus caritas est* (God Is Love), is, in a sense, a masterful synthesis of his dogmatic theology and his theology of politics. It has all the density of his earlier writings, a density that lends itself not to summary but to exposition. It must suffice here to draw attention to some of its main characteristics.

As the pope intimates in his introduction, the encyclical is a timely reminder of the primacy of love in a world threatened by religious hatred and violence (#1).[31] In the first part, however, which is speculative in nature, he corrects some deeply rooted misunderstandings about Christian love, namely the severely spiritualistic understanding of Christian love as selfless love that implies a rejection of all human loves as essentially selfish—in particular, eros, love oriented to conjugal union. The false opposition between divine love (*agape*) and human love (*eros*) is rooted in a false opposition between spirit and flesh, which is attributed to Descartes but has older, deeper roots in Gnosticism. Its effect is to banish joy from life, as Nietzsche perceived (*Jenseits von Gut und Böse*, IV, 168). Benedict XVI shows the intrinsic relationship between *eros* and *agape*, human and divine loves. Human love anticipates divine love, while divine love perfects human love. It is interesting to note that the pope takes up insights he had articulated in earlier works, such as *Introduction to Christianity*, where, for example, he describes the cross not as "the work of expiation which mankind offers to a wrathful God, but as the expression of that foolish love of God's which gives itself away to the point of humiliation in order to save man." There, too, his attempt to explain the mystery of Christ's Resurrection takes as its starting point a verse from the Song of Songs, the sublime erotic poem of the Old Testament: "Love is strong as death" (8:6). Here many of the ideas developed in the encyclical are found in seminal form.[32]

The second part of the encyclical deals with some of the practical implications of the belief in God who is love, such as the need not just for justice but for love; justice alone is not sufficient. Outlining the centrality of care for the poor and the outcast in scripture and down through the history of the church, the pope calls for an integration of charitable activity and social work of the church into the fundamental mission of the church. This would serve to bring all peoples to the knowledge of God who is love, who created and redeemed us out of love, and thus set the standard for all moral and political activity: respect for the dignity of the other and service to his or her needs. In this section, we find a synthesis of his theology of politics. The pope's theology of politics rejects all attempts to create a perfect world in the here and now—a Gnostic temptation that arises from revulsion with the real world in its murkiness—and appeals for a return to reason (in the sense of reasonableness) in political life. This implies negotiation, dialogue, and debate within generally accepted moral parameters. The courage to be imperfect is the presupposition of humane social intercourse, just as human love taken up and transformed by divine love finds its expression in the joy God intended for us when he created the world.

The collection of texts in *The Essential Pope Benedict XVI* offers both professional theologians and the broader public an opportunity to become acquainted with a writer who is not only an accomplished scholar but a thinker of the first order, someone who, because of his elevation as Pope Benedict XVI, is about to be discovered by the world at large. The editors are to be congratulated on compiling these selections, which will provide a useful introduction to the thought of a great thinker and a great pastor, now according to God's loving providence, the universal teacher of the church.

D. Vincent Twomey, SVD

Chronology of the Life of
Pope Benedict XVI

1927   On April 16, Holy Saturday, Joseph Alois Ratzinger is born in Marktl am Inn, Bavaria, Germany, to Joseph Ratzinger Sr. and Maria (Peintner) Ratzinger. He is the youngest child, having an older brother, Georg, and a sister, Maria. He is baptized at the Easter Vigil Mass on the very day he is born.

The senior Ratzinger serves in the Bavarian State Police and the German national Regular Police. He is an anti-Nazi, and his resistance to Hitler results in frequent demotions and transfers.

1929   The family moves to Tittmoning on the Austrian border.

1932   The family is again forced to relocate, this time to Auschau am Inn, at the foot of the Alps.

1937   Joseph Sr. retires and moves his family to Hufschlag, near Traunstein. Young Joseph begins his study of classical languages (Latin and Greek) in the local high school.

1939   Ratzinger enters the minor seminary in Traunstein. He has wanted to become a priest since the age of five, when he was impressed by the robes of the cardinal archbishop of Munich, who was visiting the city.

1941   At age fourteen, Ratzinger is legally required to join the Hitler Youth but refuses to attend meetings.

1943   World War II interrupts Ratzinger's studies when his seminary class is drafted to serve in the Flak, a German anti-aircraft corps. However, he is able to continue his education at the Maximilians-Gymnasium in Munich three days a week.

1944   Ratzinger is released from Flak in September and returns home. He is drafted to serve in the labor detail of the Austrian Legion on the border area to Hungary in anticipation of the Red Army offensive. Here he sees Jews being marched to death camps. He is released from service at the end of November to return home. After three weeks he is drafted into the German infantry at Munich and receives basic infantry training nearby in Traunstein. He serves at various posts around Traunstein but is not sent to the front due to illness.

1945   As the Allied front closes in that spring, Ratzinger deserts the army and heads home. When the Americans arrive and occupy the village, Ratzinger is identified as a soldier of the German army and briefly interned in a prisoner-of-war camp near Ulm. Released on June 19, he begins the seventy-five-mile walk home and eventually finds a ride in a milk truck. His brother, Georg, also returns after his release from a prisoner-of-war camp in Italy in July.

In November, Ratzinger and his brother re-enter the seminary, this time in Freising, to continue their studies for the priesthood.

1947   Ratzinger studies at the Herzogliches Georgianum of the Ludwig-Maximilian University in Munich, a theological institute. He is strongly drawn to the thought of St. Augustine and St. Bonaventure.

1951   Both Joseph and Georg Ratzinger are ordained to the priesthood on June 29, the feast of SS. Peter and Paul, by Cardinal Faulhaber of Munich in the cathedral at Freising.

1953   In July, Ratzinger receives his doctorate in theology. His thesis is titled "The People and House of God in Augustine's Doctrine of the Church."

He begins his book-length original research, required in order to teach at the university level, on St. Bonaventure's theology of history and revelation. He will complete this work in 1957.

1958   Ratzinger becomes professor of theology at Freising College.

1959   Ratzinger becomes a full professor of fundamental theology at the University of Bonn and begins lecturing there on April 15. His inaugural lecture is entitled "The God of Faith and the God of Philosophy."

On August 23, Ratzinger's father dies.

1962   Ratzinger goes to Rome with Cardinal Josef Frings of Cologne as a *peritus* (chief theological advisor) to the Second Vatican Council 1962–1965). He will be present for all four sessions of the council.

1963   Ratzinger begins teaching at the University of Münster.

On December 16, his mother dies.

1966   Ratzinger is appointed to a second chair in dogmatic theology at the University of Tübingen.

1968   Student revolutions sweep across the universities of Europe, sparking riots in April and May. At Tübingen the dominant intellectual mode is Marxist. Ratzinger is appalled by the brutal effects of this system on students and faculty alike. Scandalized by the subordination of religion to Marxist political ideology, Ratzinger determines to resist the abuse of the faith.

1969   Ratzinger accepts a position at the new University of Regensburg in Bavaria. He will soon become dean and then vice president. He is also theological advisor to the German bishops. His brother, George, is choirmaster of the chapel of the Cathedral of Regensburg.

From this year until 1980 he will be a member of the International Theological Commission of the Holy See.

1972   Ratzinger collaborates with Hans Urs von Balthasar, Henri de Lubac, Walter Kasper, and others to found the quarterly review of Catholic theology and culture, *Communio*. The journal is published in seventeen editions, including English, French, and Spanish.

1977   On March 24, Pope Paul VI (1897–1978) elects Ratzinger to be archbishop of Munich and Freising. He is ordained to the episcopal order on May 28 and takes as his motto "Co-worker of the Truth," from 3 John 8.

On June 27 he is elevated to cardinal with the titular church of St. Mary of Consolation. During his years as professor of theology, Ratzinger publishes a number of books (on eschatalogy, principles of theology, reason and revelation, tradition and revelation), but his new responsibilities interfere with his theological work.

1980   Pope John Paul II (1920–2005) names Ratzinger to chair the Synod on the Laity, then to head the Congregation for Catholic Education. He declines because he believes it is too soon to leave his post in Munich.

1981   Pope John Paul II, on November 25, appoints Ratzinger prefect for the Congregation for the Doctrine of the Faith. This makes him president of both the International Theological Commission and the Pontifical Biblical Commission.

1986   Ratzinger is made president of the Commission for Drafting the Catechism of the Catholic Church, which will take six years to complete.

1992   The Catechism of the Catholic Church is published.

1998   On November 6, Ratzinger is elected vice-dean of the College of Cardinals.

1999   Cardinal Ratzinger's sister, Maria, dies.

2002   On November 30, Pope John Paul II approves the election of Cardinal Ratzinger as dean of the College of Cardinals.

2005   Pope John Paul II dies on April 2. On Friday, April 8, Cardinal Ratzinger presides at the funeral Mass in St. Peter's Square for Pope John Paul II. On Tuesday, April 19, Cardinal Joseph Ratzinger is elected the 265th pontiff of the Roman Catholic Church. He takes the name Benedict XVI.

On May 13, Benedict XVI appoints William Joseph Levada, archbishop of San Francisco, his successor as prefect of the Congregation for the Doctrine of the Faith.

Benedict XVI's first encyclical, *Deus Caritas Est* (God Is Love), is published on December 25, the feast of the solemnity of the Nativity of the Lord.

Introduction to Christianity

Yesterday, Today, and Tomorrow

If God has truly assumed manhood,
then he participates, as man, in the presence
of God, which embraces all ages.

Since this work was first published, more than thirty years have passed, in which world history has moved along at a brisk pace. In retrospect, two years seem to be particularly important milestones in the final decades of the millennium that has just come to an end: 1968 and 1989. The year 1968 marked the rebellion of a new generation, which not only considered postwar reconstruction in Europe inadequate, full of injustice, full of selfishness and greed, but also viewed the entire course of history since the triumph of Christianity as a mistake and a failure. These young people wanted to improve things at last, to bring about freedom, equality, and justice, and they were convinced that they had found the way to this better world in the mainstream of Marxist thought. The year 1989 brought the surprising collapse of the socialist regimes in Europe, which left behind a sorry legacy of ruined land and ruined souls. Anyone who expected that the hour had come again for the Christian message was disappointed. Although the number of believing Christians throughout the world is not small, Christianity failed at that historical moment to make itself heard as an epoch-making alternative. Basically, the Marxist doctrine of salvation (in several differently orchestrated variations, of course) had taken a stand as the sole ethically motivated guide to the future that was at the same time consistent with a scientific worldview. Therefore, even after the shock of 1989, it did not simply abdicate. We need only to recall how little was said about the horrors of the Communist gulag, how isolated Solzhenitsyn's voice remained: no one speaks about any of that. A sort of shame forbids it; even

Pol Pot's murderous regime is mentioned only occasionally in passing. But there were still disappointment and a deep-seated perplexity.

People no longer trust grand moral promises, and after all, that is what Marxism had understood itself to be. It was about justice for all, about peace, about doing away with unfair master-servant relationships, and so on. Marxism believed that it had to dispense with ethical principles for the time being and that it was allowed to use terror as a beneficial means to these noble ends. Once the resulting human devastation became visible, even for a moment, the former ideologues preferred to retreat to a pragmatic position or else declared quite openly their contempt for ethics. We can observe a tragic example of this in Colombia, where a campaign was started, under the Marxist banner at first, to liberate the small farmers who had been downtrodden by the wealthy financiers.

Today, instead, a rebel republic has developed, beyond governmental control, which quite openly depends on drug trafficking and no longer seeks any moral justification for this, especially since it thereby satisfies a demand in wealthy nations and at the same time gives bread to people who would otherwise not be able to expect much of anything from the world economy. In such a perplexing situation, shouldn't Christianity try very seriously to rediscover its voice, so as to "introduce" the new millennium to its message, and to make it comprehensible as a general guide for the future?

Anyway, where was the voice of the Christian faith at that time? In 1967, when the book was being written, the fermentation of the early postconciliar period was in full swing. This is precisely what the Second Vatican Council had intended: to endow Christianity once more with the power to shape history. The nineteenth century had seen the formulation of the opinion that religion belonged to the subjective, private realm and should have its place there. But precisely because it was to be categorized as something subjective, it could not be a determining factor in the overall course of history and in the epochal decisions that must be made as part of it. Now, following the council, it was supposed to become evident again that the faith of Christians embraces all of life, that it stands in the midst of history and in time and has relevance beyond the realm of subjective notions. Christianity—at least from the viewpoint of the Catholic Church—was trying to emerge again from the ghetto to which it had been relegated since the nineteenth century and to become involved once more in the world at large. We do not need to discuss here the intra-ecclesiastical disputes and frictions that arose over the interpretation and assimilation of the council. The main thing affecting the status of Christianity in that period was the idea of a new relationship between the church and the world.

Although Romano Guardini in the 1930s had coined the expression, "*Unterscheidung des Christlichen*" (distinguishing what is Christian)—something that was extremely necessary then—such distinctions now no longer seemed to be important; on the contrary, the spirit of the age called for crossing boundaries, reaching out to the world, and becoming involved in it. It was already demonstrated upon the Parisian barricades in 1968 how quickly these ideas could emerge from the academic discussions of churchmen and find a very practical application: a revolutionary Eucharist was celebrated there, thus putting into practice a new fusion of the church and the world under the banner of the revolution that was supposed to bring, at last, the dawn of a better age. The leading role played by Catholic and Protestant student groups in the revolutionary upheavals at universities, both in Europe and beyond, confirmed this trend.

This new translation of ideas into practice, this new fusion of the Christian impulse with secular and political action, was like a lightning bolt; the real fires that it set, however, were in Latin America. The theology of liberation seemed for more than a decade to point the way by which the faith might again shape the world, because it was making common cause with the findings and worldly wisdom of the hour. No one could dispute the fact that there was in Latin America, to a horrifying extent, oppression, unjust rule, the concentration of property and power in the hands of a few, and the exploitation of the poor, and there was no disputing either that something had to be done. And since it was a question of countries with a Catholic majority, there could be no doubt that the church bore the responsibility here and that the faith had to prove itself as a force for justice. But how? Now Marx appeared to be the great guidebook. He was said to be playing now the role that had fallen to Aristotle in the thirteenth century; the latter's pre-Christian (that is, "pagan") philosophy had to be baptized, in order to bring faith and reason into the proper relation to one another. But anyone who accepts Marx (in whatever neo-Marxist variation he may choose) as the representative of worldly reason not only accepts a philosophy, a vision of the origin and meaning of existence, but also and especially adopts a practical program. For this "philosophy" is essentially a "praxis," which does not presuppose a "truth" but rather creates one. Anyone who makes Marx the philosopher of theology adopts the primacy of politics and economics, which now become the real powers that can bring about salvation (and, if misused, can wreak havoc). The redemption of mankind, to this way of thinking, occurs through politics and economics, in which the form of the future is determined. This primacy of praxis and politics meant, above all, that God could not be categorized as something "practical." The "reality" in which one had to get involved now was solely the material reality of given historical circumstances, which were to be viewed critically and reformed, redirected to the right goals by using the appropriate means, among which violence was indispensable. From this perspective, speaking about God belongs neither to the realm of the practical nor to that of reality. If it was to be indulged in at all, it would have to be postponed until the more important work had been done. What remained was the figure of Jesus, who of course no longer appeared now as the Christ, but rather as the embodiment of all the suffering and oppressed and as their spokesman, who calls us to rise up, to change society. What was new in all this was that the program of changing the world, which in Marx was intended to be not only atheistic but also antireligious, was now filled with religious passion and was based on religious principles: a new reading of the Bible (especially of the Old Testament) and a liturgy that was celebrated as a symbolic fulfillment of the revolution and as a preparation for it.

It must be admitted: by means of this remarkable synthesis, Christianity had stepped once more onto the world stage and had become an "epoch-making" message. It is no surprise that the socialist states took a stand in favor of this movement. More noteworthy is the fact that, even in the "capitalist" countries, liberation theology was the darling of public opinion; to contradict it was viewed positively as a sin against humanity and mankind, even though no one, naturally, wanted to see the practical measures applied in their own situation, because they, of course, had already arrived at a just social order. Now it cannot be denied that in the various liberation theologies there really were some worthwhile insights as well. All of these plans for an epoch-making synthesis of Christianity and the world had to step aside, however, the moment that that faith in politics as a salvific force collapsed. Man is, indeed, as Aristotle says, a "political being," but he cannot be reduced to politics and economics. I see the real and most profound problem with the liberation theologies in their effective omission of the idea of God, which, of course, also changed the figure of Christ fundamentally (as we have indicated). Not as though God had been denied—not on your life! It's just that he was not needed in regard to the "reality" that mankind had to deal with. God had nothing to do.

One is struck by this point and suddenly wonders: Was that the case only in liberation theology? Or was this theory able to arrive at such an assessment of the question about God—that the question was not a practical one for the long-overdue business of changing the world—only because the Christian world thought much the same thing, or rather, lived in much the same way, without reflecting on it or noticing it? Hasn't Christian consciousness acquiesced to a great extent—without being aware of it—in the attitude that faith in God is something subjective, which belongs in the private realm and not in the common activities of public life where, in order to be able to get along, we all have to behave now "*etsi Deus non daretur*" (as if there were no God)?

Wasn't it necessary to find a way that would be valid, in case it turned out that God doesn't exist? And indeed it happened automatically that when the faith stepped out of the inner sanctum of ecclesiastical matters into the general public, it had nothing for God to do and left him where he was: in the private realm, in the intimate sphere that doesn't concern anyone else. It didn't take any particular negligence, and certainly not a deliberate denial, to leave God as a God with nothing to do, especially since his name had been misused so often. But the faith would really have come out of the ghetto only if it had brought its most distinctive feature with it into the public arena: the God who judges and suffers; the God who sets limits and standards for us; the God from whom we come and to whom we are going. But as it was, it really remained in the ghetto, having by now absolutely nothing to do.

Yet God is "practical" and not just some theoretical conclusion of a consoling worldview that one may adhere to or simply disregard. We see that today in every place where the deliberate denial of him has become a matter of principle and where his absence is no longer mitigated at all. For at first, when God is left out of the picture, everything apparently goes on as before.

Mature decisions and the basic structures of life remain in place, even though they have lost their foundations. But, as Nietzsche describes it, once the news really reaches people that "God is dead," and they take it to heart, then everything changes. This is demonstrated today, on the one hand, in the way that science treats human life: man is becoming a technological object while vanishing to an ever-greater degree as a human subject, and he has only himself to blame. When human embryos are artificially "cultivated" so as to have "research material" and to obtain a supply of organs, which then are supposed to benefit other human beings, there is scarcely an outcry, because so few are horrified anymore. Progress demands all this, and they really are noble goals: improving the quality of life—at least for those who can afford to have recourse to such services. But if man, in his origin and at his very roots, is only an object to himself, if he is "produced" and comes off the production line with selected features and accessories, what on earth is man then supposed to think of man? How should he act toward him?

What will be man's attitude toward man, when he can no longer find anything of the divine mystery in the other, but only his own know-how? What is happening in the "high-tech" areas of science is reflected wherever the culture, broadly speaking, has managed to tear God out of men's hearts. Today there are places where trafficking in human beings goes on quite openly: a cynical consumption of humanity while society looks on helplessly. For example, organized crime constantly brings women out of Albania on various pretexts and delivers them to the mainland across the sea as prostitutes, and because there are enough cynics there waiting for such "wares," organized crime becomes more powerful, and those who try to put a stop to it discover that the hydra of evil keeps growing new heads, no matter how many they may cut off. And do we not see everywhere around us, in seemingly orderly neighborhoods, an increase in violence, which is taken more and more for granted and is becoming more and more reckless? I do not want to extend this horror-scenario any further. But we ought to wonder whether God might not in fact be the genuine reality, the basic prerequisite for any "realism," so that, without him, nothing is safe.

Let us return to the course of historical developments since 1967. The year 1989, as I was saying, brought with it no new answers, but rather deepened the general perplexity and nourished skepticism about great ideals. But something did happen. Religion became modern again. Its disappearance is no longer anticipated; on the contrary, various new forms of it are growing luxuriantly. In the leaden loneliness of a God-forsaken world, in its interior boredom, the search for mysticism, for any sort of contact with the divine, has sprung up anew. Everywhere there is talk about visions and messages from the other world, and wherever there is a report of an apparition, thousands travel there, in order to discover, perhaps, a crack in the world, through which heaven might look down on them and send them consolation. Some complain that this new search for religion, to a great extent, is passing the traditional Christian churches by. An institution is inconvenient, and dogma is bothersome. What is sought is an experience, an encounter with the Absolutely-Other. I cannot say that I am in unqualified agreement with this complaint. At the World Youth Days, such as the one recently in Paris, faith becomes experience and provides the joy of fellowship. Something of an ecstasy, in the good sense, is communicated. The dismal and destructive ecstasy of drugs, of hammering rhythms, noise, and drunkenness is confronted with a bright ecstasy of light, of joyful encounter in God's sunshine. Let it not be said that this is only a momentary thing. Often it is so, no doubt. But it can also be a moment that brings about a lasting change and begins a journey. Similar things happen in the many lay movements that have sprung up in the last few decades. Here, too, faith becomes a form of lived experience, the joy of setting out on a journey and of participating in the mystery of the leaven that permeates the whole mass from within and renews it. Eventually, provided that the root is sound, even apparition sites can be incentives to go again in search of God in a sober way. Anyone who expected that Christianity would now become a mass movement was, of course, disappointed. But mass movements are not the ones that bear the promise of the future within them. The future is made wherever people find their way to one another in life-shaping convictions. And a good future grows wherever these convictions come from the truth and lead to it.

The rediscovery of religion, however, has another side to it.

We have already seen that this trend looks for religion as an experience, that the "mystical" aspect of religion is an important part of it: religion that offers me contact with the Absolutely-Other. In our historical situation, this means that the mystical religions of Asia (parts of Hinduism and of Buddhism), with their renunciation of dogma and their minimal degree of institutionalization, appear to be more suitable for enlightened humanity than dogmatically determined and institutionally structured Christianity.

In general, however, the result is that individual religions are relativized; for all the differences and, yes, the contradictions among these various sorts of belief, the only thing that matters, ultimately, is the inside of all these different forms, the contact with the ineffable, with the hidden mystery. And to a great extent people agree that this mystery is not completely manifested in any one form of revelation, that it is always glimpsed in random and fragmentary ways and yet is always sought as one and the same thing. That we cannot know God himself, that everything which can be stated and described can only be a symbol: this is nothing short of a fundamental certainty for modern man, which he also understands somehow as his humility in the presence of the infinite.

Associated with this relativizing is the notion of a great peace among religions, which recognize each other as different ways of reflecting the One Eternal Being and which should leave up to the individual the path he will grope along to find the one who nevertheless unites them all. Through such a relativizing process, the Christian faith is radically changed, especially at two fundamental places in its essential message:

1. The figure of Christ is interpreted in a completely new way, not only in reference to dogma, but also and precisely with regard to the Gospels. The belief that Christ *is* the only Son of God, that God really dwells among us as man in him, and that the man Jesus is eternally in God, is God himself, and therefore is not a figure in which God appears, but rather the sole and irreplaceable God—this belief is thereby excluded. Instead of being the man who *is* God, Christ becomes the one who has *experienced* God in a special way. He is an enlightened one and therein is no longer fundamentally different from other enlightened individuals, for instance, Buddha. But in such an interpretation the figure of Jesus loses its inner logic. It is torn out of the historical setting in which it is anchored and forced into a scheme of things that is alien to it.

Buddha—and in this he is comparable to Socrates—directs the attention of his disciples away from himself: his own person doesn't matter, but only the path that he has pointed out. Someone who finds the way can forget Buddha. But with Jesus, what matters is precisely his Person, Christ himself. When he says, "I am he," we hear the tones of the "I AM" on Mount Horeb. The way consists precisely in following him, for "*I* am the way, the truth and the life" (Jn 14:6). He himself is the way, and there is no way that is independent of him, on which he would no longer matter. Since the real message that he brings is not a doctrine but his very Person, we must, of course, add that this "I" of Jesus refers absolutely to the "Thou" of the Father and is not self-sufficient, but rather is indeed truly a "way." "My teaching is not mine" (Jn 7:16). "I seek not my own will, but the will of him who sent me" (Jn 5:30). The "I" is important, because it draws us completely into the dynamic of mission, because it leads to the surpassing of self and to union with him by whom we have been created. If the figure of Jesus is taken out of this inevitably scandalous dimension, if it is separated from his godhead, then it becomes self-contradictory. All that is left are shreds that leave us perplexed or else become excuses for self-affirmation.

2. The concept of God is fundamentally changed. The question as to whether God should be thought of as a person or impersonally now seems to be of secondary importance; no longer can an essential difference be noted between theistic and nontheistic forms of religion. This view is spreading with astonishing rapidity. Even believing and theologically trained Catholics, who want to share in the responsibilities of the church's life, will ask the question (as though the answer were self-evident): "Can it really be that important, whether someone understands God as a person or impersonally?" After all, we should be broad-minded—so goes the opinion—since the mystery of God is in any case beyond all concepts and images. But such concessions strike at the heart of the biblical faith. The *Shema*, the "Hear, O Israel" from Deuteronomy 6:4–9, was and still is the real core of the believer's identity, not only for Israel, but also for Christianity. The believing Jew dies reciting this profession; the Jewish martyrs breathed their last declaring it and gave their lives for it: "Hear, O Israel. He is our God. He is one." The fact that this God now shows us his face in Jesus Christ (Jn 14:9)—a face that Moses was not allowed to see (Ex 33:20)—does not alter this profession in the least and changes nothing essential in this identity. Of course, the Bible does not use the term *person* to say that God is personal, but the divine personality is apparent nevertheless, inasmuch as there is a Name of God. A name implies the ability to be called on, to speak, to hear, to answer. This is essential for the biblical God, and if this is taken away, the faith of the Bible

has been abandoned. It cannot be disputed that there have been and there are false, superficial ways of understanding God as personal. Precisely when we apply the concept of person to God, the difference between our idea of person and the reality of God—as the Fourth Lateran council says about all speech concerning God—is always infinitely greater than what they have in common. False applications of the concept of person are sure to be present, whenever God is monopolized for one's own human interests and thus his Name is sullied. It is not by chance that the Second Commandment, which is supposed to protect the Name of God, follows directly after the first, which teaches us to adore him. In this respect we can always learn something new from the way in which the "mystical" religions, with their purely negative theology, speak about God, and in this respect there are avenues for dialogue. But with the disappearance of what is meant by "the Name of God," that is, God's personal nature, his Name is no longer protected and honored, but abandoned outright instead.

But what is actually meant, then, by God's Name, by his being personal? Precisely this: not only that we can experience him, beyond all [earthly] experience, but also that he can express and communicate himself. When God is understood in a completely impersonal way, for instance in Buddhism, as sheer negation with respect to everything that appears real to us, then there is no positive relationship between "God" and the world. Then the world has to be overcome as a source of suffering, but it no longer can be shaped. Religion then points out ways to overcome the world, to free people from the burden of its seeming, but it offers no standards by which we can live in the world, no forms of societal responsibility within it. The situation is somewhat different in Hinduism. The essential thing there is the experience of identity: at bottom I am one with the hidden ground of reality itself—the famous *tat tvam asi* of the Upanishads. Salvation consists in liberation from individuality, from being-a-person, in overcoming the differentiation from all other beings that is rooted in being-a-person: the deception of the self concerning itself must be put aside. The problem with this view of being has come very much to the fore in neo-Hinduism. Where there is no uniqueness of persons, the inviolable dignity of each individual person has no foundation, either. In order to bring about the reforms that are now under way (the abolition of caste laws and of immolating widows, etc.), it was specifically necessary to break with this fundamental understanding and to introduce into the overall system of Indian thought the concept of person, as it has developed in the Christian faith out of the encounter with the personal God. The search for the correct "praxis," for right action, in this case has begun to correct the "theory": we can see to some extent how "practical" the Christian belief in God is, and how unfair it is to brush these disputed but important distinctions aside as being ultimately irrelevant.

With these considerations we have reached the point from which an "Introduction to Christianity" must set out today. Before I attempt to extend a bit farther the line of argument that I have suggested, another reference to the present status of faith in God and in Christ is called for. There is a fear of Christian "imperialism," a nostalgia for the beautiful multiplicity of religions and their supposedly primordial cheerfulness and freedom. Colonialism is said to be essentially bound up with historical Christianity, which was unwilling to accept the other in his otherness and tried to bring everything under its own protection. Thus, according to this view, the religions and cultures of South America were trodden down and stamped out and violence was done to the soul of the native peoples, who could not find themselves in the new order and were forcibly deprived of the old. Now there are milder and harsher variants of this opinion. The milder version says that we should finally grant to these lost cultures the right of domicile within the Christian faith and allow them to devise for themselves an aboriginal form of Christianity. The more radical view regards Christianity in its entirety as a sort of alienation, from which the native peoples must be liberated. The demand for an aboriginal Christianity, properly understood, should be taken as an extremely important task. All great cultures are open to one another and to the truth. They all have something to contribute to the Bride's "many-colored robes" mentioned in Psalm 45:14, which patristic writers applied to the church. To be sure, many opportunities have been missed and new ones present themselves. Let us not forget, however, that those native peoples, to a notable extent, have already found their own expression of the Christian faith in popular devotions. That the suffering God and the kindly Mother in particular have become for them the central images of the faith, which have given them access to the God of the Bible, has something to say to us, too, today. But, of course, much still remains to be done.

Let us return to the question about God and about Christ as the centerpiece of an introduction to the Christian faith. One thing has already become evident: the mystical dimension of the concept of God, which the Asian religions bring with them as a challenge to us, must clearly be decisive for our thinking, too, and for our faith. God has become quite concrete in Christ, but in this way his mystery has also become still greater. God is always infinitely greater than all our concepts and all our images and names. The fact that we now acknowledge him to be triune does not mean that we have meanwhile learned everything about him. On the contrary: he is only showing us how little we know about him and how little we can comprehend him or even begin to take his measure. Today, after the horrors of the [twentieth-century] totalitarian regimes (I remind the reader of the memorial at Auschwitz), the problem of theodicy urgently and mightily [*mit brennender Gewalt*] demands the attention of us all; this is just one more indication of how little we are capable of defining God, much less fathoming him. After all, God's answer to Job explains nothing, but rather sets boundaries to our mania for judging everything and being able to say the final word on a subject, and reminds us of our limitations. It admonishes us to trust the mystery of God in its incomprehensibility. Having said this, we must still emphasize the brightness of God, too, along with the darkness. Ever since the Prologue to the Gospel of John, the concept of Logos has been at the very center of our Christian faith in God. Logos signifies reason, meaning, or even "word"—a meaning, therefore, which is Word, which is relationship, which is creative. The God who is Logos guarantees the intelligibility of the world, the intelligibility of our existence, reason's accord with God, and God's accord with reason, even though his understanding infinitely surpasses ours and to us may so often appear to be darkness. The world comes from reason and this reason is a Person, is Love—this is what our biblical faith tells us about God. Reason can speak about God, it must speak about God, or else it cuts itself short. Included in this is the concept of creation.

The world is not just *maya*, appearance, which we must ultimately leave behind. It is not merely the endless wheel of sufferings, from which we must try to escape. It is something positive. It is good, despite all the evil in it and despite all the sorrow, and it is good to live in it. God, who is the creator and declares himself in his creation, also gives direction and measure to human action. We are living today in a crisis of moral values [*Ethos*], which by now is no longer merely an academic question about the ultimate foundations of ethical theories, but rather an entirely practical matter. The news is getting around that moral values cannot be grounded in something else, and the consequences of this view are working themselves out. The published works on the theme of moral values are stacked high and almost toppling over, which on the one hand indicates the urgency of the question, but on the other hand also suggests the prevailing perplexity. Kolakowski, in his line of thinking, has very emphatically pointed out that deleting faith in God, however one may try to spin or turn it, ultimately deprives moral values of their grounding. If the world and man do not come from a creative intelligence, which stores within itself their measure and plots the path of human existence, then all that is left are traffic rules for human behavior, which can be discarded or maintained according to their usefulness. All that remains is the calculus of consequences—what is called teleological ethics or proportionalism.

But who can really make a judgment beyond the consequences of the present moment? Won't a new ruling class, then, take hold of the keys to human existence and become the managers of mankind? When dealing with a calculus of consequences, the inviolability of human dignity no longer exists, because nothing is good or bad in itself any more. The problem of moral values is back on the table today, and it is an item of great urgency. Faith in the Logos, the Word that is in the beginning, understands moral values as *responsibility*, as a response to the Word, and thus gives them their intelligibility as well as their essential orientation. Connected with this also is the task of searching for a common understanding of responsibility, together with all honest, rational inquiry and with the great religious traditions. In this endeavor there is not only the intrinsic proximity of the three great monotheistic religions, but also significant lines of convergence with the other strand of Asian religiosity we encounter in Confucianism and Taoism.

If it is true that the term *Logos*—the Word in the beginning, creative reason, and love—is decisive for the Christian image of God, and if the concept of Logos simultaneously forms the core of Christology, of faith in Christ, then the indivisibility of faith in God and faith in his incarnate Son, Jesus Christ, is only confirmed once more. We will not understand Jesus any better or come any closer to him, if we bracket off faith in his divinity. The fear that belief in his divinity might alienate him from us is widespread today. It is not only for the sake of the other religions that some would like to de-emphasize this faith as much as possible. It is first and foremost a question of our own Western fears. All of this seems incompatible with our modern worldview. It must just be a question of mythological interpretations, which were then transformed by the Greek mentality into metaphysics. But when we separate Christ and God, behind this effort there is also a doubt as to whether God is at all capable of being so close to us, whether he is allowed to bow down so low. The fact that we don't want this appears to be humility. But Romano Guardini correctly pointed out that the higher form of humility consists in allowing God to do precisely what appears to us to be unfitting, and to bow down to what he does, not to what we contrive about him and for him. A notion of God's remoteness from the world is behind our apparently humble realism, and therefore a loss of God's presence is also connected with it. If God is not in Christ, then he retreats into an immeasurable distance, and if God is no longer a God-with-us, then he is plainly an absent God and thus no God at all: a god who cannot work is not God. As for the fear that Jesus moves us too far away if we believe in his Divine Sonship, precisely the opposite is true: were he only a man, then he has retreated irrevocably into the past, and only a distant recollection can perceive him more or less clearly. But if God has truly assumed manhood and thus is at the same time true man and true God in Jesus, then he participates, as man, in the presence of God, which embraces all ages. Then, and only then, is he not just something that happened yesterday but present among us, our contemporary in our today. That is why I am firmly convinced that a renewal of Christology must have the courage to see Christ in all of his greatness, as he is presented by the four Gospels together in the many tensions of their unity.

If I had this *Introduction to Christianity* to write over again today, all of the experiences of the last thirty years would have to go into the text, which would then also have to include the context of interreligious discussions to a much greater degree than seemed fitting at the time. But I believe that I was not mistaken as to the fundamental approach, in that I put the question of God and the question about Christ in the very center, which then leads to a "narrative Christology" and demonstrates that the place for faith is in the church. This basic orientation, I think, was correct. That is why I venture to place this book once more in the hands of the reader today.

PART ONE

SERMONS AND ADDRESSES

Homily at John Paul II's Funeral Mass

APRIL 8, 2005

"Follow me." The Risen Lord says these words to Peter. They are his last words to this disciple, chosen to shepherd his flock. "Follow me"—this lapidary saying of Christ can be taken as the key to understanding the message that comes to us from the life of our late beloved Pope John Paul II. Today we bury his remains in the earth as a seed of immortality; our hearts are full of sadness, yet at the same time of joyful hope and profound gratitude.

These are the sentiments that inspire us, brothers and sisters in Christ, present here in St. Peter's Square, in neighboring streets and in various other locations within the city of Rome, where an immense crowd, silently praying, has gathered over the last few days. I greet all of you from my heart. In the name of the College of Cardinals, I also wish to express my respects to the heads of state, the heads of government, and the delegations from various countries.

I greet the authorities and official representatives of other churches and Christian communities, and likewise those of different religions. Next I greet the archbishops, bishops, priests, religious men and women, and the faithful who have come here from every continent, especially the young, whom John Paul II liked to call the future and the hope of the church. My greeting is extended, moreover, to all those throughout the world who are united with us through radio and television in this solemn celebration of our beloved Holy Father's funeral.

Follow me. As a young student Karol Wojtyla was thrilled by literature, the theater, and poetry. Working in a chemical plant, surrounded and threatened by the Nazi terror, he heard the voice of the Lord: "Follow me!" In this extraordinary setting he began to read books of philosophy and theology, and then entered the clandestine seminary established by Cardinal Sapieha. After the war he was able to complete his studies in the faculty of theology of the Jagiellonian University of Krakow.

How often, in his letters to priests and in his autobiographical books, has he spoken to us about his priesthood, to which he was ordained on November 1, 1946. In these texts he interprets his priesthood with particular reference to three sayings of the Lord.

First: "It was not you who chose me, but I who chose you and appointed you to go and bear fruit that will remain" (Jn 15:16). The second saying is: "A good shepherd lays down his life for the sheep" (Jn 10:11). And then: "As the Father loves me, so I also love you. Remain in my love" (Jn 15:9). In these three sayings we see the heart and soul of our Holy Father. He really went everywhere, untiringly, in order to bear fruit, fruit that lasts.

Rise, Let Us Be on Our Way! is the title of his next-to-last book. "Rise, let us be on our way!"—with these words he roused us from a lethargic faith, from the sleep of the disciples of both yesterday and today. "Rise, let us be on our way!" he continues to say to us even today. The Holy Father was a priest to the last, for he offered his life to God for his flock and for the entire human family, in a daily self-oblation for the service of the church, especially amid the sufferings of his final months. And in this way he became one with Christ, the Good Shepherd who loves his sheep.

Finally, "abide in my love": the pope who tried to meet everyone, who had an ability to forgive and to open his heart to all, tells us once again today, with these words of the Lord, that by abiding in the love of Christ we learn, at the school of Christ, the art of true love. Follow me! In July 1958, the young priest Karol Wojtyla began a new stage in his journey with the Lord and in the footsteps of the Lord. Karol had gone to the Masuri lakes for his usual vacation, along with a group of young people who loved canoeing. But he brought with him a letter inviting him to call on the primate of Poland, Cardinal Wyszynski. He could guess the purpose of the meeting: he was to be appointed the auxiliary bishop of Krakow.

Leaving the academic world, leaving this challenging engagement with young people, leaving the great intellectual endeavor of striving to understand and interpret the mystery of that creature which is man and of communicating to today's world the Christian interpretation of our being—all this must have seemed to him like losing his very self, losing what had become the very human identity of this young priest. Follow me—Karol Wojtyla accepted the appointment, for he heard in the church's call the voice of Christ. And then he realized how true are the Lord's words: "Whoever seeks to preserve his life will lose it, but whoever loses it will save it" (Lk 17:33).

Our pope—and we all know this—never wanted to make his own life secure, to keep it for himself; he wanted to give of himself unreservedly, to the very last moment, for Christ and thus also for us. And thus he came to experience how everything that he had given over into the Lord's hands came back to him in a new way. His love of words, of poetry, of literature became an essential part of his pastoral mission and gave new vitality, new urgency, new attractiveness to the preaching of the gospel, even when it is a sign of contradiction.

Follow me! In October 1978, Cardinal Wojtyla once again heard the voice of the Lord. Once more there took place that dialogue with Peter reported in the Gospel of this Mass: "Simon, son of John, do you love me? Feed my sheep!" To the Lord's question, "Karol, do you love me?" the archbishop of Krakow answered from the depths of his heart: "Lord, you know everything; you know that I love you." The love of Christ was the dominant force in the life of our beloved Holy Father. Anyone who ever saw him pray, who ever heard him preach, knows that. Because he was profoundly rooted in Christ, he was able to bear a burden that transcends merely human abilities: that of being the shepherd of Christ's flock, his universal church.

This is not the time to speak of the specific content of this rich pontificate. I would like only to read two passages of today's liturgy which reflect central elements of his message. In the first reading, St. Peter says—and with St. Peter, the pope himself—"In truth, I see that God shows no partiality. Rather, in every nation whoever fears him and acts uprightly is acceptable to him. You know the word he sent to the Israelites as he proclaimed peace through Jesus Christ, who is Lord of all" (Acts 10:34–36). And in the second reading, St. Paul—and with St. Paul, our late pope—exhorts us, crying out: "Therefore, my brothers, whom I love and long for, my joy and crown, in this way stand firm in the Lord, beloved" (Phil 4:1).

Follow me! Together with the command to feed his flock, Christ proclaimed to Peter that he would die a martyr's death. With those words, which conclude and sum up the dialogue on love and on the mandate of the universal shepherd, the Lord recalls another dialogue, which took place during the Last Supper. There Jesus had said: "Where I am going, you cannot come." Peter said to him, "Lord, where are you going?" Jesus replied: "Where I am going, you cannot follow me now; but you will follow me afterward" (Jn 13:33, 13:36). Jesus from the supper went toward the cross, went toward his Resurrection— he entered into the paschal mystery—and Peter could not yet follow him. Now—after the Resurrection—comes the time, comes this "afterward."

By shepherding the flock of Christ, Peter enters into the paschal mystery; he goes toward the cross and the Resurrection. The Lord says this in these words: "When you were younger, you used to dress yourself and go where you wanted; but when you grow old, you will stretch out your hands, and someone else will dress you and lead you where you do not want to go" (Jn 21:18).

In the first years of his pontificate, still young and full of energy, the Holy Father went to the very ends of the earth, guided by Christ. But afterward, he increasingly entered into the communion of Christ's sufferings; increasingly he understood the truth of the words: "Someone else will dress you." And in this very communion with the suffering Lord, tirelessly and with renewed intensity, he proclaimed the gospel, the mystery of that love which goes to the end (cf. Jn 13:1).

He interpreted for us the paschal mystery as a mystery of divine mercy. In his last book, he wrote that the limit imposed upon evil "is ultimately Divine Mercy" (*Memory and Identity,* pp. 60–61). And reflecting on the assassination attempt, he said: "In sacrificing himself for us all, Christ gave a new meaning to suffering, opening up a new dimension, a new order: the order of love.... It is this suffering which burns and consumes evil with the flame of love and draws forth even from sin a great flowering of good" (pp. 189–90). Impelled by this vision, the pope suffered and loved in communion with Christ, and that is why the message of his suffering and his silence proved so eloquent and so fruitful.

Divine Mercy: the Holy Father found the purest reflection of God's mercy in the Mother of God. He, who at an early age had lost his own mother, loved his divine mother all the more. He heard the words of the crucified Lord as addressed personally to him: "Behold your Mother." And so he did as the beloved disciple did: "He took her into his own home" (Jn 19:27)—"*Totus tuus.*" And from the Mother he learned to conform himself to Christ.

None of us can ever forget how in that last Easter Sunday of his life, the Holy Father, marked by suffering, came once more to the window of the Apostolic Palace and one last time gave his blessing "*Urbi et Orbi.*" We can be sure that our beloved pope is standing today at the window of the Father's house, that he sees us and blesses us. Yes, bless us, Holy Father. We entrust your dear soul to the Mother of God, your Mother, who guided you each day and who will guide you now to the eternal glory of her Son, our Lord Jesus Christ. Amen.

Homily at the Mass for the Election of the Roman Pontiff

ST. PETER'S BASILICA, APRIL 18, 2005

At this hour of great responsibility, we hear with special consideration what the Lord says to us in his own words. From the three readings I would like to examine just a few passages that concern us directly at this time.

The first reading gives us a prophetic depiction of the person of the Messiah, a depiction that takes all its meaning from the moment Jesus reads the text in the synagogue in Nazareth, when he says: "Today this scripture passage is fulfilled in your hearing" (Lk 4:21). At the core of the prophetic text we find a word that seems contradictory, at least at first sight. The Messiah, speaking of himself, says that he was sent "to announce a year of favor from the LORD and a day of vindication by our God" (Is 61:2). We hear with joy the news of a year of favor: divine mercy puts a limit on evil, the Holy Father told us. Jesus Christ is divine mercy in person; encountering Christ means encountering the mercy of God. Christ's mandate has become our mandate through priestly anointing. We are called to proclaim not only with our words but with our lives, and through the valuable signs of the sacraments, the "year of favor from the Lord." But what does the prophet Isaiah mean when he announces the "day of vindication by our God"? In Nazareth, Jesus did not pronounce these words in his reading of the prophet's text. Jesus concluded by announcing the year of favor. Was this, perhaps, the reason for the scandal that took place after his sermon? We do not know. In any case, the Lord gave a genuine commentary on these words by being put to death on the cross. St. Peter says: "He himself bore our sins in his body upon the cross" (1 Pt 2:24). And St. Paul writes in his letter to the Galatians: "Christ ransomed us from the curse of the law by becoming a curse for us, for it is written, 'Cursed be everyone who hangs on a tree,' that the blessing of Abraham might be extended to the Gentiles through Christ Jesus, so that we might receive the promise of the Spirit through faith" (Gal 3:13–14).

The mercy of Christ is not a cheap grace; it does not presume a trivialization of evil. Christ carries in his body and on his soul all the weight of evil, and all its destructive force. He burns and transforms evil through suffering, in the fire of his suffering love. The day of vindication and the year of favor meet in the paschal mystery, in Christ dead and risen. This is the vindication of God: he himself, in the Person of the Son, suffers for us. The more we are touched by the mercy of the Lord, the more we draw closer in solidarity with his suffering and become willing to bear in our flesh "what is lacking in the afflictions of Christ" (Col 1:24).

In the second reading, the letter to the Ephesians, we see basically three aspects: first, the ministries and charisms in the church, as gifts of the Lord risen and ascended into heaven. Then there is the maturing of faith and knowledge of the Son of God, as a condition and essence of unity in the body of Christ. Finally, there is the common participation in the growth of the body of Christ—of the transformation of the world into communion with the Lord.

Let us dwell on only two points. The first is the journey toward "the maturity of Christ" as it is said in the Italian text, simplifying it a bit. More precisely, according to the Greek text, we should speak of the "measure of the fullness of Christ," to which we are called to reach in order to be true adults in the faith. We should not remain infants in faith, in a state of minority. And what does it mean to be an infant in faith? St. Paul answers: it means "tossed by waves and swept along by every wind of teaching arising from human trickery" (Eph 4:14). This description is very relevant today!

How many winds of doctrine we have known in recent decades, how many ideological currents, how many ways of thinking? The small boat of thought of many Christians has often been tossed about by these waves, thrown from one extreme to the other: from Marxism to liberalism, even to libertinism; from collectivism to radical individualism; from atheism to a vague religious mysticism; from agnosticism to syncretism; and so forth. Every day new sects are created and what St. Paul says about human trickery comes true, with cunning that tries to draw those into error (cf. Eph 4:14). Having a clear faith, based on the Creed of the Church, is often labeled today as a fundamentalism. Whereas relativism, which is letting oneself be tossed and "swept along by every wind of teaching," looks like the only attitude (acceptable) to today's standards. We are moving toward a dictatorship of relativism, which does not recognize anything as certain and which has as its highest goal one's own ego and one's own desires.

However, we have a different goal: the Son of God, true man. He is the measure of true humanism. Being an "adult" means having a faith that does not follow the waves of today's fashions or the latest novelties. A faith that is deeply rooted in friendship with Christ is adult and mature. It is this friendship that opens us up to all that is good and gives us the knowledge to judge true from false, and deceit from truth. We must become mature in this adult faith; we must guide the flock of Christ to this faith. And it is this faith—only faith—that creates unity and takes form in love. On this theme, St. Paul offers us some beautiful words—in contrast to the continual ups and downs of those who are like infants, tossed about by the waves: (he says) make truth in love, as the basic formula of Christian existence. In Christ, truth and love coincide. To the extent that we draw near to Christ in our own life, truth and love merge. Love without truth would be blind; truth without love would be like "a resounding gong or a clashing cymbal" (1 Cor 13:1).

Looking now at the richness of the Gospel reading, I would like to make only two small observations. The Lord addresses to us these wonderful words: "I no longer call you slaves, I have called you friends" (Jn 15:15). So many times we feel like, and it is true, we are only useless servants (cf. Lk 17:10). And despite this, the Lord calls us friends, he makes us his friends, he gives us his friendship. The Lord defines friendship in a dual way. There are no secrets among friends: Christ tells us all everything he hears from the Father; he gives us his full trust, and with that also knowledge. He reveals his face and his heart to us. He shows us his tenderness for us, his passionate love, which goes to the madness of the cross. He entrusts us, he gives us power to speak in his name: "This is my body"; "I forgive you." He entrusts us with his body, the church. He entrusts our weak minds and our weak hands with his truth: the mystery of God the Father, Son, and Holy Spirit; the mystery of God who "so loved the world that he gave his only begotten Son" (Jn 3:16). He made us his friends— and how do we respond?

The second element with which Jesus defines friendship is the communion of wills. For the Romans "*idem velle idem nolle*" (same desires, same dislikes) was also the definition of friendship. "You are my friends if you do what I command you" (Jn 15:14). Friendship with Christ coincides with what is said in the third request of the Our Father: "Thy will be done on earth as it is in heaven." At the hour in the Garden of Gethsemane, Jesus transformed our rebellious human will into a will shaped and united to the divine will. He suffered the whole experience of our autonomy, and precisely bringing our will into the hands of God, he gave us true freedom: "Not my will, but your will be done." In this communion of wills our redemption takes place: being friends of Jesus to become friends of God. How much more we love Jesus, how much more we know him, how much more our true freedom grows, as well as our joy in being redeemed. Thank you, Jesus, for your friendship!

The other element of the gospel to which I would like to refer is the teaching of Jesus on bearing fruit: "I who chose you and appointed you to go and bear fruit that will remain" (Jn 15:16). It is here that is expressed the dynamic existence of the Christian, the apostle: "I chose you to go and bear fruit." We must be inspired by a holy restlessness: restlessness to bring to everyone the gift of faith, of friendship with Christ. In truth, the love and friendship of God was given to us so that it would also be shared with others. We have received the faith to give it to others; we are priests meant to serve others. And we must bring a fruit that will remain. All people want to leave a mark that lasts. But what remains? Money does not. Buildings do not, nor books. After a certain amount of time, whether long or short, all these things disappear. The only thing that remains forever is the human soul, the human person created by God for eternity. The fruit that remains, then, is that which we have sowed in human souls: love, knowledge, a gesture capable of touching the heart, words that open the soul to joy in the Lord. Let us, then, go to the Lord and pray to him, so that he may help us bear fruit that remains. Only in this way will the earth be changed from a valley of tears to a garden of God.

In conclusion, let us return to the letter to the Ephesians, which says with words from Psalm 68 that Christ, ascending into heaven, "gave gifts to men" (Eph 4:8). The victor offers gifts. And these gifts are apostles, prophets, evangelists, pastors, and teachers. Our ministry is a gift of Christ to humankind, to build up his body: the new world. We live out our ministry in this way, as a gift of Christ to humanity! But at this time, above all, we pray with insistence to the Lord, so that after the great gift of Pope John Paul II, he will again give us a pastor according to his own heart, a pastor who guides us to knowledge in Christ, to his love and to true joy. Amen.

4

First Homily of His Holiness Benedict XVI at the End of the Eucharistic Concelebration with the Cardinal Electors in the Sistine Chapel

APRIL 20, 2005

Grace and peace in abundance to all of you! In my soul there are two contrasting sentiments in these hours. On the one hand, a sense of inadequacy and human turmoil for the responsibility entrusted to me yesterday as the Successor of the Apostle Peter in this See of Rome, with regard to the universal church. On the other hand, I sense within me profound gratitude to God, who—as the liturgy makes us sing—does not abandon his flock, but leads it throughout time, under the guidance of those whom he has chosen as vicars of his Son, and made pastors.

Dear ones, this intimate recognition for a gift of divine mercy prevails in my heart in spite of everything. I consider this a grace obtained for me by my venerated predecessor, John Paul II. It seems I can feel his strong hand squeezing mine; I seem to see his smiling eyes and listen to his words, addressed to me especially at this moment: "Do not be afraid!"

The death of the Holy Father John Paul II and the days that followed were for the church and for the entire world an extraordinary time of grace. The great pain over his death and the void that it left in all of us were tempered by the action of the Risen Christ, which showed itself during long days in the choral wave of faith, love, and spiritual solidarity, culminating in his solemn funeral.

We can say it: the funeral of John Paul II was a truly extraordinary experience in which was perceived in some way the power of God, who, through his church, wishes to form a great family of all peoples, through the unifying force of Truth and Love. In the hour of death, conformed to his Master and Lord, John Paul II crowned his long and fruitful pontificate, confirming the Christian people in faith, gathering them around him and making the entire human family feel more united.

How can one not feel sustained by this witness? How can one not feel the encouragement that comes from this event of grace?

Surprising every prevision I had, Divine Providence, through the will of the venerable cardinal fathers, called me to succeed this great pope. I have been thinking in these hours about what happened in the region of Cesarea of Philippi two thousand years ago: I seem to hear the words of Peter: "You are Christ, the Son of the living God," and the solemn affirmation of the Lord: "You are Peter and on this rock I will build my church.... I will give you the keys of the kingdom of heaven."

You are Christ! You are Peter! It seems I am reliving this very Gospel scene; I, the Successor of Peter, repeat with trepidation the anxious words of the fisherman from Galilee, and I listen again with intimate emotion to the reassuring promise of the divine Master. If the weight of the responsibility that now lies on my poor shoulders is enormous, the divine power on which I can count is surely immeasurable: "You are Peter and on this rock I will build my church." Electing me as the Bishop of Rome, the Lord wanted me as his vicar, he wished me to be the "rock" upon which everyone may rest with confidence. I ask him to make up for the poverty of my strength, that I may be a courageous and faithful pastor of his flock, always docile to the inspirations of his Spirit.

I undertake this special ministry, the Petrine ministry at the service of the universal church, with humble abandon to the hands of the Providence of God. And it is to Christ in the first place that I renew my total and trustworthy adhesion: "*In te, Domine, speravi; non confundar in aeternum!*"

To you, Lord Cardinals, with a grateful soul for the trust shown me, I ask you to sustain me with prayer and with constant, active, and wise collaboration. I also ask my brothers in the episcopacy to be close to me in prayer and counsel so that I may truly be the "*servus servorum Dei*" (servant of the servants of God). As Peter and the other apostles were, through the will of the Lord, one apostolic college, in the same way the Successor of Peter and the bishops, successors of the apostles—and the council forcefully repeated this— must be closely united among themselves. This collegial communion, even in the diversity of roles and functions of the Supreme Pontiff and the bishops, is at the service of the church and the unity of faith, on which depends in a notable measure the effectiveness of the evangelizing action of the contemporary world. Thus, this path, upon which my venerated predecessors went forward,

I, too, intend to follow, concerned solely with proclaiming to the world the living presence of Christ.

Before my eyes is, in particular, the witness of Pope John Paul II. He leaves us a church that is more courageous, freer, younger. A church that, according to his teaching and example, looks with serenity to the past and is not afraid of the future. With the Great Jubilee, the church was introduced into the new millennium carrying in her hands the gospel, applied to the world through the authoritative rereading of Vatican Council II. Pope John Paul II justly indicated the council as a "compass" with which to orient ourselves in the vast ocean of the third millennium. Also in his spiritual testament he noted: "I am convinced that for a very long time the new generations will draw upon the riches that this council of the twentieth century gave us."

I, too, as I start in the service that is proper to the Successor of Peter, wish to affirm with force my decided will to pursue the commitment to enact Vatican Council II, in the wake of my predecessors and in faithful continuity with the millennia-old tradition of the church. Precisely this year is the fortieth anniversary of the conclusion of this conciliar assembly (December 8, 1965). With the passing of time, the conciliar documents have not lost their timeliness; their teachings have shown themselves to be especially pertinent to the new exigencies of the church and the present globalized society.

In a very significant way, my pontificate starts as the church is living the special year dedicated to the Eucharist. How can I not see in this providential coincidence an element that must mark the ministry to which I have been called? The Eucharist, the heart of Christian life and the source of the evangelizing mission of the church, cannot but be the permanent center and the source of the Petrine service entrusted to me.

The Eucharist makes the Risen Christ constantly present, Christ who continues to give himself to us, calling us to participate in the banquet of his body and his blood. From this full communion with him comes every other element of the life of the church, in the first place the communion among the faithful, the commitment to proclaim and give witness to the gospel, the ardor of charity toward all, especially toward the poor and the smallest.

In this year, therefore, the Solemnity of Corpus Christi must be celebrated in a particularly special way. The Eucharist will be at the center, in August, of World Youth Day in Cologne and, in October, of the ordinary Assembly of the Synod of Bishops, which will take place on the theme "The Eucharist, Source and Summit of the Life and Mission of the Church." I ask everyone to intensify in coming months love and devotion to the eucharistic Jesus and to express in a courageous and clear way the real presence of the Lord, above all through the solemnity and the correctness of the celebrations.

I ask this in a special way of priests, about whom I am thinking in this moment with great affection. The priestly ministry was born in the Cenacle, together with the Eucharist, as my venerated predecessor John Paul II under-lined so many times. "The priestly life must have in a special way a 'eucharistic form,'" he wrote in his last Letter for Holy Thursday. The devout daily celebra-tion of Holy Mass, the center of the life and mission of every priest, contrib-utes to this end.

Nourished and sustained by the Eucharist, Catholics cannot but feel stimu-lated to tend toward that full unity for which Christ hoped in the Cenacle. Peter's Successor knows that he must take on this supreme desire of the Divine Master in a particularly special way. To him, indeed, has been entrusted the duty of strengthening his brethren.

Thus, in full awareness and at the beginning of his ministry in the church of Rome that Peter bathed with his blood, the current successor assumes as his primary commitment that of working tirelessly toward the reconstitution of the full and visible unity of all Christ's followers. This is his ambition, this is his compelling duty. He is aware that to do so, expressions of good feelings are not enough. Concrete gestures are required to penetrate souls and move consciences, encouraging everyone to that interior conversion which is the basis for all progress on the road of ecumenism.

Theological dialogue is necessary. A profound examination of the histori-cal reasons behind past choices is also indispensable. But even more urgent is that "purification of memory," which was so often evoked by John Paul II and which alone can dispose souls to welcome the full truth of Christ. It is before him, supreme Judge of all living things, that each of us must stand, in the awareness that one day we must explain to him what we did and what we did not do for the great good that is the full and visible unity of all his disciples.

The current Successor of Peter feels himself to be personally implicated in this question and is disposed to do all in his power to promote the fundamen-tal cause of ecumenism. In the wake of his predecessors, he is fully determined to cultivate any initiative that may seem appropriate to promote contact and agreement with representatives from the various churches and ecclesial com-munities. Indeed, on this occasion, too, he sends them his most cordial greet-ings in Christ, the one Lord of all.

In this moment, I go back in my memory to the unforgettable experience we all underwent with the death and funeral of the lamented John Paul II. Around his mortal remains, lying on the bare earth, leaders of nations gath-ered, with people from all social classes and especially the young, in an unfor-gettable embrace of affection and admiration. The entire world looked to him with trust. To many it seemed as if that intense participation, amplified to the confines of the planet by the social communications media, was like a choral request for help addressed to the pope by modern humanity, which, wracked by fear and uncertainty, questions itself about the future.

The church today must revive within herself an awareness of the task to present the world again with the voice of the one who said: "I am the light of the world; he who follows me will not walk in darkness but will have the light of life." In undertaking his ministry, the new pope knows that his task is to bring the light of Christ to shine before the men and women of today: not his own light but that of Christ.

With this awareness, I address myself to everyone, even to those who follow other religions or who are simply seeking an answer to the fundamental questions of life and have not yet found it. I address everyone with simplicity and affection, to assure them that the church wants to continue to build an open and sincere dialogue with them, in a search for the true good of mankind and of society.

From God I invoke unity and peace for the human family and declare the willingness of all Catholics to cooperate for true social development, one that respects the dignity of all human beings.

I will make every effort and dedicate myself to pursuing the promising dialogue that my predecessors began with various civilizations, because it is mutual understanding that gives rise to conditions for a better future for everyone.

I am particularly thinking of young people. To them, the privileged interlocutors of John Paul II, I send an affectionate embrace in the hope, God willing, of meeting them at Cologne on the occasion of the next World Youth Day. With you, dear young people, I will continue to maintain a dialogue, listening to your expectations in an attempt to help you meet ever more profoundly the living, ever young Christ.

"*Mane nobiscum, Domine!*" Stay with us, Lord! This invocation, which forms the dominant theme of John Paul II's Apostolic Letter for the Year of the Eucharist, is the prayer that comes spontaneously from my heart as I turn to begin the ministry to which Christ has called me. Like Peter, I, too, renew to him my unconditional promise of faithfulness. He alone I intend to serve as I dedicate myself totally to the service of his church.

In support of this promise, I invoke the maternal intercession of Mary Most Holy, in whose hands I place the present and the future of my person and of the church. May the Holy Apostles Peter and Paul and all the saints also intercede.

With these sentiments I impart to you, venerated Brother Cardinals, to those participating in this ritual, and to all those following to us by television and radio a special and affectionate blessing.

5

Homily of His Holiness Benedict XVI at the Mass of Inauguration of His Pontificate

ST. PETER'S SQUARE, SUNDAY, APRIL 24, 2005

Your Eminences,

My dear Brother Bishops and Priests,

Distinguished Authorities and Members of the Diplomatic Corps,

Dear Brothers and Sisters,

During these days of great intensity, we have chanted the litany of the saints on three different occasions: at the funeral of our Holy Father John Paul II; as the cardinals entered the conclave; and again today, when we sang it with the response: *Tu illum adiuva*—sustain the new Successor of St. Peter. On each occasion, in a particular way, I found great consolation in listening to this prayerful chant. How alone we all felt after the passing of John Paul II—the pope who for over twenty-six years had been our shepherd and guide on our journey through life! He crossed the threshold of the next life, entering into the mystery of God. But he did not take this step alone. Those who believe are never alone—neither in life nor in death. At that moment, we could call upon the saints from every age—his friends, his brothers and sisters in the faith— knowing that they would form a living procession to accompany him into the next world, into the glory of God. We knew that his arrival was awaited. Now we know that he is among his own and is truly at home. We were also consoled as we made our solemn entrance into conclave, to elect the one whom the Lord had chosen. How would we be able to discern his name? How could 115 bishops, from every culture and every country, discover the one on whom the Lord wished to confer the mission of binding and loosing? Once again, we knew that we were not alone; we knew that we were surrounded, led, and guided by the friends of God. And now, at this moment, weak servant of God that I am, I must assume this enormous task, which truly exceeds all human capacity. How can I do this? How will I be able to do it? All of you, my dear friends, have just invoked the entire host of saints, represented by some of the great names in the history of God's dealings with mankind. In this way, I, too, can say with renewed conviction: I am not alone. I do not have to carry alone what in truth I could never carry alone. All the saints of God are there to protect me, to sustain me, and to carry me. And your prayers, my dear friends, your indulgence, your love, your faith, and your hope accompany me. Indeed, the communion of saints consists not only of the great men and women who went before us and whose names we know. All of us belong to the communion of saints, we who have been baptized in the name of the Father and of the Son and of the Holy Spirit, we who draw life from the gift of Christ's body and blood, through which he transforms us and makes us like himself. Yes, the church is alive—this is the wonderful experience of these days. During those sad days of the pope's illness and death, it became wonderfully evident to us that the church is alive. And the church is young. She holds within herself the future of the world and therefore shows each of us the way toward the future. The church is alive and we are seeing it: we are experiencing the joy that the Risen Lord promised his followers. The church is alive—she is alive because Christ is alive, because he is truly risen. In the suffering that we saw on the Holy Father's face in those days of Easter, we contemplated the mystery of Christ's Passion and we touched his wounds. But throughout these days we have also been able, in a profound sense, to touch the Risen One. We have been able to experience the joy that he promised, after a brief period of darkness, as the fruit of his Resurrection.

The church is alive—with these words, I greet with great joy and gratitude all of you gathered here, my venerable Brother Cardinals and Bishops, my dear priests, deacons, church workers, catechists. I greet you, men and women religious, witnesses of the transfiguring presence of God. I greet you, members of the lay faithful, immersed in the great task of building up the Kingdom of God, which spreads throughout the world, in every area of life. With great affection I also greet all those who have been reborn in the sacrament of baptism but are not yet in full communion with us; and you, my brothers and sisters of the Jewish people, to whom we are joined by a great shared spiritual heritage, one rooted in God's irrevocable promises. Finally, like a wave gathering force, my thoughts go out to all men and women of today, to believers and nonbelievers alike.

Dear friends! At this moment there is no need for me to present a program of governance. I was able to give an indication of what I see as my task in my message of Wednesday, April 20, and there will be other opportunities to do so. My real program of governance is not to do my own will, not to pursue my own ideas, but to listen, together with the whole church, to the word and the will of the Lord, to be guided by him, so that he himself will lead the church at this hour of our history. Instead of putting forward a program, I should simply like to comment on the two liturgical symbols which represent the inauguration of the Petrine ministry; both these symbols, moreover, reflect clearly what we heard proclaimed in today's readings.

The first symbol is the pallium, woven in pure wool, which will be placed on my shoulders. This ancient sign, which the bishops of Rome have worn since the fourth century, may be considered an image of the yoke of Christ, which the bishop of this city, the servant of the servants of God, takes upon his shoulders. God's yoke is God's will, which we accept. And this will does not weigh down on us, oppressing us and taking away our freedom. To know what God wants, to know where the path of life is found—this was Israel's joy, this was her great privilege. It is also our joy: God's will does not alienate us, it purifies us—even if this can be painful—and so it leads us to ourselves. In this way, we serve not only him but the salvation of the whole world, of all history. The symbolism of the pallium is even more concrete: the lamb's wool is meant to represent the lost, sick, or weak sheep, which the shepherd places on his shoulders and carries to the waters of life. For the fathers of the church, the parable of the lost sheep, which the shepherd seeks in the desert, was an image of the mystery of Christ and the church. The human race—every one of us—is the sheep lost in the desert that no longer knows the way. The Son of God will not let this happen; he cannot abandon humanity in so wretched a condition. He leaps to his feet and abandons the glory of heaven, in order to go in search of the sheep and pursue it, all the way to the cross. He takes it upon his shoulders and carries our humanity; he carries us all—he is the Good Shepherd who lays down his life for the sheep. What the pallium indicates first and foremost is that we are all carried by Christ. But at the same time it invites us to carry one another. Hence the pallium becomes a symbol of the shepherd's mission, of which the second reading and the gospel speak. The pastor must be inspired by Christ's holy zeal: for him it is not a matter of indifference that so many people are living in the desert. And there are so many kinds of desert. There is the desert of poverty, the desert of hunger and thirst, the desert of abandonment, of loneliness, of destroyed love. There is the desert of God's darkness, the emptiness of souls no longer aware of their dignity or the goal of human life. The external deserts in the world are growing, because the internal deserts have become so vast. Therefore the earth's treasures no longer serve to build God's garden for all to live in, but they have been made to serve the powers of exploitation and destruction. The church as a whole and all her pastors, like Christ, must set out to lead people out of the desert, toward the place of life, toward friendship with the Son of God, toward the one who gives us life, and life in abundance. The symbol of the lamb also has a deeper meaning. In the ancient Near East, it was customary for kings to style themselves shepherds of their people. This was an image of their power, a cynical image: to them their subjects were like sheep, which the shepherd could dispose of as he wished. When the shepherd of all humanity, the living God, himself became a lamb, he stood on the side of the lambs, with those who are downtrodden and killed. This is how he reveals himself to be the true shepherd: "I am the Good Shepherd. ... I lay down my life for the sheep," Jesus says of himself (Jn 10:14–15). It is not power but love that redeems us! This is God's sign: he himself is love. How often we wish that God would make himself stronger, that he would strike decisively, defeating evil and creating a better world. All ideologies of power justify themselves in exactly this way; they justify the destruction of whatever would stand in the way of progress and the liberation of humanity. We suffer on account of God's patience. And yet, we need his patience. God, who became a lamb, tells us that the world is saved by the Crucified One, not by those who crucified him. The world is redeemed by the patience of God. It is destroyed by the impatience of man.

One of the basic characteristics of a shepherd must be to love the people entrusted to him, even as he loves Christ whom he serves. "Feed my sheep," says Christ to Peter, and now, at this moment, he says it to me, as well. Feeding means loving, and loving also means being ready to suffer. Loving means giving the sheep what is truly good, the nourishment of God's truth, of God's Word, the nourishment of his presence, which he gives us in the blessed sacrament. My dear friends—at this moment I can only say: pray for me, that I may learn to love the Lord more and more. Pray for me, that I may learn to love his flock more and more—in other words, you, the holy church, each one of you and all of you together. Pray for me, that I may not flee for fear of the wolves. Let us pray for one another, that the Lord will carry us and that we will learn to carry one another.

The second symbol used in today's liturgy to express the inauguration of the Petrine ministry is the presentation of the fisherman's ring. Peter's call to be a shepherd, which we heard in the Gospel, comes after the account of a miraculous catch of fish: after a night in which the disciples had let down their nets without success, they see the Risen Lord on the shore. He tells them to let down their nets once more, and the nets become so full that they can hardly pull them in, with 153 large fish: "And although there were so many, the net was not torn" (Jn 21:11). This account, coming at the end of Jesus's earthly journey with his disciples, corresponds to an account found at the beginning: there, too, the disciples had caught nothing the entire night; there, too, Jesus had invited Simon once more to put out into the deep. And Simon, who was not yet called Peter, gave the wonderful reply: "Master, at your word I will let down the nets." And then came the conferral of his mission: "Do not be afraid. Henceforth you will be catching men" (Lk 5:1–11). Today, too, the church and the successors of the apostles are told to put out into the deep sea of history and to let down the nets, so as to win men and women over to the gospel—to God, to Christ, to true life. The fathers made a very significant commentary on this singular task. This is what they say: for a fish, created for water, it is fatal to be taken out of the sea, to be removed from its vital element to serve as human food. But in the mission of a fisher of men, the reverse is true. We are living in alienation, in the salt waters of suffering and death; in a sea of darkness without light. The net of the gospel pulls us out of the waters of death and brings us into the splendor of God's light, into true life. It is really true: as we follow Christ in this mission to be fishers of men, we must bring men and women out of the sea that is salted with so many forms of alienation and onto the land of life, into the light of God. It is really so: the purpose of our lives is to reveal God to men. And only where God is seen does life truly begin. Only when we meet the living God in Christ do we know what life is. We are not some casual and meaningless product of evolution. Each of us is the result of a thought of God. Each of us is willed, each of us is loved, each of us is necessary. There is nothing more beautiful than to be surprised by the gospel, by the encounter with Christ. There is nothing more beautiful than to know him and to speak to others of our friendship with him. The task of the shepherd, the task of the fisher of men, can often seem wearisome. But it is beautiful and wonderful, because it is truly a service to joy, to God's joy, which longs to break into the world.

Here I want to add something: both the image of the shepherd and that of the fisherman issue an explicit call to unity. "I have other sheep that are not of this fold; I must lead them too, and they will heed my voice. So there shall be one flock, one shepherd" (Jn 10:16); these are the words of Jesus at the end of his discourse on the Good Shepherd. And the account of the 153 large fish ends with the joyful statement "Although there were so many, the net was not torn" (Jn 21:11). Alas, beloved Lord, with sorrow we must now acknowledge that it has been torn! But no—we must not be sad! Let us rejoice because of your promise, which does not disappoint, and let us do all we can to pursue the path toward the unity you have promised. Let us remember it in our prayer to the Lord, as we plead with him: yes, Lord, remember your promise. Grant that we may be one flock and one shepherd! Do not allow your net to be torn; help us to be servants of unity!

At this point, my mind goes back to October 22, 1978, when Pope John Paul II began his ministry here in St. Peter's Square. His words on that occasion constantly echo in my ears: "Do not be afraid! Open wide the doors for Christ!" The pope was addressing the mighty, the powerful of this world, who feared that Christ might take away something of their power if they were to let him in, if they were to allow the faith to be free. Yes, he would certainly have taken something away from them: the dominion of corruption, the manipulation of law, and the freedom to do as they pleased. But he would not have taken away anything that pertains to human freedom or dignity, or to the building of a just society. The pope was also speaking to everyone, especially the young. Are we not perhaps all afraid in some way? If we let Christ enter fully into our lives, if we open ourselves totally to him, are we not afraid that he might take something away from us? Are we not perhaps afraid to give up something significant, something unique, something that makes life so beautiful? Do we not then risk ending up diminished and deprived of our freedom? And once again the pope said: No! If we let Christ into our lives, we lose nothing, nothing, absolutely nothing of what makes life free, beautiful, and great. No! Only in this friendship are the doors of life opened wide. Only in this friendship is the great potential of human existence truly revealed. Only in this friendship do we experience beauty and liberation. And so, today, with great strength and great conviction, on the basis of long personal experience of life, I say to you, dear young people: do not be afraid of Christ! He takes nothing away, and he gives you everything. When we give ourselves to him, we receive a hundredfold in return. Yes, open, open wide the doors to Christ— and you will find true life. Amen.

6

Message on the Twenty-fifth Anniversary of the Pontificate of Pope John Paul II from the College of Cardinals

DELIVERED BY CARDINAL JOSEPH RATZINGER, OCTOBER 18, 2003

Holy Father,

The College of Cardinals has gathered to thank the Lord and you for your twenty-five years of fruitful work as Successor of St. Peter, as it is only right to remember at this time. In these years, the bark of the church has often had to sail against the wind and on rough seas. The sea of history is agitated by conflicts between the rich and the poor, between peoples and cultures; by the prospects opened by human ability and the risk that human beings run of self-destruction because of these same possibilities. At times the sky appears to be covered by heavy clouds that conceal God from the eyes of men and women and call the faith into question.

Today more than ever, we are experiencing that the history of the world—as Augustine saw it—is a struggle between two forms of love: love of self to the point of contempt for God, and love of God to the point of being prepared to sacrifice oneself for God and for one's neighbor. And although the signs of people's presumption and of distancing themselves from God are being felt and perceived more than the witness of love, thanks be to God we can see today that his light has never been extinguished in history; the great array of saints and blesseds whom you, Holy Father, have raised to the honor of the altars, is an eloquent sign: in them we recognize with delight God's presence in history and his love, mirrored on the faces of the men and women blessed by God.

In this span of time, Your Holiness, constantly comforted by the loving presence of the Mother of Jesus, you have guided us with the joy of faith, the undaunted courage of hope, and the enthusiasm of love. You have enabled us to see God's light despite all the clouds, and made sure that the weakness of our faith, which all too easily prompts us to exclaim: "Save us, Lord; we are perishing"(Mt 8:25), does not prevail. Today we wholeheartedly thank you for this service.

As a pilgrim of the gospel, like the apostles you set out and crossed the continents bearing the proclamation of Christ, the proclamation of the Kingdom of God, the proclamation of forgiveness, of love, and of peace. Unflaggingly, you have proclaimed the gospel in season and out of season, and in its light you have reminded all people of the fundamental human values: respect for human dignity, the defense of life, the promotion of justice and peace. Above all, you have gone out to meet the young, communicating to them the fire of your faith, your love for Christ, and your willingness to dedicate yourself to him, body and soul.

You have been concerned with the sick and the suffering and have launched a passionate appeal to the world to share the goods of the earth equitably and so that the poor may have justice and love.

You have interpreted the commandment of unity that the Lord gave to his disciples as a commandment addressed to you personally; this has led you to do your utmost to make believers in Christ one, so that the benevolent power of God himself may be recognized in the miracle of unity that human beings are powerless to create. You have gone out to meet people of other religions, to reawaken in all the desire for peace and the readiness to become instruments of peace.

Thus, over and above all the barriers and divisions, you have become for all humanity a great messenger of peace. You have never ceased to appeal to the consciences of the powerful or to comfort those who are victims of the lack of peace in this world. In this way, you have obeyed the Lord who bequeathed this promise to his followers: "Peace I leave with you; my peace I give to you" (Jn 14:27). Precisely in meeting the needs of others, you have never allowed anyone to doubt that Christ is the Love of God made flesh, the Only Son and Savior of all. For you, to proclaim Christ is not to impose something foreign on anyone but to communicate to all what each one basically longs for: the eternal love that every human heart is secretly awaiting.

"The Redeemer of man is the center of the universe and of history": these opening words of your first encyclical were like a clarion call that invited us to a religious reawakening, centering all things once again in Christ.

Holy Father, the College of Cardinals, at the end of this congress during which it has recalled only a few aspects of the twenty-five years of your pontificate, desires unanimously to reaffirm its filial attachment to your person and its faithful, total loyalty to your lofty magisterium as pastor of the universal church.

"The joy of the Lord is your strength," Ezra the priest said to the people of Israel at a difficult moment (Neh 8:10). You, Holy Father, have rekindled in us this joy of the Lord. We are grateful to you for this. May the Lord always fill you with his joy.

7

Address of Cardinal Joseph Ratzinger to Pope John Paul II at a Concert Offered by the Mitteldeutscher Rundfunk Orchestra on the Twenty-fifth Anniversary of His Pontificate

OCTOBER 17, 2003

Most Holy Father,

These days, as we commemorate the twenty-five years during which you have borne in the church the burden and the grace of the pastoral office of the Successor of Peter, are marked first and foremost by sentiments of gratitude and joy. A highlight of this week of festivities is the concert with which the choir and orchestra of the Mitteldeutscher Rundfunk are now about to regale us. They will let us hear one of the great musical masterpieces, Beethoven's Ninth Symphony, which echoes the inner strife of the great maestro in the midst of the darkness of life, his passage, as it were, through dark nights in which none of the promised stars seemed any longer to shine in the heavens. But in the end, the clouds lift. The great drama of human existence that unfolds in the music is transformed into a hymn of joy for which Beethoven borrowed the words of Schiller, whose true greatness blossomed only through his music.

Since I am German, I am particularly pleased by the fact that the concert is offered by a German ensemble that is performing for the third time before you, Holy Father, and celebrating joy for us through this music. The choir and orchestra come from a part of Germany that, after the war and until the collapse of the [Berlin] Wall, experienced the wounds inflicted by the Communist dictatorship that are still being felt today. Perhaps the deepest wound is the fact that God seems to have become distant and in many hearts faith has been extinguished. But this is also the German region that gave us perhaps the greatest musical genius of all time, Johann Sebastian Bach. In the same year and in the same region Georg Friedrich Händel was also born. To him we are indebted for another incomparable hymn of joy: the great "Hallelujah Chorus," which is the crowning moment of his *Messiah*. In it he set to music promise and fulfillment, the prophecy of the Redeemer who was to come and the historical events of the life of Jesus to which it corresponds. The "Hallelujah Chorus" is the song of praise of the redeemed who, through Christ's Resurrection, can still rejoice, even amid the sufferings of this world. This great musical tradition—as we will experience in these hours—has lived on through all the vicissitudes of history, and is a ray of light in which the star of faith, the presence of Jesus Christ, continues to shine.

Compared with the intact presence of the faith that transpires in Händel's *Hymn to Joy* and which emerges in a very different way, that is, as a tranquil inner peace and the grace of reconciliation, in Bach's *Christmas Oratorio* or at the end of his *Passions,* the illuminating ode by Schiller, so impressively set to music by Beethoven, is characterized by the humanism of that time, which places man at the center and—where there is a reference to God—prefers the language of myth.

Nevertheless, we should not forget that Beethoven is also the composer of the *Missa Solemnis.* The good father of which the ode speaks is not so much a supposition, as Schiller's text might suggest, but rather an ultimate certainty. Beethoven also knew that we can entrust ourselves to the Father because in the Son he made himself close to us. And thus, we can calmly see the divine spark, of whose joy the ode speaks, as that spark of God which is communicated to us through the music and reassures us: yes, the good Father truly exists and is not utterly remote, far beyond the firmament, but thanks to the Son is here in our midst.

I greet with gratitude and joy those distinguished persons who have made this concert possible, and with you, the conductor of the ensemble, Mr. Howard Arman, the soloists as well as the choir and orchestra. We thank you because you have given us this spark of God filled with joy, which God enables to be kindled in you and in us.

8

The Assisi Day of Prayer

JANUARY 2002

This man, Francis, who responded totally to the call of the crucified Christ, continues today to glow with the splendor of the same peace that convinced the sultan, the peace that truly demolishes any wall.

When it moved off on Thursday, January 24, under a rain-laden sky, it seemed to me that the train bringing to Assisi the representatives of a great number of Christian churches and ecclesial communities together with the exponents of numerous world religions, intent on bearing witness to and praying for peace, was a symbol of our pilgrimage in history. For, are we not all passengers on the same train!

And is it not a great ambition and, at the same time, a shining beacon of hope that the train chose as its destination peace and justice, the reconciliation of peoples and religions? Everywhere as we passed through the stations a great crowd gathered to greet the pilgrims of peace. In the streets of Assisi and in the great marquee, the place of united witness, we were once again immersed in the enthusiasm and thankful joy of a large gathering of young people in particular. The people's cheers of welcome were principally for the elderly man dressed in white who was on the train. Men and women, who too often in daily life confront each other with hostility and appear to be divided by insurmountable barriers, joined to greet the pope, and he, with all the force of his personality, the profundity of his faith, and the passion he derives from it for peace and reconciliation, extracted what seemed to be the impossible from the charism of his office: he brought together the representatives of divided Christendom and the exponents of various religions in a pilgrimage of peace.

The applause, primarily for the pope, was also the spontaneous expression of assent for all those people who, with him, seek peace and justice, and it was a sign of the profound desire for peace in the hearts of individuals in the face of the devastation all around them wrought by hatred and violence. Even if the hatred seems invincible at times and appears to grow and grow in a spiral of violence, here for a moment one perceived the presence of the power of God, of the power of peace. I am reminded of the words of the Psalm: "With my God I can scale any wall" (Ps 18:30). God does not pitch us one against the other; rather, he who is One, who is the Father of all, helped us to scale the walls separating us, if even for a moment. He made us see that he is peace and that we cannot be close to God if we are far from peace.

In his address, the pope mentioned another cornerstone of the Bible—that phrase from the Letter to the Ephesians: "For he is the peace between us and has made the two peoples into one entity and broken down the barrier which used to keep them apart ... the hostility" (Eph 2:14). In the New Testament, peace and justice are the names of Christ (for "Christ, our justice," see, for example, 1 Cor 1:30). As Christians, we must not conceal this conviction of ours: the confession of Christ our peace on the part of the pope and of the ecumenical patriarch resounded clear and solemn. But then again, it is this that unites us over and beyond the frontiers: the pilgrimage for peace and justice.

The words a Christian should put to anyone setting out for these same destinations are the Lord's own words in reply to the scribe who had recognized a synthesis of the Old Testament message in Christ's twofold commandment to love God and one's neighbor. Jesus said: "You are not far from the kingdom of God" (Mk 12:34).

For a proper understanding of the Assisi event, I think it important that we do not see it as a representative array of supposedly interchangeable religions.

It was not the affirmation of any equality of the religions, which does not exist. Assisi was more the expression of a journeying, of a seeking, of the pilgrimage for peace that is only possible if peace be united with justice. For, wherever there is no justice, wherever individuals are denied their rights, the absence of war may be just a veil behind which are hidden injustice and oppression.

With their witness for peace, with their commitment to peace in justice, the representatives of religions, as far as it was possible for them, embarked on a journey that for everyone must be a journey of purification. That holds for us Christians, too. We will only truly attain Christ if we have attained his peace and his justice. Assisi, the city of St. Francis, is probably the best interpreter of this thinking. Francis was Christian even before his conversion, as were his fellow townspeople. And the victorious army of Perugia that cast him into prison, a captive, a beaten man, was also made up of Christians. It was only then, beaten, a prisoner, suffering, that he began to think of Christianity in a new way.

And it was only after this experience that it became possible for him to hear and understand the voice of the Crucified One who spoke to him in the tiny St. Damian's Church, which was in ruins, the very symbol therefore of the church of the time, profoundly rotten and decadent. Only then did he see how great was the contrast between the nudity of the Crucified One, his poverty and humiliation, and the luxury and violence that had once seemed normal to him. And only then did he truly know Christ and understand, too, that the Crusades were not the way to defend the rights of Christians in the Holy Land. He saw, rather, that one had to take the message literally in imitation of the Crucified One.

This man, Francis, who responded totally to the call of the crucified Christ, continues today to glow with the splendor of the same peace that convinced the sultan, the peace that truly demolishes any wall. If we as Christians embark on the journey to peace following St. Francis's example, we cannot fear any loss of our identity. For it will be only then that we find it. And if others join with us in seeking peace and justice, neither they nor we ourselves can have any fear that the truth will be crushed under polished, prepackaged phraseology. No, if we seriously set out toward peace, then we will be on the right road because we will be on God's own road to peace (Rom 15:33), God whose face was made visible to us as Christians through faith in Christ.

9

The Feeling of Things, the Contemplation of Beauty

Message to the Communion and Liberation Meeting at Rimini

AUGUST 24–30, 2002

Every year, in the Liturgy of the Hours for the Season of Lent, I am struck anew by a paradox in Vespers for Monday of the Second Week of the Psalter. Here, side by side, are two antiphons, one for the Season of Lent, the other for Holy Week. Both introduce Psalm 44 [45], but they present strikingly contradictory interpretations. The psalm describes the wedding of the king, his beauty, his virtues, his mission, and then becomes an exaltation of his bride. In the season of Lent, Psalm 44 is framed by the same antiphon used for the rest of the year. The third verse of the psalm says: "You are the fairest of the children of men and grace is poured upon your lips."

Naturally, the church reads this psalm as a poetic-prophetic representation of Christ's spousal relationship with his church. She recognizes Christ as the fairest of men, the grace poured upon his lips points to the inner beauty of his words, the glory of his proclamation. So it is not merely the external beauty of the Redeemer's appearance that is glorified: rather, the beauty of Truth appears in him, the beauty of God himself, who draws us to himself and at the same time captures us with the wound of Love, the holy passion (*eros*), that enables us to go forth together, with and in the church, his Bride, to meet the Love who calls us.

On Monday of Holy Week, however, the church changes the antiphon and invites us to interpret the Psalm in the light of Isaiah 53:2: "He had neither beauty, no majesty, nothing to attract our eyes, no grace to make us delight in him." How can we reconcile this? The appearance of the "fairest of the children of men" is so wretched that no one desires to look at him. Pilate presented him to the crowd, saying, "Behold the man!" to rouse sympathy for the crushed and battered Man, in whom no external beauty remained.

Augustine, who in his youth wrote a book on the Beautiful and the Harmonious [De pulchro et apto] and who appreciated beauty in words, in music, in the figurative arts, had a keen appreciation of this paradox and realized that in this regard, the great Greek philosophy of the beautiful was not simply rejected but rather dramatically called into question, and what the beautiful might be, what beauty might mean, would have to be debated anew and suffered. Referring to the paradox contained in these texts, he spoke of the contrasting blasts of "two trumpets" produced by the same breath, the same Spirit. He knew that a paradox is contrast and not contradiction. Both quotes come from the same Spirit who inspires all scripture, but sounds different notes in it. It is in this way that he sets us before the totality of true Beauty, of Truth itself.

In the first place, the text of Isaiah supplies the question that interested the fathers of the church, whether or not Christ was beautiful. Implicit here is the more radical question of whether beauty is true or whether it is not ugliness that leads us to the deepest truth of reality. Whoever believes in God, in the God who manifested himself, precisely in the altered appearance of Christ crucified as Love "to the end" (Jn 13:1), knows that beauty is truth and truth beauty; but in the suffering Christ he also learns that the beauty of truth also embraces offense, pain, and even the dark mystery of death, and that this can only be found in accepting suffering, not in ignoring it.

Certainly, the consciousness that beauty has something to do with pain was also present in the Greek world. For example, let us take Plato's *Phaedrus.* Plato contemplates the encounter with beauty as the salutary emotional shock that makes man leave his shell and sparks his "enthusiasm" by attracting him to what is other than himself. Man, says Plato, has lost the original perfection that was conceived for him. He is now perennially searching for the healing primitive form. Nostalgia and longing impel him to pursue the quest; beauty prevents him from being content with just daily life. It causes him to suffer. In a Platonic sense, we could say that the arrow of nostalgia pierces man, wounds him, and in this way gives him wings, lifts him upward toward the transcendent. In his discourse on the *Symposium,* Aristophanes says that lovers do not know what they really want from each other. From the search for what is more than their pleasure, it is obvious that the souls of both are thirsting for something other than amorous pleasure. But the heart cannot express this "other" thing; "it has only a vague perception of what it truly wants and wonders about it as an enigma."

In the fourteenth century, in the book *The Life in Christ* by the Byzantine theologian Nicholas Cabasilas, we rediscover Plato's experience in which the ultimate object of nostalgia, transformed by the new Christian experience, continues to be nameless. Cabasilas says: "When men have a longing so great that it surpasses human nature, and eagerly desire and are able to accomplish things beyond human thought, it is the Bridegroom who has smitten them with this longing. It is he who has sent a ray of his beauty into their eyes. The greatness of the wound already shows the arrow which has struck home, the longing indicates who has inflicted the wound" (cf. *The Life in Christ*, Book II, p. 15).

The beautiful wounds, but this is exactly how it summons man to his final destiny. What Plato said, and more than 1,500 years later, Cabasilas, has nothing to do with superficial aestheticism and irrationalism or with the flight from clarity and the importance of reason. The beautiful is knowledge certainly but in a superior form, since it arouses man to the real greatness of the truth. Here Cabasilas has remained entirely Greek, since he puts knowledge first when he says, "In fact it is knowing that causes love and gives birth to it.... Since this knowledge is sometimes very ample and complete and at other times imperfect, it follows that the love potion has the same effect."

He is not content to leave this assertion in general terms. In his characteristically rigorous thought, he distinguishes between two kinds of knowledge. One is knowledge through instruction, which remains, so to speak, "secondhand" and does not imply any direct contact with reality itself. The second type of knowledge is knowledge through personal experience, through a direct relationship with the reality. "Therefore we do not love it to the extent that it is a worthy object of love, and since we have not perceived the very form itself we do not experience its proper effect."

True knowledge is being struck by the arrow of Beauty that wounds man, moved by reality, "how it is Christ himself who is present and in an ineffable way disposes and forms the souls of men" (cf. *The Life in Christ*, Book II, p. 15).

Being struck and overcome by the beauty of Christ is a more real, more profound knowledge than mere rational deduction. Of course, we must not underrate the importance of theological reflection, of exact and precise theological thought; it remains absolutely necessary. But to move from here to disdain or to reject the impact produced by the response of the heart in the encounter with beauty as a true form of knowledge would impoverish us and dry up our faith and our theology. We must rediscover this form of knowledge; it is a pressing need of our time.

Starting with this concept, Hans Urs von Balthasar built his magnum opus, *Theological Aesthetics*. Many of its details have passed into theological work, while his fundamental approach, in truth the essential element of the whole work, has not been so readily accepted. Of course, this is not just, or principally, a theological problem, but a problem of pastoral life, which has to foster the person's encounter with the beauty of faith. All too often arguments fall on deaf ears because in our world too many contradictory arguments compete with one another, so much so that we are spontaneously reminded of the medieval theologians' description of reason, that it "has a wax nose": in other words, it can be pointed in any direction, if one is clever enough. Everything makes sense, is so convincing, whom should we trust?

The encounter with the beautiful can become the wound of the arrow that strikes the heart and in this way opens our eyes, so that later, from this experience, we take the criteria for judgment and can correctly evaluate the arguments. For me an unforgettable experience was the Bach concert that Leonard Bernstein conducted in Munich after the sudden death of Karl Richter. I was sitting next to the Lutheran Bishop Hanselmann. When the last note of one of the great Thomas Kantor cantatas triumphantly faded away, we looked at each other spontaneously and right then we said: "Anyone who has heard this knows that the faith is true." The music had such an extraordinary force of reality that we realized, no longer by deduction but by the impact on our hearts, that it could not have originated from nothingness, but could only have come to be through the power of the Truth that became real in the composer's inspiration. Isn't the same thing evident when we allow ourselves to be moved by the icon of the Trinity of Rublëv? In the art of the icons, as in the great Western paintings of the Romanesque and Gothic periods, the experience described by Cabasilas, starting with interiority, is visibly portrayed and can be shared.

In a rich way, Pavel Evdokimov has brought to light the interior pathway that an icon establishes. An icon does not simply reproduce what can be perceived by the senses, but rather it presupposes, as he says, "a fasting of sight." Inner perception must free itself from the impression of the merely sensible and in prayer and ascetical effort acquire a new and deeper capacity to see, to perform the passage from what is merely external to the profundity of reality, in such a way that the artist can see what the senses as such do not see, and what actually appears in what can be perceived: the splendor of the glory of God, the "glory of God shining on the face of Christ" (2 Cor 4:6).

To admire the icons and the great masterpieces of Christian art in general leads us on an inner way, a way of overcoming ourselves; thus in this purification of vision that is a purification of the heart, it reveals the beautiful to us, or at least a ray of it. In this way we are brought into contact with the power of the truth. I have often affirmed my conviction that the true apology of Christian faith, the most convincing demonstration of its truth against every denial, is to be found in the saints and the beauty that the faith has generated. Today, for faith to grow, we must lead ourselves and the persons we meet to encounter the saints and to enter into contact with the Beautiful.

Now, however, we still have to respond to an objection. We have already rejected the assumption which claims that what has just been said is a flight into the irrational, into mere aestheticism.

Rather, it is the opposite that is true: this is the very way in which reason is freed from dullness and made ready to act.

Today another objection has even greater weight: the message of beauty is thrown into complete doubt by the power of falsehood, seduction, violence, and evil. Can the beautiful be genuine, or in the end, is it only an illusion? Isn't reality perhaps basically evil? The fear that in the end it is not the arrow of the beautiful that leads us to the truth and that falsehood, all that is ugly and vulgar, may constitute the true "reality" has at all times caused people anguish. At present this is expressed in the assertion that after Auschwitz it was no longer possible to write poetry; after Auschwitz it is no longer possible to speak of a God who is good. People wondered: where was God when the gas chambers were operating? This objection, which seemed reasonable enough before Auschwitz when one became aware of all the atrocities of history, shows that in any case a purely harmonious concept of beauty is not enough. It cannot stand up to the confrontation with the gravity of the questioning about God, truth, and beauty. Apollo, who for Plato's Socrates was "the God" and the guarantor of unruffled beauty as "the truly divine," is absolutely no longer sufficient.

In this way, we return to the "two trumpets" of the Bible with which we started, to the paradox of being able to say of Christ: "You are the fairest of the children of men," and "He had no beauty, no majesty to draw our eyes, no grace to make us delight in him." In the Passion of Christ, the Greek aesthetic, which deserves admiration for its perceived contact with the divine but which remained inexpressible for it, is not removed but overcome. The experience of the beautiful has received new depth and new realism. The one who is Beauty itself let himself be slapped in the face, spat upon, crowned with thorns; the shroud of Turin can help us imagine this in a realistic way. However, in his face, which is so disfigured, there appears genuine, extreme beauty: the beauty of love that goes "to the very end"; for this reason it is revealed as greater than falsehood and violence. Whoever has perceived this beauty knows that truth, not falsehood, is the real aspiration of the world. It is not the false that is "true" but, indeed, the Truth. It is, as it were, a new trick of what is false to present itself as "truth" and to say to us: over and above me there is basically nothing, stop seeking or even loving the truth; in doing so you are on the wrong track. The icon of the crucified Christ sets us free from this deception that is so widespread today. However, it imposes a condition: that we let ourselves be wounded by him, and that we believe in the Love who can risk setting aside his external beauty to proclaim, in this way, the truth of the beautiful.

Falsehood, however, has another stratagem. A beauty that is deceptive and false, a dazzling beauty that does not bring human beings out of themselves to open them to the ecstasy of rising to the heights but indeed locks them entirely into themselves. Such beauty does not reawaken a longing for the Ineffable, readiness for sacrifice, the abandonment of self, but instead stirs up the desire, the will for power, possession, and pleasure. It is that type of experience of beauty of which Genesis speaks in the account of the Original Sin. Eve saw that the fruit of the tree was "beautiful" to eat and "delightful to the eyes." The beautiful, as she experienced it, aroused in her a desire for possession, making her, as it were, turn in upon herself. Who would not recognize, for example in advertising, the images made with supreme skill that are created to tempt the human being irresistibly, to make him want to grab everything and seek the passing satisfaction rather than be open to others.

So it is that Christian art today is caught between two fires (as perhaps it always has been): it must oppose the cult of the ugly, which says that everything beautiful is a deception, and only the representation of what is crude, low, and vulgar is the truth, the true illumination of knowledge. And it has to counter the deceptive beauty that makes the human being seem diminished instead of making him great, and for this reason is false.

Is there anyone who does not know Dostoyevsky's often quoted sentence: "The Beautiful will save us"? However, people usually forget that Dostoyevsky is referring here to the redeeming Beauty of Christ. We must learn to see him. If we know him, not only in words, if we are struck by the arrow of his paradoxical beauty, then we will truly know him, and know him not only because we have heard others speak about him. Then we will have found the beauty of Truth, of the Truth that redeems. Nothing can bring us into close contact with the beauty of Christ himself other than the world of beauty created by faith and light that shines out from the faces of the saints, through whom his own light becomes visible.

Guardini on Christ in Our Century

Romano Guardini's book *The Lord* has helped more than one generation of Christians enter into a deeper relationship with Jesus Christ. When the book first appeared, it offered a new approach to the spiritual interpretation of scripture for which young people in particular longed—a longing, I might add, that is being felt again in our own day.

The First World War was everywhere experienced as the collapse of the liberal dream of ever-advancing progress engendered by reason alone. This crisis of liberalism had great consequences for the church and theology. Every "rational Christianity" that the liberal theologians had managed to develop was affected by it. Liberal biblical interpretation, or exegesis, had actually prepared the ground for this crisis by its attempt to discover behind the "veneer of dogma" the true "historical" Jesus. Naturally, by the liberals' way of thinking, the historical Jesus could only be a mere man. The liberals thought that everything supernatural, everything pertaining to the mystery of God that surrounded Jesus, was merely the embellishment and exaggeration of believers. Only with everything supernatural removed could the true figure of Jesus finally come into view! Already by the turn of the century, however, Albert Schweitzer had established that such an attempt would result only in contradictions: such a "sanitized" Jesus would be not an actual person but the product of a historian.

As a student, Romano Guardini had himself experienced the drama of liberalism and its collapse, and with a few friends he set out to find a new path for theology. What came to impress him in the course of this search was the experience of the liturgy as the place of encounter with Jesus. It is above all in the liturgy that Jesus is among us; here he speaks to us, here he lives.

Guardini recognized that the liturgy is the true, living environment for the Bible and that the Bible can be properly understood only in this living context within which it first emerged. The texts of the Bible, this great book of Christ, are not to be seen as the literary products of some scribes at their desks, but rather as the words of Christ himself delivered in the celebration of Holy Mass. The scriptural texts are thoroughly imbued with the awe of divine worship resulting from the believer's interior attentiveness to the living voice of the present Lord. In the preface to his book, Guardini himself tells us of the way in which these texts have arisen: "We can only reverently pause before this or that word or act, ready to learn, adore, obey."

Guardini did not view his book as theology in the strict sense of the word, but more as a kind of proclamation or preaching. Nonetheless, he did not fail to take into account the theological significance of what he had to say. Throughout *The Lord,* Guardini struggled to come to the correct understanding of Jesus: all attempts to "cleanse" the figure of Jesus of the supernatural result in contradictions and meaningless constructions. One simply cannot strip "the wholly other," the mysterious, the divine from this individual. Without this element, the very Person of Jesus himself dissolves. There simply is no psychological portrait of Jesus which can render his different features comprehensible solely from a human perspective. Repeatedly the analysis of this man takes us into a realm that is incomprehensible, "an incomprehensibility, however, full of measureless promise." The figure and mission of Jesus are "forever beyond the reach of history's most powerful ray," because "their ultimate explanations are to be found only in that impenetrable territory which he calls 'my Father's will.'"

Guardini spoke in a similar way in 1936 in a small but invaluable book entitled *The Picture of Jesus the Christ in the New Testament,* the result of characteristically methodical reflections:

> Perhaps we will not even succeed in arriving at a "person," but rather only at a series of sketches which stretch out beyond our range of vision. Perhaps we will experience that the Ascension was not simply a unique occurrence in the life of Jesus, but rather above all, the manner in which He is given to us: as one vanishing into heaven, into the Unconditional which is God. However, if that is the case, then these bare sketches are most precious: They are sign-posts pointing us to the "stepping beyond" of faith; and insofar as they go beyond our vision, in fact, precisely because they go beyond our vision, they teach us to worship.

From such a way of thinking, the meditations arose that together make up this book. For Guardini the first step is always attentive listening to the message of the scriptural text. In this way the real contribution of exegesis to an understanding of Jesus is fully acknowledged. But in this attentiveness to the text, the listener, according to Guardini's understanding, does not make himself to be master of the Word. Rather, the listener makes himself the believing disciple who allows himself to be led and enlightened by the Word. It is precisely by repudiating a closed, merely human logic that the greatness and uniqueness of this person becomes apparent to us. It is precisely in this way that the prison of our prejudice is broken open; it is in this way that our eyes are slowly opened and that we come to recognize what is truly human, since we have been touched by the very humanity of God himself.

One of Guardini's favorite expressions was "that which is truly real will arise from the rich, varied expansiveness of our existence, of our being fully Christian, and will lead us to the One who is truly real." As we are taught by Guardini, the essence of Christianity is not an idea, not a system of thought, not a plan of action. The essence of Christianity is a person: Jesus Christ himself. That which is essential is the one who is essential. To become truly real means to come to know Jesus Christ and to learn from him what it means to be human.

Our time is in many respects far different from that in which Romano Guardini lived and worked. But it is as true now as in his day that the peril of the church, indeed of humanity, consists in bleaching out the image of Jesus Christ in an attempt to shape a Jesus according to our own standards, so that we do not follow him in obedient discipleship but rather recreate him in our own image! Yet still in our own day, salvation consists only in our becoming "truly real." And we can do that only when we discover anew the true reality of Jesus Christ and through him discover the way to an upright and just life. Guardini's book *The Lord* has not grown old, precisely because it still leads us to that which is essential, to that which is truly real, Jesus Christ himself. That is why this book still has a great mission today.

Christ the Liberator

An Easter Homily

The Eastern church's picture of Easter has taken a different path from that of the Western world and the images that are familiar to us. She does not show the Lord having burst from the grave, suspended in a brilliant, divine glory above the world, as in Grunewald's impressive and masterful painting. Since scripture itself does not portray the Resurrection event, Eastern believers, too, refrained from depicting it. The icon, by contrast, represents as it were the mysterious inner dimension of the event of Easter, which is indicated by a few words of scripture and which we profess in the Creed when we say, "He descended into hell." In the perspective of the icon, this is an affirmation concerning Jesus's victory. The icon shows him having shattered the bolt of this world, having torn its gates from their hinges. It depicts him as the "stronger man" who has opened and penetrated the domain of the "strong man." It portrays him as the Victor, having burst through the supposedly impregnable fortress of death, such that death is now no longer a place of no return; its doors lie open. Christ, in the aura of his wounded love, stands in this doorway, addresses the still somnolent Adam, and takes him by the hand to lead him forth. The liturgy of Holy Saturday circles around this event.[1]

In an ancient Easter Vigil homily ascribed to Epiphanius, which is also read in our liturgy now, we hear what we may imagine to be the words of Jesus Christ.[2] He says to Adam, "I am your God, yet I have become your son. I am in you, and you are in me. We together are a single, indivisible person." Thus it is clear that this Adam does not signify an individual in a dim and distant past: the Adam addressed by the victorious Christ is we ourselves—"I am in you, and you are in me." Having taken human nature, he is now present in human flesh, and we are present in him, the Son. Epiphanius quotes and expands a passage from the Letter to the Ephesians: "Awake, O sleeper, and arise from the dead, and Christ shall give you light. I have not created you to be in prison forever. I did not make you for the dungeon."[3] This pronouncement contains the whole Christian message of Easter. Again, we see that this prison which Christ opens is not somewhere or other in the unknown depths of the earth. It can be anywhere—in the prisons of this world but also in the midst of luxury and apparent freedom. A theologian of the ancient church once wrote, "Christ descended into hell when he spoke with Caiaphas."[4] What a terrible dictum! But how many Caiaphases are there in the world? How much of Caiaphas is there in each of us? Truly, the prison that alienates us from ourselves can be anywhere and everywhere. What, then, makes this prison, this alienation, which robs man of freedom and against which he rebels in a thousand different ways? What makes man a prisoner, incapable of being himself?

What is the specific characteristic of a prison? On reflection, it is surely the deprivation of freedom, and at a deeper level, it is that the human being is denied communication, that is, normal fellowship and relationship with others, along with normal participation in activity in the world. I am reminded of the phrase in which the Bishops' Conference in Puebla summed up their strategy of liberation: *comuniori y participation* (fellowship and participation). These two give substance to man. Where both are cut off, his own selfhood is denied him. Yet if we see our freedom solely in these two elements, fellowship and participation, we shall be forgetting a third fundamental element, which is actually the first, the basis for all real freedom, without which man can never genuinely discover his dignity and his freedom. This third element is mentioned in the words of Ephesians we have just heard: "Awake ... and Christ shall give you light." In ancient times the really terrible thing about prisons was that they cut people off from the light of day and plunged them into darkness. So, at a deeper level, the real alienation, unfreedom, and imprisonment of man consists in his want of truth. If he does not know truth, if he does not know who he is, why he is there, and what the reality of this world consists in, he is only stumbling around in the dark. He is a prisoner; he is not "being's freedman." The first and most fundamental of all human rights is the right to God, the Holy Father said on his visit to Ireland. Without this basic right, which is also the right to truth, the other human rights are not enough. Without this fundamental right to truth and to God, man becomes degraded to the level of a mere creature of needs. And the deep darkness and alienation of our times are shown in the fact that we have powers and abilities but do not know what they are for; we have so much knowledge that we are no longer able to believe and see truth; we are no longer able to embrace the totality. Our philosophy is that of Pilate: what is truth? This only looks like a question: in fact, it is a statement, to the effect that there is no truth, and only idiots and fanatics imagine they have it or argue about it. But if this is how things are, if man has no truth, only abilities, he is fundamentally alienated, and "participation" is only an empty playacting in the dark, deluding man with the notion of freedom and hurting him deeply. There is nothing fortuitous about the strident protests against such empty freedom: man, deprived of truth, has been dishonored.

"I did not make you for the dungeon. Arise, and Christ shall give you light!" The ancient church used these words of Christ to Adam as a baptismal hymn, as the believing church's summons to the candidate. Thus it expresses the fact that Easter, the victory in which Jesus Christ breaks down the walls of alienation and leads us out into the open air, is to be heard continually in the sacrament of baptism. In this sacrament he takes us by the hand; in it, Truth speaks to us and shows us to the way to freedom. Wherever baptism is celebrated, the reality of Easter takes place here and now. So the annual feast of Easter is an invitation to us to return to our own baptism, to seize the hand of Truth, which reaches out to lead us to the light. To renew our baptism, and hence genuinely to celebrate Easter, the feast of liberation, means that we renew our acceptance of the truth of faith; it means entering into the light of this truth and, as believers, overcoming the darkness of truth's absence. In this way we discover the real core of our freedom.

"Arise, Christ shall give you light!" The church's real ministry of liberation is to hold aloft the flame of truth in the world. Liberation is our continual and fresh acceptance of truth as the path of life set before us.

We must acknowledge, however, that faith is seriously weakened and threatened within the church. Even we in the church have lost courage. We feel it to be arrogance or triumphalism to assume that the Christian faith tells us the truth. We have picked up the idea that all religions are the product of history, some developing this way and others that, and that every person is as he is because of the accident of birth. Such a view reduces religion from the level of truth to the level of habit. It becomes an empty flux of inherited traditions that no longer have any significance. But this view also eliminates a crucial affirmation from the Christian faith, namely Christ's "I am the Truth"—and hence the Way, hence also the Life. There is a great temptation to say, "But there is so much suffering in the world!—let's suspend the question of truth for a while. First let's get on with the great social tasks of liberation; then, one day, we will indulge in the luxury of the question of truth." In fact, however, if we postpone the question of truth and declare it to be unimportant, we are emasculating man, depriving him of the very core of his human dignity. If there is no truth, everything is a matter of indifference. Then social order swiftly becomes compulsion, and participation becomes violation. The church's real contribution to liberation, which she can never postpone and which is most urgent today, is to proclaim truth in the world, to affirm that

Truth =

God is, that God knows us, and that God is as Jesus Christ has revealed him, and that, in Jesus Christ, he has given us the path of life. Only then can there be such a thing as conscience, man's receptivity to truth, which gives each person direct access to God and makes him greater than every imaginable world system.

"I did not make you for the dungeon." In this Easter hour let us ask the Lord to visit the dungeons of this world, all the prisons that are hushed up by a propaganda that knows no truth, by a strategy of disinformation, keeping us in the dark and constituting our dungeon. Let us ask him to enter into the spiritual prisons of this age, into the darkness of our lack of truth, revealing himself as the Victor who tears down the gates and says to us, "I, your God, have become your Son. Come out! I have not created you to be in prison forever. I did not make you for the dungeon." In his play *No Exit,* Jean-Paul Sartre portrays man as a being who is hopelessly trapped. He sums up his gloomy picture of man in the words, "Hell is other people." This being so, hell is everywhere, and there is no exit, the doors are everywhere closed.

Christ, however, says to us, "I, your God, have become your Son. Come out!" Now the exact opposite is true: heaven is other people. Christ summons us to find heaven in him, to discover him in others and thus to be heaven to each other. He calls us to let heaven shine into this world, to build heaven here. Jesus stretches out his hand to us in his Easter message, in the mystery of the sacraments, so that Easter may be now, so that the light of heaven may shine forth in this world and the doors may be opened. Let us take his hand! Amen.

PART TWO

THE CHURCH

At the Root of the Crisis

The Idea of Church

VITTORIO MESSORI INTERVIEWS
JOSEPH CARDINAL RATZINGER (1985)

CHAPTER 3 OF *THE RATZINGER REPORT*

So, it's a crisis.[1] *But where, in your opinion, is the principal point of rupture, the crack that, by widening, threatens the stability of the whole edifice of the Catholic faith?*

No doubts exist in Cardinal Ratzinger's mind: the alarm must focus before all else on the crisis of the understanding of the church, on ecclesiology: "Herein lies the cause of a good part of the misunderstandings or real errors that endanger theology and common Catholic opinion alike."

He explains: "My impression is that the authentically Catholic meaning of the reality 'church' is tacitly disappearing, without being expressly rejected. Many no longer believe that what is at issue is a reality willed by the Lord himself. Even with some theologians, the church appears to be a human construction, an instrument created by us and one that we ourselves can freely reorganize according to the requirements of the moment. In other words, in many ways a conception of church is spreading in Catholic thought, and even in Catholic theology, that cannot even be called Protestant in a 'classic' sense. Many current ecclesiological ideas, rather, refer to the model of certain North American 'free churches,' in which in the past believers took refuge from the oppressive model of the 'state church' produced by the Reformation. Those refugees, no longer believing in an institutional church willed by Christ, and wanting at the same time to escape the state church, created their *own* church, an organization structured according to their needs."

How is it with Catholics instead?

"For a Catholic," he explains, "the church is indeed composed of men who organize her external visage. But behind this, the fundamental structures are willed by God himself, and therefore they are inviolable. Behind the *human* exterior stands the mystery of a *more than human* reality, in which reformers, sociologists, organizers have no authority whatsoever. If the church instead is viewed as a human construction, the product of our own efforts, even the contents of the faith end up assuming an arbitrary character: the faith, in fact, no longer has an authentic, guaranteed instrument through which to express itself. Thus, without a view of the mystery of the church that is also *supernatural* and not only *sociological,* Christology itself loses its reference to the divine in favor of a purely human structure, and ultimately it amounts to a purely human project: the gospel becomes the *Jesus-project,* the social-liberation project, or other merely historical, immanent projects that can still seem religious in appearance, but which are atheistic in substance."

During Vatican II there was a great emphasis—in the interventions of some bishops, in the statements of their theological advisors, but also in the final documents—on the concept of the church as "People of God," a conception that subsequently seemed to dominate in the postconciliar ecclesiologies.

"That's true. There was and there still is this emphasis, which in the council texts, however, is balanced with others that complete it. A balance that has been lost with many theologians. Yet, contrary to what the latter think, in this way there is the risk of moving backward rather than forward. Here, indeed, there is even the danger of abandoning the New Testament in order to return to the Old. 'People of God' in scripture, in fact, is a reference to Israel in its relationship of prayer and fidelity to the Lord. But to limit the definition of the church to that expression means not to give expression to the New Testament understanding of the church in its fullness. Here 'People of God' actually refers always to the Old Testament element of the church, to her continuity with Israel. But the church receives her New Testament character more distinctively in the concept of the 'body of Christ.' One is church and one is a member thereof, not through a sociological adherence but precisely through incorporation in this body of the Lord through baptism and the Eucharist. Behind the concept of the church as the People of God, which has been so exclusively thrust into the foreground today, hide influences of ecclesiologies that de facto revert to the Old Testament; and perhaps also political, partisan, and collectivist influences. In reality, there is no truly New Testament, Catholic concept of church without a direct and vital relation not only with sociology but first of all with Christology. The church does not exhaust herself in the 'collective' of the believers: being the 'body of Christ' she is much more than the simple sum of her members."

For the prefect, the gravity of the situation is accentuated by the fact that—on so vital a point as ecclesiology—it does not seem possible to bring about a clarification through promulgations. And although these have not been lacking, in his view what would be necessary is a work in depth. "It is necessary to recreate an authentically *Catholic* climate, to find again the meaning of the church as Church of the Lord, as the locus of the real presence of God in the world. That mystery of which Vatican II speaks when it writes those awesomely challenging words, which correspond nonetheless to the whole Catholic tradition: 'The church, or, in other words, *the Kingdom of Christ now present in mystery*'" (*Lumen Gentium*, no. 3).

"IT IS NOT OURS; IT IS HIS"

In confirmation of the "qualitative" difference of the church with respect to any other human organization whatsoever, he recalls that "only the church, in this world, goes beyond even the radically impassable frontier: the frontier of death. Living or dead, the members of the church live in association with the same life that proceeds from the incorporation of all in the body of Christ."

It is the reality, I observe, that Catholic theology has always called communio sanctorum, *the communion of "saints," in which all the baptized are "saints."*

"Of course," he says. "But it must not be forgotten that the Latin expression does not mean only the union of the members of the church, living or dead. *Communio sanctorum* means also to have 'holy things' in common, that is to say, the grace of the sacraments that pours forth from the dead and resurrected Christ. It is precisely this mysterious yet real bond, this union in Life, that is also the reason why the church is not *our* church, which we could dispose of as we please. She is, rather, *his* church. All that which is only *our* church is not church in the deep sense; it belongs to her human—hence secondary, transitory—aspect."

Does the modern forgetfulness or rejection of this Catholic concept of the church, I ask, not also involve consequences in the relation with the ecclesial hierarchy?

"Certainly. And among the gravest. Here lies the origin of the decline of the authentic concept of 'obedience.' According to some, it would no longer even be a Christian virtue but a heritage of an authoritarian, dogmatic past, hence one to be overcome. If the church, in fact, is *our* church, if *we alone* are the church, if her structures are not willed by Christ, then it is no longer possible to conceive of the existence of a hierarchy as a service to the baptized established by the Lord himself. It is a rejection of the concept of an authority willed by God, an authority therefore that has its legitimation in God and not—as happens in political structures—in the consensus of the majority of the members of an organization. But the church of Christ is not a party, not an association, not a club. Her deep and permanent structure is not *democratic* but *sacramental, consequently hierarchical*. For the hierarchy based on the apostolic succession is the indispensable condition to arrive at the strength, the reality of the sacrament. Here authority is not based on the majority of votes; it is based on the authority of Christ himself, which he willed to pass on to men who were to be his representatives until his definitive return. Only if this perspective is acquired anew will it be possible to rediscover the necessity and fruitfulness of obedience to the legitimate ecclesiastical hierarchies."

FOR A REAL REFORM

Yet alongside the traditional expression *communio sanctorum* (in that comprehensive meaning), I remark, there is also another Latin phrase that has always enjoyed validity among Catholics: *Ecclesia semper reformanda*, the church is always needful of reform. The council has clearly expressed itself on this score:

> By the power of the Holy Spirit, the Church is the faithful spouse of the Lord and will never fail to be a sign of salvation in the world; but she is by no means unaware that down through the centuries there have been among her members, both clerical and lay, some who were disloyal to the Spirit of God. Today as well, the Church is not blind to the discrepancy between the message she proclaims and the human weakness of those to whom the Gospel has been entrusted. Whatever is history's judgment on these shortcomings, we cannot ignore them, and we must combat them earnestly, lest they hinder the spread of the Gospel. (*Gaudium et spes,* no. 43)

Even respecting the mystery, are we not also called to make efforts to change the church?

"To be sure," he replies, "in her human structures the church is *semper reformanda,* but one must be clear in this question as to how and up to what point.

The text cited from Vatican II already gives a quite precise indication, by speaking of the 'fidelity of the Bride of Christ,' which is not called in question by the infidelities of her members. But in order to make this clearer, I shall refer to the Latin formula that the Roman liturgy had the celebrant pronounce in every Mass, at the 'sign of peace' preceding Communion. That prayer read: *Domine Jesu Christe ... ne respicias peccata mea, sed fidem Ecclesiae tuae*. That is to say: 'Lord Jesus Christ, look not upon *my sins*, but upon the faith of *your* church.' Now in many translations of the Ordinary of the Mass into the languages of different countries (but also in the renewed Latin text), the formula has been changed from this 'I' form to a 'We' form: 'Look not upon *our sins*.' A change of this kind may appear irrelevant at first, but it is of great significance."

Why attribute such importance to the change from "I" to "We"?

"Because," he explains, "the use of the singular is an allusion to the necessity of a *personal* admission of one's own fault, to the requisiteness of *personal* conversion, which today is very often hidden in the anonymous mass of 'We,' of the group, of the 'system,' of humanity. Hence, in the end, where all have sinned, nobody seems to have sinned. In this way the sense of personal responsibility, of the faults of each one, is dissolved. Naturally the new version of the text can be understood in a correct manner, because the *I* and the *We* are always intertwined in sin—and, of course, in the Lord's Prayer itself we pray, 'Forgive us *our trespasses*.' But the alteration here does nevertheless reinforce the contemporary tendency to diminish personal responsibility. What is important is that in the new emphasis on the *We*, the *I* not disappear."

This point, I remark, is important, and it will be worthwhile to come back to it later. But for the moment let us go back where we were: to the connection between the axiom Ecclesia semper reformanda *and the invocation to Christ for personal forgiveness.*

"Agreed, let us go back to that prayer which liturgical wisdom inserted at the most solemn moment of the Mass, to that moment of physical, intimate union with Christ who has transformed himself into bread and wine. The church presumed that anyone who celebrated the Eucharist would need to say: *I* have sinned, Lord, look not upon *my sins*. It was the obligatory invocation of every priest: each bishop, the pope himself, like the least priest, had to pronounce it in his daily Mass. And also the laity, all the other members of the church, were called to unite themselves to that recognition of guilt. Therefore, *everybody* in the church, with no exception, had to confess himself to be a sinner, beseech forgiveness, and then set out on the path of his real reform. But this in no way means that the church as such was also a sinner. The church—as we have seen—is a reality that surpasses, mysteriously and infinitely, the sum of her members. In fact, in order to obtain Christ's forgiveness, *my sin* was set over against the *faith of his church*."

And today?

"Today this seems to have been forgotten by many theologians, priests, and laymen. It is not only the change from the *I* to the *We*, from personal to collective responsibility. One even gets the impression that some, although unconsciously, may reverse the prayer by understanding it in this way: 'Look not upon the *sins of the church* but upon *my faith*....' Should this really happen, the consequences will be grave: the faults of individuals become the faults of the church, and faith is reduced to a personal event, to *my way* of understanding and of accepting God and his demands. I really fear that today this is a widespread manner of feeling and thinking. It is another sign of how greatly in many places the common Catholic consciousness has distanced itself from an authentic conception of the church."

wow

What is to be done, then?

"We must," he replies, "go back to saying to the Lord: 'We sin, but the church that is yours and the bearer of faith does not sin.' Faith is the answer of the church to Christ. It is church in the measure that it is an act of faith. This faith is not an individual, solitary act, a response of the individual. Faith means to believe *together*, with all the church."

Where, then, can those "reforms" that we are always enjoined to introduce to our community of believers, who live in history, address themselves?

He says, "We must always bear in mind that the church is not ours but his. Hence the 'reform,' the 'renewals'—necessary as they may be—cannot exhaust themselves in a zealous activity on our part to erect new, sophisticated structures. The most that can come from a work of this kind is a church that is 'ours,' to our measure, which might indeed be interesting but which, by itself, is nevertheless not the true church, that which sustains us with the faith and gives us life with the sacrament. I mean to say that what we can do is infinitely inferior to him who does. Hence, true 'reform' does not mean to take great pains to erect new façades (contrary to what certain ecclesiologies think). Real 'reform' is to strive to let what is ours disappear as much as possible so what belongs to Christ may become more visible. It is a truth well known to the saints. Saints, in fact, reformed the church in depth, not by working up plans for new structures, but by reforming themselves. What the church needs in order to respond to the needs of man in every age is holiness, not management."

Eucharist, Communion, and Solidarity

Lecture Given at the Eucharistic Congress of the Archdiocese of Benevento, Italy

JUNE 2, 2002

Dear friends, after preparing for your Eucharistic Congress with prayer, reflection, and charitable activities under the guidance of your pastor, Archbishop Serafino Sprovieri, the archdiocese of Benevento decided to undertake a twofold investigation. It began an in-depth exploration of the relationship between the deepest sacramental mystery of the church—the Holy Eucharist—and the church's most practical, down-to-earth commitment: her charitable work of sharing, reconciling, and unifying. The diocese proposed this exploration the better to celebrate the sacrament and to live more fruitfully Christ's "new commandment" that we "love one another."

"AGAPE, PAX," ORTHODOXY, ORTHOPRAXIS

Often, in the primitive church, the Eucharist was called simply "*agape*," that is, "love," or even simply "*pax*," that is, "peace." The Christians of that time thus expressed in a dramatic way the unbreakable link between the mystery of the hidden presence of God and the praxis of serving the cause of peace, of Christians being peace. For the early Christians, there was no difference between what today is often distinguished as orthodoxy and orthopraxis, as right doctrine and right action. Indeed, when this distinction is made, there generally is a suggestion that the word *orthodoxy* is to be disdained: those who hold fast to right doctrine are seen as people of narrow sympathy, rigid, potentially intolerant. In the final analysis, for those holding this rather critical view of orthodoxy, everything depends on "right action," with doctrine regarded as something always open to further discussion. For those holding this view, the chief thing is the fruit doctrine produces, while the way that leads to our just action is a matter of indifference. Such a comparison would have been incomprehensible and unacceptable for those in the ancient church, for they rightly understood the word *orthodoxy* not to mean "right doctrine" but to mean the authentic adoration and glorification of God.

They were convinced that everything depended on being in the right relationship with God, on knowing what pleases him and what one can do to respond to him in the right way. For this reason, Israel loved the law: from it, they knew God's will, they knew how to live justly and how to honor God in the right way: by acting in accord with his will, bringing order into the world, opening it to the transcendent.

CHRIST TEACHES HOW GOD IS GLORIFIED, THE WORLD IS MADE JUST

This was the new joy Christians discovered: that now, beginning with Christ, they understood how God ought to be glorified and how precisely through this the world would become just. That these two things should go together—how God is glorified and how justice comes—the angels had proclaimed on the holy night: "Glory to God in the highest, and peace on earth, goodwill toward men," they had said (Lk 2:14). God's glory and peace on earth are inseparable. Where God is excluded, there is a breakdown of peace in the world; without God, no orthopraxis can save us. In fact, there does not exist an orthopraxis that is simply just, detached from a knowledge of what is good. The will without knowledge is blind, and so action, orthopraxis, without knowledge is blind and leads to the abyss. Marxism's great deception was to tell us that we had reflected on the world long enough, that now it was at last time to change it. But if we do not know in what direction to change it, if we do not understand its meaning and its inner purpose, then change alone becomes destruction—as we have seen and continue to see. But the inverse is also true: doctrine alone, which does not become life and action, becomes idle chatter and so is equally empty. The truth is concrete. Knowledge and action are closely united, as are faith and life. This awareness is precisely what your theme seeks to state, "Eucharist, Communion, and Solidarity." I should like to dwell on the three key words you have chosen for your Eucharistic Congress so as to clarify them.

Eucharist

"Eucharist" is today—and it is entirely right that it be so—the most common name for the sacrament of the body and blood of Christ, which the Lord instituted on the night before his Passion. In the early church there were other names for this sacrament—*agape* and *pax* we have already mentioned. Along with these there was, for example, also *synaxis*—assembly, reunion of the many. Among Protestants this sacrament is called "Supper," with the intent—following the lead of Luther, for whom scripture alone was valid—to return totally to the biblical origins. And in fact, in St. Paul, this sacrament is called "the Lord's Supper." But it is significant that this title very soon disappeared, and from the second century it was used no longer. Why? Was it perhaps a moving away from the New Testament, as Luther thought, or something else? Certainly the Lord instituted his sacrament in the context of a meal, more precisely that of the Jewish Passover supper, and so at the beginning it was also linked with a gathering for a meal. But the Lord had not ordered a repetition of the Passover supper, which constituted the framework. That was not his sacrament, his new gift. In any event, the Passover supper could only be celebrated once a year. The celebration of the Eucharist was therefore detached from the gathering for the supper to the degree that the detachment from the law was beginning to take place, along with the passage to a church of Jews and Gentiles, but above all, of Gentiles. The link with the supper was thus revealed as extrinsic—indeed, as the occasion for ambiguities and abuses, as Paul amply described in his First Letter to the Corinthians.

LITURGY OF WORD, PRAYER OF THANKSGIVING, WORDS OF INSTITUTION

Thus the church, assuming her own specific configuration, progressively freed the specific gift of the Lord, which was new and permanent, from the old context and gave it its own form. This took place thanks to the connection with the liturgy of the Word, which has its model in the synagogue; and thanks to the fact that the Lord's words of institution formed the culminating point of the great prayer of thanksgiving—that thanksgiving, also derived from the synagogue traditions and so ultimately from the Lord, who clearly had rendered thanks and praise to God in the Jewish tradition. But he had emphatically enriched that prayer of thanksgiving with a unique profundity by means of the gift of his body and his blood.

Through this action, the early Christians had come to understand that the essence of the event of the Last Supper was not the eating of the lamb and the *essence*

other traditional dishes, but the great prayer of praise that now contained as its center the very words of Jesus. With these words he had transformed his death into the gift of himself, in such a way that we can now render thanks for this death. Yes, only now is it possible to render thanks to God without reserve, because the most dreadful thing—the death of the Redeemer and the death of all of us—was transformed through an act of love into the gift of life.

death thru act of love => gift of life

EUCHARIST, EUCHARISTIC PRAYER

Accordingly, the Eucharist was recognized as the essential reality of the Last Supper, what we call today the Eucharistic Prayer, which derives directly from the prayer of Jesus on the eve of his Passion and is the heart of the new spiritual sacrifice, the motive for which many fathers designated the Eucharist simply as *oratio* (prayer), as the "sacrifice of the Word," as a spiritual sacrifice, but which becomes also material and matter transformed: bread and wine become the body and blood of Christ, the new food, which nourishes us for the resurrection, for eternal life. Thus, the whole structure of words and material elements becomes an anticipation of the eternal wedding feast. At the end, we shall return once more to this connection. Here it is important only to understand better why we as Catholic Christians call this sacrament not "Supper" but "Eucharist." The infant church slowly gave to this sacrament its specific form, and precisely in this way, under the guidance of the Holy Spirit, she clearly identified and correctly represented in signs the true essence of the sacrament, which the Lord really "instituted" on that night.

Precisely by examining the process by which the eucharistic sacrament progressively took on its form, one understands in a beautiful way the profound connection between scripture and tradition. The Bible considered solely in historical context does not communicate sufficiently to us the vision of what is essential. That insight only comes through the living practice of the church that lived scripture, grasped its deepest intention, and made it accessible to us.

non sola Scriptura

"Communio"

The second word in the title of your eucharistic congress—*Communion*—has become fashionable these days. It is, in fact, one of the most profound and characteristic words of the Christian tradition. Precisely for this reason it is very important to understand it in the whole depth and breadth of its meaning. Perhaps I may make an entirely personal observation here. When with a few friends—in particular, Henri de Lubac, Hans Urs von Balthasar, Louis Bouyer, and Jorge Medina—I had the idea of founding a magazine in which we intended to deepen and develop the inheritance of the council, we looked for an appropriate name, a single word that could fully convey the purpose of this publication. Already, in the last year of the Second Vatican Council, 1965, a review was begun, to serve as the permanent voice of the council and its spirit, called *Concilium*. Hans Küng thought he had discovered an equivalence between the words *ekklesia* (church) and *concilium*. The root of both terms was the Greek word *kalein* (to call), the first word, *ekklesia*, meaning to convoke, the second word, *concilium*, to summon together. Therefore both words essentially signify the same thing. From such an etymological relationship one could say the terms *church* and *council* were almost synonymous and see the church by her very nature as being the continuing council of God in the world. Therefore, the church was to be conceived of in this "conciliar" sense and "actualized" in the form of a council; and, vice versa, the council was seen as the most intense possible realization of "church," namely, the church in her highest form.

In the years following the council, for a time, I followed this concept—the church as the permanent council of God in the world—which seemed at first glance rather enlightening. The practical consequences of this conception should not be overlooked; its attractiveness is immediate. Still, though I came to the conclusion that the vision of Hans Küng certainly contained something true and serious, I also saw that it needed considerable correction. I would like to try to summarize very briefly the result of my studies at that time. My philological and theological research into the understanding of the words *church* and *council* in ancient times showed that a council can certainly be an important, vital manifestation of the church, but that in reality the church is something more, that her essence goes deeper.

"*KOINONIA*" LIVES THE WORD OF LIFE

The council is something that the church holds, but the church is not a council. The church does not exist primarily to deliberate, but to live the Word that has been given to us. I decided that the word that best expressed this fundamental concept, which conveyed the very essence of the church itself, was *koinonia*—communion. Her structure, therefore, is not to be described by the term *concilial*, but rather with the word *communional*. When I proposed these ideas publicly in 1969 in my book *The New People of God*, the concept of communion was not yet widespread in public theological and ecclesial discussions. As a result, my ideas on this matter were also given little consideration. These ideas, however, were decisive for me in the search for a title for the new journal, and led to our later calling the journal *Communio* (Communion).

The concept itself received wide public recognition only with the Synod of Bishops in 1985. Until then the phrase "People of God" had prevailed as the chief new concept of the church, and was widely believed to synthesize the intentions of Vatican II itself. This belief might well have been true, if the words had been used in the full profundity of their biblical meaning and in the broad, accurate context in which the council had used them. When, however, the main word becomes a slogan, its meaning is inevitably diminished; indeed, it is trivialized.

SYNOD OF 1985

As a consequence, the Synod of 1985 sought a new beginning by focusing on the word *communion,* which refers first of all to the eucharistic center of the church, and so again returns to the understanding of the church as the most intimate place of the encounter between Jesus and mankind, in his act of giving himself to us.

It was unavoidable that this great fundamental word of the New Testament, isolated and employed as a slogan, would also suffer diminishment—indeed, might even be trivialized. Those who speak today of an "ecclesiology of communion" generally tend to mean two things: (1) they support a "pluralist" ecclesiology, almost a "federative" sense of union, opposing what they see as a centralist conception of the church; (2) they want to stress, in the exchanges of giving and receiving among local churches, their culturally pluralistic forms of worship in the liturgy, in discipline, and in doctrine.

Even where these tendencies are not developed in detail, *communion* is nonetheless generally understood in a horizontal sense—communion is seen as emerging from a network of multiple communities. This conception of the communal structure of the church is barely distinguishable from the conciliar vision mentioned above. The horizontal dominates. The emphasis is on the idea of self-determination within a vast community of churches. Naturally, there is here much that is true. However, fundamentally the approach is not correct, and in this way the true depth of what the New Testament and Vatican II and also the Synod of 1985 wanted to say would be lost. To clarify the central meaning of the concept of *communio,* I would like briefly to turn to two great texts on *communio* from the New Testament. The first is found in I Corinthians 10:16ff., where Paul tells us: "The chalice of blessing, which we bless, is it not a participation ["communion" in the Italian text] in the blood of Christ? The bread which we break, is it not a participation in the body of Christ? Because there is but one bread, we who are many are one body, for we all partake of the one bread."

THE VERTICAL DIMENSION IN THE EUCHARIST

The concept of communion is above all anchored in the holy sacrament of the Eucharist, the reason why, still today in the language of the church, we rightly designate the reception of this sacrament simply as "to Communicate." In this way, the very practical social significance of this sacramental event also immediately becomes evident, and this in a radical way that cannot be achieved in exclusively horizontal perspectives. Here we are told that by means of the sacrament we enter in a certain way into a communion with the blood of Jesus Christ, where blood, according to the Hebrew perspective, stands for "life." Thus, what is being affirmed is a commingling of Christ's life with our own.

In the context of the Eucharist, blood clearly stands also for "gift," for an existence that pours itself out, gives itself for us and to us. Thus the communion of blood is also insertion into the dynamic of this life, into this "blood poured out." Our existence is "dynamized" in such a way that each of us can become a being for others, as we see obviously happening in the open Heart of Christ.

From a certain point of view, the words over the bread are even more stunning. They tell of a "communion" with the body of Christ that Paul compares to the union of a man and a woman (cf. 1 Cor 6:17ff.; Eph 5:26–32). Paul also expresses this from another perspective when he says it is one and the same bread, which all of us now receive. This is true in a startling way: the "bread"—the new manna, which God gives to us—is for all one and the same Christ.

THE LORD UNITES US WITH HIMSELF

It is truly the one, identical Lord whom we receive in the Eucharist, or better, it is the Lord who receives us and assumes us into himself. St. Augustine expressed this in a short passage that he perceived as a sort of vision: eat the bread of the strong; you will not transform me into yourself, but I will transform you into me. In other words, when we consume bodily nourishment, it is assimilated by the body, becoming itself a part of ourselves. But this bread is of another type. It is greater and higher than we are. It is not we who assimilate it, but it assimilates us to itself, so that we become in a certain way "conformed to Christ," as Paul says, members of his body, one in him.

We all "eat" the same person, not only the same thing; we all are in this way taken out of our closed individual persons and placed inside another, greater one. We all are assimilated into Christ and so, by means of communion with

Christ, united among ourselves, rendered the same, sole thing in him, members of one another.

To communicate with Christ is essentially also to communicate with one another. We are no longer each alone, each separate from the other; we are now each part of the other; each of those who receive communion is "bone of my bone and flesh of my flesh" (Gn 2:23).

SOCIAL UNIVERSAL UNION

A true spirituality of communion seen in its Christological profundity, therefore, necessarily has a social character, as Henri de Lubac brilliantly described more than a half-century ago in his book *Catholicism*.

For this reason, in my prayer at communion, I must look totally toward Christ, allowing myself to be transformed by him, even to be burned by his enveloping fire. But, precisely for this reason, I must always keep clearly in mind that in this way he unites me organically with every other person receiving him—with the one next to me, whom I may not like very much; but also with those who are far away, in Asia, Africa, America, or any other place.

Becoming one with them, I must learn to open myself toward them and to involve myself in their situations. This is the proof of the authenticity of my love for Christ. If I am united with Christ, I am together with my neighbor, and this unity is not limited to the moment of communion; it only begins here. It becomes life, becomes flesh and blood, in the everyday experience of sharing life with my neighbor. Thus, the individual realities of my communicating and being part of the life of the church are inseparably linked to one another. The church is not born as a simple federation of communities. Her birth begins with the one bread, with the one Lord and from him from the beginning and everywhere, the one body, which derives from the one bread. She becomes one not through a centralized government but through a common center open to all, because it constantly draws its existence from a single Lord, who forms her by means of the one bread into one body. Because of this, her unity has a greater depth than that which any other human union could ever achieve. Precisely when the Eucharist is understood in the intimacy of the union of each person with the Lord, it becomes also a social sacrament to the highest degree.

MARTIN DE PORRES, MOTHER TERESA

The great social saints were, in reality, always the great eucharistic saints. I would like to mention just two examples chosen entirely at random.

First of all, the beloved figure of St. Martin de Porres, who was born in 1569 in Lima, Peru, the son of an Afro-American mother and a Spanish nobleman. Martin lived from the adoration of the Lord present in the Eucharist, passing entire nights in prayer before the crucified Lord in the tabernacle, while during the day he tirelessly cared for the sick and assisted the socially outcast and despised, with whom he identified as a mulatto. The encounter with the Lord, who gives himself to us from the cross, makes all of us members of the one body by means of the one bread, which when responded to fully moves us to serve the suffering, to care for the weak and the forgotten.

In our time, we can recall the person of Mother Teresa of Calcutta. Wherever she opened the houses of her sisters to the service of the dying and outcast, the first thing she asked for was a place for the tabernacle, because she knew that only beginning from there would come the strength for such service.

Whoever recognizes the Lord in the tabernacle recognizes him in the suffering and the needy; they are among those to whom the world's judge will say: "I was hungry and you gave me food; I was thirsty and you gave me drink; I was naked and you clothed me; I was sick and you visited me; I was in prison and you came to me" (Mt 25:35).

Briefly, I would like to recall a second important New Testament text concerning the word *communion* (*koinonia*). It is found right at the beginning of the first Letter of John (1:3–7), where he speaks of the encounter granted him with the Word made flesh. John says that he is transmitting what he has seen with his own eyes and what he has touched with his own hands. This encounter has given him the gift of *koinonia*—communion—with the Father and his Son, Jesus Christ. It has become a true "communion" with the living God. As John expresses it, the communion has opened his eyes and he now lives in the light, that is, in the truth of God, which is expressed in the unique new commandment that encompasses everything—the commandment to love. And so the communion with the "Word of life" becomes the just life, becomes love. In this way it also becomes reciprocal communion: "If we walk in the light, as he is in the light, we are in communion one with another" (1 Jn 1:7).

The text shows the same logic of *communio* that we already found in Paul: communion with Jesus becomes communion with God himself, communion with the light and with love; it becomes in this way an upright life, and all of this unites us with one another in the truth. Only when we regard communion in this depth and breadth do we have something to say to the world.

We arrive finally at the third key word, *solidarity*. While the first two words come from the Bible and from Christian tradition, this word comes to us from outside. The concept of "solidarity"—as Archbishop Paul Cordes has shown— was developed initially among the early socialists by P. Lerou (died 1871) in contraposition to the Christian idea of love, as the new, rational, and effective response to social problems.

WITHOUT CHRIST, THERE ARE NO SOLUTIONS

Karl Marx held that Christianity had had a millennium and a half to demonstrate its capacity to deal with poverty, inequality, and injustice, and had only succeeded in proving its incapacity to do so.

Therefore, Marx claimed, new ways had to be employed. And for decades many were convinced that the Marxist socialist system, centered around the concept of "solidarity," was now the way finally to achieve human equality, to eliminate poverty, and to bring peace to the world. Today, we can see what horrors and massacres were left behind by a social theory and policies that took no account of God.

It is undeniable that the liberal model of the market economy, especially as moderated and corrected under the influence of Christian social ideas, has in some parts of the world led to great success. All the sadder are the results, especially in places like Africa, where clashing power blocs and economic interests have been at work. Behind the apparent beneficial models of development, there has all too often been hidden the desire to expand the reach of particular powers and ideologies in order to dominate the market. In this situation, ancient social structures and spiritual and moral forces have been destroyed, with consequences that echo in our ears like a single great cry of sorrow.

No, without God things cannot go well. Because only in Christ has God shown us his face, spoken his name, entered into communion with us; without Christ there is no ultimate hope.

CHRISTIANS HAVE EXEMPLIFIED SOLUTIONS
DESPITE TERRIBLE FAILURES

It is clear that Christians in past centuries have been stained with serious sins. Slavery and the slave trade remain a dark chapter that show how few Christians were truly Christian and how far many Christians were from the faith and message of the gospel, from true communion with Jesus Christ.

On the other hand, lives full of faith and love, as seen in the humble willingness of so many priests and sisters to sacrifice themselves, have provided a positive counterweight and left an inheritance of love, which, even if it cannot eliminate the horror of exploitation, can help to lessen it. On this witness we can build; along this path we can proceed farther.

It was in this situation, in recent decades, that the understanding of the concept of solidarity—thanks above all to the ethical studies of the Holy Father—has been slowly transformed and Christianized, so that now we can justly place it next to the two key Christian words *Eucharist* and *Communion*. Solidarity in this context signifies people who feel responsible for one another, the healthy for the sick, the rich for the poor, the countries of the North for those of the South. It means a sense of individual awareness, of reciprocal responsibility; it means we are conscious that when we give we receive, that we can always give only what has been given to us, that what we have been given never belongs to us for ourselves alone.   *nemo dat quod non habet*

SPIRITUALITY HAS TO ACCOMPANY SCIENTIFIC AND TECHNICAL FORMATION

Today we see that it is not enough to transmit technical skills, scientific knowledge and theories, nor the praxis of certain political structures. Those things not only do not help but even end up causing harm, if the spiritual forces which give meaning to these technologies and structures are not also reawakened so as to make their responsible use possible. It was easy to destroy with our rationality the traditional religions, which now survive as subcultures, remnants of superstition that have been deprived of their better elements and now are practices that can harm people in mind and body. It would have been better to expose their healthy nucleus to the light of Christ and so lead them to the fulfillment of the tacit expectations within them. Through such a process of purification and development, continuity and progress would have been united in a fruitful way.

Where missions were successful, they generally followed this path and so helped to develop those forces of faith that are so urgently needed today.

In the crisis of the 1960s and 1970s, many missionaries came to the conclusion that missionary work—that is, the proclamation of the gospel of Jesus Christ—was no longer appropriate today.

They thought the only thing that still made sense was to offer help in social development. But how can positive social development be carried out if we become illiterate with regard to God?

GOSPEL AND SOCIAL ADVANCEMENT GO TOGETHER

The fundamental idea tacitly agreed upon, that the peoples or tribes needed to preserve their own religions and not concern themselves with ours, shows only that the faith in the hearts of such men had grown cold despite their great goodwill; it shows that communion with the Lord was no longer seen as vital. Otherwise how could they have thought that it was a good thing to exclude others from these things?

Basically it is a matter here—often without realizing it—of thinking poorly of religion in general and of not esteeming other religions. A person's religion is considered an archaic relic to be left alone because ultimately it is thought to have nothing to do with the true greatness of progress. What religions say and do appears totally irrelevant; they are not even a part of the world of rationality; their contents ultimately count for nothing. The "orthopraxis" that we then look forward to will truly be built on sand.

It is high time to abandon this erroneous way of thinking. We need faith in Jesus Christ if for no other reason than because it brings together reason and religion. It offers us in this way the criteria of responsibility and releases the strength necessary to live according to this responsibility. Sharing on all levels, spiritual, ethical, and religious, is part of solidarity between peoples and nations.

GLOBALIZATION MEANS SEEKING THE WELFARE OF ALL THE CONTINENTS

It is clear that we must develop our economy further such that it no longer operates only in favor of the interests of a certain country or group of countries, but rather for the welfare of all the continents. This is difficult and is never fully realized. It requires that we make sacrifices. But if a spirit of solidarity truly nourished by faith is born, then this could become possible, even if only in an imperfect way.

The theme of globalization arises in this context, but here I am unable to address it. It is clear today that we all depend on each other. But there is a globalization that is conceived of unilaterally in terms of personal interests. There ought to exist a globalization that requires nations to be responsible for one another and to bear one another's burdens. All of this cannot be realized in a neutral way, with reference only to market mechanisms. For decisions about market value are determined by many presuppositions. Thus, our religious and moral horizon is always decisive. If globalization in technology and economy is not accompanied by a new opening of the conscience to God, before whom all of us have a responsibility, then there will be a catastrophe. This is the great responsibility that weighs today on Christians.

Christianity, from the one Lord, the one bread, which seeks to make of us one body, has from the beginning aimed at the unification of humanity. If we, precisely at the moment when the exterior unification of humanity, previously unthinkable, becomes possible, withdraw ourselves as Christians, believing we cannot or should not give anything further, we would burden ourselves with a serious sin. In fact, a unity that is built without God, or indeed against him, ends up like the experiment of Babylon: in total confusion and total destruction, in hatred and total chaos of all against all.

THE EUCHARIST AS THE SACRAMENT OF TRANSFORMATION

Let us return to the Holy Eucharist. What really happened on the night when Christ was betrayed? Let us listen to the Roman Canon—the heart of the "Eucharist" of the church in Rome: "The day before he suffered, he took bread into his sacred hands, and looking up to heaven, to you, his almighty Father, he gave you thanks and praise, broke the bread, gave it to his disciples and said: 'Take this all of you, and eat it. This is my body which will be given up for you.' When supper was ended, he took the cup, again he gave you thanks and praise, gave the cup to his disciples and said: 'Take, all of you, and drink from it. This is the cup of my blood the blood of the new and everlasting covenant, it will be shed for you and for all so that sins may be forgiven. Do this in memory of me'" (ICEL translation).

TRANSUBSTANTIATION

What is happening in these words?

In the first place we are confronted by the word *transubstantiation*. The bread becomes the body, his body. The bread of the earth becomes the bread of God, the "manna" of heaven, with which God nourishes men not only in their earthly life but also in the prospect of the resurrection—which prepares for the Resurrection, or rather, already makes it begin. The Lord, who would have been able to transform stones into bread, who was able to raise up from rocks the sons of Abraham, wishes to transform the bread into a body, his body. Is this possible? How can it happen?

BODY GIVEN, BLOOD POURED OUT

We cannot avoid the questions that the people posed in the synagogue of Capernaum. He is there before his disciples, with his body; how can he say over the bread: this is my body? It is important to pay close attention to what the Lord really said. He does not say only, "This is my body," but: "This is my body, which is given up for you." It can become gift, because it is given. By means of the act of giving it becomes "capable of communicating," has transformed itself into a gift. We may observe the same thing in the words over the cup. Christ does not say simply, "This is my blood," but: "This is my blood, which is shed for you." Because it is shed, inasmuch as it is shed, it can be given.

THE REAL TRANSFORMATION OF VIOLENCE
INTO AN ACT OF LOVE

But now a new question emerges: what do "it is given" and "it is shed" mean? In truth, Jesus is killed; he is nailed to a cross and dies amid torment. His blood is poured out, first in the Garden of Olives due to his interior suffering for his mission, then in the flagellation, the crowning with thorns, the Crucifixion, and after his death in the piercing of his heart. What occurs is above all an act of violence, of hatred, torture, and destruction.

At this point we run into a second, more profound level of transformation: he transforms, from within, the act of violent men against him into an act of giving on behalf of these men—into an act of love. This is dramatically recognizable in the scene of the Garden of Olives. What he teaches in the Sermon on the Mount, he now does: he does not offer violence against violence, as he might have done, but puts an end to violence by transforming it into love. The act of killing, of death, is changed into an act of love; violence is defeated by love. This is the fundamental transformation upon which all the rest is based. It is the true transformation that the world needs and which alone can redeem the world. Since Christ in an act of love has transformed and defeated violence from within, death itself is transformed: love is stronger than death. It remains forever.

TRANSFORMATION OF DEATH INTO LIFE

And so in this transformation is contained the broader transformation of death into resurrection, of the dead body into the risen body. If the first man was a living being, as St. Paul says, the new Adam, Christ, will become by this spiritual event the giver of life (1 Cor 15:45). The Risen One is gift, is spirit who gives his life, "communicates," indeed, is communication. This means that there is no farewell here to material existence; rather, in this way material existence achieves its goal: without the actual event of death (with its interior transcendence), all this complex transformation of material things would not be possible. And so in the transformation of the Resurrection, all the fullness of Christ continues to subsist but transformed in this way; now being a body and the gift of self are no longer mutually exclusive, but are implicit in each other.

Before going on, let us first seek to sum this up once more in order to understand this whole complex reality. At the moment of the Last Supper, Jesus has already anticipated the event of Calvary. He accepts the death on the cross and with his acceptance transforms the act of violence into an act of giving, of self-giving poured forth, "Even if I am to be poured out as a libation on the sacrificial offering of your faith," St. Paul says on the basis of this and in regard to his own imminent martyrdom in Philippians 2:17. At the Last Supper the cross is already present, accepted, and transformed by Jesus.

This first and fundamental transformation draws to itself all the others—the mortal body is transformed into the resurrected body: it is "the spirit which gives life."

THE TRANSFORMATION OF BREAD AND WINE

On the basis of this, the third transformation becomes possible: the gifts of bread and wine, which are the gifts of Creation and at the same time fruits of human labor and the "transformation" of the Creation, are transformed so that in them the Lord who gives himself becomes present, in his gift of self-giving. His gift is himself—since he is the gift. The act of self-giving is not something from him, but it is himself.

And on this basis the prospect opens onto two further transformations that are essential to the Eucharist from the instant of its institution: the transformed bread, the transformed wine.

Through them the Lord himself gives himself as spirit that gives life, to transform us men, so that we become one bread with him and then one body with him. The transformation of the gifts, which is only the continuation of the fundamental transformations of the cross and the Resurrection, is not the final point, but in its turn only a beginning.

TRANSFORMATION OF COMMUNICANTS INTO ONE BODY

The purpose of the Eucharist is the transformation of those who receive it in authentic communion. And so the end is unity, that peace which we—separate individuals who live beside one another or in conflict with one another—become with Christ and in him, as one organism of self-giving, to live in view of the Resurrection and the new world.

THE TRANSFORMATION OF CREATION INTO
A DWELLING PLACE FOR GOD

The fifth and final transformation that characterizes this sacrament thus becomes visible: by means of us, the transformed, who have become one body, one spirit that gives life, the entire creation must be transformed. The entire creation must become a "new city," a new paradise, the living dwelling place of God: "God all in all" (1 Cor 15:28)—thus Paul describes the end of Creation, which must be conformed to the Eucharist.

Thus the Eucharist is a process of transformations, drawing on God's power to transform hatred and violence, his power to transform the world. We must therefore pray that the Lord will help us to celebrate and to live the Eucharist in this way. We pray that he transform us, and together with us the world, into the new Jerusalem.

The Ecclesiology of the Constitution on the Church: *Lumen Gentium*

At the time of the preparation for the Second Vatican Council and during the council itself, Cardinal Frings often told me of a small episode that moved him deeply. Pope John XXIII had not personally decided on themes for the council, but invited the world's bishops to make their suggestions, so that the subjects to be treated by the council might emerge from the lived experience of the universal church. In the German Bishops' Conference, topics were presented for the council, but not only in Germany but throughout the Catholic Church, it was felt that the theme of the council should be the church. The First Vatican Council had been unable to complete its ecclesiological synthesis because it was cut short by the Franco-Prussian War and had to leave the chapter on the primacy and infallibility of the Roman pontiff to stand by itself. To offer a comprehensive vision of the church seemed to be the urgent task of the coming Second Vatican Council. The focus on the church flowed from the cultural atmosphere of the time. The end of the First World War had brought a profound theological upheaval. Liberal theology with its individualistic orientation had been completely eclipsed, and a new sensitivity to the church was arising. Not only did Romano Guardini speak of a reawakening of the church in souls. The Evangelical bishop Otto Dibelius coined the formula "the century of the church," and Karl Barth gave to his dogmatic synthesis of the reformed (Calvinist) tradition the programmatic title *Kirchliche Dogmatik* (Church Dogmatics). He explained that a dogmatic theology presupposes the church; without the church it does not exist. Among the members of the German Episcopal Conference there was consequently a broad consensus that the theme of the council should be the church.

SPEAKING OF THE CHURCH WITHIN THE DISCOURSE ON GOD

But the senior bishop of Regensburg, Bishop Buchberger, was esteemed and respected far beyond his diocese for having conceived the ten-volume *Lexikon für Theologie und Kirche,* now in its third edition. He asked to speak—as the archbishop of Cologne told me—and said: "Dear brothers, at the council you should first of all speak about God. This is the most important theme." The bishops were deeply impressed; they could not ignore the seriousness of his suggestion. Of course, they could not make up their minds simply to propose the theme of God. But an unspoken concern lingered, at least in Cardinal Frings, who continued to ponder how the bishops might satisfy this imperative.

The episode came to mind when I read the text of the conference given by Johann Baptist Metz in 1993 at the time he retired from his chair in Münster. I would like to quote at least a few significant phrases of his important address. Metz says: "The crisis reached by European Christianity is no longer primarily or at least exclusively an ecclesial crisis.... The crisis is more profound: it is not only rooted in the situation of the church: the crisis has become a crisis of God. To sum up, one could say 'religion yes,' 'God no,' where this 'no,' in turn, is not meant in the categorical sense of the great forms of atheism. There are no longer any great forms of atheism. Today's atheism can effectively return to speaking of God—distractedly or calmly—without really intending him [his person].... Furthermore, the church has her own concept of immunization against the crisis of God. She no longer speaks today of God—as, for example, she still did at the Second Vatican Council—but only (as she did at the council) of God proclaimed through the church. The crisis of God is codified ecclesiologically." Words like this from the mouth of the creator of political theology cannot fail to capture our attention. They rightly remind us that the Second Vatican Council was not only an ecclesiological council, but that first and foremost, it spoke of God—and this not only within Christianity but to the world—of the God who is the God of all, who saves all and is accessible to all. Perhaps the Second Vatican Council, as Metz seems to say, only accepted half the legacy of the First Vatican Council? Obviously a treatment of the ecclesiology of the council has to deal with this question.

THE BASIC THESIS

Right now I want to state my basic thesis: the Second Vatican Council clearly wanted to speak of the church within the discourse on God, to subordinate the discourse on the church to the discourse on God and to offer an ecclesiology that would be theological in a true sense. Until now, however, the way the council was received has ignored this qualifying characteristic in favor of individual ecclesiological affirmations; it has highlighted single phrases that are easy to repeat and has thus fallen away from the broad horizons of the council fathers. Something similar can be said about the first text on which the Second Vatican Council focused—the Constitution on the Sacred Liturgy. The fact that it was placed at the beginning was basically due to pragmatic motives. But retrospectively, it must be said that it has a deeper meaning within the structure of the council: adoration comes first. Therefore God comes first. This introduction corresponds to the norm of the Benedictine Rule: *Operi Dei nihil praeponatur* (Let nothing be placed before the work of God, the divine office). As the second text of the council, the Constitution on the Church should be considered inwardly connected with the text on the liturgy. The church is guided by prayer, by the mission of glorifying God. By its nature, ecclesiology is connected with the liturgy. It is, therefore, logical that the third constitution should speak of the Word of God, which convokes the church and renews her in every age. The fourth constitution shows how the glorification of God is realized in the active life, since the light received from God is carried into the world and only in this way becomes fully the glorification of God. In the history of the postconciliar period, the Constitution on the Liturgy was certainly no longer understood from the viewpoint of the basic primacy of adoration, but rather as a recipe book of what we can do with the liturgy. In the meantime, the fact that the liturgy is actually "made" for God and not for ourselves seems to have escaped the minds of those who are busy pondering how to give the liturgy an ever more attractive and communicable shape, actively involving an ever greater number of people. However, the more we make it for ourselves, the less attractive it is, because everyone perceives clearly that the essential focus on God has increasingly been lost.

PARTIAL INTERPRETATIONS

As regards the ecclesiology of *Lumen gentium,* certain key words continue to be kept in mind: the idea of the "People of God," the collegiality of the bishops as a reappraisal of the bishops' ministry in relation to the primacy of the pope, the reappraisal of the local churches in relation to the universal church, the ecumenical openness of the concept of church and openness to other religions, lastly, the question of the specific position of the Catholic Church, expressed in the formula which holds that the church, defined in the Creed as one, holy, catholic, and apostolic, *subsistit in Ecclesia catholica.* For now I will leave the famous formula untranslated, because—as was foreseen—it has received the most contradictory explanations, which range from the idea that it expresses the uniqueness of the Catholic Church united to the pope to the idea that it expresses the equivalency of the other Christian churches with the Catholic Church and that the Catholic Church has given up her claim of being distinctive. In the early stages of the reception of the council, the concept of "People of God" predominated together with the theme of collegiality; the term *people* was understood in terms of ordinary political usage, later in the context of liberation theology it was understood in terms of the Marxist use of the term *people* as opposed to *the dominating classes,* and even more widely, in the sense of the sovereignty of the people, which would now finally be applied to the church. This, in turn, gave rise to broad discussions about her structures, in which *People of God* was interpreted, according to the situation, either in a more Western way as "democratization," or in the Eastern European way as "popular democracy." Gradually these "verbal fireworks" (N. Lohfink) around the concept of the People of God burned out, above all because the power games became empty and had to make room for ordinary work in parish councils, but also because sound theological work has incontrovertibly shown that the politicization of a concept that comes from a totally different context cannot be supported. As a result of his careful exegetic analyses, the exegete of Bocum, Werner Berg, to take one example, states: "Despite the small number of passages that contain the expression 'People of God,' from this point of view 'People of God' is a rare biblical expression, but nevertheless a common idea emerges: the phrase 'People of God' expresses 'kinship' with God, a relationship with God, the link between God and what is designated as 'People of God,' hence a 'vertical orientation.' The expression lends itself less to describe the hierarchical structure of this community, especially if the 'People of God' is described as a 'counterpart' to the ministers.... Nor, starting with its biblical significance, does the expression lend itself to a cry of protest against the ministers: 'We are the People of God.'" Josef Meyer zu Schlotern, the professor of fundamental theology of Paderborn, concludes the examination of the discussion about the concept of "People of God" by observing that the Constitution on the Church of the Second Vatican Council ends the pertinent chapter in such a way as "to outline the Trinitarian structure as the foundation of the ultimate definition of the church...." Thus the discussion is led back to the essential point: the church does not exist for herself but must be God's instrument, in order to gather man to himself to prepare for the moment when "God will be all in all" (1 Cor 15:28). It was the concept of God that lost out in the "fireworks" sparked by the expression, and in this way the expression *People of God* lost its meaning. In fact, a church that exists for herself alone is superfluous. And people notice it immediately. The crisis of the church as it is reflected in the concept of "People of God" is a "crisis of God"; it is the consequence of abandoning the essential. What remains is merely a struggle for power. There is enough of this elsewhere in the world; there is no need of the church for this.

ECCLESIOLOGY OF COMMUNION

It can certainly be said that, at the time of the extraordinary Synod of 1985, which was to attempt an evaluation of the twenty years following the council, there appeared a new effort to sum up conciliar ecclesiology in a basic concept: the ecclesiology of *communio*. I received this new focus of ecclesiology with joy and did my best to prepare it. Even so, it should be recognized first of all that the word *communio* does not have a central position in the council. But if it is properly understood, it can serve as a synthesis for the essential elements of conciliar ecclesiology. All of the essential elements of the Christian concept of *communio* are combined in the famous text of I John 1:3, which can be taken as the criterion for the correct Christian understanding of communion: "That which we have seen and heard we proclaim also to you, so that you also may have fellowship with us; and our fellowship is with the Father and with his Son Jesus Christ. And we are writing this that our joy may be complete." Here the starting point of *communio* is brought to the fore: the encounter with the Son of God, Jesus Christ, who comes to men and women through the church's proclamation. So there arises communion among human beings, which in turn is based on *communio* with the Triune God. We have access to communion with God through the realization of the communion of God with man, which is Christ in person; the encounter with Christ creates communion with him and thus with the Father in the Holy Spirit, and from this point unites human beings with one another. The purpose of all this is full joy: the church carries an eschatological dynamic within her. In the words *full joy*, we can glimpse a reference to the farewell discourse of Jesus, to the Easter mystery, and to the return of the Lord in his Easter appearances, which prepare for his full return in the new world: "You will weep and lament, but the world will rejoice; you will be sorrowful, but your sorrow will turn into joy.... I will see you again and your hearts will rejoice.... [A]sk, and you will receive, that your joy may be full" (Jn 16:20, 22, 24). If the last sentence is compared with Luke 11:13—the invitation to prayer in Luke—it clearly appears that "joy" and "Holy Spirit" are one and the same, and that the word *joy* in I John 1:3 conceals the Holy Spirit, who is not expressly mentioned here. The word *communio*, therefore, based on the biblical context, has a theological, Christological, salvation historical, and ecclesiological character. It, therefore, has within it the sacramental dimension that appears explicitly in Paul: "The cup of blessing which we bless, is it not a participation in the blood of Christ? The bread which we break, is it not a participation in the body of Christ? Because there is one Bread, we who are many are one body" (1 Cor 10:16f.). The ecclesiology of communion is a profoundly eucharistic ecclesiology. It is thus very close to the eucharistic ecclesiology that Orthodox theologians have developed convincingly in our century. Ecclesiology becomes more concrete and at the same time remains totally spiritual, transcendent, and eschatological. In the Eucharist, Christ, present in the bread and wine and giving himself ever anew, builds the church as his body, and through his risen body unites us to the Triune God and to one another. The Eucharist is celebrated in different places, yet at the same time it is universal, because there is only one Christ and only one body of Christ. The Eucharist includes the priestly service of the *repraesentatio Christi* and thus the network of service, the synthesis of unity and multiplicity that is already expressed in the word *communio*. Thus it can be said without a doubt that the concept incorporates an ecclesiological synthesis, which unites the discourse on the church with the discourse on God and life from God and with God, a synthesis that takes up all the essential intentions of the Second Vatican Council's ecclesiology and connects them in the right way.

For these reasons I was grateful and pleased when the Synod of 1985 made the concept of communion once again the focus of reflection. However, the years that followed show that no word is safe from misunderstandings, not even the best and most profound.

PARTIAL INTERPRETATIONS

To the extent that *communio* became an easy slogan, it was devalued and distorted. As with the concept of "People of God," here, too, a gradual "horizontalism" should be pointed out, with the giving up of the idea of God. The ecclesiology of communion began to be reduced to the theme of the relationship between the local church and the universal church, which, in turn, degenerated gradually into the problem of the division of the areas of competence between them. Of course, the egalitarian cause, which claimed that there could only be complete equality in *communio*, was again disseminated. Thus once again the disciples' discussion on who was the greatest became operative, which, of course, will not be settled in any generation. Mark mentions it with the greatest insistence. On the way to Jerusalem, Jesus had spoken for the third time to the disciples about his forthcoming Passion. On arriving in Capernaum he asked them what they had been discussing on the way. "But they were silent," for they had been discussing which of them was the greatest—a sort of discussion of primacy (Mk 9:33–37). Isn't it still the same today? As the Lord walks toward his Passion and the church, he himself within her, suffering, we reflect on our favorite theme, the discussion of our rights of precedence. And if he were to come among us and ask us what we were discussing along the way, how embarrassed and silent we would have to be!

This does not mean that the church should not also discuss the proper order and designation of responsibilities; and naturally, imbalances will always be found in her that will require correction. Of course, there can be an excessive Roman centralism, which must be identified and purified. But such matters cannot detract from the church's true task: the church must speak primarily not of herself but of God; and so that this may happen with integrity, there are also certain intra-ecclesial criticisms for which the connecting of her discourse on God and on common service must provide the proper direction. Finally, it is not by accident that what Jesus said about the last becoming first and the first becoming last returns in various contexts of the evangelical tradition—as a mirror that always reflects everyone.

THE CDF LETTER ON COMMUNION

To confront the reduction of the concept of *communio* that has taken place since 1985, the Congregation for the Doctrine of the Faith saw fit to prepare a Letter to the Bishops of the Catholic Church entitled "Some Aspects of the Church Understood as Communion," which was published on June 28, 1992.

Since it now seems to have become obligatory for theologians who want to make a name for themselves to offer a negative appraisal of the documents of the Congregation for the Doctrine of the Faith, theologians created a storm of criticism over it from which it could hardly recover. The sentence that said that the universal church is a reality that in its essential mystery is logically and ontologically prior to the particular churches was singled out for criticism. In the text, this was supported concisely by recalling that, according to the fathers, the church, which is one and unique, precedes Creation and gives birth to the particular churches (n. 9). Thus the fathers take up a rabbinical theology that had conceived of the Torah and Israel as pre-existent: Creation was considered to be so conceived that there would be room in it for God's will, but this would require a people who would live in accord with God's will and make it the light of the world. Since the fathers were convinced of the ultimate identity between the church and Israel, they could not see in the church something that took place by chance at the last hour, but recognized in the gathering of the peoples in accord with God's will the internal purpose of creation. The image is broadened and deepened on the basis of Christology: history—again in relation to the Old Testament—is explained as a love story between God and man. God finds and prepares a Bride for his Son, the single Bride who is the unique church. Starting from the word of Genesis, that the man and his wife will become "one flesh" (Gn 2:24), the image of the bride is united with the idea of the church as the body of Christ, a metaphor that in turn comes from the eucharistic liturgy. The one body of Christ is prepared; Christ and the church will be two "in one flesh," one body, and thus "God will be all in all." This ontological precedence of the universal church, the one church, the one body, the one Bride, over the concrete empirical realizations in the particular churches seems to me so obvious that I find it hard to understand the objections to it. Indeed it seems to me that they are only possible if one does not want to see, or no longer succeeds in seeing, the great church conceived by God—perhaps out of desperation at her earthly inadequacy; she now appears as a theological fancy, so all that remains is the empirical image of the church in the mutual relations and conflicts of the particular churches. But this means that the church as a theological subject has been obliterated. If from now on the church can only be recognized in her human organization, then, in fact, all that is left is desolation. But then one has not only abandoned the ecclesiology of the fathers, but also that of the New Testament and the conception of Israel in the Old Testament. In the New Testament, however, it is not necessary to wait for the Deutero-Pauline Epistles and the Apocalypse to find the ontological priority—reaffirmed by the Congregation for the Doctrine of the Faith—of the universal church in relation to the particular churches. In the heart of the great Pauline letters, in the Letter to the Galatians, the apostle does not speak to us of the heavenly Jerusalem as a great eschatological reality, but as of one that precedes us: "But the Jerusalem above is our mother" (Gal 4:26). In this regard, H. Schlier points out that for Paul, as for the Jewish tradition from which he draws inspiration, the heavenly Jerusalem is the new aeon. However, for the apostle, this new aeon is already present "in the Christian Church. This is for him the heavenly Jerusalem in her children."

THE LUCAN VISION OF THE CHURCH

Even though the ontological priority of the one church cannot seriously be denied, the question concerning her temporal priority is certainly more difficult. The Letter of the Congregation for the Doctrine of the Faith is referring here to the Lucan image of the birth of the church at Pentecost through the work of the Holy Spirit. There is no intention to discuss the question of the historical aspect of this account. What matters is the theological affirmation, which Luke has at heart. The Congregation for the Doctrine of the Faith called attention to the fact that the church began in the community of the 120 gathered around Mary, especially in the renewed community of the Twelve, who are not members of a local church, but the apostles who will take the gospel to the ends of the earth. As a further clarification, one can add that in their number, twelve, they are both the old and the new Israel, the one Israel of God, which now—as at the outset was fundamentally implied in the concept of the "People of God"—is extended to all the nations and founds the unique "People of God" among all peoples. This reference is reinforced by two other elements: the church at the time of her birth already speaks all languages. The fathers of the church have rightly interpreted this account of the miracle of tongues as an anticipation of the Catholica—the church from the very first moment is oriented *kat'holon*: she embraces the whole universe. The counterpart to this is Luke's description of the multitude of those who listened as pilgrims coming from all over the earth on the basis of the table of twelve peoples, by which he intends to allude to the all-inclusiveness of the hearers. Luke has enriched this Hellenistic table of peoples with a thirteenth name: the Romans, an idea through which he doubtless wanted to stress once more the idea of the Orbis. The precise meaning of the text of the Congregation for the Doctrine of the Faith is not fully conveyed when a German theologian says of it that the original community of Jerusalem was, in fact, the universal church and the local church at the same time, and then continues: "This certainly represents a Lucan elaboration, in fact, in the historical perspective presumably several communities existed from the very start, with communities in Galilee alongside the community of Jerusalem." Here it is not a matter of the question, ultimately insoluble for us, of when and exactly where Christian communities came into being for the first time, but of the interior beginning of the church, which Luke wants to describe and which he attributes, over and apart from any empirically verifiable fact, to the power of the Holy Spirit. However, it does not do justice to the Lucan account to say that the original community of Jerusalem was simultaneously the universal church and the local church. The first reality in St. Luke's account is not an indigenous community of Jerusalem; rather, the first reality is that in the Twelve, the old Israel, which is unique, becomes the new one, and this one Israel of God, through the miracle of tongues, even before it becomes the representation of the local church of Jerusalem, is now revealed as a unity that embraces all time and places. In the pilgrims present who came from all countries, it immediately encompasses all the peoples of the world. Perhaps it is not necessary to overemphasize the question of the temporal priority of the

universal church, which Luke clearly presents in his account. What is important is that at the beginning the church is generated in the Twelve by the one
Spirit for all peoples, hence even from the first moment, she is directed to
being in all cultures, and thus to being the one "People of God:" she is not a
local community that grows gradually but the leaven that is always destined to
permeate the whole and, consequently, embodies universality from the first
instant.

Resistance to the affirmations of the pre-eminence of the universal church
in relation to the particular churches is difficult to understand and even impossible to understand theologically. It only becomes understandable on the
basis of a suspicion: "The formula becomes totally problematic if the one universal church is tacitly identified with the Roman Church, de facto with the
pope and the curia. If this occurs, then the Letter of the Congregation for the
Doctrine of the Faith cannot be understood as an aid to the clarification of
the ecclesiology of communion, but must be understood as its abandonment
and an endeavor to restore the centralism of Rome." In this text the identification of the universal church with the pope and the curia is first introduced as
a hypothesis, as a risk, but then seems de facto to have been attributed to the
Letter of the Congregation for the Doctrine of the Faith, which thus appears
as a kind of theological restoration, thereby diverging from the Second Vatican Council. This interpretative leap is surprising but obviously represents a
widespread suspicion; it gives voice to an accusation heard everywhere, and
expresses succinctly a growing inability to portray anything concrete under
the name of universal church, under the elements of the one, holy, catholic of
the church. The pope and the curia are the only elements that can be identified, and if one exalts them inordinately from the theological point of view, it
is understandable that some may feel threatened.

THE COUNCIL ON THE UNIVERSAL CHURCH

Thus we find ourselves concretely, after what is only apparently an excursus,
facing the question of the interpretation of the council. We now ask the following question: what really was the idea of the council on the universal
church? It cannot be rightly said that the Letter of the Congregation for the
Doctrine of the Faith tacitly identifies the universal church with the Roman
Church, or de facto with the pope and the curia. The temptation to do so
arises if at the start the local church of Jerusalem and the universal church
have already been identified, that is, if the concept of church has been reduced
to that of the communities that are empirically discernible, and if one has lost
sight of its theological depth. It is helpful to return with these questions to the

text of the council itself. The first sentence of the Constitution on the Church immediately explains that the council does not consider the church to be a reality closed in on herself, but sees her in a Christological perspective: "Christ is the light of the nations; and it is, accordingly, the heartfelt desire of this sacred council, being gathered together in the Holy Spirit, that ... the light of Christ, reflected on the face of the church, may enlighten all men." With this background we can understand the image used in the theology of the fathers, who see the church as the moon that does not shine with its own light but re-flects the light of Christ, the sun. Ecclesiology is shown to be dependent upon Christology and connected with it. But since no one can speak correctly of Christ, of the Son, without at the same time speaking of the Father, and since it is impossible to speak correctly of the Father and the Son without listening to the Holy Spirit, the Christological vision of the church necessarily expands to become a Trinitarian ecclesiology (*Lumen gentium,* nn. 2–4). The discourse on the church is a discourse on God, and only in this way is it correct. In this Trinitarian overture, which offers the key to a correct interpretation of the whole text, we learn what the one holy church is, starting with and in all her concrete historical phenomena, and what "universal church" should mean. This is further explained when we are subsequently shown the church's inner dynamism toward the Kingdom of God. Precisely because the church is to be theologically understood, she is always transcending herself; she is the gather-ing for the Kingdom of God, the breaking-in of the kingdom. Then the differ-ent images of the church are briefly presented, which all describe the unique church, whether she is described as the Bride, the house of God, his family, the temple, the holy city, our mother, the Jerusalem that is above, or God's flock. This, ultimately, becomes even more concrete. We are given a very practical answer to the question, What is this, this one universal church that ontologi-cally and temporally precedes the local churches? Where is she? Where can we see her act?

BAPTISM AND EUCHARIST

The Constitution answers, speaking to us of the sacraments. First comes bap-tism: it is a Trinitarian event, in other words, totally theological, far more than a socialization bound up with the local church; this, unfortunately, is a common distortion. Baptism does not derive from the local community; rather, through baptism the door of the one church is opened to us. It is the presence of the one church and can only flow from her, from the heavenly Je-rusalem, from the new mother. In this regard, the well-known ecumenist Vinzenz Pfnur recently said: "Baptism is being incorporated into the 'one'

one

body of Christ, opened up for us through the cross (Eph 2:16), in which we ... are all baptized by means of the one Spirit (1 Cor 12:13), that is, it is essentially more than the baptismal announcement in use in many places: 'We have received into our community....' We come to belong to this one body through baptism, which should not be replaced by membership in a local church. The 'one' bride and the 'one' episcopate also belong to it ... in which one participates, according to Cyprian, only within the communion of bishops." In baptism the universal church continuously precedes the local church and builds her. Because of this, the Letter of the Congregation for the Doctrine of the Faith on *communio* can say that there are no strangers in the church: everyone is at home everywhere and is not just a guest. The church is always the one church, one and the same. Whoever is baptized in Berlin is as much at home in the church in Rome or New York or Kinshasa or Bangalore or in any other place, as he is in the church where he was baptized. He does not have to register for baptism again; the church is one. Baptism comes from her and gives birth within her. Whoever speaks of baptism speaks of and, by that very fact, treats of the Word of God, which for the whole church is one and continuously precedes her in all places, summons her, and builds her up. This Word is above the church, yet it is in her, entrusted to her as a living subject. To be effectively present in history, the Word needs this subject, but this subject on her part does not subsist without the vital life-giving force of the Word, which first makes her a subject. When we speak of the Word of God, we also mean the Creed, which is at the heart of the baptismal event; it is also the way in which the church receives the Word and makes it her own; in a certain way it is a word and also a response. Here, too, the universal church, the one church, is present in a concrete way, and can be perceived as such.

The conciliar text passes from baptism to the Eucharist, in which Christ gives his body and thus makes us his body. This body is one, and so again for every local church the Eucharist is the place of incorporation into the one Christ, the becoming-one of all communicants in the universal *communio*, which unites heaven and earth, the living and the dead, past, present and future, and opens up into eternity. The Eucharist is not born from the local church and does not end in her. It continuously shows that Christ comes to us from outside, through our closed doors; the church comes to us continuously from outside, from the total, unique body of Christ, and leads us into it. This *extra nos* of the sacrament is also revealed in the ministry of the bishop and of the priest: the truth that the Eucharist needs the sacrament of priestly service is founded precisely in the fact that the community cannot give itself the Eucharist; it must receive it from the Lord through the mediation of the one church. Apostolic succession, which constitutes the priestly ministry, implies at the same time the synchronic and diachronic aspects of the concept of church: belonging to the whole history of the faith from the apostles and being in communion with all who let themselves be gathered by the Lord in his body. The Constitution on the Church has notably treated the episcopal ministry in chapter 3, and explained its meaning starting with the fundamental concept of the collegium. This concept, which appears only marginally in tradition, serves to illustrate the interior unity of the episcopal ministry. The bishop is not a bishop as an individual, but by belonging to a body, a college, which in turn represents the historical continuity of the *collegium apostolorum*. In this sense, the episcopal ministry derives from the one church and leads into it. Precisely here it becomes evident that there is no opposition between the local church and the universal church. The bishop represents the one church in the local church, and builds up the one church while he builds up the local church and awakens her particular gifts for the benefit of the whole body. The ministry of the Successor of Peter is a particular form of episcopal ministry connected in a special way with responsibility for the unity of the whole church. But Peter's ministry and responsibility would not even exist had the universal church not existed first. In fact, he would have been moving in a void and representing an absurd claim. Without a doubt, the right relationship between episcopate and primacy must be continuously rediscovered, even at the cost of hard work and suffering. However, this quest is correctly formulated only when it is seen in relation to the primacy of the church's specific mission and, in every age, when it is oriented to and subordinated to it: that is, to the duty to bring God to men and men to God. The church's goal is the gospel, around which everything else must revolve.

"SUBSISTIT IN": THE CHURCH OF CHRIST "SUBSISTS IN" THE CATHOLIC CHURCH

At this point I would like to interrupt my analysis of the concept of *communio* and at least briefly take a stance regarding the most disputed point of *Lumen gentium*: the meaning of the disputed sentence, n. 8, which teaches that the unique church of Christ, which we confess in the Creed as one, holy, catholic, and apostolic, "subsists" in the Catholic Church, which is governed by the Successor of Peter and by the bishops in communion with him. In 1985 the Congregation for the Doctrine of the Faith was forced to adopt a position with regard to this text, because of a book by Leonardo Boff in which he supported the idea that the one church of Christ as she subsists in the Roman Catholic Church could also subsist in other Christian churches. It is superfluous to say that the statement of the Congregation for the Doctrine of the Faith was met with stinging criticism and then later put aside.

In the attempt to reflect on where we stand today in the reception of the council's ecclesiology, the question of the interpretation of the *subsistit* is inevitable, and on this subject the postconciliar magisterium's single official pronouncement, that is, the notification I just mentioned, cannot be ignored. Looking back from the perspective of fifteen years, it emerges more clearly that it was not so much the question of a single theological author, but rather a vision of the church that was put forward in a variety of ways and is still current today. The clarification of 1985 presented the context of Boff's thesis at great length. We do not need to examine these details further, because we have something more fundamental at heart. The thesis, which at the time had Boff as its proponent, could be described as ecclesiological relativism. It finds its justification in the theory that the "historical Jesus" would not have conceived the idea of a church as such, much less have founded one. The church, as a historical reality, would have come into existence only after the Resurrection, on account of the loss of the eschatological anticipation of the immediate coming of the kingdom, caused in its turn by the inevitable sociological needs of institutionalization. In the beginning, a universal Catholic Church would certainly not have existed, but only different local churches with different theologies, different ministers, and so on. No institutional church could, therefore, say that she was that one church of Jesus Christ desired by God himself; all institutional forms thus stem from sociological needs and as such are human constructions that can and even must be radically changed again in new situations. In their theological quality they are only different in a very secondary way, so one might say that in all of them or at least in many, the "one church of Christ" subsists; with regard to this hypothesis the question naturally arises: in this vision, what right does one have to speak at all of the one church of Christ?

Instead, Catholic tradition has chosen another starting point: it puts its confidence in the Evangelists and believes in them. It is obvious then that Jesus, who proclaimed the Kingdom of God, would gather disciples around him for its realization; he not only gave them his Word as a new interpretation of the Old Testament, but in the sacrament of the Last Supper he gave them the gift of a new unifying center, through which all who profess to be Christians can become one with him in a totally new way, so that Paul could designate this communion as being one body with Christ, as the unity of one body in the Spirit. It then becomes obvious that the promise of the Holy Spirit was not a vague announcement but that it brought about the reality of Pentecost, hence the church was not conceived of and established by men but created by means of the Holy Spirit, whose creation she is and continues to be.

As a result, however, the institution and the Spirit have a very different relationship in the church than that which the trends of thought I just mentioned would like to suggest to us. The institution is not merely a structure
that can be changed or demolished at will, which would have nothing to do
with the reality of faith as such. This form of bodiliness [body of Christ] belongs to the church herself. Christ's church is not hidden invisibly behind the
manifold human configurations, but really exists, as a true and proper church,
which is manifest in the profession of faith, in the sacraments, and in apostolic succession.

The Second Vatican Council, with the formula of the *subsistit*—in accord
with Catholic tradition—wanted to teach the exact opposite of "ecclesiological relativism": the church of Jesus Christ truly exists. He himself willed her,
and the Holy Spirit has continuously created her since Pentecost, in spite of
being faced with every human failing, and sustains her in her essential identity. The institution is not an inevitable but theologically unimportant or even
harmful externalization, but belongs in its essential core to the concrete character of the Incarnation. The Lord keeps his word: "The gates of hell shall not
prevail against her."

THE COUNCIL: "SUBSISTIT IN" EXPLAINS THE CHURCH
AS A CONCRETE SUBJECT

At this point it becomes necessary to investigate the word *subsistit* somewhat
more carefully. With this expression, the council differs from the formula of
Pius XII, who said in his encyclical *Mystici Corporis Christi*: "The Catholic
Church 'is' (*est*) the one mystical body of Christ." The difference between *subsistit* and *est* conceals within itself the whole ecumenical problem. The word
subsistit derives from ancient philosophy as later developed in Scholastic philosophy. The Greek word *hypostasis* has a central role in Christology to describe the union of divine and human nature in the Person of Christ.
Subsistere is a special case of *esse*, It is being in the form of a subject who has
an autonomous existence. Here it is a question precisely of this. The council
wants to tell us that the church of Jesus Christ as a concrete subject in this
world can be found in the Catholic Church. This can take place only once,
and the idea that the *subsistit* could be multiplied fails to grasp precisely the
notion that is being intended. With the word *subsistit*, the council wished to
explain the unicity of the Catholic Church and the fact of her inability to be
multiplied: the church exists as a subject in historical reality.

The difference between *subsistit* and *est*, however, contains the tragedy of
ecclesial division. Although the church is only one and "subsists" in a unique

subject, there are also ecclesial realities beyond this subject—true local churches and different ecclesial communities. Because sin is a contradiction, this difference between *subsistit* and *est* cannot be fully resolved from the logical viewpoint. The paradox of the difference between the unique and concrete character of the church, on the one hand, and on the other, the existence of an ecclesial reality beyond the one subject reflects the contradictory nature of human sin and division. This division is totally different from the relativistic dialectic described above, in which the division of Christians loses its painful aspect and, in fact, is not a rupture but only the manifestation of multiple variations on a single theme, in which all the variations are in a certain way right and wrong. An intrinsic need to seek unity does not then exist, because in any event the one church really is everywhere and nowhere. Thus Christianity would actually exist only in the dialectic correlation of various antitheses. Ecumenism consists in the fact that in some way all recognize one another, because all are supposed to be only fragments of Christian reality. Ecumenism would therefore be the resignation to a relativistic dialectic, because the Jesus of history belongs to the past, and the truth in any case remains hidden.

The vision of the council is quite different: the fact that in the Catholic Church is present the *subsistit* of the one subject, the church, is not at all the merit of Catholics but is solely God's work, which he makes endure despite the continuous unworthiness of the human subjects. They cannot boast of anything but can only admire the fidelity of God, with shame for their sins and at the same time great thanks. But the effect of their own sins can be seen: the whole world sees the spectacle of the divided and opposing Christian communities, reciprocally making their own claims to truth and thus clearly frustrating the prayer of Christ on the eve of his Passion. Whereas division as a historical reality can be perceived by each person, the subsistence of the one church in the concrete form of the Catholic Church can be seen as such only through faith.

Since the Second Vatican Council was conscious of this paradox, it proclaimed the duty of ecumenism as a search for true unity, and entrusted it to the church of the future.

CONCLUSION: THE CALL TO HOLINESS

I come to my conclusion. Anyone who desires to understand the approach of the council's ecclesiology cannot ignore chapters 4 to 7 of the constitution, which speak of the laity, the universal call to holiness, religious, and the eschatological orientation of the church. In these chapters the intrinsic purpose once again comes to the fore—that is, all that is most essential to her existence: it is contingent on holiness, conformity to God, that there be room in the world for God, that he dwell in it, and thus that the world become his "kingdom." Holiness is something more than a moral quality. It is the dwelling of God with men, and of men with God, God's "tent" among us and in our midst (Jn 1:14). It is the new birth—not of flesh and blood but of God (Jn 1:13). The movement toward holiness is identical with the eschatological movement and, indeed, from the standpoint of Jesus's message, is now fundamental to the church. The church exists so that she may become God's dwelling place in the world and thus be "holiness": it is this for which one should compete in the church—not for a given rank in rights of precedence or to occupy the first places. All this is taken up and formed into a synthesis in the last chapter of the Constitution, which presents Mary, the Mother of the Lord.

MARIAN VISION

At first sight the insertion of Mariology in ecclesiology that the council decided upon could seem accidental. In fact, it is true from the historical viewpoint that a rather small majority of the fathers voted for the inclusion of Mariology. But from the inner logic of their vote, their decision corresponds perfectly to the movement of the whole constitution: only if this correlation is grasped can one correctly grasp the image of the church that the council wished to portray. In this decision the research of Hugo Rahner, A. Muller, R. Laurentin, and Karl Delahaye played a great part, and thanks to them, Mariology and ecclesiology were both renewed and more deeply expounded. Hugo Rahner, in particular, showed in a magnificent way from the sources that Mariology in its entirety was first thought of and established by the fathers as ecclesiology: the church is virgin and mother, she was conceived without sin and bears the burden of history; she suffers, and yet she is taken up into heaven. Very slowly there develops later the notion that the church is anticipated in Mary, she is personified in Mary, and Mary is not an isolated individual closed in on herself but carries within her the whole mystery of the church. The person is not closed individualistically nor is the community understood as a collectivity in an impersonal way: both inseparably overlap. This already applies to the woman in the Apocalypse, as she appears in chapter 12: it is not right to limit this figure exclusively and individualistically to Mary, because in her we contemplate together the whole People of God, the old and new Israel, which suffers and is fruitful in suffering; nor is it right to exclude from this image Mary, the Mother of the Redeemer. Thus the overlapping of individual and community, as we find it in this text, anticipates the identification of Mary and the church that was gradually developed in the theology of the fathers and finally taken up by the council. The fact that the two were later separated, that Mary was seen as an individual filled with privileges and therefore infinitely beyond our reach, where the church [was seen] in an impersonal and purely institutional manner has caused equal damage to both Mariology and ecclesiology. Here are active the divisions brought about by Western thought in particular, which otherwise would have their own good reasons. But if we want to understand the church and Mary properly, we must go back to the time before these divisions, in order to understand the supra-individual nature of the person and the supra-institutional nature of the community, precisely where person and community are taken back to their origins, grounded in the power of the Lord, the new Adam. The Marian vision of the church and the ecclesial, salvation-historical vision of Mary take us back ultimately to Christ and to the Trinitarian God, because it is here that we find revealed what holiness means, what is God's dwelling in man and in the world, and what we should understand by the "eschatological" tension of the church. Thus only the chapter on Mary leads conciliar ecclesiology to its fulfillment and brings us back to its Christological and Trinitarian starting point.

To give a taste of the fathers' theology, I would like as a conclusion to propose a text of St. Ambrose, chosen by Hugo Rahner:

> So stand on the firm ground of your heart!... What standing means, the Apostle taught us, Moses wrote it: "The place on which you stand is holy ground." No one stands except the one who stands firm in the faith ... and yet another word is written: "But you, stand firm with me." You stand firm with me, if you stand in the Church. The Church is holy ground on which we must stand.... So stand firm, stand in the Church, stand there, where I want to appear to you. There I will stay beside you. Where the Church is, there is the stronghold of your heart. On the Church are laid the foundations of your soul. Indeed I appeared to you in the Church as once in the burning bush. You are the bush; I am the fire. Like the fire in the bush I am in your flesh. I am fire to enlighten you; to burn away the thorns of your sins, to give you the favor of my grace.

The Local Church and the Universal Church

The editors of *America* have kindly invited me to respond to an article (April 23, 2001) by Cardinal Walter Kasper, the president of the Council for Promoting Christian Unity, in which he reacted to remarks of mine that, in turn, were a reply to an earlier text by Kasper in which he sharply criticized a crucial statement from a document by the Congregation for the Doctrine of the Faith. For a long while I hesitated to accept this invitation because I do not want to foster the impression that there is a long-standing theological dispute between Cardinal Kasper and myself, when in fact none exists.

After much reflection, however, I was finally moved to take up *America*'s offer after all. My first reason is that the article by Cardinal Kasper is a response to texts that are largely unknown to both German and American readers. The article by Walter Kasper that set off the dispute is tucked away in a Festschrift read only by specialists. My own piece, which covers a much broader thematic gamut and in which only two of its twenty-three pages deal with Kasper, has been published in German only in excerpts, and thus far in English (to my knowledge) not at all. Even though Cardinal Kasper sincerely strove in his "friendly exchange" to inform readers about what he was responding to, his necessarily sketchy allusions can hardly provide a clear picture of those previous texts, although they are the focus of his article.

Of course, I cannot give the reader a really satisfactory notion of them, either; but it may nonetheless be useful to shed some light on the prehistory of this disagreement from a different perspective, to get a better understanding of the general shape and significance of the discussion. Above all, however, I would like to invite people to read the original texts.

The second reason why I finally decided to write is a pleasant one: Kasper's response to my statements has led to clarifications whose scope readers will hardly be able to appreciate clearly unless they are familiar with what went before. Pointing out the progress made in this debate strikes me as significant.

It all began, as mentioned, not with anything I wrote, but with a "Letter to the Bishops of the Catholic Church on Some Aspects of the Church as *Communio,*" which was published, with the pope's approval, by the Congregation for the Doctrine of the Faith on June 28, 1992. The term *communio,* which played a rather marginal role in the texts of the Second Vatican Council, was moved to the center of the question of the church by the Extraordinary Synod of Bishops of 1985—and in so doing the synod was surely following the council's intentions. Since this word had been used, and misused, in many different ways, an explanation by the magisterium of the essential elements of *communio*-ecclesiology seemed appropriate; and such was the purpose of the letter from the congregation.

In that letter, then, we also find the principle that the universal church (*ecclesia universalis*) is in its essential mystery a reality that takes precedence, ontologically and temporally, over the individual local churches. This principle was given a sharp critique by Walter Kasper, who at the time was bishop of Rottenburg, Germany, culminating in the statement, "The formula becomes thoroughly problematic if the universal church is being covertly identified with the church of Rome, and de facto with the pope and the curia. If that happens, the letter from the Congregation for the Doctrine of the Faith cannot be read as an aid in clarifying *communio*-ecclesiology, but as a dismissal of it and as an attempt to restore Roman centralism."

The attack on the doctrinal letter from the congregation sounds at first, from a linguistic point of view, hypothetical: were one to identify the universal church with the pope and the curia, then the restoration of Roman centralism would be at hand. But in the second half of the statement, the attack clearly takes on the tone of an affirmation, because the claim that there is a will to bring on a Roman "restoration" makes sense only if Rome itself is thinking and acting that way, not if such interpretations are merely proposed, so to speak, by a third party.

As a matter of fact, in the same article Kasper writes as follows, nonhypothetically: "This determination by the council has undergone, after the council ... a further development by the Congregation for the Doctrine of the Faith that practically amounts, more or less, to a reversal of it." Thus Kasper's text was quite rightly understood everywhere as a warning cry against a new, theologically veiled form of Roman centralism and as an emphatic criticism of the Congregation for the Doctrine of the Faith.

A warning like this from the mouth of a bishop with solid theological credentials carries weight. If theology or any interpretation of the faith by the magisterium is misused to introduce a strategy for gaining power or to reverse the council, that is a serious matter. Kasper's critique, as has no doubt become obvious, was not directed against me personally, but against a text from the Congregation for the Doctrine of the Faith, which is the office of the Holy See in charge of doctrine. Some sort of clarification was therefore unavoidable.

As prefect of the Congregation for the Doctrine of the Faith, I tried to find the least polemical way to clear up the problem. An opportunity to do so arose when I was invited in the spring of 2000 to speak at a symposium, on the thirty-fifth anniversary of the conclusion of Vatican II, about the ecclesiological vision of its "Dogmatic Constitution on the Church" (*Lumen Gentium*). In so doing I tried above all to spotlight the link between the church and the question of God: the church is not there for itself, but to serve God's presence in the world.

In this broad context I addressed the relationship between the universal church and the local churches and, in the process, briefly explained that the letter from the congregation never dreamt of identifying the reality of the universal church with the pope and curia, and hence that the fears voiced by Kasper were groundless. In order to do this, I mainly tried to shed light on the rich implications of the term *universal church*, which may at first sound abstract.

The most positive feature of Cardinal Kasper's response to my talk is that he tacitly dropped the reproach from his first article and now assigned to our argument the rank of a "controversy over a scholastic dispute." The thesis of the ontological and temporal priority of the universal church to individual churches was now treated as a question "not of church doctrine but of theological opinions and of the various related philosophies." The statement by the Congregation for the Doctrine of the Faith was categorized as my personal theology and tied in with my "Platonism," while Kasper traced his own view back to his more Aristotelian (Thomistic) approach. By reframing the dispute in this way, the question was basically blunted and shifted to another level. The charge was no longer that the Congregation for the Doctrine of the Faith was intent on centralism, restoration, and turning the church around. Instead, Cardinal Kasper now noted two different theological points of view separating his theology and mine, which can and perhaps should coexist peacefully.

Above and beyond that, Kasper's "friendly exchange" had two further positive results. He unambiguously emphasized—and I am very grateful to him for this—our common ecclesiological foundations, and he modified his own rejection of the ontological and temporal precedence of the universal church over the individual churches, when he characterized the "pre-existence" (properly understood) of the church as indispensable for understanding it.

To be sure, he claims that this pre-existence applies not only to the universal church but also to the concrete church, which is composed "in and of" local churches. As opposed to the notion of the "primacy" of the universal church, he defends the "thesis of the simultaneity of the universal church and the particular churches." What he means by this becomes clearer when he writes: "The local church and the universal church are internal to one another; they penetrate each other and are perichoretic."

I can certainly accept this formula; it is valid for the church as it lives in history. But it misses the actual point at issue as seen in the reference to the "pre-existence" of the church. In order to clarify what is at stake here, let me quote a few sentences from my talk on this topic. In it I argued that the fathers of the church saw the church as a greater Israel, now become universal; and from that standpoint they also adopted the rabbinical view of the meaning of Creation, which is based on the Bible itself: "Thus creation is conceived in such a way that there is a place in it for God's will. But this will needs a people that lives for God's will and makes it the light of the world."

From the standpoint of Christology, the picture is expanded and deepened. History is, once again in connection with the Old Testament, interpreted as a love story between God and humanity. God finds and prepares for himself the Bride of the Son, the one Bride, which is the one church. On the strength of the saying in Genesis that a man and his wife become "two in one flesh" (Gn 2:24), the image of the bride fused with the idea of the church as the body of Christ, which for its part is based on eucharistic piety. The one body of Christ is made ready; Christ and the church will be "two in one flesh," one body; and thus God will be all in all.

The basic idea of sacred history is that of gathering together, of uniting—uniting human beings in the one body of Christ, the union of human beings and through human beings of all creation with God. There is only one Bride, only one body of Christ, not many brides, not many bodies. The Bride is, of course, as the fathers of the church said, drawing on Psalm 44, dressed "in many-colored robes"; the body has many organs. But the superordinate principle is ultimately unity. That is the point here. Variety becomes richness only through the process of unification.

I can only repeat what I said in that talk. I cannot understand how my position can be refuted by means of biblical theology. The inner priority of unity, of the one Bride to her essential variety, seems to be plainly evident.

At the same time, in my talk I tried to understand where the resistance to this self-evident biblical view of history comes from; and I came up with two closely interrelated motives. The first is that mentioning the universal church and its ontological (or should we say teleological?) precedence over the individual churches leads people to think immediately about the pope and the curia, and the need to avert centralism. Hence, the problem of centralism and of the role of the local bishops also lies at the root of Cardinal Kasper's reaction to my thoughts.

Forgive me if I say quite candidly that this linkage, objectively speaking, makes no sense. The church of Rome is a local church and not the universal church—a local church with a peculiar, universal responsibility, but still a local church. And the assertion of the inner precedence of God's idea of the one church, the one Bride, over all its empirical realizations in particular churches has nothing whatsoever to do with the problem of centralism.

Once this has been made clear, another question arises: why does this same association keep coming up everywhere, even with so great a theologian as Walter Kasper? What makes people suspect that the thesis of the internal priority of the one divine idea of the church over the individual churches might be a ploy of Roman centralism?

This brings us to the second reason why the plain biblical evidence is not, in fact, functional today. The term *universal church* is understood to refer only to the pope and the curia. It seems, as Kasper says in his response, echoing Henri de Lubac, to be a pure abstraction. That is why in my talk I made a deliberate effort to present the practical reality of the Catholic Church and how it actually works, in close conjunction with the "Dogmatic Constitution on the Church."

To my astonishment, Cardinal Kasper said not a word about this extensive and central passage of my text. Here I can only make the briefest of allusions to my remarks. I showed that the council answers the question, where one can see the universal church as such, by speaking of the sacraments:

There is, first of all, baptism. It is a Trinitarian, that is, a thoroughly theological event, and means far more than being socialized into the local church.... Baptism does not arise from the individual community; rather, in baptism the door to the one church is opened to us; it is the presence of the one church, and it can come only from her—from the Jerusalem that is above, our new mother. In baptism the universal church continually precedes and creates the local church.

On this basis the letter of the Congregation for the Doctrine of the Faith can say that there are no strangers in the church. Everyone in it is at home everywhere.... Anyone baptized in the church in Berlin is always at home in the church in Rome or in New York or in Kinshasa or in Bangalore or wherever, as if he or she had been baptized there. He or she does not need to file a change-of-address form; it is one and the same church. Baptism comes out of it and delivers (gives birth to) us into it.

To my pleasure, I was recently on hand when Cardinal Kasper made this very argument in a discussion about the church and cited an example from his own life. Early on, he and his parents had left the parish where he was baptized—yet in baptism he had not been socialized into this particular community, but born into the one church. As far as I am concerned, this statement clears up the controversy—for that is the issue here. I would like to make just one more point, taken from the longer discussion in my talk, about the concrete content of the phrase "universal church," specifically, about the Word of God. I said: Anyone who speaks of baptism is automatically dealing with the Word of God, which for the entire church is only one, and which always precedes the church in all places, calls it together, and builds it up. This one Word is above the church and yet in it, entrusted to it as to a living subject. In order to be really present in history, the Word of God needs this subject; but this subject cannot subsist without the vivifying power of the Word, which makes it a subject to begin with. When we speak of the Word of God we also mean the Creed, which stands at the center of the baptismal event. It is a way the church receives and appropriates the Word, which is in a sense both word and response. Here, too, the universal church, the one church, is quite concretely and palpably present. If one strips away all the false associations with church politics from the concept of the universal church and grasps it in its true theological (and hence quite concrete) content, then it becomes clear that the argument about church politics misses the heart of the matter. It becomes clear that the problem is not Platonism or Aristotelianism, but the key notion of salvation history in the Bible. And then one can no longer also say that the "universalistic view" of the church is "ecumenically off-putting."

I would really like to go on and address many other points that Kasper makes—for example, his objections to my analysis of the account of Pentecost in the Acts of the Apostles. But perhaps I had better leave that to a future personal conversation.

Let me, if I may, add only one rather humorous little note. In the section "Historical Perspectives," which supplies in a few sentences some very good information about the essential issues, Cardinal Kasper, invoking J. Gnilka, observes that "in Paul the local community is the focus." But in Rudolf Bultmann we can read the exact opposite. According to Bultmann:

The church's organization grew primarily out of the awareness that the community as a whole takes precedence over the individual communities. A symptom of this is that the word *ekklesia* [church] is used to refer, in the first instance, by no means to the individual community but to the "people of God."... The notion of the priority of the church as a whole over the individual community is further seen in the equation of the *ekklesia* with the *soma Christou* [body of Christ], which embraces all believers.[1]

This conflict between Gnilka and Bultmann shows, first of all, the relativity of exegetical judgments. But for that very reason it is especially instructive in our case, because Bultmann, who vigorously defended the thesis of the precedence of the universal church over the local church, could certainly never be accused of Platonism or of a bias in favor of bringing back Roman centralism. Perhaps it was simply because he stood outside these controversies that he was able to read and expound the texts with a more open mind.

The Canon of Criticism

PETER SEEWALD INTERVIEWS
JOSEPH CARDINAL RATZINGER (1996)[1]

Referring to criticism of the church, you once spoke of a classical "canon of issues": women's ordination, contraception, celibacy, the remarriage of divorced persons. This list is from 1984. The "Petition of the People of the Church" of 1995 in Austria, Germany, and Switzerland shows that this canon of issues hasn't changed one iota. The discussion seems to be going wearyingly in circles. Perhaps a few clarifications would help get beyond this impasse. It seems to me that many don't know exactly what they're talking about when they speak of the papacy and priesthood, that they actually don't know the meaning of these terms.

I would stress again that all of these are certainly genuine issues, but I also believe that we go astray when we raise them to *the* standard questions and make them the only concerns of Christianity. There is a very simple reflection that argues against this (which, by the way, Johann Baptist Metz has mentioned in an article entitled "Petition of the People of the Church"). These issues are resolved in Lutheran Christianity. On these points it has taken the other path, and it is quite plain that it hasn't thereby solved the problem of being a Christian in today's world and that the problem of Christianity, the effort of being a Christian, remains just as dramatic as before. Metz, if I recall correctly, asks why we ought to make ourselves a clone of Protestant Christianity. It is actually a good thing, he says, that the experiment was made. For it shows that being Christian today does not stand or fall on these questions. That the resolution of these matters does not make the gospel more attractive or being Christian any easier. It does not even achieve the agreement that will better hold the church together. I believe we should finally be clear on this point, that the church is not suffering on account of these questions.

THE DOGMA OF INFALLIBILITY

Let us begin, then, with a point that the Protestants crossed off the list quite early on, the dogma of infallibility. Now, what does this dogma really mean? Is it correctly or falsely translated when we assume that everything the Holy Father says is automatically sacred and correct? I would like to put this question at the beginning of the canon of criticism because it seems especially to agitate people, for whatever reasons.

You have in fact touched upon an error. As a matter of fact, this dogma does not mean that everything the pope says is infallible. It simply means that in Christianity, at any rate, as Catholics believe, there is a final decision-making authority, that ultimately there can be binding decisions about essential issues and we can be certain that they correctly interpret the heritage of Christ. In one form or another, this authority is present in every Christian faith community, but it is not associated with the pope.

For the Orthodox Church, too, it is clear that conciliar decisions are infallible in the sense that I can be confident that here the inheritance of Christ is correctly interpreted; this is our common faith. It's not necessary for each person, as it were, to distill it and extract it from the Bible anew; rather, the church has been given the possibility of reaching communal certainty. The difference from Orthodoxy is only that Roman Christianity recognizes another level of assurance in addition to the ecumenical council, namely, the Successor of Peter, who can likewise provide this assurance. The pope is, of course, bound to certain conditions in this matter, conditions that guarantee—and in addition put him under the deepest obligation—that he decides not out of his own subjective consciousness but in the great communion of the tradition.

It did take a long time, though, to find this solution.

Well, councils were also held before there was any theory of councils. The fathers of the Council of Nicaea, the first council, which was held in 325, didn't have any idea what a council was; in fact, it was the emperor who had convoked it. Nevertheless, they were already clear that not only had they spoken but they were entitled to say, "It has seemed good to the Holy Spirit and to us" (Acts 15:28), which the council of the apostles also says. This means: the Holy Spirit has decided with us and through us. The Council of Nicaea then speaks of three primatial sees in the church, namely, Rome, Antioch, and Alexandria, thus naming jurisdictions connected with the Petrine tradition. Rome and Antioch are the episcopal sees of St. Peter, and Alexandria, as Mark's see, was, as it were, tied to the Petrine tradition and subsumed into this triad.

Very early on, the bishops of Rome knew clearly that they were in this Petrine tradition and that, together with the responsibility, they also had the promise that helped them to live up to it. This subsequently became very clear in the Arian crisis, when Rome was the only authority that could face up to the emperor. The Bishop of Rome, who naturally has to listen to the whole church and does not creatively produce the faith himself, has a function that is in continuity with the promise to Peter. To be sure, only in 1870 was it given its definitive conceptual formulation.

Perhaps we ought also to note that in our day an understanding is emerging even outside Catholic Christianity that a guarantor of unity is necessary for the whole. This has emerged in the dialogue with the Anglicans, for example. The Anglicans are ready to acknowledge, as it were, providential guidance in tying the tradition of primacy to Rome, without wanting to refer the promise to Peter directly to the pope. Even in other parts of Protestant Christianity there is an acknowledgment that Christianity ought to have a spokesman who can express it in person. And also the Orthodox Church has voices that criticize the disintegration of the church into autocephalies (national churches) and, instead of this, regard recourse to the Petrine principle as meaningful. That is not an acknowledgment of the Roman dogma, but convergences are becoming increasingly clear.

THE GOSPEL: AFFIRMATION OR CONDEMNATION?

The traditional morality of the church, according to one criticism, is really based on guilt feelings. It is above all negative in its evaluation of sexuality. The church, it is said, has also imposed burdens that have nothing to do with revelation. Now there is the idea that we ought to cease basing Christian theology on sin and contrition. It is necessary and possible, they say, to rediscover the mystery of religious experience beyond religious norms.

The sloganlike opposition between "condemnation" and "affirmation" [*Droh-Botschaft/Froh-Botschaft*: threatening news/good news] is one that I have never thought highly of. For whoever reads the gospel sees that Christ preached the Good News but that the message of judgment is a part of it. There are quite dramatic words of judgment in the gospel that can really make one shudder. We ought not to stifle them. The Lord himself in the gospel obviously sees no contradiction between the message of judgment and the Good News. On the contrary. That there is a judgment, that there is justice, at least for the oppressed, for those who are unjustly treated—that is the real hope and, in that sense, good news. Those who belong to the oppressors and the workers of injustice are primarily the ones who feel threatened.

Even Adorno said that there can really be justice only if there is a resurrection of the dead, so that past wrongs can be settled retroactively, as it were. There must, in other words, somewhere, somehow, be a settling of injustices, the victory of justice; that is what we are awaiting, at least. Nor are Christ and his judgment a victory for evil. No, *he* is the victory of the good, and in this sense, the fact that God is righteous and is the judge is profoundly good news. Naturally, this Good News puts me under an obligation. But when I conceive of the Good News only as self-affirmation, in the final analysis it is meaningless; there is an anesthetization going on somewhere. For this reason, we must become familiar again with the dimension of judgment, precisely with a view to those who suffer and those who have received no justice but who have a right to it—and then also agree to put ourselves under this standard and not to belong to the doers of injustice.

Of course, there is an unsettling element in the message of judgment, and that is a good thing. I mean, when you see how the medieval rulers committed injustice but then, when judgment was approaching, tried to make amends by benefactions and good deeds, you see that consciousness of judgment was also a political and social factor. The awareness that I really mustn't leave the world in this state, that I have to put things right somehow, in other words, that there was an even higher threat hanging over the powerful, was extremely salutary. That benefits everyone concretely.

However, we have to add that we know that as judge, Christ is not a cold legalist but that he is familiar with grace and that ultimately we may approach him without fear. But I think that everyone must find this inner balance, must feel that he is under judgment and recognize: I can't simply muddle along as I please, there is a judgment over me—without, however, surrendering to scruples and anxiety.

This, it seems to me, also suggests an orientation for the church's preaching and pastoral ministry. She must also be able to threaten the powerful; she must also be able to threaten those who neglect, squander, even destroy their lives, for the sake of the right and the good and their own well-being, their own happiness. But she must not become a power that instills fear; she must also know with whom she is speaking. There are sensitive, almost sick souls, who are quickly plunged into fear. They have to be retrieved from the zone of fear; the word of grace has to shine powerfully into the soul. I believe that both aspects must be kept together in a whole, but in such a way that judgment is also Good News, because it assures us that the world makes sense and good triumphs.

WE ARE THE PEOPLE OF GOD

The term "People of God" is understood today as the idea of an autonomy vis-à-vis the official church. The motto is "we are the people," and what the people say has to be done. On the other hand, there is also the expression "vox populi, vox Dei." How do you understand this term?

If we are theologians and believers, we listen first to what the Bible says. In other words, we ourselves can't invent the major concepts: "Who is God?" "What is the church?" "grace," and so forth. The gift of faith consists precisely in the fact that there is a prior given. The term "People of God" is a biblical one. The biblical use is thus also normative for how we might use it. It is first and essentially an Old Testament term; the term *people* comes long before the era of nations and is connected more with the clan, with the family.

Above all, it is a relational term. More recent exegesis has made this very clear. Israel is not the people of God when it acts simply as a political nation. It becomes the people of God by turning to God. It is the people of God only in relation, in turning to God, and in Israel turning to God consists in submission to the Torah. In this sense, the idea of "People of God" in the Old Testament includes, first, the election of Israel by God, who chooses it for no merit of its own—despite the fact that it is not a great or significant people but one of the smallest of the peoples—who chooses it out of love and thus bestows his love upon it. Second, it includes the acceptance of this love, and concretely this means submission to the Torah. Only in this submission, which places Israel in relation to God, is it the people of God.

In the New Testament, the concept "People of God" (with perhaps one or two exceptions) refers only to Israel, that is, to the people of the Old Covenant. It is not a concept that applies directly to the church. However, the church is understood as the continuation of Israel, although Christians don't descend directly from Abraham and thus actually don't belong to this people. They enter into it, says the New Testament, by their descent from Christ and thereby also become children of Abraham. Thus, whoever belongs to Christ belongs to the "People of God." One could say that the term *Torah* is replaced by the Person of Christ, and, in this sense, the "People of God" category, though not applied directly to the new people, is tied to communion with Christ and to living like Christ, or, as St. Paul says, "hav[ing] the mind of Christ" (Phil 2:5). Paul goes on to describe the "mind of Christ" with the words: "*He* became obedient unto death on the cross." Only when we understand the term "People of God" in its biblical usage do we use it in a Christian way. Everything else is extra-Christian construction that misses the real core and is, in my opinion, a product of arrogance. Which of us can say that we are the people of God, while the others perhaps are not?

But regarding the statement "we are the people," I would add a very practical consideration. The "we are the people" functions as the premise for the conclusion "we decide." For example, if in Germany all the members of a certain association got together and said, "We are the people, and therefore we decide that now it is thus and so," all the people would just laugh. Every nation has its institutions; everyone knows that it's not the town council but the parliament, in other words, an institution that really represents the whole—that votes on federal laws. And in this way not just anyone is the comprehensive "we" of the church with the corresponding authority to make decisions, but only everyone together is this "we," and the individual group is this "we" only insofar as it lives in the whole. It would, in fact, be completely absurd, even in the purely popular understanding of democracy, if groups pretended to vote about the whole themselves. A parish council or a diocesan forum should take in hand *its* affairs. But it cannot claim to decide the affairs of the universal church as such.

In the church, there is another element in addition to the example given us by the law of the state (which also has significance for the church), namely, the fact that the church lives not only synchronically but diachronically, as well. This means that it is always all—even the dead—who live and are the whole church, that it is always all who must be considered in any majority in the church. In the state, for example, one day we have the Reagan administration, and the next day the Clinton administration, and whoever comes next always throws out what his predecessor did and said; we always begin again from scratch. That's not the way it is in the church. The church lives her life precisely from the identity of all the generations, from their identity that overarches time, and her real majority is made up of the saints. Every generation tries to join the ranks of the saints, and each makes its contribution. But it can do that only by accepting this great continuity and entering into it in a living way.

But, of course, there is also a continuity of the state that is independent of individual presidents.

Correct. What I said just now was a bit exaggerated. It's also the case in the state that not every government starts all over again from the beginning. Each of them is in the great tradition of the state and, being bound to the constitution, can't reconstruct the state from zero, as it were. So what holds for a state holds also for the church, only in an even stricter and more far-reaching way.

Now, there are "we are the people" movements that no longer group themselves around the traditional laws, rules, parliaments, but simply go off on their own.

In the state, you mean? Yes, yes. In that sense, the phenomenon is also nothing peculiar to the church. But these popular democratic movements show us that this really doesn't work in the state. The Soviet Union began like that. The "base" was supposed to decide things via the councils; all were supposed to take an active part in governing. This allegedly direct democracy, dubbed "people's democracy," which was contrasted with representative (parliamentary) democracy, became, in reality, simply a lie. It would be no different in a church made up of such councils.

The slogan "we are the people" is also attractive because in our most recent past it proved to be successful in the protest movements in the former East Germany.

That's quite true. But in that case the people obviously stood behind it. By now, the consensus has fallen apart again. It was sufficient for a great protest, but it's not enough for the positive task of governing a commonwealth.

SACRED RULE AND BROTHERHOOD

Why must the church continue to operate even today with authoritarian methods and be organized according to "totalitarian" structures? Many people have the idea that democratic models could be possible in the church, too. It's argued that you can't sue for democracy and human rights in society and then leave them at the door of your own house. You can't go around demanding a sense of fellowship and then operate yourself predominantly with accusations of guilt, laws, and a pointing finger.

First, to the word *hierarchy*. The correct translation of this term is probably not "sacred rule" but "sacred origin." The word *archē* can mean both things, origin and rule. But the likelier meaning is "sacred origin." In other words, it communicates itself in virtue of an origin, and the power of this origin, which is sacred, is, as it were, the ever-new beginning of every generation in the church. It doesn't live by the mere continuum of generations but by the presence of the ever-new source itself, which communicates itself unceasingly through the sacraments. That, I think, is an important, different way of looking at things: the category that corresponds to the priesthood is not that of rule. On the contrary, the priesthood has to be a conduit and a making present of a beginning and has to make itself available for this task. When priesthood, episcopacy, and papacy are understood essentially in terms of rule, then things are truly wrong and distorted.

We know from the Gospels that the disciples argued about their rank, that the temptation to turn discipleship into lordship was there from the first and also always is there. Therefore, there is no denying that this temptation exists in every generation, including today's. At the same time, however, there is the gesture of the Lord, who washes the feet of his disciples and thereby makes them fit to sit at table with him, with God himself. When he makes this gesture, it is as if he were saying: "This is what I mean by priesthood. If you don't like that, then you are no priests." Or, as he says to the mother of the Zebedees: the prior condition is drinking the cup, that is, suffering with Christ. Whether they then sit at the right or at the left or anywhere else, that has to remain open. So that this is another way of saying that to be a disciple means to drink the chalice, to enter into a communion of destiny with the Lord, to wash another's feet, to lead the way in suffering, to share another's suffering. This, then, is the first point, namely, that the origin of hierarchy, in any event its true meaning, is not to construct a structure of domination but to keep something present that doesn't come from the individual. No one can forgive sins on his own initiative; no one can communicate the Holy Spirit on his own initiative; no one can transform bread into the presence of Christ or keep him present on his own initiative. In this sense one has to perform a service in which the church doesn't become a self-governing business but draws her life again and anew from her origin.

A second general preliminary remark. The word *brotherhood* is, to be sure, a fine word, but we ought not forget its ambiguity. The first pair of brothers in the history of the world were, according to the Bible, Cain and Abel, and the one murdered the other. And that is an idea that also occurs elsewhere in the history of religions. The mythology surrounding the origin of Rome has the same thing: Romulus and Remus. It also begins with two brothers, and one murders the other. So, siblings are not automatically the quintessence of love and equality. Just as fatherhood can turn into tyranny, we also have sufficient examples of negative brotherhood in history. Even brotherhood must be redeemed, as it were, and pass through the cross in order to find its proper form.

Now to the practical questions. Perhaps there really is too much decision-making and administration in the church at the present time. In reality, office by nature ought to be a service to ensure that the sacraments are celebrated, that Christ can come in, and that the Word of God is proclaimed. Everything else is only ordered to that. It ought not be a standing governing function but should have a bond of obedience to the origin and a bond to the life lived in this origin. The office holder ought to accept responsibility for the fact that he does not proclaim and produce things himself but is a conduit for the Other and therefore ought to step back himself—we have already touched on that. In this sense, he should be in the very first place one who obeys, who does not say, "I would like to say this now," but asks what Christ says and what our faith is and submits to that. And in the second place, he ought to be one who serves, who is available to the people and who, following Christ, keeps himself ready to wash their feet. This is marvelously illustrated in St. Augustine. We have already spoken of the fact that he was constantly busy with trivial affairs, with foot-washing, and that he was ready to spend his great life on the little things, if you will, but in the knowledge that he wasn't squandering it by doing so. That would, then, be the true image of the priesthood. When it is lived *correctly,* it cannot mean finally getting one's hands on the levers of power but rather renouncing one's own life project in order to give oneself over to service.

Part of that, of course—and here I am citing Augustine again—is to reprimand and rebuke and thereby to cause problems for oneself. Augustine illustrates this in a homily in the following terms: *You* want to live badly; you want to perish. *I,* however, am not allowed to want this; I have to rebuke you, even though it displeases you. He then uses the example of the father with sleeping sickness whose son keeps waking him up because that is the only chance of his being cured. But the father says: Let me sleep, I'm dead tired. And the son says: No, I'm not allowed to let you sleep. And that, he says, is precisely the function of a bishop. I am not permitted to let you sleep. I know that you would like to sleep, but that is precisely what I may not allow. And in this sense the church must also raise her index finger and become irksome. But in all this it must remain perceptible that the church is not interested in harassing people but that she herself is animated by the restless desire for the good. I must not allow you to sleep, because sleep would be deadly. And in the exercise of this authority she must also take Christ's suffering upon herself. What—let's put it in a purely human way—gives Christ credibility is, in fact, that he suffered. And that is also the credibility of the church. For this reason, she also becomes most credible where she has martyrs and confessors. And where things go comfortably, she loses credibility.

CELIBACY

Curiously, nothing enrages people more than the question of celibacy. Even though it concerns directly only a tiny fraction of the people in the church. Why is there celibacy?

It arises from a saying of Christ. There are, Christ says, those who give up marriage for the sake of the kingdom of heaven and bear testimony to the kingdom of heaven with their whole existence. Very early on, the church came to the conviction that to be a priest means to give this testimony to the kingdom of heaven. In this regard, the practice could go back analogously to an Old Testament parallel of another nature. Israel marches into the land. Each of the eleven tribes gets its land, its territory. Only the tribe of Levi, the priestly tribe, gets an inheritance; its inheritance is God alone. This means in practical terms that its members live on the cult offerings and not, like the other tribes, from the cultivation of land. The essential point is that they have no property. In Psalm 16 we read: "You are my assigned portion; I have drawn you as my lot; God is my land." This figure—that is, the fact that in the Old Testament the priestly tribe is landless and, as it were, lives on God, and thereby also really bears witness to him—was later translated, on the basis of Jesus's words, to this: The land where the priest lives is God.

We have such difficulty understanding this renunciation today because the relationship to marriage and children has clearly shifted. To have to die without children was once synonymous with a useless life: the echoes of my own life die away, and I am completely dead. If I have children, then I continue to live in them; it's a sort of immortality through posterity. For this reason the ultimate condition of life is to have posterity and thereby to remain in the land of the living.

The renunciation of marriage and family is thus to be understood in terms of this vision: I renounce what, humanly speaking, is not only the most normal but also the most important thing. I forgo bringing forth further life on the tree of life, and I live in the faith that my land is really God—and so I make it easier for others, also, to believe that there is a kingdom of heaven. I bear witness to Jesus Christ, to the gospel, not only with words, but also with this specific mode of existence, and I place my life in this form at his disposal.

In this sense, celibacy has a Christological and an apostolic meaning at the same time. The point is not simply to save time—so I then have a little bit more time at my disposal because I am not a father of a family. That would be too primitive and pragmatic a way to see things. The point is really an existence that stakes everything on God and leaves out precisely the one thing that normally fulfills a human existence with a promising future.

On the other hand, it's certainly not a dogma. Couldn't the question perhaps be negotiated one day in the direction of a free choice between a celibate and a noncelibate form of life?

No, it's certainly not a dogma. It is an accustomed way of life that evolved very early in the church on good biblical grounds. Recent studies show that celibacy goes back much farther than the usually acknowledged canonical sources would indicate, back to the second century. In the East, too, it was much more widespread than we have realized up until now. In the East it isn't until the seventh century that there is a parting of the ways. Today, as before, monasticism in the East is still the foundation that sustains the priesthood and the hierarchy. In that sense, celibacy also has a major significance in the East.

It is not a dogma. It is a form of life that has grown up in the church and that naturally always brings with it the danger of a fall. When one aims so high, there are failures. I think that what provokes people today against celibacy is that they see how many priests really aren't inwardly in agreement with it and either live it hypocritically, badly, not at all, or only live it in a tortured way. So people say ...

... it ruins them ...

The poorer an age is in faith, the more frequent the falls. This robs celibacy of its credibility and obscures the real point of it. People need to get straight in their minds that times of crises for celibacy are always times of crisis for marriage, as well. For, as a matter of fact, today we are experiencing not only violations of celibacy; marriage itself is becoming increasingly fragile as the basis of our society. In the legislation of Western nations we see that it is increasingly placed on the same level as other forms and is thereby largely "dissolved" as a legal form. Nor is the hard work needed really to live marriage negligible. Put in practical terms, after the abolition of celibacy we would only have a different kind of problem, with divorced priests. That is not unknown in the Protestant churches. In this sense, we see, of course, that the lofty forms of human existence involve great risks.

The conclusion that I would draw from this, however, is not that we should now say, "We can't do it anymore," but that we must learn again to believe. And that we must also be even more careful in the selection of candidates for the priesthood. The point is that someone ought really to accept it freely and not say, well now, I would like to become a priest, so I'll put up with this. Or: Well then, I'm not interested in girls anyway, so I'll go along with celibacy. That is not a basis to start from. The candidate for the priesthood has to recognize the faith as a force in his life, and he must know that he can live celibacy only in faith. Then celibacy can also become again a testimony that says something to people and that also gives them the courage to marry. The two institutions are interconnected. If fidelity in the one is no longer possible, the other no longer exists: one fidelity sustains the other.

Is that a conjecture when you say that there is a connection between the crisis of celibacy and the crisis of marriage?

That seems quite apparent to me. In both cases the question of a definitive life decision is at the center of one's own personality: Am I already able, let's say at age twenty-five, to arrange my whole life? Is that something appropriate for man at all? Is it possible to see it through and in doing so to grow and mature in a living way—or must I not rather keep myself constantly open for new possibilities? Basically, then, the question is posed thus: Does the possibility of a definitive choice belong in the central sphere of man's existence as an essential component? In deciding his form of life, can he commit himself to a definitive bond? I would say two things. He can do so only if he is really anchored in his faith. Second, only then does he also reach the full form of human love and human maturity. Anything less than monogamous marriage is too little for man.

But if the figures about the breakdowns of celibacy are correct, then celibacy collapsed de facto a long time ago. To say it again: is this question perhaps one day negotiable in the sense of a free choice?

The point is that, in any case, it has to be free. It's even necessary to confirm by an oath before ordination one's free consent and desire. In this sense, I always have a bad feeling when it's said afterward that it was a compulsory celibacy and that it was imposed on us. That goes against one's word given at the beginning. It's very important that in the education of priests we see to it that this oath is taken seriously. This is the first point. The second is that where there is living faith, and in the measure in which a church lives faith, the strength to do this is also given.

I think that giving up this condition basically improves nothing; rather, it glosses over a crisis of faith. Naturally, it is a tragedy for a church when many lead a more or less double life. Unfortunately, this is not the first time that has happened. In the late Middle Ages we had a similar situation, which was also one of the factors that caused the Reformation. That is a tragic event indeed that calls for reflection, also for the sake of the people, who also really suffer deeply. But I think that, according to the findings of the last synod of bishops, it is the conviction of the great majority of bishops that the real question is the crisis of faith and that we won't get better and more priests by this "uncoupling" but will only gloss over a crisis of faith and falsely obtain solutions in a superficial way.

Back to my question: do you think that perhaps one day priests will be able to decide freely between celibate and noncelibate life?

I understood your question. I simply had to make it clear that in any event, at least according to what every priest says before his ordination, celibacy is not a matter of compulsion. Someone is accepted as a priest only when he does it of his own accord. And that is now the question, of course: how deeply do priesthood and celibacy belong together? And is not the wish to have only one [without the other] a lower view of the priesthood? Nor do I think that in this matter it's enough simply to point to the Orthodox churches and Protestant Christianity. Protestant Christianity has per se a completely different understanding of office: it is a function, it is a ministry coming out of the community, but it is not a sacrament in the same sense; it is not priesthood in this proper sense. In the Orthodox churches we have, on the one hand, the full form of the priesthood, the priest monks, who alone can become bishops. Alongside them are the "people's priests," who, if they want to marry, must marry before ordination but who exercise little pastoral care and are really only liturgical ministers. This is also a somewhat different conception of priesthood. We, on the other hand, are of the opinion that everyone who is a priest at all must be so in the way that the bishop is and that there cannot be such a division.

One ought not to declare that any custom of the church's life, no matter how deeply anchored and well founded, is wholly absolute. To be sure, the church will have to ask herself the question again and again; she has now done so in two synods. But I think that given the whole history of Western Christianity and the inner vision that lies at the basis of the whole, the church should not believe that she will easily gain much by resorting to this uncoupling; rather in any case she will lose if she does so.

Can one say, then, that you do not believe that one day the Catholic Church will have married priests?

At least not in the foreseeable future. To be quite honest, I must say that we do have married priests, who came to us as converts from the Anglican Church or from various Protestant communities. In exceptional cases, then, it is possible, but they are just that: exceptional situations. And I think that these will also remain exceptional cases in the future.

Mustn't celibacy be dropped for the simple reason that otherwise the church won't get any more priests?

I don't think that the argument is really sound. The question of priestly vocations has many aspects. It has, first of all, to do with the number of children. If today the average number of children is 1.5, the question of possible priests takes on a very different form from what it was in ages when families were considerably larger. And there are also very different expectations in families. Today we are experiencing that the main obstacles to the priesthood often come from parents. They have very different expectations for their children. That is the first point. The second point is that the number of active

Christians is much smaller, which means, of course, that the selection pool has become much smaller. Looked at relative to the number of children and the number of those who are believing churchgoers, the number of priestly vocations has probably not decreased at all. In this sense, one has to take the proportion into account. The first question, then, is: are there believers? And only then comes the second question. Are priests coming from them?

CONTRACEPTION

Your Eminence, many Christians do not understand the church's position on contraception. Do you understand that they don't understand it?

Yes, I can understand that quite well; the question is really complicated. In today's troubled world, where the number of children cannot be very high given living conditions and so many other factors, it's very easy to understand. In this matter, we ought to look less at the casuistry of individual cases and more at the major objectives that the church has in mind.

I think that it's a question of three basic options. The first and most fundamental is to insist on the value of the child in society. In this area, in fact, there has been a remarkable change. Whereas in the simple societies of the past up to the nineteenth century, the blessing of children was regarded as *the* blessing, today children are conceived of almost as a threat. People think that they rob us of a place for the future, they threaten our own space, and so forth. In this matter a primary objective is to recover the original, true view that the child, the new human being, is a blessing. That by giving life we also receive it ourselves and that going out of ourselves and accepting the blessing of creation is good for man.

The second is that today we find ourselves before a separation of sexuality from procreation such as was not known earlier, and this makes it all the more necessary not to lose sight of the inner connection between the two.

Meanwhile, even representatives of the sixties generation who tried it are making some astonishing statements. Or perhaps that's just what we should expect. Rainer Langhans, for example, who once explored "orgasmic sexuality" in his communes, now proclaims that "the pill severed sexuality from the soul and led people into a blind alley." Langhans complains that now there "is no longer any giving, no longer any devoted dedication." "The highest" aspect of sexuality, he now professes, is "parenthood," which he calls "collaboration in God's plan."

It really is true that increasingly we have the development of two completely separated realities. In Huxley's famous futuristic novel *Brave New World*, we see a vision of a coming world in which sexuality is something completely detached from procreation. He had good reason to expect this, and its human tragedy is fully explored. In this world, children are planned and produced in a laboratory in a regulated fashion. Now, that is clearly an intentional caricature, but like all caricatures, it does bring something to the fore: that the child is going to be something that tends to be planned and made, that he lies completely under the control of reason, as it were. And that signals the self-destruction of man. Children become products in which we want to express ourselves and are robbed in advance of their own life's projects. And sexuality once again becomes something replaceable. And, of course, in all this the relationship of man and woman is also lost. The developments are plain to see.

In the question of contraception, precisely such basic options are at stake. The church wants to keep man human. For the third option in this context is that we cannot resolve great moral problems simply with techniques, with chemistry, but must solve them morally, with a lifestyle. It is, I think—independently now of contraception—one of our great perils that we want to master even the human condition with technology, that we have forgotten there are primordial human problems that are not susceptible of technological solutions but that demand a certain lifestyle and certain life decisions. I would say that in the question of contraception, we ought to look more at these basic options, in which the church is leading a struggle for man. The point of the church's objections is to underscore this battle. The way these objections are formulated is perhaps not always completely felicitous, but what is at stake are such major cardinal points of human existence.

The question remains whether you can reproach someone, say a couple who already has several children, for not having a positive attitude toward children.

No, of course not, and that shouldn't happen, either.

But must these people nevertheless have the idea that they are living in some sort of sin if they...

I would say that those are questions that ought to be discussed with one's spiritual director, with one's priest, because they can't be projected into the abstract.

ABORTION

The church, says the pope, will continue her vehement opposition to all measures that "in any way promote abortion, sterilization, and contraception." Such measures wound, he says, the dignity of man as an image of God and thereby undermine the basis of society. The fundamental issue is the protection of life. On the other hand, why is the death penalty, as the Catechism says, "not excluded as a right of the state"?

In the death penalty, when it is legitimately applied, someone is punished who has been proved guilty of the most serious crimes and who also represents a threat to the peace of society. In other words, a guilty person is punished. In the case of abortion, on the other hand, the death penalty is inflicted on someone who is absolutely innocent. And those are two completely different things that you cannot compare with one another.

It is true that the unborn child is regarded by not a few people as an unjust aggressor who narrows the scope of my life, who forces his way into my life, and whom I must kill as an unjust attacker. But that is nothing less than the vision we spoke of earlier, in which the child is no longer considered a distinct creature of God, created in the image of God, with his own right to life but, at least as long as he is yet unborn, suddenly appears as a foe or as an inconvenience I can do with as I please. I think that the point is to clarify the awareness that a conceived child is a human being, an individual.

The child, though needing the protection of the mother's bodily communion, is still a distinct person in his own right, and he must be treated as a human being because he is a human being. I think that if we give up the principle that every man as man is under God's protection, that as a man he is beyond the reach of our arbitrary will, we really do forsake the foundation of human rights.

But can one then say that someone who finds herself in a great moral dilemma and decides to terminate pregnancy is a conspirator against life?

How guilt is assigned to individual persons is always a question that cannot be decided abstractly. But let's say that the act itself—whoever has brought about the situation; it can also be due to pressure from men—remains by its nature an attempt to resolve a conflict situation by killing a human being. We also know from psychology how deeply something like this can stick in the mother's psyche, because she knows, at some level, that there was a human being in her, that it would have been her child, and that it might have turned out to be someone she would have been proud of. Needless to say, society must also help to ensure the availability of other possibilities for dealing with difficult situations and to end pressure on expectant mothers and to reawaken a new love for children.

Excommunication in the case of married people who divorce and live in a new civil marriage not recognized by the church is something that today probably only especially loyal Catholics can agree with. It seems unjust, humiliating, and, in the end, unChristian, as well. You yourself observed in 1972: "Marriage is a sacrament.... [T]his does not rule out that the church's communion also embraces those people who recognize this doctrine and this principle of life but are in an exceptionally difficult situation in which they especially need full communion with the body of the Lord."

First of all, I must make a purely canonical clarification, namely, that these married people are not excommunicated in the formal sense. Excommunication is a whole cluster of ecclesiastical penalties; it is a restriction of church membership. This ecclesiastical penalty is not imposed on them, even though what you might call the core that immediately catches the eye, the fact of not being able to receive Communion, does affect them. But, as I said, they are not excommunicated in the juridical sense. They are, indeed, members of the church who, because of a specific situation in their lives, cannot go to Communion. It is beyond doubt that this is a great burden especially in our world, in which the percentage of broken marriages is increasing.

I think that this burden can be carried if it becomes clear that there are also other people who may not receive Communion. The real reason why the problem has become so dramatic is that Communion has become a sort of social rite and that one is really stigmatized if one doesn't participate in it. If it becomes plain again that many people should be saying to themselves, I've got a few things to answer for, I can't go up to Communion as I am now; and if, as St. Paul puts it, the discernment of the body of Christ is once more practiced in this way, the situation will immediately take on a different look. That is one condition. The second is that they have to feel that, in spite of everything, they are accepted by the church, that the church suffers with them.

But that sounds like a pious wish.

Of course, that would have to find some expression in the life of a community. And conversely, by taking this renunciation upon oneself, one does something for the church and for humanity, in that one bears a kind of witness to the uniqueness of marriage. I think that this, in turn, also has a very important aspect, namely, the recognition that suffering and renunciation can be something positive and that we have to find a new appreciation for these things. And finally that we also recover the awareness that one can meaningfully and fruitfully participate in the celebration of the Mass, of the Eucharist, without going to Communion each time. So it remains a difficult matter, but I think that when a few connected factors get straightened out again, this will also become easier to bear.

Still, the priest does say the words, "Happy are those who are called to the Lord's Supper." Consequently, the others ought to feel that they are unhappy.

Unfortunately, this has been somewhat obscured by the translation. The words do not refer directly to the Eucharist. They are, in fact, taken from the Book of Revelation and refer to the invitation to the eternal marriage feast that is represented in the Eucharist. Therefore, someone who cannot receive Communion at the moment is not necessarily excluded from the eternal wedding feast. There has to be, as it were, a constant examination of conscience. I have to think about being fit for this eternal meal and communicate now so that that actually happens. Even someone who cannot receive Communion now is, like all the others, exhorted by this call to think, while he is on the way, that he will one day be admitted to the eternal marriage banquet. And perhaps, because he has suffered, that he can be even more acceptable.

Is discussion of this question still open, or is it already decided and settled once and for all?

The principles have been decided, but factual questions, individual questions, are of course always possible. For example, perhaps in the future there could also be an extrajudicial determination that the first marriage did not exist. This could perhaps be ascertained locally by experienced pastors. Such juridical developments, which can make things less complicated, are conceivable. But the principle that marriage is indissoluble and that someone who has left the valid marriage of his life, the sacrament, and entered into another marriage cannot communicate does, in fact, hold definitively.

Everything revolves again and again on this point: what must the church salvage from her tradition and what must she, if the need arises, discard? How is this question decided? Is there a list with two columns? On the right: always valid; on the left: capable of renewal?

No, it's obviously not that simple. But there are various degrees of importance in the tradition. It was once customary in theology to speak of degrees of certitude, and that was not so wrong. Many say that we have to go back to that. The term *hierarchy of truths* does seem to point in this direction, namely, that not everything has the same weight, that there are, so to speak, essentials, for example, the great conciliar decisions or what is stated in the Creed. These things are the Way and as such are vital to the church's existence; they belong to her inner identity. And then there are ramifications that are connected with these essentials and certainly belong to the whole tree but that are not all of the same importance. The identity of the church has clear distinguishing marks, so that it is not rigid but the identity of something living, which remains true to itself in the midst of development.

WOMEN'S ORDINATION

On another issue, women's ordination, an absolute "no" has been "promulgated by the Magisterium in an infallible way." This was reconfirmed by the pope in the fall of 1995. "We do not have the right to change this," reads the statement. So here, too, it is the historical argument that counts. But if one takes that seriously, there ought never to have been a St. Paul, for everything new also does away with holy and venerable things. Paul did new things. The questions are: When can you put an end to a particular [disciplinary] regulation? How can new things come into being? And: Can't the foreshortenings of history also be an idolatry that is incompatible with the freedom of a Christian?

Here, I think, it is necessary to state a few things more precisely. The first point is that St. Paul did new things in the name of Christ but not in his own name. And he emphasized explicitly that anyone who acknowledges Old Testament revelation as valid but then alters a few things without authorization is acting unjustly. There could be new things because God had done new things in Christ. And as a servant of this newness, he knew that he hadn't invented it but that it came out of the newness of Jesus Christ himself. Which then, in turn, has its conditions, and in that matter he was very strict. If you think, for example, of the account of the Last Supper, he says expressly: "I received myself what I have handed on to you," thus clearly declaring that he is bound to what the Lord did on the last night and what has come down to him by way of tradition. Or think of the message of Easter, where he says once more: This I received, and I also encountered him myself. And so we teach, and so we all teach; and whoever doesn't do that estranges himself from Christ. Paul distinguished very clearly between the new things that come from Christ and the bond to Christ, which alone authorizes him to do these new things. That is the first point.

The second is that in all areas that aren't really defined by the Lord and the apostolic tradition there are in fact constant changes—even today. The question is just this: Does it come from the Lord or not? And how does one recognize this? The answer, confirmed by the pope, that we, the Congregation for the Doctrine of the Faith, gave to the issue of women's ordination does not say that the pope has performed an infallible act of teaching. The pope established rather that the church, the bishops of all places and times, have always taught and acted in this way. The Second Vatican Council says: what bishops teach and do in unison over a very long time is infallible; it is the expression of a bond that they themselves did not create. The *responsum* appeals to this passage of the council (*Lumen Gentium, 25*). It is not, as I said, an infallible act of the pope, but the binding authority rests upon the continuity of the tradition. And, as a matter of fact, this continuity with the origin is already significant. For it was never self-evident. The ancient religions, without exception, had priestesses, and it was so in the Gnostic movements, as well. An Italian scholar recently discovered that in southern Italy, around the fifth or sixth century, various groups instituted priestesses, and the bishops and the pope immediately took steps against this. Tradition emerged not from the surrounding world but from within Christianity.

But I would now add a further piece of information that I find very interesting. I am referring to the diagnosis that one of the most important Catholic feminists, Elisabeth Schüssler Fiorenza, has given in this matter. She is a German, an important exegete, who studied exegesis in Münster, where she married an Italian-American from Fiorenza, and who now teaches in America. At first she took a vehement part in the struggle for women's ordination, but now she says that that was a wrong goal. The experience with female priests in the Anglican Church has, she says, led to the realization that "ordination is not a solution; it isn't what we wanted." She also explains why. She says, "Ordination is subordination, and that's exactly what we don't want." And on this point, her diagnosis is completely correct.

To enter into an *ordo* always also means to enter into a relationship of subordination. But in our liberation movement, says Schüssler Fiorenza, we don't want to enter into an *ordo*, into a *subordo*, a "subordination," but rather to overcome the very phenomenon itself. Our struggle, she says, therefore mustn't aim at women's ordination; that is precisely the wrong thing to do. Rather, it must aim at the cessation of ordination altogether and at making the church a society of equals in which there is only a "shifting leadership." Given the motivations behind the struggle for women's ordination, which does, in fact, aim at power-sharing and liberation from subordination, she has seen that correctly. But then one must really say there is a whole question behind this: What is the priesthood actually? Does the sacrament exist, or should there be only a shifting leadership in which no one is allowed permanent access to "power"? I think that in this sense perhaps the discussion will also change in the near future.

All these questions that we have just touched upon have for years been constantly reorchestrated, sometimes with more, sometimes with less response from the people. How do you judge undertakings like the "Petition of the People of the Church" in Germany?

I already said a few things about that when we were talking about the situation of the church in Italy and in other countries. I find that Metz's remarks in many respects are right on the mark. If I recall correctly, he points out that this movement merely tries to cure the symptoms, whereas it excludes the question that is really at the core of the crisis in the church, which he terms—and the expression is perhaps not entirely felicitous—a "God-crisis." As far as the content is concerned, he has indicated exactly the decisive point. And when we spoke earlier of the modern consensus that is opposed to faith, I described it in these terms: God no longer counts, even if he should exist. If we live in this way, then the church becomes a club, which now has to search for substitute goals and meanings. And then all the things that can't be explained without God are vexatious. In other words, the precise point that is centrally at issue is bracketed out. Metz then—I'm still following my memory—points out that the "Petition of the People of the Church" is on the whole met in the Protestant churches. It is quite obvious that this does not protect them from the crisis. So the question is raised—he says something more or less like this—why do we want to make ourselves a clone of Protestant Christianity? I can only agree with all that.

It seems that something like a Western-liberal civilizational Christianity has formed, a sort of secularized faith that regards many things as one and the same. This culture, which often no longer really has much to do with the essence of Christianity—or of Catholicism—clearly seems to be becoming more attractive. One has the impression that the official church has hardly anything, at least theologically, to say against this philosophy, which is represented especially by Eugen Drewermann.

The Drewermann craze [*Welle*] is already beginning to abate. What he proposes is indeed just a variant of that general culture of secularized faith of which you spoke. I would say that people don't want to do without religion, but they want it only to give, not to make its own demands on man. People want to take the mysterious element in religion but spare themselves the effort of faith. The diverse forms of this new religion, of its religiosity and its philosophy, all largely converge today under the heading "New Age." A sort of mystical union with the divine ground of the world is the goal to which various techniques are supposed to lead. So there is the idea that it is possible to experience religion in its highest form and at the same time to remain completely within the scientific picture of the world. In contrast to this, the Christian faith seems complicated. It is doubtless in a difficult situation. But, thank God, great Christian thinkers and exemplary figures of Christian life have not been lacking even in this very century. They show the relevance of Christian faith and make evident that this faith helps one attain the fulfillment of humanity. For this reason there are most definitely new movements toward a decisive Christian life precisely in the younger generation, even if this can't become a mass movement.

The "canon of criticism" just treated is apparently not so easy to be rid of. If that is so, how must one deal with it? Is it possible to wait out all these questions? Will we ever be rid of them?

In any case, they will lose their urgency as soon as the church is no longer looked upon as a final end, an end in itself, and as a place for gaining power. As soon as celibacy is once again lived convincingly out of a strong faith. As soon as we see, as the goal of Christianity, eternal life instead of ensconcing ourselves in a group in which one can exercise power, I am convinced that a spiritual turning point will come sometime and that then these questions will lose their urgency as suddenly as they arose. After all, in the end, they are not man's real questions, either.

The Basis of Christian Brotherhood: Faith

FROM *THE MEANING OF CHRISTIAN BROTHERHOOD*

Christian brotherhood, unlike the purely secular brotherhood of Marxism, is, above all, brotherhood based on the common paternity of God. Unlike the impersonal Stoic idea of God the father and the vague paternal idea of the Enlightenment, the fatherhood of God is a fatherhood mediated by the Son and including brotherly union in the Son.

If, therefore, Christian brotherhood is to be vitally realized, both a vital knowledge of the fatherhood of God and a vital joining with Jesus Christ in a unity of grace are necessary.

The fatherhood of God gives Christian brotherhood its firm foundation. It is important here to understand fully the new knowledge that the Christian faith has given us of God's paternity. Mythical religion, Plato and the Stoics, and eighteenth-century deism all speak of God as a father. And yet it is something quite different when the Christian says "Our Father." Early mythical thought conceived of the sky as the world-creating force which, together with Mother Earth, produced all the life of the world. In this naturalistic sense, then, the sky can be called the "father" of men.[1] Greek philosophy spiritualized this idea without completely removing its basic assumption. In the eternal, transcendent idea of the good, Plato sees the father and the lord, but its quality as "person" remains in doubt, and there is no question of a personal relationship with the creatures of the world.[2] With the Stoics the return to naturalism is quite clear. Their doctrine of the fatherhood of God depends on a reinterpretation in terms of natural philosophy of the old myth of the *hieros gamos* (sacred marriage) of Zeus and Hera. Thus it remains ultimately a proposition of natural philosophy when man appears in Epictetus as *idios huios tou theou* (God's own son).[3] It certainly does not mean that he is seen in relation to a personal, caring and loving, angry and forgiving, paternal God. He is merely the culminating point of the cosmos, the one most filled by its sublime powers. The uncosmic, strictly personalist idea of Father, which gives to the paternity of God the seriousness of a true claim on us and to the fraternity of his children life and significance, is revealed only in the words of the Bible and is thus apparent only to the eyes of faith. Insight into the brotherhood of men is given ultimately only to him who has seen, in faith, the full paternity of God.

At the same time, the concreteness of God, his personal relation to man, also undergoes an increasing spiritualization in the language of scripture—an increasing spiritualization that does not, however, lead to increasing rarification (as is always the danger) but, on the contrary, serves to intensify the concreteness and the living reality of his fatherhood. This God never becomes a God of the philosophers; he remains the living God, the God of Abraham, of Isaac, and of Jacob; more, he becomes the God of Jesus Christ and thus the God who has taken on our flesh and blood and our whole human nature. In Jesus Christ, God has not only spoken to men but has also finally and radically made it possible for them to speak to him; for in him God became man and, as man, finally stepped out of his totally different being and entered into the dialogic situation of all men. Jesus the *man* stands as such within the community of discourse that unites all men as beings of the same order. The man Jesus can be addressed by every man, but in him it is God who is addressed. Thus the question of how changeable man can address a totally different, unchangeable God is resolved. In Christ, God has taken a piece of this world's time and of changeable creatureliness, drawn it to himself, and finally thrown open the door between himself and his creatures. In Christ, God has become God more concretely, more personally, and more "addressably," "a partner of men." We are better placed to understand the importance of this for the Christian conception of fatherhood and brotherhood if we consider more closely the biblical growth of the idea. We have already seen that the Old Testament distinguishes two kinds of divine paternity and, correspondingly, two kinds of human childhood: the sonship of all peoples because of Creation, and the sonship of Israel because of its election. The Old Testament expresses Israel's priority by (among other things) calling Israel the "firstborn son of God" (Ex 4:22).

At the time of the kings, an important development takes place in Israel's understanding of itself. The king now became virtually the personification of all Israel; he represented, as it were, its "total person." (Since the research work by Pedersen, this expression of Max Scheler's can be used to describe Israelite thinking on this question.)[4] Thus the name "the son of God" is transferred to the king (2 Sm 7:14; Ps 2:7; 89:27). He is the son of God in the sense described, inasmuch as he represents Israel, which has a special elective sonship in relation to God. When the idea of a king passed into the eschatological hope of salvation and the idea of the Messiah was formulated concretely, the title of sonship went with it and became an honorific designation for the king of the last times, the Messiah, as the fulfilled image of the true Israel. Exegesis of the last few decades has confirmed the view that nearly all the synoptic texts that call Jesus *huios tou theou* (Son of God) are not to be understood in the sense of a metaphysical statement about the eternal inner-trinitarian divine sonship of Jesus, but reproduce the messianic title of honor, designating him as the epitome of the true Israel.[5] This accords with the fact that Jesus saw himself expressly as the founder of a new Israel already founded in his person—a conception that John expresses by having Jesus describe himself in two places in suggestive imagery as the new Jacob-Israel (Jn 1:51 [cf. Gn 28:12] and 4:6, 11–12).

If we compare these exegetical findings with our dogmatic acknowledgment of the divine sonship of Jesus, we can say that Christ is the fulfillment of what Israel only foreshadowed. He is truly the "Son." Thus he is ultimately the true and real Israel because he possesses the highest distinction of Israel, the sonship of God, in an infinitely more real way than was the case with the old People of God. At the same time, the fact that he has himself become a man, "Israel," shows that he does not regard his divine sonship as reserved only for himself: the meaning of the Incarnation is rather to make what is his available to all. Man can be "in Christ," enter into him, and become one with him; and whoever is in Jesus Christ shares his sonship and is able to say with him, "Abba," "my father."[6] The new Israel, which is composed of all the faithful, is no longer a son merely because of the choosing and summoning call of God, the ultimate concrete form of which is the Torah; she is a "son in the son" (Eckhart); she is a son through being planted in the innate Son of the Father (Jn 1:18), with whom we are *one single* body, one single "seed of Abraham." "You are all one in Christ Jesus," Paul emphasizes in Galatians 3:28, after (in 3:16) he had emphasized that the promise given to Abraham referred not to many but only to one man, Christ Jesus, with whom, however, we are united in the unity of a single man. Thus the ideas of fatherhood, sonship, and brotherhood acquire a completely new ring, the ring of reality. Behind the word *Father* there stands the *fact* of our true childhood in Christ Jesus (Gal 4:6; Rom 8:15f.). What is new about the New Testament statements concerning the Father is not a new psychological atmosphere, nor a new subjective intensity, nor a new idea, but the new fact created by Christ. The mood of trusting love and pure devotion may be found in late Jewish prayers or in the texts of the Hermes mystery cult.[7] But in these it is ultimately *only* a question of atmosphere. What is expressed by them is valuable and profound and can be largely taken over by the Christian. But it acquires in Christianity a new meaning by being founded firmly on fact—the fact of our real embodiment in Christ, which includes our becoming truly sons. What is true of the ideas of "fatherhood" and "sonship" is no less true of "brotherhood." This is the fundamental dogmatic basis for the brotherliness of Christians among one another; for this brotherliness is founded on our being incorporated in Christ Jesus, in the uniqueness of a new man. Like the fatherhood of God, the brotherhood of Christians in the Lord is raised—through the Christ-event—above the realm of ideas to the dignity of true actuality. We also find here the concrete realization and the constant source of Christian brotherliness. It rests on the fact of our being embodied in Christ. The act that does this for us is baptism (which is renewed in penance). The celebration of the Eucharist is the constant reestablishment of our bodily unity with the Lord and with one another. But with this idea we are already on the way toward realizing Christian brotherhood concretely, and that we shall pursue later on. Summing up what we have said so far, we can assert that Christian brotherhood differs from all other brotherhoods that transcend the sphere of blood brotherhood precisely in its character as real and actual. This is grasped in faith and acquired through the sacraments.

From these dogmatic conclusions, we can deduce the Christian attitudes that are able to provide the basis for an ethos of true brotherhood. In general terms, these consist, as we have seen, in the conscious spiritual acceptance of the fatherhood of God and union with the life of Christ. We shall now endeavor to explore these two relationships a little further.

Christian brotherhood is ultimately founded on the faith that gives us our assurance of our real sonship in relation to the heavenly Father and of our brotherhood among one another. But here it is necessary to emphasize the social dimension of faith more than is generally done. To take only one example: when theologians today interpret the opening words of the Our Father, they usually restrict themselves to an analysis of the word *father,* and this is in tune with our contemporary religious awareness. But a theologian such as Cyprian, on the other hand, chose to give special attention to the word *our*.[8] In fact, this word does have great importance, for only one man has the right to say "*my* Father" to God, and that is Jesus Christ, the only-begotten Son. All other men must say "*our* Father," for the Father is God for us only so long as we are part of the community of his children. For "me" he becomes a Father only through my being in the "we" of his children. The Christian prayer to the Father "is not the call of a soul that knows nothing outside God and itself,"[9] but is bound to the community of brothers. Together with these brothers we make up the one Christ, in whom and through whom alone we are able to say "Father," because only through Christ and in Christ are we his "children." Thus, strictly speaking, we should not say that Christ taught men to call God "Father," but rather that it was he who taught them to say "*our* Father"—and the *our* is no less important than the *Father,* for it *locates* faith and prayer, assigning them their Christological component. When we see this, Harnack's view that the "Son" does not form part of the gospel proclaimed by Christ is shown to be obviously false.[10] Its place is firmly fixed in the word *our* and, in a logically developing *kerygma,* could not fail to emerge as the social dimension of faith. It is important that this social dimension be brought once more to the consciousness of the faithful, that Christian belief in God the Father should be shown necessarily to involve the affirmation of our brothers, the brotherhood of all Christians.

Living faith in the spirit of the Our Father will necessarily lead to a new relationship to God and to our fellow man, whom we recognize as our brother. Toward God it includes the attitudes of trust and love. God has accepted us as his children in Christ Jesus and has thus become our Father; he is the absolutely faithful and dependable God who has remained true to his covenant in spite of the sin of men—indeed, has been moved by this sin and faithlessness to an even greater outpouring of grace and forgiveness. He is the exact opposite of the Homeric "father of the gods and of men." That god was a domineering and unpredictable despot—not despite his fatherhood, but precisely because of it: there is a despotic quality in the Greek idea of fatherhood.[11] And yet this despotic father was not himself the highest power, for above, or beside him, stood *moira* (fate) and *themis* (the law of the cosmos), against which even he could do nothing.[12] Against this background the biblical idea of fatherhood acquires its true greatness. For this God is the ultimate power, power itself, *Pantocrator,* and at the same time, the most reliable, unfailing fidelity. Both these qualities are able to move man to an ultimate, unshakable trust that is love and worship in one.

A second attitude that faith produces in us is in relation to our fellow men. One might call it, with Dietrich von Hildebrand, "the true loss of oneself."[13] To become a Christian means to become incorporated in the Son, in Christ, so that we become "sons in the Son." This is a sacramental but also an ethical process. Its ethical nature is illuminated by one of Eckhart's thoughts, which, when taken to its logical conclusion, is dogmatically incorrect but can still help us to see the present point more clearly. Eckhart wrongly interprets the dogmatic teaching that Christ possessed human nature but not human personality, by saying that, in that case, Christ was "man in general," possessing humanity without any individuality or particular qualities. In one of his German sermons, he expresses the doctrine of the two natures and the one person like this: "The eternal Word did not take upon himself this or that man, but rather did it take upon itself a free, undivided human nature."[14] This is an ethical reinterpretation of the doctrine of the hypostatic union. Eckhart seeks to make the dogmatic statement yield a basic ethical principle. For Christ is the goal of man, nay more: it is for man to be himself "in Christ," to grow into Christ. To the question of how man can grow into Christ, Eckhart's suggestion offers a surprisingly clear and simple answer. Christ is man, humanity free from any particular individuality. Accordingly, man grows into Christ the more that he becomes "man in himself"—the more that he loses himself, his own particular ego. What separates him from Christ is his own individuality, the self-assertion of his ego. What unites him with Christ is his general humanity. The measure of his share in the hypostatic union, his being "in Christ," is the extent to which he has destroyed his own ego; so that, according to Eckhart, if he were able to rid himself entirely of his ego, he would become identical with Christ. It is not necessary here to enter on a discussion of this ethic, which is an ethic of the mystical body of Christ and yet runs the danger of turning into pure humanism. The important thing here is to see the truth that lies at the heart of it: to become one with Christ means to lose one's "oneself," to cease to regard one's own ego as an absolute. It is consistent with this basic view that Eckhart's ethic has a marked social character and emphasizes service to our neighbor rather than the joys of contemplation.[15] The belief that we have all become a single new man in Jesus Christ will always call us to let the separating particularity of our own egos, the self-assertion of human selfhood, melt into the community of the new man Jesus Christ. Whoever believes in Jesus Christ has not only found an ethical model to be imitated privately but is called to break up his own merely private ego and merge into the unity of the body of Christ.

The ethic of Christ is essentially an ethic of the body of Christ. Inevitably, therefore, it means losing one's own ego and becoming one in brotherhood with all those who are in Christ. As an ethic of true self-loss, it necessarily includes the brotherhood of all Christians.

PART THREE

THE LITURGY

Theology of the Liturgy

Lecture Delivered During the
Journées Liturgiques de Fontgombault

JULY 22–24, 2001

The Second Vatican Council defined the liturgy as "the work of Christ the Priest and of His Body which is the Church."

The work of Jesus Christ is referred to in the same text as the work of the redemption that Christ accomplished especially by the paschal mystery of his Passion, his Resurrection from the dead, and his glorious Ascension.

"By this Mystery, in dying He has destroyed our death, and in rising He has restored life." At first sight, in these two sentences, the phrase "the work of Christ" seems to have been used in two different senses. "The work of Christ" refers first of all to the historical, redemptive actions of Jesus, his death and his Resurrection; at the same time, the celebration of the liturgy is called "the work of Christ."

In reality, the two meanings are inseparably linked: the death and Resurrection of Christ, the paschal mystery, are not just exterior, historic events. In the case of the Resurrection this is very clear. It is joined to and penetrates history but transcends it in two ways: it is not the action of a man, but an action of God, and in that way carries the risen Jesus beyond history, to that place where he sits at the right hand of the Father. But the cross is not a merely human action, either. The purely human aspect is present in the people who led Jesus to the cross. For Jesus himself, the cross is not primarily an action but a passion, and a passion which signifies that he is but one with the Divine Will—a union, the dramatic character of which is shown to us in the Garden of Gethsemane. Thus the passive dimension of being put to death is transformed into the active dimension of love: death becomes the abandonment of himself to the Father for men. In this way, the horizon extends, as it does in the Resurrection, well beyond the purely human aspect and well beyond the fact of having been nailed to a cross and having died. This element added to the mere historical event is what the language of faith calls a "mystery," and it has condensed into the term *paschal mystery* the innermost core of the redemptive event. If we can say from this that the "paschal mystery" constitutes the core of "the work of Jesus," the connection with the liturgy is immediately clear: it is precisely this "work of Jesus" that is the real content of the liturgy. In it, through the faith and prayer of the church, the "work of Jesus" is continually brought into contact with history in order to penetrate it. Thus, in the liturgy, the merely human historical event is transcended over and over again and is part of the divine and human action that is the Redemption. In it, Christ is the true subject/bearer: it is the work of Christ; but in it he draws history to himself, precisely in this permanent action in which our salvation takes place.

SACRIFICE CALLED INTO QUESTION

If we go back to Vatican II, we find the following description of this relationship: "In the liturgy, through which, especially in the divine Sacrifice of the Eucharist, 'the work of our Redemption is carried on,' the faithful are most fully led to express and show to others the mystery of Christ and the real nature of the true Church."

All that has become foreign to modern thinking and, only thirty years after the council, has been brought into question even among Catholic liturgists. Who still talks today about "the divine Sacrifice of the Eucharist"? Discussions about the idea of sacrifice have again become astonishingly lively, as much on the Catholic side as on the Protestant. People realize that an idea which has always preoccupied, under various forms, not only the history of the church but the entire history of humanity must be the expression of something basic that concerns us, as well. But, at the same time, the old Enlightenment positions still live on everywhere: accusations of magic and paganism, contrasts drawn between worship and the service of the Word, between rite and ethos, the idea of a Christianity that disengages itself from worship and enters into the profane world, Catholic theologians who have no desire to see themselves accused of antimodernity. Even if people want, in one way or another, to rediscover the concept of sacrifice, embarrassment and criticism are the end result. Thus, Stefan Orth, in the vast panorama of a bibliography of recent works devoted to the theme of sacrifice, believed he could make the following statement as a summary of his research: "In fact, many Catholics themselves today ratify the verdict and the conclusions of Martin Luther, who says that to speak of sacrifice is 'the greatest and most appalling horror' and a 'damnable impiety': this is why we want to refrain from all that smacks of sacrifice, including the whole canon, and retain only that which is pure and holy." Then Orth adds: "This maxim was also followed in the Catholic Church after Vatican II, or at least tended to be, and led people to think of divine worship chiefly in terms of the feast of the Passover related in the accounts of the Last Supper." Appealing to a work on sacrifice edited by two modern catholic liturgists, he then said, in slightly more moderate terms, that it clearly seemed that the notion of the sacrifice of the Mass—even more than that of the sacrifice of the cross—was at best an idea very open to misunderstanding.

I certainly don't need to say that I am not one of the "numerous Catholics" who consider it the most appalling horror and a damnable impiety to speak of the sacrifice of the Mass. It goes without saying that the writer did not mention my book on the spirit of the liturgy, which analyzes the idea of sacrifice in detail. His diagnosis remains dismaying. Is it true? I do not know these numerous Catholics who consider it a damnable impiety to understand the Eucharist as a sacrifice. The second, more circumspect diagnosis, according to which the sacrifice of the Mass is open to misunderstandings is, on the other hand, easily shown to be correct. Even if one leaves to one side the first affirmation of the writer as a rhetorical exaggeration, there remains a troubling problem, which we should face up to. A sizable party of Catholic liturgists seems to have practically arrived at the conclusion that Luther, rather than Trent, was substantially right in the sixteenth-century debate; one can detect much the same position in the postconciliar discussions on the priesthood. The great historian of the Council of Trent, Hubert Jedin, pointed this out in 1975, in the preface to the last volume of his history of the Council of Trent: "The attentive reader … in reading this will not be less dismayed than the author, when he realizes that many of the things—in fact, almost everything— that disturbed the men of the past [are] being put forward anew today." It is only against this background of the effective denial of the authority of Trent, that the bitterness of the struggle against allowing the celebration of Mass according to the 1962 Missal, after the liturgical reform, can be understood. The possibility of so celebrating constitutes the strongest and thus (for them) the most intolerable contradiction of the opinion of those who believe that the faith in the Eucharist formulated by Trent has lost its value.

It would be easy to gather proofs to support this statement of the position. I leave aside the extreme liturgical theology of Harald Schützeichel, who departs completely from Catholic dogma and expounds, for example, the bold assertion that it was only in the Middle Ages that the idea of the Real Presence was invented. A modern liturgist such as David N. Power tells us that through the course of history, not only the manner in which a truth is expressed but also the content of what is expressed can lose its meaning. He links his theory in concrete terms with the statements of Trent. Theodore Schnitker tells us that an up-to-date liturgy includes both a different expression of the faith and theological changes. Moreover, according to him, there are theologians, at least in the circles of the Roman Church and her liturgy, who have not yet grasped the full import of the transformations put forward by the liturgical reform in the area of the doctrine of the faith. R. Messner's certainly respectable work on the reform of the Mass carried out by Martin Luther and on the Eucharist in the early church, which contains many interesting ideas, arrives nonetheless at the conclusion that the early church was better understood by Luther than by the Council of Trent.

The serious nature of these theories comes from the fact that frequently they pass immediately into practice. The thesis according to which it is the community itself that is the subject of the liturgy serves as an authorization to manipulate the liturgy according to each individual's understanding of it. So-called new discoveries and the forms that follow from them are diffused with astonishing rapidity and with a degree of conformity that has long ceased to exist where the norms of ecclesiastical authority are concerned. Theories, in the area of the liturgy, are transformed very rapidly today into practice, and practice, in turn, creates or destroys ways of behaving and thinking.

Meanwhile the problem has been aggravated by the fact that the most recent movement of "enlightened" thought goes much further than Luther: where Luther still took literally the accounts of the institution and made them, as the *norma normans,* the basis of his efforts at reform, the hypotheses of historical criticism have, for a long time, been causing a broad erosion of the texts. The accounts of the Last Supper appear as the product of the liturgical construction of the community; a historical Jesus is sought behind the texts who could not have been thinking of the gift of his body and blood, nor understood his cross as a sacrifice of expiation; we should, rather, imagine a farewell meal that included an eschatological perspective. The authority not only of the ecclesiastical magisterium, but scripture, too, is downgraded in the eyes of many; in its place are put changing pseudohistorical hypotheses, which are immediately replaced by any arbitrary idea, thus placing the liturgy at the mercy of fashion. Where, on the basis of such ideas, the liturgy is manipulated ever more freely, the faithful feel that, in reality, nothing is celebrated, and it is understandable that they desert the liturgy and with it the church.

THE PRINCIPLES OF THEOLOGICAL RESEARCH

Let us return to the fundamental question: is it correct to describe the liturgy as a divine sacrifice, or is it a damnable impiety? In this discussion, one must first of all establish the principal presuppositions that, in any event, determine the reading of scripture, and thus the conclusions which one draws from it. For the Catholic Christian, two lines of essential hermeneutic orientation assert themselves here. The first: we trust scripture and we base ourselves on scripture, not on hypothetical reconstructions that go behind it and, according to their own taste, reconstruct a history in which the presumptuous idea of our knowing what can or cannot be attributed to Jesus plays a key role; which, of course, means attributing to him only what a modern scholar is happy to attribute to a man belonging to a time that the scholar himself has reconstructed.

The second is that we read scripture in the living community of the church, and therefore on the basis of the fundamental decisions thanks to which it has become historically efficacious, namely, those that laid the foundations of the church. One must not separate the text from this living context. In this sense, scripture and tradition form an inseparable whole, and it is this that Luther, at the dawn of the awakening of historical awareness, could not see. He believed that a text could only have one meaning, but such univocity does not exist, and modern historiography has long since abandoned the idea. That in the nascent church, the Eucharist was, from the beginning, understood as a sacrifice, even in a text such as the Didache, which is so difficult and marginal vis-à-vis the great tradition, is an interpretative key of primary importance.

But there is another fundamental hermeneutical aspect in the reading and interpretation of biblical testimony. The fact that I can, or cannot, recognize a sacrifice in the Eucharist as our Lord instituted it depends most essentially on the question of knowing what I understand by sacrifice, therefore on what is called precomprehension. The precomprehension of Luther, for example, in particular his conception of the relation between the Old and New Testaments, his conception of the event and of the historic presence of the church, was such that the category of sacrifice, as he saw it, could not appear other than as an impiety when applied to the Eucharist and the church. The debates to which Stefan Orth refers show how confused and muddled is the idea of sacrifice among almost all authors, and clearly shows how much work must be done here. For the believing theologian, it is clear that scripture itself must teach him the essential definition of sacrifice, and that will come from a "canonical" reading of the Bible, in which the scripture is read in its unity and its dynamic movement, the different stages of which receive their final meaning from Christ, to whom this whole movement leads. By this same standard, the hermeneutic here presupposed is a hermeneutic of faith, founded on faith's internal logic. Ought not the fact to be obvious? Without faith, scripture itself is not scripture, but rather an ill-assorted ensemble of bits of literature that cannot claim any normative significance today.

SACRIFICE AND EASTER

The task alluded to here far exceeds, obviously, the limits of one lecture; so allow me to refer you to my book *The Spirit of the Liturgy,* in which I have sought to give the main outlines of this question. What emerges from it is that, in its course through the history of religions and biblical history, the idea of sacrifice has connotations that go well beyond the area of discussion we habitually associate with the idea of sacrifice. In fact, it opens the doorway to a global understanding of worship and the liturgy: these are the great perspectives that I would like to try to point out here. Also I necessarily have to omit here particular questions of exegesis, in particular the fundamental problem of the accounts of the Institution, on the subject of which, in addition to my book on the liturgy, I have tried to provide some thoughts in my contribution "The Eucharist and Mission."

There is, however, a remark that I cannot refrain from making. In the bibliographic review mentioned, Stefan Orth says that the fact of having avoided, after Vatican II, the idea of sacrifice has "led people to think of divine worship in terms of the feast of the Passover related in the accounts of the Last Supper." At first sight this wording appears ambiguous: is one to think of divine worship in terms of the Last Supper narratives or in terms of the Passover, to which those narratives refer in giving a chronological framework but which they do not otherwise describe. It would be right to say that the Jewish Passover, the institution of which is related in Exodus 12, acquires a new meaning in the New Testament. A great historical movement is manifested there that goes from the beginnings right up to the Last Supper, the cross, and the Resurrection of Jesus. But what is astonishing above all in Orth's presentation is the opposition posited between the idea of sacrifice and the Passover. The Jewish Old Testament deprives Orth's thesis of meaning, because from the law of Deuteronomy on, the slaughtering of lambs is linked to the temple; and even in the earliest period, when the Passover was still a family feast, the slaughtering of lambs already had a sacrificial character. Thus, precisely through the tradition of the Passover, the idea of sacrifice is carried over into the words and gestures of the Last Supper, where it is present also on the basis of a second Old Testament passage, Exodus 24, which relates the conclusion of the Covenant at Sinai. There, it is related that the people were sprinkled with the blood of the victims brought previously, and that Moses said on this occasion: "This is the blood of the Covenant which Yahweh makes with you in accordance with all these provisions." (Ex 24:8) The new Christian Passover is thus expressly interpreted in the accounts of the Last Supper as a sacrificial event, and on the basis of the words of the Last Supper, the nascent church knew that the cross was a sacrifice, because the Last Supper would be an empty gesture without the reality of the cross and the Resurrection, which is anticipated in it and made accessible for all time in its interior content.

I mention this strange opposition between the Passover and sacrifice, because it represents the architectonic principle of a book recently published by the Society of St. Pius X claiming that a dogmatic rupture exists between the new liturgy of Paul VI and the preceding Catholic liturgical tradition. This rupture is seen precisely in the fact that everything is interpreted henceforth on the basis of the "paschal mystery," instead of the redeeming sacrifice of expiation of Christ; the category of the paschal mystery is said to be the heart of the liturgical reform, and it is precisely that which appears to be the proof of the rupture with the classical doctrine of the church. It is clear that there are authors who lay themselves open to such a misunderstanding; but that it is a misunderstanding is completely evident to those who look more closely. In reality, the term *paschal mystery* clearly refers to the realities that took place in the days following Holy Thursday up until the morning of Easter Sunday: the Last Supper as the anticipation of the cross, the drama of Golgotha, and the Lord's Resurrection. In the expression *paschal mystery,* these happenings are seen synthetically as a single, united event, as "the work of Christ," as we heard the council say at the beginning, which took place historically and at the same time transcends that precise point in time. As this event is, inwardly, an act of worship rendered to God, it could become divine worship and in that way be present to all times. The paschal theology of the New Testament, upon which we have cast a quick glance, gives us to understand precisely this: the seemingly profane episode of the Crucifixion of Christ is a sacrifice of expiation, a saving act of the reconciling love of God made man. The theology of the Passover is a theology of the redemption, a liturgy of expiatory sacrifice. The Shepherd has become a Lamb. The vision of the lamb, which appears in the story of Isaac—the lamb that gets entangled in the undergrowth and ransoms the son—has become a reality: the Lord became a Lamb; he allows himself to be bound and sacrificed, to deliver us.

All this has become very foreign to contemporary thought. Reparation ("expiation") can perhaps mean something within the limits of human conflicts and the settling of guilt that holds sway among human beings, but its transposition to the relationship between God and man cannot work. This, surely, is largely the result of the fact that our image of God has grown dim, has come close to deism. One can no longer imagine that human offenses can wound God, and even less that they could necessitate an expiation such as the cross of Christ. The same applies to vicarious substitution: we can hardly still imagine anything in that category—our image of man has become too individualistic for that. Thus the crisis of the liturgy has its basis in central ideas about man. To overcome it, it does not suffice to banalize the liturgy and transform it into a simple gathering at a fraternal meal. But how can we escape from these disorientations? How can we recover the meaning of this immense thing that is at the heart of the message of the cross and the Resurrection? In the final analysis, not through theories and scholarly reflections but only through conversion, by a radical change of life. It is, however, possible to single out some things that open the way to this change of heart, and I would like to put forward some suggestions in that direction, in three stages.

LOVE, THE HEART OF SACRIFICE

The first stage should be a preliminary question on the essential meaning of the word *sacrifice*. People commonly consider sacrifice as the destruction of something precious in the eyes of man; in destroying it, man wants to consecrate this reality to God, to recognize his sovereignty. In fact, however, a destruction does not honor God. The slaughtering of animals or whatever else can't honor God. "If I am hungry, I will not tell you, because the world is mine and all it contains. Am I going to eat the flesh of bulls, shall I drink the blood of goats? Offer to God a sacrifice of thanksgiving, fulfill your vows to the Most High," says God to Israel in Psalm 50 (49):12–14. What, then, does sacrifice consist of? Not in destruction, not in this or that thing, but in the transformation of man. In the fact that he becomes himself conformed to God. He becomes conformed to God when he becomes love. "That is why true sacrifice is every work which allows us to unite ourselves to God in a holy fellowship," as Augustine puts it.

With this key from the New Testament, Augustine interprets the Old Testament sacrifices as symbols pointing to this sacrifice properly so called, and that is why, he says, worship had to be transformed, the symbol had to disappear in favor of the reality. "All the divine prescriptions of scripture which concern the sacrifices of the tabernacle or of the temple, are figures which refer to the love of God and neighbor" (*City of God,* X:5). But Augustine also knows that love only becomes true when it leads a man to God, and thus directs him to his true end; it alone can likewise bring about unity of men among themselves. Therefore the concept of sacrifice refers to community, and the first definition that Augustine attempted is broadened by the following statement: "The whole redeemed human community, that is to say the assembly and the community of the saints, is offered to God in sacrifice by the High Priest Who offered Himself" (X:6). And even more simply: "This sacrifice is ourselves," or again: "Such is the Christian sacrifice: the multitude—a single body in Christ" (X:6). Sacrifice consists then—we shall say it once more—in a process of transformation, in the conformity of man to God, in his theiosis, as the fathers would say. It consists, to express it in modern phraseology, in the abolition of difference—in the union between God and man, between God and creation: "God all in all" (1 Cor 15:28).

But how does this process that makes us become love and one single body with Christ, which makes us become one with God, take place? How does this abolition of difference happen? There exists here first of all a clear boundary between the religions founded on the faith of Abraham on one hand, and on the other hand, the other forms of religion, such as we find them particularly in Asia, and also those based, probably, on Asiatic traditions—in the Plotinian style of Neoplatonism. There, union signifies deliverance as far as finitude (self-awareness) is concerned, which in the final analysis is seen to be a façade, the abolition of myself in the ocean of the completely other, which, as compared to our world of façades, is nothingness but nonetheless is the only true being. In the Christian faith, which fulfills the faith of Abraham, union is seen in a completely different way: it is the union of love, in which differences are not destroyed but are transformed in a higher union of those who love each other, just as it is found, as in an archetype, in the trinitarian union of God. Whereas, for example in Plotinus, finitude is a falling away from unity, and so to speak of the kernel of sin and therefore at the same time of the kernel of all evil, the Christian faith sees finitude not as a negation but as a creation, the fruit of a divine will that creates a free partner, a creature who does not have to be destroyed but must be completed, must insert itself into the free act of love. Difference is not abolished, but becomes the means to a higher unity. This philosophy of liberty, which is at the basis of the Christian faith and differentiates it from the Asiatic religions, includes the possibility of the negative. Evil is not a mere falling away from being, but the consequence of a freedom used badly. The way of unity, the way of love, is then a way of conversion, a way of purification: it takes the shape of the cross, it passes through the paschal mystery, through death and resurrection. It needs the Mediator, who, in

sacrifice holy
make holy
transform

his death and Resurrection becomes for us the way, draws us all to himself, and thus fulfills us (Jn 12:32).

Let us cast a glance back over what we have said. In his definition, sacrifice equals love; Augustine rightly stresses the saying, which is present in different variations in the Old and New Testaments, which he cites from Hosea: "It is love that I want, not sacrifices" (6:6; St. Augustine, *City of God*, X:5). But this saying does not merely place an opposition between ethos and worship—then Christianity would be reduced to a moralism. It refers to a process that is more than a moral philosophy—a process in which God takes the initiative. He alone can arouse man to start out toward love. It is the love with which God loves that alone makes our love for him increase. This fact of being loved is a process of purification and transformation, in which we are not only open to God but united to each other. The initiative of God has a name: Jesus Christ, the God who himself became man and gives himself to us. That is why Augustine could synthesize all that by saying, "Such is the sacrifice of Christians: the multitude is one single body in Christ. The church celebrates this mystery by the sacrifice of the Altar, well known to believers, because in it, it is shown to her that in the things which she offers, it is she herself who is offered" (X:6). Anyone who has understood this will no longer be of the opinion that to speak of the sacrifice of the Mass is at least highly ambiguous, or even an appalling horror. On the contrary: if we do not remember this, we lose sight of the grandeur of that which God gives us in the Eucharist.

THE NEW TEMPLE

I would now like to mention, again very briefly, two other approaches. An important indication is given, in my opinion, in the scene of the purification of the temple, in particular in the form handed down by John. John, in fact, relates a phrase of Jesus's that doesn't appear in the Synoptics except in the trial of Jesus, on the lips of false witnesses and in a distorted way. The reaction of Jesus to the merchants and money changers in the temple was practically an attack on the immolation of animals, which were offered there, hence an attack on the existing form of worship and the existing form of sacrifice in general. That is why the competent Jewish authorities asked him, with good reason, by what sign he justified an action that could only be taken as an attack against the law of Moses and the sacred prescriptions of the Covenant. Thereupon Jesus replies: "Destroy [dissolve] this sanctuary; in three days I will build it up again" (Jn 2:19). This subtle formula evokes a vision that John himself says the disciples did not understand until after the Resurrection, in remembering what had happened, and which led them to "believe the scripture and the word of Jesus" (Jn 2:22). For they now understand that the temple had been abolished at the moment of the Crucifixion of Jesus: Jesus, according to John, was crucified exactly at the moment when the paschal lambs were immolated in the sanctuary. At the moment when the Son makes himself the Lamb, that is, gives himself freely to the Father and hence to us, an end is made of the old prescriptions of a worship that could only be a sign of the true realities. The temple is "destroyed." From now on his resurrected body—he himself—becomes the true temple of humanity, in which adoration in spirit and in truth takes place (Jn 4:23). But spirit and truth are not abstract philosophical concepts—he is himself the truth, and the spirit is the Holy Spirit who proceeds from him. Here, too, it thus becomes apparent that worship is not replaced by a moral philosophy, but that the ancient worship comes to an end, with its substitutes and its often tragic misunderstandings, because the reality itself is manifested, the new temple: the resurrected Christ who draws us, transforms us, and unites us to himself. Again it is clear that the Eucharist of the church—to use Augustine's term—is the *sacramentum* of the true *sacrificium*: the sacred sign in which that which is signified is produced.

THE SPIRITUAL SACRIFICE

Finally, I would like to point out very briefly a third way in which the passage from the worship of substitution—the immolation of animals—to the true sacrifice, the communion with the offering of Christ, becomes progressively clearer. Among the prophets before the exile, there was an extraordinarily harsh criticism of temple worship, which Stephen, to the horror of the doctors and priests of the temple, resumes in his great discourse, with some citations, notably this verse of Amos: "Did you offer victims and sacrifices to me, during forty years in the desert, house of Israel? But you have carried the tent of Moloch and the star of the god Rephan, the images which you had made to worship" (Am 5:25–26; Acts 7:42). This critique that the prophets had made provided the spiritual foundation that enabled Israel to get through the difficult time following the destruction of the temple, when there was no worship. Israel was obliged at that time to bring to light more deeply and in a new way what constitutes the essence of worship, expiation, sacrifice. In the time of the Hellenistic dictatorship, when Israel was again without temple and without sacrifice, the book of Daniel gives us this prayer: "Lord, see how we are the smallest of all the nations.... There is no longer, at this time, leader nor prophet ... nor holocaust, sacrifice, oblation, nor incense, no place to offer you the first fruits and find grace close to you. But may a broken soul and a humbled spirit be accepted by you, like holocausts of rams and bulls, like thousands of fattened lambs; thus may our sacrifice be before you today, and may it please you that we may follow you wholeheartedly, because there is no confounding for those who hope in you. And now we put our whole heart into following you, to fearing you and seeking your face" (Dn 3:37–41).

Thus gradually there matured the realization that prayer, the Word, the man at prayer and becoming himself word, is the true sacrifice. The struggle of Israel could here enter into fruitful contact with the search of the Hellenistic world, which itself was looking for a way to leave behind the worship of substitution, of the immolation of animals, in order to arrive at worship properly so called, at true adoration, at true sacrifice. This path led to the idea of *logike tysia*—of the sacrifice [consisting] in the Word—which we meet in the New Testament in Romans 12:1, where the apostle exhorts the believers "to offer themselves as a living sacrifice, holy and pleasing to God": it is what is described as *logike latreia,* as a divine service according to the Word, engaging the reason. We find the same thing, in another form, in Hebrews 13:15: "Through him—Christ—let us offer ceaselessly a sacrifice of praise, that is to say the fruit of the lips which confess his name." Numerous examples coming from the fathers of the church show how these ideas were extended and became the point of junction between Christology, eucharistic faith, and the putting into existential practice of the paschal mystery. I would like to cite, by way of example, just a few lines of Peter Chrysologos; really, one should read the whole sermon in question in its entirety in order to be able to follow this synthesis from one end to the other:

> It is a strange sacrifice, where the body offers itself without the body, the blood without the blood! I beg you—says the Apostle—by the mercy of God, to offer yourselves as a living victim.
>
> Brothers, this sacrifice is inspired by the example of Christ, who immolated His Body, so that men may live.... Become, man, become the sacrifice of God and his priest.... God looks for faith, not for death. He thirsts for your promise, not your blood. Fervor appeases Him, not murder.

Here, too, it is a question of something quite different from a mere moralism, because man is so caught up in it with the whole of his being: sacrifice [consisting] in words—this, the Greek thinkers had already put in relation to the Logos, to the Word itself, indicating that the sacrifice of prayer should not be mere speech but the transmutation of our being into the Logos, the union of ourselves with it. Divine worship implies that we ourselves become beings of the Word, that we conform ourselves to the creative Intellect. But once more, it is clear that we cannot do this of ourselves, and thus everything seems to end again in futility—until the day when the Word comes, the true, the Son, when he becomes flesh and draws us to himself in the exodus of the cross. This true sacrifice, which transforms us all into sacrifice, that is to say, unites us to God, makes of us beings conformed to God, is indeed fixed and founded on an historical event, but is not situated as a thing in the past behind us—on the contrary, it becomes contemporary and accessible to us in the community of the believing and praying church, in its sacrament: that is what is meant by the "sacrifice of the Mass."

The error of Luther lay, I am convinced, in a false idea of historicity, in a poor understanding of unicity. The sacrifice of Christ is not situated behind us as something past. It touches all times and is present to us. The Eucharist is not merely the distribution of what comes from the past, but rather the presence of the paschal mystery of Christ, who transcends and unites all times. If the Roman Canon cites Abel, Abraham, Melchizedek, including them among those who celebrate the Eucharist, it is in the conviction that in them also, the great offerers, Christ was passing though time, or perhaps better, that in their search they were advancing toward a meeting with Christ. The theology of the fathers such as we find it in the Canon did not deny the futility and insufficiency of the pre-Christian sacrifices; the Canon includes, however, with the figures of Abel and Melchizedek, the "holy pagans" themselves in the mystery of Christ. What is happening is that everything that went before is seen in its insufficiency as a shadow, but also that Christ is drawing all things to himself, that there is, even in the pagan world, a preparation for the gospel, that even imperfect elements can lead to Christ, however much they may stand in need of purification.

CHRIST, THE SUBJECT OF THE LITURGY

Which brings me to the conclusion. Theology of the liturgy means that God acts through Christ in the liturgy and that we cannot act but through him and with him. Of ourselves, we cannot construct the way to God. This way does not open up unless God himself becomes the way. And again, the ways of man that do not lead to God are non-ways. Theology of the liturgy means furthermore that in the liturgy, the Logos himself speaks to us; and not only does he speak, he comes with his body, and his soul, his flesh and his blood, his divinity, and his humanity, in order to unite us to himself, to make of us one single "body." In the Christian liturgy, the whole history of salvation—even more, the whole history of human searching for God—is present, assumed, and brought to its goal. The Christian liturgy is a cosmic liturgy—it embraces the whole of Creation, which "awaits with impatience the revelation of the sons of God" (Rom 8:19).

Trent did not make a mistake; it leant for support on the solid foundation of the tradition of the church. It remains a trustworthy standard. But we can and should understand it in a more profound way in drawing from the riches of biblical witness and from the faith of the church of all the ages. There are true signs of hope that this renewed and deepened understanding of Trent can, in particular through the intermediary of the Eastern churches, be made accessible to Protestant Christians.

One thing should be clear: the liturgy must not be a terrain for experimenting with theological hypotheses. Too rapidly, in these last decades, the ideas of experts have entered into liturgical practice, often also bypassing ecclesiastical authority, through the channel of commissions that have been able to diffuse at an international level their "consensus of the moment," and practically turn it into laws for liturgical activity. The liturgy derives its greatness from what it is, not from what we make of it. Our participation is, of course, necessary, but as a means of inserting ourselves humbly into the spirit of the liturgy and of serving him who is the true subject of the liturgy: Jesus Christ. The liturgy is not an expression of the consciousness of a community, which, in any case, is diffuse and changing. It is revelation received in faith and prayer, and its measure is consequently the faith of the church in which revelation is received. The forms that are given to the liturgy can vary according to place and time, just as the rites are diverse. What is essential is the link to the church, which, for her part, is united by faith in the Lord. The obedience of faith guarantees the unity of the liturgy, beyond the frontiers of place and time, and so lets us experience the unity of the church, the church as the homeland of the heart.

The essence of the liturgy is finally summarized in the prayer that St. Paul (1 Cor 16:22) and the Didache (10:6) have handed down to us: *Maran atha*— "our Lord is there—Lord, come!" From now on, the parousia is accomplished in the liturgy, but that is so precisely because it teaches us to cry: "Come, Lord Jesus," while reaching out toward the Lord who is coming. It always brings us to hear his reply yet again and to experience its truth: "Yes, I am coming soon" (Rv 22:17, 20).

On the Theological Basis of Prayer and Liturgy

FROM *THE FEAST OF FAITH*

THE END OF RELIGION?

A Contemporary Dispute

A few years ago those interested in the debate about Christianity could have followed a characteristically confusing dispute that appeared in the *Süddeutsche Zeitung*.[1] The Dominican Father Anselm Hertz published an article entitled "Have We Come to the End of All Religion?" in which he presented a totally irresponsible picture of the course of history, albeit one that has gained wide currency. In former times, so he maintained, religion had been the public and private bond linking society and the individual to God or the gods; it was manifest in pious conduct and in cultic behavior. No doubt as a rhetorical ploy, he illustrates his argument (with references to Augustine) by citing the prayer made by both sides in war for victory or preservation. (Thus the reader is encouraged to associate the issue of prayer with that of war.) His supposedly logical conclusion with regard to the phenomenon of war is evidently meant to be of general application: "The metaphysical, transcendental reference of all causes has been dismantled; and if the cause can no longer be interpreted metaphysically, a metaphysical view of the effects becomes superfluous too."[2] This general proposition is then reapplied to the concrete case, yielding the characteristic aside: "Prayer for victory or preservation in battle has become meaningless, even if now and then armies and weapons continue to be blessed."[3]

According to Fr. Hertz's scheme of history, private piety was able to keep going for a long time after the demise of public religion. God was no longer responsible "for the events of war as a whole but only for the fate of his faithful ones." It is thus an easy matter to describe this phase of religious history as schizophrenia and go on to make the reader aware that the time for private piety, too, has run out.[4] At this point he goes beyond the topic of war, which up to now provided the argument: a God who "was primarily seen as a God of the weather, of protection and blessing" has disappeared, and this means that a God of transcendence, standing over against immanence, belongs "to the magical and mythical substrata of human religiosity," which has been "nowadays largely overcome."[5] Now the new form of religion heaves in sight, the third phase of this view of history, in which modern man is ensconced, finally, above all the errors and false starts of the past: now the criterion of religion is no longer "in what forms man's attachment to God is expressed, but whether man is ready and able to transcend himself."[6] No doubt all men may aspire to this readiness, this capacity, especially as what it implies is left totally vague.

However, while the good Dominican was endeavoring to console the reader for the loss of a personal God (albeit by too obvious a sleight-of-hand in the matter of prayer in time of war), the political theorist Lobkowicz was pulling the veil from his somewhat confused arguments. Not mincing matters, he simply asked what this "self-transcendence" meant: "What good is it for Hertz to urge us to transcend ourselves? Apropos, it is noticeably those who think they are too superior to talk simply and concretely of God who are in the habit of talking about 'transcendence'.... Suppose I had achieved this transcendence and come face to face with the 'ultimate ground of being' which 'is manifest everywhere in the world, wherever man is searching for the abiding meaning of his existence.' What then? Do I respectfully salute this 'ground of being' and simply return to the hardness of my daily life?—or does this encounter become a fundamental experience causing me to see everything differently and revolutionizing my behavior?"[7] With refreshing clarity Lobkowicz has expressed the fact that "every theology which no longer facilitates petitionary prayer, and hence thanksgiving, is a fraud."[8] This drama, in which theology keeps talking although the God who can speak and listen has long ago submerged together with the myths, is fascinating in the way it seems to spread, presenting itself quietly, piously, without the least trumpeting of heresy, as the most natural thing in the world. It is impossible to read without deep sadness the "prayer," expressive of this approach, with which G. Hasenhüttl concludes his "Introduction to the Doctrine of God"—a prayer that no longer addresses anyone, desperately trying to convince itself that man still has access to meaning and love and that the experience of this is "God" for man. Let us read a little of it to see what "transcendence" means in this kind of theology—a somber dialogue with the void, trying to keep up its courage and calling itself "prayer":

It was easy to pray when in simplicity of heart I could still kneel down and know that there was a God in heaven to see me. I could lay my anxieties and joys before him and know that he heard me, even if I could not always experience that he did.

Today I am part of a social order in which the relation of lord to servant has finally been abolished, and this means that I can no longer feel that God is Lord and I am his unworthy servant. It would be meaningless now to fall down in worship with eyes full of tears of joy or sorrow. It is hard now to address God as "Thou," for the only "Thou" I know is the human "Thou" in all its ambivalence. I am a partner to my fellow men in society, but God is not my partner....

So I know, here and now, stripped of all illusions, that I am affirmed, that there is meaning in the absurdity of life, a meaning that brings happiness. I am affirmed every time I give love, when I collaborate in the making of the society of the future, for all its provisional character. So, even today, I can cry out like the psalmist thousands of years ago and say: Yes, he is; I am affirmed; God is! And if you want to dispense with the word *God*, well and good, but keep its place open, for the reality it signifies will come to you, will force you to decide, and in love it will be revealed to you and you will find yourself crying out: "Yes, do you see? God is when men love one another!"

It often happens nowadays that we can no longer call upon God because he is not the powerful Lord; similarly we cannot live in hope of a paradisal future, since it is only a creation of man's imagination. But we can thank and pray, knowing, in all our brokenness, that today itself gives us hope for the future; we live today believing in new possibilities; today we can love, we will love, for it is only today that we can experience God, it is only today that he is near to us.[9]

Where Does the Bible Stand?

We do not know what human experiences, sufferings, and crises lie behind words such as these; we must respect them: it is not our business to judge. On the other hand, we are obliged to state firmly that this is not Christian theology. For the prime characteristic of Christian faith is that it is faith in God—furthermore, that this God is someone who speaks, someone to whom man can speak. The Christian God is characterized by revelation, that is, by the words and deeds in which he addresses man, and the goal of revelation is man's response in word and deed, which thus expands revelation into a dialogue between Creator and creature that guides man toward union with

God.[10] So prayer is not something on the periphery of the Christian concept of God; it is a fundamental trait. The whole Bible is dialogue: on the one side, revelation, God's words and deeds, and on the other side, man's response in accepting the Word of God and allowing himself to be led by God. To delete prayer and dialogue, genuine two-way dialogue, is to delete the whole Bible.

We must insist, however, that the Bible in no way needs to be "rescued" from a mythical worldview that supposedly encapsulates it; it does not need to be "helped" on the way toward its fuller development. The reverse is the case: Greek philosophy had come to the conclusion that it was impossible to pray to God, since the Eternal One, by being eternal, cannot enter into time relations. This led to such an utter separation of philosophy and religion, of reason and piety, that it heralded the end of ancient religion. Later indeed it did try to rescue the old religions by acknowledging in them a demythologized meaning, in the way many theologians today try to demythologize dogma and sacrament. We can see in this endeavor the last traces of nostalgia for the lost world of the religions—the attempt to save what has been lost, even if its original meaning can no longer be entertained. This romantic reaction may have been able to slow down the decline of the gods, but it could not stop it. It simply lacked truth.

In this process, which involved all the questions raised in the current debate, the Christian faith took up a unique position. With regard to the concept of God, it held to the enlightened view of the philosophers: the gods are illusory; they do not exist. What Christians call "God" is what the philosophers call "being," "ground," or (also) "God." They are not afraid to say that it is this God of the philosophers who is their God, too. What is unique about their position is that they attribute to the God of the philosophers the fundamental trait of the gods of the old religions, namely, the relationship with men, albeit now in an absolute form insofar as they call God the Creator. This paradoxical conjunction constitutes the Christian synthesis, its outstanding novelty; it is the source of the basic difficulty and vulnerability of the Christian position in the history of religions: only "the Absolute" can be God, but this very Absolute has the attribute of being "relative," relationship, Creator, and Revealer, or as later tradition would put it, "Person," someone who addresses the creature and to whom the creature can turn. This synthesis also distinguishes the Christian faith from the "mythical" religions like those of Asia and connects it with Judaism and Islam, although Christianity exhibits a unique and distinct form in its belief in the Trinity. Ultimately all questions come back to the enormous tension created by *this* synthesis; the modern situation has not really introduced anything radically new. In the end, of course, whether this synthesis can be affirmed depends not on philosophical considerations but on whether one has been given the degree of spiritual tension that corresponds to the tension of the Christian idea of God.[11]

Arguments Against Prayer

Consequently, in our efforts to work out the theological and anthropological basis of prayer, it is not a question of proving the validity of Christian prayer by the standards of some neutral reasonableness. It is a case of uncovering the inner logic of faith itself, with its own distinct reasonableness. Our first step, however, must be to ask briefly what are the substantial reasons that seem to militate against prayer's reasonableness. I observe three kinds, occurring naturally in countless variations and combinations.

Firstly there is the general rejection of a metaphysical approach, corresponding to the main thrust of contemporary thought. Karl Jaspers has clothed this rejection in a religious form in his philosophy; his explicit aim is to continue religion without metaphysics, or rather to see the farewell to metaphysics as a better way of legitimizing faith and spirituality. From what we have said so far it should be clear that the results of this approach are, in fact, very different from what is envisaged by the Bible and the faith of the church. For Christian faith it is essential that it address the God who really exists, the Creator of all things and the ground of all being, and that this God has spoken to us. To reject metaphysics is to reject creation and hence the Christian concept of God itself. Conversely, now as always, it is the belief in Creation that is the strongest rational foundation for the Christian idea of God and its metaphysical implications, as is very clear from J. Monod's consistent line of thought.[12]

Even if metaphysical questions are not rejected in principle, there is a second objection to a God of revelation. This was already formulated in the philosophy of the ancients, but it has acquired far greater force in the modern scientific and technological world. It can be put like this: a rationally constructed world is determined by rationally perceived causality. To such a scheme the notion of personal intervention is both mythical and repugnant. But if this approach is adopted, it must be followed consistently, for what applies to God applies equally to man. If there is only one kind of causality, man, too, as a person is excluded and reduced to an element in mechanical causality, in the realm of necessity; freedom, too, in this case, is a mythical idea. In this sense it can be said that the personalities of God and of man cannot be separated. If personality is not a possibility, that is, not present, with the "ground" of reality, it is not possible at all. Either freedom is a possibility inherent in the ground of reality or it does not exist. Thus the issue of prayer is intimately linked with those of freedom and personality: the question of prayer decides whether the world is to be conceived as pure "chance and necessity" or whether freedom and love are constitutive elements of it.

Finally, there is a real theological objection to a God who operates *ad extra* in creation and revelation. Aristotle was the first to put it in its most pointed form; it has always been behind the scenes in Christian theology, and to this day it has probably not been fully dealt with. According to this objection, eternity by its very nature cannot enter into relationship with time, and similarly time cannot affect eternity. Eternity implies immutability, the concentrated fullness of being, removed from the vicissitudes of time. Time is essentially changeable and changing. If it were to initiate anything new in eternity, eternity would have become time. And if eternity were to get involved with the changing stream of time, it would forfeit its nature as eternity. Here we cannot go into the question of whether the concept of eternity employed in these undoubtedly logical trains of thought is adequate. So far, the debate on that particular issue has not come up with any convincing results; it needs to be continued. It will be essential to probe more deeply into the concept of "relation" if progress is to be made at this point; furthermore, instead of the negative "timelessness" of eternity, we need to work out a concept of the creativity that eternity exercises with regard to time.[13]

There is a further aspect, which brings us directly to the Christian answer. I would like to put forward this thesis: a non-Trinitarian monotheism can hardly meet Aristotle's objection. In the end it will simply have to leave eternity and time as isolated opposites. But if they cannot communicate with one another, that is, if there cannot be a reciprocal influence between time and eternity, then eternity (if there is an eternity) can be of no significance to men. For it has no power in the world, no influence on human life. It is this feeling that caused the monotheism underlying ancient religion to die out in favor of the idea of the *Deus otiosus*. There is such a God, people thought, but he is separated from man by an unbridgeable chasm. Since he has no power with regard to man, he cannot matter to him, either. This feeling is fundamental to the separation of philosophy and religion that we have observed in ancient times. Thus in a rational world, where faith is reduced to rational monotheism, the notion of God simply fades away: it becomes irrelevant. The Enlightenment dissolved the Christian mystery and left it with an ephemeral monotheism. Deism is not a new creation of the Enlightenment: it is merely the return of the *Deus otiosus* of the mythical religions. It either invokes the old gods or heralds the total rejection of the notion of God, or at least the rejection of a praying religion and the transition to a religiously tinged "self-transcendence." This, it seems to me, is the deepest cause of the crisis in theology that we have observed in men like Hertz and Hasenhüttl. Initially what happens is that people become uncertain about the Christological and Trinitarian mystery; its relationship to exegesis is felt to be problematical; it is regarded as a Hellenistic scheme projected into the universe of linear time, a necessary element of its age but now no longer intelligible. But the retreat to a rationally presentable monotheism is always merely the first step. Next comes the abandonment of the relational categories of creation and revelation. Thus this God himself fades into the concept of "transcendence." The possibility of prayer being "heard" dwindles, and faith becomes "self-transcendence."

Life with a Religious Flavor but Without a God Who Hears

Before turning to the positive side we must investigate a little more closely what kind of religion is still possible under the presupposition of a God who cannot "relate." In accord with those who follow Jaspers, we have termed such a possibility the religion of "self-transcendence." History, however, allows us to be more precise. In fact we can speak of two major basic possibilities.

Aristotle ascribes significance to the prayer that fails to reach God in that it "fosters what is best in us."[14] At bottom this is identical with what modern theologians mean by "self-transcendence." Karl Barth would see it as that "religion" which is the very opposite of faith. It is strange indeed: whereas two decades ago, in the enthusiasm for Bonhoeffer, people pleaded for a religionless faith, now everything is reversed: everything now tends toward the preservation of religion and a religious flavor to life, even though its original content, faith, is represented as untenable. This pseudoreligiosity cannot be expected to last, however, all the more since its content is too unstable, following every wind of change because it is not oriented to truth, being merely a matter of "relation," addressing a something that does not reciprocate that relation. It is trying to be a *relatio pura*, which no longer contains anything that can be objectified.[15] But in reality this "pure relation" is spurious: relation without reciprocity has no meaning.

By contrast, the path of the Asiatic religions seems logically consistent and religiously profound: they start from the ultimate identity of the "I," which is in reality not an "I," with the divine ground of the world. Here prayer is the discovery of this identity, in which, behind the surface illusion, I find my own, serene identity with the ground of all being and thus am liberated from the false identity of the individualized "I." Prayer is letting myself be absorbed into what I really am; it is the gradual disappearance of what, to the separate "I," seems to be the real world. It is liberation in that one bids farewell to the empirical, experienced world with its chaos of illusion and enters the pure nothingness, which is truly divine.

There can be no doubt that this is a path of impressive proportions; moreover, it appeals strongly to man's painful experience, which causes him to wish to abandon what seems to be the illusory surface of being. Only a radical abandonment of being, in favor of nothingness, seems to offer hope of real freedom. It is no accident, therefore, that the way of Asia presents itself as the way of salvation wherever the content of faith is relegated to the level of an untenable piece of Western metaphysics or mythology yet where there is still a deep spiritual and religious will. I believe that as far as religion is concerned, the present age will have to decide ultimately between the Asiatic religious worldview and the Christian faith. I have no doubt that both sides have a great deal to learn from each other. The issue may be which of the two can rescue more of the other's authentic content. But in spite of this possibility of mutual exchange, no one will dispute the fact that the two ways are different. In a nutshell one could say that the goal of Asiatic contemplation is the escape from personality, whereas biblical prayer is essentially a relation between persons and hence ultimately the affirmation of the person.

THE STRUCTURE AND CONTENT OF CHRISTIAN PRAYER

In this second part, our task is to develop the positive basis of Christian prayer. As we have already said, it is not enough to approach it with external proofs; we must attempt, at least in outline, to reveal its intrinsic logic.[16]

The Formal Structure of Christian Prayer

The basic reason that man can speak with God is because God himself is speech, word. His nature is to speak, to hear, to reply, as we see particularly in Johannine theology, where Son and Spirit are described in terms of pure "hearing"; they speak in response to what they have first heard. Only because there is already speech, "Logos," in God can there be speech, "Logos," to God. Philosophically we could put it like this: the Logos in God is the ontological foundation for prayer. The prologue of John's Gospel speaks of this connection in its very first sentences: "In the beginning was the Word, and the Word was in communication with God" (1:1)—as a more precise translation of the Greek *prós* suggests, rather than the usual "with God." It expresses the act of turning to God, of relationship. Since there is relationship within God himself, there can also be a participation in this relationship. Thus we can relate to God in a way that does not contradict his nature.

In God, we have said, there is speech and the intercourse of partners in dialogue. Man could speak with God if he himself were drawn to share in this internal speech. And this is what the Incarnation of the Logos means: he who is speech, Word, Logos, in God and to God, participates in human speech. This has a reciprocal effect, involving man in God's own internal speech. Or we could say that man is able to participate in the dialogue within God himself because God has first shared in human speech and has thus brought the two into communication with one another. The Incarnation of the Logos brings eternity into time and time into eternity. It is not that God is time, but he *has* time.[17] As a result of the Incarnation, human speech has become a component in divine speech; it has been taken up, unconfusedly and inseparably, into that speech that is God's inner nature.

Through the Spirit of Christ, who is the Spirit of God, we can share in the human nature of Jesus Christ; and in sharing in his dialogue with God, we can share in the dialogue that God is. This is prayer, which becomes a real exchange between God and man.

The locus of this identification with Christ, facilitated by the Spirit, which necessarily implies that those involved are also identified with one another in Christ, is what we call "church." We could, in fact, define *church* as the realm of man's discovery of his identity through the identification with Christ, which is its source.

The Content of Christian Prayer

A fundamental word in the mouth of "the Son" is *Abba*. It is no accident that we find this word characterizing the figure of Jesus in the New Testament. It expresses his whole being, and all that he says to God in prayer is ultimately only an explication of his being (and hence an explication of this one word); the Our Father is this same *Abba* transposed into the plural for the benefit of those who are his.

Let us try to ascertain the content, the inner intentionality, of this basic act of prayer (which is the Son's act of being, as Son, and thus is rooted in the ultimate ontological depths of reality). First we can say that it is an act of consent. Its basic tenor is affirmatory. Essentially it means this: I can affirm the world, being, myself, because I can affirm the ground of my being, for this ground is good. It is good to *be*. Josef Pieper has interpreted the nature of the "feast," the festival (in general terms) as affirmation of the world:[18] whenever I am able to say yes, I can celebrate a feast; whenever I am able to say yes, I am (to that extent) free, liberated. Christian prayer holds the key to making the whole world a celebration, a feast, namely, affirmation. Asiatic contemplation is not affirmation but liberation through the renunciation of being. The Marxist approach is not affirmation but outrage, opposition to being because it is bad and so must be changed. Prayer is an act of being; it is affirmation, albeit not affirmation of myself as I am and of the world as it is, but affirmation of the ground of being and hence a purifying of myself and of the world from this ground upward. All purification (every *via negationis*) is only possible on the rocklike basis of affirmation, of consent: Jesus Christ is Yes (cf. 2 Cor 1:19–20). Conversely, in the purification that issues from this fundamental yes, we discover the active power of prayer, which yields a deep security in the affirmation of being, as a foil to the hectic world of self-made man, yet is by no means a flight from the world but rather entrusts people with the task of purifying the world and empowers them to carry it out.

The next step is this: we can only say *Abba* together with Christ; only in fellowship with him can we recognize the world's ground in a way that invites our Yes. Apart from the Son, the Father remains ambivalent and strange; it is Jesus who turns the scales of the Old Testament and makes its message clear. "Patrocentrism," that is, the *Abba*, presupposes the Christological character of prayer.[19] It is the Son who guides us along the path of purification, which leads to the door of the Yes. So Christian prayer depends on our continually looking to Christ, talking with him, being silent with him, listening to him, doing and suffering with him.

Let us go a step further. We cannot reach Christ through historical reconstruction. It may be helpful, but it is not sufficient and, on its own, becomes mere necrophilia. We encounter him as a living person only in the foretaste of his presence, which is called "church." At this point we begin to see how it may be possible to purify and accept the inheritance of Asia. The latter is correct in refusing to see individual identity as an encapsulated "I" over against a similarly encapsulated "Thou" of God, ignoring the existence of other "I's," which are themselves related individually and separately to this divine Thou. Here we see the limitation of the kind of personalism that was developed between the wars by Ebner, Buber, Rosenzweig, E. Brunner, Steinbüchel, and others. Here God is portrayed in a way that conflicts with his nature as the ground of all being. Partnership between God and man is conceived in I-Thou terms in a way which deprives God of his infinity and excludes each individual "I" from the unity of being. By comparison with God, man's identity is not simply in himself but outside himself, which is why he can only attain it by "transcendence." The Christian believer discovers his true identity in him who, as "the firstborn of all creation," holds all things together (Col 1:15ff.), with the result that we can say that our life is hidden with him in God (Col 3:3).[20] Through identification with Christ I discover my own entirely personal identity.

The church as a whole presents the model of this kind of "identity." The church is so identified with Christ that she can be called his "body." But this bodily unity is to be understood against the biblical concept of man and wife: they are to become two in one flesh (Gn 2:24; Eph 5:3 cf.; cf. 1 Cor 6:16–17). It is a unity through the unifying power of love, which does not destroy the two-ness of I and Thou but welds it into a profound oneness. In finding my own identity by being identified with Christ, I am made one with him; my true self is restored to me, I know that I am accepted, and this enables me to give myself back to him. On this basis the theology of the Middle Ages proposed that the aim of prayer (and the movement of being in which it consists) was that, through it, man should become an *anima ecclesiastica*—a personal em-bodiment of the church. This is both identity and purification; it is a surren-dering of oneself and a being drawn into the innermost nature of what we mean by "church." In this process the language of our Mother becomes ours; we learn to speak it along with her, so that, gradually, her words on our lips become our words. We are given an anticipatory share in the church's peren-nial dialogue of love with him who desired to be one flesh with her, and this gift is transformed into the gift of speech. And it is in the gift of speech, and not until then, that I am really restored to my true self; only thus am I given back to God, handed over by him to all my fellow men; only thus am I free.

At this point everything becomes very practical: How can I learn to pray? By praying in fellowship. Prayer is always a praying *with* someone. No one can pray to God as an isolated individual and in his own strength. Isolation and the loss of a basic sense of fellowship in prayer constitute a major reason for the lack of prayer. I learn to pray by praying with others, with my mother for instance, by following her words, which are gradually filled out with meaning for me as I speak, live, and suffer in fellowship with her. Naturally I must be always asking what these words mean. Naturally, too, I must continually "cash" these words into the small change of daily life. And having done so, I must try to repossess them in exchange for my small coin, little by little, as I draw nearer the fullness of the mystery and become more capable of speaking of it. And that is precisely why it is impossible to start a conversation with Christ alone, cutting out the church: a Christological form of prayer that excludes the church also excludes the Spirit and the human being himself. I need to feel my way into these words in everything I do, in prayer, life, suffering, in my thoughts. And this very process transforms me. But I must not try to dispense with the example of the words, for they are alive, a growing organism, words that are lived and prayed by countless people.

Of course, this applies to all the various modes of prayer: repetition, si-lence, speech, singing, and so on. All the dimensions of the human psyche are involved; we must never make rational understanding the only criterion. How could reason grow and develop if it regarded its own premature limitations as normative![21]

Answers to Prayer

Christian prayer is addressed to a God who hears and answers. But in what way? What can the witness of the New Testament and the tradition of faith tell us?

First, let us examine what is meant by answers to prayer.[22] Luke transmits one of the Lord's words, which puts it very precisely: "If you then, who are evil, know how to give good gifts to your children, how much more will the heavenly Father give the Holy Spirit to those who ask him?" (Lk 11:13). What we are to ask of God is the gift of the *pneuma,* his Spirit. God gives himself. We are to ask no less than this. We find the same thing put in different terms in Jesus's farewell discourses in John. Here the gift of God, promised unconditionally to those who ask, is joy, that "full" joy which is the expression and the presence of a love that has become "full" (Jn 16:24). The reality is the same in each case. Prayer, because of the transformation of being that it involves, means growing more and more into identity with the *pneuma* of Jesus, the Spirit of God (becoming an *anima ecclesiastica*); borne along by the very breath of his love, we have a joy that cannot be taken from us.

But how are we to conceive of God answering prayer? Put in the briefest possible form, we can say something like this: in Jesus, God participates in time. Through this participation he operates in time in the form of love. His love purifies men; through purification (and not otherwise) men are identified and united with him. Or we could say this: as a result of God's participation in time in Jesus, love becomes the causality operating in the world to transform it; in any place, at any time, it can exercise its influence. As a cause, love does not vitiate the world's mechanical causality but uses and adopts it. Love is the power that God exercises in the world. To pray is to put oneself on the side of this love-causality, this causality of freedom, in opposition to the power of necessity. As Christians, as those who pray, this is our very highest task.

The Regensburg Tradition and the Reform of the Liturgy

This essay was originally a sermon on the occasion of the retirement of his brother, Monsignor Georg Ratzinger, as choirmaster of Regensburg cathedral.

In the autumn of 1992, after an unforgettable helicopter flight over the mountains of South Tyrol, I visited the monastery of Mount St. Mary (Marienberg) in the valley of the Etsch.

The monastery was founded in that magnificent natural setting to the praise and glory of God, thus responding in its own way to the invitation expressed in the Canticle of the Three Young Men: "Ye mountains and heights, praise the Lord!" (Dn 3:75).

The real treasure of this monastery is the crypt (dedicated July 13, 1160) with its glorious frescoes, which in recent years have been almost completely cleared, restored, and laid open to view.[1] As is true of all medieval art, these images had no merely aesthetic meaning. They conceive of themselves as worship, as a part of the great liturgy of Creation and of the redeemed world in which this monastery was intended to join. Therefore, the pictorial program reflects that common basic understanding of the liturgy that was then still alive and well in the church universal, Eastern and Western. On the one hand these images show a strong Byzantine influence while remaining at bottom quite biblical; on the other hand they are essentially determined by the monastic tradition—concretely, the Rule of Saint Benedict.

And so the real focus of attention is the *majestas Domini*, the risen and glorified Lord in all his majesty—seen also and indeed chiefly as the one who is to come, who cometh even now in the Eucharist. In celebrating the divine liturgy, the church goes forth to meet him—in truth, liturgy *is* the act of this going forth to meet him who cometh. He always anticipates in the liturgy his promised coming: liturgy is anticipated *parousia,* or second coming; it is the entry of the "already" into our "not yet," as John presented it in the story of the wedding at Cana. The hour of the Lord has not yet come, and everything that must happen has not yet been fulfilled. But at the request of Mary and of the church, he nonetheless gives now the new wine, and pours out now in advance, the gift of his "hour."

The Risen Lord is not alone in these Mount St. Mary's frescoes. We see him in the images that the Apocalypse uses to depict the heavenly liturgy—surrounded by the four winged creatures and above all by a great throng of singing angels. Their singing is an expression of that joy which no one can take from them, of the dissolution of existence into the rejoicing of freedom fulfilled. From the very beginning, monastic living was understood as a life lived after the manner of the angels, which is simply adoration. Entering or assuming the lifestyle of the angels means forming one's whole life into an act of adoration, as far as that is possible for human weakness.[2] Celebrating the liturgy is the very heart of monachism [monastic life], but in that respect monachism simply makes visible to all the deepest reason for Christian—indeed, for human—existence!

As they gazed upon these frescoes, the monks of Mount St. Mary surely thought of the nineteenth chapter of the Rule of Saint Benedict, which treats the discipline of psalm singing and the manner of saying the divine office. There, the father of Western monasticism reminds them, among other things, of the verse of Psalm 147 (Vulgate): "*In conspectu angelorum psallam tibi*" (In the sight of the angels I will sing to Thee). And Benedict goes on: "Let us then consider how we ought to behave ourselves in the presence of God and His angels, and so sing the psalms that mind and voice may be in harmony, *ut mens nostra concordet voci nostrœ.*"

It is, therefore, not at all the case that man contrives something and then sings it, but rather the song comes to him from the angelic choirs, and he must raise his heart on high so that it can harmonize with the tone that comes to him.

But one fact is of fundamental importance: the sacred liturgy is not something the monks manufacture or produce. It existed before they were there; it is an entering into heavenly liturgy that was already taking place. Only in and through this fact is earthly liturgy a liturgy at all: in that it be—takes itself into—that greater and grander liturgy that is already being celebrated.

And thus the meaning of these frescoes becomes completely clear. Through them, the genuine reality, the heavenly liturgy, shines through into this space. The frescoes are, as it were, a window through which the monks peer out into that great choir, of which membership is the very heart and center of their own vocation. "In the sight of the angels I will sing to Thee." This standard is constantly present to the gaze of the monks, in their frescoes.

A SIDELIGHT ON THE POSTCONCILIAR DISPUTE OVER THE LITURGY

Let us descend from Mount St. Mary and the wondrous panorama that those heights opened to us, and come down to the level of liturgical reality in today's world. Here, the panorama is much more confused and disordered. A contemporary observer has described the present situation as one of "already and not yet," by which he does not mean the eschatological anticipation of Christ who is to come in a world still marked by death and its difficulties. This author is simply saying that the "new" that is "already" there is the reform of the liturgy, but the "old" (namely the "Tridentine" order) is in fact "not yet" overcome.[3] And so the age-old question, "Whither shall I turn?" no longer refers, as it once did, to our search for the countenance of the living God. That question becomes instead a description of the perplexity and embarrassment that typifies the situation of church music, said to have resulted from the half-hearted realization of the liturgical reform.

To put the matter in terms of today's trendy expression: a profoundly radical "paradigm shift" has quite obviously taken place. A great abyss divides the history of the church into two irreconcilable worlds: the preconciliar and postconciliar worlds. As a matter of fact, many believe that it is impossible to utter a more fearful verdict over an ecclesiastical decision, a text, a liturgical form, or even a person, than to say that it is "preconciliar." If that be true, then Catholic Christendom must have been in a truly frightful condition—until 1965.

Now, let us apply that to our practical instance: a cathedral choirmaster who held his post from 1964 until 1994 at the cathedral church in Regensburg was really, if matters are really so, in a rather hopeless situation. When he began his duties, the liturgy constitution of Vatican II had not yet been promulgated. When he took office, he very definitely followed the proud standard of the Regensburg tradition, or more precisely the standard of the *motu proprio, Tra le sollecitudini* on church music, issued by Saint Pius X on November 22, 1903.[4]

Nowhere was this *motu proprio* received with such rejoicing, and so unreservedly accepted as the norm and standard to be followed, as in the cathedral at Regensburg, which, of course, with this attitude set an example that was followed by many a cathedral and parish church in Germany, as well as in other lands. In this reform of church music, Pius X had put to good use his own liturgical knowledge and experience. At the major seminary he had already conducted a Gregorian chant *schola,* and as bishop of Manuta and later patriarch of Venice he fought to eliminate the operatic church-music style that was then dominant in Italy. Insistence upon Gregorian chant as the genuine music of the liturgy was for him but a part of that greater program of reform which was aimed at restoring to liturgical worship its pristine dignity, shaping and forming Catholic cult on the basis of its inner requirements.[5] During the course of these efforts, he had come to know the Regensburg tradition, which, one might say, was something of a godparent to the *motu proprio,* without implying that the "Regensburg tradition" as such was thereby "canonized" in its entirety. In Germany (but not only there!) Pius X is today often remembered chiefly as the "antimodernist" pope, but Giampaolo Romanato has clearly shown, in his critical biography, the great extent to which this pontiff was a reforming pope precisely because he was a pastor of souls.[6]

He who reflects upon all of this and spends a little time examining it more closely will soon notice that the chasm separating "preconciliar" and "postconciliar" has already grown smaller. And the historian will add another insight. The liturgy constitution of the last council indeed laid the foundations for a reform that was then shaped by a postconciliar committee and in its concrete details cannot without further ado be attributed to the council itself. That sacred synod was an open beginning whose broad parameters permitted a number of concrete realizations. When one duly reflects upon these facts, then one will be disinclined to describe that broad arc of tensions which manifested itself in these decades, in terms like "preconciliar tradition" and "conciliar reform." It would be better to speak of the confrontation or contrast between the reform of St. Pius X and that introduced by the council in other words, to speak about stages of reform instead of a deep trench between two opposing worlds. And if we broaden our perspective even more, we can say that the history of the liturgy always involves a certain degree of tension between continuity and renewal.

The history of the liturgy is constantly growing into an ever-new now, and it must also repeatedly prune back a present that has become the past, so that what is essential can reappear with new vigor. The liturgy needs growth and development as well as purgation and refining and in both cases needs to preserve its identity and that purpose without which it would lose the very reason for its existence. And if that is really the case, then the alternative between "traditionalists" and "reformers" is woefully inadequate to the situation. He who believes that he can only choose between old and new has already traveled a good way along a dead-end street.

The real question is rather: What is the essential nature of the liturgy? What standard does the liturgy set for itself? Only when this question has been answered can one ask: What must remain? What is permanent? What can and perhaps must change?

Our reflection upon the frescoes at Mount St. Mary's in South Tyrol have by anticipation given a preliminary answer to the question about the essence of the liturgy. It is time to examine the question in greater depth.

As we begin to do so, we at once encounter another of those alternatives which derive from that dualistic view of history which divides the world into pre- and postconciliar ages. In this view, the priest alone "did" the liturgy before the council, while now, after the synod, the assembled community "does" liturgy, indeed "causes" it. Hence, some conclude, the celebrating community is the true subject of the liturgy and determines what occurs in the liturgy.[7]

Now, it is, of course, true that the priest celebrant never had the right to determine by himself what was to be done, or how, in the Sacred Liturgy. For him, the liturgy was not at all a matter of acting according to his own liking. The liturgy existed before the priest, as rite, as the objective form of the church's common prayer.

The polemic alternative "Priest or Congregation Source and Support of the Liturgy?" is unreasonable because it prevents instead of promoting a correct understanding of worship, and because it creates that false chasm between "preconciliar" and "postconciliar," which rends asunder the overall continuity of the living history of faith. Such a false alternative is rooted in superficial thinking that does not penetrate to the heart of the matter. On the other hand, when we open the *Catechism of the Catholic Church* we find a masterfully luminous summary of the best insights of the liturgical movement and thus of the permanently valid elements of the great tradition. First of all, we are reminded that liturgy means "service of and for the people."[8]

When Christian theology adapted from the Greek Old Testament this word formed in the pagan world, it naturally was thinking of the "People of God," which the Christians had become through the fact that Christ had broken down the barrier between Jews and heathens in order to unite them all in the peace of the one God. "Service for the people"—Christians thought of the basic truth that this people did not exist of itself, for instance as a community by ancestral descent through bloodlines, but rather came into existence through the paschal service of Jesus Christ—was based, in other words, solely upon the ministry or service of someone else: the Son. "People of God" do not simply exist the way Germans, Frenchmen, Italians, Americans, or other peoples "exist." They always come into being only through the ministry or service of the Son and by virtue of the fact that he raises us up to fellowship with God on a level we cannot attain by our own efforts. Accordingly, the *Catechism* continues:

In Christian tradition [the word *liturgy*] means the participation of the people of God in "the work of God" (*opus Dei*). Through the liturgy, Christ our Redeemer and High Priest continues the work of our redemption in, with, and through His Church.

The Catechism quotes the Liturgy Constitution of Vatican II which stresses that every liturgical celebration, because it is an action of Christ the Priest, and of His body, which is the church, is a sacred action surpassing all others [*actio præcellenter sacra*].[9]

And now, matters already look very different. The sociological reduction, which can only oppose human actors to each other, has been burst open. As we have seen, the sacred liturgy presupposes that heaven has been flung open, and only when that is the case can there be any liturgy at all. If heaven has not been opened, then what formerly was liturgy will atrophy into a mere playing of roles, an ultimately insignificant search for community self-confirmation in which at bottom nothing really transpires. In other words, the primacy of Christology is decisive. The liturgy is God's work—*opus Dei*—or it is nothing. The primacy of God and his activity, which seeks us in earthly signs, also includes the universality and the universal publicity of all liturgy, which cannot be comprehended in the categories of community or congregation, but only on the basis of categories like "People of God" and "body of Christ."

It is only in this great structural framework that the mutual relationship of priest and congregation can be correctly understood. In the Divine Liturgy the priest does and says what by himself he cannot say or do—he acts, as the traditional expression has it, *in persona Christi*, which is to say he acts on the strength of the sacrament that guarantees the presence of the Other of Christ himself. The priest does not represent himself, neither is he the delegate of the congregation that has invested him with a special role. No, his position in the sacrament of succession or following of Christ manifests precisely that primacy of Jesus which is the basic and indispensable condition of all liturgy. Because the priest depicts and indeed embodies the truth that "Christ comes first!" his ministry points every assembly above and beyond itself into the larger totality, for Christ is one and undivided, and insofar as he opens the heavens he is also the One who breaks down all earthly boundaries.

The new *Catechism* presents its theology of the liturgy according to a Trinitarian scheme. It is, I think, very important that the community or the assembly appears in the chapter on the Holy Spirit, in these words:

In the liturgy of the New Covenant every liturgical action, especially the celebration of the Eucharist and the sacraments, is an encounter between Christ and the Church. The liturgical assembly derived its unity from the "community of the Holy Spirit," who gather the children of God into the one Body of Christ. This assembly transcends racial, cultural, social, indeed, all human affinities.... [T]he assembly should prepare itself to encounter its Lord and to become "a people well disposed."[10]

Here we must recall that the word *congregation* (which originates in the tradition of the so-called Reformation) cannot be translated in most languages. In the Romance tongues, for instance, the equivalent expression is *assemblée*, or gathering, which already imparts a slightly different nuance or accent.

Both expressions (*congregation, assembly*) indisputably manifest two important facts: first, that the participants in a liturgical celebration are not mere individuals totally unrelated to each other, but are joined together through the liturgical event to constitute a concrete representation of God's people; and secondly, that these participants as the people of God gathered here are genuine actors in the liturgical celebration, by the Lord's will.

But we must firmly oppose the "hypostasizing" of the congregation that is so widely bandied about today. As the *Catechism* quite rightly says, those assembled become a unity only on the strength of the communion of the Holy Spirit: of themselves, as a sociologically closed group, they are not a unity. And when they are united in a fellowship that comes from the Spirit, then that is always an openhanded unity whose transcending of national, cultural, and social boundaries expresses itself in concrete openness for those who do not belong to its core group.

To a large extent, contemporary talk about "community" presupposes a homogeneous group that is able to plan common activities and jointly carry them out. And then, of course, this community may perhaps be asked to "tolerate" none but a priest with whom it is mutually acquainted. All of that, of course, has nothing to do with theology. For instance, when at a solemn service in a cathedral church a group of men gather who from a sociological point of view do not form a unified congregation and who find it very difficult to join in congregational singing, for example, do they constitute a "community" or not? Indeed they do, because in common they turn toward the Lord, and he approaches them interiorly in a way that draws them together much more intimately than any mere social togetherness could ever do.

We can summarize these thoughts by saying that neither the priest alone nor the congregation alone "does" the liturgy. Rather, the divine liturgy is celebrated by the whole Christ, head and members: the priest, the congregation, the individuals insofar as they are united with Christ and to the extent that they represent the total Christ in the communion of head and body. The whole church, heaven and earth, God and man, takes part in every liturgical celebration, and that not just in theory but in actual fact. The meaning of liturgy is realized all the more concretely the more each celebration is nourished by this awareness and this experience.

These reflections appear to have taken us far away from the subject of Regensburg tradition and postconciliar reform, but that only *seems* to be the case. It was necessary to describe the great overall context, which constitutes the standard by which any reform is measured. And only in terms of that standard can we appropriately describe the inner location and the correct type of church music.

Now we can briefly depict the essential tendency of the reform chosen by the council. In opposition to modern individualism and the moralism connected with it, the dimension of the *mysterium* was to appear once more, that is, the cosmic character of the liturgy, which encompasses heaven and earth. In its sharing in the paschal mystery of Christ, the liturgy transcends the boundaries of places and times in order to gather all into the hour of Christ, which is anticipated in the liturgy and thus opens up history to its final goal.[11]

The conciliar Constitution on the Liturgy adds two other important aspects.

First, in Christian faith the concept of the *mysterium* is inseparable from the concept of the Logos. In contrast to many heathen mystery cults, the Christian mysteries are Logos-mysteries. They reach beyond the limits of human reason, but they do not lead into the formlessness of frenzy or the dissolution of rationality in a cosmos understood as irrational. Rather, the Christian mysteries lead to the Logos—the Word—that is, to creative reason, in which the meaning of all things is finally grounded. And that is the source and origin of the ultimate sobriety, the thorough-going rationality, and the verbal character of the liturgy.

With this there is connected a second fact: the Word became flesh in history. Hence, for the Christian to be oriented toward the Logos always means being oriented toward the historical origins of the faith, toward the word of scripture and its authoritative development and explanation in the church of the fathers. As a result of contemplating the *mysterium* of a cosmic liturgy (which is a Logos-liturgy), it becomes necessary to describe in a visible and concrete way the community aspect of worship, the fact that it is an action to be performed, its formulation in words.

This is the key to understanding all the individual directives about the revision of the liturgical books and rites. When one keeps this in mind, it becomes clear that in spite of the outward differences, both the Regensburg tradition and the *motu proprio* of Saint Pius X intend the same goal and point in the same direction. The de-emphasizing of orchestral accompaniment, which above all in Italy had developed opera-like qualities, was meant to put church music once again at the service of the liturgical text, and of adoration. Church music was to be no longer a performance on the occasion of a liturgical service but rather the liturgy itself, that is, joining in with the choir of angels and saints.

Thus it was to be made clear that liturgical music was to lead the faithful into the glorification of God, into the sober intoxication of the faith. The emphasis upon Gregorian chant and classical polyphony was therefore ordered at once to the "mystery" aspect of the liturgy and its Logos-like character and to its link with the Word in history. That emphasis was, one might say, intended to stress anew the authoritative nature of the patristic standard for liturgical music, which some had occasionally conceived in a manner too exclusively historical. Such an authoritative standard, correctly understood, does not mean exclusion of anything new, but rather means pointing out the direction that leads into open spaces. Here, progress into new territory is made possible precisely because the right path has been found.

Only when one appreciates the essential elements of intention and tendency, which are common to the reforms of both Saint Pius X and Vatican II, can one correctly evaluate the differences in their practical suggestions. And from that position we can turn the proposition around and assert that any view of the liturgy that loses sight of its character as "mystery," and its cosmic dimension, must result in the deformation of worship instead of its reform.

THE REASON FOR MUSIC AND ITS ROLE IN WORSHIP

By itself, the question of the liturgy's essence and the standards of the reform has brought us back to the question of music and its position in the liturgy. And as a matter of fact one cannot speak about worship at all without also speaking of the music of worship. Where the liturgy deteriorates, *musica sacra* degenerates, too. And where worship is correctly understood and lived out in practice, there, too, will good church music grow and thrive. We noted earlier that the concept of "congregation" (or "assembly") appears in the new *Catechism* for the first time at the point when the Holy Spirit is described as the one who shapes or forms the liturgy, and we had said that it is a precise description of the congregation's inner location. Similarly, it is no accident that in the *Catechism* we find the verb *to sing* for the first time in the section that deals with the cosmic character of the liturgy, in a quotation from the conciliar constitution on the liturgy:

In the earthly liturgy we take part in a foretaste of that heavenly liturgy which is celebrated in the holy city of Jerusalem toward which we journey as pilgrims.... With all the warriors of the heavenly army we sing a hymn of glory to the Lord.[12]

A recent author has found a very good way to express that state of affairs by modifying the famous aphorism of Ludwig Wittgenstein, who wrote, "One must remain silent about that which one cannot utter." This now becomes: That which one cannot utter can and must be expressed in song and music when silence is not permissible.[13] And the author adds that "Jews and Christians agree in viewing their singing and music-making as referring heavenward or coming from heaven, as eavesdropped from on high."[14]

In these few sentences we find set forth the fundamental principles of liturgical music. Faith comes from hearing God's Word. And whenever God's Word is translated into human words, there remains something unspoken and unutterable, which calls us to silence, into a stillness that ultimately allows the Unutterable to become song and even calls upon the voices of the cosmos to assist in making audible what had remained unspoken. And that implies that church music, originating in the Word and in the silence heard in that Word, presupposes a constantly renewed listening to the rich plenitude of the *Logos*.

While some maintain that in principle any kind of music can be used in a worship service,[15] others point to the deeper and essential relationships between certain vital activities and forms of musical expression that are fitting and appropriate to them: "I am convinced that there is also a type of music particularly appropriate (or, as the case may be, inappropriate) ... for man's encounter with the mystery of faith."[16] And as a matter of fact, music meant to serve the Christian liturgy must be appropriate and fitting for the Logos, which means, concretely: such music must be meaningfully related to the Word in which the Logos has found utterance.

Even in its purely instrumental form, such music cannot disengage itself from the inner direction or orientation of this Word, which opens up an infinite space but also draws certain boundaries and establishes criteria of distinction. In its essence, such music must be different from a music that is meant to lead the listener into rhythmic ecstasy or stupefied torpor, sensual arousal, or the dissolution of the ego in nirvana, to mention but a few of the attitudes that are possible. St. Cyprian has a fine observation in this connection, in his commentary on the Lord's Prayer:

But let our speech and petition when we pray be under discipline, observing quietness and modesty. Let us consider that we are standing in

God's sight [*sub conspectu Dei*]. We must please the divine eyes both
with the habit of body and with the measure of voice. For as it is characteristic of a shameless man to be noisy with his cries, so on the other
hand, is it fitting to the modest man to pray with moderated petitions....
And when we meet together with the brethren in one place, and celebrate divine sacrifices with God's priest, we ought to be mindful ... not
to throw abroad our prayers indiscriminately, with unsubdued voices,
nor to cast to God with tumultuous wordiness a petition that ought to
be commended to God by modesty ... for God ... need not be clamor-
ously reminded. ...[17]

It goes without saying that this interior standard of a music appropriate to
the Logos must be related to life in this world: it must introduce men into
the fellowship of Christ as fellow suppliants at prayer here and now, in this
era and in a specific location. It must be accessible to them while at the same
time leading them onward in the direction that the divine liturgy itself formulates with unsurpassable brevity at the beginning of the Canon: *sursum
corda*—lift up your hearts! Lift up the heart, meaning the inner man, the
totality of the self, to the heights of God himself, to the sublimity that is
God and that in Christ touches the earth, drawing it with and upward
toward itself.

Before I attempt to apply these principles to a few specific problems of
church music in the cathedral of Regensburg, something must be said about
the subjects of liturgical music and the language of the chants.

Wherever an exaggerated concept of "community" predominates, a concept
that is (as we have already seen) completely unrealistic precisely in a highly
mobile society such as ours, there only the priest and the congregation can be
acknowledged as legitimate executors or performers of liturgical song.

Today, practically everyone can see through the primitive activism and the
insipid pedagogic rationalism of such a position, which is why it is now asserted so seldom. The fact that the *schola* and the choir can also contribute to
the whole picture is scarcely denied anymore, even among those who errone-
ously interpret the council's phrase about "active participation" as meaning
external activism.

However, a few exclusions remain, and about them we shall speak presently. They are rooted in an insufficient interpretation of liturgical cooperative action in community, in which the congregation that actually happens to
be present can never be the sole subject but may only be understood as an assembly open toward and from above, synchronically and diachronically, into
the breadth of divine history.

A recent author has stressed an important aspect of the question by speaking of highly developed forms that are not lacking in the liturgy as a feast of God, but which cannot be filled by the congregation as a whole. He reminds us that "the choir, in other words, is not related to a listening congregation as it is to a concert audience which allows something to be performed for it. Rather the choir is itself part of the congregation and sings *for* it as legitimate delegate."[18] The concept of delegation is one of the basic categories of all Christian faith and applies to all levels of faith-filled reality, and precisely for this reason it is essential in the liturgical assembly.[19]

The insight here regarding delegation in fact resolves the apparent conflict of opposites. The choir acts on behalf of the others and includes them in the purpose of its own action. Through the singing of the choir, everyone can be conducted into the great liturgy of the communion of saints and thus into that interior prayer which pulls our hearts on high and permits us to join with the heavenly Jerusalem in a manner far beyond all earthly expectations.

But can one really sing in Latin when the people do not understand it? Since the council, there has arisen in many places a fanaticism for the vernacular that is, in fact, very difficult to comprehend in a multicultural society, just as in a mobile society it is not very logical to hypostasize the congregation. And for the moment let us pass over the fact that a text translated into the vernacular is not thereby automatically comprehensible to everyone; this touches upon an entirely different question of no little importance.

A point that is essential for Christian liturgy in general was recently expressed in splendid fashion:

> This celebration is not interrupted whenever a song is sung or an instrumental piece is played ..., but it shows by that very fact its nature as "feast" or "celebration." But this requirement does not demand unity of liturgical language nor of style in the various musical parts. The traditional, so-called "Latin Mass" always had parts in Aramaic (*Amen, Alleluia, Maranatha*), Greek (*Kyrie eleison, Trisagion*) and the vernacular (the sermon, as a rule). Real life knows little of stylistic unity and perfection. On the contrary, a thing which is really alive will always exhibit formal and stylistic diversity ...; the unity is organic.[20]

It was on the basis of insights such as these that in the three decades of theological and liturgical turmoil during which the retiring choirmaster [Cardinal Ratzinger's brother, Monsignor Georg Ratzinger—Ed.] did his duty, supported by the confidence both of Bishop Graber and of his successor, Bishop Manfred Müller, and the auxiliary bishops Flügel, Guggenberger, and Schraml. He steered a course of continuity in development and development in continuity, often in spite of the difficulty caused by powerful contrary currents.

Thanks to the profound agreement between the choirmaster and the responsible prelates and their collaborators, he was in a position unswervingly, but at the same time in an open way, to make an essential contribution to the preservation of the dignity and grandeur of liturgical worship in the cathedral of Regensburg, which maintained its transparency toward the cosmic liturgy of the Logos within the unity of the worldwide church, without becoming a museum piece or petrifying into a nostalgic byway.

CONTINUITY AND DEVELOPMENT IN LITURGY

And now, in conclusion, I should like to discuss briefly two characteristic examples of this struggle to maintain continuity while still developing, even in the face of published opinion. I refer to the question of the *Sanctus* and *Benedictus,* and the question of the meaningful position of the *Agnus Dei.*

It was my friend and former colleague in Münster, Monsignor Emil Joseph Lengeling, who said that when one understood the *Sanctus* as an authentic part intended for the congregation celebrating the service, "then there result not only compelling conclusions for new compositions, but the exclusion of most Gregorian and all polyphonic settings of the *Sanctus,* because they exclude the congregation from singing and ignore the acclamatory character of the *Sanctus*."[21]

With all due respect to the renowned liturgist, that quotation shows that even great experts can err egregiously. First of all, mistrust is always in order when the greater part of living history must be tossed into the dustbin of old misunderstandings now happily clarified. That is all the more true of the Christian liturgy, which lives out of the continuity and the inner unity of prayer based on faith.

As a matter of fact, the alleged acclamatory character of the *Sanctus,* to which only the congregation could do justice, is totally unfounded. In the entire liturgical tradition of East and West, the preface always concludes with a reference to the heavenly liturgy and invites the assembled congregation to join in the hymn of heavenly choirs. And it was precisely the conclusion of the preface that had such a decisive influence upon the iconography of the *majestas Domini,* which we mentioned at the beginning of our reflections.[22]

Compared with the biblical matrix of Isaiah 6, the liturgical text of the *Sanctus* shows three new accents.[23] [Isaiah 6:3: "And one cried unto another (the seraphim), Holy, holy, holy, is the LORD of Hosts: the whole earth is full of his glory." Cf. Rv 4:8.—Ed.]

First, the scene of the action is no longer the temple at Jerusalem, as in the case of the prophet, but rather heaven, which in the *mysterium* opens itself toward the earth. Hence it is no longer merely the seraphs who cry out, but all the legions of the heavenly hosts, in whose cry to us from Christ (who unites heaven and earth) the entire church, all of redeemed mankind, can join in chorus.

And that, finally, is the reason why the *Sanctus* was transposed from the "he" to the "thou" form: heaven and earth are filled with *thy* glory. The *Hosanna,* originally a cry for help, thus becomes a song of praise.

He who ignores the mystery character and the cosmic nature of this summons to join in the praise of the heavenly choirs has already failed to grasp the meaning of the whole.

THE CHOIR AND ACTIVE CONTEMPLATION

This joining in can take place in different ways, but it always has something to do with deputyship. The congregation gathered in one particular locality opens itself out to the whole. It also represents those absent; it is united with those far away and those very near. And when in this congregation a choir exists, which can draw the congregation into the cosmic praise and the wide open space of heaven and earth more strongly than the congregation's own stammering is able to do, then precisely in that moment the delegated, representative function of the choir is especially appropriate and fitting.

Through the choir, a greater transparency toward the praise of angels is rendered possible, and therefore a more profound interior participation in the singing than would be possible in many places through one's own crying and singing.

I suspect, however, that the real reproach cannot consist in the "acclamatory character" and in the demand for unison singing. That would seem too banal, I think. In the background there surely lurks the fear that a choral *Sanctus* is regarded as a kind of concert piece, even more so when it is made obligatory to follow with the *Benedictus* precisely at the moment of entering into the Canon of the Mass—which produces a break or a pause in the prayer at the point where it is least desirable, and thus insupportable.

As a matter of fact, if one presupposes that there is no such thing as delegation or representation and that it is not possible to sing and pray interiorly while remaining outwardly silent, then this reproach is quite justified. If all those not singing during the *Sanctus* simply await its conclusion, or merely listen to a religious concert piece, then the choir's performance is hard to justify, if not intolerable.

But does that have to be the case? Have we not forgotten something here that we urgently need to relearn? Perhaps it is helpful here to recall that the silent recitation of the Canon [Eucharistic Prayer] by the priest did not begin during the singing of the *Sanctus* in order to save time because it lasted so long. The real succession of events was the exact opposite. Certainly since the Carolingian epoch, but very probably also earlier, the celebrant entered the sanctuary of the Canon "silently." The Canon is the time of pure silence as "worthy preparation for God's approach."[24] And then for a time an "office of accompanying petitionary prayers, akin to the Eastern *ektene* ... [was laid] like an outer veil to cover the silent praying of the canon by the celebrant."[25] And later on, it was the singing of the choir that (as Jungmann put it) "continues to maintain the old dominant note of the Canon, thanksgiving and praise, and unfolds it musically to the ear of the participant over the entire canon."[26]

Even though we may not wish to restore that state of affairs, it can none-theless give us a useful hint: Would we not do well, before moving on into the center of the *mysterium*, to be gifted with a period of well-filled silence in which the choir recollects us interiorly and leads each individual into silent prayer and, precisely in that way, into a union that can take place only on the interior level? Must we not relearn precisely this silent interior praying to-gether and with the angels and saints, the living and the dead, with Christ himself, so that the words of the Canon do not become mere tired formulas, which we then try in vain to replace by constantly new and different word-montages in which we attempt to conceal the absence of any real inner experi-ence of the liturgy, any movement beyond human talk into actual contact with the Eternal?

The exclusion alleged by Lengeling and repeated by many others after him is meaningless. Even after Vatican II, the *Sanctus* sung by the choir is perfectly justified. But what about the *Benedictus*? The assertion that it may not, under any circumstance, be separated from the *Sanctus* has been put forth with such emphasis and seeming competence that only a few strong souls were able to oppose it. But the assertion cannot be justified, either historically or theologi-cally or liturgically. Of course, it makes good sense to sing both movements together when the composition makes this relationship clear, for it is a very ancient one and very well founded. But here again, what must be rejected is the exclusionary alternative.

SANCTUS AND BENEDICTUS ORIGINS

Both the *Sanctus* and the *Benedictus* have their own separate points of depar-ture in Holy Writ, which is why they developed separately at first. Although we already find the *Sanctus* in the First Letter of Clement (34:5 ff.),[27] that is, in the age of the apostles, we first find the *Benedictus* (as far as I can see) in the apostolic constitutions—in other words, in the second half of the fourth century—as a cry or acclamation before the distribution of Holy Communion, in response to the call "Holy things to the holy ones!"

Since the sixth century, we find the *Benedictus* again in Gaul. There it had been joined to the *Sanctus*, as also happened in the oriental tradition.[28] While the *Sanctus* developed out of Isaiah 6 and then was transferred from the earthly to the heavenly Jerusalem and thus became a song of the church, the *Benedictus* is based upon a New Testament rereading of a verse from Psalm 117 (118).[29]

In the Old Testament this verse ["Blessed is He that cometh in the name of the Lord" —Ed.] is a blessing upon the arrival of the festive procession in the temple; on Palm Sunday [Matthew 21:9] it received a new meaning—which admittedly was already prepared for in the development of Jewish prayer. After all, the expression "He comes" had become a name for the Messiah. When on Palm Sunday the young people of Jerusalem shouted out this verse at Jesus, they were greeting him as the Messiah, the King of the end times who entered into the holy city and the temple in order to take possession of them.

The *Sanctus* is directed to the eternal glory of God; the *Benedictus*, on the other hand, refers to the coming of the God made flesh in our midst. Christ, the one who has come, is always the one who is coming, too! His eucharistic coming, the anticipation of his "hour," makes promise become present and brings the future into our today.

Consequently, the *Benedictus* is meaningful both as moving toward the consecration and as an acclamation to the Lord become present in the eucharistic species. The great moment of his coming, the prodigy of his Real Presence in the elements of earth, expressly calls for due response: the elevation, the genuflection, the ringing of bells are all stammering attempts to respond.[30]

Following a parallel in the Byzantine rite, the liturgy reform has constructed a congregational acclamation: "Christ has died. ..." But now the question has been raised of other possible cries of greeting to the Lord who is coming and has come. And for me it is plain that there is no more profoundly appropriate and no more truly traditional "acclamation" than this one: "Blessed is He that cometh in the name of the Lord."

The separation of the *Sanctus* from the *Benedictus* is, of course, not necessary, but it is extremely meaningful. When the *Sanctus* and *Benedictus* are sung by the choir without a break, then the caesura between Preface and Canon can, in fact, become too long, so that it no longer serves to promote that silently participatory entry into the praise of the whole cosmos because the interior tension cannot be maintained. But when, on the other hand, during a well-filled silence, one once again joins in an interior greeting to the Lord after the Consecration has taken place, then that corresponds most profoundly to the inner structure of the event. The pedantically censorious proscription of such a division (which developed organically for good reasons) should be consigned as soon as possible to the scrap heap of mere memories.

WHY THE *AGNUS DEI?*

And finally, a word about the *Agnus Dei.* At the cathedral of Regensburg it has become customary that after the kiss of peace, the priest and people together recite the threefold *Agnus Dei.* And then it is continued by the choir during the distribution of Holy Communion. It was, of course, objected that the *Agnus Dei* belongs to the rite of the breaking of the bread, the *fractio panis.* From this original function as accompaniment for the time it took for the breaking of the bread, only a completely petrified archaism can conclude that the *Agnus Dei* may only and exclusively be sung at this point. In actual fact, when the old rites of *fractio panis* became superfluous because of the new small hosts coming into use during the ninth and tenth centuries, the *Agnus Dei* indeed became a communion song.

No less an expert than the late J. A. Jungmann points out that already in the early Middle Ages, oftentimes only one *Agnus Dei* was sung after the kiss of peace, while the second and third invocations found their place after Communion, thus accompanying the distribution of Holy Communion (when it took place).[31] And does it not make very good sense to beseech Christ, the Lamb of God, for mercy at the precise moment in which he gives himself anew as defenseless Lamb into our hands—he who is the Lamb, sacrificed but also triumphant, the Lamb who bears the key of history (Rv 5)? And is it not particularly appropriate, at the moment of receiving Holy Communion, to direct our request for peace to him, the defenseless one who, as such, was victorious? After all, in the ancient church, "peace" was actually one of the names used to designate the Eucharist, because it flings open the boundaries between heaven and earth, between nations and states, and unites all men in the unity of Christ's body.

At first glance, the Regensburg tradition and the reform, conciliar and postconciliar, may seem like two contrary worlds that clash like diametrical opposites. The man who stood between them for three decades has the scars to prove how difficult were the questions raised. But where this tension can be endured, it gradually becomes clear that all these are but states on one single path. It is only when they are held together and endured that they are correctly understood, and then there can unfold and develop a true reform in the spirit of the Second Vatican Council—a reform that is not synonymous with rupture or breach and destruction, but rather purification, cleansing, and growth to new maturity and abundance. Thanks are due the cathedral choirmaster who bore this tension: that was not only a service to Regensburg and its cathedral church, but a service to the whole church!

Music and Liturgy

How Does Music Express the Word of God, the Vision of God?

The importance of music in biblical religion is shown very simply by the fact that the verb *to sing* (with related words such as *song*) is one of the most commonly used words in the Bible. It occurs 309 times in the Old Testament and thirty-six in the New. When man comes into contact with God, mere speech is not enough. Areas of his existence are awakened that spontaneously turn into song. Indeed, man's own being is insufficient for what he has to express, and so he invites the whole of creation to become a song with him: "Awake, my soul! Awake, O harp and lyre! I will awake the dawn! I will give thanks to you, O Lord, among the peoples; I will give thanks to you, O Lord, among the peoples; I will sing praises to you among the nations. For your steadfast love is great to the heavens, your faithfulness to the clouds" (Ps 57:9ff.).

We find the first mention of singing in the Bible after the crossing of the Red Sea. Israel has now been definitively delivered from slavery. In a desperate situation, it has had an overwhelming experience of God's saving power. Just as Moses as a baby was taken from the Nile and only then really received the gift of life, so Israel now feels as if it has been "taken out of the water": it is free, newly endowed with the gift of itself from God's own hands.

Year by year at the Easter Vigil, Christians join in the singing of this song, because they know that they have been "taken out of the water" by God's power, set free by God for authentic life.

The Apocalypse of St. John draws the bow back even farther. The final enemies of the People of God have stepped onto the stage of history: the Satanic trinity, consisting of the Beast, its image, and the number of its name. But then the Seer is given the vision of the conquerors, "standing beside the sea of glass with harps of God in their hands. And they sing the song of Moses, the servant of God, and the song of the Lamb" (Rv 15:3).

Liturgical singing is established in the midst of this great historical tension. For Israel, the event of salvation in the Red Sea will always be the main reason for praising God, the basic theme of the songs it sings before God. For Christians, the Resurrection of Christ is the true exodus. He has stridden through the Red Sea of death itself, descended into the world of shadows, and smashed open the prison door. In baptism this exodus is made ever present. To be baptized is to be made a partaker, a contemporary, of Christ's descent into hell and of his rising up therefrom, in which he takes us up into the fellowship of new life.

The man who believes in the Resurrection of Christ really does know what definitive salvation is. He realizes that Christians, who find themselves in the "New Covenant," now sing an altogether new song, which is truly and definitively new in view of the wholly new thing that has taken place in the Resurrection of Christ.

The definitively new song has been intoned, but still all the sufferings of history must be endured, all pain gathered in and brought into the sacrifice of praise, in order to be transformed there into a song of praise.

Here, then, is the theological basis for liturgical singing. We need to look more closely at its practical reality. With regard to the singing of the church, we notice the same pattern of continuity and renewal that we have seen in the nature of the liturgy in general, in church architecture, and in sacred images.

The Holy Spirit is love, and it is he who produces the singing. He is the Spirit of Christ, the Spirit who draws us into love for Christ and so leads to the Father. In the musical sphere, biblical faith created its own form of culture, an expression appropriate to its inward essence, one that provides a standard for all later forms of enculturation.

The question of how far enculturation can go soon became a very practical one for early Christianity, especially in the area of music. The Christian community had grown out of the synagogue and, along with the Christologically interpreted Psalter, had taken over the synagogue's way of singing. Very soon new Christian hymns and canticles came into being: first, with a wholly Old Testament foundation, the *Benedictus* and *Magnificat,* but then Christologically focused-on texts, preeminently the prologue of St. John's Gospel (1:1–18), the hymn of Christ in the Epistle to the Philippians (2:6–11), and the song of Christ in the First Epistle to Timothy (3:16). But historically there have been various errors, and tension between faith and culture.

During the nineteenth century, the century of self-emancipating subjectivity, this led in many places to obscuring the sacred by the operatic. Pope Pius X tried to remove the operatic element from the liturgy and declared Gregorian chant and the great polyphony of the age of the Catholic Reformation to be the standard for liturgical music.

A clear distinction was made between liturgical music and religious music in general, just as visual art in the liturgy has to conform to different standards from those employed in religious art in general. Art in the liturgy has a very specific responsibility, and precisely as such does it serve as a wellspring of culture, which in the final analysis owes its existence to cult.

After the cultural revolution of recent decades, we are faced with a challenge no less great than that of the three moments of crisis that we have encountered in our historical sketch: the Gnostic temptation, the crisis at the end of the Middle Ages and the beginning of modernity, and the crisis at the beginning of the twentieth century, which formed the prelude to the still more radical questions of the present day.

Three developments in recent music epitomize the problems that the church has to face when she is considering liturgical music.

First of all, there is the cultural universalization that the church has to undertake if she wants to get beyond the boundaries of the European mind. This is the question of what enculturation should look like in the realm of sacred music if, on the one hand, the identity of Christianity is to be preserved and, on the other, its universality is to be expressed in local forms.

Then there are two developments in music itself that have their origins primarily in the West but that for a long time have affected the whole of mankind in the world culture that is being formed. Modern so-called classical music has maneuvered itself, with some exceptions, into an elitist ghetto, which only specialists may enter—and even they do so with what may sometimes be mixed feelings. The music of the masses has broken loose from this and treads a very different path.

On the one hand, there is pop music, which is certainly no longer supported by the people in the ancient sense (*populus*). It is aimed at the phenomenon of the masses, is industrially produced, and ultimately has to be described as a cult of the banal. "Rock," on the other hand, is the expression of elemental passions, and at rock festivals it assumes a cultic character, a form of worship, in fact, in opposition to Christian worship. People are, so to speak, released from themselves by the emotional shock of rhythm, noise, and special lighting effects. However, in the ecstasy of having all their defenses torn down, the participants sink, as it were, beneath the elemental force of the universe. The music of the Holy Spirit's sober inebriation seems to have little chance when self has become a prison, the mind is a shackle, and breaking out from both appears to be a true promise of redemption that can be tasted at least for a few moments.

What is to be done? Theoretical solutions are perhaps even less helpful here. There has to be renewal from within. Nevertheless, I am going to try to sum up the principles that have emerged from our look at the inner foundations of Christian sacred music.

The music of Christian worship is related to Logos in three senses:

1. It is related to the events of God's saving action to which the Bible bears witness and which the liturgy makes present. God's action continues in the history of the church, but it has its unshakable center in the paschal mystery of Jesus Christ, his cross, Resurrection, and Ascension. This takes up, interprets, and brings to fulfillment the history of salvation in the Old Testament, as well as the hopes and experiences of deliverance in the religious history of mankind. In liturgical music, based as it is on biblical faith, there is, therefore, a clear dominance of the Word; this music is a higher form of proclamation. Ultimately, it rises up out of the love that responds to God's love made flesh in Christ, which for us went unto death. After the Resurrection, the cross is by no means a thing of the past, and so this love is always marked by pain at the hiddenness of God, by the cry that rises up from the depths of anguish, *Kyrie eleison* (Lord, have mercy), by hope and by supplication. But it also has the privilege, by anticipation, of experiencing the reality of the Resurrection, and so it brings with it the joy of being loved, that gladness of heart that Haydn said came upon him when he set liturgical texts to music.

Thus the relation of liturgical music to Logos means, first of all, simply its relation to words. That is why singing in the liturgy has priority over instrumental music, though it does not in any way exclude it.

It goes without saying that the biblical and liturgical texts are the normative words from which liturgical music has to take its bearings. This does not rule out the continuing creation of "new songs," but instead inspires them and assures them of a firm grounding in God's love for mankind and his work of redemption.

2. St. Paul tells us that of ourselves we do not know how to pray as we ought but that the Spirit himself intercedes for us "with sighs too deep for words" (Rom 8:26). Prayer is a gift of the Holy Spirit, both prayer in general and that particular kind of prayer which is the gift of singing and playing before God. The Holy Spirit is love. He enkindles love in us and thus moves us to sing. Now the Spirit of Christ "takes what is [Christ's]" (cf. Jn 16:14), and so the gift that comes from him, the gift that surpasses all words, is always related to Christ, the Word, the great Meaning that creates and sustains all life.

Words are superseded, but not the Word, the Logos. This is the second, deeper sense in which liturgical music is related to Logos. The church's tradition has this in mind when it talks about the sober inebriation caused in us by the Holy Spirit. There is always an ultimate sobriety, a deeper rationality, resisting any decline into irrationality and immoderation.

We can see what this means in practice if we look at the history of music. The writings of Plato and Aristotle on music show that the Greek world in their time was faced with a choice between two kinds of worship, two different images of God and man. Now what this choice came down to concretely was a choice between two fundamental types of music.

On the one hand, there is the music that Plato ascribes, in line with mythology, to Apollo, the god of light and reason. This is the music that draws senses into spirit and so brings man to wholeness. It does not abolish the senses, but inserts them into the unity of this creature that is man. It elevates the spirit precisely by wedding it to the senses, and it elevates the senses by uniting them with the spirit. Thus this kind of music is an expression of man's special place in the general structure of being. But then there is the music that Plato ascribes to Marsyas, which we might describe, in terms of cultic history, as "Dionysian." It drags man into the intoxication of the senses, crushes rationality, and subjects the spirit to the senses. The way Plato (and more moderately, Aristotle) allots instruments and keys to one or other of these two kinds of music is now obsolete and may in many respects surprise us. But the Apollonian/Dionysian alternative runs through the whole history of religion and confronts us again today. Not every kind of music can have a place in Christian worship. It has its standards, and that standard is the Logos. If we want to know whom we are dealing with, the Holy Spirit or the unholy spirit, we have to remember that it is the Holy Spirit who moves us to say, "Jesus is Lord" (1 Cor 12:3). The Holy Spirit leads us to the Logos, and he leads us to a music that serves the Logos as a sign of the *sursum corda,* the lifting up of the human heart. Does it integrate man by drawing him to what is above, or does it cause his disintegration into formless intoxication or mere sensuality? That is the criterion for a music in harmony with Logos, a form of that *logike latreia* (reasonable, Logos-worthy worship) of which we spoke in the first part of this book.

3. The Word incarnate in Christ, the Logos, is not just the power that gives meaning to the individual, not even just the power that gives meaning to history. No, he is the creative Meaning from which the universe comes and which the universe, the cosmos, reflects. That is why this Word leads us out of individualism into the communion of saints spanning all times and places. This is the "broad place" (Ps 31:9), the redemptive breadth into which the Lord places us. But its span stretches still farther. As we have seen, Christian liturgy is always a cosmic liturgy. What does this mean for our question? The Preface, the first part of the Eucharistic Prayer, always ends with the affirmation that we are singing "Holy, Holy, Holy" together with the cherubim and seraphim and with all the choirs of heaven. The liturgy is echoing here the vision of

God in Isaiah chapter 6. In the Holy of Holies in the temple, the prophet sees the throne of God, protected by the seraphim, who call to one another: "Holy, holy, holy is the Lord of hosts; the whole earth is full of His glory" (Is 6:1–3). In the celebration of Holy Mass, we insert ourselves into this liturgy that always goes before us. All our singing is a singing and praying with the great liturgy that spans the whole of creation.

Among the fathers, it was especially St. Augustine who tried to connect this characteristic view of the Christian liturgy with the worldview of Greco-Roman antiquity. In his early work "On Music" he is still completely dependent on the Pythagorean theory of music. According to Pythagoras, the cosmos was constructed mathematically, a great edifice of numbers. Modern physics, beginning with Kepler, Galileo, and Newton, has gone back to this vision and, through the mathematical interpretation of the universe, has made possible the technological use of its powers. For the Pythagoreans, this mathematical order of the universe (*cosmos* means "order"!) was identical with the essence of beauty itself. Beauty comes from meaningful inner order. And for them this beauty was not only optical but also musical. Goethe alludes to this idea when he speaks of the singing contest of the fraternity of the spheres: the mathematical order of the planets and their revolutions contains a secret timbre, which is the primal form of music. The courses of the revolving planets are like melodies, the numerical order is the rhythm, and the concurrence of the individual courses is the harmony. The music made by man must, according to this view, be taken from the inner music and order of the universe, be inserted into the "fraternal song" of the "fraternity of the spheres." The beauty of music depends on its conformity to the rhythmic and harmonic laws of the universe. The more that human music adapts itself to the musical laws of the universe, the more beautiful will it be.

St. Augustine first took up this theory and then deepened it. In the course of history, transplanting it into the worldview of faith was bound to bring with it a twofold personalization. Even the Pythagoreans did not interpret the mathematics of the universe in an entirely abstract way. In the view of the ancients, intelligent actions presupposed an intelligence that caused them. The intelligent, mathematical movements of the heavenly bodies were not explained, therefore, in a purely mechanical way; they could only be understood on the assumption that the heavenly bodies were animated, were themselves "intelligent." For Christians, there was a spontaneous turn at this point from stellar deities to the choirs of angels that surround God and illuminate the universe. Perceiving the "music of the cosmos" thus becomes listening to the song of the angels, and the reference to Isaiah chapter 6 naturally suggests itself.

But a further step was taken with the help of Trinitarian faith, faith in the Father, the Logos, and the *pneuma*. The mathematics of the universe does not exist by itself, nor, as people now came to see, can it be explained by stellar deities. It has a deeper foundation: the mind of the Creator. It comes from the Logos, in whom, so to speak, the archetypes of the world's order are contained. The Logos, through the Spirit, fashions the material world according to these archetypes. In virtue of his work in creation, the Logos is, therefore, called the "art of God" (*ars = techne!*). The Logos himself is the great artist, in whom all works of art and the beauty of the universe have their origin.

To sing with the universe means, then, to follow the track of the Logos and to come close to him. All true human art is an assimilation to the artist, to Christ, to the mind of the Creator. The idea of a music of the cosmos, of singing with the angels, leads back again to the relation of art to Logos, but now it is broadened and deepened in the context of the cosmos. Yes, it is the *cosmic context* that gives art in the liturgy both its measure and its scope. A merely subjective "creativity" is no match for the vast compass of the cosmos and for the message of its beauty. When a man conforms to the measure of the universe, his freedom is not diminished but expanded to a new horizon.

One final point follows from this. The cosmic interpretation remained alive, with some variations, well into the early modern age. Only in the nineteenth century was there a move away from it, because "metaphysics" seemed so outdated. Hegel now tried to interpret music as just an expression of the subject and of subjectivity. But whereas Hegel still adhered to the fundamental idea of reason as the starting point and destination of the whole enterprise, a change of direction took place with Schopenhauer that was to have momentous consequences. For him, the world is no longer grounded in reason but in "will and idea" (*Wille und vorstellung*). The will precedes reason. And music is the primordial expression of being human as such, the pure expression of the will anterior to reason, which creates the world. Music should not, therefore, be subjected to the Word, and only in exceptional cases should it have any connection with the Word. Since music is pure will, its origin precedes that of reason. It takes us back behind reason to the actual foundation of reality. [Schopenhauer's view] is reminiscent of Goethe's recasting of the prologue of St. John: no longer "in the beginning was the Word," but now "in the beginning was the Deed."

In our own times this continues in the attempt to replace "orthodoxy" by "orthopraxy": there is no common faith anymore (because truth is unattainable), only common praxis. By contrast, for Christian faith, as Guardini shows so penetratingly in his masterly early work, *The Spirit of the Liturgy*, Logos takes precedence over ethos. When this is reversed, Christianity is turned upside down. The cosmic character of liturgical music stands in opposition to the two tendencies of the modern age that we have described: music as pure subjectivity, and music as the expression of mere will. We sing with the angels. But this cosmic character is grounded ultimately in the ordering of all Christian worship to Logos.

Let us have one last brief look at our own times. The dissolution of the subject, which coincides for us today with radical forms of subjectivism, has led to "deconstructionism," the anarchistic theory of art. Perhaps this will help us to overcome the unbounded inflation of subjectivity and recognize once more that a relationship with the Logos, who was at the beginning, brings salvation to the subject, that is, to the person. At the same time it puts us into a true relationship of communion that is ultimately grounded in trinitarian love.

As we have seen, the problems of the present day pose without doubt a grave challenge to the church and the culture of the liturgy. Nevertheless, there is no reason at all to be discouraged. The great cultural tradition of the faith is home to a presence of immense power. What in museums is only a monument from the past, an occasion for mere nostalgic admiration, is constantly made present in the liturgy in all its freshness.

But the present day is not condemned to silence where the faith is concerned. Anyone who looks carefully will see that, even in our own time, important works of art, inspired by faith, have been produced and are being produced in visual art as well as in music (and indeed literature).

Today, too, joy in the Lord and contact with his presence in the liturgy has an inexhaustible power of inspiration. The artists who take this task upon themselves need not regard themselves as the rear guard of culture. They are weary of the empty freedom from which they have emerged. Humble submission to what goes before us releases authentic freedom and leads us to the true summit of our vocation as human beings.

Sacred Places

The Significance of the Church Building

Even the staunchest opponents of sacred things—of sacred space, in this case—accept that the Christian community needs a place to meet, and on that basis they define the purpose of church buildings in a nonsacral, strictly functional sense. Church buildings, they say, make it possible for people to get together for the liturgy. This is without question an essential function of church buildings, and it distinguishes them from the classical form of the temple in most religions. In the Old Covenant, the high priest performed the rite of atonement in the Holy of Holies. None but he was allowed to enter, and even he could do so only once a year. Similarly, the temples of all the other religions are usually not meeting places for worshipers but cultic spaces reserved to the deity. The Christian church building soon acquired the name *domus ecclesiae* (the house of the church, the assembly of the People of God), and then, as an abbreviation, the word *ecclesia* ("assembly," "church") came to be used, not just of the living community but also of the building that housed it. This development is accompanied by another idea: Christ himself offers worship as he stands before the Father. He becomes his members' worship as they come together with him and around him. This essential difference between the Christian place of worship and the temples of the other religions must not, of course, be exaggerated into a false opposition. We must not suggest a break in the inner continuity of mankind's religious history, a continuity that, for all the differences, the Old and New Testaments never abolish. In his eighteenth catechesis (23–25), St. Cyril of Jerusalem makes an interesting point about the word *convocatio* (*synagogē-ekklēsia*, the assembly of the people called together and made his own by God). He rightly points out that in the Pentateuch, when the word first makes its appearance with the appointment of Aaron, it is ordered toward worship. Cyril shows that this applies to all the later passages in the Torah, and even in the transition to the New Testament, this ordering is not forgotten. The calling together, the assembly, has a purpose, and that purpose is worship. The call comes from worship and leads back to worship. It is worship that unites the people called together and gives their being together its meaning and worth: they are united in that "peace" which the world cannot give. This also becomes clear in relation to that great Old and New Testament archetype of the *ekklçsia,* the community on Sinai. They come together to hear God's Word and to seal everything with sacrifice. That is how a "covenant" is established between God and man.

But instead of continuing with these theoretical considerations, let us look more closely at the process by which church buildings took concrete form. Using the research of E. L. Sukenik, Louis Bouyer has shown how the Christian house of God comes into being in complete continuity with the synagogue and thus acquires a specifically Christian newness, without any dramatic break, through communion with Jesus Christ, the Crucified and Risen Lord. This close connection with the synagogue, with its architectural structure and liturgical form, does not in any way contradict what we said above about the Christian liturgy not just continuing the synagogue but also incorporating the temple. For the Jews saw the synagogue in relation to the temple. The synagogue was never just a place for instruction, a kind of religious classroom, as Bouyer puts it. No, its orientation was always toward the presence of God. Now, for the Jews, this presence of God was (and is) indissolubly connected with the temple. Consequently, the synagogue was characterized by two focal points. The first is the "seat of Moses," of which the Lord speaks in the gospel (cf. Mt 23:2). The rabbi does not speak from his own resources. He is not a professor, analyzing and reflecting on the Word of God in an intellectual way. No, he makes present the Word that God addressed and addresses to Israel. God speaks through Moses today. What the seat of Moses stands for is this: Sinai is not just a thing of the past. It is not mere human speech that is happening here. God is speaking.

The seat of Moses, then, does not stand for itself and by itself, nor is it simply turned toward the people. No, the rabbi looks—as does everyone else in the synagogue—toward the ark of the covenant, or rather the shrine of the Torah, which represents the lost ark. Up to the Exile, the ark of the covenant was the only "object" allowed inside the Holy of Holies. That is what gave the Holy of Holies its special dignity. The ark was seen as an empty throne, upon which the Shekinah—the cloud of God's presence—came down. The cherubim—representing, as it were, the elements of the world—served as "assistants at the throne." They were not self-subsistent deities but an expression of the created powers that worship the only God. God is addressed as "thou who art enthroned between the cherubim." The heavens cannot contain him, but he has chosen the ark as the "footstool" of his presence. In this sense, the ark embodies something like the real presence of God among his own. At the same time it is an impressive sign of the absence of images from the liturgy of the Old Testament, which maintains God in his sovereignty and holds out to him, so to speak, only the footstool of his throne. During the Exile, the ark of the covenant was lost, and from then on the Holy of Holies was empty. That is what Pompeius found when he strode through the temple and pulled back the curtain. He entered the Holy of Holies full of curiosity and there, in the very emptiness of the place, discovered what is special about biblical religion. The empty Holy of Holies had now become an act of expectation, of hope, that God himself would one day restore his throne.

The synagogue, in its shrine of the Torah, contains a kind of ark of the covenant, which means it is the place of a kind of "real presence." Here are kept the scrolls of the Torah, the living Word of God, through which he sits on his throne in Israel among his own people. The shrine is surrounded, therefore, with signs of reverence befitting the mysterious presence of God. It is protected by a curtain, before which burn the seven lights of the menorah, the seven-branch candlestick. Now the furnishing of the synagogue with an "ark of the covenant" does not in any way signify that the local community has become, so to speak, independent, self-sufficient. No, it is the place where the local community reaches out beyond itself to the temple, to the commonality of the one People of God as defined by the one God. The Torah is in all places one and the same. And so the ark points beyond itself, to the one place of its presence that God chose for himself—the Holy of Holies in the temple in Jerusalem. This Holy of Holies remained, as Bouyer puts it, "the ultimate focus of the synagogal worship" (p. 15). "Thus have all the synagogues, at the time of Our Lord and since that time, been oriented" (p. 15). The rabbi and the people gaze at the "ark of the covenant," and in so doing, they orient themselves toward Jerusalem, turn themselves toward the Holy of Holies in the temple as the place of God's presence for his people. This remained the case even after the destruction of the temple. The empty Holy of Holies had already been an expression of hope, and so, too, now is the destroyed temple, which waits for the return of the Shekinah, for its restoration by the Messiah when he comes.

This orientation toward the temple, and thus the connection of the synagogue's liturgy of the Word with the sacrificial liturgy of the temple, can be seen in its form of prayer. The prayers said at the unrolling and reading of the scrolls of scripture developed out of the ritual prayers originally linked to the sacrificial actions in the temple and now regarded, in accord with the tradition of the time outside the temple, as an equivalent of sacrifice. The first of the two great prayers of the synagogue rite comes to a climax in the common recitation of the *Kid-dush,* of which the hymn of the seraphim in Isaiah chapter 6 and the hymn of the cherubim in Ezekiel chapter 3 are a part. Bouyer makes this comment: "But the truth must be that the association of men with these heavenly canticles, in the worship of the Temple, had probably been a central feature of the offering of the sacrifice of incense morning and evening of every day" (p. 22). Who would not be reminded of the Trisagion of the Christian liturgy, the "thrice holy" hymn at the beginning of the Canon? Here the congregation does not offer its own thoughts or poetry but is taken out of itself and given the privilege of sharing in the cosmic song of praise of the cherubim and seraphim. The other great prayer of the synagogue culminates in "the recitation of the *Abodah* which, according to the rabbis, was formerly the consecration prayer of the daily burnt offering in the Temple" (p. 22). The petition added to it about the coming of the Messiah and the final restoration of Israel may be seen, according to Bouyer, "as the expression of the essence of the sacrificial worship" (p. 22). Let us remind ourselves here of that transition from animal sacrifices to "worship in harmony with Logos," which characterizes the path from the Old Testament into the New. Finally, we must mention the fact that no special architectural form was created for the synagogue. The "typical Greek building for public meetings: the basilica," was used (p. 17). Its aisles, divided off by rows of columns, enabled people entering the building to circulate around it.

I have lingered over this description of the synagogue because it exhibits already the essential and constant features of Christian places of worship. Once again we see clearly the essential unity of the two testaments. Not surprisingly, in Semitic, non-Greek Christianity, the original form of church buildings generally retains the close connection of church with synagogue, a pattern of religious continuity and innovation. (I am thinking here of the Monophysite and Nestorian Churches of the Near East, which broke away from the church of the Byzantine Empire during the Christological debates of the fifth century.) The Christian faith produced three innovations in the form of the synagogue as we have just sketched it. These give Christian liturgy its new and proper profile. First of all, the worshiper no longer looks toward Jerusalem. The destroyed temple is no longer regarded as the place of God's earthly presence. The temple built of stone has ceased to express the hope of Christians; its curtain is forever. Christians look toward the east, the rising sun.... This is not a case of Christians worshiping the sun, but of the cosmos speaking of Christ. The song of the sun in Psalm 19 (18) is interpreted as a song about Christ when it says: "[The sun] comes forth like a bridegroom leaving his chamber.... Its rising is from the end of the heavens and its circuit to the end of them" (vv. 5ff.). This psalm proceeds directly from applauding

Creation to praising the law. Christians interpret it in terms of Christ, who is the living Word, the eternal Logos, and thus the true light of history, who came forth in Bethlehem from the bridal chamber of the Virgin Mother and now pours out his light on all the world. The east supersedes the Jerusalem temple as a symbol. Christ, represented by the sun, is the place of the Shekinah, the true throne of the living God. In the Incarnation, human nature truly becomes the throne and seat of God, who is thus forever bound to the earth and accessible to our prayers. In the early church, prayer toward the east was regarded as an apostolic tradition. We cannot date exactly when this turn to the east, the diverting of the gaze from the temple, took place, but it is certain that it goes back to the earliest times and was always regarded as an essential characteristic of Christian liturgy (and indeed of private prayer). This "orientation"[1] of Christian prayer has several different meanings. Orientation is, first and foremost, a simple expression of looking to Christ as the meeting place between God and man. It expresses the basic Christological form of our prayer.

The fact that we find Christ in the symbol of the rising sun is an indication of a Christology defined eschatologically. Praying toward the east means going to meet the coming Christ. The liturgy, turned toward the east, effects entry, so to speak, into the procession of history toward the future, the New Heaven and the New Earth, which we encounter in Christ. It is a prayer of hope, the prayer of the pilgrim as he walks in the direction shown us by the life, Passion, and Resurrection of Christ. Thus very early on, in parts of Christendom, the eastward direction for prayer was given added emphasis by a reference to the cross. This may have come from linking Revelation 1:7 with Matthew 24:30. In the first of these, the Revelation of St. John, it says: "Behold, he is coming with the clouds, and every eye will see him, every one who pierced him; and all tribes of the earth will wail on account of him. Even so. Amen." Here the seer of the Apocalypse depends on John 19:37, where, at the end of the account of the Crucifixion, the mysterious text of the prophet Zechariah (12:10) is quoted, a text that suddenly acquires a wholly new meaning: "They shall look on him whom they have pierced." Finally, in Matthew 24:30 we are given these words of the Lord: "Then [on the Last Day] will appear the sign of the Son of man in heaven, and then all the tribes of the earth will mourn [cf. Zech 12:10], and they will see the Son of man coming on the clouds of heaven [cf. Dn 7:13] with power and great glory." The sign of the Son of Man, of the Pierced One, is the cross, which has now become the sign of victory of the Risen One. Thus the symbolism of the cross merges with that of the east. Both are an expression of one and the same faith, in which the remembrance of the Pasch of Jesus makes it present and gives dynamism to the hope that goes out to meet the One who is to come. But, finally, this turning toward the east also signifies that cosmos and saving history belong together. The cosmos is praying with us. It, too, is waiting for redemption. It is precisely this cosmic dimension that is essential to Christian liturgy. It is never performed solely in the self-made world of man. It is always a cosmic liturgy. The theme of Creation is embedded in Christian prayer. It loses its grandeur when it forgets this connection. That is why, wherever possible, we should definitely take up again the apostolic tradition of facing the east, both in the building of churches and in the celebration of the liturgy. We shall come back to this later, when we say something about the ordering of liturgical prayer.

The second innovation in regard to the synagogue is as follows. A new element has appeared that could not exist in the synagogue. At the east wall, or in the apse, there now stands an altar on which the eucharistic sacrifice is celebrated. As we saw, the Eucharist is an entry into the liturgy of heaven; by it we become contemporaries with Jesus Christ's own act of worship, into which, through his body, he takes up worldly time and straightway leads it beyond itself, snatching it out of its own sphere and enfolding it into the Communion of eternal love. Thus the altar signifies the entry of him who is the Orient into the assembled community, and the going out of the community from the prison of this world through the curtain now torn open, a participation in the Pasch, the "passing over" from the world to God that Christ has opened up. It is clear that the altar in the apse both looks toward the *Oriens* and forms part of it. In the synagogue the worshipers looked beyond the ark of the covenant, the shrine of the Word, toward Jerusalem. Now, with the Christian altar comes a new focal point. Let us say it again: on the altar, what the temple had in the past foreshadowed is now present in a new way. Yes, it enables us to become the contemporaries of the sacrifice of the Logos. Thus it brings heaven into the community assembled on earth, or rather it takes that community beyond itself into the communion of saints of all times and places. We might put it this way: the altar is the place where heaven is opened up. It does not close off the church, but opens it up—and leads it into the eternal liturgy. We shall have more to say about the practical consequences of the significance of the Christian altar, because the question of the correct position for the altar is at the center of the postconciliar debate.

But first we must finish what we were saying about the different ways in which Christian faith transformed the synagogue. The third point to be noted is that the shrine of the Word remained, even with regard to its position in the church building. However, of necessity, there is a fundamental innovation here. The Torah is replaced by the Gospels, which alone can open up the meaning of the Torah. "Moses," says Christ, "wrote of me" (Jn 5:46). The shrine of the Word, the ark of the covenant, now becomes the throne of the gospel. The gospel does not, of course, abolish the "scriptures," nor push them to one side, but rather interprets them, so that henceforth and forever they are the scriptures of Christians, without which the gospel would have no foundation. The practice in the synagogue of covering the shrine with a curtain to express the sacredness of the Word is retained. Quite spontaneously, the new, second holy place, the altar, is surrounded by a curtain, from which in the Eastern church, the Iconostasis develops. The fact that there are two holy places had significance for the celebration of the liturgy. During the Liturgy of the Word, the congregation gathered around the shrine of the Sacred Books, or around the seat associated with it, which evolved quite spontaneously from the seat of Moses to the bishop's throne. Just as the rabbi did not speak by his own authority, so the bishop expounds the Bible in the name, and by the mandate, of Christ. Thus, from being a written word from the past, it again becomes what it is: God's addressing us here and now. At the end of the Liturgy of the Word, during which the faithful stand around the bishop's seat, everyone walks together with the bishop to the altar, and now the cry resounds: "*Conversi ad Dominum,*" "Turn toward the Lord!" In other words, look toward the east with the bishop, in the sense of the words from the epistle to the Hebrews: "[Look] ... to Jesus the pioneer and perfecter of our faith" (12:2). The Liturgy of the Eucharist is celebrated as we look up to Jesus. It is our looking up to Jesus. Thus, in early church buildings, the liturgy has two places. First, the Liturgy of the Word takes place at the center of the building. The faithful are grouped around the *bema,* the elevated area where the throne of the gospel, the seat of the bishop, and the lectern are located. The eucharistic celebration proper takes place in the apse, at the altar, which the faithful "stand around." Everyone joins with the celebrant in facing east, toward the Lord who is to come.

Finally, we must mention one last difference between the synagogue and the earliest church buildings. In Israel only the presence of men was deemed to be necessary for divine worship. The common priesthood described in Exodus chapter 19 was ascribed to them alone. Consequently, in the synagogue, women were only allowed into the tribunes or galleries. As far as the apostles were concerned, as far as Jesus himself is concerned, there was no such discrimination in the church of Christ. Even though the public Liturgy of the Word was not entrusted to women, they were included in the liturgy as a whole in exactly the same way as men. And so now they had a place—albeit separated from men—in the sacred space itself, around both the *bema* and the altar.

The Beginning of the Council and the Transfer to Münster

While my relationship with Cardinal Wendel, the archbishop of Munich, had not been wholly without complications, a very straightforward and even affectionate understanding developed at once between the archbishop of Cologne, Cardinal Frings, and me. This was due in part to the fact that his secretary, Hubert Luthe, now bishop of Essen, was a friend of mine from the years in Fürstenried, where I had had a friendly rapport with several other theology students from Cologne, for instance, Bishop Dick, the present auxiliary bishop. Meanwhile, John XXIII had announced the Second Vatican Council and thereby reanimated and, for many, intensified even to the point of euphoria the atmosphere of renewal and hope that had reigned in the church and in theology since the end of the First World War despite the perils of the National Socialist era. Cardinal Frings heard a conference on the theology of the council that I had been invited to give by the Catholic Academy of Bensberg, and afterward he involved me in a long dialogue that became the starting point of a collaboration that lasted for years. As a member of the Central Preparatory Commission, the cardinal was sent the drafts of texts ("schemata") that were to be presented to the council fathers for their discussion and vote after the assembly had convened. He now began to send me these texts regularly to have my criticism and suggestions for improvement. Naturally I took exception to certain things, but I found no grounds for a radical rejection of what was being proposed, such as many demanded later on in the council and actually managed to put through. It is true that the documents bore only weak traces of the biblical and patristic renewal of the last decades, so that they gave an impression of rigidity and narrowness through their excessive dependency on scholastic theology. In other words, they reflected more the thought of scholars than that of shepherds. But I must say that they had a solid foundation and had been carefully elaborated.

Finally the great hour for the council arrived. Cardinal Frings took his secretary, Father Luthe, and me, as his theological advisor, to Rome. He worked things so that I was named a *peritus* (official council theologian) toward the end of the first session. I cannot and will not enter here into a detailed portrayal of those very special years, during which we lived in the cozy Anima, the residence for German and Austrian priests near the Piazza Navona, cannot recount the many encounters that were now granted me—with great men like Henri de Lubac, Jean Daniélou, and Gerard Philips, to name only a few prominent names—cannot report on the meetings with bishops from all continents or on personal conversations with only a few of them. Nor does the theological and ecclesial drama of those years belong in these memoirs.

But the reader will allow me two exceptions. The first question was what the council should begin with, what its proximate task ought to be. The pope had given only a very wide-ranging description of his purpose in calling a council, and this left the fathers with an almost unlimited freedom to give things concrete shape. The pope's view basically amounted to this: the faith, while remaining the same in its contents, was to be proclaimed to our era in a new way, and after a period of demarcations and defensive maneuvers, we were now no longer to condemn but to apply the "medicine of mercy." There was implicit agreement that the church herself should be the main theme of the gathering, which would thus take up again and conclude the work of the First Vatican Council, which had been prematurely interrupted in 1870 by the Franco-Prussian War. Cardinals Montini and Suenens presented plans for a vast theological outline of the work of the council, in which the theme of the church was to be divided into two parts: "the interior life of the church" and "the church vis-à-vis the world." This second part would permit the great questions of the present to come to the fore under the perspective of the relationship between church and "world."

The reform of the liturgy in the spirit of the liturgical movement was not a priority for the majority of the fathers, and for many not even a consideration. Thus, for example, in his outline of themes after the beginning of the council, Cardinal Montini—who as Paul VI would be the real pope of the council—said quite clearly that he did not see the reform of the liturgy as a substantial task in the council. The liturgy and its reform had, since the end of World War I, become a pressing question only in France and Germany, and indeed above all from the perspective of the purest possible restoration of the ancient Roman liturgy, to which belonged the active involvement of the people in the liturgical event. These two countries, which at that time enjoyed theological leadership in the church (and we must, of course, add Belgium and the Netherlands), had during the preparation phase succeeded in putting through a schema on the sacred liturgy, which quite naturally found its place in the general theme of the church. The fact that this text became the first subject for the council's discussions really had nothing to do with the majority of the fathers having an intense interest in the liturgical question. Quite simply, no great disagreements were expected in this area, and the undertaking was viewed as a kind of practical exercise to learn and test the method of conciliar work. It would not have occurred to any of the fathers to see in this text a "revolution" signifying the "end of the Middle Ages," as some theologians felt they should interpret it subsequently. The work was seen as a continuation of the reforms introduced by Pius X and carried on carefully but resolutely by Pius XII. General expressions, such as "the liturgical books should be revised as soon as possible" (no. 25), were understood in this sense: as the uninterrupted continuation of that development which had always been there and which, since Popes Pius X and Pius XII, had received a definite profile from the rediscovery of the classical Roman liturgical tradition, which was, of course, to overcome certain tendencies of Baroque liturgy and nineteenth-century devotional piety and to promote a new humble and sober centering of the authentic mystery of Christ's presence in his church. In this context it is not surprising that the "model Mass" now proposed, which was supposed to (and, in fact, did) take the place of the traditional *Ordo missae,* was in 1967 rejected by the majority of the fathers who had been called together to a special synod on the matter. Some publications now tell us that some liturgists (or perhaps many?) who were working as advisors had had more far-reaching intentions from the outset. Their wishes would surely not have received the approval of the fathers. Nor were such wishes expressed in any way in the text of the council, although one can subsequently read them into some general statements.

The debate on the liturgy had taken place calmly and without serious tension. A dramatic controversy did begin, however, when "The Sources of Revelation" was presented for discussion. By "sources of revelation" was meant scripture and tradition; their relationship to one another and to the Magisterium had been dealt with solidly in the forms of post-Tridentine scholasticism according to the custom of the textbooks then in use. In the meantime, the historical-critical method of biblical interpretation had made itself at home in Catholic theology. By its very nature, this method has no patience with any restrictions imposed by an authoritative magisterium; it can recognize no authority but that of the historical argument. From its perspective, the concept of "tradition" had itself become questionable, since this method will not allow for an oral tradition running alongside scripture and reaching back to the apostles—and hence offering another source of historical knowledge besides the Bible. This impasse is indeed what made the dispute on the dogma of Mary's bodily Assumption into heaven so difficult and insoluble.

Thus, with this text, the whole problem of modern biblical interpretation was up for debate and, beyond it, also the fundamental question of the relationship between history and spirit [*Geist*] within the context of faith. The concrete form of the debate was determined by an alleged historical discovery that the Tübingen dogma specialist J. R. Geiselmann believed he had made in the 1950s. In the Acts of the Council of Trent he had found that the initial formulation suggested for the decree issued at that time had stated that revelation was contained "partially in scripture and partially in tradition." The definitive text, however, avoided this "partially/partially," replacing it with an *and*: in other words, scripture and tradition *together* communicate revelation to us. From this, Geiselmann concluded that Trent had wanted to teach that there can be no distribution of the contents of faith into scripture, on the one hand, and tradition on the other, but rather that both scripture and tradition, each on its own, contain the whole of revelation, hence that each is complete in itself. At this point what interested people was not the alleged or real completeness of tradition; the interesting thing was the announcement that, according to Trent, scripture contains the deposit of faith whole and entire. There was talk of the "material completeness" of the Bible in matters of faith. This catchword, which was immediately on everybody's lips and was regarded as a great new realization, just as quickly became detached from its point of departure in the interpretation of the Tridentine decree. It was now asserted that the inevitable consequence of this realization was that the church could not teach anything that was not expressly contained in scripture, since scripture was complete in matters of faith. And, since the interpretation of scripture was identified with the historical-critical method, this meant that nothing could be taught by the church that could not pass the scrutiny of the historical-critical method. With this, Luther's *sola scriptura* ("scripture alone"), which had been the main focus in Trent, was completely overshadowed. This new theory, in fact, meant that exegesis now had to become the highest authority in the church, and since, by the very nature of human reason and historical work, no agreement among interpreters can be expected in the case of such difficult texts (where acknowledged or unacknowledged prejudices are always at work), all of this meant that faith had to retreat into the region of the indeterminate and continual changing that characterizes historical or would-be historical hypotheses. In other words, believing now amounted to having opinions and was in need of continual revision. The council, naturally, had to oppose a theory developed in this manner, but the catchword "material completeness," along with all its consequences, now remained in the church's public awareness much more firmly than the council's actual final document. The drama of the postconciliar era has been largely determined by this catch-word and its logical consequences.

I had personally become acquainted with Geiselmann's thesis early in 1956 at the Königstein Congress of systematic theologians. It was here that this scholar from Tübingen first proposed his alleged discovery (which, inciden-tally, he did not himself extend to all the consequences just described, a devel-opment that emerged only with the propaganda surrounding the council). At first I, too, was fascinated, but soon I came to see that the great theme of scripture and tradition could not be solved in so simple a manner. I then un-dertook a thorough study of the Acts of Trent and came to see that the redac-tional change that Geiselmann had made the main point was only an insignificant aspect of the fathers' efforts, which searched much more deeply and extensively into the fundamental question of how revelation could be contained, first, in human words and, finally, in written words. In this I was helped by the knowledge I had gained while studying Bonaventure's concept of revelation. I found that the basic direction taken by the fathers of Trent in their conception of revelation had essentially remained the same as in the High Middle Ages. On the basis of these principles, which I naturally cannot develop at any greater length here, my objections to the proposed conciliar schema were of a very different kind from either Geiselmann's theses or the cruder versions of them that circulated in the council's increasingly heated atmosphere.

But I would at least like to sketch the essence of my thoughts on the matter. Revelation, which is to say, God's approach to man, is always greater than what can be contained in human words, greater even than the words of scrip-ture. As I have already said in connection with my work on Bonaventure, both in the Middle Ages and at Trent it would have been impossible to refer to scripture simply as "revelation," as is the normal linguistic usage today. Scrip-ture is the essential witness of revelation, but revelation is something alive, something greater and *more:* proper to it is the fact that it *arrives* and is *per-ceived*—otherwise it could not have become revelation. Revelation is not a meteor fallen to earth that now lies around somewhere as a rock mass from which rock samples can be taken and submitted to laboratory analysis. Reve-lation has instruments, but it is not separable from the living God, and it always requires a living person to whom it is communicated. Its goal is always to gather and unite men, and this is why the church is a necessary aspect of revelation. If, however, revelation is more than scripture, if it transcends scrip-ture, then the "rock analysis"—which is to say, the historical-critical method—cannot be the last word concerning revelation; rather, the living organism of the faith of all ages is then an intrinsic part of revelation. And what we call tradition is precisely that part of revelation that goes above and beyond scripture and cannot be comprehended within a code of formulas. In the general atmosphere dominant in 1962, which had taken over Geiselmann's theses in the form I have described, it was impossible for me to explain the perspective I had gained from the sources—a perspective, moreover, that had already been misunderstood in 1956. My position was simply aligned with the general opposition to the official schema and considered to be one more vote in favor of Geiselmann.

At the request of Cardinal Frings, I wrote up at that time a brief schema in which I attempted to express my viewpoint. I had occasion to read my text, with Cardinal Frings present, to a number of highly regarded cardinals, who found it interesting but naturally neither wanted to nor could at that moment give any judgment concerning it. My small effort had been composed in great haste and so naturally could not in any way compete in solidity and thoroughness with the official schema, which had been elaborated in a long process and had gone through many revisions by competent scholars. It was clear that the text had to be reworked and deepened. For this, other eyes and hands were needed. Thus, it was agreed that Karl Rahner and I together would produce a second, more developed version. This second text, much more Rahner's work than my own, was then distributed among the fathers and evoked some rather bitter reactions. As we worked together, it became obvious to me that, despite our agreement in many desires and conclusions, Rahner and I lived on two different theological planets. In questions such as liturgical reform, the new place of exegesis in the church and in theology, and many other areas, he stood for the same things as I did but for entirely different reasons. Despite his early reading of the fathers, his theology was totally conditioned by the tradition of Suarezian scholasticism and its new reception in the light of German idealism and Heidegger. His was a speculative and philosophical theology in which scripture and the fathers in the end did not play an important role and in which the historical dimension was really of little significance. For my part, my whole intellectual formation had been shaped by scripture and the fathers and profoundly historical thinking. The great difference between the Munich school, in which I had been trained, and Rahner's became clear to me during those days, even though it still took a while for our parting of ways to become outwardly visible.

It now became clear that Rahner's schema could not be accepted, but the official text, too, was rejected by a narrow margin of votes. The theme, therefore, had to be postponed. The Constitution on Divine Revelation could be completed only in the final period of the council after some very complex debates, but the final product was one of the outstanding texts of the council and one that has yet to be truly received. Practically the only thing that had any effect was what trickled down into popular opinion as the allegedly new viewpoint of the fathers. We still have before us the task of communicating what the council actually said to the church at large and, beyond that, of developing its implications. In the meantime I had to make a difficult personal decision. The great dogma specialist from Münster, Hermann Volk, who despite the difference in our ages had become my friend, had been made bishop of Mainz in 1962. Now I was being invited to take his chair. I loved the Rhineland, and I loved my students and my work at the University of Bonn; because of Cardinal Frings I was even more committed to this work. But Bishop Volk was pressuring me, and friends advised me very emphatically, that dogma was the correct road for me because it would open up a much wider sphere of influence than fundamental theology. They also argued that my formation in scripture and the fathers could be applied much more effectively in the area of dogma. Such an apparently simple decision nevertheless became difficult, and after much vacillation I decided to decline the Münster offer. This should have been the final word on the matter; but a splinter had remained in me that now began to hurt as I ran into considerable opposition within our tension-filled faculty in Bonn in connection with two doctoral dissertations. Such opposition would probably result in the failing of the two young scholars in question. I remembered the drama of my own *habilitation* and saw in Münster the way Providence was pointing out to me that I could help these two candidates. That became even clearer when I realized that similar difficulties were also likely in other cases and that I had no reason to fear the same thing in Münster, given the circumstances there. Together with the arguments concerning my greater involvement in dogma, which I had previously discounted, these other reasons now amounted to a force to which I yielded. Of course, I had discussed all these things with Cardinal Frings and can even now feel only gratitude for his fatherly understanding and personal generosity. Thus, in the summer of 1963, I took up my post lecturing in Münster, where both the personal and material situations granted me were generous. My reception by colleagues in the faculty was very warm, and conditions could hardly have been more favorable. But I must admit that I retained a certain nostalgia for Bonn, the city on the river, for its cheerfulness and intellectual dynamism.

The year 1963 brought yet another deep wound to my life. Already since January my brother had noticed that Mother was eating less and less. In mid-August her physician announced to us with sad certainty that she had cancer of the stomach, which would follow its course quickly and relentlessly. With what was left of her energies she kept house for my brother until the end of

October, even though she was already reduced to skin and bones. Then one day she collapsed in a shop, and then was never again able to leave her sickbed. Our experience with her now was very similar to what we had lived with Father. Her goodness became even purer and more radiant and continued to shine unchanged, even through the weeks of increasing pain. On the day after Gaudete Sunday, December 16, 1963, she closed her eyes forever, but the radiance of her goodness has remained, and for me it has become more and more a confirmation of the faith by which she had allowed herself to be formed. I know of no more convincing proof for the faith than precisely the pure and unalloyed humanity that the faith allowed to mature in my parents and in so many other persons I have had the privilege to encounter.

PART FOUR

THEOLOGY

On the Meaning of Faith

Let me begin with a brief story from the early postconciliar period. The council documents—particularly the Constitution on the Church in the Modern World, but also the decrees on ecumenism, on mission, on non-Christian religions, and on freedom of religion—had opened up broad vistas of dialogue for the church and theology. New issues were appearing on the horizon, and it was becoming necessary to find new methods. It seemed self-evident that a theologian who wanted to be up to date and who rightly understood his task should temporarily suspend the old discussions and devote all of his energies to the new questions pressing in from every side.

At about this time, I sent a small piece of mine to Hans Urs von Balthasar. Balthasar replied by return mail on a correspondence card, as he always did, and after expressing his thanks, added a terse sentence that made an indelible impression on me: do not presuppose the faith but propose it. This was an imperative that hit home. Wide-ranging exploration of new fields was good and necessary, but only so long as it issued from, and was sustained by, the central light of faith. Faith is not maintained automatically. It is not a "finished business" that we can simply take for granted. The life of faith has to be constantly renewed. And since faith is an act that comprehends all the dimensions of our existence, it also requires constantly renewed reflection and witness. It follows that the chief points of faith—God, Christ, the Holy Spirit, grace and sin, sacraments and church, death and eternal life—are never outmoded. They are always the issues that affect us most profoundly. They must be the permanent center of preaching and therefore of theological reflection. The bishops present at the 1985 Synod called for a universal catechism of the whole church because they sensed precisely what Balthasar had put into words in his note to me. Their experience as shepherds had shown them that the various new pastoral activities have no solid basis unless they are irradiations and applications of the message of faith. Faith cannot be presupposed; it must be proposed. This is the purpose of the *Catechism*. It aims to propose the faith in its fullness and wealth, but also in its unity and simplicity.

What does the church believe? This question implies another: who believes, and how does someone believe? The *Catechism* treats these two main questions, which concern, respectively, the "what" and the "who" of faith, as an intrinsic unity. Expressed in other terms, the *Catechism* displays the act of faith and the content of faith in their indivisible unity. This may sound somewhat abstract, so let us try to unfold a bit what it means.

We find in the creeds two formulas: "I believe" and "We believe." We speak of the faith of the church, of the personal character of faith, and finally of faith as a gift of God—as a "theological act," as contemporary theology likes to put it. What does all of this mean?

Faith is an orientation of our existence as a whole. It is a fundamental option that affects every domain of our existence. Nor can it be realized unless all the energies of our existence go into maintaining it. Faith is not a merely intellectual, or merely volitional, or merely emotional activity—it is all of these things together. It is an act of the whole self, of the whole person in his concentrated unity. The Bible describes faith in this sense as an act of the "heart" (Rom 10:9).

Faith is a supremely personal act. But precisely because it is supremely personal, it transcends the self, the limits of the individual. Augustine remarks that nothing is so little ours as our self. Where man as a whole comes into play, he transcends himself; an act of the whole self is at the same time always an opening to others, hence, an act of being together with others [*Mitsein*]. What is more, we cannot perform this act without touching our deepest ground, the living God who is present in the depths of our existence as its sustaining foundation.

Any act that involves the whole man also involves not just the self but the we-dimension—indeed, the wholly other "thou," God, together with the self. But this also means that such an act transcends the reach of what I can do alone. Since man is a created being, the deepest truth about him is never just action but always passion, as well; man is not only a giver but also a receiver. The *Catechism* expresses this point in the following words: "No one can believe alone, just as no one can live alone. You have not given yourself faith as you have not given yourself life."[1] Paul's description of his experience of conversion and baptism alludes to faith's radical character: "It is no longer I who live, but Christ lives in me" (Gal 2:20). Faith is a perishing of the mere self and precisely a resurrection of the true self. To believe is to become oneself through liberation from the mere self, a liberation that brings us into communion with God mediated by communion with Christ.

So far, we have attempted, with the help of the *Catechism*, to analyze "who" believes, hence, to identify the structure of the act of faith. But in so doing we have already caught sight of the outlines of the essential content of faith. In its core, Christian faith is an encounter with the living God. God is, in the proper and ultimate sense, the content of our faith. Looked at in this way, the content of faith is absolutely simple: I believe in God. But this absolute simplicity is also absolutely deep and encompassing. We can believe in God because he can touch us, because he is in us, and because he also comes to us from the outside. We can believe in him because of the one whom he has sent. "Because he has 'seen the Father,'" says the *Catechism,* referring to John 6:56, "Jesus Christ is the only one who knows him and can reveal him."[2] We could say that to believe is to be granted a share in Jesus's vision. He lets us see with him in faith what he has seen.

This statement implies both the divinity of Jesus Christ and his humanity. Because Jesus is the Son, he has an unceasing vision of the Father. Because he is man, we can share this vision. Because he is both God and man at once, he is neither merely a historical person nor simply removed from all time in eternity. Rather, he is in the midst of time, always alive, always present.

But in saying this, we also touch upon the mystery of the Trinity. The Lord becomes present to us through the Holy Spirit. Let us listen once more to the *Catechism:* "One cannot believe in Jesus Christ without sharing in his Spirit.... Only God knows God completely: we believe in the Holy Spirit because he is God."[3]

It follows from what we have said that, when we see the act of faith correctly, the single articles of faith unfold by themselves. God becomes concrete for us in Christ. This has two consequences. On the one hand, the triune mystery of God becomes discernible; on the other hand, we see that God has involved himself in history to the point that the Son has become man and now sends us the Spirit from the Father. But the Incarnation also includes the mystery of the church, for Christ came to "gather into one the children of God who are scattered abroad" (Jn 11:52). The "we" of the church is the new communion into which God draws us beyond our narrow selves (cf. Jn 12:32). The church is thus contained in the first movement of the act of faith itself. The church is not an institution extrinsically added to faith as an organizational framework for the common activities of believers. No, she is integral to the act of faith itself. The "I believe" is always also a "We believe." As the *Catechism* says, "'I believe' is also the Church, our mother, responding to God by faith as she teaches us to say both 'I believe' and 'We believe.'"[4]

We observed just now that the analysis of the act of faith immediately displays faith's essential content, as well: faith is a response to the triune God: the Father, the Son, and the Holy Spirit. We can now add that the same act of faith also embraces God's incarnation in Jesus Christ, his theandric mystery, and thus the entirety of salvation history. It further becomes clear that the People of God, the church as the human protagonist of salvation history, is present in the very act of faith. It would not be difficult to demonstrate in a similar fashion that the other items of belief are also explications of the one fundamental act of encountering the living God. For by its very nature, relation to God has to do with eternal life. And this relation necessarily transcends the merely human sphere. God is truly God only if he is the Lord of all things. And he is the Lord of all things only if he is their Creator. Creation, salvation history, and eternal life are thus themes that flow directly from the question of God. In addition, when we speak of God's history with man, we also imply the issue of sin and grace. We touch upon the question of how we encounter God, hence, the question of the liturgy, of the sacraments, of prayer and morality. But I do not want to develop all of these points in detail now; my chief concern has been precisely to get a glimpse of the intrinsic unity of faith, which is not a multitude of propositions but a full and simple act whose simplicity contains the whole depth and breadth of being. He who speaks of God speaks of the whole; he learns to discern the essential from the inessential, and he comes to know, albeit only fragmentarily and "in a glass, darkly" (1 Cor 13:12) as long as faith is faith and not yet vision, something of the inner logic and unity of all reality.

Finally, I would like to touch briefly on the question we mentioned at the beginning of our reflections. I mean the question of how we believe. Paul furnishes us with a remarkable and extremely helpful statement on this matter when he says that faith is an obedience "from the heart to the form of doctrine into which you were handed over" (Rom 6:17). These words ultimately express the sacramental character of faith, the intrinsic connection between confession and sacrament. The apostle says that a "form of doctrine" is an essential component of faith. We do not think up faith on our own. It comes not from us as an idea of ours but to us as a word from outside. It is, as it were, a word about the Word; we are "handed over" into this Word, which reveals new paths to our reason and gives form to our life.

We are "handed over" into the Word that precedes us through an immersion in water, symbolizing death. This recalls the words of Paul cited earlier: "I live, yet not I"; it reminds us that what takes place in the act of faith is the destruction and renewal of the self. Baptism as a symbolic death links this renewal to the death and Resurrection of Jesus Christ. To be handed over into the doctrine is to be handed over into Christ. We cannot receive his word as a theory in the same way that we learn, say, mathematical formulas or philosophical opinions. We can learn it only in accepting a share in Christ's destiny. But we can become sharers in Christ's destiny only where he has permanently committed himself to sharing in man's destiny: in the church. In the language of this church, we call this event a "sacrament." The act of faith is unthinkable without the sacramental component.

These remarks enable us to understand the concrete literary structure of the *Catechism*. To believe, as we have heard, is to be handed over into a form of doctrine. In another passage, Paul calls this form of doctrine a confession (cf. Rom 10:9). A further aspect of the faith event thus emerges. That is, the faith that comes to us as a word must also become a word in us, a word that is simultaneously the expression of our life. To believe is always also to confess the faith. Faith is not private but something public that concerns the community. The word of faith first enters the mind, but it cannot stay there: thought must always become word and deed again.

The *Catechism* refers to the various kinds of confessions of faith that exist in the church: baptismal confessions, conciliar confessions, confessions formulated by popes.[5] Each of these confessions has a significance of its own, but the primordial type that serves as a basis for all further developments is the baptismal creed. When we talk about catechesis, that is, initiation into the faith and adaptation of our existence to the church's communion of faith, we must begin with the baptismal creed. This has been true since apostolic times, and it, therefore, imposed itself as the method of the *Catechism*, which, in fact, unfolds the contents of faith from the baptismal creed. It thus becomes apparent how the *Catechism* intends to teach the faith: catechesis is catechumenate. It is not merely religious instruction but also the act whereby we surrender ourselves and are received into the word of faith and communion with Jesus Christ. Adaptation to God's ways is an essential part of catechesis. St. Irenaeus says a propos of this that we must accustom ourselves to God, just as in the Incarnation God accustomed himself to us men. We must accustom ourselves to God's ways so that we can learn to bear his presence in us. Expressed in theological terms, this means that the image of God—which is what makes us capable of communion of life with him—must be freed from its encasement of dross. The tradition compares this liberation to the activity of the sculptor who chisels away at the stone bit by bit until the form that he beholds emerges into visibility.

Catechesis should always be such a process of assimilation to God. After all, we can only know a reality if there is something in us corresponding to it. Goethe, alluding to Plotinus, says that "the eye could never recognize the sun were it not itself sunlike."[6] The cognitional process is a process of assimilation, a vital process. The "we," the "what," and the "how" of faith belong together.

This brings to light the moral dimension of the act of faith, which includes a style of humanity we do not produce by ourselves, but which we gradually learn by plunging into our baptismal existence. The sacrament of penance is one such immersion into baptism, in which God again and again acts on us and draws us back to himself. Morality is an integral component of Christianity, but this morality is always part of the sacramental event of "Christianization" [Christwerdung]—an event in which we are not the sole agents but are always, indeed primarily, receivers. And this reception entails transformation.

The Catechism, therefore, cannot be accused of any fanciful attachment to the past when it unfolds the contents of faith using the baptismal creed of the church of Rome, the so-called "Apostles' Creed." Rather, this option brings to the fore the authentic core of the act of faith and thus of catechesis as existential training in existence with God.

Equally apparent is that the Catechism is wholly structured according to the principle of the hierarchy of truths as understood by the Second Vatican Council. For, as we have seen, the creed is in the first instance a confession of faith in the triune God developed from and bound to the baptismal formula. All of the "truths of faith" are explications of the one truth that we discover in them. And this one truth is the pearl of great price that is worth staking our lives on: God. He alone can be the pearl for which we give everything else. Dios solo basta[7]—he who finds God has found all things. But we can find him only because he has first sought and found us. He is the one who acts first, and for this reason faith in God is inseparable from the mystery of the Incarnation, of the church, and of the sacraments. Everything that is said in the Catechism is an unfolding of the one truth that is God himself—the "love that moves the sun and all the stars."[8]

Liberation Theology

PRELIMINARY NOTES

1. Liberation theology is a phenomenon with an extraordinary number of layers. There is a whole spectrum, from radically Marxist positions to the efforts that are being made within the framework of a correct and ecclesial theology, a theology that stresses the responsibility Christians necessarily bear for the poor and oppressed, as we see in the documents of the Latin American Bishops' Conference (CELAM) from Medellín to Puebla. In what follows, the concept of liberation theology will be understood in a narrower sense: it will refer only to those theologies that, in one way or another, have embraced the Marxist fundamental option. Here, too, there are many individual differences, which cannot be dealt with in a general discussion of this kind. All I can do is attempt to illuminate certain trends that are widespread, notwithstanding the different nuances they exhibit, and exert a certain influence even where liberation theology in this more restricted sense does not exist.

2. An analysis of the phenomenon of liberation theology reveals that it constitutes a fundamental threat to the faith of the church. At the same time it must be borne in mind that no error could persist unless it contained a grain of truth. Indeed, an error is all the more dangerous the greater that grain of truth is, for then the temptation it exerts is all the greater.

Furthermore, the error concerned would not have been able to wrench that piece of the truth to its own use if that truth had been adequately lived and witnessed to in its proper place (in the faith of the church). So, in denouncing error and pointing to dangers in liberation theology, we must always be ready to ask what truth is latent in the error and how it can be given its rightful place, how it can be released from error's monopoly.

3. Liberation theology is a universal phenomenon in three ways:

a. It does not intend to add a new theological treatise to those already existing; that is, it does not wish to develop new aspects of the church's social ethics. Rather it sees itself as a new hermeneutics of the Christian faith, a new way of understanding Christianity as a whole and implementing it. Thus it affects theology in its basic constitution, not merely in aspects of its content. So, too, it alters all forms of church life: the church's constitution, liturgy, catechesis, moral options.

b. While liberation theology today has its center of gravity in Latin America, it is by no means an exclusively Latin American phenomenon. It is unthinkable apart from the governing influence of European and North American theologians. But it is also found in India, Sri Lanka, the Philippines, Taiwan, and Africa, though in the latter case the search for an "African theology" is in the foreground. The Union of Third World Theologians is strongly characterized by an emphasis on the themes of liberation theology.

c. Liberation theology goes beyond denominational borders: from its own starting point it frequently tries to create a new universality for which the classical church divisions are supposed to have become irrelevant.

I. The Concept of Liberation Theology and Its Origins and Preconditions

These preliminary remarks have brought us right to the heart of the subject, without, however, dealing with the central question: what is liberation theology? Initially we said that liberation theology intends to supply a new total interpretation of the Christian reality; it explains Christianity as a praxis of liberation and sees itself as the guide to this praxis. However, since in its view all reality is political, liberation is also a political concept and the guide to liberation must be a guide to political action: "Nothing lies outside ... political commitment. Everything has a political color." A theology that is not "practical"—that is, not essentially political—is regarded as "idealistic" and thus lacking in reality, or else it is condemned as a vehicle for the oppressors' maintenance of power.

A theologian who has learned his theology in the classical tradition and has accepted its spiritual challenge will find it hard to realize that an attempt is being made, in all seriousness, to recast the whole Christian reality in the categories of politico-social liberation praxis. This is all the more difficult because many liberation theologians continue to use a great deal of the church's classical ascetical and dogmatic language while changing its signification. As a result, the reader or listener who is operating from a different background can gain the impression that everything is the same as before, apart from the addition of a few somewhat unpalatable statements, which, given so much spirituality, can scarcely be all that dangerous.

The very radicalness of liberation theology means that its seriousness is often underestimated, since it does not fit into any of the accepted categories of heresy; its fundamental concern cannot be detected by the existing range of standard questions. I would like to try, therefore, to approach the basic orientation of liberation theology in two steps: first by saying something about its presuppositions, which make it possible, and then by referring to some of its basic concepts, which reveal something of its structure.

What could have led to that complete new orientation of theological thought that is expressed in liberation theology? In the main I see three factors that made it possible.

1. After the council a new theological situation had arisen, characterized by three assertions:

a. The view arose that the existing theological tradition was largely no longer adequate, and that as a result, an entirely new theological and spiritual orientation needed to be sought directly from scripture and from the signs of the times.

b. The idea of a turning to the world, of responsibility for the world, frequently deteriorated into a naïve belief in science that accepted the human sciences as a new gospel without wanting to see their limitations and endemic problems. Psychology, sociology, and the Marxist interpretation of history seemed to be scientifically established and hence to become unquestionable arbiters of Christian thought.

c. The criticism of tradition applied by modern Evangelical exegesis, in particular by Rudolf Bultmann and his school, similarly became a firm theological authority, cutting off the path to theology in its prior form and so encouraging people all the more to produce new constructions.

2. This changed theological situation coincided with a changed intellectual situation. At the end of the phase of reconstruction after the Second World War, which corresponded roughly to the end of the council, a tangible vacuum of meaning had arisen in the Western world to which the still dominant existentialist philosophy could give no answer. In this situation the various brands of neo-Marxism became a moral impulse, holding out a promise of meaning that was practically irresistible to the academic youth. Bloch's Marxism, with its religious veneer, and the strictly scientific appearance of the philosophies of Adorno, Horkheimer, Habermas, and Marcuse offered models of action by which people believed they could respond to the moral challenge of misery in the world and seize the proper meaning of the biblical message.

3. The moral challenge of poverty and oppression presented itself in an ineluctable form at the very moment when Europe and North America had attained a hitherto unknown affluence. This challenge evidently called for new answers, which were not to be found in the existing tradition. The changed theological and philosophical situation was a formal invitation to seek the

answer in a Christianity that allowed itself to be guided by the models of hope—apparently scientifically grounded—put forward by Marxist philosophies.

II. The Basic Structure of Liberation Theology

This answer takes very different shapes, depending on the particular form of liberation theology, theology of revolution, political theology, and so on. No overall description can be given, therefore. Yet there are certain basic concepts that recur in various modifications and express fundamental intentions held in common.

Before examining the content of these basic concepts we must make an observation concerning the cardinal structural elements of liberation theology, taking up what we have already said about the changed theological situation in the wake of the council. As I explained, the exegesis of Bultmann and his school now came to be read as the verdict of "science" on Jesus, a verdict that simply had to be accepted as valid. But Bultmann's "historical Jesus" is separated from the Christ of faith by a great gulf (Bultmann himself speaks of a "chasm"). In Bultmann, though Jesus is part of the presuppositions of the New Testament, he himself is enclosed in the world of Judaism.

Now the crucial result of this exegesis was to shatter the historical credibility of the Gospels: the Christ of the church's tradition and the Jesus of history put forward by science evidently belong to two different worlds. Science, regarded as the final arbiter, had torn the figure of Jesus from its anchorage in tradition; on the one hand, consequently, tradition hangs in a vacuum, deprived of reality, while on the other hand, a new interpretation and significance must be sought for the figure of Jesus.

Bultmann's importance, therefore, was less because of his positive discoveries than because of the negative result of his criticism: the core of faith, Christology, was open to new interpretations because its previous affirmations had perished as being historically no longer tenable. It also meant that the church's teaching office was discredited, since she had evidently clung to a scientifically untenable theory, and thus ceased to be regarded as an authority where knowledge of Jesus was concerned. In the future her statements could only be seen as futile attempts to defend a position that was scientifically obsolete.

Another key word made Bultmann important for future developments. He had reinstated the old concept of hermeneutics and given it a new thrust. The word *hermeneutics* expresses the insight that a real understanding of historical texts does not come about by mere historical interpretation and, indeed, that every historical interpretation already includes certain prior decisions. Once the historical material has been established, it is the task of hermeneutics to "actualize" scripture. In classical terminology, it is to "dissolve the horizon" between then and now. It asks the question: what significance do these past events hold for today? Bultmann himself had answered this question with the help of Heidegger's philosophy and had interpreted the Bible in a correspondingly existentialist manner. This answer attracted no interest then, nor does it now; to that extent Bultmann has been superseded in the exegesis currently acceptable. Yet what has remained is the abstraction of the figure of Jesus from the classical tradition, as well as the idea that, using a new hermeneutics, we can and must bring this figure into the present in a new way.

At this point we come to the second element of our situation, to which we have already referred: the new philosophical climate of the late sixties. In the meantime, the Marxist analysis of history and society was largely accepted as the only "scientific" one. This means that the world must be interpreted in terms of the class struggle and that the only choice is between capitalism and Marxism. It also means that all reality is political and has to justify itself politically. The biblical concept of the "poor" provides a starting point for fusing the Bible's view of history with Marxist dialectic; it is interpreted by the idea of the proletariat in the Marxist sense and thus justifies Marxism as the legitimate hermeneutics for understanding the Bible.

Since, according to this view, there are and can only be two options, any objection to this interpretation of the Bible is an expression of the ruling class's determination to hold on to its power. A well-known liberation theologian asserts: "The class struggle is a fact; neutrality on this point is simply impossible."

This approach also takes the ground from under the feet of the church's teaching office: if she were to intervene and proceed against such an interpretation of Christianity, she would only prove that she is on the side of the rich and the rulers against the poor and suffering—that is, against Jesus himself: she would show that she had taken the negative side in the dialectic of history.

This decision, apparently unavoidable in "scientific" and "historical" terms, automatically determines how Christianity shall be interpreted in the future, as regards both the activities of this interpretation and its content.

As far as the arbiters are concerned, the crucial concepts are people, community, experience, and history. Previously it was the church, namely the Catholic Church in her totality—a totality that spanned time and space and embraced laity (*sensus fidei*) and hierarchy (magisterium)—that constituted the hermeneutical criterion; now it is the "community." The experience of the "community" determines the understanding and the interpretation of scripture.

Again it can be said, in a way that seems strictly scientific, that the Gospels' picture of Jesus is itself a synthesis of event and interpretation based on the experience of the individual communities, in which interpretation was far more important than the no longer ascertainable event.

This original synthesis of event and interpretation can be dissolved and reformed continually: the community "interprets" the events on the basis of its "experience" and thus discovers what its "praxis" should be. The same idea appears in a somewhat modified form in connection with the concept of the people, where the conciliar emphasis on the "People of God" is transformed into a Marxist myth. The experiences of the "people" elucidate scripture. Here *people* is the antithesis of the hierarchy, the antithesis of all institutions, which are seen as oppressive power. Ultimately anyone who participates in the class struggle is a member of the "people," and the "church of the people" becomes the antagonist of the hierarchical church.

Finally the concept of history becomes a crucial interpretative category. The view, accepted as scientifically certain and incontrovertible, that the Bible speaks exclusively in terms of salvation history (and thus, antimetaphysically), facilitates the fusing of the biblical horizon with the Marxist idea of history, which progresses in a dialectical manner and is the real bringer of salvation. History is accordingly a process of progressive liberation; history is the real revelation and hence the real interpreter of the Bible. Sometimes this dialectic of progress is supported by pneumatology. In any case the latter also makes a teaching office that insists on abiding truths into an authority inimical to progress, thinking "metaphysically" and hence contradicting "history." We can say that the concept of history swallows up the concepts of God and Revelation. The "historicality" of the Bible must justify its absolute dominance and thus legitimize the transition to materialist-Marxist philosophy, in which history has taken over the role of God.

III. Central Concepts of Liberation Theology

So we have arrived at the basic concepts of the new interpretation of Christian reality. Since the individual concepts occur in different contexts, I will simply discuss them one after another, without any systematization. Let us begin with the new meaning of faith, hope, and love. Concerning faith, one South American theologian says, for instance, that Jesus's experience of God is radically historical. "His faith is transformed into fidelity." Thus faith is fundamentally replaced by "fidelity to history." Here we see that fusion between God and history which makes it possible to keep the Chalcedonian formula for Jesus, albeit with a totally changed meaning: it is clear that the classical tests for orthodoxy are of no avail in analyzing this theology. It is asserted "that Jesus is God, but it is immediately added that the true and only God is he who reveals himself historically and as a stumbling block in Jesus, and in the poor who prolong his presence. Only the person who holds together these two affirmations is orthodox."

Hope is interpreted as "confidence in the future" and working for the future, and thus is subordinated once more to the history of class conflict.

Love consists in the "option for the poor"; that is, it coincides with opting for the class struggle. In opposition to "false universalism," the liberation theologians emphasize very strongly the partiality and partisan nature of the Christian option; in their view, taking sides is the fundamental presupposition for a correct hermeneutics of the biblical testimony. Here, I think, one can see very clearly that amalgam between a basic truth of Christianity and an un-Christian fundamental option that makes the whole thing so seductive: the Sermon on the Mount is indeed God taking sides with the poor. But to interpret the "poor" in the sense of the Marxist dialectic of history and "taking sides with them" in the sense of the class struggle is a wanton attempt to portray as identical things that are contrary.

The fundamental concept of the preaching of Jesus is the "Kingdom of God." This concept is also at the center of the liberation theologies, but read against the background of Marxist hermeneutics. According to one of these theologians, the kingdom must not be understood in a spiritualist or universalist manner, not in the sense of an abstract eschatological eventuality. It must be understood in partisan terms and with a view to praxis. The meaning of the kingdom can only be defined by reference to the praxis of Jesus, not theoretically: it means working at the historical reality that surrounds us in order to transform it into the kingdom.

Here we must mention another basic idea of a particular postconciliar theology that has led in this direction. People said that after the council every dualism must be overcome: the dualism of body and soul, of natural and supernatural, of this world and the world beyond, of then and now. Once these supposed dualisms had been eliminated, it only remained to work for a kingdom to be realized in present history and in politico-economic reality. This meant, however, that one had ceased to work for the benefit of people in this present time and had begun to destroy the present in the interests of a supposed future: thus the real dualism had broken loose.

In this connection I would like to mention the interpretation of death and resurrection given by one of the leading liberation theologians. First of all he once again opposes "universalist" conceptions by asserting that resurrection is in the first place a hope for those who are crucified, who make up the majority of men: all the millions who are subjected to a slow crucifixion by structural injustice. But faith also participates in Jesus's lordship over history by setting up the kingdom, that is, by fighting for justice and integral liberation, by transforming unjust structures into more human ones. This lordship over history is exercised by repeating in history the gesture by which God raised Jesus—that is, by giving life to those who are crucified in history. Man has taken over God's gesture—this manifests the whole transformation of the biblical message in an almost tragic way, when one thinks how this attempted imitation of God has worked out in practice and continues to do so.

As to other reinterpretations of biblical concepts: the Exodus becomes the central image of salvation history; the paschal mystery is understood as a revolutionary symbol, and consequently the Eucharist is interpreted as a celebration of liberation in the sense of politico-messianic hope and praxis. The word *redemption* is largely replaced by *liberation,* which is seen, against the background of history and the class struggle, as a process of progressive liberation. Absolutely fundamental, finally, is the stress on praxis: truth must not be understood metaphysically, for that would be "idealism." Truth is realized in history and its praxis. Action is truth. Hence even the ideas that are employed in such action are ultimately interchangeable. Praxis is the sole deciding factor. The only true orthodoxy is therefore orthopraxy. It follows that the biblical texts can be treated more loosely, for historical criticism has loosed scripture from the traditional interpretation, which now appears to be unscientific. Tradition itself is treated with the greatest possible scientific strictness, along the lines of Bultmann. But as for the historically transmitted content of the Bible, it cannot be exclusively binding. Ultimately, what is normative for interpretation is not historical research but the hermeneutic of history experienced in the community or the political group.

In trying to arrive at an overall evaluation, it must be said that if one accepts the fundamental assumptions that underlie liberation theology, it cannot be denied that the whole edifice has an almost irresistible logic. By adopting the position of biblical criticism and a hermeneutics that grows through experience, on the one hand, and of the Marxist analysis of history, on the other, liberation theologians have succeeded in creating a total picture of Christian reality, and this total view seems to respond fully both to the claims of science and to the moral challenges of our time, urging people to make Christianity an instrument of concrete world transformation; it seems to have united Christianity, in this way, with all the "progressive forces" of our era. One can understand, therefore, that this new interpretation of Christianity should have exercised an increasing fascination over theologians, priests, and religious, particularly against the background of Third World problems.

To say "no" to it must seem to them to be a flight from reality as well as a denial of reason and morality. On the other hand, if one considers how radical this reinterpretation of Christianity is, it is all the more pressing to find the right answer to the challenge it presents. We shall survive this crisis only if we succeed in making the logic of faith visible in an equally compelling manner and in presenting it as a logic of reality, that is, manifesting the concrete force of a better answer attested in lived experience. Since it is so, since thought and experience, interpretation and realization are equally called for, it is a task for the whole church. Theology alone is insufficient; church authority alone is insufficient. Since the phenomenon of liberation theology indicates a lack of conversion in the church, a lack of radical faith, only an increase in conversion and faith can arouse and elicit those theological insights and decisions on the part of the shepherds that will give an answer to the magnitude of the question.

Relativism: The Central Problem for Faith Today

Address to the Presidents of the Doctrinal Commissions of the Bishops' Conferences of Latin America

GUADALAJARA, MEXICO, MAY 1996

In the 1980s, the theology of liberation in its radical forms seemed to be the most urgent challenge to the faith of the church. It was a challenge that required both a response and a clarification because it proposed a new, plausible, and at the same time practical response to the fundamental question of Christianity: namely, the problem of redemption.

The very word *liberation* was used to explain in a different and more understandable way that which in the traditional language of the church was called "redemption." In fact, in the background there is always the same observation: We experience a world that does not correspond to a good God. Poverty, oppression, all kinds of unjust domination, the suffering of the just and the innocent constitute the signs of the times and of all times. And we all suffer: no one can readily say to this world and to his or her own life, "Stay as you are, you are so beautiful." From this the theology of liberation deduced that the situation, which must not continue, could only be overcome through a radical change in the structures of this world, which are structures of sin and evil. If sin exerts its power over the structures and impoverishment is programmed beforehand by them, then its overthrow will come about not through individual conversions but through struggle against the structures of injustice. It was said, however, that this struggle ought to be political because the structures are consolidated and preserved through politics. Redemption thus became a political process for which Marxist philosophy provided the essential guidelines. It was transformed into a task that people themselves could and even had to take into their own hands, and at the same time it became a totally practical hope: faith, in theory, became praxis, concrete redeeming action, in the process of liberation.

The fall of the European governmental systems based on Marxism turned out to be a kind of twilight of the gods for that theology of redeeming political praxis. Precisely in those places where the Marxist liberating ideology had been applied consistently, a radical lack of freedom had been produced, the horror of which now appeared out in the open before the eyes of world public opinion. The fact is that when politics are used to bring redemption, they promise too much. When they presume to do God's work, they become not divine but diabolical.

For this reason, the political events of 1989 have also changed the theological scenario. Until then, Marxism had been the last attempt to provide a universally valid formula for the right configuration of historical action. Marxism believed it knew the structure of world history, and from there it tried to show how history could be led definitively along the right path. The fact that the presumption was based on what was apparently a strictly scientific method that totally substituted science for faith and made science the praxis gave it a strong appeal. All the unfulfilled promises of religions seemed attainable through a scientifically based political praxis.

The nonfulfillment of this hope brought a great disillusionment with it, which is still far from being assimilated. Therefore, it seems probable to me that new forms of the Marxist conception of the world will appear in the future. For the moment, we cannot but be perplexed: the failure of the only scientifically based system for solving human problems could only justify nihilism or, at the least, total relativism.

RELATIVISM: THE PREVAILING PHILOSOPHY

Relativism has thus become the central problem for the faith at the present time. No doubt it is not presented only with its aspects of resignation before the immensity of the truth. It is also presented as a position defined positively by the concepts of tolerance and knowledge through dialogue and freedom, concepts that would be limited if the existence of one valid truth for all were affirmed.

In turn, relativism appears to be the philosophical foundation of democracy. Democracy, in fact, is supposedly built on the basis that no one can presume to know the true way, and it is enriched by the fact that all roads are mutually recognized as fragments of the effort toward that which is better. Therefore, all roads seek something common in dialogue, and they also compete regarding knowledge that cannot be compatible in one common form. A system of freedom ought to be essentially a system of positions that are connected with one another because they are relative, as well as being dependent on historical situations open to new developments. Therefore, a liberal society would be a relativist society: only with that condition could it continue to be free and open to the future.

In the area of politics, this concept is considerably right. There is no one correct political opinion. What is relative—the building up of liberally ordained coexistence between people—cannot be absolute. Thinking in this way was precisely the error of Marxism and the political theologies.

However, with total relativism, everything in the political area cannot be achieved, either. There are injustices that will never turn into just things (such as, for example, killing an innocent person, denying an individual or groups the right to their dignity or to life corresponding to that dignity), while, at the same time, there are just things that can never be unjust. Therefore, although a certain right to relativism in the social and political area should not be denied, the problem is raised at the moment of setting its limits. There has also been the desire to apply this method in a totally conscious way in the area of religion and ethics. I will now try to briefly outline the developments that define the theological dialogue today on this point.

The so-called pluralist theology of religion has been developing progressively since the 1950s. Nonetheless, only now has it come to the center of the Christian conscience.[1] In some ways this conquest occupies today—with regard to the force of its problematic aspect and its presence in the different areas of culture—the place occupied by the theology of liberation in the preceding decade. Moreover, it joins in many ways with it and tries to give it a new, updated form. Its means and methods are varied; therefore, it is not possible to synthesize it into one short formula or present its essential characteristics briefly. On the one hand, relativism is a typical offshoot of the Western world and its forms of philosophical thought, while on the other it is connected with the philosophical and religious intuitions of Asia especially and, surprisingly, with those of the Indian subcontinent. Contact between these two worlds gives it a particular impulse at the present historical moment.

RELATIVISM IN THEOLOGY:
THE ATTENUATION OF CHRISTOLOGY

The situation can be clearly seen in one of its founders and eminent representatives, the American Presbyterian John Hick. His philosophical departure point is found in the Kantian distinction between phenomenon and noumenon: We can never grasp ultimate truth in itself, but only its appearance in our way of perceiving through different "lenses." What we grasp is not really and properly reality in itself but a reflection on our scale.

At first Hick tried to formulate this concept in a Christ-centered context. After a year's stay in India, he transformed it—after what he himself calls a Copernican turn of thought—into a new form of theocentrism. The identification of only one historical person, Jesus of Nazareth, with what is "real," the living God, is now relegated as a relapse into myth. Jesus is consciously relativized as one religious leader among others. The Absolute cannot come into history, but only models and ideal forms that remind us of what can never be grasped as such in history. Therefore, concepts such as the *church, dogma,* and *sacraments* must lose their unconditional character. To make an absolute of such limited forms of mediation or, even more, to consider them real encounters with the universally valid truth of God who reveals himself would be the same as elevating oneself to the category of the Absolute, thereby losing the infiniteness of the totally other God.

From this point of view, which is present not only in the works of Hick but also in other authors, affirming that there is a binding and valid truth in history in the figure of Jesus Christ and the faith of the church is described as fundamentalism. Such fundamentalism, which constitutes the real attack on the spirit of modernity, is presented in different ways as the fundamental threat emerging against the supreme good of modernity: tolerance and freedom.

On the other hand, the notion of *dialogue*—which has maintained a position of significant importance in the Platonic and Christian traditions— changes meaning and becomes both the quintessence of the relativist creed and the antithesis of conversion and the mission. In the relativist meaning, *to dialogue* means to put one's own position, that is, one's faith, on the same level as the convictions of others, without recognizing in principle more truth in it than that which is attributed to the opinion of the others. Only if I suppose in principle that the other can be as right or more right than I am, can an authentic dialogue take place.

According to this concept, dialogue must be an exchange between positions that have fundamentally the same rank and therefore are mutually relative.

Only in this way will the maximum cooperation and integration between the different religions be achieved.[2] The relativist dissolution of Christology, and even more of ecclesiology, thus becomes a central commandment of religion. To return to Hick's thinking, faith in the divinity of one concrete person, as he tell us, leads to fanaticism and particularism, to the dissociation between faith and love, and it is precisely this which must be overcome.[3]

RECOURSE TO ASIAN RELIGIONS

In the thinking of Hick, whom we are considering here as an eminent representative of religious relativism, there is a strange closeness between Europe's postmetaphysical philosophy and Asia's negative theology. For the latter, the divine can never enter unveiled into the world of appearances in which we live; it always manifests itself in relative reflections and remains beyond all worlds and notions in an absolute transcendence.[4]

The two philosophies are fundamentally different both in their departure point and in the orientation they imprint on human existence. Nonetheless, they seem to mutually confirm one another in their metaphysical and religious relativism. The a-religious and pragmatic relativism of Europe and America can get a kind of religious consecration from India, which seems to give its renunciation of dogma the dignity of a greater respect before the mystery of God and man.

In turn, the support of European and American thought to the philosophical and theological vision of India reinforces the relativism of all the religious forms proper to the Indian heritage. In this way it also seems necessary to Christian theology in India to set aside the image of Christ from its exclusive position—which is considered typically Western—in order to place it on the same level as the Indian saving myths. The historical Jesus—it is now thought—is no more the absolute Logos than any other saving figure of history.[5]

Under the sign of the encounter of cultures, relativism appears to be the real philosophy of humanity. As we pointed out earlier, this fact, both in the East and the West, visibly gives it a strength before which it seems that there is no room for any resistance.

Anyone who resists not only opposes democracy and tolerance—the basic imperatives of the human community—but also persists obstinately in giving priority to one's Western culture and thus rejects the encounter of cultures, which is well known to be the imperative of the present moment. Those who want to stay with the faith of the Bible and the church see themselves pushed from the start to a no-man's-land on the cultural level and must as a first measure rediscover the "madness of God" (1 Cor 1:18) to recognize the true wisdom in it.

ORTHODOXY AND ORTHOPRAXIS

In order to help us in this effort to penetrate the hidden wisdom contained in the madness of the faith, it will be good for us to try to know better the relativist theory of Hick's religion and discover where it leads man. In the end, for Hick, religion means that man goes from "self-centeredness," the existence of the old Adam, to "reality-centeredness," the existence of the new man, thus extending from oneself to the otherness of one's neighbor.[6] It sounds beautiful, but when it is considered in depth it is as empty and vacuous as the call to authenticity proposed by Bultmann, who, in turn, had taken that concept from Heidegger. For this, religion is not necessary.

Aware of these limits, the former Catholic priest Paul Knitter tried to overcome the void of a theory of religion reduced to the categorical imperative by means of a new synthesis between Asia and Europe that should be more concrete and internally enriched.[7] His proposal gives religion a new concrete expression by joining the theology of pluralist religion with the theologies of liberation. Interreligious dialogue must be simplified radically and become practically effective by basing it on only one principle: "the primacy of orthopraxis with regard to orthodoxy."[8]

Putting praxis above knowledge in this way is also a clearly Marxist inheritance. However, whereas Marxism makes only what comes logically from renouncing metaphysics concrete—when knowledge is impossible, only action is left—Knitter affirms: the absolute cannot be known, but it can be made. The question is why? Where do I find a just action if I cannot know what is just in an absolute way? The failure of the communist regimes is due precisely to the fact that they tried to change the world without knowing what is good and what is not good for the world, without knowing in what direction the world must be changed in order to make it better. Mere praxis is not light.

This is the moment for a critical examination of the notion of orthopraxis. The previous history of religion had shown that the religions of India did not have an orthodoxy in general, but rather an orthopraxis. From there the notion probably entered into modern theology. However, in the description of the religions of India this had a very precise meaning: it meant that those religions did not have a general, compulsory catechism, and belonging to them was not defined by the acceptance of a particular creed. On the other hand, those religions have a system of ritual acts that they consider necessary for salvation and that distinguish a "believer" from a "nonbeliever."

In those religions, a believer is recognized not by certain knowledge but by scrupulous observance of a ritual that embraces the whole of life. The meaning of *orthopraxis*, right acting, is determined with great precision: it is a code of rituals. On the other hand, the word *orthodoxy* originally had almost the same meaning in the early church and in the Eastern churches. In the suffix *doxia, doxa* was not understood in the sense of "opinion" (real opinion). From the Greek viewpoint, opinions are always relative; *doxa* was understood rather in its meaning of "glory, glorification." To be *orthodox* thus meant to know and practice the right way in which God wants to be glorified. It refers to the cult and, based on the cult, to life. In this sense here there would be a solid point for a fruitful dialogue between East and West.

But let us return to the meaning of the term *orthopraxis* in modern theology. No one thinks any longer about following a ritual. The word has taken on a new meaning that has nothing to do with the authentic Indian concept. To tell the truth, something does remain from it: if the requirement of orthopraxis has a meaning and does not wish to be the lid over its not being obligatory, then a common praxis must also be given that is recognizable by all, which surpasses the general wordiness of "centering on self" and "reference to another." If the ritual meaning given to it in Asia is excluded, praxis can only be understood as *ethics* or *politics*. In the first case, orthopraxis would imply an *ethos* that is clearly defined with regard to its content. This is no doubt excluded in the relativist ethical discussion since there is no longer anything good or evil in itself.

However, if orthopraxis is understood in a social and political sense, it again raises the question of the nature of correct political action. The theologies of liberation, animated by the conviction that Marxism clearly points out to us what good political praxis is, could use the notion of orthopraxis in its proper sense. In this case it was not a question of being obligatory; instead, a form was set down for everyone defining correct practice, or *orthopra*, which brought the community together and distinguished it from those who rejected the correct way of acting. To this extent, the Marxist theologies of liberation were, in their own way, logical and consistent.

As we can see, however, this kind of orthopraxis rests on a certain orthodoxy—in the modern sense: a framework of obligatory theories regarding the path to freedom. Knitter is close to this principle when he affirms that the criterion for differentiating orthopraxis from pseudopraxis is freedom.[9] Nonetheless, he still has to explain to us in a convincing and practical way what freedom is and what the purpose of real human liberation is: surely not Marxist orthopraxis, as we have seen. Nonetheless, something is clear: the relativist theories all flow into a state of not being obligatory, and thus become superfluous, or else they presume to have an absolute standard that is not found in the praxis, by elevating it to an absolutism that really has no place. Actually, it is a fact that in Asia concepts of the theology of liberation are also proposed today as forms of Christianity that are presumably more suitable to the Asian spirit, and they place the nucleus of religious action in the political sphere. When mystery no longer counts, politics must be converted into religion. And there is no doubt that this is deeply opposed to the original Asian religious vision.

NEW AGE

The relativism of Hick, Knitter, and related theorists is ultimately based on a rationalism which declares that reason—in the Kantian meaning—is incapable of metaphysical cognition.[10] The new foundation of religion comes about by following a pragmatic path with more ethical or political overtones. However, there is also a consciously antirationalist response to the experience of the slogan "Everything is relative," which comes together under the pluriform denomination *New Age*.[11]

For the supporters of the New Age, the solution to the problem of relativity must be sought not in a new encounter of the self with another or others but by overcoming the subject in an ecstatic return to the cosmic dance. Like the old gnosis, this way pretends to be totally attuned to all the results of science and to be based on all kinds of scientific knowledge (biology, psychology, sociology, physics). But on the basis of this presupposition, it offers at the same time a considerably antirationalist model of religion, a modern "mystic": the Absolute is not to be believed but to be experienced. God is not a person to be distinguished from the world but a spiritual energy present in the universe. Religion means the harmony of myself with the cosmic whole, the overcoming of all separations.

K. H. Menke characterizes very well this change in history that is taking place, when he states: "The subject that wanted to submit everything to himself now wants to be placed into 'the whole.'"[12] Objective reason closes off the path for us to the mystery of reality; the self isolates us from the richness of cosmic reality, destroys the harmony of the whole, and is the real cause of our unredemption. Redemption is found in unbridling of the self, immersion in the exuberance of that which is living, and a return to the Whole. Ecstasy is sought; the inebriety of the infinite, which can be experienced in inebriating music, rhythm, dance, frenetic lights and dark shadows, and the human mass.

This is renouncing not only modernity but man himself. The gods return. They have become more believable than God. The primitive rites, in which the self is initiated into the mystery of the Whole and liberated from itself, must be renewed.

There are many explanations for the re-editing of pre-Christian religions and cultures that is attempted frequently today. If there is no common truth in force precisely because it is true, then Christianity is only something imported from outside, a spiritual imperialism that must be thrown off with no less force than political imperialism. If no contact with the living God of all men takes place in the sacraments, then they are empty rituals, which tell us nothing and give us nothing. At most, they let us perceive what is numinous, which prevails in all religions.

Even in that case it seems more sensible to look for what is originally one's own instead of letting something alien and antiquated be imposed upon oneself. Above all, if the "sober inebriety" of the Christian mystery cannot elevate us to God, then we must seek the true inebriety of real ecstasies, whose passion sweeps us away and transforms us—at least for a moment—into gods and lets us perceive for a moment the pleasure of the infinite and forget the misery of the finite. The more manifest the uselessness of political absolutism, the stronger the attraction will be to what is irrational and to the renunciation of the reality of everyday life.[13]

PRAGMATISM IN THE CHURCH'S DAILY LIFE

Together with these radical solutions and the great pragmatism of the theologies of liberation, there is also the gray pragmatism of the daily life of the church, in which everything apparently continues normally, but in reality the faith is being consumed and falling into meanness. I am thinking of two phenomena that I consider with concern.

First, there is the intention, with different degrees of intensity, to extend the principle of the majority to the faith and customs, in order to ultimately "democratize" the church in a decisive way. What does not seem obvious to the majority cannot be obligatory. This is what seems to be. But which majority? Will there be a majority tomorrow like the one today? A faith that we ourselves can decide about is not a faith in the absolute. And no minority has any reason to let faith be imposed on it by a majority.

The faith, together with its praxis, either comes to us from the Lord through his church and the sacramental ministry or it does not exist in the absolute. The abandonment of the faith by many is based on the fact that it seems to them that the faith should be decided by some requests, which would be like a kind of party program: whoever has power decides what must be part of the faith. Therefore, it is important within the church itself to arrive at power or, on the contrary—which is more logical and obvious—to not believe.

The other point to which I wished to draw your attention refers to the liturgy. The different phases of liturgical reform have let the opinion be introduced that the liturgy can be changed arbitrarily. From being something unchangeable in any case, it is a question of the words of consecration; all the rest could be changed.

The following thinking is logical: if a central authority can do this, why not a local one? And if the local ones can do this, why not the community itself? Community should be expressed and come together in the liturgy. Following the rationalist and puritanical tendency of the 1970s and even the 1980s, today there is weariness with the pure, spoken liturgy, and a living liturgy is sought that does not delay in coming closer to the New Age tendencies: the inebriating and ecstatic is sought, and not the *logike latreia*, the *rationabilis oblatio* about which Paul speaks and with him the Roman liturgy (cf. Rom 12:1).

I admit that I am exaggerating. What I am saying does not describe the normal situation of our communities. But the tendencies are there. For this reason, vigilance is required so that a gospel will not be surreptitiously introduced to us—a stone instead of bread—different from the one that the Lord gave us.

TASKS OF THEOLOGY

We find ourselves, all told, in a unique situation. The theology of liberation tried to give Christianity, which was tired of dogmas, a new praxis whereby redemption would finally take place. But that praxis has left ruin in its aftermath instead of freedom. Relativism remains and the attempt to conform to it, but what it offers us is so empty that the relativist theories are looking for help from the theology of liberation in order to be able to put it into practice. The New Age says finally: it is better for us to leave the failed experiment of Christianity and return to the gods, because we live better in this way.

Many questions come up. Let us take the most practical one: why has classical theology appeared to be so defenseless in the face of these happenings? Where is its weak point, and why has it lost credibility?

I would like to mention two evident points in the writings of Hick and Knitter. Both authors, for their attenuated faith in Christ, refer to exegesis. They state that exegesis has proven that Jesus did not consider himself absolutely the Son of God, the incarnate God, but that he was made such afterward, in a gradual way, by his disciples.[14] Both Hick, in a clearer way, and

Knitter also refer to philosophical evidence. Hick assures us that Kant proved beyond dispute that what is absolute or the Absolute can neither be recognized in history nor appear in history as such.[15] Because of the structure of our cognition, what the Christian faith maintains cannot be, according to Kant. Therefore, miracles, mysteries, and sacraments are superstitions, as Kant clarifies for us in his work *Religion Within the Limits of Reason Alone*.[16]

It seems to me that the questions from exegesis and the limits and possibilities of our reason, that is, the philosophical premises of the faith, indicate, in fact, the crucial point of the crisis of contemporary theology whereby the faith—and more and more the faith of simple persons, as well—is heading toward crisis.

Now I would only like to outline the task before us. First, with regard to exegesis, let it be said from the outset that Hick and Knitter cannot be supported by exegesis in general, as if there were a clear result shared by all. This is impossible in historical research, which does not have this type of certainty, and it is even more impossible with regard to a question that is not purely historical or literary but includes value choices that go beyond a mere verification of the past and a mere interpretation of texts. However, it is certain that an overall glance at modern exegesis can leave an impression that is close to Hick's and Knitter's.

What type of certainty corresponds to this? Let us suppose—which can be doubted—that most exegetes think in this way. Nonetheless, the question still remains, To what point is that majority opinion grounded?

My thesis is the following: many exegetes think like Hick and Knitter and reconstruct the history of Jesus as they do because they share the same philosophy. It is not the exegesis that proves the philosophy, but the philosophy that generates the exegesis.[17] If I know a priori (to speak like Kant) that Jesus cannot be God and that miracles, mysteries, and sacraments are three forms of superstition, then I cannot discover what cannot be a fact in the sacred books. I can only describe why and how such affirmations were arrived at and how they were gradually formed.

Let us look at this more precisely. The historical-critical method is an excellent instrument for reading historical sources and interpreting texts. But it contains its own philosophy, which in general—for example, when I try to study the history of medieval emperors—is hardly important. And this is because in that case I want to know the past and nothing more. But even this cannot be done in a neutral way, and so there are also limits to the method.

But if it is applied to the Bible, two factors come clearly to light that would not be noted otherwise. First, the method wants to find about the past as something past. It wants to grasp with the greatest precision what happened at a past moment, closed in its past situation, at the point where it was found in time. Furthermore, it supposes that history is, in principle, uniform; therefore, man with all his differences and the world with all its distinctions are determined by the same laws and limitations, so that I can eliminate whatever is impossible. What cannot happen today in any way could not happen yesterday nor will it happen tomorrow.

If we apply this to the Bible, it means the following: a text, a happening, a person will be strictly fixed in his or her past. There is the desire to verify what the past author said at that time and what he could have said or thought. This is what is "historical" about the "past." Therefore, historical-critical exegesis does not bring the Bible to today, to my current life. This is impossible. On the contrary, it separates it from me and shows it strictly fixed in the past.

This is the point on which Drewermann rightly criticized historical-critical exegesis to the extent that it presumes to be self-sufficient. Such exegesis, by definition, expresses reality, not today's or mine, but yesterday's, another's reality. Therefore, it can never show the Christ of today, tomorrow, and always, but only—if it remains faithful to itself—the Christ of yesterday.

To this a second supposition must be added: the homogeneity of the world and history—that is, what Bultmann calls the modern image of the world. Michael Waldstein has shown through a careful analysis that Bultmann's theory of knowledge was totally influenced by the neo-Kantianism of Marburg.[18] Thanks to Marburg, he knew what could and could not exist. In other exegetes, the philosophical conscience is less pronounced, but the foundation based on the theory of Kantian cognition is always implicitly present as an unquestionable, hermeneutic access to criticism. This being as it is, the authority of the church can no longer impose from without that a Christology of divine filiation should be arrived at. But it can and must invite a critical examination of one's method.

In short, in the revelation of God, he, the living and true One, bursts into our world and also opens the prison of our theories, with whose nets we want to protect ourselves against God's coming into our lives. Thank God, in the midst of the current crisis of philosophy and theology, a new meaning of foundation has been set in motion in exegesis itself and, not in the last term, through knowledge attained from the careful historical interpretation of texts.[19] This helps break the prison of previous philosophical decisions that paralyze interpretation: the amplitude of the Word is opening up again.

The problem of exegesis is connected, as we have seen, with the problem of philosophy. The indigence of philosophy, the indigence to which paralyzed positivist reason has led itself, has turned into the indigence of our faith. The faith cannot be liberated if reason itself does not open up again. If the door to metaphysical cognition remains closed, if the limits of human knowledge set by Kant are impassable, faith is destined to atrophy: it simply lacks air to breathe.

When a strictly autonomous reason, which does not want to know anything about the faith, tries to get out of the bog of uncertainty "by pulling itself up by its hair," to express it in some way, it will be difficult for this effort to succeed. For human reason is not autonomous in the absolute. It is always found in a historical context. The historical context disfigures its vision (as we have seen). Therefore, it also needs historical assistance to help it cross over its historical barriers.[20]

I am of the opinion that neo-Scholastic rationalism failed because—with reason totally independent from faith—it tried to reconstruct the *pre-ambula fidei* with pure rational certainty. All attempts that presume to do the same will have the same result. Yes, Karl Barth was right to reject philosophy as a foundation of the faith independent from the faith. If it were such, our faith would be based from the beginning to the end on changing philosophical theories.

But Barth was wrong when, for this same reason, he proposed the faith as a pure paradox that can only exist against reason and totally independent from it. It is not the lesser function of the faith to care for reason as such. It does not do violence to it; it is not external to it; rather, it makes it come to itself. The historical instrument of the faith can again liberate reason as such, so that by introducing it to the path it can see by itself once again. We must make efforts toward a new dialogue of this kind between faith and philosophy because both need one another reciprocally. Reason will not be saved without the faith, but the faith without reason will not be human.

PERSPECTIVE

If we consider the present cultural situation, about which I have tried to give some indications, frankly it must seem a miracle that there is still Christian faith despite everything, and not only in the surrogate forms of Hick, Knitter, and others, but the complete, serene faith of the New Testament and of the church of all times.

Why, in brief, does the faith still have a chance? I would say the following: because it is in harmony with what man is. Man is something more than what Kant and the various post-Kantian philosophers wanted to see and concede. Kant himself must have recognized this in some way with his postulates.

In man there is an inextinguishable yearning for the infinite. None of the answers attempted are sufficient. Only the God who became finite in order to open our finiteness and lead us to the breadth of his infiniteness responds to the question of our being. For this reason, the Christian faith finds man today, too. Our task is to serve the faith with a humble spirit and the whole strength of our heart and understanding.

PART FIVE

SCRIPTURE

Biblical Interpretation in Crisis

On the Question of the Foundations and Approaches of Exegesis Today

ST. PETER'S CHURCH, NEW YORK CITY,
JANUARY 27, 1988

In Wladimir Solowjew's *History of the Antichrist,* the eschatological enemy of the Redeemer recommended himself to believers, among other things, by the fact that he had earned his doctorate in theology at Tübingen and had written an exegetical work that was recognized as pioneering in the field. The Antichrist, a famous exegete! With this paradox Solowjew sought to shed light on the ambivalence inherent in biblical exegetical methodology for almost a hundred years now. To speak of the crisis of the historical-critical method today is practically a truism. This, despite the fact that it had gotten off to so optimistic a start.

Within that newfound freedom of thought into which the Enlightenment had launched headlong, dogma or church doctrine appeared as one of the real impediments to a correct understanding of the Bible itself. But freed from this impertinent presupposition, and equipped with a methodology that promised strict objectivity, it seemed that we were finally going to be able to hear again the clear and unmistakable voice of the original message of Jesus. Indeed, what had been long forgotten was to be brought into the open once more: the polyphony of history could be heard again, rising from behind the monotone of traditional interpretations. As the human element in sacred history became more and more visible, the hand of God, too, seemed larger and closer.

Gradually, however, the picture became more and more confused. The theories increased and multiplied and separated one from the other and became a veritable fence that blocked access to the Bible for all the uninitiated. Those who were initiated were no longer reading the Bible anyway, but were dissecting it into the various parts from which it had to have been composed. The methodology itself seems to require such a radical approach: it cannot stand still when it "scents" the operation of man in sacred history. It must try to remove all the irrational residue and clarify everything. Faith itself is not a component of this method. Nor is God a factor to be dealt with in historical events. But since God and divine action permeate the entire biblical account of history, one is obliged to begin with a complicated anatomy of the scriptural word. On one hand there is the attempt to unravel the various threads (of the narrative) so that in the end one holds in one's hands what is the "really historical," which means the purely human element in events. On the other hand, one has to try to show how it happened that the idea of God became interwoven through it all. And so it is that another "real" history is to be fashioned in place of the one given. Underneath the existing sources—that is to say, the biblical books themselves—we are supposed to find more original sources, which, in turn, become the criteria for interpretation. No one should really be surprised that this procedure leads to the sprouting of ever more hypotheses until finally they turn into a jungle of contradictions. In the end, one no longer learns what the text says, but what it should have said, and by which component parts this can be traced back through the text.[1]

Such a state of affairs could not but generate a counterreaction. Cautious systematic theologians began a search for a theology that was as independent as possible from exegesis.[2] But what possible value can a theology have which is cut off from its own foundations? So it was that a radical approach called "fundamentalism" began to win supporters, who brand as false in itself and contradictory any application of the historical-critical method to the Word of God. They want to take the Bible again in its literal purity, just as it stands and just as the average reader understands it to be. But when do I really take the Bible "literally"? And which is the "normative" understanding that holds for the Bible in all its particularity? Certainly fundamentalism can take as a precedent the position of the Bible itself, which has selected as its own hermeneutical perspective the viewpoint of the "little ones," the "pure of heart."[3] The problem still remains, however, that the demand for "literalness" and "realism" is not at all as univocal as it might first appear. In grappling with the problem of hermeneutics, an alternative process presents itself: the explanation of the historical process of the development of forms is only one part of the duty of the interpreter; his understanding within the world of today is the other. According to this idea, one should investigate the conditions for understanding itself in order to come to a visualization of the text that would get beyond this historical "autopsy."[4] In fact, as it stands, this is quite correct, for one has not really understood something in its entirety simply because one knows how to explain the circumstances surrounding its beginning.

But how is it possible to come to an understanding that is not based on some arbitrary choice of particular aspects, but nonetheless allows me to hear the message of the text and not something coming from my own self? Once the methodology has picked history to death by its dissection, who can re-awaken it so that it can live and speak to me? Let me put it another way: if "hermeneutics" is ever to become convincing, the inner harmony between historical analysis and hermeneutical synthesis must first be found.

To be sure, great strides have already been made in this direction, but I must honestly say that a truly convincing answer has yet to be formulated.[5] If Rudolph Bultmann used the philosophy of Martin Heidegger as a vehicle to represent the biblical word, then that vehicle stands in accord with his reconstruction of the essence of Jesus's message. But was this reconstruction itself not likewise a product of his philosophy? How great is its credibility from a historical point of view? In the end, are we listening to Jesus or to Heidegger with this kind of an approach to understanding? Still, one can hardly deny that Bultmann seriously grappled with the issue of increasing our access to the Bible's message. But today, certain forms of exegesis are appearing which can only be explained as symptoms of the disintegration of interpretation and hermeneutics. Materialist and feminist exegesis, whatever else may be said about them, do not even claim to be an understanding of the text itself in the manner in which it was originally intended. At best they may be seen as an expression of the view that the Bible's message is in and of itself inexplicable, or else that it is meaningless for life in today's world. In this sense, they are no longer interested in ascertaining the truth, but only in whatever will serve their own particular agenda. They go on to justify this combination of agenda with biblical material by saying that the many religious elements help strengthen the vitality of the treatment. Thus historical method can even serve as a cloak for such maneuvers insofar as it dissects the Bible into discontinuous pieces, which are then able to be put to new use and inserted into a new montage altogether different from the original biblical context.[6]

THE CENTRAL PROBLEM

Naturally, this situation does not occur everywhere with the same starkness. The methods are often applied with a good deal of prudence, and the radical hermeneutics of the kind I have just described have already been disavowed by a large number of exegetes. In addition, the search for remedies to the basic errors of modern methods has been going on for some time now. The scholarly search to find a better synthesis between the historical and theological methods, between higher criticism and church doctrine, is hardly a recent phenomenon. This can be seen from the fact that hardly anyone today would assert that a truly pervasive understanding of this whole problem has yet been found that takes into account the undeniable insights uncovered by the historical method, while overcoming its limitations and disclosing them in a thoroughly relevant hermeneutic. At least the work of a whole generation is necessary to achieve such a thing. What follows, therefore, is an attempt to sketch out a few distinctions and to point out a few first steps that might be taken toward an eventual solution.

There should be no particular need to demonstrate that it is useless to take refuge in an allegedly pure, literal understanding of the Bible. However, a merely positivistic and rigid ecclesiasticism will not do, either. Just to challenge individual theories, especially the more daring and dubious ones, is likewise insufficient. Likewise dissatisfying is the middle-ground position of trying to pick out in each case as soon as possible the answers from modern exegesis that are more in keeping with tradition. Such foresight may sometimes prove profitable, but it does not grasp the problem at its root and, in fact, remains somewhat arbitrary if it cannot make its own arguments intelligible. In order to arrive at a real solution, we must get beyond disputes over details and press on to the foundations. What we need might be called a criticism of criticism. By this I mean not some exterior analysis, but a criticism based on the inherent potential of all critical thought to analyze itself.

We need a self-criticism of the historical method that can expand to an analysis of historical reason itself, in continuity with and in development of the famous critique of reason by Immanuel Kant. Let me assure you at once that I do not presume to accomplish so vast an undertaking in the short time we have together. But we must make some start, even if it is just by way of preliminary explorations in what is still a largely uncharted land. The self-critique of historical method would have to begin, it seems, by reading its conclusions in a diachronic manner so that the appearance of a quasi-clinical-scientific certainty is avoided. It is this appearance of certainty that has caused its conclusions to be accepted so far and wide.

In fact, at the heart of the historical-critical method lies the effort to establish in the field of history a level of methodological precision that would yield conclusions of the same certainty as in the natural sciences. But what one exegete takes as definite can only be called into question by other exegetes. This is a practical rule that is presupposed as plainly and self-evidently valid. Now, if the natural science model is to be followed without hesitation, then the importance of the Heisenberg principle should be applied to the historical-critical method as well. Heisenberg has shown that the outcome of a given experiment is heavily influenced by the point of view of the observer. So much so that both the observer's questions and the observations continue to change in the natural course of events.[7] When applied to the witness of history, this means that interpretation can never be just a simple reproduction of history's being, "as it was." The word *interpretation* gives us a clue to the question itself: every exegesis requires an "inter"—an entering in and a being "inter," or between things; this is the involvement of the interpreter himself. Pure objectivity is an absurd abstraction. It is not the uninvolved who comes to knowledge; rather, interest itself is a requirement for the possibility of coming to know.

Here, then, is the question: how does one come to be interested, not so that the self drowns out the voice of the other, but in such a way that one develops a kind of inner understanding of things of the past, and ears to listen to the word they speak to us today?[8]

This principle Heisenberg enunciated for experiments in the natural sciences has a very important application to the subject-object relationship. The subject is not to be neatly isolated in a world of its own apart from any interaction. One can only try to put it in the best possible state. This is all the more the case with regard to history, since physical processes are in the present and repeatable. Moreover, historical processes deal with the impenetrability and the depths of the human being himself, and are thus even more susceptible to the influence of the perceiving subject than are natural events. But how are we to reconstruct the original historical context of a subject from the clues that survive?

We need to introduce at this point what I have already called the diachronic approach to exegetical findings. After about two hundred years now of exegetical work on the texts, one can no longer give all the results equal weight. Now one has to look at them within the context of their particular history. It then becomes clear that such a history is not simply one of progress from imprecise to precise and objective conclusions. It appears much more as a history of subjectively reconstructed interrelationships whose approaches correspond exactly to the developments of spiritual history. In turn, these developments are reflected in particular interpretations of texts. In the diachronic reading of an exegesis, its philosophic presuppositions become quite apparent. Now, at a certain distance, the observer determines to his surprise that these interpretations, which were supposed to be strictly and purely "historical," reflect their own overriding spirit, rather than the spirit of times long ago. This insight should not lead us to skepticism about the method, but rather to an honest recognition of what its limits are, and perhaps how it might be purified.

A SELF-CRITICISM OF THE HISTORICAL-CRITICAL METHOD ON THE MODEL OF HOW THE METHOD WAS TAUGHT BY MARTIN DIBELIUS AND RUDOLPH BULTMANN

In order not to let the general rules of the method and their presuppositions remain altogether abstract, I would like to illustrate what I have been saying thus far with an example. I am going to follow here the doctoral dissertation written by Reiner Blank at the University of Basel, entitled *Analysis and Criticism of the Form-Critical Works of Martin Dibelius and Rudolph Bultmann*.[9] This book seems to me to be a fine example of a self-critique of the historical-critical method. This kind of self-critical exegesis stops building "conclusions" on top of conclusions, and constructing and opposing hypotheses. It looks for a way to identify its own foundations and to purify itself by reflections on those foundations. This does not mean that it is pulling itself up by its own bootstraps. On the contrary, by a process of self-limitation, it marks out for itself its own proper space. It goes without saying that the form-critical works of Dibelius and Bultmann have in the meantime been surpassed and in many respects corrected in their details. But it is likewise true that their basic methodological approaches continue even today to determine the methods and procedures of modern exegesis. Their essential elements underlie more than their own historical and theological judgments, and to be sure, these have widely achieved an authority like unto dogma.

For Dibelius, like Bultmann, it was a matter of overcoming the arbitrary manner in which the preceding phase of Christian exegesis, so-called liberal theology, had been conducted. This was imbued with judgments about what was "historical" or "unhistorical." Both of these scholars then sought to establish strict *literary* criteria that would reliably clarify the process by which the texts were developed, and would thus provide a true picture of the tradition. With this outlook, both were in search of the pure form and the rules that governed the development from the initial forms to the text as we have it before us today. As is well known, Dibelius proceeded from the view that the secret of history discloses itself as one sheds light on its development.[10] But how does one arrive at this first premise and develop the ground rules for further development? Even with all their particular differences, one can discover here a series of fundamental presuppositions common to Dibelius and Bultmann, which both considered trustworthy beyond question. Both proceed from the priority of what is preached over the event in itself: in the beginning was the Word. Everything in the Bible develops from the proclamation. This thesis is so vigorously promoted by Bultmann that for him only the Word can be original: the Word generates the scene.[11] All events, therefore, are already secondary, mythological developments.

And so a further axiom is formulated that has remained fundamental for modern exegesis since the time of Dibelius and Bultmann: the notion of discontinuity. Not only is there no continuity between the pre-Easter Jesus and the formative period of the church, but discontinuity applies to all phases of the tradition. This is so much the case that Reiner Blank could state, "Bultmann wanted incoherence at any price."[12]

To these two theories—the pure originality of the simple word and the discontinuity between particular phases of development—there is joined the further notion that what is simple is original, and what is more complex must be a later development. This idea affords an easily applied parameter to determine the stages of development: the more theologically considered and sophisticated a given text is, the more recent it is; and the simpler something is, the easier it is to reckon it original.[13] The criterion according to which something is considered more or less developed, however, is not as evident as it first seems. In fact, the judgment essentially depends upon the theological values of the individual exegete. There remains considerable room for arbitrary choice.

First and foremost, one must challenge that basic notion dependent upon a simplistic transferal of science's evolutionary model to spiritual history. Spiritual processes do not follow the rule of zoological genealogies. In fact, it is frequently the opposite: after a great breakthrough, generations of descendants may come who reduce what was once a courageous new beginning to an academic commonplace. They bury it and disguise it by all kinds of variations of the original theory until it finally comes to have a completely different application.

One can easily see how questionable the criteria have been by using a few examples. Who would hold that Clement of Rome is more developed or complex than Paul? Is James any more advanced than the Epistle to the Romans? Is the Didache more encompassing than the Pastoral Epistles? Take a look at later times: whole generations of Thomistic scholars have not been able to take in the greatness of his thought. Lutheran orthodoxy is far more medieval than was Luther himself. Even between great figures there is nothing to support this kind of developmental theory.

Gregory the Great, for example, wrote long after Augustine and knew of him, but for Gregory, the bold Augustinian vision is translated into the simplicity of religious understanding. Another example: what standard could one use to determine whether Pascal should be classified as before or after Descartes? Which of their philosophies should be mentioned to illustrate the whole of human history? All judgments based on the theory of discontinuity in the tradition and on the assertion of an evolutionary priority of the "simple" over the "complex" can thus be immediately called into question as lacking foundation.

But now we must explain in an even more concrete way what criteria have been used to determine what is "simple." In this regard there are standards as to form and content. In terms of form, the search was for the original forms. Dibelius found them in the so-called paradigm, or example narrative in oral tradition, which can be reconstructed behind the proclamation. Later forms would be the anecdote, the legend, the collections of narrative materials, and the myth.[14]

Bultmann saw the pure form in the apothegm, "the original specific fragment which would sum things up concisely; interest would be concentrated on the word [spoken by] Jesus at the end of a scene; the details of the situation would lie far from this kind of form; Jesus would never come across as the initiator ... everything not corresponding to this form Bultmann attributed to development."[15] The arbitrary nature of these assessments, which would characterize theories of development and judgments of authenticity from then on, is obvious. To be honest, though, one must also say that these theories are not as arbitrary as they may first appear. The designation of the "pure form" is based on a loaded idea of what is original, which we must now put to the test.

One element is what we have just encountered: the thesis of the priority of the word over the event. But this thesis conceals two further pairs of opposites: the pitting of word against cult, and eschatology against apocalyptic. In close harmony with these is the antithesis between Judaic and Hellenistic. Hellenistic was, for example, in Bultmann, the notion of the cosmos, the mystical worship of the gods, and cultic piety. The consequence is simple: what is Hellenistic cannot be Palestinian, and therefore it cannot be original. Whatever has to do with cult, cosmos, or mystery must be rejected as a later development. The rejection of the "apocalyptic," the alleged opposite of eschatology, leads to yet another element: the supposed antagonism between the prophetic and the "legal," and thus between the prophetic and the cosmic and cultic. It follows, then, that ethics is seen as incompatible with the eschatological and the prophetic. In the beginning there was no ethics, but simply an ethos.[16] What is surely at work is the by-product of Luther's fundamental distinction: the dialectic between the law and the gospel. According to this dialectic, ethics and cult are to be relegated to the realm of the law and put in dialectical contrast with Jesus, who, as bearer of the Good News, brings the long line of promise to completion and thus overcomes the law. If we are ever to understand modern exegesis and critique it correctly, we must simply return and reflect anew on Luther's view of the relationship between the Old and New Testaments. For the analogy model that was then current, he substituted a dialectical structure.

However, for Luther all of this remained in a very delicate balance, whereas for Dibelius and Bultmann the whole degenerates into a developmental scheme of well-nigh intolerable simplicity, even if this has contributed to its attractiveness.

With these presuppositions, the picture of Jesus is determined in advance. Thus Jesus has to be conceived in strongly "Judaic" terms. Anything "Hellenistic" has to be removed from him. All apocalyptic, sacramental, mystical elements have to be pruned away. What remains is a strictly "eschatological" prophet, who really proclaims nothing of substance. He only cries out "eschatologically" in expectation of the "wholly other," of that transcendence which he powerfully presents before men in the form of the imminent end of the world.

From this view emerged two challenges for exegesis: it had to explain how one got from the unmessianic, unapocalyptic, prophetic Jesus to the apocalyptic community that worshiped him as Messiah; to a community in which were united Jewish eschatology, stoic philosophy, and mystery religion in a wondrous syncretism. This is exactly how Bultmann described early Christianity.[17]

The second challenge consists in how to connect the original message of Jesus to Christian life today, thus making it possible to understand his call to us.

According to the developmental model, the first problem is relatively easy to solve in principle, even though an immense amount of scholarship had to be dedicated to working out the details. The agent responsible for the contents of the New Testament was to be found not in persons but in the collective, in the "community." Romantic notions of the "people" and its importance in shaping traditions play a key role here.[18] Add to this the thesis of Hellenization and the appeal to the history of religions school. The works of Gunkel and Bousset exerted decisive influence in this area.[19] The second problem was more difficult. Bultmann's approach was his theory of demythologization, but this did not achieve quite the same success as his theories on form and development. If one were allowed to characterize somewhat roughly Bultmann's solution for a contemporary appropriation of Jesus's message, one might say that the scholar from Marburg had set up a correspondence between the non-apocalyptic-prophetic and the fundamental thought of the early Heidegger. Being a Christian, in the sense Jesus meant it, is essentially collapsed into the mode of existing in openness and alertness that Heidegger described. The question has to arise whether one cannot come by some simpler way to such general and sweeping formal assertions.[20]

Still, what is of interest to us here is not Bultmann the systematician, whose activities came to an abrupt halt in any case with the rise of Marxism. Instead, we should examine Bultmann the exegete, who is responsible for an ever more solid consensus regarding the methodology of scientific exegesis.

THE PHILOSOPHIC SOURCE OF THE METHOD

At this point the question arises, how could Dibelius and Bultmann's essential categories for judgment—that is, pure form, the opposition between apocalyptic and eschatology and so on—present such evidence to them that they believed they had at their disposal the perfect instrument for gaining a knowledge of history? Why, even today in large part, is this system of thought taken without question and applied? Since then, most of it has simply become an academic commonplace that precedes individual analysis and appears to be legitimized almost automatically by application. But what about the founders of the method? Certainly, Dibelius and Bultmann already stood in a tradition. Mention has already been made of their dependence on Gunkel and Bousset. But what was their dominant idea? With this question, the self-critique of the historical method passes over to a self-criticism of historical reason, without which our analysis would get stuck in superficialities.

In the first place, one can note that in the history of religions school, the model of evolution was applied to the analysis of biblical texts. This was an effort to bring the methods and models of the natural sciences to bear on the study of history. Bultmann laid hold of this notion in a more general way and thus attributed to the so-called scientific worldview a kind of dogmatic character. Thus, for example, for him the nonhistoricity of the miracle stories was no question whatever anymore. The only thing one needed to do yet was to explain how these miracle stories came about. On one hand, the introduction of the scientific worldview was indeterminate and not well thought out. On the other hand, it offered an absolute rule for distinguishing between what could have been and what had to be explained only by development. To this latter category belonged everything that is not met with in common daily experience.[21] There could only have been what now is. For everything else, therefore, historical processes are invented, whose reconstruction became the particular challenge of exegesis.

But I think we must go yet a step further to appreciate the fundamental decision of the system that generated these particular categories for judgment. The real philosophical presupposition of the whole system seems to me to lie in the philosophical turning point proposed by Immanuel Kant. According to him, the voice of being-in-itself cannot be heard by human beings. Man can hear it only indirectly in the postulates of practical reason, which have remained as it were the small opening through which he can make contact with the real—that is, his eternal destiny. For the rest, as far as the content of his intellectual life is concerned, he must limit himself to the realm of the categories. Thence comes the restriction to the positive, to the empirical, to "exact" science, which by definition excludes the appearance of what is "wholly other," the one who is wholly other, or a new initiative from another plane.

In theological terms, this means that revelation must recede into the pure formality of the eschatological stance, which corresponds to the Kantian split.[22] As far as everything else is concerned, it all needs to be "explained." What might otherwise seem like a direct proclamation of the divine can only be myth, whose laws of development can be discovered. It is with this basic conviction that Bultmann, with the majority of modern exegetes, reads the Bible. He is certain that it cannot be the way it is depicted in the Bible, and he looks for methods to demonstrate the way it really had to be. To that extent there lies in modern exegesis a reduction of history to philosophy, a revision of history by means of philosophy.

The real question before us then is: can one read the Bible any other way? Or perhaps better: must one agree with the philosophy that requires this kind of reading? At its core, the debate about modern exegesis is not a dispute among historians; it is rather a philosophical debate. Only in this way can it be carried on correctly. Otherwise it is like a battle in a mist. The exegetical problem is identical in the main with the struggle for the foundations of our time. Such a struggle cannot be conducted casually, nor can it be won with a few suggestions. It will demand, as I have already intimated, the attentive and critical commitment of an entire generation. It cannot simply retreat back to the Middle Ages or to the fathers, and place them in blind opposition to the spirit of the present age. But neither can it renounce the insights of the great believers of the past and pretend that the history of thought seriously began only with Kant.

In my opinion the more recent debate about biblical hermeneutics suffers from just such a narrowing of our horizon. One can hardly dismiss the exegesis of the fathers by calling it mere allegory or set aside the philosophy of the Middle Ages by branding it "precritical."

THE BASIC ELEMENTS OF A NEW SYNTHESIS

After these remarks on the challenge of a self-critique of the historical method, we find ourselves confronted with the positive side of the problem: how to join its tools with a better philosophy, which would entail fewer drawbacks foreign to the text, which would be less arbitrary, and which would offer greater possibilities for a true listening to the text itself. The positive task is without a doubt even more difficult than the critical one. I can only conclude these remarks by trying to carve out a few narrow footpaths in the thicket, which may perhaps point out where the main road lies and how it is to be found.

In the midst of the theological, methodological debate of his day, Gregory of Nyssa called upon the rationalist Eunomius not to confuse theology with the science of nature. (*Theologein* is not *physiologein*.)[23] "The mystery of theology is one thing," he said, "the scientific investigation of nature is quite another." One cannot then "encompass the unembraceable nature of God in the palm of a child's hand." Gregory was here alluding to a famous saying of Zeno: "The open hand is perception, the clapping hand is the agreement of the intellect, the hand fully closed upon something is the recording of judgment, the one hand clasped by the other is systematic science."[24]

Modern exegesis, as we have seen, completely relegated God to the incomprehensible, the otherworldly, and the inexpressible in order to be able to treat the biblical text itself as an entirely worldly reality according to natural-scientific methods.

Contrary to the text itself, *physiologein* is practiced. As a "critical science," it claims an exactness and certitude similar to natural science. This is a false claim because it is based upon a misunderstanding of the depth and dynamism of the word. Only when one takes from the word its own proper character as word and then stretches it onto the screen of some basic hypothesis can one subject it to such exact rules. Romano Guardini commented in this regard on the false certainty of modern exegesis, which he said "has produced very significant individual results, but has lost sight of its own particular object and generally has ceased being theology."[25] The sublime thought of Gregory of Nyssa remains a true guidepost today: "These gliding and glittering lights of God's word which sparkle over the eyes of the soul ... but now let what we hear from Elijah rise up to our soul and would that our thoughts, too, might be snatched up into the fiery chariot ... so we would not have to abandon hope of drawing close to these stars, by which I mean the thoughts of God."[26]

Thus the Word should not be submitted to just any kind of enthusiasm. Rather, preparation is required to open us up to the inner dynamism of the

Word. This is possible only when there is a certain sym-*pathia*, or understanding, a readiness to learn something new, to allow oneself to be taken along a new road. It is not the closed hand that is required, but the opened eye....

Thus the exegete should not approach the text with a ready-made philosophy, nor in accordance with the dictates of a so-called modern or scientific worldview, which determines in advance what may or may not be. He may not exclude a priori that (almighty) God could speak in human words in the world. He may not exclude that God himself could enter into and work in human history, however improbable such a thing might at first appear.

He must be ready to learn from the extraordinary. He must be ready to accept that the truly original may occur in history, something which cannot be derived from precedents but which opens up out of itself.[27] He may not deny to humanity the ability to be responsive beyond the categories of pure reason, and to reach beyond ourselves toward the open and endless truth of being.

We must likewise reexamine the relationship between event and the Word. For Dibelius, Bultmann, and the mainstream of modern exegesis, the event is the irrational element. It lies in the realm of mere facticity, which is a mixture of accident and necessity. The fact as such, therefore, cannot be a bearer of meaning. Meaning lies only in the Word, and where events might seem to bear meaning, they are to be considered illustrations of the Word, to which they have to be referred. Judgments which derive from such a point of view are certainly persuasive for people of today, since they fit nicely into their own patterns of expectations. There is, however, no evidence in reality to support them. Such evidence is admissible only under the presupposition that the principle of scientific method, namely that every effort which occurs can be explained in terms of purely immanent relationships within the operation itself, is not only valid methodologically but is true in and of itself. Thus, in reality there would be only "accident and necessity," nothing else, and one may look upon only these elements as brute facts.

But what is useful as a methodological principle for the natural sciences is a foregone banality as a philosophical principle; and as a theological principle it is a contradiction. (How can any or all of God's activity be considered either accidental or necessary?) It is here, for the sake of scientific curiosity, too, that we must experiment with the precise contrary of this principle—namely, that things can indeed be otherwise.

To put it another way: the event itself can be a "word," in accord with the biblical word terminology.[28] From this flow two important rules for interpretation.

(a) First, both word and event have to be considered equally original, if one wishes to remain true to the biblical perspective. The dualism that banishes the event into wordlessness, that is meaninglessness, would rob the Word of its power to convey meaning as well, for it would then stand in a world without meaning.

It also leads to a docetic Christology in which the reality—that is, the concrete fleshly existence of Christ and especially of man—is removed from the realm of meaning. Thus the essence of the biblical witness fails in its purpose.

(b) Second, such a dualism splits the biblical Word off from Creation and would substitute the principle of discontinuity for the organic *continuity* of meaning that exists between the Old and New Testaments. When the continuity between Word and event is allowed to disappear, there can no longer be any unity within the scripture itself. A New Testament cut off from the Old is automatically abolished since it exists, as its very title suggests, because of the unity of the two. Therefore the principle of discontinuity must be counterbalanced by the interior claim of the biblical text itself, according to the principle of the *analogia scripturae*: the mechanical principle must be balanced by the teleological principle.[29]

Certainly texts must first of all be traced back to their historical origins and interpreted in their proper historical context. But then, in a second exegetical operation, one must look at them also in light of the total movement of history and history's central event, Jesus Christ. Only the *combination of both* of these methods will yield a correct understanding of the Bible. If the first exegetical operation by the fathers and in the Middle Ages is found to be lacking, so, too, is the second, since it easily falls into arbitrariness. Thus, the first was fruitless, but the rejection of any coherence of meaning leads to an opinionated methodology.

To recognize the inner self-transcendence of the historical word, and thus the inner correctness of subsequent rereadings, in which event and meaning are gradually interwoven, is the task of interpretation properly so-called, for which appropriate methods can and must be found. In this connection, the exegetical maxim of Thomas Aquinas is quite to the point: "The duty of every good interpreter is to contemplate not the words, but the *sense* of the words."[30]

In the last hundred years, exegesis has had many great achievements, but it has brought forth great errors, as well. These latter, moreover, have in some measure grown to the stature of academic dogmas. To criticize them at all would be taken by many as tantamount to sacrilege, especially if it were to be done by a nonexegete. Nevertheless, so prominent an exegete as Heinrich Schlier previously warned his colleagues: "Do not squander your time on trivialities."[31] Johann Gnilka gave concrete expression to this warn-

ing when he reacted against an exaggerated emphasis by the history of traditions school.[32]

Along the same lines, I would like to express the following hopes:

(a) The time seems to have arrived for a new and thorough reflection on
exegetical method. Scientific exegesis must recognize the philosophic element
present in a great number of its ground rules, and it must then reconsider the
results that are based on these rules.

(b) Exegesis can no longer be studied in a unilinear, synchronic fashion, as
is the case with scientific findings, which depend not upon their history but
only upon the precision of their data. Exegesis must recognize itself as an historical discipline. Its history belongs to itself. In a critical arrangement of its
respective positions within the totality of its own history, it will be able, on
one hand, to recognize the relativity of its own judgments (where, for example, errors may have crept in). On the other hand, it will be in a better position
to achieve an insight into our real, if always imperfect, comprehension of the
biblical Word.

(c) Philological and scientific literary methods are and will remain critically important for a proper exegesis. But for their actual application to the
work of criticism—and for an examination of their claims—an understanding of the philosophic implications of the interpretative process is required.
The self-critical study of its own history must also imply an examination of
the essential philosophic alternatives for human thought. Thus, it is not sufficient to scan simply the last 150 years. The great outlines of patristic and medieval thought must also be brought into the discussion. It is equally
indispensable to reflect on the fundamental judgments made by the Reformers and the critical importance they have had in the history of exegesis.

(d) What we need now is not new hypotheses on the *Sitz im Leben,* on possible sources, or on the subsequent process of handing down the material.
What we *do* need is a critical look at the exegetical landscape we now have, so
that we may return to the text and distinguish between those hypotheses that
are helpful and those that are not. Only under these conditions can a new and
fruitful collaboration between exegesis and systematic theology begin. And
only in this way will exegesis be of real help in understanding the Bible.

(e) Finally, the exegete must realize that he does not stand in some neutral
area, above or outside history and the church. Such a presumed immediacy
regarding the purely historical can only lead to dead ends. The first presupposition of all exegesis is that it accepts the Bible as a book. In so doing, it
has already chosen a place for itself that does not simply follow from the
study of literature. It has identified *this particular literature* as the product

of a coherent history, and this history as the proper space for coming to understanding. If it wishes to be theology, it must take a further step. It must recognize that the faith of the church is that form of *sympathia* without which the Bible remains a *closed* book. It must come to acknowledge this faith as a hermeneutic, the space for understanding, which does not do dogmatic violence to the Bible but precisely allows the solitary possibility for the Bible to be itself.

Sin and Salvation

Now the serpent was more subtle than any other wild creature that the Lord God had made. He said to the woman, "Did God say, 'You shall not eat of any tree of the garden'?" And the woman said to the serpent, "We may eat of the fruit of the trees of the garden; but God said, 'You shall not eat of the fruit of the tree which is in the midst of the garden, neither shall you touch it, lest you die.'" But the serpent said to the woman, "You will not die. For God knows that when you eat of it your eyes will be opened, and you will be like God, knowing good and evil." So when the woman saw that the tree was good for food, and that it was a delight to the eyes, and that the tree was to be desired to make one wise, she took of its fruit and ate; and she also gave some to her husband, and he ate. Then the eyes of both were opened, and they knew that they were naked; and they sewed fig leaves together and made themselves aprons. And they heard the sound of the Lord God walking in the garden in the cool of the day, and the man and his wife hid themselves from the presence of the Lord God among the trees of the garden. But the Lord God called to the man, and he said to him, "Where are you?" And he said, "I heard the sound of thee in the garden, and I was afraid, because I was naked; and I hid myself." He said, "Who told you that you were naked? Have you eaten of the tree of which I commanded you not to eat?" The man said, "The woman whom thou gavest to be with me, she gave me fruit of the tree, and I ate...." And to Adam he said, "Because you have listened to the voice of your wife, and have eaten of the tree of which I commanded you, 'You shall not eat of it,' cursed is the ground because of you; in toil you shall eat of it all the days of your life; thorns and thistles it shall bring forth to you; and you shall eat the plants of the field. In the sweat of your face you shall eat bread till you return to the ground, for out of it you were taken; you are dust, and to dust you shall return." ... Therefore the Lord God sent him forth from the garden of Eden, to till the ground from which he was taken. He drove out the man;

and at the east of the garden of Eden he placed the cherubim, and a flaming sword which turned every way, to guard the way to the tree of life.

GENESIS 3:1–12, 17–19, 23–24

ON THE SUBJECT OF SIN

After the end of the bishops' synod that was devoted to the subject of the family, we were discussing in a small group possible themes for the next synod, and Jesus's words at the beginning of Mark's Gospel came to mind.[1] These words summarize Jesus's whole message: "The time is fulfilled, and the kingdom of God is at hand; repent, and believe in the gospel" (Mk 1:15). One of the bishops reflected on these words and said he had the impression that we had long ago actually halved Jesus's message as it is thus summarized. We speak a great deal—and like to speak—about evangelization and the Good News, in such a way as to make Christianity attractive to people. But hardly anyone, according to this bishop, dares nowadays to proclaim the prophetic message: Repent! Hardly anyone dares to make to our age this elementary evangelical appeal, with which the Lord wants to induce us to acknowledge our sinfulness, do penance, and become other than what we are. Our confrere added that Christian preaching today sounded to him like the recording of a symphony that was missing the initial bars of music, so that the whole symphony was incomplete and its development incomprehensible. With this he touched a weak point of our present-day spiritual situation.

Sin has become, almost everywhere today, one of those subjects that are not spoken about. Religious education of whatever kind does its best to evade it. Theater and films use the word ironically or in order to entertain. Sociology and psychology attempt to unmask it as an illusion or a complex. Even the law is trying to get by more and more without the concept of guilt. It prefers to make use of sociological language, which turns the concept of good and evil into statistics, and in its place distinguishes between normative and nonnormative behavior. Implicit here is the possibility that the statistical proportions will themselves change; what is presently nonnormative could one day become the rule; indeed, perhaps one should even strive to make the nonnormative normal. In such an atmosphere of quantification, the whole idea of the moral has been generally abandoned. This is a logical development if there is no standard for human beings to use as a model—something not discovered by us but coming from the inner goodness of Creation.

With this we have arrived at the real heart of the matter. People today know of no standard; to be sure, they do not want to know of any because they see standards as threats to their freedom. Here one is made to think of some words of the French Jew Simone Weil, who said that "we experience good only by doing it.... When we do evil we do not know it, because evil flies from the light.[2] People recognize the good only when they themselves do it. They recognize the evil only when they do not do it.

Thus sin has become a suppressed subject, but everywhere we can see that although it is suppressed, it has nonetheless remained real. What is remarkable to me is the aggressiveness, always on the verge of pouncing, that we experience openly in our society—the lurking readiness to demean the other person, to hold others guilty whenever misfortune occurs to them, to accuse society, and to want to change the world by violence. It seems to me that all of this can be understood only as an expression of the suppressed reality of guilt, which people do not want to admit. But since it is still there, they have to attack it and destroy it. As long as the situation remains thus—that is, as long as people suppress the truth but do not succeed in doing away with it, and as long as they are suffering from this suppressed truth—it will be one of the tasks of the Holy Spirit to "convince the world of sin" (Jn 16:8). It is not a question here of making people's lives unpleasant and of fettering them with restrictions and negations, but rather simply of leading them to the truth and thus healing them. Human beings can be healthy only when they are true and when they stop suppressing and destroying the truth. The third chapter of the Book of Genesis, on which this meditation is based, is of a piece with this task of the Holy Spirit, which he pursues throughout history. He convinces the world and us of sin—not to humiliate us, but to make us true and healthy, to "save" us.

LIMITATIONS AND FREEDOM OF THE HUMAN BEING

This text proclaims its truth, which surpasses our understanding, by way of two great images in particular—that of the garden, to which the image of the tree belongs, and that of the serpent. The garden is an image of the world, which to humankind is not a wilderness, a danger, or a threat, but a home that shelters, nourishes, and sustains. It is an expression for a world that bears the imprint of the Spirit, for a world that came into existence in accordance with the will of the Creator. Thus two movements are interacting here. One is that of human beings who do not exploit the world and do not want to detach it from the Creator's governance and make it their own property; rather they recognize it as God's gift and build it up in keeping with what it was created for. Conversely, we see that the world, which was created to be at one with its Lord, is not a threat but a gift, a sign of the saving and unifying goodness of God.

The second movement involves the image of the serpent, which is taken from the Eastern fertility cults. These fertility religions were severe temptations to Israel for centuries, tempting it to abandon the covenant and enter into the religious milieu of the time. Through the fertility cults, the serpent speaks to the human being: Do not cling to this distant God, who has nothing to offer you. Do not cling to this covenant, which is so alien to you and which imposes so many restrictions on you. Plunge into the current of life, into its delirium and its ecstasy, and thus you will be able to partake of the reality of life and its immortality.[3]

At the moment when the paradise narrative took its final literary form, there was a great danger that Israel would succumb to the many seductive elements of these religions and the God of the promise and of Creation, who seemed so far off, would disappear and be forgotten. Against its historical background, which we know, for example, from events in the life of the prophet Elijah, we can understand this text much better. "The woman saw that the tree was good for food, and that it was a delight to the eyes, and that the tree was to be desired to make one wise" (Gn 3:6). In that religious setting, the serpent was a symbol of that wisdom which rules the world and of the fertility through which human beings plunge into the divine current of life and for a few moments experience themselves fused with its divine power. Thus the serpent also serves as a symbol of the attraction these religions exerted over Israel, in contrast to the mystery of the God of the covenant.

It is with Israel's temptation in mind that holy scripture portrays Adam's temptation and, in general, the nature of temptation and sin in every age. Temptation does not begin with the denial of God and a fall into outright atheism. The serpent does not deny God; it starts out, rather, with an apparently reasonable request for information, which in reality, however, contains an insinuation that provokes the human being and lures him or her from trust to mistrust: "Did God say, 'You shall not eat of any tree of the garden'?" (Gn 3:1). The first thing is not the denial of God but rather doubt about his covenant, about the community of faith, prayer, the commandments—all of which are the context for living God's covenant. There is indeed a great deal of enlightenment when one doubts the covenant, experiences mistrust, demands freedom, and renounces obedience to the covenant as a straitjacket that prevents one from enjoying the real promises of life. It is so easy to convince people that this covenant is not a gift, but rather an expression of envy of humankind and that it is robbing human beings of their freedom and the most precious things of life. With this doubt, people are well on their way to building their own worlds. In other words, they then make the decision not to accept the limitations of their existence; they then decide not to be bound by the limitations imposed by good and evil, or by morality in general, but quite simply to free themselves by ignoring these limits.[4]

This doubt about the covenant and the accompanying invitation to human beings to free themselves from their limitations have appeared in various forms throughout history and also shape the present-day scene.[5] I mention here only two variations—the aesthetic and the technical. Let us treat the aesthetic variation first. It begins with the question: what may art do? The answer seems perfectly clear: it may do anything that it "artistically" can. It needs only one rule—itself, artistic ability. And only one error can be made with respect to it—artistic error, artistic incompetence. From this it follows that there are no good and bad artworks, but only well-written or poorly written books, only well-produced or poorly produced films, and so on. The good and the moral no longer count, it seems, but only what one can do. Art is a matter of competence, so it is said; anything else is a violation. That is enlightening! But it means, if one is to be consistent, that there is an area where human beings can ignore their limitations: when they create art, they may do what they can do; they have no limitations. And that means, in turn, that the measure of human beings is what they can do and not what they are, not what is good or bad. What they can do they may do.

The significance of this is far more evident today with respect to the second variation, the technical. But it is only another version of the same way of thinking and the same reality, because the Greek word *techne* stands for the English word *art*, and the same idea of "being able" is implied here. Hence the same question pertains: what may technology do? For a long time, the answer was perfectly clear: it may do what it can do. The only error it knows is that of incompetence. Robert Oppenheimer relates that when the atomic bomb became a possibility, nuclear physicists were fascinated by "the technically sweet." The technically possible, the desire to do and the actual doing of what it was possible to do, was like a magnet to which they were involuntarily attracted. Rudolf Höss, the last commandant of Auschwitz, declared in his diary that the concentration camp was a remarkable technical achievement. If one took into account the pertinent transportation schedules, the capacity of the crematories, and their burning power, seeing how all of these worked together so smoothly, this was clearly a fascinating and well-coordinated program, and it justified itself.[6] One could continue at length with similar examples. All the productions of horrible things, whose multiplication we look on nowadays with incomprehension and ultimately with helplessness, have their common basis here. But in the consequences of this principle we should finally recognize today that it is a trick of Satan, who wants to destroy human beings and the world. We should see that human beings can never retreat into the realm of what they are capable of. In everything that they do, they constitute themselves. Therefore they themselves, and Creation with its good and evil, are always present as their standard, and when they reject this standard they deceive themselves. They do not free themselves, but place themselves in opposition to the truth. And that means that they are destroying themselves and the world. This, then, is the first and most important thing that appears in the story of Adam, and it has to do with the nature of human guilt and thus with our entire existence. The order of the covenant—the nearness of the God of the covenant, the limitations imposed by good and evil, the inner standard of the human person, creatureliness: all of this is placed in doubt. Here we can at once say that at the very heart of sin lies human beings' denial of their creatureliness, inasmuch as they refuse to accept the standard and limitations that are implicit in it. They do not want to be creatures, do not want to be subject to a standard, do not want to be dependent. They consider their dependence on God's creative love to be an imposition from without. But that is what slavery is, and from slavery one must free oneself. Thus human beings themselves want to be God. When they try this, everything is thrown topsy-turvy. The relationship of human beings to themselves is altered, as well as their relationships to others. The other is a hindrance, a rival, a threat to the person who wants to be God. The relationship with the other becomes one of mutual recrimination and struggle, as is masterfully shown in Genesis 3:8–13, which presents God's conversation with Adam and Eve. Finally, the relationship to the world is altered in such a way as to become one of destruction and exploitation. Human beings who consider dependence on the highest love as slavery and who try to deny the truth about themselves, which is their creatureliness, do not free themselves; they destroy truth and love. They do not make themselves gods, which, in fact, they cannot do, but rather caricatures, pseudogods, slaves of their own abilities, which then drag them down.

So it is clear now that sin is, in its essence, a renunciation of the truth. Now we can also understand the mysterious meaning of the words: "When you eat of it [that is, when you deny your limitations, when you deny your finitude], then you will die" (cf. Gn 3:3). This means that human beings who deny the limitations imposed on them by good and evil, which are the inner standard of Creation, deny the truth. They are living in untruth and unreality. Their lives are mere appearance; they stand under the sway of death. We who are surrounded by a world of untruths, of unlife, know how strong this sway of death is, which even negates life itself and makes it a kind of death.

ORIGINAL SIN

In the Genesis story that we are considering, a further characteristic of sin is described. Sin is spoken of in general not as an abstract possibility but as a deed, as the sin of a particular person, Adam, who stands at the origin of humankind and with whom the history of sin begins. The account tells us that sin begets sin, and that, therefore, all the sins of history are interlinked. Theology refers to this state of affairs by the certainly misleading and imprecise term *original sin*. What does this mean? Nothing seems to us today to be stranger or, indeed, more absurd than to insist upon original sin, since, according to our way of thinking, guilt can only be something very personal, and God does not run a concentration camp in which one's relatives are imprisoned, because he is a liberating God of love who calls each one by name. What does *original sin* mean, then, when we interpret it correctly?

Finding an answer to this requires nothing less than trying to understand the human person better. It must once again be stressed that no human being is closed in upon himself or herself and that no one can live of or for himself or herself alone. We receive our life not only at the moment of birth but every day from without—from others who are not ourselves but who nonetheless somehow pertain to us. Human beings have their selves not only in themselves but also outside of themselves: they live in those whom they love and in those who love them and to whom they are present. Human beings are relational, and they possess their lives—themselves—only by way of relationship. I alone am not myself, but only in and with you am I myself. To be truly a human being means to be related in love, to be *of* and *for*. But sin means the damaging or destruction of relationality. Sin is a rejection of relationality because it wants to make the human being a god. Sin is loss of relationship, a disturbance of relationship, and, therefore, it is not restricted to the individual. When I destroy a relationship, then this event—sin—touches the other person involved in the relationship. Consequently sin is always an offense that touches others, that alters the world and damages it. To the extent that this is true, when the network of human relationships is damaged from the very beginning, then every human being enters into a world that is marked by relational damage. At the very moment when a person begins human existence, which is a good, he or she is confronted by a sin-damaged world. Each of us enters into a situation in which relationality has been hurt. Consequently each person is, from the very start, damaged in relationships and does not engage in them as he or she ought. Sin pursues the human being, and he or she capitulates to it.

But from this it is also clear that human beings alone cannot save themselves. Their innate error is precisely that they want to do this by themselves.

We can only be saved—that is, be free and true—when we stop wanting to be God and renounce the madness of autonomy and self-sufficiency. We can only be saved—that is, become ourselves—when we engage in the proper relationship. But our interpersonal relationships occur in the context of our utter creatureliness, and it is there that the damage lies. Since the relationship with Creation has been damaged, only the Creator himself can be our savior. We can be saved only when he from whom we have cut ourselves off takes the initiative with us and stretches out his hand to us. Only being loved is being saved, and only God's love can purify damaged human love and radically reestablish the network of relationships that have suffered from alienation.

THE RESPONSE OF THE NEW TESTAMENT

Thus the Old Testament account of the beginnings of humankind points, questioningly and hopefully, beyond itself to the One in whom God endured our refusal to accept our limitations and who entered into those limitations in order to restore us to ourselves. The New Testament response to the account of the Fall is most briefly and urgently summarized in the pre-Pauline hymn that Paul incorporated into the second chapter of his Letter to the Philippians. The church has therefore correctly placed this text at the very center of the Easter Triduum, the holiest time of the church year. "Have this in mind among yourselves, which was in Christ Jesus, who, though he was in the form of God, did not count equality with God a thing to be grasped, but emptied himself, taking the form of a servant, being born in the likeness of men. And being found in human form he humbled himself and became obedient unto death, even death on a cross. Therefore God has highly exalted him and bestowed on him the name which is above every name, that at the name of Jesus every knee would bow, in heaven and on earth and under the earth, and every tongue confess that Jesus Christ is Lord, to the glory of God the Father" (Phil 2:5–11; cf. Is 45:23).

We cannot consider this extraordinarily rich and profound text in detail. We want to limit ourselves here to its connection with the story of the Fall, even though it seems to have a somewhat different version in mind than the one that is related in Genesis 3 (cf., e.g., Jb 15:7–8).[7] Jesus Christ goes Adam's route, but in reverse. In contrast to Adam he is really "like God." But this being like God, this similarity to God, is being a Son, and hence it is totally relational. "I do nothing on my own authority" (Jn 8:28). Therefore the one who is truly like God does not hold graspingly to his autonomy, to the limitlessness of his ability and his willing. He does the contrary: he becomes completely dependent; he becomes a slave. Because he does not go the route of power but that of love, he can descend into the depths of Adam's lie, into the depths of death, and there raise up truth and life.

Thus Christ is the new Adam, with whom humankind begins anew. The Son, who is by nature relationship and relatedness, reestablishes relationships. His arms, spread out on the cross, are an open invitation to relationship, which is continually offered to us. The cross, the place of his obedience, is the true tree of life. Christ is the antitype of the serpent, as is indicated in John 3:14. From this tree there comes not the word of temptation but that of redeeming love, the word of obedience, which an obedient God himself used, thus offering us his obedience as a context for freedom. The cross is the tree of life, now become approachable. By his Passion, Christ, as it were, removed the fiery sword, passed through the fire, and erected the cross as the true pole of the earth, by which it is itself once more set aright. Therefore the Eucharist, as the presence of the cross, is the abiding tree of life, which is ever in our midst and ever invites us to take the fruit of true life. This means that the Eucharist can never be merely a kind of community builder. To receive it, to eat of the tree of life, means to receive the crucified Lord and consequently to accept the parameters of his life, his obedience, his "yes," the standard of our creatureliness. It means to accept the love of God, which is our truth—that dependence on God which is no more an imposition from without than is the Son's sonship. It is precisely this dependence that is freedom, because it is truth and love.

May this Lent help us to free ourselves from our refusals and our doubt concerning God's covenant, from our rejection of our limitations and from the lie of our autonomy. May it direct us to the tree of life, which is our standard and our hope. May we be touched by the words of Jesus in their entirety. "The kingdom of God is at hand; repent, and believe in the gospel" (Mk 1:15).

Meditation on the Priesthood

In the last twenty years there has been a good deal of thinking on the priest-hood, but there has also been much adverse debate. In such discussions the fact has increasingly been apparent that many hasty arguments are seeking to eliminate the priesthood as ill-informed sacralization and to substitute for it simple temporary offices, functional in character. Slowly premises are becom-ing evident that at first seemed to make such arguments almost unopposable. The overcoming of prejudice once again makes possible a deeper understand-ing of the biblical data in their intrinsic unity of Old and New Testaments, Bible and church, so that we are no longer constrained to draw water from cisterns, only for it to leak rapidly through cracks of hypothesis and suddenly collect again in little scattered patches, but can now find access to the living fountain of the church's faith throughout the ages.

It can easily be seen that in the future it will be most essential to solve this precise problem: what is the authentic reading of scripture? In that period when the Canon was being drawn up, which corresponds moreover to the period of formation of the church and its catholicity, Irenaeus of Lyons was the first to engage in this question. On the solution of this question depends the possibility or impossibility of continued life for the church. Irenaeus rec-ognized in his time that the breaking of the Bible to bits and the separation of Bible and church were the elements in Christianity and the Enlightenment (so-called Gnosis) that threatened to destroy the church of the time at its foundations. Earlier, before such fundamental divisions, there had been an internal subdivision of the church into communities, which, in turn, managed to legitimize themselves by means of a selective use of sources. Splitting up the sources of the faith brings with it divisions in communion and vice versa. Gnosis, which seeks to introduce, as an authentic rational principle, separation of the testaments, separation of scripture from tradition, and division of en-lightened Christians from the nonenlightened is in reality a product of deca-dence. Unity of the church, on the other hand, makes visible the unity of that which constitutes the reason of its existence, and conversely, in order to live it needs the strength drawn from the totality, from the multiform unity of the

Old and New Testaments, scriptural tradition, and faithful realizations of the Word. Once it has yielded to the logic of decadence, however, it is no longer possible to connect things again.

Nevertheless, it is not opportune to tackle this theological dispute here, though it must be done elsewhere; instead, I will limit myself to making a spiritual meditation, starting from the biblical testimonies, which I intend to expound without making use of any scientific critical apparatus, but accentuating the aspects that seem to me to belong to the priestly life.

REFLECTIONS OF A PRIESTLY IMAGE IN THE ACCOUNTS OF THE CALL IN LUKE 5:1–11 AND JOHN 1:35–42

For my first text I have selected Luke 5:1–11.[1] Here we are told that crowds were pressing around Jesus because they wanted to hear the Word of God. He is standing at the edge of the lake, the fishermen are washing their nets, and Jesus goes out in one of the two boats that are there, in Peter's boat. Jesus asks him to pull out a little from the land, sits down in the boat, and teaches. Peter's boat becomes the cathedra of Jesus Christ. Then he tells Simon to row out to deep water and let down the nets for a catch. The fishermen have tried on their own, all night, without success; it would seem useless to start fishing again, now in the morning. But Jesus has already become so important, so overriding, to Peter that he risks saying: "At your word I will do it!" The word of Jesus has become more real than what appears sure and real empirically. The Galilean morning, its freshness breathing through this description, becomes the image of the new gospel morning after the night of delusions in which our work, our good will, are continually entangled.

When, then, Peter and his companions returned to the shore with the boats laden and had managed to haul in the results of the catch—but only *together* because of the superabundance of the gift that was breaking their nets—Peter had not only made a journey outwardly and completed a job of work; this trip had become for him an interior journey, the extent of which is expressed by Luke in two words. What the evangelist tells us is that before the miraculous draught of fish Peter had called the Lord "*Epistata,*" master, rabbi, someone who teaches. But on his return he falls on his knees before Jesus and no longer calls him rabbi but "*Kyrie,*" Lord, giving him the title reserved for God. Peter had made the journey from rabbi to lord, from master to Son of God. After this interior pilgrimage he is in a position to receive his call.

Here a comparison with John 1:35–42, the first account of the calling in the fourth Gospel, seems necessary. There we are told how the two first disciples—Andrew and another whose name is not recorded—join Jesus, struck by the Baptist's words: "Behold the Lamb of God!" They are struck either by the recognition of being sinners that resounds in these words, or by the hope that the Lamb of God saves sinners. Their sense of unsureness is clearly visible: that they will follow him is as yet uncertain, doubtful. They come up to him guardedly, without saying anything; it seems that they do not have the courage to ask. So it is he who turns to them, saying: "What do you seek?" Their answer still sounds embarrassed, a little hesitant and troubled, but it goes straight to the essential: "Rabbi, where do you live?" or rather, in a more precise translation, "Where are you *staying?*" Where is your dwelling, your abode, where are you, so that we can join you? And here it comes to mind that the word *stay* is one of the more meaningful expressions in St. John's Gospel.

Jesus's reply is commonly translated: "Come and see!" More exactly it means: "Come, and you shall *become* people that see!" They would, that is, be made capable of seeing. This corresponds also to the conclusion of the second account of the call, that of Nathanael, who hears it said at the end: "You shall see greater things than these" (1:50). Becoming capable of seeing is therefore the point of the coming; to come means to enter his presence, to be seen by him and to see together with him. Over his dwelling in fact the heavens open, the secret place where God is (1:51); there we can dwell in the holiness of God. "Come and you will be introduced to vision," which corresponds also to the church's Communion psalm: "Taste and see that the Lord is good" (Ps 34:9). The coming, and only the coming, leads on to sight. Tasting opens the eyes. As once in paradise the taste of the forbidden fruit had unhappily opened the eyes, so now we have the contrary, that to savor the truth opens the eyes so as to see the goodness of God. Only by coming, by dwelling with Jesus, is sight realized. Without taking the risk of coming, it is not possible to see. John notes: it was about the tenth hour, the fourth hour of the afternoon (1:39), so already a late hour, a time at which it might be thought it was no longer possible to start anything; an hour at which, however, something decisive occurs not to be deferred. According to an apocalyptic calculation, this hour was considered the last hour. Anyone coming to Jesus enters into something definitive, the fullness of time, the definitive hour, the end of time; attains to the parousia, the already present reality of the Resurrection and the Kingdom of God.

In the "coming," therefore, is realized the "seeing." In John this is unfolded in the same way as in Luke, as we have noticed. To Jesus's first words, both replied, "Rabbi." When they return after being with him, Andrew says to his brother Simon: "We have found the Christ" (1:41). Coming to Jesus, staying with him, he, too, had covered the road from rabbi to Christ; in the master he had learned to see the Christ, and this cannot be learnt except by staying with him. Thus is evident the close unity between the third and fourth Gospels: both times, trusting in the word of the Lord, which opens the dialogue, they dare to go with him. Both times life is experienced by relying on his word, and both times the interior journey follows in such a way that from "come" is born "see," which makes of the coming a seeing of the Lord.

Unlike the apostles' journey, we have already started our journey with the *full* testimony of the church, which believes in the Son of God, but the condition of our seeing remains for us, too, a similar coming, always to be renewed "at your word," like going toward him where he dwells. And only one who sees in person, not only through the witness of others, can call others. This coming, the daring to trust oneself to his word, is still today and always will be the indispensable condition of apostleship, of the call to priestly service. We will always need to ask him afresh: where do you dwell? We will always need to start out again spiritually on the road to where he is. We, too, will always have to cast the nets over again at his word, even when it seems senseless. The principle will always remain true that his word must be held more real than any reality that we consider real: statistics, technology, public opinion. Often we will have the feeling that it is now the tenth hour and that we have to postpone Jesus's hour. But precisely then can it become the time when he is near.

Let us consider again those elements that are common to the *two* accounts of the call. Both the disciples John speaks of let themselves be called at the word "Lamb." Evidently they have had some experience and *know* themselves to be sinners. And this is not a vague religious expression for them but something that moves them to their depths; it is a reality for them. It is precisely because they know this that, therefore, the Lamb becomes their hope, and, therefore, they begin to follow him. When Peter returns with the abundance of fish, something unexpected happens. He does not, as might be imagined, throw his arms around Jesus's neck for the good success of the undertaking, but throws himself at Jesus's feet. He does not hold on to him so as to have a guarantee of success later on, as well, but distances himself from him because he fears the power of God. "Depart from me, for I am a sinful man" (Lk 5:8). Where God is experienced, human beings recognize their condition as sinners and only then, while they are truly recognizing this and admitting it, do they see themselves in truth. But precisely so do they become true. Only when one knows oneself to be a sinner and has understood the tragedy of sin can one then understand also the call: "Repent, and believe in the Gospel" (Mk 1:15).

Without conversion, however, we cannot come to Jesus, nor arrive at the gospel. There is a paradoxical saying of Chesterton's that expresses this circumstance exactly: "A saint can be recognised by the fact that he knows himself to be a sinner." Weakening in experience of God is shown today by the disappearance of any feeling of sin and vice versa: when this disappearance takes place, it distances a person from God. Without relapsing into a false system of fear, we should precisely return to learning the truth of this word: "The fear of the Lord is the beginning of wisdom" (Sir 1:12; "the root of wisdom" in 1:18; "the fullness of wisdom" in 1:14). Wisdom, true understanding, begins with the right fear of God. We should start learning this again so as also to be able to grasp and understand true love, what it means that we can love him and that he loves us. Also this experience of Peter, Andrew, John, is then a fundamental condition of apostleship and thus of the priesthood, also. *Conversion* is the first word in Christianity: only someone who has had personal experience of the need of it can proclaim it well, as a consequence of having understood the greatness of the grace.

The sacramental structure of the church appears to be of the same type as what we have seen in these texts of the fundamental elements in the spiritual itinerary of an apostle. As the experience of sin is to baptism and confession, so becoming seeing people, making for the place where Jesus dwells, is to the mystery of the Eucharist. Prior to the Last Supper, the realism that could assume Jesus's abode to be in our midst was certainly unimaginable. "Here you will become seeing people"—the Eucharist is the mystery in which is fulfilled the promise made to Nathanael: that we can see the heavens open and the angels of God ascending and descending (Jn 1:51). Jesus dwells and "*stays*" in the Sacrifice, in the act of love, during which he goes to the Father and by way of his love restores us also to *him*.

The Communion psalm (Ps 34), which speaks of tasting and seeing, contains also the other words: "Look to him and you will be radiant" (34:6). To communicate with the Lord is to communicate with "the true light that enlightens every man coming into the world" (cf. Jn 1:9).

Let us consider yet another point common to the two accounts with which we are concerned. The abundance of fish tears the nets. Peter and his men can no longer make it out. What is said, then, is very much to the point: "They beckoned to their partners in the other boat to come and help them. And they came and filled both the boats, so that they began to sink" (Lk 5:7). The call from Jesus is at the same time a call to come together (a calling together), a call to *syl-labethai,* as the Greek text says, to hold one another by the hand, support one another, one helping the other, in order to bring the two boats together.

The same thing is evident also in St. John. Andrew, on his return from "Jesus's hour," cannot keep his discovery hidden. He calls his brother Simon to Jesus and does the same with Philip, who in his turn calls Nathanael (cf. Jn 1:41–45). The call leads one along *with* another. It incorporates them in the following and demands sharing. Every call has in it that human element: the aspect of fraternity, the feeling of being spoken to by another. If we think over the road we have traveled, each of us knows full well that there was no beam of bright light from God shed directly on us, but that somehow there had been an invitation from someone faithful, a being carried along by someone. Certainly a vocation can sustain us only if ours is not a secondhand belief— "because this or that person said I should"—but when, led by others, we personally find the Lord (cf. Jn 4:42). Equally necessary are the inviting, the leading, the carrying, on the one side, and one's own "coming and seeing" on the other. Thus it seems to me that we ought nowadays to have rather more courage in inviting one another and not to hold it of little account, to walk along together following each other's example. The "with" appertains to the humanity of faith: it is an essential element of it. In it we bring to maturity our own personal encounter with Jesus. Just as in leading to him and carrying along with us, it is equally important to leave others free, allowing them the liberty for their particular call, even when this appears to be different from what we would have envisaged.

In Luke these ideas are extended to a whole vision of the church. The sons of Zebedee, James and John, are called by him *koinonoi* of Simon, partners, if it can be properly so translated. This means that the three are presented as a little fishing company, a cooperative with Peter as manager and chief proprietor. Jesus, at first, calls this group *koinonia* (*communio*), Simon's company. In the words of his call, however, Simon's secular profession is transformed into an image of the future and the new. The fishing company becomes Jesus's *communio*. The Christians will be the *communio* of that fishing boat, united in their call from Jesus, united in the miracle of grace that gives the riches of the sea after a night without hope. United in making up a single gift, they are likewise united for the mission.

In St. Jerome we find a fine explanation of the title "fishers of men," which, in this case, in this inner transformation of their profession, contributes to a vision of the future church.[2] St. Jerome says that to take the fish out of the water means to draw them out of the jaws of death, and the night without stars means to give them the air and light of heaven. It means to transfer them to the kingdom of life, which, at the same time, is light and gives the vision of the truth. Light is life, since its element, by which human beings live in their inmost selves, is truth, which is at the same time love. Naturally people swimming in the waters of this present life are not conscious of that. That is why they furiously oppose anyone trying to pull them out of the water. They think they are, as it were, a kind of fish, which will die soon after being drawn out of deep water. That, of course, would be truly mortal. But this death leads to the true life, in which one truly begins to find the meaning of one's life. To be a disciple means to let oneself be caught by Jesus, by him, the Fish wrapped in mystery, who came down into the waters of this world, into the waters of death, who has become even a fish to let himself be caught by us so as to become for us the food of life. He lets himself be caught so that we will let ourselves be seized by him and find the courage to let ourselves be drawn with him out of the waters of our habits and comforts. Jesus has become a fisher of men by the fact that he himself has taken on himself the dark night of the sea and come down in person into the depths of his Passion. We can only become fishers of men when we give ourselves totally, as he did. But we cannot do this except when we trust ourselves to the bark of Peter, when we enter personally into Peter's *communio*. Vocation is not a private matter; it is not a pursuing of the reality of Jesus for our own sake. The place for it is the whole church, which can only subsist in communion with Peter and in that way with the apostles of Jesus Christ.

PRIESTLY SPIRITUALITY IN PSALM 16

Secondly, since I deem important the unity of the two testaments, I should like to take now a text of the Old Testament, Psalm 16 (15 according to the Greek numbering). Verse 5 of this psalm was pronounced, by the older ones among us, at the giving of the Tonsure, at reception into the clerical state, almost as if it were the watchword for having assumed the full undertaking. When I go through the psalm (it is to be found now in Compline of Thursday), it always makes me think again of how I sought then in my understanding of this text to study the procedure of what I was undertaking, so as to carry it out with a deeper understanding. So I treasure this verse for the light it gives me, and it has remained to this day a personal motto signifying the essence of the priestly state and the way to live it. This verse runs thus in the Vulgate translation: "*Dominus pars hereditatis meae et calicis mei: Tu es qui restitues hereditatem meam mihi*" ("The Lord is the portion of my inheritance and of my cup. It is you who will give back to me my inheritance").

This passage makes more concrete what was expressed in verse 2: "I have no good [no happiness] apart from thee!" It does it indeed in worldly language, pragmatically, and I would almost say not in theological language at all—that is in the language of the land proprietor and the distribution of holdings in Israel, as it is described in the Pentateuch or in the Book of Joshua.

In this distribution to the tribes of Israel, the tribe of Levi, the priestly tribe, were excluded. They were given no land. For them was the saying: "Yahweh [the Lord God] is his inheritance" (Dt 10:9; Jo 13:33). "I [Yahweh] am your portion and your inheritance" (Nm 18:20). Here it is a question, at first, of a simple, concrete law of preservation: the Israelites lived on the land assigned to them; their land is the physical basis for their existence. Through the possession of the physical earth on which they exist through the possession of the soil, there is, so to speak, life assigned to each one of them. Only the priests do not draw their living from the agricultural work of a countryman on his own plot. The sole foundation of their life, even physically, is Yahweh himself. To put it in concrete terms, they lived on their share of the sacrificial offerings and the other cultic gifts; they lived on what was offered to God, in which they were made sharers because they were entrusted with the divine service.

Thus two forms of physical support are expressed at first. In the general context of the thinking of Israel, however, these necessarily bear on something deeper. The land is for an Israelite not only the guarantee of a livelihood; it is the way in which he shares in God's promise made to Abraham, of his inclusion, that is, in the future vital context of the chosen people. Thus it becomes at the same time a pledge of sharing in the very living power of God. By contrast, the Levite is one who has no land, and in this sense, one who is not supported, who is excluded from the earthly guarantees. He is projected directly and exclusively on Yahweh, as it says in Psalm 22:10.

Although it could seem, at least at first sight, that land is being substituted for God as a guarantee of subsistence, almost as offering an independent form of security, this view is, however, alien to the levitical concept of life. God alone is the direct guarantee of life; even earthly physical life is founded on him. If there were no longer divine worship, there would no longer be sustenance for life. Thus the life of the Levite is at the same time privilege and risk. Nearness to God is the one and only and direct means of life.

Here we have an important consideration to make. The terminology of verses 5 and 6 is evidently the terminology of land appropriation and the different apportioning to the tribe of Levi of what was necessary for their subsistence. It means that this psalm is the song of a priest who is expressing in it the physical and spiritual focus of his life. The one praying here has what has been established by the law: deprivation of external property, with subsistence from the divine service and for the divine service, not explained only in this sense of a defined mode of subsistence but lived in its true basic principle. He has spiritualized the law, transposed it to Christ, precisely because he fully realized its true content. What for us is important in this psalm is firstly the fact that it is a priestly prayer; secondly that we find here the inner self-surmounting of the Old Testament moving toward Christ, the Old Testament drawing near to the New, and thus we can admire the unity in the history of salvation. To live not by virtue of possessions but by the sacrifice means for the one praying is to live in the presence of God, in intimate recourse to him, thus giving stability to one's existence. Hans Joachim Kraus observes very aptly that here the Old Testament allows an understanding of what is required for mystical communion with God, as it develops from the uniqueness of the levitical prerogative.[3]

Yahweh has become, therefore, the "holding" of the one praying. The dimension this reality assumes concretely in daily life appears clearly in the following verses. There it says: "The Lord is always at my right hand." To journey with God, to know him to be always at one's side, to speak with him, look to him, and to lay oneself open to his scanning look—this is shown to be at the heart of this prerogative of the Levites. In this way God truly becomes a property, the land of one's life. Thus we dwell and "stay" with him. Here the psalm tallies with what we have found in John. It follows, therefore, that to be a priest means to walk with him, and so to learn to see; it is to stay with him where he dwells.

How this is so is still clearer in the verses that follow. The one praying here blesses Yahweh, who has "counseled" him, and thanks him because at night he has "instructed" him. The Septuagint and the Vulgate are with this formulation evidently thinking of the physical laws that "educate" a person. "Education" is understood as being correctly adjusted to the true dimensions of a human being, which is not to be realized without suffering. The word *education* would be, in this case, a comprehensive expression for the direction of a person along the way of salvation; through that process of transformation by which from being clay we become an image of God, and so are able to receive God for eternity. The rod of the one who corrects is here replaced by the sufferings of life, by which God leads us, brings us to live close to him. All this is recalled to us also by the great psalm of the word of God, Psalm 119, which we recite at the Midday Office during the week. Its construction is built precisely around the basic existential affirmation of the Levite's life: "The LORD is my portion" (v. 57; cf. v. 14). And in this assertion, the motifs with which Psalm 16 expounds this reality return with manifold variations. "Thy testimonies ... are my counsellors" (v. 24). "It is good for me that I was afflicted, that I might learn thy statutes" (v. 71). "In faithfulness thou hast afflicted me. Let thy steadfast love be ready to comfort me" (v. 75). So we begin to understand the depth of the invocation that runs through the whole psalm like a refrain: "Teach me thy statutes" (vv. 12, 26, 29, 33, 64). Where life becomes truly anchored like this in the Word of God, we find that the Lord "counsels" us. The biblical word is no longer an indifferent expression, distant and general, but a term that affects life directly. It leaves history's distance behind and becomes a personal word for me. "The Lord counsels me": my life now becomes a word originating from him. So the saying comes true: "Thou dost show me the path of life" (Ps 16:11). Life ceases to be a dark enigma. We learn what it means to live. Life unfolds its meaning and, in the very midst of the pain of "being educated," it becomes joy. "Thy statues have been my songs," says Psalm 119 (v. 54), and Psalm 16 expresses it no differently: "Therefore my heart is glad and my soul rejoices" (v. 9); "In thy presence there is fullness of joy, in thy right hand are pleasures for evermore" (v. 11).

When such readings from the Old Testament are put into practice and the Word of God is accepted as the ground of life, then comes the contact with him whom we believe to be the living Word of God. It seems to me that it was not by chance that this psalm became in the ancient church the great prophecy of the Resurrection, the description of the new David and the one true Priest, Jesus Christ. To know life does not mean applying some technique or another, but going beyond death. The mystery of Jesus Christ, his death and Resurrection, shine out where the suffering of the Word and its indestructible force of life become a living experience.

For this there is no need to make any great transposition in our own spiritual life. Fundamental parts of the priesthood are something like the status of the Levites, exposed, without land, projected on God. The account of vocation in Luke 5:1–11, which we considered first, ends not without reason with the words: "They left everything and followed him" (v. 11). Without such a forsaking on our part, there is no priesthood. The call to follow is not possible without this sign of freedom and renunciation of any kind of compromise. I think that from this point of view, celibacy acquires its great significance as the foregoing of a future earthly home and a life in chosen and familiar surroundings, and thus it becomes truly indispensable, in order that being given over to God may remain fundamental and become truly realized. This means—it is clear—that celibacy imposes its demands in any setting up of one's life. Its full significance cannot be attained if for everything else we follow the rules of property and of life's game, as commonly accepted today. It is above all not possible for celibacy to have stability if we do not make remaining close to God the center of our life. Psalm 16, like Psalm 119, is a strong pointer to the necessity for continual meditation to make the Word of God our own, for only in this way can we be at home with it and can it become our home. The community aspect of liturgical prayer and worship necessarily connected with this comes out here, where Psalm 16 speaks of the Lord as "my cup" (v. 5). In accordance with the language usual in the Old Testament, this reference is to the festive cup that was passed from hand to hand at the sacrificial meal, or to the fatal cup, the cup of wrath or salvation. The

New Testament praying person can find indicated here in a special way that chalice by means of which the Lord becomes in the deepest sense our land, our inheritance: the eucharistic chalice, in which he shares himself with us as our life. The priestly life in the presence of God thus takes on actuality in our life in virtue of the eucharistic mystery. In the most profound sense, the Eucharist is the land that has become our portion and of which we can say: "The lines have fallen for me in pleasant places; yea, I have a goodly heritage" (v. 6).

THE TWO FUNDAMENTAL CONSEQUENCES ARISING FROM THESE BIBLICAL TEXTS

The Unity of the Two Testaments

Particularly important in this priestly prayer of the Old and New Testaments is, in my opinion, the unity between the two testaments; thus the unity of biblical spirituality with its fundamental exemplifications appears clearly realizable. This is highly important, because one of the main reasons for the crisis in the priestly image, from the point of view of both exegesis and theology, is the casting off of the Old Testament. The Old Testament is seen only in the light of the dialectical opposition between law and gospel. It is taken for granted that the New Testament ministry would have nothing in common with the Old Testament ministry. It is an unacceptable refutation of the Catholic concept of the priesthood that this could be presented as a reversion to the Old Testament. Christology would mean the abolition of any priesthood, the attenuation of the boundaries between the sacred and the profane, the setting aside of the whole history of the religion, abandoning its concept of priesthood—as some have actually said. Everywhere in the image of the church's priest, links can be found with the Old Testament or with the religious patrimony of the history of religion, the fact counted as a sign of the decline of the Christian message toward some ecclesiasticism and as proof against the image of the church's priest. Thus there was complete separation from the well-head of all biblical piety and of human experience in general, and relegation to being a profanation, whose spasmodic Christonomonism has in reality destroyed even the image of the Christ of the Bible. This, in its turn, depended on the fact that the Old Testament itself was constructed as a contraposition of the law and the prophets, where however the law was identified with the cultic and priestly element, and the prophetic dimension with criticism of the cult and a pure ethic of the human community, finding God not in the temple but in the neighbor. At the same time, the cultic element could be stylized on the example of the legal element, and prophetic piety characterized instead as faith in the grace of God. In all this, the position of the New Testament was relegated to the anticultic, to pure common humanity, and later attempts to open a door to the priesthood could not achieve consistent and convincing results.

The theological controversy on this whole thought complex has yet to take place. Anyone reciting the priestly Psalm 16 together with the psalms connected with it, especially Psalm 119, sees clearly that a fundamental contraposition of cult and prophets, priesthood and prophecy, relative to Christology, disappears completely, since this psalm is at the same time and in the same measure as much a priestly prayer as a prophetic prayer. In this psalm the purer and more profound aspect of prophetic piety appears evident, precisely as priestly piety. It is, then, a Christological text. And precisely for this reason, Christianity in its earliest formation interpreted it as a prayer of Jesus Christ, and believed that Christ, in turn, applies it to us, so that we in our turn can recite it with him (cf. Acts 2:25–29). In it is shown prophetically the new priesthood of Christ, and from this it is clear that the New Testament priesthood subsists in virtue of Christ in the unity of the history of salvation, and must continue to exist. Beginning with him, it can be understood that he does not abolish the law, but rather fulfills it and, after having transmitted it anew to the church, exalts it in the church as an expression of grace. The Old Testament belongs to Christ and, in Christ, to us. Only in the unity of the two testaments can the faith continue to live.

The Sacred and the Profane

Here we arrive at the second consideration. Along with the recapture of the Old Testament, we must overcome the anathematization of the sacral and the mystification of the profane. By its nature Christianity is a ferment and a leaven; the sacral is not closed and completed but dynamic. The priest has received the mandate: "Go, therefore, and make disciples of all nations" (Mt 28:19). But this dynamic of mission, this inner opening out and ampleness of the gospel, cannot be translated by the formulas "Go into the world and become world yourselves" and "Go into the world and conform yourselves to its worldliness": the contrary is true. There is God's holy mystery, the Gospels' grain of mustard seed, which does not identify with the world, but is destined to be the ferment for the whole world. Therefore we ought to find the courage again to return to the sacral, the courage to look in Christian reality, not to set limits but to transform, to be truly dynamic. Eugene Ionesco, a founder of the theater of the absurd, expressed this in 1975 in an interview, with all the strong feeling of a man of our time seeking and thirsting after truth. I quote a few sentences: "The church does not want to lose her clients, she wants to acquire new members. This produces a kind of secularization which is truly deplorable." "The world is going astray, the church is going astray in the world, priests are stupid and mediocre, happy to be only mediocre people like the rest, to be little proletarians of the left. I heard a parish priest in one church saying: 'Let's all be happy together, let's shake hands all round … Jesus jovially wishes you a lovely day, have a good day!' Before long there will be a bar with bread and wine for Communion; and sandwiches and Beaujolais will be handed round. It seems to me incredible stupidity, a total absence of spirit. Fraternity is neither mediocrity nor fraternisation. We need the eternal; because … what is religion? what is the Holy? We are left with nothing; with no stability everything is fluid. And yet what we need is a rock."[4] In this context there are some provocative sentences to be found in Peter Handke's new work, *On Villages*, that also come to my mind. There we read: "No one wants us, and no one has ever wanted us…. Our homes are empty shells of despair…. We are not on the wrong path, we are not on any path…. How abandoned is humankind!"[5] I think that if we listen to the voices of people who are conscious of living in this world, it will be clear to us that we cannot serve this world by means of trite compliance. The world does not need us to agree with it, but for us to transform it with radical evangelization.

To conclude, I wish to refer to yet another text: Mark 10:28–31. It is the part when Peter says to Jesus: "Lo, we have left everything and followed you." Matthew explains the point of the query by adding: "What then shall we have in exchange?" (Mt 19:27). We have already spoken of forsaking everything. It is an indispensable element in apostolic and priestly spirituality. Let us, therefore, consider Jesus's reply, which is surprising. He in no way rejects Peter's request because Peter is expecting a reward, but says he is right: "Truly, I say to you, there is no one who has left house or brothers or sisters or father or mother or children or lands, for my sake and for the gospel, who will not receive a hundredfold now in this time, houses and brothers and sisters and mothers and lands, with persecutions, and in the age to come eternal life" (Mk 10:29ff). God is generous, and if we look at our lives with sincerity, we can see that whatever we have given up he has truly repaid a hundred to one. He does not let himself be overtaken by us in generosity. He does not wait for the next life to give us our reward, but he gives us the hundredfold right now, even if this world does remain a world of persecutions, sorrows, and sufferings. St. Teresa of Avila has reduced this passage to the simple form: "Already in this life God gives a hundred for one."[6] We only need the initial courage to be the first to give that "one," just like Peter who on the word of the Lord pushes out again in the morning—he gives one and receives a hundred.

Even today the Lord invites us to push out into the deep, and I am sure we will have the same surprise as Peter: the fish will be in abundance, because the Lord dwells in Peter's boat—the boat that has become his cathedra and throne of mercy.

The Place of Mariology in the Bible

A discriminating observer of the church's life today will discover a peculiar dichotomy in the church's Marian belief and devotion. On the one hand, the impression is given that Mariology is a scaled-down duplicate of Christology that somehow arose on irrational grounds; or even more, it appears to be but the echo of ancient models found in the history of religions, which ineradicably returns to claim its position and value even in Christianity, although closer examination shows that there are neither historical nor theological grounds to support it. Historical support is lacking because Mary obviously plays scarcely any role in Jesus's career; she appears, rather, under the sign of misunderstanding. Theological support is lacking because the Virgin-Mother has no place in the structure of the New Testament credo. Indeed, many find no embarrassment in identifying the non-Christian origin of Marian belief and devotion: from Egyptian myths, from the cult of the Great Mother, from Diana of Ephesus, who, entirely on her own, became "Mother of God" (Øeotókos) at the council convened in Ephesus.... On the other hand, there are those who plead for a magnanimity with regard to diverse types of piety: without puritanical tendencies, we should just leave the Romans their madonnas.[1] Behind this generosity can be seen an attitude that becomes noticeably stronger as a result of the trend toward rationalization of Christianity—namely, the longing for a response in the religious sphere to the demands of emotion, and after that, the longing for the image of woman as virgin and mother to have a place in religion, as well. Of course, mere tolerance in the face of manifold customs will not suffice to justify Marian piety. If its basis was as negligible as might appear from the considerations just mentioned, then the continued cultivation of Marian piety would be nothing but a custom contrary to truth. Such customs either wither away because their root, the truth, has dried up, or they continue to proliferate contrary to conviction, and thus destroy the correlation between truth and life. They thereby lead to a poisoning of the intellectual-spiritual organism, the results of which are incalculable.

Thus there is need of deeper reflection. Before entering into an examination of individual texts, we must direct our attention to the whole picture, the question of structure. Only in this way can a meaningful arrangement of individual elements be obtained. Is there any place at all for something like Mariology in holy scripture, in the overall pattern of its faith and prayer? Methodologically, one can approach this question in one of two ways, backwards or forwards, so to speak: one can either read back from the New Testament into the Old or, conversely, feel one's way slowly from the Old Testament into the New. Ideally both ways should coincide, permeating one another, to produce the most exact image possible. If one begins by reading backwards—or, more precisely, from the end to the beginning—it becomes obvious that the image of Mary in the New Testament is woven entirely of Old Testament threads. In this reading, two or even three major strands of tradition can be clearly distinguished that were used to express the mystery of Mary. First, the portrait of Mary includes the likeness of the great mothers of the Old Testament: Sarah and especially Hannah, the mother of Samuel. Second, into that portrait is woven the whole theology of the daughter of Zion, in which, above all, the prophets announced the mystery of election and covenant, the mystery of God's love for Israel. A third strand can perhaps be identified in the Gospel of John: the figure of Eve, the "woman" par excellence, is borrowed to interpret Mary.[2]

These first observations, which we will have to pursue later, offer us a guide to the Old Testament; they indicate where those elements lie that are pregnant with the future. All consequent Marian piety and theology is fundamentally based upon the Old Testament's deeply anchored theology of woman, a theology indispensable to its entire structure. Contrary to a widespread prejudice, the figure of woman occupies an irreplaceable place in the overall texture of Old Testament faith and piety.[3] This fact is seldom taken into sufficient consideration. Consequently, a one-sided reading of the Old Testament opens no door for an understanding of the Marian element in the church of the New Testament. Usually only one side is taken into consideration: the prophets conducted a relentless battle for the uniqueness of God against the temptation to polytheism, and as matters then stood this was a battle against the goddess of heaven, a battle against the fertility religion, which imagined God to be man and woman. In practice it was a resolute battle against the cultic representation of the divine woman in temple prostitution, a battle against a cult that celebrated fertility by imitating it in ritual fornication. For this reason, idolatry is usually referred to in the literature of the Old Testament as "fornication." The rejection of these representations apparently led to the result that Israel's cult is primarily an affair of men, since the women certainly stay in the outer court of the temple.[4]

From the above considerations, it has been concluded that women had no role at all in the faith of the Old Testament, and that there is and can be no theology of woman because the Old Testament's chief concern is precisely the opposite: to exclude woman from theology, from the language of God. This would then mean that Mariology de facto could only be seen as the infiltration of a nonbiblical model. Consistent with this view is the contention that at the Council of Ephesus (431), which confirmed and defended Mary's title as "Mother of God," the previously rejected "Great Mother" of pagan piety had, in reality, secured a place for herself in the church. This view's presuppositions about the Old Testament, however, are false. For even though the prophetic faith rejects the model of deities set in "syzygies," in pairs, and the cultic expression of this model in sacred prostitution, it gives to woman, in its own way, an indispensable place in its own model of belief and life, corresponding to marriage on the human level.[5] One could even say that whereas the worldwide fertility cults provide the immediate theological basis for prostitution, Israel's belief in God with respect to the relation of man and woman expresses itself as marriage. Here, marriage is the immediate "translation" of theology, the consequence of an image of God; here and only here does there exist in the true sense a theology of marriage, just as in the fertility cults there exists a theology of prostitution.[6] This is admittedly obscured in the Old Testament by many compromises, but what Jesus maintains in Mark 10:1–12 and what Ephesians 5 then further explains theologically is entirely the consequence of Old Testament theology. In addition, the idea and reality of virginity also emerge. For virginity is most intimately connected to the theological foundation of marriage; it does not stand in opposition to marriage, but rather signifies its fruit and confirmation.

But let us attempt, at long last, to get down to details. By tracing back to the Old Testament those elements by means of which the New Testament theologically interprets the figure of Mary, we have already hit upon three strands of a theology of woman.

1. In the first place we have to mention the figure of Eve. She is depicted as the necessary opposite pole of man, Adam. His being without her would be "not good" (Gn 2:18). She comes, not from the earth but from himself: in the "myth" or "legend" of the rib is expressed the most intimate reference of man and woman to each other. In that mutual reference, the wholeness of humanity is first realized. The necessary condition for the creation of mankind, to be fulfilled in the oneness of man and woman, is apparent here, just as previously Genesis 1:27 had portrayed mankind from the very beginning as masculine and feminine in its likeness to God, and had mysteriously, cryptically, linked its resemblance to God with the mutual reference of the sexes to each other.

Admittedly the text also makes clear the ambivalence of this reference: woman can become a temptation for man, but simultaneously she is the mother of all life, whence she receives her name. In my opinion it is significant that her name is bestowed in Genesis 3:20 *after* the Fall, *after* God's words of judgment. In this way the undestroyed dignity and majesty of woman are expressed. She preserves the mystery of life, the power opposed to death; for death is like the power of nothingness, the antithesis of Yahweh, who is the creator of life and the God of the living. She, who offers the fruit that leads to death, whose task manifests a mysterious kinship with death, is nonetheless from now on the keeper of the seal of life and the antithesis of death. The woman, who bears the key of life, thus touches directly the mystery of being, the living God, from whom in the last analysis all life originates and who, for that reason, is called "life," the "living one."[7] We will see how precisely these relationships are taken up again in the dogma of the Assumption.

2. In the Old Testament's history of promises, it is true that the patriarchs stand in the foreground as the true bearers of that history. Yet the mothers also played a specific role. In the history of the patriarchs, Sarah-Hagar, Rachel-Leah, and Hannah-Penina are pairs of women in whom the extraordinary element in the path of the promises stands out. In each case the fertile and the infertile stand opposite each other, and in the process a remarkable reversal in values is reached.[8] In archaic modes of thought, fertility is a blessing; infertility is a curse. Yet here all is reversed: the infertile one ultimately turns out to be truly blessed, while the fertile one recedes into the ordinary or even has to struggle against the curse of repudiation, of being unloved. The theological implication of this overthrow of values becomes clear only gradually; from it Paul developed his theology of spiritual birth: the true son of Abraham is not the one who traces his physical origin to him, but the one who, in a new way beyond mere physical birth, has been conceived through the creative power of God's word of promise. Physical life as such is not really wealth; this promise, which endures beyond life, is what first makes life fully itself (cf. Rom 4; Gal 3:1–14; 4:21–31).

At an earlier stage of the Old Testament's evolution, a theology of grace was developed from this reversal of values in the song of Hannah, which is echoed in Mary's *Magnificat:* the Lord raises the humble from the dust; he lifts the poor from the ashes (1 Sm 2:7–8). God bends down to the humble, the powerless, the rejected, and in this condescension the love of God, which truly saves, shines forth both for Hannah and for Mary, in the remarkable phenomenon of unblessed-blessed women. The mystery of the last place (Lk 14:10), the exchange between the first and the last place (Mk 10:31), the reversal of values in the Sermon on the Mount, the reversal of earthly values founded upon *hubris*—all of this is intimated. Here also the theology of virginity finds its first, still hidden formulation: earthly infertility becomes true fertility....

3. Near the end of the Old Testament Canon, in the late writings, a new and, again, entirely original type of theology of woman is developed. The great salvific figures of Esther and Judith appear, taking up again the most ancient tradition as it was embodied, for example, in the figure of the judge Deborah. Esther and Judith have an essential characteristic in common with the great mothers: one is a widow, the other a harem-wife at the Persian court, and thus both find themselves—in different ways—in an oppressed state. Both embody the defeated Israel: Israel who has become a widow and wastes away in sorrow; Israel who has been abducted and dishonored among the nations, enslaved to their arbitrary desires. Yet both personify at the same time the unconquered spiritual strength of Israel, which cannot boast as do the worldly powers and for that very reason knows how to scorn and overcome the mighty. The woman as savior, the embodiment of Israel's hope, thereby takes her place alongside the unblessed-blessed mothers. It is significant that the woman always figures in Israel's thought and belief not as a priestess but as prophetess and judge-savior. What is specifically hers, the place assigned to her, emerges from this.[9] The essence of what has previously been seen is repeated and strengthened: the infertile one, the powerless one becomes the savior because it is there that the locus for the revelation of God's power is found. After every fall into sin, the woman remains "mother of life."

4. In the theological short-story type of the woman-savior, one finds already presupposed and newly expressed what the prophetic preaching had developed with theological profundity from the image of the great maternal women, and what is considered the proper center of the Old Testament's theology of woman: Israel herself, the chosen people, is interpreted simultaneously as woman, virgin, beloved, wife, and mother. The great women of Israel represent what their people is. The history of these women becomes the theology of God's people and, at the same time, the theology of the covenant. By making the covenant comprehensible and by giving it meaning and spiritual orientation, the figure of the woman enters the most intimate reaches of Old Testament piety, of the Old Testament relationship with God. Probably the notion of covenant was at first largely patterned after the model of ancient Eastern vassal indentures, in which the sovereign king assigns rights and duties.[10] This political and legal notion of the covenant, however, is continually deepened and surpassed in the theology of the prophets: the covenant of Yahweh to Israel is a covenant of marital love, which—as in Hosea's magnificent vision—moves and stirs Yahweh himself to his heart. He has loved the young maiden Israel with a love that has proved indestructible, eternal. He

can be angry with the wife of his youth on account of her adultery. He can punish her, but all this is simultaneously directed against himself and pains him, the lover, whose "bowels churn." He cannot repudiate her without rendering judgment against himself. It is on this, on his personal, innermost bewilderment as lover, that the covenant's eternal and irrevocable character is based. "How could I betray you, Ephraim, or hand you over, Israel ...? My heart turns against me, my mercy catches fire all at once. I do not act according to the fire of my anger, I no longer annihilate Ephraim, for I am God and not man, the Holy One in your midst. I do not come to destroy all in flames" (Hos 11:8ff.).[11] God's divinity is no longer revealed in his ability to punish but in the indestructibility and constancy of his love.

This means that the relationship between God and Israel includes not only God but also Israel as woman, who, in this relationship with God, is at once virgin and mother. For this reason, the covenant, which forms the very basis of the existence of Israel as a nation and the existence of each individual as an Israelite, is expressed interpersonally in the fidelity of the marriage covenant and in no other way. Marriage is the form of the mutual relationship between husband and wife that results from the covenant, the fundamental human relationship upon which all human history is based. It bears a theology within itself, and indeed it is possible and intelligible only theologically. But above all, this also means that to God, the One, is joined not a goddess but, as in his historical revelation, the chosen creature, Israel, the daughter of Zion, the woman. To leave woman out of the whole of theology would be to deny creation and election (salvation history) and thereby nullify revelation. In the women of Israel, the mothers and the saviors, in their fruitful infertility is expressed most purely and most profoundly what creation is and what election is, what "Israel" is as God's people. And because election and revelation are one, what ultimately becomes apparent in this for the first time is who and what God is.

Of course, this line of development in the Old Testament remains just as incomplete and open as all the other lines of the Old Testament. It acquires its definitive meaning for the first time in the New Testament—in the woman who is herself described as the true holy remnant, as the authentic daughter of Zion, and who is thereby the mother of the Savior, yes, the mother of God. In passing, one might mention that the acceptance of the Canticle of Canticles into the Canon of scripture would have been impossible if this theology of love and woman had not existed. The Canticle is certainly, on technical grounds, a collection of profane love songs with a heavily erotic coloring. But once the songs have entered the Canon, they serve as an expression of God's dialogue with Israel, and to that extent such an interpretation of them is anything but mere allegory.[12]

5. In the last layers of the Old Testament, a further, remarkable line of development comes to light, which likewise does not lend itself to interpretation within the context of the Old Testament alone. The figure of wisdom (Sophia) attains central significance. She was probably taken over from Egyptian prototypes and then adapted to Israel's belief. "Wisdom" appears as the mediatrix of Creation and salvation history, as God's first creature, in whom both the pure, primordial form of his creative will and the pure *answer* that he discovers find their expression; indeed, one can say that precisely this concept of the answer is formative for the Old Testament idea of wisdom. Creation answers, and the answer is as close to God as a playmate, a lover.[13]

We have previously noted that in order to interpret Mary, the New Testament refers back to the mothers of the Old Testament, to the theology of the daughter of Zion, and probably also to Eve, and then ties these three lines of development together. We must now add that the church's liturgy expands this Old Testament theology of woman insofar as it interprets the woman-saviors, Esther and Judith, in terms of Mary and refers the Wisdom texts to Mary. This has been sharply criticized by this century's liturgical movement in view of its Christocentric theology; it has been argued that these texts can and should allow only a Christological interpretation. After years of wholehearted agreement with this latter view, it is ever clearer to me that it actually misjudges what is most characteristic in those Wisdom texts. While it is correct to observe that Christology assimilated essential elements of the wisdom idea, so that one must speak of a Christological strand in the New Testament's continuation of the notion of wisdom, a remainder nevertheless resists total integration into Christology. In both Hebrew and Greek, *wisdom* is a feminine noun, and this is no empty grammatical phenomenon in antiquity's vivid awareness of language. *Sophia*, a feminine noun, stands on that side of reality which is represented by the woman, by what is purely and simply feminine. It signifies the answer that emerges from the divine call of Creation and election. It expresses precisely this: that there is a pure answer and that God's love finds its irrevocable dwelling place within it. In order to deal with the full complexity of the facts of the case, one must certainly consider that the word for "Spirit" in Hebrew (not, however, in Greek) is feminine. In that respect, because of the teaching about the Spirit, one can, as it were, practically have a presentiment of the primordial type of the feminine, in a mysterious, veiled manner, within God himself. Nevertheless, the doctrine of the Spirit and the doctrine of wisdom represent separate strands of tradition. From the viewpoint of the New Testament, wisdom refers, on one side, to the Son as the Word in whom God creates, but, on the other side, to the creature, the true Israel, who is personified in the humble maid whose whole existence is marked by the attitude of *Fiat mihi secundum verbum tuum*. Sophia refers to the Logos, the Word who establishes wisdom, and also to the womanly answer, which receives wisdom and brings it to fruition. The eradication of the Marian interpretation of Sophiology ultimately leaves out an entire dimension of the biblical and Christian mystery.

Thus we can now say the figure of the woman is indispensable for the structure of biblical faith. She expresses the reality of Creation, as well as the fruitfulness of grace. The abstract outlines for the hope that God will turn toward his people receive, in the New Testament, a concrete, personal name in the figure of Jesus Christ. At that same moment, the figure of the woman, until then seen only typologically in Israel although provisionally personified by the great women of Israel, also emerges with a name: Mary. She emerges as the personal epitome of the feminine principle in such a way that the principle is true only in the person, but the person as an individual always points beyond herself to the all-embracing reality that she bears and represents.[14] To deny or reject the feminine aspect in belief, or more concretely, the Marian aspect, leads finally to the negation of Creation and the invalidation of grace. It leads to a picture of God's omnipotence that reduces the creature to a mere masquerade and that also completely fails to understand the God of the Bible, who is characterized as being the creator and the God of the covenant—the God for whom the beloved's punishment and rejection themselves become the passion of love, the cross. Not without reason did the church fathers interpret the Passion and cross as marriage, as that suffering in which God takes upon himself the pain of the faithless wife in order to draw her to himself irrevocably in eternal love.[15]

PART SIX

THE
PRIESTHOOD

The Nature of the Priesthood

Speech Given at the Opening of
the VIIIth Ordinary Assembly of the
Synod of Bishops on Priestly Formation

OCTOBER 1, 1990

The Catholic conception of priesthood, defined by the Council of Trent and reiterated by the Second Vatican Council with fresh attention to the testimony of sacred scripture, has come into crisis in the postconciliar era. The great number of those who have left the priesthood and the enormous decline in priestly vocations in many countries certainly cannot be attributed to theological causes alone. The extra-ecclesial causes, however, would not have been nearly so influential if the theological foundations of the priestly ministry had not been discredited among many priests and young people.

In the new cultural situation that has evolved since the council, the old arguments of the sixteenth-century Reformation, together with more recent findings of modern biblical exegesis—which, moreover, was nourished by the presuppositions of the Reformation—acquired a certain plausibility, and Catholic theology was unable to respond to them adequately.

What are these arguments? We might first of all mention a terminological consideration that emerges from a more careful study of sacred scripture. The early church employed profane rather than sacral terminology when referring to its ministries. There is no evident continuity between these ministries and the priesthood of the Mosaic Law. Moreover, these ministries, which for a long time were not very clearly defined, assumed a variety of names and forms. Only toward the end of the first century was some clarity reached regarding the form and content of the ministries, although the process of definition had not yet come to an end. It is, however, of great significance that the cultic function of these ministries is nowhere explicitly mentioned. These ministries are never explicitly linked with the eucharistic celebration. The preaching of the gospel appears as their primary function, together with a variety of other services for the life of the Christian community.

The theory has been derived from this fact: the ministries of the nascent church were at that time viewed not in terms of sacrament but only in terms of function. To these observations may easily be linked a theory that says that the Christian faith restores the profane world, that its real intention was to thoroughly remove everything sacred—a theory whose aim is to develop fully and apply the views of Karl Barth and Dietrich Bonhoeffer on the opposition between faith and religion.

Not uncommonly cited as a biblical basis for these views were the words of the Letter to the Hebrews, where it is said that Jesus suffered outside the gate and that he is inviting us to go out to him there (Heb 13:12–13). Against the real intent of these words, which express a profound theology of the cross, it was rather said: At the moment of Jesus's death, the veil of the temple was rent. There was no longer any separation between temple and world, between the sacred and the profane. The death of Christ in the midst of the world shows us that acts of love performed in the midst of life can be the only legitimate liturgy in the New Testament era.

Such views, derived from modern exegesis, somehow presuppose hermeneutical decisions developed in the period of the Protestant Reformation and endow them with new force. A basic key in the new reading of scripture that has been born in these times must be found in the opposition between law and gospel that was deduced from Pauline theology. The law that has been abolished is opposed to the gospel. Priesthood and cult (sacrifice) would seem to belong to the category of law: the gospel is said to express itself in the figure of the prophets and in the preaching of the Word. For this reason, the categories law-priesthood-sacrifice-cult acquire a negative connotation because they lead man to the letter that kills and to works that cannot justify. The essence of the gospel, on the contrary, would consist in the hearing of the Word and in faith, which alone can render a man just. Thus the figures of the prophet and of preaching are alone congruent with the gospel, while priesthood would pertain to the law and should be thoroughly excluded from the church of the New Testament.

It was this perspective that thoroughly determined the course of modern exegesis, and it shows through at every point. The above-mentioned terminological observations took their force from it. Catholic theology, which since the council has accepted modern exegesis almost without argument, was unaware of its hermeneutical key and thus unable to respond to the great questions to which it would give rise. And so the crisis we spoke about at the beginning was born.

In the meantime, the work of theologians is beginning to acquire a more balanced view of these questions. It should not be forgotten that already in the sixteenth century, after the initial conflicts, the beginnings of a new balance appeared. The ordination to the ministry of preaching among Protestants began after a short time to be seen analogously to a sacrament. Likewise, the connection of the ministry of preaching with the ministry of the eucharistic celebration once again came to light. Even though the term *priesthood* was avoided in the tradition of the confessions of faith that sprang from the Reformation, the ministry of the Word as sacrament was restored in various ways on the basis of New Testament evidence. For this reason, ecumenical dialogue has indeed opened a path by which the hermeneutical key for a correct understanding of sacred scripture can be better defined and the foundations of the Catholic doctrine of priesthood are brought to light in a new way. In this sense, I would like to show briefly how this doctrine clearly emerges from the witness of scripture.

BASIS OF NEW TESTAMENT MINISTRY: THE APOSTOLATE AS PARTICIPATION IN CHRIST'S MISSION

We must acknowledge the novelty of the New Testament to understand the Gospel as gospel, as Good News, but it is also necessary to learn to perceive properly the unity of salvation history as it progresses in the Old and New Covenants. In its very novelty, the message of Christ and his works together fulfill everything that went before and form a visible center that brings God's action and us together. If we seek the true novelty of the New Testament, Christ himself stands before us. This novelty consists not so much in new ideas or conceptions—the novelty is a person, God, who becomes man and draws human beings to himself.

Even the question regarding what the New Testament has to say about priesthood should begin with Christology. The so-called Liberal Age interpreted the figure of Christ on the basis of its own presuppositions. According to its interpretation, Jesus set up pure ethics in opposition to ritually distorted religion; to communal and collective religion he contrasted the freedom and responsibility of the individual person. He himself is portrayed as the great teacher of morals who frees man from the bonds of cult and of rite and without other mediations sets him before God alone with his personal conscience. In the second half of our century, such views have become wedded to the ideas diffused by Marx: Christ is now described as a revolutionary who sets himself against the power of institutions that lead people into slavery, and in this conflict—primarily against the arrogance of the priests—he dies. In this way, he is seen primarily as the liberator of the poor from the oppression of the rich, one who wants to establish the "kingdom," that is, the new society of the free and equal.

The image of Christ that we encounter in the Bible is a very different one. It is clear that we can consider here only those elements that immediately pertain to our problem. The essential factor in the image of Christ handed down by the writings of the New Testament consists in his unique relationship with God. Jesus knows that he has a direct mission from God; God's authority is at work in him (cf. Mt 7:29, 21:25; Mk 1:27, 11:28; Lk 20:2, 24:19, etc.). He proclaims a message that he has received from the Father: he has been "sent" with an office entrusted to him by the Father.

The Evangelist John clearly presents this theme of the "mission" of the Son who proceeds from the Father—a theme that is always present, however, even in the so-called Synoptic Gospels. A "paradoxical" moment of this mission clearly appears in the formula of John that Augustine so profoundly interpreted: "My doctrine is not mine ..." (7:16). Jesus has nothing of his own except the Father. His doctrine is not his own, because for his entire existence he is, as it were, Son from the Father and directed toward the Father. But for the same reason, because he has nothing of his own, everything that the Father has belongs to him as well: "I and the Father are one" (10:30). The giving back of his whole existence and activity to the Father, an act through which he did not seek his own will (5:30), made him credible, because the Word of the Father shone through him like light. Here the mystery of the divine Trinity shines forth, which is also the model for our own existence.

Only from this Christological center can we understand the ministry of the apostles to which the priesthood of Christ's church traces its origin. Toward the beginning of his public life, Jesus created the new figure of twelve chosen men, a figure that is continued after the Resurrection in the ministry of the apostles—that is, of the ones sent. Of great importance for our question is the fact that Jesus gave his power to the apostles in such a way that he made their ministry, as it were, a continuation of his own mission. "He who receives you receives me," he himself says to the Twelve (Mt 10:40; cf. Lk 10:16, Jn 13:10). Many other texts in which Jesus gives his power to the disciples could here be cited: Matthew 9:8, 10:1, 21:23; Mark 8:7, 13:34; Luke 9:1, 10:19. The continuity between the mission of Jesus and that of the apostles is once again illustrated with great clarity in the Fourth Gospel: "As the Father has sent me, even so I send you" (20:21, cf. 13:20, 17:18).

The weight of this sentence is evident if we recall what we said above concerning the structure of the mission of Jesus. As we saw, Jesus himself, sent in the totality of his Person, is indeed mission and relation from the Father and to the Father. In this light, the great importance of the following parallelism appears: "The Son can do nothing of his own accord" (Jn 5:19–30).

"APART FROM ME YOU CAN DO NOTHING" (JOHN 15:5)

This "nothing" that the disciples share with Jesus expresses at one and the same time both the power and the infirmity of the apostolic ministry. By themselves, of their own strength, they can do none of those things that apostles must do. How could they of their own accord say, "I forgive you your sins"? How could they say, "This is my body"? How could they perform the imposition of hands and say, "Receive the Holy Spirit"? None of those things that constitute apostolic activity are done by one's own authority. But this expropriation of their very powers constitutes a mode of communion with Jesus, who is wholly from the Father, with him all things and nothing without him. Their own "*nihil posse*," their own inability to do anything, draws them into a community of mission with Jesus. Such a ministry, in which a man does and gives through a divine communication what he could never do and give on his own, is called by the tradition of the church a sacrament.

If church usage calls ordination to the ministry of priesthood a sacrament, the following is meant: this man is in no way performing functions for which he is highly qualified by his own natural ability, nor is he doing the things that please him most and that are most profitable. On the contrary: the one who receives the sacrament is sent to give what he cannot give of his own strength; he is sent to act in the person of another, to be his living instrument. For this reason, no human being can declare himself a priest; for this reason, too, no community can promote a person to this ministry by its own decree. Only from the sacrament, which belongs to God, can priesthood be received. Mission can only be received from the one who sends—from Christ in his sacrament, through which a person becomes the voice and the hands of Christ in the world. This gift of himself, this renunciation and forgetfulness of self, does not, however, destroy the man; rather, it leads to true human maturity because it assimilates him to the Trinitarian mystery and it brings to life the image according to which we were created. Since we were created in the image of the Trinity, he who loses himself will find himself.

But here we have got somewhat ahead of ourselves. In the meantime we have acquired a number of conclusions of great importance. According to the Gospels, Christ himself handed on the essential structure of his mission to the apostles, to whom he granted his power and whom he associated with his power. This association with the Lord, by which a man receives the power to do what he cannot do alone, is called a sacrament. The new mission created in the choosing of twelve men has a sacramental nature. This structure flows, therefore, from the center of the biblical message.

It is obvious that this ministry created by Christ is altogether new and is in no way derived from the Old Testament, but arises from Jesus Christ with new power. The sacramental ministry of the church expresses the novelty of Jesus Christ and his presence in all phases of history.

APOSTOLIC SUCCESSION

After this brief exposition of the origin and the nucleus of the new ministry founded in Christ, we pose the question: how was all of this received in apostolic times? And above all: how did the transition evolve from the apostolic period into the postapostolic period? Or, in other words: how do we see reflected in the New Testament that apostolic succession which, after the Christological foundation, constitutes the second pillar of Catholic doctrine on New Testament priesthood?

We can treat the first question briefly, because the testimony of St. Paul above all is clear enough on this matter. With great clarity, his vision of the apostolic office appears in that famous statement found in the Second Letter to the Corinthians: "So we are ambassadors for Christ, God making his appeal through us. We beseech you on behalf of Christ, be reconciled to God" (2 Cor 5:20). God exhorts through the apostle, who is the ambassador of Christ. Here clearly appears that nature of the apostolic ministry which we have already learned constitutes the essence of "Sacrament." This structure of speaking and acting not in one's own name but from divine authority appears again when Paul says: "As servants of God we commend ourselves in every way" (6:4).

The substance of the apostolic ministry is also summed up when Paul speaks confidently of the "ministry of reconciliation" given to him (5:18). Reconciliation with God emanates from the cross of Christ, and for this reason it has a "sacramental" nature. Paul presupposes that humankind is living in a state of "alienation" from itself (Eph 2:12). Only by union with the crucified love of Jesus Christ can this alienation of man from God and from himself be overcome, can man find "reconciliation." This process of reconciliation took place on the cross of Christ. The death of Christ as a historical event is past; it becomes present to us in "sacrament." In his First Letter to the Corinthians, the apostle shows the enormously important role that the sacraments of baptism and the Eucharist play in this process, together with the word of reconciliation, which arouses faith and gives us a new birth.

In the light of these observations, it is clear that the apostolic ministry is distinguished by the apostles in the scriptures from the common gifts of Christian existence. With great clarity this specific difference also comes to light when Paul says in the first letter to the Corinthians: "This is how one should regard us, as servants of Christ and stewards of the mysteries of God" (4:1).

This specific difference logically implies the authority of the apostle with respect to the community, an authority he frequently expresses—even in vehement terms, when, for example, he asks the Corinthians: "Shall I come to you with a rod, or with love in a spirit of gentleness?" (4:21). On the basis of this authority, the apostle may even make use of excommunication, "that the spirit may be saved in the day of the Lord Jesus" (5:5). The figure of the apostle explained in this way has nothing in common with that "pneumatic anarchy" that some contemporary theologians attempt to deduce from the First Letter to the Corinthians and to present as the true image of the church.

From our analysis it is clear that the testimony of St. Paul as to the apostolic ministry is in full accord with that which we have already found in the Gospels; in the office of the "New Testament ministries" (2 Cor 3:6) that we are speaking about, we see the same sacramental structure, which is made known to us from the words of the Lord: the apostle acts from an authority that is not his own; he acts from the authority of Christ, not as a member of the community but as one who stands before the community and addresses it in the name of Christ. This dialogical structure pertains to the essence of revelation. Faith is not something that man thinks up on his own; man does not make himself a Christian by his own meditation or by his moral rectitude. Conversion to the faith always comes from without: it is a gift that always comes from another, from Christ, who comes forward to meet us. Where this "divine outside" is obscured, an essential structure of the Christian faith is in danger.

Any community that would set itself up as church or as ecclesial community would thereby destroy the dialogical mystery of revelation and the gift of grace, which is always received from an "other," from outside. In all the sacraments, the gift of God and man's reception of this gift stand opposite each other. The same structure also applies with respect to the Word of God: faith arises not from reading but from hearing; the preaching of the Word through one who has been sent to preach belongs to the structure of the act of faith.

Let us go on now to our second question: does this ministry of the apostles continue after their death in an "apostolic succession," or is this office something unique, which becomes extinct with the death of the apostles? As we look for a response to this highly disputed question, we should first of all remark that the meaning of the term *apostle* was still rather broad in the earliest days of the nascent church. Only in the theology of St. Luke, toward the end of the first Christian generation, is this title reserved to the twelve men chosen by the Lord. Other ministries found at this time had not yet acquired a definitive shape. Certain ministries appear that transcend the boundaries of the local community—prophets and teachers, for example.

At the same time, we see offices that serve the local church. Among Christians who come from a Jewish tradition, the men who hold these offices are called "presbyters," while for the church that arises from the pagan world, we find "bishops and deacons" for the first time in the Letter to the Philippians (1:1).

Little by little, from these beginnings, there emerges a clearly defined structure of the ministries, which by the end of the apostolic era had achieved initial maturity. This emerging maturity is attested above all by two famous texts of the New Testament, about which I would like to speak briefly. In the first place, we should interpret the speech of St. Paul to the presbyters of Asia Minor. This speech was given in Miletus, and in the narrative of Luke it appears as the apostle's last will and testament. In the words here handed down, the principle of apostolic succession is clearly established. The apostle says, according to the tradition of St. Luke: "Keep watch over yourselves and all the flock of which the Holy Spirit has made you overseers. Be shepherds of the Church of God which he bought with his own blood" (Acts 20:28).

Various elements should be looked at here. First of all, two notions that up until this point were unconnected, *presbyter* and *bishop*, are here equated; the traditions of Christians stemming from a Jewish background and those of Christians who entered from paganism coalesce and are explained as a single ministry of apostolic succession.

It is the Holy Spirit who introduces one into this ministry, which in no way comes from the delegation of the community but is, rather, the gift of God, who through his Spirit "sets up bishops." Because this gift is conferred by the Spirit, it has the dignity of sacrament. The duty of the apostles to feed the flock of Christ is thus continued. The apostolic structure sends us back to the mystery of Christ, the true Shepherd, who bought his flock "with his own blood." In these words not only do the traditions of Jewish and Gentile Christians coalesce, but above all—and this is of even greater importance—the ministry of priests and bishops as to their spiritual essence is clearly shown to be the same as the ministry of the apostles. St. Luke distinguishes this essential identity, which constitutes the principle of apostolic succession by means of a formal difference: because he designates only the Twelve by the term *apostle*, we are able to distinguish between the unique nature of the original office and the permanent nature of the succession.

In this sense, the ministry of the presbyters and bishops is different from the mission of the twelve apostles. Presbyters/bishops are successors, but the apostles themselves are not. A certain "once" and also a certain "always" pertain to the structure of revelation and of the church. The power given by Christ to reconcile, to feed, and to teach continues unaltered in the successors, but these are true successors only if "they devote themselves to the apostles' teaching" (Acts 2:42).

The same principles found in the speech of St. Paul at Miletus, which he addressed to the presbyters, are put forward in the First Letter of St. Peter (5:1–4): "So I exhort the elders among you, as a fellow elder and a witness of the sufferings of Christ as well as a partaker in the glory that is to be revealed: Tend the flock of God that is your charge, not by constraint but willingly, not for shameful gain but eagerly, not as domineering over those in your charge but being examples to the flock. And when the Chief Shepherd is manifested, you will obtain the unfading crown of glory." Already in the first words of this apostolic admonition we find an expression of the identity of the apostolic and the presbyteral ministry, which is of great importance: the apostle calls himself "copresbyter," and in this way establishes a theological link between the ministry of the apostles and that of the presbyters.

The theology of the apostolate, which we looked at in the first section, is here transferred to the presbyterate, and in this way a genuine New Testament theology of priesthood is born. By calling himself copresbyter with the presbyters, the apostle is acknowledging that they are constituted in the same ministry as he, and he is thus clearly establishing the principle of apostolic succession.

Another aspect of great importance in answering our question may be found in this short text. Just as in the speech at Miletus, about which we spoke above, here, too, the nature of the apostolic office is summarized in the term *feed*, which is taken from the imagery of the pastor, the shepherd. The significance of this expression is illuminated by the fact that the apostle toward the end of the second chapter (2:25) designates the Lord as the "shepherd and bishop of your souls." Here in the fifth chapter, he follows the same mode of speaking when he calls Christ the chief of shepherds. The apostle, aware of the etymological meaning of the term *bishop*, that is, guard, one who is in charge, who provides, sees this meaning as coinciding with the term *pastor*, shepherd. In this way the formerly secular term *bishop* begins to refer to Christ the Shepherd, and a new Christian terminology appears together with a new "sacrality" of the Christian faith. Just as the term *copresbyter* linked the apostles and their successors the presbyters together, so the term *bishop* refers those successors to Christ and reveals the Christological foundation of the episcopal and presbyteral ministry. It must be said, therefore, that toward the end of the apostolic era in the writings of the New Testament an explicit theology of New Testament priesthood appears. This theology is entrusted to the faithful hands of the church and constitutes the inalienable core of every theology of Christian priesthood for the rest of time.

COMMON PRIESTHOOD AND PARTICULAR PRIESTHOOD: OLD TESTAMENT AND NEW TESTAMENT

As we conclude our reflections, we must discuss the relationship of this new priestly office, born of the mission of Christ to the priesthood of all the faithful. In the writings of the New Testament the notion of the common priesthood is set forth in two places: in the ancient baptismal catechesis that we find in the First Letter of St. Peter and in the greeting to the seven churches in the beginning of the Apocalypse of John (1 Pt 2:9; Rv 1:6). The expression of the common priesthood employed in these texts is taken from the Book of Exodus (19:6). Here the context is that of a divine utterance in which God speaking with Moses on Mount Sinai is offering a covenant to the people of Israel, that they may be God's inheritance and may become "a kingdom of priests" in the midst of the nations. As the Chosen People, they are to be the locus of true worship and, at the same time, a priesthood and temple for the whole world. The baptismal catechesis handed on to us in the Letter of St. Peter transfers this vocation of the people of the Old Covenant to the baptized, thus suggesting that Christians become partakers through baptism of the privileges of the People of God.

What happened on Mount Sinai becomes present in a new way in the sacrament of baptism. The church of Christ in her totality is the living temple where God dwells and is rightly worshiped. Through the ministry of the church, the world is united for the worship of the true God. St. Paul says the same thing in other words in his Letter to the Romans, where he himself speaks as the "minister [leitourgon] of Christ Jesus to the Gentiles in the priestly service [hierourgounta] of the gospel of God, so that the offering [he prosphora] of the Gentiles may be acceptable, sanctified by the Holy Spirit" (Rom 15:16).

It is clear, then, that the common priesthood of the baptized, which follows from their entrance into the history of God's covenant initiated on Mount Sinai and renewed in the cross of Christ, is in no way opposed to the ministerial priesthood, just as the common priesthood of the people of Israel was never set in opposition to its priestly orders. From these observations it is also clear in what sense the ministry of apostolic succession is something truly new, and in what sense this Christian novelty incorporated the preparatory figures of the Old Testament. On the one hand, the apostolic ministry of the church is new, because Christ is new, from whose words, life, and death this ministry flowed. On the other hand, Christ, who makes all things new, at the same time fulfills all the figures that throughout history led up to him. For this reason the new priesthood of the apostles of Jesus Christ and of their successors carries within itself everything which was prophetically contained in the Old Testament. This becomes very clear when we consider the formula that John Colson, after a very careful analysis of the sources, employs to define the nature of Old Testament priesthood. "The essential function of the *kohanim* (*hiereis,* priests) is this: to keep the people aware of its priestly character and to labor that it may live as such and glorify God by its whole existence."

How close this formula is to the words of St. Paul mentioned above is evident. However, the new missionary force proper to the Christian priesthood follows from the fact that Christ on his cross "has broken down the dividing wall" (Eph 2:14), bringing near in his blood those who once were far off (2:15–17). The priesthood of the New Testament, therefore, has this as its aim: that the whole world may become a temple and a sacrifice pleasing to God, that in the end God may be all in all (cf. 1 Cor 15:28).

CONCLUSIONS REGARDING THE PRIESTLY MINISTRY OF TODAY

How these biblical foundations of the ministerial priesthood are to be applied to priestly formation in the circumstances of today is a topic to be discussed by the synod. I cannot anticipate its conclusions, nor do I wish to do so. I take the liberty of offering but a few brief suggestions. We have seen that the priesthood of the New Testament, which appeared first in the apostles, presupposes a true communion with the mission of Jesus Christ. The person who becomes a priest is grafted into his mission.

For this reason, an intimate personal relationship with Christ is fundamental for priestly life and ministry. All priestly formation should lead to the fostering of this relationship. The priest should be a person who knows Jesus intimately, has met him and learned to love him. The priest should therefore be a man of prayer, a truly "spiritual" man. Without strong spiritual substance, he cannot last in his ministry. From the mystery of Christ he should also learn in his life not to seek himself nor his own promotion. He should learn to spend his life for Christ and for his flock.

Such a way of living is opposed to our natural inclination, but little by little it becomes clear that only he who is capable of forgetting himself is truly free. One who works for Christ learns by experience that one sows and another reaps (cf. Jn 4:37). He has no need to look for success and thus has to rely on himself. Since he is working for the Lord, he leaves the outcome to the Lord, and in joyfulness of spirit he places his concerns in the hands of the Lord. When we seek our own success, the priesthood begins to appear as a burden that surpasses our strength, and burdens too heavy for our shoulders to bear are the inevitable result. But Christ carries us in faith, and from our union with Christ an invincible joy arises, which proceeds from the victory of Christ, who conquers the world (Jn 16:33) and is with us to the very end of time (Mt 28:20).

From an intimate union with Christ, there automatically arises also a participation in his love for human beings, in his will to save them and to bring them help. He who knows Christ from within wishes to communicate to others the joy of the redemption that has opened up for him in the Lord: pastoral labor flows from this communion of love and even in difficult situations is always nourished by this motivation and becomes life-fulfilling.

He who loves wishes to know. A true love of Christ, therefore, expresses itself also in the will to know him and everything that pertains to him. Since the love of Christ necessarily becomes love of human beings, education to the ministry of Christ includes also education to the natural human virtues. Since to love him means to know him, it follows that a will that is eager to study carefully and diligently is a sign of a solid vocation. Because Christ is never alone but comes to gather human beings into his body, a love for the church must necessarily accompany a love for Christ. Christ has willed to come to us in the community of his church. In a person's zealous love for the church, his relationship with the Lord himself is revealed as intimate and strong.

I would like to conclude with the words of Pope St. Gregory the Great in which he shows from Old Testament images the essential connection between the interior life and ministry: "What else are the rivers of holy men which water the dry ground of the carnal heart? But ... they dry up quickly, unless by the intention of the heart they keep diligently returning to the place from which they came. If they do not return inwardly to the heart, and bind themselves in love for their Creator with the bonds of holy desires, the tongue goes dry. But they do always return inside through love, and what they pour forth in public as they work and speak, they draw in secret from the fountain of love. They learn through love what they proclaim through teaching" (*Hom. in Ez. lib I, hom V*, 16 *PL* 76, 828 B).

The Ministry and Life of Priests

The priest's function, finally, is very simple:
to be a voice for the Word,
"He must increase and I must decrease" (John 3:30).

When the fathers of the Second Vatican Council set to work on the *Decree on the Ministry and Life of Priests,* they had already finished major debates on the nature of the episcopacy, and had made important statements on the position of the laity in the church and on the religious life.[1] It was now time to provide a word of encouragement to priests, who day by day must bear the burden of working in the Lord's vineyard. Of course, no merely pious exhortation would be enough: once the bishops had clarified the meaning and theological foundation of their own ministry, the words addressed to the priests, too, would require comparable theological depth. For only in this way could the work of priests be convincingly recognized and their efforts encouraged.

But such a message to priests was needed for more reasons than to give proportionate attention to the various "states" in the church. When the council fathers had worked out the special significance of the bishops' office in relation to the ministry of St. Peter's successor, they could count on a wide-ranging consensus in the public opinion of both church and world, especially within the Christian *oikoumene.* But it was otherwise when it came to the Catholic concept of the priesthood, the meaning of which was no longer self-evident, even in the consciousness of the church. To be sure, the crisis over that concept, which would quickly come into the open after the council and lead to further crises concerning the very existence of the priesthood and the priestly vocation, was at the moment only in its first stages. One of its causes was an altered approach to life, in which the "sacred" was understood less and less, and the "functional" elevated as the only valid category. But there were also theological roots, which gained unexpected nourishment from the new conditions of society. The very exegesis of the New Testament seemed to establish a nonsacral view of ecclesial tasks, removing all continuity between the sacral functions of the Old Testament and the new ministries of the infant church. Still less could any connection be discerned with pagan conceptions of the priesthood. The very novelty of Christianity appeared to consist precisely in the desacralization of ministries. The servants of the Christian community were called not *hiereis* (the Greek equivalent of Latin *sacerdotes*) but *presbyteroi,* or "elders." Now although the Protestant origins of modern exegesis were essentially operative in this manner of interpreting the New Testament, nothing could change the evidence that appeared to justify the conclusion: on the contrary, the burning question at the time was whether Luther, and not the Council of Trent, was right after all.

Two opposing concepts of priestly ministry stood—and still stand—face to face. On one side, the social-functional view defines priesthood in terms of "service"—a service performed for the community, through carrying out a function of the church in its social dimension. On the other side, the sacramental-ontological view, without denying the aspect of service, sees priesthood as rooted in the minister's being, and this being, in turn, as determined through a gift, known as a sacrament, bestowed by the Lord through the church. The functional view is also connected with a shift in terminology: expressions like *priest* and *priesthood,* with their sacral connotations, are avoided, and replaced by the neutral, functional words *minister* and *ministry,* until now hardly used in Catholic theology.

This difference in understanding the nature of the priesthood corresponds, to a certain extent, with a change of emphasis in the definition of the priest's role: the classically Catholic centering of the priesthood on the Eucharist (*sacerdos, sacrificium*), as against the typically Protestant priority given to the Word. Now, a view of the priesthood that places primacy on the Word does not have to be antisacramental. The Vatican II *Decree on Priests* proves the contrary. But the question arises whether the two concepts must be mutually exclusive, or whether they might not reciprocally enrich each other and resolve their discord from within. This, then, was the question faced by the Second Vatican Council: how far could the classical, post-Tridentine image of the priest be broadened—that is, how far could it satisfy the demands proposed by the Reformation, by critical exegesis, and by the modern attitude to life—without losing its essentials and vice versa: how far could the Protestant idea of the "minister" open itself up to the living tradition of the church, both East and West, for (likewise, since the Council of Trent) there has been no essential difference between Catholic and Orthodox notions of the priesthood.

THE NATURE OF THE PRIESTLY MINISTRY

Vatican II did not enter into these problems, which were then just beginning to surface. After the great debates on episcopal collegiality, on ecumenism, on religious freedom, and on the issues of the modern world, neither time nor energy were available for the council fathers. Since then, the 1971 and 1990 synods have studied the subject of the priesthood and expanded on the council's declarations, while the pope's "Holy Thursday Letters" to priests and the Directory of the Congregation of the Clergy have been applying the theme more concretely to everyday priestly life. And if the conciliar decree does not explicitly take up positions in regard to present-day controversies, it provides the foundation for any further elaboration.

What, then, are the answers to the problems we have described? To put it briefly, the council teaching cannot be reduced to either of the alternatives. The decree's first definition of the priesthood states that by their consecration, priests are ordained for the service of Christ as teacher, priest, and king; they share in his ministry, by virtue of which the church here on earth is constantly being built up into the People of God, the body of Christ, and the temple of the Holy Spirit (no. 1). In subsequent paragraphs, mention is made of the priest's power to offer sacrifice and forgive sins (no. 2). But this special task of the priest is emphatically inserted into a dynamic, historical vision of the church, in which all the faithful "participate in the mission" of the whole body, though "all have not the same function" (cf. Rom. 12:4). To sum up the thinking thus far, we can state that the first chapter of the decree (nos. 2 and 3) heavily underlines the ontological aspect of priestly existence, and thereby emphasizes the power to offer sacrifice. Both elements are again stressed at the beginning of no. 3: "Priests, taken from among the people, and ordained on their behalf in the things that pertain to God for the purpose of offering up gifts and sacrifices for sins (cf. Heb. 5:1), live with them as with their brothers." In contrast to the Council of Trent, there is a new emphasis on the lived unity and common path of the whole church, into which the traditional conception of the priesthood has been inserted.

All the more, then, is our attention drawn to the beginning of the second chapter, where the concrete duties of the priest are described: "It is the first task of priests, as co-workers of the bishops, to preach the Gospel of God to all" (no. 4). This seems to affirm clearly the primacy of the Word, or the ministry of preaching. The question then arises, What is the relationship between these two statements: a priest is "ordained ... for the purpose of offering up gifts and sacrifices," and his "first task" (*primum ... officium*) is to "preach the Gospel" (*Evangelium ... evangelizandi*)"?

The Christological Foundation

To find a solution to this problem, we should first ask ourselves, What does it mean to "evangelize"? What really happens when someone does this? And just what is this gospel? The council could certainly have referred to the Gospels to establish the primacy of preaching. I have in mind here a short but significant episode from the beginning of Mark. Everyone was seeking out our Lord for his miraculous powers, but he goes off to a remote place to pray (Mk 1:35–39); when he is pressed by "Simon and those who were with him," our Lord says, "Let us go on to the nearby villages, so that I may preach there also, for this is what I have come out to do" (1:38). Jesus says that the purpose of his coming is to preach the Kingdom of God. Therefore this should also be the defining priority of all his ministers: they come out to proclaim the kingdom, and that means to make the living, powerful, ever-present God take first place in our lives. Now, for the correct understanding of this priority, two further insights can be gained from this brief pericope. First, this evangelization is to go hand-in-hand with a withdrawal into the solitude of personal prayer; such interior recollection appears, in fact, to be a necessary precondition for the preaching. Second, the preaching is connected with the "casting out of devils" (1:39): it is a matter not just of speech but of effective action. And the preaching takes shape in no bright, happy world, but in a world tyrannized by demons, into which it intervenes so as to liberate.

But we must take a further step, beyond the brief but meaningful passage of Mark, and take a look over the entire gospel, for a correct understanding of Jesus's own priorities. He preaches the Kingdom of God, and he does so especially with parables but also with signs, in which the living presence of the kingdom draws near to men. Word and sign are inseparable. Whenever the signs are seen merely as wonders but without meaning, Jesus ceases to perform them. But neither does he allow his evangelizing to be taken for a merely intellectual affair, a matter for discussion alone. His words demand decision; they bring reality. In this sense, his word is "incarnate": the mutual relation of word and sign expresses a "sacramental" structure.[2]

But we must go a step further. Jesus does not convey a knowledge that is independent from his own person, as any teacher or storyteller would do. He is different from and more than a rabbi. As his preaching unfolds, it becomes ever clearer that his parables refer to himself, that the "kingdom" and his person belong together, that the kingdom comes in his person. The decision he demands is a decision about how one stands in relation to him, as when Peter says, "You are the Christ" (Mk 8:29). Ultimately, the message of his preaching about the Kingdom of God turns out to be quite clearly Jesus's own paschal mystery, his destiny of death and Resurrection. We see this, for example, in the parable of the murderous vine-dressers (Mk 12:1–11). Word and reality are here intertwined in a new way: the parable arouses the anger of his adversaries, who do everything the parable says. They kill the son. This means that the parables would be void of meaning were it not for the living person of the incarnate Son, who has "come out [*exēlthon*] for this" (Mk 1:38), who "was sent" from the Father (Mk 12:6). The parables would be empty without a confirmation of his Word by the cross and the Resurrection. We now understand that Jesus's preaching can be called "sacramental" in a deeper sense than we could have seen before. His Word contains in itself the reality of the Incarnation and the theme of the cross and the Resurrection. It is "deed/word" in this very profound sense, instructing the church in the mutual dependence of preaching and the Eucharist, as well as in the mutual dependence of preaching and an authentic, living witness.

We take yet another step forward with the paschal vision St. John presents in his Gospel. Peter had said that Jesus was the Christ. John now adds that Jesus Christ is the Logos. He himself is the eternal Word of the Father, who is with God and who is God (Jn 1:1). In him, this Word became flesh and dwelt among us (Jn 1:14). In Christian preaching, one is not dealing with words, but with the Word. "When we speak of the ministry of the word of God, the inter-Trinitarian relation is also understood."[3] Yet at the same time, "this ministry participates in the function of the Incarnation."[4] It has rightly been pointed out that the fundamental difference between the preaching of Jesus and the lessons of the rabbis consists precisely in the fact that the "I" of Jesus—that is, he himself—is at the center of his message.[5] But we must also remember that Jesus himself understood that what especially characterized his speaking was that he was not speaking "in his own name" (cf. Jn 5:43, 7:16). His "I" is totally open to the "thou" of the Father; it does not remain in itself but takes us inside the very life of the Trinity. This means that the Christian preacher does not speak about himself, but becomes Christ's own voice, by making way for the Logos and leading, through communion with the man Jesus, to communion with the living God.

This brings us back to the Vatican II Decree on the Priesthood. It emphasizes a common characteristic of all forms of preaching. The priest should never teach his own wisdom. What always matters is the Word of God, which impels toward truth and holiness (no. 4). With St. Paul as a model, the ministry of the Word demands that the priest divest himself profoundly of his own self: "It is no longer I who live, but Christ who lives in me" (Gal 2:20).

I would like to recall now an episode from the early days of Opus Dei, which illustrates the point. A young woman had the opportunity to listen for the first time to a talk given by Fr. Escriva, the founder of Opus Dei. She was very curious to hear a famous preacher, but after participating in a Mass he celebrated, she no longer wanted to listen to a human orator. She recounted later that from that moment on, her only interest was to discover the Word and will of God.

The ministry of the Word requires that the priest share in the kenosis of Christ, in his "increasing and decreasing." The fact that the priest does not speak about himself, but bears the message of another, certainly does not mean that he is not personally involved, but precisely the opposite: it is a giving-away-of-the-self in Christ that takes up the path of his Easter mystery and leads to a true finding-of-the-self, and communion with him who is the Word of God in person. This paschal structure of the "not-self," which turns out to be the "true self" after all, shows, in the last analysis, that the ministry of the Word reaches beyond all "functions" to penetrate the priest's very being, and presupposes that the priesthood is a sacrament.

Development in Tradition (St. Augustine)

Since we have now reached the central point of our discussion, I would like to illustrate it with two series of images taken from the works of St. Augustine. These images, which are taken from his biblical commentaries, have also had an important influence on the traditional teaching of the Catholic Church.

First of all, the priest is described as *servus Dei* or *servus Christi*.[6] This expression, "the servant of Christ," which is taken from the ecclesiastical language of his time, has a background in the Christological hymn of the Letter to the Philippians (2:5–11): Christ, the Son who is equal to God, took on the condition of a servant and became a slave for us. Here we must leave to one side Augustine's profound theology on freedom and service, as developed in the passage. What is pertinent to our theme is that "servant" is a relational concept. One is a servant only in relation to another. If the priest is defined as a servant of Jesus Christ, this means that his existence is essentially determined as relational. The essence of his ministry consists in his having been ordained for the service of the Lord, and this reaches into his very own being. He is a servant of Christ in order to be from him, through him, and with him, a servant of men. His being in relation to Christ is not opposed to his being ordained for the service of the community (of the church); rather, it is the foundation that alone gives depth to that service. Being related to Christ means being taken up into his existence as servant and staying with him at the service of the "body," that is, the church. Precisely because the priest belongs to Christ, he belongs, in a thoroughly radical sense, to men. Otherwise, he would be unable to dedicate himself profoundly and absolutely to them. This means, in turn, that the ontological concept of the priesthood, which affects the priest's being, is not opposed to his important function as a minister to the community. In fact, the ontological aspect creates a service too radical to be conceived in merely profane terms.

This image of the servant is linked with the image of the indelible character, which has become part of the patrimony of the church's faith. In the language of late antiquity, the word *character* designated the permanent mark of ownership that was impressed upon an object, an animal, or even a person. The property was assigned irrevocably and "called to its owner" (*clamat ad dominum*). One could say that *character* signifies a "belonging" impressed on the very being of an object. To this extent, then, *character* expresses that "being in relation," and "being in reference to" another that we have mentioned. And such belonging is not simply at one's own disposal, to acquire or use as one pleases. The initiative comes from the owner, from Christ. This makes the sacramental nature obvious: I cannot simply "declare" that I belong to our Lord. He must first appropriate me as his own. Only then can I enter into the state of belonging, which I can accept and try to live as my own. The word *character* describes the ontological nature of the service to Christ that lies in the priesthood, while illustrating what is meant by sacramentality. Only from this perspective can we understand why St. Augustine describes the character—both functionally and ontologically—as "the right of giving" (*ius dandi*), the necessary precondition for valid administration of the sacraments.[7] To belong to our Lord, who has become a servant, is to belong to those who are his. This means that now the servant can, under the sacred sign, give what he could never give on his own. In fact, he can give the Holy Spirit, absolve from sins, make present the sacrifice of Christ and Christ himself in his sacred body and blood, which are all rights reserved to God that no man can acquire by himself or by delegation from any community. So if *character* is an expression of community service, it shows that it is ultimately always our Lord who is acting, and that he nevertheless acts in the visible church by means of men. Character thus guarantees the "validity" of a sacrament, even in the case of an unworthy servant, but at the same time stands in judgment on the servant and obliges him to live the sacrament.

We can briefly touch on a second series of images St. Augustine used in his attempts to explain the nature of priestly service to himself and his faithful. They arose from his meditation on John the Baptist, whom he saw as prefiguring the priesthood.[8] Augustine points out that in the New Testament John is described, with an expression taken from Isaiah, as a "voice," whereas Christ, in St. John's Gospel, is called "the Word." The relationship between "voice" (*vox*) and "word" (*verbum*) helps to clarify the relationship between Christ and the priest. A word exists in the heart before it is grasped by someone else's sense of hearing. Through the conveyance of the voice, it enters into another's perception and is then present in the other person's heart, without being lost by the one who speaks the word. The audible sound—that is, the voice—which bears the word from one person to another (or to others), passes away, but the word remains. The priest's function, finally, is very simple: to be a voice for the Word ("he must increase and I must decrease"). The only purpose of the voice is to transmit the word and then disappear. Here we see both the sublimity and the humility of the priesthood. Like John the Baptist, the priest is only a precursor, a servant and minister of the Word. The focus is not on himself but on the Other. Yet he is *vox*, voice, with all his being. It is his mission to become a voice for the Word. It is precisely in this radical relatedness to another that he takes part in the grandeur of the Baptist's mission, in the mission of the Logos himself. It is also in this context that Augustine calls the priest the friend of the bridegroom (Jn 3:29), who does not take the bride but shares, as a friend, in the joy of the wedding: the Lord has made the servant into a friend (Jn 15:15), who now belongs to his household and remains in his house, no longer as a servant but as a free man (Gal 4:7, 4:21–5:1).[9]

CHRISTOLOGY AND ECCLESIOLOGY: THE ECCLESIAL CHARACTER OF THE PRIESTHOOD

Up to this point, we have been speaking about the Christological character of the priesthood, which always has a Trinitarian character, as well, because the Son, by nature, comes from the Father and returns to him. He communicates himself in the Holy Spirit, who is love and giving personified. But the conciliar decree rightly goes a step further in emphasizing the ecclesial character of the priesthood, which is inseparable from its Christological-Trinitarian foundation. The Incarnation of the Word signifies that God does not simply wish to come, by way of the Spirit, directly to the spirit of man, but rather that he seeks man by means of the material world and wants to move man as a social and historical being. God chooses to come to us through other human beings. God has come to us such that we find our way to one another through him and starting from him. The Incarnation thus brings with it a faith that is both communal and historical. The way "through the body" signifies that time and human sociability become factors in man's relationship to God, and these, in turn, are based on the antecedent relationship of God to men. Consequently, Christology and ecclesiology are inseparable: God's action creates the "People of God," and it is through Christ that the "People of God" become the "body of Christ," according to St. Paul's profound interpretation, in the Letter to the Galatians, of the promise made to Abraham. As Paul knew from the Old Testament, this promise is made "to the seed" of Abraham—that is, not to many but to a single one. The action of God, therefore, makes us, the many, become not simply "one thing" but "One," in bodily communion with Jesus Christ (Gal 3:16ff., 28).

Now, it is from this profoundly ecclesiological aspect of Christology that the council derives the world-historical dynamic of the Christ-event, to whose service priests are ordained. The ultimate goal, for all of us, is to become happy. But happiness is only to be found in togetherness, and togetherness is only to be found in the infinitude of love. Happiness is found only in the opening of self to the divine—that is, in divinization. In this sense, the council says, with Augustine, that the goal of history is for humanity to become love, and that means adoration, living worship, the City of God (*civitas Dei*); thus the deepest longing of Creation will be realized: "That God may be all in all" (1 Cor. 15:28; *Presbyterorum ordinis* no. 2, ll. 44–45; St. Augustine, *De Civitate Dei*, 10.6). Only in this broad perspective can we really understand what worship is or what the sacraments are.

This vision, which directs our attention on a large scale to ultimate questions, can also lead us back to very concrete matters. As we have seen, Christian faith is never purely spiritual and interior, and can never be a purely subjective or private personal relationship to Christ and his Word. Rather, it is a concrete, ecclesial reality. For this reason the council, perhaps forcing the matter a bit, underlines the bond priests have with their bishop. They represent him, act in his name, and receive their mission from him. The great Christological obedience, which reverses Adam's disobedience, is concretized in ecclesial obedience, which, for the priest, means obedience to his own bishop. Certainly the council could have insisted more strongly that there must first be a common obedience of all to the Word of God and his example, as presented in the living tradition of the church. This common bond of obedience is also common freedom: it offers protection against arbitrariness and guarantees the authentically Christological character of ecclesial obedience. Ecclesial obedience is not positivistic; it is paid not to a merely formal authority but rather to someone who obeys on his own part, too, and personifies the obedient Christ. And yet such obedience does not, of course, depend on the virtue and holiness of the officeholder, precisely because it refers to the objectivity of faith, a gift from our Lord that transcends all subjectivity. In this sense, obedience to one's bishop always transcends the local church: it is a Catholic obedience. The bishop is obeyed because he represents the universal church in this specific place. And such obedience also points beyond the current moment, since it is directed to the totality of the history of the faith. It is based on all that has grown to maturity in the *communio sanctorum,* and thus opens itself up to the future, in which God will be all in all and we will all be one. From this point of view, the demand of obedience makes a very serious demand on the one who holds authority. This does not mean, again, that obedience is conditional. It is concrete. I do not obey a Jesus that I or some others have constructed out of sacred scripture; in that case, I would only be obeying my own favorite notions: by adoring the image of Jesus I have invented, I would be adoring myself. No! To obey Christ means to obey his body, to obey him in his body.

Ever since the Letter to the Philippians, Jesus's obedience, understood as victory over the disobedience of Adam, has been at the center of the history of salvation. In the priest's life, this obedience should be incarnated in obedience to the church's authority; concretely, that means to the bishop. Only then is there a real rejection of the idolatry of self. Only then will the Adam within us be overcome and the new humanity formed. Today, when emancipation is considered the essence of redemption and freedom is presented as the right for me to do everything I want to do and nothing I don't want to do, the very concept of obedience has, so to speak, been anathematized. It has been eliminated not only from our vocabulary but also from our thinking. But this erroneous notion of freedom makes unity and love impossible. It makes man a slave. A rightly understood obedience must be rehabilitated and assume once more its true value at the center of Christian and priestly spirituality.

SPIRITUAL APPLICATIONS

Christology, when approached from a pneumatological and Trinitarian standpoint and thus taken in an ecclesial sense, naturally leads to spirituality, to the way faith is lived in practice. Since the Constitution on the Church had already provided the dogmatic basis, the council's decree on priestly life and ministry could attend directly to this aspect and give concrete instruction on priestly spirituality. I would like to develop one aspect of this. In no. 14, the decree deals with the difficult problem faced by the priest who finds himself torn between a great number of very different tasks. How can he preserve the interior unity of his life? Given the diminishing number of priests, this problem threatens to become the principal crisis in priestly life. A pastor today, with three or four parishes in his charge, will have to be constantly on the move. Missionaries are very familiar with this situation, but it is beginning to become something of a norm even in countries that have been Christian for centuries. The priest has to try to guarantee the celebration of the sacraments in the communities. He is harried by administrative tasks. He is challenged by issues of every kind, together with the personal problems of so many individuals, for whom he often cannot find the time. Pulled in all directions by these activities, the priest feels empty and less and less able to find time for the recollection that could provide him with fresh energy and inspiration. Scattered on the outside and empty on the inside, the priest can lose the joy of his vocation and end up regarding it as a burden too heavy to endure. The only solution is to flee.

The council offers three ways to overcome this situation. They are based on intimate communion with Christ, whose food was to do the will of the Father (Jn 4:34). The first one serves as a foundation: the priest needs to develop a living awareness of his ontological union with Christ, which is then expressed in his activity: Everything I do, I do in communion with him. Precisely in doing it, I am with him. No matter how multiple or even contradictory my activities may seem to others, they still constitute a single vocation: it is all being together with Christ, acting as an instrument in communion with him.

A second indication follows from the first. Priestly asceticism should not be placed alongside pastoral action as if it were an additional burden, just one more assignment added to an already overwhelming day. It is precisely in action that I learn to overcome myself, to lose and give my life. In disappointments and failure I learn renunciation, acceptance of suffering, and detachment from self. With the joy of success I learn gratitude. In the celebration of the sacraments, I inwardly benefit. In fact, there is no external work I perform in which I do not speak with Christ, and with the triune God through Christ. Thus I pray with others and for others. This *askesis* of service, or my ministry itself as the true asceticism of my life, is, without any doubt, a very important idea, but it requires constant, conscious exercise, an interior ordering of priestly action that comes from being a priest.

But there is still a third indispensable element. Even if I strive to approach service as asceticism and see sacramental action as a personal encounter with Christ, there have to be some moments when I can take time out and "catch my breath" from activity, to ensure this interior orientation. The conciliar decree says that priests will achieve this only by penetrating deeply, with their own lives, into the mystery of Christ. In this connection, it is very moving to read what St. Charles Borromeo says, based on his own experience: If he wishes to attain a truly priestly life, a priest must employ the appropriate means—that is, fasting, prayer, and the avoidance of both bad company and harmful and dangerous familiarity. "If a tiny spark of God's love already burns within you, do not expose it to the wind, for it may get blown out.... Stay quiet with God.... Are you in charge of the souls of the parish? If so, do not neglect your own soul, do not give yourself to others so completely that you have nothing left for yourself. You have to be mindful of your people without becoming forgetful of yourself.... When you administer the sacraments, meditate on what you are doing. When you celebrate Mass, meditate on the sacrifice you are offering. When you pray the office, meditate on the words you are saying and the Lord to whom you are speaking. When you take care of your people, meditate on whose blood has washed them clean."[10] The verb *meditate,* repeated four times, shows the importance, for this great pastor of souls, of the deepening of our inner life as a basis for action. And we know very well how much Charles Borromeo gave himself to his people. He died at forty-six, worn out by his dedication to his ministry. This man who was truly consumed for Christ, and through him for his fellow men, teaches us that such dedication is impossible without the regimen—and refuge—of an authentic, faithful interiority. This is a lesson we must learn, over and over again.

In recent decades, having interior life has been widely mistrusted as "escapism," as an excessive search for privacy. Yet ministry without spirituality, without interior life, leads to empty activism. Not a few priests who set out on their mission with great idealism fail in the end because of a mistrust for spirituality. To have time for God, to face him personally and intimately, is a pastoral priority of equal or even greater importance than all the other priorities. It is not an added duty but the soul's very breath, without which we would be "out of breath"—drained of the spiritual breath, or "breathing" (*spiritus*), of the Holy Spirit within us. Although there are other important and appropriate ways to recuperate spiritually, the fundamental way to recover from activity and to learn to love it again is the interior search for the face of God, which always restores our joy in God. One of the greatest and most humble parish priests of our century, Fr. Didimo Mantiero (1912–92) from Bassano del Grappa [Italy], wrote in his spiritual diary: "Converts have always been made through the prayer and sacrifice of unknown faithful. Christ won souls, not by the force of his marvelous words, but by the power of his constant prayer. He preached by day, but at night he prayed."[11] Souls— that is, living men and women—cannot be drawn to God simply by convincing arguments or discussions. They have to be won through prayer—by God and for God. Christian interior life is also the most important pastoral activity. In our pastoral plans this point ought to be given much greater importance. We must learn, again and again, that we need less discussion—and more prayer.

A LOOK AHEAD: THE UNITY OF THE OLD AND
NEW TESTAMENTS IN CHRIST

In conclusion, I would like to turn once more to the problem I sketched out in the introduction. What does the New Testament tell us about the priesthood of the church? Does such a thing really exist? Or were the Reformers right when they accused the church of betraying the newness of Christianity, of nullifying the change Christ brought, by turning the elder (*presbyter*) back into a priest (*sacerdos*)? Shouldn't the church have remained strictly faithful to the function of the elder without any sacralization or sacramentalization? We cannot get the correct answer merely by studying the terms *priest* (*presbyter*) and *hiereus* (*sacerdos*), terms originally different but later united. One has to go deeper, since the whole question of the relationship between the Old and New Testaments is at stake. Does the New Testament constitute what is essentially a break with the past or, rather, a fulfillment in which the old continues but is completely transformed and, really, restored in the new? Is grace opposed to the law, or is there an inner connection between the two?

Historically, it should be pointed out first of all that in the year 70 AD the Temple of Jerusalem was destroyed, and with it disappeared the whole sector of sacrifice and priesthood that had been, in certain respects, at the heart of the "law." Judaism sought to preserve what had been lost by applying the prescription of the holiness of the temple to the life of the Jewish people in general.[12] And it anchored the lost heritage of the temple in its spirituality, through the prayerful hope of reestablishing worship in Jerusalem. The synagogue, which is above all a gathering place for prayer, for preaching and hearing the Word, is but a fragment living in expectation of something much bigger. A strict Reformation interpretation of Christian ministry and worship reduces Christianity to the image of the synagogue, that is, to meeting, Word, and prayer. The historicist reading of the uniqueness of Christ's sacrifice banishes sacrifice and cult to the past and excludes from the present both priesthood and sacrifice. Meanwhile, it is being increasingly observed, even by those within churches that began at the Reformation, that this reading misses the grandeur and depth of the New Testament event. And it could even imply that the Old Testament was not, in fact, fulfilled.

In Christ's Resurrection, however, the temple is reconstructed by God's own power (Jn 2:19). Christ, the living Temple, is himself the new sacrifice, which continues today in the body of Christ, the church. Coming from this sacrifice, and oriented toward it, we have the true, priestly ministry of the new worship, in which all the "figures" have been fulfilled.

We must, therefore, reject the view that the church's worship and priesthood entails a clean break with the history of pre-Christian salvation, a view that consequently denies any continuity from the priesthood of the Old Testament to the priesthood of the New. For in this view, the New Testament would not be a fulfillment of the Old Covenant but would stand in opposition to it. This would effectively destroy the internal unity of the history of salvation. By means of the sacrifice of Christ and its acceptance in the Resurrection, the entire heritage of worship and priesthood of the Old Covenant is handed over to the church. The fullness of the Christian "yes" counters any attempt to reduce the church to the synagogue. This is the only way to understand fully, and in depth, the ministry of the apostolic succession. In this way we should not feel ashamed or make any excuses for affirming that, yes, the priesthood of the church continues and renews the priesthood of the Old Testament, which finds its true fulfillment precisely in this radical and transforming newness.

This position is important even for relations between Christianity and other world religions. Although Christianity is a new beginning—the greatest and most radically new reality that has come from God—it does not negate the efforts of other religions, in their Advent-like gestures toward the meaning of man's existence; however much distorted and deformed, their search is not in vain.

This concept of the priesthood in no way implies a devaluation of the common priesthood of the baptized. Once again, it is Augustine who has beautifully expressed this by calling all the faithful "servants of God" and priests "servants of the servants," thus designating the faithful as their masters.[13] The priesthood of the New Testament means following in the footsteps of our Lord, who washes the feet of his disciples: his greatness cannot subsist except in humility. Greatness and self-abasement have been intertwined ever since Christ—who is the greatest—became the least; ever since the One who is first took the last place. To be a priest means to enter into this communion of self-abasement, in order to share in the universal glory of the redemption.

The Sacrament of Reconciliation

The Apostolic Letter in the form of a *motu proprio misericordia Dei* published on May 2, 2002, reaffirms the teaching of the Church that it is necessary "by divine decree" to confess each and every mortal sin. The Church has always seen an essential link between the judgment entrusted to the priest in the sacrament and the need for penitents to name their own sins, except where this is not possible. Cardinal Ratzinger addresses the sacramental and doctrinal sources of the decree.

The fact that humanity needs purification and forgiveness is something that is most evident at this historical moment. For this very reason the Holy Father in his Apostolic Letter *Novo Millennio ineunte* placed among the priorities of the mission of the church for the new millennium "a renewed pastoral courage in proposing in an attractive and effective way the practice of the Sacrament of Reconciliation" (no. 37).

THE PERSONALIST NATURE OF CHRISTIAN LIFE

The new *motu proprio misericordia Dei* is linked to this invitation and makes theologically, pastorally, and juridically concrete a few important aspects of the practice of this sacrament. Above all, the *motu proprio* emphasizes the personalist nature of the sacrament of penance: as the sin, despite all our bonds with the human community, is ultimately something totally personal, so also our healing with forgiveness has to be something that is totally personal. God does not treat us as part of a collectivity. He knows each one by name; he calls him/her personally and saves him if he has fallen into sin. Even if in all the sacraments, the Lord addresses the person as an individual, the personalist nature of the Christian life is manifested in a particularly clear way in the sacrament of penance. That means that the personal confession and the forgiveness directed to this person are constitutive parts of the sacrament. Collective absolution is an extraordinary form that is possible only in strictly determined cases of necessity; it also supposes, as something that belongs to the nature of the sacrament, the will to make a personal confession of sins, as soon as it will be possible to do so. The strongly personalist nature of the sacrament of penance was overshadowed in the last decade by the ever more frequent recourse to general absolution, which was increasingly considered a normal form of the sacrament of penance, an abuse that contributed to the gradual disappearance of this sacrament in some parts of the church.

TRENT UNDERSTANDS THAT THE POWER TO FORGIVE SINS GIVEN TO THE APOSTLES AND THEIR SUCCESSORS REQUIRES A JUDGMENT

If the pope now reduces again the extent of this possibility, the objection might be made: but has not the sacrament of penance undergone many transformations in history, why not this one? In this regard one needs to say that, in reality, the form manifests notable variations, but the personalist component was always essential.

The church had and has the consciousness that only God can forgive sins (cf. Mk 2:7). For that reason she had to learn to discern carefully and almost with reverent awe which powers the Lord transmitted to her and which he did not. After a long journey of historical maturation, the Council of Trent expounded in an organic form the ecclesial doctrine on the sacrament of penance (DS 1667–1693; 1701–1715).

The fathers of the Council of Trent understood the words of the Risen One to his disciples in John 20:22f as the specific words of the institution of the sacrament: "Receive the Holy Spirit, whose sins you shall forgive they are forgiven them, whose sins you shall retain, they are retained" (DS 1670, 1703, 1710). Starting with John 20 they interpreted Matthew 16:19 and 18:18 and understood the power of the keys of the church as the power for the remission of sins (DS 1692, 1710). They were fully conscious of the problems of the interpretation of these texts and established their interpretation in terms of the sacrament of penance with the help of "the understanding of the church" that is expressed in the universal consensus of the fathers (1670, 1679, 1683; 1703 is important for this).

The decisive point in these words of institution lies in the fact that the Lord entrusts to the disciples the choice between loosing and binding, retaining or forgiving: the disciples are not simply a neutral instrument of divine forgiveness; rather, a power of discernment is entrusted to them and with it a duty of discernment for individual cases. The fathers saw in this the judicial nature of the sacrament. Two aspects belong essentially to the sacrament of penance: on the one hand the sacramental aspect, namely the mandate of the Lord, which goes beyond the real power of the disciples and of the community of disciples of the church; on the other hand, the commission to make the decision, which must be founded objectively and therefore must be just, and in this sense has a judicial nature. "Jurisdiction" belongs to the sacrament, and it requires a juridical order in the church that is always directed to the essence of the sacrament, to the saving will of God (1686f.).

Trent is clearly differing from the position of the Reformers, in which the sacrament of penance signifies only the manifestation of a forgiveness already granted through faith, and so does not do anything new but only announces what always already exists in faith.

THE JUDICIAL NATURE OF THE SACRAMENT IMPLIES THE NECESSITY TO CONFESS EACH MORTAL SIN

This juridical-sacramental character of the sacrament has two important implications: if this is the reality, we must speak of a sacrament that is different from baptism, of a specific sacrament that supposes a special sacramental power, that is linked with the sacrament of orders (1684). If, however, there is also a judicial evaluation, then it is clear that the judge has to know the facts of the case on which he is to judge. The necessity of the personal confession with the telling of the sins, for which one must ask pardon of God and of the church because they have broken the unity of love with God that is given by baptism, is implicit in the juridical aspect. At this point the council can say that it is necessary *iure divino* (by divine law) to confess each and every mortal sin (canon 7, 1707). So the council teaches that the duty of confession was instituted by the Lord himself and is constitutive of the sacrament, and so not left to the disposition of the church.

THE CHURCH DOES NOT HAVE THE POWER TO REPLACE PERSONAL CONFESSION WITH GENERAL ABSOLUTION

Therefore, it is not in the power of the church to replace personal confession with general absolution: the pope reminds us of this in the new *motu proprio,* which expresses the church's consciousness of the limits of her power; it expresses the bond with the Word of the Lord, which is binding even on the pope. Only in situations of necessity, in which the human being's final salvation is at stake, can absolution be anticipated and confession left for a time in which it will be possible to make it. This is what in a rather obscure way is meant by the words *collective absolution*. It is also the mission of the church to define when one is in the presence of such a situation of necessity. After, as we said, hearing in the last decades expansive and for many reasons unsustainable interpretations of the concept of necessity, in this document the pope gives precise determinations that must be applied in their particulars by the bishops.

CONFESSION OFFERS AN EXPERIENCE OF LIBERATION BY GOD FROM THE PAST WEIGHT OF SINS

Does this document place a new burden on the backs of Christians? Precisely the contrary: the totally personal character of Christian life is defended. Of course, the confession of one's own sin can seem heavy to the person, because it humbles his pride and confronts him with his poverty. It is what we need; we suffer exactly for this reason: we shut ourselves up in our delirium of guiltlessness, and for this reason we are closed to others and to any comparison with them. In psychotherapeutic treatment a person is made to bear the burden of profound and often dangerous revelations of his inner self. In the sacrament of penance, the simple confession of one's guilt is presented with confidence in God's merciful goodness. It is important to do this without falling into scruples, with the spirit of trust proper to the children of God. In this way confession can become an experience of deliverance, in which the weight of the past is removed from us and we feel rejuvenated by the merit of the grace of God, who each time gives back the youthfulness of the heart.

PART SEVEN

CHRISTIAN MORALITY

Europe's Crisis of Culture

Lecture Given in the Convent of Saint Scholastica in Subiaco, Italy, the Day Before Pope John Paul II Died, When Then Cardinal Ratzinger Received the St. Benedict Award for the Promotion of Life and the Family in Europe

APRIL 1, 2005

We are living in a time of great dangers and great opportunities for man and the world, a time of great responsibility for us all. During the past century, man's possibilities and his dominion over matter grew by truly unthinkable measures. However, his power to dispose of the world has been such as to allow his capacity for destruction to reach dimensions that at times horrify us. In this connection, the threat of terrorism comes spontaneously to mind— this new war without boundaries or fronts.

The fear that a terrorist might soon get hold of nuclear or biological weapons is not unfounded and has made it necessary for lawful states to adopt internal security systems similar to those that previously existed only in dictatorships. The feeling remains, nevertheless, that, in reality, all these precautions are not enough, as global control is neither possible nor desirable.

Less visible but no less disquieting are the possibilities of self-manipulation that man has acquired. He has plumbed the depths of being, deciphered the components of the human being, and is now capable, so to speak, of constructing man himself, who thus comes into the world no longer as a gift of the Creator but as a product of our action, a product that, therefore, can also be selected according to the exigencies we have established.

Thus, the splendor of being an image of God no longer shines over man, which is what confers on him his dignity and inviolability, and he is left only to the power of his own human capacities. He is no more than the image of man—of what man?

To this are added the great global problems: inequality in the distribution of the goods of the earth, growing poverty, and the more threatening impoverishment and exhaustion of the earth and its resources, hunger, sicknesses that threaten the whole world, and the clash of cultures. All this shows that the growth of our possibilities has not been matched by a comparable development of our moral energy. Moral strength has not grown together with the development of science; rather, it has diminished, because the technical mentality relegates morality to the subjective realm, while we have need, precisely, of a public morality, a morality that can respond to the threats that weigh on the existence of us all. The real and grave danger in these times lies, precisely, in this imbalance between technical possibilities and moral energy.

The security we need as a precondition for freedom and dignity cannot come, in the last analysis, from technical systems of control, but can spring only from man's moral strength; whenever the latter is lacking or is insufficient, the power man has will be transformed increasingly into a power of destruction.

A NEW MORALISM

It is true that a new moralism exists today whose key words are *justice, peace,* and *conservation of Creation*—words that call for essential moral values, of which we are in real need. But this moralism remains vague and thus slides, almost inevitably, into the political-party sphere. It is, above all, a dictum addressed to others, and too little a personal duty of our daily life. In fact, what does justice mean? Who defines it? What serves peace?

Over the last decades we have amply seen in our streets and squares how pacifism can deviate toward a destructive anarchism and terrorism. The political moralism of the 1970s, the roots of which are anything but dead, succeeded in attracting even young people full of ideals. But it was a moralism with a mistaken direction, inasmuch as it was deprived of serene rationality and, in the last analysis, placed the political utopia above the dignity of the individual man, showing itself even capable of contempt for man in the name of great objectives.

Political moralism, as we have lived it and are still living it, does not open the way to regeneration, and even blocks it. The same is true, consequently, for a Christianity and a theology that reduces the heart of Jesus's message, the "Kingdom of God," to the "values of the kingdom," identifying these values with the great key words of political moralism and proclaiming them, at the same time, to be a synthesis of the religions.

Nonetheless, God is neglected in this way, notwithstanding the fact that precisely he is the subject and cause of the Kingdom of God. In his stead, great words (and values) remain, which lend themselves to all kinds of abuse.

This brief look at the situation of the world leads us to reflect on today's situation of Christianity and, therefore, on the foundations of Europe, which at one time, we can say, was the Christian continent but also the starting point of the new scientific rationality, which has given us great possibilities, as well as great threats. Christianity, it is true, did not start in Europe, and, therefore, it cannot even be classified as a European religion, the religion of the European cultural realm. But it received precisely in Europe its most effective cultural and intellectual imprint and remains, therefore, identified in a special way with Europe.

Furthermore, it is also true that Europe, since the time of the Renaissance and in a fuller sense since the time of the Enlightenment, has developed precisely that scientific rationality which not only led in the era of the discoveries to the geographic unity of the world, to the meeting of continents and cultures, but which today—much more profoundly, thanks to the technical culture made possible by science—imprints itself on the whole world, and even more than that, in a certain sense gives it uniformity.

GODLESS SOCIETY

And in the wake of this form of rationality, Europe has developed a culture that, in a manner unknown to humanity before now, excludes God from the public conscience, either by denying him altogether or by judging that his existence is not demonstrable, uncertain, and therefore belongs to the realm of subjective choices—something, in any case, irrelevant to public life.

This purely functional rationality, so to speak, has implied a disorder of the moral conscience altogether unknown in cultures existing up to now, as it deems rational only that which can be proved with experiments. As morality belongs to an altogether different sphere, it disappears as a category unto itself and must be identified in another way, inasmuch as it must be admitted, in any case, that morality is essential.

In a world based on calculation, it is the calculation of consequences that determines what must be considered moral. And thus the category of the good, as was clearly pointed out by Kant, disappears. Nothing is good or bad in itself; everything depends on the consequences that an action allows one to foresee.

Although Christianity has found its most effective form in Europe, it is necessary to say that in Europe a culture has developed that constitutes the absolutely most radical contradiction not only of Christianity but of the religious and moral traditions of humanity.

From this, one understands that Europe is experiencing a true and proper "test of tension"; from this, one also understands the radicalism of the tensions that our continent must face. However, from this emerges also and above all the responsibility that we Europeans must assume at this historical moment in the debate on the definition of Europe, on its new political shape. It is a question not of a nostalgic rearguard battle of history being played out but rather of a great responsibility for today's humanity.

Let us take a closer look at this opposition between the two cultures that have characterized Europe. In the debate on the Preamble of the European Constitution, this opposition was seen in two controversial points: the question of the reference to God in the Constitution and the mention of the Christian roots of Europe. Given that in article 52 of the Constitution the institutional rights of churches are guaranteed, we can be at peace, it is said.

But this means that in the life of Europe, the churches find a place in the realm of political commitment, whereas in the realm of the foundations of Europe the imprint of their content has no place. The reasons given in the public debate for this clear "no" are superficial, and it is obvious that more than indicating the real motivation, they conceal it. The affirmation that the mention of the Christian roots of Europe injures the sentiments of many nonChristians who are in Europe is not very convincing, given that it relates, first of all, to a historical fact that no one can seriously deny.

Naturally, this historical mention has reference to the present. To mention the roots indicates, as well, residual sources of moral orientation, which is a factor in Europe's identity. Who would be offended? Whose identity is threatened?

The Muslims, who in this respect are often and willingly brought in, feel threatened not by our Christian moral foundations but by the cynicism of a secularized culture that denies its own foundations. Neither are our Jewish fellow citizens offended by the reference to the Christian roots of Europe, inasmuch as these roots go back to Mount Sinai: they bear the sign of the voice that made itself heard on the mountain of God and unite with us in the great fundamental orientations that the Decalogue has given humanity. The same is true for the reference to God: it is not the mention of God that offends those who belong to other religions, but rather the attempt to build the human community absolutely without God.

The motivations of this twofold "no" are more profound than one would think from the reasons offered. They presuppose the idea that only radical Enlightenment culture, which has reached its full development in our time, could be constitutive for European identity. Next to this culture, then, different religious cultures can coexist with their respective rights, on the condition and to the degree in which they respect the criteria of Enlightenment culture and are subordinated to it.

THE CULTURE OF RIGHTS

This Enlightenment culture is essentially defined by the rights of freedom. It stems from freedom as a fundamental value that measures everything: freedom of religious choice, which includes the religious neutrality of the state; freedom to express one's own opinion, as long as it does not cast doubt specifically on this canon; democratic ordering of the state, that is, parliamentary control over state organisms; the free formation of parties; the independence of the judiciary; and finally, safeguarding of the rights of man, and the prohibition of discrimination. Here the Canon is still in the process of formation, given that there are also rights of man that are in opposition, as for example, in the case of the conflict between a woman's desire for freedom and the right of the unborn to live.

The concept of discrimination is ever more extended, and so the prohibition of discrimination can be increasingly transformed into a limitation of the freedom of opinion and religious liberty. Very soon it will not be possible to state that homosexuality, as the Catholic Church teaches, is an objective disorder in the structuring of human existence. And the fact that the church is convinced of not having the right to confer priestly ordination on women is considered by some up to now as being irreconcilable with the spirit of the European Constitution.

It is evident that this canon of Enlightenment culture, less than definitive, contains important values that we, precisely as Christians, do not want and cannot renounce; however, it is also obvious that the ill-defined or undefined concept of freedom that is at the base of this culture inevitably entails contradictions; it is obvious that precisely because of its use (a use that seems radical), it has implied limitations of freedom that a generation ago we could not even imagine. A confused ideology of freedom leads to dogmatism, which is showing itself increasingly hostile to freedom.

We must, without a doubt, focus again on the question of the internal contradictions of the present form of Enlightenment culture. But we must first finish describing it. It is part of its nature as a culture of reason that, finally, has complete awareness of itself, to boast a universal pretense and conceive itself as complete in itself, not in need of some completion through other cultural factors.

Both these characteristics are clearly seen when the question is posed about who can become a member of the European community and, above all, in the debate about Turkey's entry into this community. It is a question of a state or, perhaps better, of a cultural realm that does not have Christian roots but was influenced by Islamic culture. Then, Ataturk tried to transform Turkey into a secular state, attempting to implant in Muslim terrain the secularism that had matured in the Christian world of Europe.

UNIVERSAL CULTURE?

We can ask ourselves if that is possible. According to the thesis of the Enlightenment and the secular culture of Europe, only the norms and contents of Enlightenment culture will be able to determine Europe's identity, and consequently, every state that makes these criteria its own will be able to belong to Europe. It does not matter, in the end, in what plot of ground this culture of freedom and democracy is implanted.

And, precisely because of this, it is affirmed that the roots cannot enter into the definition of the foundations of Europe, it being a question of dead roots that are not part of the present identity. As a consequence, this new identity, determined exclusively by the Enlightenment culture, also implies that God does not enter at all into public life and the foundations of the state.

Thus everything becomes logical and also, in some sense, plausible. In fact, what could we desire as being more beautiful than knowing that everywhere democracy and human rights are respected? Nevertheless, the question must be asked if this secular Enlightenment culture is really the culture, finally proposed as universal, that can give a common cause to all men; a culture that will be accessible from everywhere, even though it is on a humus that is historically and culturally differentiated. And we also ask ourselves if it is really complete in itself, to the degree that it has no need of roots outside itself.

Let us address these last two questions. To the first, that is, to the question as to whether a universally valid philosophy has been reached that is finally wholly scientifically rational, which expresses the cause common to all men, we must respond that undoubtedly we have arrived at important acquisitions that can pretend to universal validity. These include: the acquisition that religion cannot be imposed by the state but can only be accepted in freedom, respect of the fundamental rights of man equal for all, and the separation of powers and control of power.

It cannot be thought, however, that these fundamental values, recognized by us as generally valid, can be realized in the same way in every historical context. Not all societies have in place the sociological assumptions for a democracy based on parties, as occurs in the West; therefore, total religious neutrality of the state, in the majority of historical contexts, has to be considered an illusion.

And so we come to the problems raised by the second question. But let us clarify first whether the modern Enlightenment philosophies, considered as a whole, can contain the last word on the cause common to all men. These philosophies are characterized by the fact that they are positivist and, therefore, antimetaphysical, so much so that, in the end, God cannot have any place in them. They are based on the self-limitation of rational positivism, which can be applied in the technical realm but which, when it is generalized, entails instead a mutilation of man. It succeeds in having man no longer admit any moral claim beyond his calculations, and as we saw, the concept of freedom, which at first glance would seem to extend in an unlimited manner, in the end leads its own destruction.

It is true that the positivist philosophies contain important elements of truth. However, these are based on imposed limitations of reason, characteristic of a specific cultural situation—that of the modern West—and are, therefore, not the last word of reason. Nevertheless, though they might seem totally rational, they are not the voice of reason itself but are identified culturally with the present situation in the West.

For this reason they are in no way that philosophy which one day could be valid throughout the world. But, above all, it must be said that this Enlightenment philosophy, like its respective culture, is incomplete. It consciously severs its own historical roots, depriving itself of the regenerating forces from which it sprang, from that fundamental memory of humanity, so to speak, without which reason loses its orientation.

KNOWING IS DOING

In fact, the principle is now valid according to which man's capacity is measured by his action. What one knows how to do may also be done. There no longer exists a knowing how to do separated from a being able to do, because it would be against freedom, which is the absolute supreme value. But man knows how to do many things and knows increasingly how to do more things;

if this knowing how to do does not find its measure in a moral norm, it becomes, as we can already see, a power of destruction.

Man knows how to clone men, and so he does it. Man knows how to use men as a store of organs for other men, and so he does it; he does it because this seems to be an exigency of his freedom. Man knows how to construct atomic bombs, and so he makes them, being, in line of principle, also disposed to use them. In the end, terrorism is also based on this modality of man's self-authorization, and not on the teachings of the Qur'an.

The radical detachment of Enlightenment philosophy from its roots becomes, in the last analysis, contempt for man. Man, deep down, has no freedom, we are told by the spokesmen of the natural sciences, in total contradiction with the starting point of the whole question. Man must not think that he is something more than all other living beings and, therefore, should be treated like them, we are told by even the most advanced spokesmen of a philosophy clearly separated from the roots of humanity's historical memory.

We asked ourselves two questions: if rationalist (positivist) philosophy is strictly rational and, consequently, universally valid, and if it is complete. Is it self-sufficient? Can it, or more directly must it, relegate its historical roots to the realm of the pure past and, therefore, to the realm of what can only be valid subjectively?

We must respond to both questions with a definitive "no." This philosophy expresses not man's complete reason but only a part of it, and because of this mutilation of reason it cannot be considered entirely rational. For this reason, it is incomplete and can only be fulfilled by reestablishing contact with its roots. A tree without roots dries up.

REMOVING GOD

By stating this, one does not deny all that is positive and important in this philosophy, but one affirms, rather, its need to complete itself, its profound deficiency. And so we must again address the two controversial points of the Preamble of the European Constitution. The banishment of Christian roots does not reveal itself as the expression of a higher tolerance, which respects all cultures in the same way, not wishing to privilege any, but, rather, as the absolutizing of a pattern of thought and of life that are radically opposed, among other things, to other historical cultures of humanity.

The real opposition that characterizes today's world is not that between various religious cultures but that between the radical emancipation of man from God, from the roots of life, on one hand, and from the great religious cultures on the other. If there were to be a clash of cultures, it would be not because of a clash of the great religions—which have always struggled against one another but in the end have also always known how to live with one another—but because of the clash between this radical emancipation of man and the great historical cultures.

Thus, even the rejection of the reference to God is not the expression of a tolerance that desires to protect the nontheistic religions and the dignity of atheists and agnostics, but rather the expression of a conscience that would like to see God cancelled definitively from the public life of humanity and relegated to the subjective realm of residual cultures of the past.

Relativism, which is the starting point of all this, thus becomes a dogmatism that believes itself to be in possession of the definitive scope of reason, with the right to regard all the rest only as a stage of humanity, in the end surmounted, that can be appropriately relativized. In reality, this means that we have need of roots to survive and that we must not lose sight of God, if we do not want human dignity to disappear.

THE PERMANENT SIGNIFICANCE OF THE CHRISTIAN FAITH

Is this a simple rejection of the Enlightenment and modernity? Absolutely not. From the beginning, Christianity has understood itself as the religion of the Logos, as the religion according to reason. In the first place, it has identified its precursors not in other religions but in that philosophical enlightenment that has cleared the path of traditions to turn to the search for the truth and toward the good, toward the one God who is above all gods.

As a religion of the persecuted, a universal religion beyond the different states and peoples, it has denied the state the right to regard religion as a part of state ordering, thus postulating freedom of faith. It has always defined men, all men without distinction, as creatures and images of God, proclaiming for them, in terms of principle, although within the imperative limits of social ordering, the same dignity.

In this connection, the Enlightenment is of Christian origin, and it is no accident that it was born precisely and exclusively in the realm of the Christian faith, whenever Christianity, against its nature and unfortunately, had become a tradition and religion of the state. Notwithstanding philosophy, insofar as the search for rationality—also for our faith—was always a prerogative of Christianity, the voice of reason had become too domesticated.

It was and is the merit of the Enlightenment to have again proposed these original values of Christianity and of having given back to reason its own voice. In the pastoral constitution *On the Church in the Modern World,* Vatican Council II underlined again this profound correspondence between Christianity and the Enlightenment, seeking to come to a true conciliation between the church and modernity, which is the great heritage that both sides must defend.

Given all this, it is necessary that both sides engage in self-reflection and be willing to correct themselves. Christianity must always remember that it is the religion of the Logos. It is faith in the "Creator Spiritus," in the Creator Spirit, from which proceeds everything that exists. Today, this should be precisely its philosophical strength, insofar as the problem is whether the world comes from the irrational and reason is not, therefore, a "subproduct," on occasion even harmful to its development—or whether the world comes from reason and is, as a consequence, its criterion and goal.

The Christian faith inclines toward this second thesis, and thus has, from the purely philosophical point of view, really good cards to play, despite the fact that many today consider the first thesis as the only modern and rational one. However, reason that springs from the irrational and is, in the final analysis, itself irrational, does not constitute a solution for our problems. Only creative reason, which in the crucified God is manifested as love, can really show us the way. In the so-necessary dialogue between secularists and Catholics, we Christians must be very careful to remain faithful to this fundamental line: to live a faith that comes from the Logos, from creative reason, which, because of this, is also open to all that is truly rational.

"AS IF GOD EXISTED"

But at this point, in my capacity as believer, I would like to make a proposal to the secularists. At the time of the Enlightenment there was an attempt to understand and define essential moral norms, saying that they would be valid "*etsi Deus non daretur*," even in the case that God did not exist. Given the opposition of the confessions and the pending crisis of the image of God, an attempt was made to keep the essential values of morality outside the contradictions and to seek for them an evidence that would render them independent of the many divisions and uncertainties of the different philosophies and confessions. In this way, they wanted to ensure the basis of coexistence and, in general, the foundations of humanity. At that time, this was thought possible, as the great deep convictions created by Christianity to a large extent remained. But this is no longer the case.

The search for such a reassuring certainty, which could remain uncontested beyond all differences, failed. Not even the truly grandiose effort of Kant was able to create the necessary shared certainty. Kant had denied that God could be known in the realm of pure reason, but at the same time he had represented God, freedom, and immortality as postulates of practical reason, without which, coherently, for him no moral behavior was possible.

Does not the world's situation today make us think perhaps that he might have been right? I would like to express it in a different way: The attempt, carried to the extreme, to manage human affairs while disdaining God completely leads us increasingly to the edge of the abyss, to an ever greater isolation from reality. We must reverse the axiom of the Enlightenment and say: even one who does not succeed in finding the way of accepting God, should, nevertheless, seek to live and direct his life *"veluti si Deus daretur,"* as if God existed. This is the advice Pascal gave to his friends who did not believe. In this way, no one is limited in his freedom, but all our affairs find the support and criterion of which they are in urgent need.

Above all, we are in need at this moment in history of men who, through an enlightened and lived faith, render God credible in this world. The negative testimony of Christians who speak about God and live against him has darkened God's image and opened the door to disbelief. We need men who have their gaze directed to God, to understand true humanity. We need men whose intellects are enlightened by the light of God, and whose hearts God opens, so that their intellects can speak to the intellects of others and their hearts are able to appeal to the hearts of others.

Only through men who have been touched by God can God come near to men. We need men like Benedict of Nursia, who, during a time of dissipation and decadence, plunged into the most profound solitude, succeeding, after all the purifications he had to suffer, in ascending again to the light, and returning and founding Monte-Casino, the city on the mountain that, with so many ruins, gathered together the forces from which a new world was formed.

In this way Benedict, like Abraham, became the father of many nations. The recommendations to his monks presented at the end of his "Rule" are guidelines that show us also the way that leads on high, beyond the crisis and the ruins.

Just as there is a bitter zeal that removes one from God and leads to hell, so there is a good zeal that removes one from vices and leads to God and to eternal life. It is in this zeal that monks must exercise themselves with most ardent love: May they outdo one another in rendering each other honor, may they support, in turn, with utmost patience their physical and moral infirmities.... May they love one another with fraternal affection.... Fear God in love.... Put absolutely nothing before Christ who will be able to lead all to eternal life.[1]

Truth and Freedom

Man is God's image precisely insofar as being "from," "with," and "for" constitute the fundamental anthropological pattern.

THE QUESTION

In the mind of contemporary man, freedom appears to a large extent to be the absolutely highest good to which all other goods are subordinate. Court decisions consistently accord artistic freedom and freedom of opinion primacy over every other moral value. Values that compete with freedom, or which might necessitate its restriction, seem to be fetters or "taboos," that is, relics of archaic prohibitions and fears. Political policy must show that it contributes to the advancement of freedom in order to be accepted. Even religion can make its voice heard only by presenting itself as a liberating force for man and humanity. In the scale of values on which man depends for a humane existence, freedom serves as the basic value and as the fundamental human right. In contrast, we are inclined to react with suspicion to the concept of truth: we recall that the term *truth* has already been claimed for many opinions and systems, and that the assertion of truth has often been a means of suppressing freedom. In addition, natural science has nourished a skepticism with regard to everything that cannot be explained or proved by its exact methods: all such things seem in the end to be a mere subjective assignment of value, which cannot pretend to be universally binding. The modern attitude toward truth is summed up most succinctly in Pilate's question, "What is truth?" Anyone who maintains that he is serving the truth by his life, speech, and action must prepare himself to be classified as a dreamer or a fanatic. For "the world beyond is closed to our gaze"; this sentence from Goethe's *Faust* characterizes our common sensibility today.

Doubtless, the prospect of an all-too-self-assured passion for the truth suggests reasons enough to ask cautiously, "What is truth?" But there is just as much reason to pose the question "What is freedom?" What do we actually mean when we extol freedom and place it at the pinnacle of our scale of

values? I believe that the content people generally associate with the demand
for freedom is very aptly explained in the words of a passage of Karl Marx in
which he expresses his own dream of freedom. The state of the future Communist society will make it possible, he says, "to do one thing today and another tomorrow; to hunt in the morning, fish in the afternoon, breed cattle in
the evening and criticize after dinner, just as I please."[1] This is exactly the sense
in which average opinion spontaneously understands freedom: as the right
and opportunity to do just what we wish and not to have to do anything we
do not wish to do. In other terms: freedom would mean that our own will is
the sole norm of our action and that the will not only can desire anything but
also would have the opportunity to carry out its desire. At this point, however,
questions begin to arise: How free is the will after all? And how reasonable is
it? Is an unreasonable will truly a free will? Is an unreasonable freedom truly
freedom? Is it really a good? To prevent the tyranny of unreason, must we not
complete the definition of freedom as the capacity to will and to do what we
will by placing it in the context of reason, of the totality of man? And will not
the interplay between reason and will also involve a search for the common
reason shared by all men and thus for the compatibility of liberties? It is obvious that the question of truth is implicit in the question of the reasonableness
of the will and of the will's link with reason.

It is not merely abstract philosophical considerations but rather the concrete situation of our society that compels us to ask such questions. In this
situation, the demand for freedom remains undiminished, yet doubts about
the forms of struggle for liberation movements and the systems of freedom
that have existed until now are coming more and more dramatically to the
fore. Let us not forget that Marxism began its career as the one great political
force of our century with the claim that it would usher in a new world of freedom and human liberation. It was precisely Marxism's assurance that it knew
the scientifically guaranteed way to freedom and that it would create a new
world which drew to it many of the boldest minds of our epoch. Eventually,
Marxism even came to be seen as the power by which the Christian doctrine
of redemption could finally be transformed into a realistic praxis of liberation—as the power whereby the Kingdom of God could be concretely realized
as the true kingdom of man. The collapse of "real socialism" in the nations of
Eastern Europe has not entirely extirpated such hopes, which quietly survive
here and there while searching for a new face. The political and economic collapse was not matched by any real intellectual defeat, and in that sense the
question posed by Marxism is still far from being resolved. Nevertheless, the
fact that the Marxist system did not function as had been promised is plain
for all to see. No one can still seriously deny that this ostensible liberation

movement was, alongside National Socialism, the greatest system of slavery in modern history. The extent of its cynical destruction of man and the environment is rather shamefacedly kept quiet, but no one can any longer dispute it.

These developments have brought out the moral superiority of the liberal system in politics and economics. Nevertheless, this superiority is no occasion for enthusiasm. The number of those who have no part in the fruits of this freedom—indeed, who are losing their freedom altogether—is too great: unemployment is once again becoming a mass phenomenon, and the feeling of not being needed, of superfluity, tortures men no less than material poverty. Unscrupulous exploitation is spreading; organized crime takes advantage of the opportunities of the free and democratic world, and in the midst of all this we are haunted by the specter of meaninglessness. At the Salzburg University Weeks of 1995, Polish philosopher Andrej Szizypiorski unsparingly described the dilemma of freedom that has arisen after the fall of the Berlin Wall; it is worth listening to him at somewhat greater length:

> It admits of no doubt that capitalism made a great step forward. And it also admits of no doubt that it has not lived up to what was expected of it. The cry of the huge masses whose desire has not been fulfilled is a constant refrain in capitalism.... The downfall of the Soviet conception of the world and of man in political and social praxis was a liberation of millions of human lives from slavery. But in the intellectual patrimony of Europe, in the light of the tradition of the last two hundred years, the anti-Communist revolution also signals the end of the illusions of the Enlightenment, hence, the destruction of the intellectual conception which was at the basis of the development of early modern Europe.... A remarkable, hitherto unprecedented epoch of uniform development has begun. And it has suddenly become apparent—probably for the first time in history—that there is only one recipe, one way, one model and one method of organizing the future. And men have lost their faith in the meaning of the revolutions which are occurring. They have also lost their hope that the world can be changed at all and that it is worthwhile changing it.... Today's lack of any alternative, however, leads people to pose completely new questions. The first question: was the West wrong after all? The second question: if the West was not right, who, then, was? Because there is no one in Europe who can doubt that Communism was not right, the third question arises: can it be that there is no such thing as right? But if this is the case, the whole intellectual inheritance of the Enlightenment is worthless.... Perhaps the worn-out steam engine of the Enlightenment, after two centuries of profitable, trouble-free labor

has come to a standstill before our eyes and with our cooperation. And the steam is simply evaporating. If this is the way things are in fact, the prospects are gloomy.[2]

Although many questions could also be posed here in response, the realism and logic of Szizypiorski's fundamental queries cannot be brushed aside. At the same time, his diagnosis is so dismal that we cannot stop there. Was no one right? Is there perhaps no "right" at all? Are the foundations of the European Enlightenment, upon which the historical development of freedom rests, false, or at least deficient? The question "What is freedom?" is in the end no less complicated than the question "What is truth?" The dilemma of the Enlightenment, into which we have undeniably fallen, constrains us to repose these two questions, as well as to renew our search for the connection between them. In order to make headway, we must, therefore, reconsider the starting point of the career of freedom in modernity; the course correction that is plainly needed before paths can reemerge from the darkening landscape before us must go back to the starting points themselves and begin its work there. Of course, in the limited framework of an article I can do no more than try to highlight a few points. My purpose in this is to convey some sense of the greatness and perils of the path of modernity and thereby to contribute to a new reflection.

THE PROBLEM: THE HISTORY AND
CONCEPT OF FREEDOM IN MODERNITY

There is no doubt that from the very outset freedom has been the defining theme of the epoch we call modern. The sudden break with the old order to go off in search of new freedoms is the sole reason that justifies such a periodization. Luther's polemical writing *Von der Freiheit eines Christenmenschen* [On the Freedom of a Christian] boldly struck up this theme in resounding tones.[3] It was the cry of freedom that made men sit up and take notice, triggered a veritable avalanche, and turned the writings of a monk into the occasion for a mass movement that radically transformed the face of the medieval world. At issue was the freedom of conscience vis-à-vis the authority of the church, hence the most intimate of all human freedoms. It is not the order of the community that saves man, but his wholly personal faith in Christ. That the whole ordered system of the medieval church ultimately ceased to count was felt to be a massive impulse of freedom. The order that was in reality meant to support and save seemed a burden; it was no longer binding—that is, it no longer had any redemptive significance. Redemption now meant liberation, liberation from the yoke of a supra-individual order. Even if it would not be right to speak of the individualism of the Reformation, the new importance of the individual and the shift in the relation between individual conscience and authority are nonetheless among its dominant traits. However, this liberation movement was restricted to the properly religious sphere. Every time it was extended into a political program, as in the Peasant War and the Anabaptist movement, Luther vigorously opposed it. What came to pass in the political sphere was quite the contrary of liberation: with the creation of territorial and national churches, the power of the secular authority was augmented and consolidated. In the Anglo-Saxon world the free churches subsequently broke out of this new fusion of religious and political government and thus became precursors of a new construction of history, which later took on clear features in the second phase of the modern era, the Enlightenment.

Common to the whole Enlightenment is the will to emancipation, first in the sense of Kant's "*sapere aude*"—dare to use your reason for yourself. Kant is urging the individual reason to break free of the bonds of authority, which must all be subjected to critical scrutiny. Only what is accessible to the eyes of reason is allowed validity. This philosophical program is by its very nature a political one, as well: reason shall reign, and in the end no other authority is admitted than that of reason. Only what is accessible to reason has validity; what is not reasonable—that is, not accessible to reason—cannot be binding, either. This fundamental tendency of the Enlightenment shows up, however, in diverse, even antithetical, social philosophies and political programs. It seems to me that we can distinguish two major currents. The first is the Anglo-Saxon current with its predominantly natural-rights orientation and its proclivity for constitutional democracy, which it conceives as the only realistic system of freedom. At the opposite end of the spectrum is the radical approach of Rousseau, which aims ultimately at complete autarchy. Natural-rights thinking critically applies the criterion of man's innate rights both to positive law and to the concrete forms of government. These rights are held to be prior to every legal order and are considered its measure and basis. "Man is created free, and is still free, even were he born in chains," says Friedrich Schiller in this sense. Schiller is not making a statement that consoles slaves with metaphysical notions but is offering a principle for fighters, a maxim for action. A juridical order that creates slavery is an order of injustice. From Creation man has rights that must be enforced if there is to be justice. Freedom is not bestowed upon man from without. He is a bearer of rights because he is created free. Such thinking gave rise to the idea of human rights, which is the Magna Carta of the modern struggle for freedom. When nature is spoken of in this context, what is meant is not simply a system of biological processes. Rather, the point is that rights are naturally present in man himself prior to all legal constructs. In this sense, the idea of human rights is in the first place a revolutionary one: it opposes the absolutism of the state and the caprice of positive legislation. But it is also a metaphysical idea: there is an ethical and legal claim in being itself. Being is not blind materiality, which can then be formed in accord with pure functionality. Nature contains spirit, ethos, and dignity, and in this way is a juridical claim to liberation, as well as its measure. In principle, what we find here is very much the concept of nature in Romans 2. According to this concept, which is inspired by the Stoa and transformed by the theology of Creation, the Gentiles know the law "by nature" and are thus a law unto themselves (Rom 2:14).

The element specific to the Enlightenment and to modernity in this line of thought may be seen in the notion that the juridical claim of nature vis-à-vis the existing forms of government is, above all, a demand that state and other institutions respect the rights of the individual. Man's nature is, above all, to possess rights against the community, rights that must be protected from the community; institution seems to be the polar opposite of freedom, whereas the individual appears as the bearer of freedom, whose goal is his full emancipation.

This is a point of contact between the first current and the second, which is far more radical in orientation. For Rousseau, everything that owes its origin to reason and will is contrary to nature, and corrupts and contradicts it. The concept of nature is not itself shaped by the idea of a right supposedly preceding all our institutions as a law of nature. Rousseau's concept of nature is antimetaphysical; it is correlative to his dream of total, absolutely unregimented freedom.[4] Similar ideas resurface in Nietzsche, who opposes Dionysian frenzy to Apollonian order, thus conjuring up primordial antitheses in the history of religions: the order of reason, whose symbolic representation is Apollo, corrupts the free, unrestrained frenzy of nature.[5] Klages reprises the same motif with his idea that the spirit is the adversary of the soul: the spirit is not the great new gift wherein alone freedom exists but, with its passion and freedom, is corrosive of the pristine origin.[6] In a certain respect this declaration of war on the spirit is inimical to the Enlightenment, and to that extent National Socialism, with its hostility toward the Enlightenment and its worship of "blood and soil," could appeal to currents such as these. But even here the fundamental motif of the Enlightenment, the cry for freedom, not only is operative but occurs in its most radically intensified form. In the radical politics of both the past and the present century, various forms of such tendencies have repeatedly erupted against the democratically domesticated form of freedom. The French Revolution, which had begun with the idea of a constitutional democracy, soon cast off these fetters and set out on the path of Rousseau and the anarchic conception of freedom; precisely by this move it became inevitably a bloody dictatorship.

Marxism, too, is a continuation of this radical line: it consistently criticized democratic freedom as a sham and promised a better, more radical freedom. Indeed, its fascination derived precisely from its promise of a grander and bolder freedom than is realized in democracies. Two aspects of the Marxist system seem to me particularly relevant to the problem of freedom in the modern period and to the question of truth and freedom.

(1) Marxism proceeds from the principle that freedom is indivisible, hence, that it exists as such only when it is the freedom of all. Freedom is tied to equality. The existence of freedom requires before anything else the establishment of equality. This means that it is necessary to forgo freedom in order to attain the goal of total freedom. The solidarity of those struggling for the freedom of all comes before the vindication of individual liberties. The citation from Marx that served as the starting point for our reflections shows that the idea of the unbounded freedom of the individual reappears at the end of the process. For the present, however, the norm is the precedence of community, the subordination of freedom to equality, and therefore the right of the community vis-à-vis the individual.

(2) Bound up with this notion is the assumption that the freedom of the individual depends upon the structure of the whole and that the struggle for freedom must be waged not primarily to secure the rights of the individual but to change the structure of the world. However, in the question of how this structure was supposed to look and what the rational means to bring it about were, Marxism came up short. For, at bottom, even a blind man could see that none of its structures really makes possible that freedom for whose sake men were being called upon to forgo freedom. But intellectuals are blind when it comes to their intellectual constructs. For this reason they could forswear every realism and continue to fight for a system incapable of honoring its promises. They took refuge in mythology: the new structure, they claimed, would bring forth a new man—for, as a matter of fact, Marxism's promises could work only with new men who are entirely different from what they are now. If the moral character of Marxism lies in the imperative of solidarity and the idea of the indivisibility of freedom, there is an unmistakable lie in its proclamation of the new man, a lie that paralyzes even its inchoate ethics. Partial truths are correlative to a lie, and this fact undoes the whole: any lie about freedom neutralizes even the elements of truth associated with it. Freedom without truth is no freedom at all.

Let us stop at this point. We have arrived once more at the very problems that Szizypiorski formulated so drastically in Salzburg. We now know what the lie is—at least with respect to the forms in which Marxism has occurred until now. But we are still far from knowing what the truth is. Indeed, our apprehension intensifies: is there perhaps no truth at all? Can it be that there simply is no right at all? Must we content ourselves with a minimal stopgap social order? But may it be that even such an order does not work, as the latest developments in the Balkans and in so many other parts of the world show? Skepticism is growing, and the grounds for it are becoming more forcible. At the same time, the will for the absolute cannot be done away with.

The feeling that democracy is not the right form of freedom is fairly common and is spreading more and more. The Marxist critique of democracy cannot simply be brushed aside: How free are elections? To what extent is the outcome manipulated by advertising, that is, by capital, by a few men who dominate public opinion? Is there not a new oligarchy who determine what is modern and progressive, what an enlightened man has to think? The cruelty of this oligarchy, its power to perform public executions, is notorious enough. Anyone who might get in its way is a foe of freedom, because, after all, he is interfering with the free expression of opinion. And how are decisions arrived at in representative bodies? Who could still believe that the welfare of the community as a whole truly guides the decision-making process? Who could doubt the power of special interests, whose dirty hands are exposed with increasing frequency? And in general, is the system of majority and minority really a system of freedom? And are not interest groups of every kind appreciably stronger than the proper organ of political representation, the parliament? In this tangled power play, the problem of ungovernability arises ever more menacingly: the will of individuals to prevail over one another blocks the freedom of the whole.

There is doubtless a flirtation with authoritarian solutions and a flight from a runaway freedom. But this attitude does not yet define the mind of our century. The radical current of the Enlightenment has not lost its appeal; indeed, it is becoming even more powerful. It is precisely in the face of the limits of democracy that the cry for total freedom gets louder. Today as yesterday, indeed, increasingly so, law and order is considered the antithesis of freedom. Today as yesterday, institution, tradition, and authority as such appear to be polar opposites of freedom. The anarchist trend in the longing for freedom is growing in strength because the ordered forms of communal freedom are unsatisfactory. The grand promises made at the inception of modernity have not been kept, yet their fascination is unabated. The democratically ordered form of freedom can no longer be defended merely by this or that legal reform. The question goes to the very foundations themselves: it concerns what man is and how he can live rightly both individually and collectively.

We see that the political, philosophical, and religious problem of freedom has turned out to be an indissoluble whole; whoever is looking for ways forward must keep this whole in view and cannot content himself with superficial pragmatism. Before attempting in the last part to outline some directions that I see opening up, I would like to glance briefly at perhaps the most radical philosophy of freedom in our century, that of J. P. Sartre, inasmuch as it brings out clearly the full magnitude and seriousness of the question. Sartre regards man as condemned to freedom. In contrast to the animal, man has no "nature." The animal lives out its existence according to laws it is simply born with; it does not need to deliberate what to do with its life. But man's essence is undetermined. It is an open question. I must decide myself what I understand by "humanity," what I want to do with it, and how I want to fashion it. Man has no nature, but is sheer freedom. His life must take some direction or another, but in the end it comes to nothing. This absurd freedom is man's hell. What is unsettling about this approach is that it is a way through the separation of freedom from truth to its most radical conclusion: there is no truth at all. Freedom has no direction and no measure.⁷ But this complete absence of truth, this complete absence of any moral and metaphysical bond, this absolutely anarchic freedom—which is understood as an essential quality of man—reveals itself to one who tries to live it not as the supreme enhancement of existence but as the frustration of life, the absolute void, the definition of damnation. The isolation of a radical concept of freedom, which for Sartre was a lived experience, shows with all desirable clarity that liberation from the truth does not produce pure freedom but abolishes it. Anarchic freedom, taken radically, does not redeem but makes man a miscarried creature, a pointless being.

TRUTH AND FREEDOM

On the Essence of Human Freedom

After this attempt to understand the origin of our problems and to get a clear view of their inner tendency, it is now time to search for answers. It has become evident that the critical point in the history of freedom in which we now find ourselves rests upon an unclarified and one-sided idea of freedom. On the one hand, the concept of freedom has been isolated and thereby falsified: freedom is a good, but only within a network of other goods together with which it forms an indissoluble totality. On the other hand, the notion itself has been narrowly restricted to the right of individual liberty and has thus been robbed of its human truth. I would like to illustrate the problem posed by this understanding of freedom with the help of a concrete example. At the same time this example can open the way to a more adequate view of freedom. I mean the question of abortion. In the radicalization of the individualistic tendency of the Enlightenment, abortion appears as a right of freedom: the woman must be able to take charge of herself. She must have the freedom to decide whether she will bring a child into the world or rid herself of it. She must have the power to make decisions about her own life, and no one else can—so we are told—impose from the outside any ultimately binding norm. What is at stake is the right to self-determination. But is it really the case that the woman who aborts is making a decision about her own life? Is she not deciding precisely about someone else—deciding that no freedom shall be granted to another and that the space of freedom, which is life, must be taken from him, because it competes with her own freedom? The question we must, therefore, ask is this: exactly what sort of freedom has the right to annul another's freedom as soon as it begins?

Now, let it not be said that the issue of abortion concerns a special case and is not suited to clarify the general problem of freedom. No, it is this very example that brings out the basic figure of human freedom and makes clear what is typically human about it. For what is at stake here? The being of another person is so closely interwoven with the being of this person, the mother, that for the present it can survive only by physically being with the mother, in a physical unity with her. Such unity, however, does not eliminate the otherness of this being or authorize us to dispute its distinct selfhood. However, to be oneself in this way is to be radically from and through another. Conversely, this being-with compels the being of the other—that is, the mother—to become a being-for, which contradicts her own desire to be an independent self and is thus experienced as the antithesis of her own freedom. We must now add that even once the child is born and the outer form of its being-from and -with changes, it remains just as dependent on, and at the mercy of, a being-for. One can, of course, send the child off to an institution and assign it to the care of another "for," but the anthropological figure is the same, since there is still a "from" that demands a "for." I must still accept the limits of my freedom, or rather, I must live my freedom not out of competition but in a spirit of mutual support. If we open our eyes, we see that this, in turn, is not only true of the child, but that the child in the mother's womb is simply a very graphic depiction of the essence of human existence in general. Even the adult can exist only with and from another, and is thus continually thrown back on that being-for which is the very thing he would like to shut out. Let us say it even more precisely: man quite spontaneously takes for granted the being-for of others in the form of today's network of service systems, yet if he had his way he would prefer not to be forced to participate in such a "from" and "for," but would like to become wholly independent, and to be able to do and not to do just what he pleases. The radical demand for freedom, which has proved itself more and more clearly to be the outcome of the historical course of the Enlightenment, especially of the line inaugurated by Rousseau, and which today largely shapes the public mentality, prefers to have neither a whence nor a whither, to be neither from nor for, but to be wholly at liberty. In other words, it regards what is actually the fundamental figure of human existence itself as an attack on freedom that assails it before any individual has a chance to live and act. The radical cry for freedom demands man's liberation from his very essence as man, so that he may become the "new man." In the new society, the dependencies that restrict the I and the necessity of self-giving would no longer have the right to exist.

"Ye shall be as gods." This promise is quite clearly behind modernity's radical demand for freedom. Although Ernst Topitsch believed he could safely say that today no reasonable man still wants to be like or equal to God, if we look more closely we must assert the exact opposite: the implicit goal of all of modernity's struggles for freedom is to be at last like a god who depends on nothing and no one, whose own freedom is not restricted by that of another. Once we glimpse this hidden theological core of the radical will to freedom, we can also discern the fundamental error that still spreads its influence even where such radical conclusions are not directly willed or are even rejected. To be totally free, without the competing freedom of others, without a "from" and a "for"—this desire presupposes not an image of God but an idol. The primal error of such a radicalized will to freedom lies in the idea of a divinity conceived as a pure egoism. The god thought of in this way is not a God, but an idol. Indeed, it is the image of what the Christian tradition would call the devil—the anti-God—because it harbors exactly the radical antithesis to the real God. The real God is by his very nature entirely being-for (Father), being-from (Son), and being-with (Holy Spirit). Man, for his part, is God's image precisely insofar as the "from," "with," and "for" constitute the fundamental anthropological pattern. Whenever there is an attempt to free ourselves from this pattern, we are on our way not to divinity but to dehumanization, to the destruction of being itself through the destruction of the truth. The Jacobin variant of the idea of liberation (let us call the radicalisms of modernity by this name) is a rebellion against man's very being, a rebellion against truth, which consequently leads man—as Sartre penetratingly saw—into a self-contradictory existence that we call hell.

The foregoing has made it clear that freedom is tied to a measure, the measure of reality: the truth. Freedom to destroy oneself or to destroy another is not freedom but its demonic parody. Man's freedom is shared freedom, freedom in the conjoint existence of liberties that limit and thus sustain one another. Freedom must measure itself by what I am, by what we are—otherwise it annuls itself. But having said this, we are now ready to make an essential correction of the superficial image of freedom that largely dominates the present: if man's freedom can consist only in the ordered coexistence of liberties, this means that order—right[8]—is not the conceptual antithesis of freedom but rather its condition, indeed, a constitutive element of freedom itself. Right is not an obstacle to freedom but constitutes it. The absence of right is the absence of freedom.

Freedom and Responsibility

Admittedly, this insight immediately gives rise to new questions, as well: which right accords with freedom? How must right be structured so as to constitute a just order of freedom? For there doubtless exists a counterfeit right, which enslaves and is, therefore, not right at all but a regulated form of injustice. Our criticism must not be directed at right—self, inasmuch as right belongs to the essence of freedom; it must unmask counterfeit right for what it is and serve to bring to light the true right—that right which is in accord with the truth and consequently with freedom.

But how do we find this right order? This is the great question of the true history of freedom, posed at last in its proper form. As we have already done so far, let us refrain from setting to work with abstract philosophical considerations. Rather, let us try to approach an answer inductively, starting from the realities of history as they are actually given. If we begin with a small community of manageable proportions, its possibilities and limits furnish some basis for finding out which order best serves the shared life of all the members, so that a common form of freedom emerges from their joint existence. But no such small community is self-contained; it has its place within larger orders, which, along with other factors, determine its essence. In the age of the nation-states it was customary to assume that one's own nation was the standard unit—that its common good was also the right measure of its freedom as a community. Developments in our century have made it clear that this point of view is inadequate. Augustine had said on this score that a state which measures itself only by its common interests and not by justice itself, by true justice, is not structurally different from a well-organized robber band. After all, the robber band typically takes as its measure the good of the band independently of the good of others. Looking back at the colonial period and the ravages it bequeathed to the world, we see today that even well-ordered and

civilized states were, in some respects, close to the nature of robber bands because they thought only in terms of their own good and not of the good itself.
Accordingly, freedom guaranteed in this way accordingly has something of
the brigand's freedom. It is not true, genuinely human freedom. In the search
for the right measure, the whole of humanity must be kept in mind and
again—as we see ever more clearly—the humanity not only of today but of
tomorrow, as well.

The criterion of real right—right entitled to call itself true right, which accords with freedom—can, therefore, only be the good of the whole, the good
itself. On the basis of this insight, Hans Jonas has defined responsibility as the
central concept of ethics.[9] This means that in order to understand freedom
properly, we must always think of it in tandem with responsibility. Accordingly, the history of liberation can never occur except as a history of growth in
responsibility. Increased freedom can no longer lie simply in giving more and
more latitude to individual rights—which leads to absurdity and the destruction of those individual freedoms themselves. Increase in freedom must be an
increase in responsibility, which includes acceptance of the ever greater bonds
required both by the claims of humanity's shared existence and by conformity
to man's essence. If responsibility is answering to the truth of man's being,
then we can say that an essential component of the history of liberation is
ongoing purification for the sake of the truth. The true history of freedom
consists in the purification of individuals and institutions through this truth.

The principle of responsibility sets up a framework that needs to be filled
by some content. This is the context in which we have to look at the proposal
for the development of a planetary ethos, for which Hans Küng has been the
preeminent and passionately committed spokesman. It is no doubt sensible,
indeed, in our present situation necessary, to search for the basic elements
common to the ethical traditions of the various religions and cultures. In this
sense, such an endeavor is by all means important and appropriate. On the
other hand, the limits of this sort of enterprise are evident; Joachim Fest,
among others, has called attention to these limits in a sympathetic but also
very pessimistic analysis, whose general drift comes quite close to the skepticism of Szizypiorski.[10] For this ethical minimum distilled from the world
religions lacks first of all the bindingness, the intrinsic authority, that is a prerequisite of ethics. Despite every effort to reach a clearly understandable position, it lacks the obviousness to reason that, in the opinion of the authors,
could and should replace authority; it also lacks the concreteness without
which ethics cannot come into its own.

One idea, which is implicit in this experiment, seems to me correct: reason
must listen to the great religious traditions if it does not wish to become deaf,

dumb, and blind precisely to what is essential about human existence. There is no great philosophy that does not draw life from listening to and accepting religious tradition. Wherever this relation is cut off, philosophical thought withers and becomes a mere conceptual game.[11] The very theme of responsibility—that is, the question of anchoring freedom in the truth of the good, man, and the world—reveals clearly the necessity of such attentive listening. For, although the general approach of the principle of responsibility is very much to the point, it is still a question of how we are supposed to get a comprehensive view of what is good for all: good not only for today but also for tomorrow. A twofold danger lies in wait here. On the one hand there is the risk of sliding into consequentialism, which Pope John Paul II rightly criticizes in his moral encyclical (Veritas Splendor, 1993, nn. 71–83). Man simply overreaches himself if he believes that he can assess the whole range of consequences resulting from his action and make them the norm of his freedom. In doing so he sacrifices the present to the future, while also failing even to construct the future. On the other hand, who decides what our responsibility enjoins? When the truth is no longer seen in the context of an intelligent appropriation of the great traditions of belief, it is replaced by consensus. But once again we must ask: whose consensus? The common answer is the consensus of those capable of rational argument. Because it is impossible to ignore the elitist arrogance of such an intellectual dictatorship, it is then said that those capable of rational argument would also have to engage in "advocacy" on behalf of those who are not. This whole line of thought can hardly inspire confidence. The fragility of consensuses and the ease with which, in a certain intellectual climate, partisan groups can assert their claim to be the sole rightful representatives of progress and responsibility are plain for all to see. It is all too easy here to drive out the devil with Beelzebub; it is all too easy to replace the demon of bygone intellectual systems with seven new and worse ones.

The Truth of Our Humanity

How we are to establish the right relationship between responsibility and freedom cannot be settled simply by means of a calculus of effects. We must return to the idea that man's freedom is a freedom in the coexistence of freedoms; only thus is it true, that is, in conformity with the authentic reality of man. It follows that it is by no means necessary to seek outside elements in order to correct the freedom of the individual. Otherwise, freedom and responsibility, freedom and truth, would be perpetual opposites, which they are not. Properly understood, the reality of the individual itself includes reference to the whole, to the other. Accordingly, our answer to the question above is that there is a common truth of a single humanity present in every man. The tradition has called this truth man's "nature." Basing ourselves on faith in Creation, we can formulate this point even more clearly: there is one divine idea, "man," to which it is our task to answer. In this idea, freedom and community, order and concern for the future, are a single whole.

Responsibility would thus mean to live our being as an answer—as a response to what we are in truth. This one truth of man, in which freedom and the good of all are inextricably correlative, is centrally expressed in the biblical tradition in the Decalogue, which, by the way, coincides in many respects with the great ethical traditions of other religions. The Decalogue is at once the self-presentation and self-exhibition of God and the exposition of what man is, the luminous manifestation of his truth. This truth becomes visible in the mirror of God's essence, because man can be rightly understood only in relation to God. To live the Decalogue means to live our Godlikeness, to correspond to the truth of our being and thus to do the good. Said in yet another way, to live the Decalogue means to live the divinity of man, which is the very definition of freedom: the fusion of our being with the divine being and the resulting harmony of all with all (CCC, nn. 2052–82).

In order to understand this statement aright, we must add a further remark. Every significant human word reaches into greater depths beyond what the speaker is immediately conscious of saying: in what is said there is always an excess of the unsaid, which allows the words to grow as the ages go forward. If this is true even of human speech, it must a fortiori be true of the Word that comes out of the depths of God. The Decalogue is never simply understood once and for all. In the successive, changing situations where responsibility is exercised historically, the Decalogue appears in ever new perspectives, and ever new dimensions of its significance are opened. Man is led into the whole of the truth, truth that could by no means be born in one historical moment alone (cf. Jn 16:12f.). For the Christian, the exegesis of the Decalogue accomplished in the words *life, Passion,* and *Resurrection of Christ* is the decisive interpretive authority, which a hitherto unsuspected depth opens up. Consequently, man's listening to the message of faith is not the passive registering of otherwise unknown information, but the resuscitation of our choked memory and the opening of the powers of understanding, which await the light of the truth in us. Hence, such understanding is a supremely active process, in which reason's entire quest for the criteria of our responsibility truly comes into its own for the first time. Reason's quest is not stifled, but is freed from circling helplessly in impenetrable darkness and set on its way. If the Decalogue, unfolded in rational understanding, is the answer to the intrinsic requirements of our essence, then it is not the counterpole of our freedom, but its real form. It is, in other words, the foundation of every just order of freedom and the true liberating power in human history.

Summary of the Results

"Perhaps the worn-out steam engine of the Enlightenment, after two centuries of profitable, trouble-free labor has come to a standstill before our eyes and with our cooperation. And the steam is simply evaporating." This is Szizypiorski's pessimistic diagnosis, which we encountered at the beginning as an invitation to reflection. Now, I would say that the operation of this machine was never trouble-free: let us think only of the two world wars of our century and of the dictatorships we have witnessed. But I would add that we by no means need to retire the whole inheritance of the Enlightenment as such from service and pronounce it a worn-out steam engine. What we do need, however, is a course correction on three essential points, with which I would like to sum up the yield of my reflections.

(1) An understanding of freedom that tends to regard liberation exclusively as the ever more sweeping annulment of norms and the constant extension of individual liberties to the point of complete emancipation from all order is false. Freedom, if it is not to lead to deceit and self-destruction, must orient itself by the truth—that is, by what we really are—and must correspond to our being. Since man's essence consists in being-from, being-with, and being-for, human freedom can exist only in the ordered communion of freedoms. Right is, therefore, not antithetical to freedom, but is a condition—indeed, a constitutive element of freedom itself. Liberation lies not in the gradual abolition of right and norms but in the purification of ourselves and the norms so that they will make possible the humane coexistence of freedoms.

(2) A further point follows from the truth of our essential being: there will never be an absolutely ideal state of things within our human history, and the definitive order of freedom will never be established. Man is always underway and always finite. Szizypiorski, considering both the notorious injustice of the socialist order and all the problems of the liberal order, had posed the doubt-filled question: what if there is no right order at all? Our response must now be that, in fact, the absolutely ideal order of things that is right in all respects will never exist.[12] Whoever claims that it will is not telling the truth. Faith in progress is not false in every respect. What is false, however, is the myth of the liberated world of the future, in which everything will be different and good. We can erect only relative orders, which can never be and embody right except in their relative way. But we must strive precisely for this best possible ap-

proximation to what is truly right. Nothing else, no inner-historical eschatology, liberates; rather, it deceives and therefore enslaves. For this reason, the mythic luster attached to concepts like change and revolution must be demythologized. Change is not good in itself. Whether it is good or bad depends upon its concrete contents and points of reference. The opinion that the essential task in the struggle for freedom is to change the world is—I repeat—a myth. History will always have its vicissitudes. When it comes to man's ethical nature in the strict sense, things proceed not in a straight line but in cycles. It is our task always to struggle in the present for the comparatively best constitution of man's shared existence and in so doing to preserve the good we have already achieved, overcome existing ills, and resist the incipient forces of destruction.

(3) We must also lay to rest once and for all the dream of the absolute autonomy and self-sufficiency of reason. Human reason needs the support of the great religious traditions of humanity. It will, of course, examine critically individual religious traditions. The pathology of religion is the most dangerous sickness of the human mind. It exists in religions, but it also exists where religion as such is rejected and the status of an absolute is assigned to relative goods; the atheistic systems of modernity are the most terrifying examples of a religious passion alienated from its nature, creating a life-threatening sickness of the human mind. Where God is denied, freedom is not built up, but robbed of its foundation and thus distorted.[13] Where the purest and deepest religious traditions are entirely discarded, man severs himself from his truth, lives contrary to it, and becomes unfree. Even philosophical ethics cannot be unqualifiedly autonomous. It cannot renounce the idea of God or the idea of a truth of being having an ethical character.[14] If there is no truth about man, man also has no freedom. Only the truth makes us free.

The Church's Teaching

Authority, Faith, Morals

AN OUTLINE OF THE PROBLEM

The crisis of faith that is increasingly making itself felt by Christian people is revealing itself with increasing clarity as a crisis regarding awareness of fundamental values of human life. It is nourished by the moral crisis of mankind, and at the same time it intensifies this crisis. When trying to come to an appreciation of the whole sweep of current discussion on this question, however, one meets with notions that, though strangely contrary, are all the same closely connected. On the one hand, particularly since the formation of the World Council of Churches in Uppsala, there is an increasingly clear trend to view Christianity primarily not as orthodoxy but as orthopraxy. Many factors have contributed to this trend. There is, for instance, the question of racial equality in America, which has had a serious influence on Christianity there, since it is evident that the existence of a common confession of faith has done nothing to break down the wall of division. Thus, the concrete value of the confession of faith has become questionable, as it has no power to arouse love, which is the root of the gospel. Here we see a practical question becoming the touchstone for the truth of doctrine, a test case for the Christian position; where orthopraxy is so scandalously lacking, orthodoxy becomes questionable.

Another factor in the trend toward praxis lies in the various strands of political theology, which are, in turn, variously motivated. They are all deeply affected by the questions raised by Marxism. Here, the concept of truth is itself under suspicion, if not devoid of content. To that extent, this mode of thought is one with the sentiment that gives rise to positivism. Truth is felt to be unattainable, and the insistence on truth is regarded as the ploy of interest groups seeking to confirm their position. According to this view, only praxis can decide the value or worthlessness of theories. If Christianity, therefore, wishes to contribute to a better world, it must come up with a better praxis— not seeking truth as a theory but producing it as a reality. Here, the demand that Christianity must become an "orthopraxy" of common action toward a more human future, leaving orthodoxy behind as unfruitful or even harmful, is far more radical than the purely pragmatic positions mentioned earlier. At the same time, it is clear that the two approaches tend to combine operations and reinforce one another. Neither has much space left for a teaching authority, although, if these views were carried through consistently, it would inevitably reemerge in a different form. But a teaching authority that would formulate an already given truth concerning man's authentic praxis and measure man's performance against this truth would be banished to the negative side of reality as a hindrance to creative and forward-looking praxis. It would be regarded as a symptom of particular interests hiding behind the slogan of orthodoxy and opposing the onward march of the history of freedom. On the other hand, it is admitted that praxis needs reflection and tactics resulting from reflection, so the linking of Marxist praxis to the party's "teaching authority" is completely logical.

At the opposite end from the view that would define and realize Christianity in terms of orthopraxy, there is a position (often, unaccountably, embracing the former) that affirms that there is no such thing as a specifically Christian morality and that Christianity must take its norms of conduct from the anthropological insights of its time. Faith does not supply any independent source of moral norms, but points insistently to the future. Nothing that is not ratified by the future can be maintained by faith. This view is substantiated by indicating that, even in its historical roots, faith does not develop a morality of its own, but adopts the practical reason of contemporary men and women.[1] This can already be seen in the Old Testament, where there is continual change in values from the time of the patriarchs to the Wisdom literature, determined by the encounter with the developing moral ideas of surrounding cultures. There is no moral proposition found exclusively in the Old Testament that can be regarded solely as the fruit of faith in Yahweh; in moral matters everything is taken from elsewhere. This applies to the New Testament, as well: the lists of virtues and vices in the apostolic letters reflect the Stoic ethos and thus represent the adoption of what was at that time reason's guide for human conduct. Consequently it is not their content but their structure that is significant, in that they point to reason as the only source of moral norms. We need hardly say that, here, too, there is no place for a church teaching authority in moral matters; to set up detailed norms of conduct on the basis of the tradition of faith would be to act on the misconception that the statements of the Bible have an abiding validity in terms of content, whereas, according to this view, they only point to the particular stage reached at the time by rational human understanding.

Both approaches clearly raise fundamental problems regarding the nature of the Christian position that cannot be fully dealt with in a few pages. In the first case, where Christianity is interpreted as orthopraxy, not only pragmatically but in principle, the basic issue is the question of truth, of reality. Ultimately, the question of being is inextricably involved with the first article of faith, even if, in particular instances, people are not always aware of it, and the positions adopted are rarely carried through with absolute consistency. At first sight, the second case seems to revolve around a single historical problem— that is, the historical origin of certain biblical statements. But if we look closer, we find that it rests on a more fundamental problem—namely, the question of how what is specifically Christian can be defined vis-à-vis the changing historical forms it adopts. It also involves the problem of how faith communicates with reason, with universally human aspects, and ultimately the question of reason's sphere of action and limitations in matters of faith.[2]

AN INITIAL RESPONSE

Let us begin with the most immediate aspect, which is simplest to deal with, and thus come to grips with the problem of the historical origins of biblical utterances on moral issues. First of all, there is a general question of methodology, for it is quite simply wrong to say that things inherited from elsewhere can never attain separate and distinctive existence. Our own life tells us this; the theological affirmation "What have you that you did not receive?" can be demonstrated even at a purely human level. We know it, too, from the whole history of civilization: the greatness of a civilization is seen in its ability to communicate, its ability to give and receive, but in particular to receive, to assimilate elements into itself. The originality of Christianity does not consist in the number of propositions for which no parallel can be found elsewhere (if there *are* such propositions, which is highly questionable). It is impossible to distill out what is specifically Christian by excluding everything that has come about through contact with other milieus. Christianity's originality consists rather in the new total form into which human searching and striving have been forged under the guidance of faith in the God of Abraham, the God of Jesus Christ. The fact that the Bible's moral pronouncements can be traced to other cultures or to philosophical thought in no way implies that morality is a function of mere reason—this is a premature conclusion we should no longer allow to pass unchallenged. What is important is not that such utterances can be found elsewhere, but the particular position they have or do not have in the spiritual edifice of Christianity. This is what we must now examine.

Let us begin with an absolutely simple observation. Historically speaking, it is incorrect to say that biblical faith simply adopted the morality of the surrounding world—that is, the particular stage of rational moral awareness that had been reached at the time—for there was no "surrounding world," no "environment" as such, nor was there a single "morality" that could have been adopted. What we find is that, guided by Israel's perception of Yahweh, an often highly dramatic struggle took place between those elements of the surrounding legal and moral tradition that could be assimilated by Israel and those that Israel was bound to reject. In the final analysis, this is what the prophets are fighting for. Thus Nathan forbids David to adopt the manner of an absolute oriental potentate who would take someone else's wife if he so desired. Thus Elijah, in championing Naboth's rights, is defending the rights of the nation, guaranteed by the God of Israel, against royal absolutism. So, too, Amos, in fighting for the rights of the hired laborer and of all dependent people, is vindicating the vision of the God of Israel. It is always the same story. Similarly, the many-sided struggle between Yahweh and Baal cannot be reduced to a merely "dogmatic" question; what is at stake here is the indivisible unity of faith and life. Deciding for or against the one God or the many gods is always a life decision.

THREE EXAMPLES OF THE INTERRELATION OF FAITH AND MORALS

The Ten Commandments

We come now to a more detailed discussion, which will be clarified somewhat by three characteristic examples. First let us consider the Ten Commandments (Ex 20:1–17; Dt 5:6–21), one of the central formulations of Yahweh's will for Israel, which has always been a formative influence on the ethos of Israel and the church. No doubt it can be shown that there are precedents, both in Egyptian lists of transgressions to be avoided and in the interrogations of Babylonian exorcisms. Even the introductory formula, "I am the Lord your God," is not entirely new. Yet it imparts a new face to the "Ten Words," linking them to the God of the Covenant and his covenant will. The "Ten Words" show in practical terms what it means to believe in Yahweh, to accept the covenant with Yahweh. At the same time they define the figure of God himself, whose nature is manifested through them. This situates the Ten Commandments in the context of God's decisive self-revelation in Exodus 3, for there, too, God's self-portrayal is expressed in practical terms by setting forth his moral will: he has heard the groaning of the oppressed and has come to liberate them. The introduction to the Ten Commandments, both in the Exodus 20 version and in Deuteronomy, links up with this revelation: Yahweh introduces himself as the God who brought Israel out of Egypt, out of the house of bondage. In other words, for Israel, the Ten Commandments are part of the concept of God. They are not supplementary to faith, to the covenant; they show who this God is, with whom Israel stands in a covenant relationship.[3]

Connected with this is the concept of the holy, as it has developed in the religion of the Bible. In the history of religions in general, holiness is simply the divinity's total otherness, the specific atmosphere of divinity, yielding particular rules for encountering it. Initially, Israel is no different in this regard, as many passages show. Since Yahweh, however, reveals what is special about him, his complete otherness, through the "Ten Words," it becomes clear (and the prophets increasingly call it to mind) that Yahweh's total otherness, his holiness, is a moral dimension; to it corresponds man's moral action in accord with the "Ten Words." In the ancient layers of tradition to which the Ten Commandments belong, the concept of the holy as the specific category of the divine has already coalesced with the concept of the moral: that is, what is new and unique about this God and his holiness. It is also what imparts a new status to the category of the moral, and it provides criteria of selection in the debate with the ethos of the nations, eventually attaining the heights of the concept of holiness in the Old Testament that anticipates Jesus's own picture of God: "I will not execute my fierce anger ... for I am God and not man, the Holy One in your midst" (Hos 11:9). "Now there can be no doubt that it is the proclamation of the Decalogue over her which puts Israel's election into effect," as Gerhard von Rad formulates it in his *Old Testament Theology;* he also illustrates this connection by showing its effects upon liturgical life.[4] This by no means implies that the Ten Commandments were understood right from the outset in the fullness of their significance, nor that the mere word alone communicates fundamental moral understanding in a definitive form; on the contrary, the history of interpretation, from the earliest strands of tradition right up to the recasting of the Ten Commandments in the Sermon on the Mount, shows that this word could (and was bound to) ignite an ever-deeper understanding of the will of God, and hence of God and of man. At the same time, as we have said, the fact that particular elements of the Ten Commandments can be traced to non-Israelite origins tells us nothing about whether or not they can be separated off from the core of covenant faith. Such a view can only be maintained if one assumes that there is no analogy between the nations' reason and God's revelation, and that the two phenomena confront each other in a pure paradox—that is, if one has a particular concept of the relationship between revelation and reason, a concept that is not verified by the biblical texts, but rather is falsified by them.

The Name "Christian"

Let us take another example, this time from the early Christian period—namely, the significance of the words *Christian* and *Christianity* in the church's initial development.[5] Here again, as with the Ten Commandments in Israel, it is the central core itself that is speaking. From Acts 11:26, we know that this name was first applied in Antioch to the community of believers. Though the occasion that gave rise to this epithet is lost to us and its original signification is disputed (and will remain so, given the sources available to us), there was clearly something ironic about it in the beginning. Moreover, in Roman law it denoted a punishable offense: the *christiani* were members of Christ's band of conspirators. From the time of Hadrian, therefore, bearing the name *Christian* was a crime. Peterson has shown that the charges laid against Christians—in Suetonius and Tacitus, for instance—are an integral part of political propaganda "against real or alleged conspirators."[6] Yet in Ignatius of Antioch we already find Christians applying this dangerous title to themselves; indeed, they are proud to bear it and eager to prove worthy of it. What does it mean, therefore, when people deliberately adopt a term of abuse, a criminal title?

The answer is twofold. First of all, we find in Ignatius a strongly marked theology of martyrdom, which leads to the adoption of a word that itself evokes martyrdom. Fellowship with Jesus Christ, which faith is, signifies to the eyes of the world a participation in a conspiracy punishable by death. The bishop of Antioch realizes that this "external" verdict somehow or other actually hits upon a central truth, although the way in which it is true is internal: fellowship with Jesus is in fact a participation in his death, and thus (only thus) in his life.[7] The idea that Christians are united in a conspiracy with Christ is correct insofar as Christians do not merely adopt a theory about Jesus but enter into his way of living and dying and make it their own. "Since we have become his disciples, we must learn how to live in accordance with Christianity."[8] In this sense, so far as the Syrian martyr-bishop is concerned, Christianity is most definitely an orthopraxy—it is a realization of Jesus Christ's manner of life. But what form does that take? To answer this question, we must go one step farther. For the pagan, the word *christianus* meant a conspirator, represented in the stereotypes of political propaganda as a person characterized by evil *flagitia* (crimes)—in particular, by "hatred against the human race" and *stuprum* (licentiousness).[9] In response, Ignatius uses a play

connection of faith and life

on words that came to have a long history in Christian apologetics. In Greek phonetics, the word *chrestos* (good) was, and is, pronounced *christos*. Ignatius seizes on this association when he prefaces the words "we must learn how to live in accordance with Christianity [*christianismos*]" with the admonition "let us not be unfeeling toward his goodness [*chrestotes*, pronounced *christotes*]."[10] The conspiracy of the *Christos* is a conspiracy of those who are *chrestos*, a conspiracy of goodness. Thus Tertullian, a hundred years later, will assert that "the word *Christ* comes from the word for goodness."[11] Here, the link we found in the Ten Commandments between the concept of God and the moral idea is repeated at a most sublime and exacting level in the Christian context: the name *Christian* implies fellowship with Christ, and hence the readiness to take upon oneself martyrdom in the cause of goodness. Christianity is a conspiracy to promote the good; the theological and moral aspects are fused inseparably, both in the word itself and deeper, in the basic concept of what Christian reality is.[12]

The Apostolic Exhortation

Thus Ignatius and the early Christian theology that follows him stand foursquare on the foundation of apostolic preaching, which brings us to our third example. In Pauline preaching, in particular, there is an intimate connection between faith and "imitating" the apostle, who, in turn, "imitates" Jesus Christ. This is put especially clearly in 1 Thessalonians: "As you learned from us how you ought to live ... do so more and more. For you know what instructions we gave you through the Lord Jesus" (1 Thes 4:1ff.). This manner of life, this "walking" (AV), is part of the transmitted tradition. Paul's instruction does not come from just anywhere; it comes from the Lord Jesus. His subsequent remarks are loosely related to the Ten Commandments and applied in a Christian sense to the particular situation of the Thessalonians.

Now, it might be objected that what is at stake here is simply the formal intention toward the good, which is, no doubt, characteristic of Christianity, but as to the question of what this goodness involves, that is something to be decided by reason and in the light of the times, not on the basis of internal theological sources. This seems to be suggested, for instance, by a text such as Philippians 4:8: "Finally, brethren, whatever is true, whatever is honorable, whatever is just, whatever is pure, whatever is lovely, whatever is gracious, if there is any excellence, if there is anything worthy of praise, think about these things." What we have here, it might be said, are current notions of popular philosophy; accepted notions of what is good are being commended to Christians for their acceptance, too. To this we could immediately reply that the passage goes on: "What you have learned and received and heard and seen in me, do" (4:9). We could point out that this is ultimately an interpretation of 2:5: "Have this mind among yourselves, which was in Christ Jesus"—which reveals the same connection between the attitude of Jesus (as the standard of behavior) and Christian existence that we met in Ignatius.

But we must probe a little deeper. No doubt it is correct that, here as elsewhere, Paul is referring to the moral awareness that conscience has awakened among the pagans, and he identifies this awareness with the true law of God, according to the principles developed in Romans 2:15. This does not mean, however, that the kerygma shrinks to a nonspecific pointer to whatever contemporary reason regards as good. In the first place, there has never been this kind of "contemporary reason," nor will there be. Paul was confronted not with a particular scholarly consensus on the subject of the "good" to be simply adopted, but with a maze of conflicting positions, in which Epicurus and Seneca are only two examples of the whole spectrum. The only way to proceed here was not to accept the given but to apply resolute critical discernment. It was a case of the Christian faith making its new decisions on the basis of the Old Testament tradition and, in concrete terms, of the "mind of Christ"; from outside this was condemned as conspiracy, whereas from inside it was proclaimed all the more insistently as the genuine good. Second, it is not true to say that, for Paul, conscience and reason are variables, one thing today and something else tomorrow. Conscience is shown to be what it is precisely because it says the same thing that God proclaimed to the Jews in the word of the covenant. Conscience, as such, uncovers what is constant and thus necessarily leads to the "mind of Christ." Paul's real view of things comes to light most clearly, perhaps, in the first chapter of Romans, where we find that same connection between moral issues and the concept of God that we saw to be characteristic of the Old Testament: a faulty concept of God leads to faulty moral behavior in the pagan world; returning to God in Jesus Christ is identical with a return to the manner of life of Jesus Christ. Paul had already put forward this view in 1 Thessalonians: the pagans' unholiness is connected with the fact that they do not know God; the will of God is for their "sanctification," and the gospel of grace understands this morally. Anyone who reads the Pauline letters carefully will see that the apostolic exhortation is not some moralizing appendix with a variable content, but a very practical setting forth of what faith means; thus, it is inseparable from faith's core. The apostle is, in fact, only following the pattern of Christ, who, in this central theme of his preaching, linked admission to the Kingdom of God and exclusion from it with fundamental moral decisions, which are consequences intimately related to the way God is conceived.[13]

FAITH, MORALS, TEACHING AUTHORITY

In mentioning the apostolic exhortation, we have gone beyond the connection of faith and morals and raised the question of teaching authority, for the apostolic letters are instances of the exercise of teaching authority. Here Paul is also putting forward "official" teaching about the moral form that faith takes; the same applies to the other New Testament letters, as well as the Gospels, which are full of moral instruction, and finally the Book of Revelation. Paul does not offer theories about what is human and reasonable; what he does is explicate the inner demands of grace, as H. Schlier has shown in his fine article on the uniqueness of Christian moral exhortation.[14] True, the apostle does not use express commands very often (1 Thes 4:10f.), although he is aware that he has the authority to do so (2 Cor 8:8); he does not want to approach the Christian communities as the pedagogues of the ancient world treated their pupils, with threats and force, but prefers to admonish them as a father within the Christian family. In doing so, he shows clearly that it is the mercy of God that is calling to them through his words. It is grace; it is God exhorting them through Paul's exhortation; it is not some supplementary variable added to the gospel: it is clothed with the Lord's authority, even when it does not appear in the form of a command or an official doctrinal decision.[15] The same thing is observable if we examine the central themes of his exhortation: the saving events we have from Christ's life, baptism, fellowship of the body of Christ, the prospect of the Last Judgment.[16] There is a clearly drawn line between grace and the manner of life of those who do not know God; it is described as a turning away from licentiousness, covetousness, idolatry, envy, and quarrelsomeness, and a turning toward obedience, patience, truth, freedom from anxiety, and joy. The fundamental commandment of love expresses itself in these attitudes.[17]

What we observe in Paul is continued in the writings of those taught by the apostles; here the apostolic exhortation, as a normative tradition, is expounded as it applies to the particular situation.[18] This means that, so far as the New Testament is concerned, the church's official teaching does not come to an end with the age of the apostles; it is a permanent gift to the church. The church remains apostolic in the postapostolic age, in that the authentic followers of the apostles bear responsibility to see that the church abides in the teaching of the apostles. Luke stresses this in the crisis of transition, when he portrays the primitive Jerusalem community "remaining in the teaching of the apostles" (Acts 2:42) as the standard form of the church for all time, with its presbyters as the guardians of this "remaining" (Acts 20:17–38).[19] In this context, it is not necessary to develop a detailed theory of the church's teaching office centered on the teaching office of the Successor of Peter, although it would not be difficult to indicate the New Testament lines running in this direction. (On the one hand, there is the ever-clearer idea of tradition and succession, and on the other hand, the development of Petrine theology.) It is manifest that the fundamental content of apostolic succession consists precisely in the authority to preserve apostolic faith; also, that the plenitude of teaching authority that goes with this includes the task of making concrete the moral demands of grace and of working them out in detail with regard to the contemporary situation.[20]

Thus, our reflections have returned to their starting point. Christian faith does indeed involve a praxis on the part of faith; orthodoxy without orthopraxy fails to reach the core of the Christian reality, namely, love proceeding from grace. This also implies that Christian praxis is nourished by the core of Christian faith, that is, the grace that appeared in Christ and that is appropriated in the sacrament of the church. Faith's praxis depends on faith's truth, in which man's truth is made visible and lifted up to a new level by God's truth. Hence, it is fundamentally opposed to a praxis that first wants to produce facts and so establish truth. By holding on to the Creator, faith's praxis protects Creation against such a total manipulation of reality. By looking to the example of Jesus Christ, faith recognizes fundamental human values and rescues them from all manipulation. It protects man by protecting Creation; the apostles' successors have an indestructible commission to maintain apostolic teaching and make it present. Since grace refers to both Creation and the Creator, apostolic exhortation (as a continuation of Old Testament admonitions) is involved with human reason. Contrary to appearances, the flight into pure orthopraxy and the attempt to banish substantive morals from the realm of faith (with the teaching authority that is an integral part of the realm of faith) turn reason into a heresy. In the one case, reason's ability to recognize truth is denied and the renunciation of truth is elevated into a method; in the other case, faith is lifted out of the realm of reason, and rational considerations are not admitted as possible components of the world of faith. Either faith is declared to be irrational or reason is made out to be unbelieving—or both. Either reason is imagined to speak with a single voice at any one time—which, of itself, it cannot do—or its message is bound to what is contemporary in such a way that truth disappears behind the values of the age. Thus, every age sees reason differently, which ultimately leads to opting for the absolute dominance of practical reason. The faith of the apostles, as we see it in Romans 1 and 2 for instance, thinks more highly of reason. This faith is convinced that reason is capable of embracing truth and that, therefore, faith does not have to erect its edifice apart from the tradition of reason but finds its language in communication with the reason of the nations through a process of reception and dialectic. This means that both the process of assimilation and that of negation and criticism must be pursued on the basis of faith's fundamental options and must be firmly rooted in the latter. Reason's ability to embrace truth also implies that truth's content is constant and coincident with the constancy of faith.

The task of the church's teaching office in moral matters follows automatically from what has been said. As we have seen, faith involves fundamental decisions (with definite content) in moral matters. The first obligation of the teaching office is to continue the apostolic exhortation and to protect these fundamental decisions against reason's capitulation to the age, as well as against reason's capitulation in the face of almighty praxis. There must be a correspondence with basic insights of human reason, although these insights have been purified, deepened, and broadened through contact with the way of faith. As we have said, the positive, critical dialogue with reason is something that must go on for all time. There is never a clear-cut division between genuine reason and what merely appears "reasonable"; however, the two things—that is, the "appearance" of reason and the manifestation of truth through reason—coexist in all ages. The whole church is involved in the process of assimilating what is genuinely rational and rejecting what is only superficially reasonable. It cannot be done by an isolated teaching authority, with oracular infallibility in every detail. The life and suffering of Christians, living out their faith in the midst of the times, is just as much a part of it as the reflections and questionings of the scholars. Indeed, the latter is nothing but idle verbiage unless it is backed up by a Christian existence that has learned to discern the spirits in the "Passion" of everyday life. The faith experience of the whole church and the research and questioning, in faith, on the part of scholars represent two factors; a third factor is the watchful attention, listening, and deciding undertaken by the teaching authority. Right from the first century, it has been the church's experience that there is nothing automatic about the maintenance of right doctrine; responsible shepherds are needed in the church to "exhort and admonish." That is why it has fashioned the office of those who are called, through prayer and the imposition of hands, to be successors of the apostles. Today, equally, this office is indispensable. Those who fundamentally deny that it has any competence to make detailed and practical decisions for or against an interpretation on the morality that springs from grace are trying to overturn the very basic form of apostolic tradition.

Culture and Truth: Some Reflections on the Encyclical Letter *Fides et Ratio*

I would like to begin my reflections on the encyclical letter *Fides et Ratio* of Pope John Paul II with a brief quotation from *The Screwtape Letters* by C. S. Lewis. This short book, which appeared in 1942, presents the questions and dangers faced by modern man in a spirited and ironic way, through a series of imaginary letters of instruction written by a higher demon, Screwtape, to his nephew, a junior demon and a beginner in the work of human seduction.

At one point it seems that the junior demon may have expressed some concern to his uncle over the fact that intelligent people are especially prone to read books containing the wisdom of the ancients, and by doing so, they may come upon traces of the truth. Screwtape responds by reassuring him that the spirits from below have succeeded in inculcating among educated people something which makes that very unlikely. It is called "the Historical Point of View," and it works this way:

> The Historical Point of View, put briefly, means that when a learned man is presented with any statement from an ancient author, the one question he never asks is whether it is true. He asks who influenced the ancient writer, and how far the statement is consistent with what he said in other books, and what phase in the writer's development, or in the general history of thought, it illustrates ... and so on.[1]

In his study of interpretation, Josef Pieper cites this passage from C. S. Lewis and relates how, for example, in the editions of Plato or Dante that were produced in countries under Communist domination, an introduction to the text was systematically added to give the reader a "historical" understanding of the writing, and thereby exclude the question of truth. In this way, scholarship becomes an immunization against the truth.

The question of whether and to what extent the author's statements are true is viewed as a question that is not scholarly; indeed, it is a question that leads beyond what can be documented and demonstrated, and causes one to fall back into the naïveté of the precritical world. In this way, also, the reading of the Bible is neutralized: we can explain when and under what conditions a phrase came into being and we can classify it historically, which does not really concern us in an ultimate way.

Behind this form of "historical interpretation" lies a philosophy, a fundamental perspective on reality, which says that it is, in fact, pointless to ask about what is; we can only ask ourselves what we are able to do with things. The issue is not truth, but praxis, the domination of things for our needs. In the face of such an apparently enlightened limitation of human thought, the questions naturally arise: What really is useful to us? Why is it useful? Why do we exist?

One who observes carefully will see that the modern attitude reveals at once a false humility and a false presumption: a false humility that does not recognize in the human person the capacity for the truth, and a false presumption by which one places oneself above things, above truth itself, while making the extension of one's power, one's domination over things, the objective of one's thought.

Viewed against the background of this fundamental orientation of modern thought, the intention of the encyclical and its significance for our historical moment can be better understood. *Fides et Ratio* seeks to restore to humanity the courage to seek the truth, that is, to encourage reason once again in the adventure of searching for truth. It does this when, referring to the task of interpretation, it contradicts all of Screwtape's instructions and states: "The interpretation of this word [that is, the word of God] cannot merely keep referring us to one interpretation after another, without ever leading us to a statement which is simply true" (*FR* 84).

Man is not trapped in a hall of mirrors of interpretations; one can and must seek a breakthrough to what is really true. Man must ask who he really is and what he is to do. He must ask whether there is a God, who God is, and what the world is. The one who no longer poses these questions is, by that very fact, bereft of any standard or path. Allow me to give an example.

The position is gaining ground which maintains that human rights are a cultural product of the Judeo-Christian world that, outside this world, would be unintelligible and without foundation. But what then? What happens if we can no longer recognize common standards that transcend individual cultures? What happens if the unity of mankind is no longer recognizable to man?

Will not division into separate races, classes, and nationalities become insurmountable? The person who can no longer recognize a common human nature in others, beyond all such boundaries, has lost his identity. Precisely as a human being, he is in peril. Thus, for philosophy in its classical and original sense, the question of truth is not a frivolity to be enjoyed by affluent cultures that can afford the luxury, but rather a question that concerns the existence or nonexistence of man.

And therefore the pope earnestly asks us to break down the barriers of eclecticism, historicism, scientism, pragmatism, and nihilism, and he exhorts us not to allow ourselves to be caught up in a form of postmodernism that, in a decadent desire for negativity, abdicates all meaning and seeks to grasp only what is provisional and ephemeral (cf. FR 91).

Whoever poses the question of truth today, as we already mentioned, is necessarily directed to the problem of cultures and their mutual openness. Christianity's claim to universality, which is based on the universality of truth, is often countered in our day with the argument of the relativity of cultures. It is maintained that, in fact, the Christian missionary effort did not disseminate a truth that is the same for all people, but instead subjugated indigenous cultures to the particular culture of Europe, thus damaging the richness of those cultures that had evolved among a variety of peoples.

The Christian missionary effort thus appears as another of the great European sins, as the original form of colonialism and thus as the spiritual despoiling of other peoples. To this argument, we must reply first of all by noting that in the history of evangelization, there were certainly mistakes; about this no one would disagree. Moreover, that the cultural multiplicity of humanity must find a place in the church, the common home for all people, is today recognized without exception.

But in the radical critique of the Christian missionary effort from the standpoint of cultures, there is something deeper at work: the question of whether there can be a communion of cultures within the truth that unites them, the question of whether truth can be expressed for all people beyond cultural forms, or instead whether, finally, behind the diversity of cultures, truth only appears asymptotically because of its importance. The pope dedicates several paragraphs of the encyclical to this question (FR 69–72). He underscores the fact that when cultures are deeply rooted in what is human, they bear witness in themselves to the human person's "characteristic openness to the universal and the transcendent" (FR 70).

Therefore, cultures, the expression of man's one essence, are characterized by the human dynamic, which is to transcend all boundaries. Thus, cultures are not fixed once and for all in a single form; they have the capacity to make progress and to be transformed, as they also face the danger of decadence. Cultures are predisposed to the experience of encounter and reciprocal enrichment. As man's inner openness to God leaves its mark on a culture to the extent to which that culture is great and pure, so there is written in such cultures an inner openness to the revelation of God. Revelation is not extraneous to cultures; rather, it responds to an inner expectation within cultures themselves.

It was in this connection that Theodor Hacher spoke of the advent character of pre-Christian cultures, and since that time, many studies in the history of religions have demonstrated quite impressively this advance of cultures toward the Logos of God, who in Jesus Christ became flesh. In this context, the Holy Father makes reference to the listing of peoples in the Pentecost account in the Acts of the Apostles (Acts 2:7–11), which narrates for us how, through all languages and in all languages, that is, in all cultures that manifest themselves in language, the testimony about Jesus Christ becomes understandable.

In all of them, the human word becomes the bearer of God's language, of God's Logos. The encyclical puts it in this way: "While it demands of all who hear it the adherence of faith, the proclamation of the gospel in different cultures allows people to preserve their own cultural identity. This in no way creates division because the community of the baptized is marked by a universality which can embrace every culture" (FR 71).

Taking as his starting point the encounter with the culture of India, the Holy Father develops the fundamental principles for the relationship between Christian faith and pre-Christian cultures. He refers briefly to the great spiritual quest of Indian thought, which struggles for the liberation of the spirit from the confines of space and time, and so manifests in practice the metaphysical openness of man.

This quest for liberation, then, takes on an intellectual form in the great philosophical systems (FR 72). With this reference, the universalistic tendency of the great cultures becomes evident: their transcending of place and time, and so, too, the way in which they advance man's being and his highest possibilities. Here the capacity for reciprocal dialogue between cultures finds its foundation in this specific case, the dialogue between Indian culture and those cultures that have grown up on the soil of the Christian faith.

Thus, from a profound contact with Indian culture, a first criterion emerges almost spontaneously: "The universality of the human spirit, whose basic needs are the same in the most disparate cultures" (FR 72). From this, a second criterion immediately follows: "In engaging great cultures for the first time, the church cannot abandon what she has gained from her enculturation in the world of Greco-Latin thought" (FR 72).

Finally, the encyclical specifies a third criterion, which derives from the re-flections up to this point on the nature of culture: one must take care lest "contrary to the very nature of the human spirit, the legitimate defense of the uniqueness and originality of Indian thought be confused with the idea that a particular cultural tradition should remain closed in its difference and affirm itself by opposing other traditions" (FR 72).

When the pope insists upon the inalienability of an acquired cultural in-heritance that has become a vehicle for the common truth about God and man, the question naturally arises as to whether this does not amount to a canonization of Eurocentrism in the Christian faith, a Eurocentrism that would not seem susceptible to being superseded by a new patrimony and, in fact, has entered into the permanent identity of the faith. The question is un-avoidable: how Latin or Greek is the Christian faith in reality, a faith that, of course, originated neither in the Greek nor the Latin world, but in the Semitic world of the Middle East, where Asia, Africa, and Europe come together?

The encyclical takes a position on this problem above all in the second chapter, which treats the development of philosophical thought within the Bible, and in the fourth chapter, which presents the decisive meeting of the wisdom of reason that has matured within the faith and the Greek wisdom of philosophy. On this question, I would make the following brief observations.

Already within the Bible, a pluralistic inheritance of religious and philo-sophical thought deriving from various cultural worlds is developed. The Word of God unfolds in a process of encounters with man's search for an answer to his ultimate questions. It does not simply fall straight from heaven, but is, in reality, a synthesis of cultures. It allows us, on deeper inspection, to recognize a process in which God struggles with man and slowly opens him to his deeper Word, to himself, to the Son who is the Logos. The Bible is not simply the expression of the culture of the people of Israel, but rather mani-fests a constant conflict with the completely natural desire of the people of Israel to be only themselves, to shut themselves in their own culture.

Faith in God and their "yes" to the will of God is wrested from them against their own ideas and wishes. God places himself against certain expressions of the religiosity and religious culture of Israel, which sought to assert itself in worship on the high places, in the worship of the "Queen of heaven," and in the claim to power of its own kingdom. From the anger of God and of Moses regarding the worship of the golden calf at Sinai to the late Post-Exilic proph-ets, Israel must constantly be drawn away from elements of its own cultural identity and religious desires; it must leave the worship of its own nationality, the worship of "Blood and Land," in order to submit to God, who is completely other, a God who is not of Israel's own making, the God who created the heavens and the earth and who is God of all peoples.

Israel's faith requires continual self-transcendence, overcoming of its own culture, in order to open itself and enter into the expansiveness of a truth common to all. The books of the Old Testament may appear in many respects less pious, less poetic, less inspired than certain passages of the sacred books of other peoples. But they possess their own originality in this struggle of faith against particularity, the process of taking leave of what is their own, which begins with Abraham's departure on his journey.

In a sense, when St. Paul departs from the law, a departure based on his encounter with the Risen Lord, this fundamental trajectory of the Old Testament is brought to its logical conclusion; it expresses fully the universalization of the faith of Israel, released from the particularity of an ethnic structure. Now all peoples are invited to join in this process of self-transcendence of their own particularity, the process that began in Israel. All people are invited to direct themselves to the God who has gone beyond himself in Jesus Christ and, in him, has broken down the "wall of hostility" (Eph 2:14) that was between us, and who leads us to one another through the self-emptying of the cross.

Faith in Jesus Christ is of its nature a continual opening of the self: it is God's breaking into the world of human beings and the response of human beings breaking out toward God, who at the same time leads them to one another. Everything particular now belongs to everyone, and everything that belongs to others becomes also our own. The "everything" referred to in the parable of the prodigal son, when the father says to the elder son, "everything which is mine is yours," later reappears in the high-priestly prayer of Jesus as the Son's address to the Father: "Everything of mine is yours and everything of yours is mine."

This fundamental pattern also shapes the encounter of the Christian message with Greek culture, an encounter that did not begin with the proclamation of the gospel but had already developed within the writings of the Old Testament, above all when these were translated into Greek, and which continued in early Judaism. The encounter was made possible because at the same time a similar process of transcending the particular had begun in the Greek world.

The fathers of the church did not simply mix an autonomous Greek culture into the gospel. They were able to take up the dialogue with Greek philosophy and use it as an instrument for the gospel, because in the Greek world a form of auto-criticism of their own culture, which had arisen through the search for God, was already underway. Beginning with the Germanic and Slavic peoples—who in the period of the great migrations came into contact with the Christian message and later with the peoples of Asia, Africa, and America—the Christian faith introduced these people not to Greek culture as such, but rather to its capacity for self-transcendence, which was the true connecting point for interpreting the Christian message.

It drew them into the dynamic of self-transcendence. On this question, Richard Schaffler has recently stated in a striking way that, from the very outset, the proclamation of the Christian message required from the European peoples (who incidentally did not exist as such before the Christian missionary effort) "the abandonment ... of every aboriginal God of the Europeans, long before the extra-European cultures came on the scene."

Thus, we can understand why it was that the Christian proclamation sought a connection with philosophies and not with religions. Where it did seek to connect with religions—for example, where Christ was interpreted as the true Dionysius, Asclepius, or Hercules—such attempts were quickly superseded. That a connection was sought not with religions but with philosophies was itself linked to the fact that there was no intention to canonize a particular culture as such, but rather an effort to enter into it at the point where it had begun to transcend itself, at the point where it had begun to open itself to universal truth and thus to lead it out of the enclosure of pure particularity.

This is a fundamental point of reference also today for the question of connection and contact with other peoples and cultures. Certainly, the Christian faith cannot utilize philosophies that exclude the question of truth, but it can connect with those movements that seek to escape from the prison of relativism. Surely, it cannot reestablish a connection with the ancient religions: there was such an attempt in early Christianity, when, for example, the mystery religions gave new content to the worship of the ancient gods, or when certain schools of philosophy interpreted in a new way the ancient teachings about the gods.

However, religions can offer forms and structures, and especially attitudes—for example, reverence, humility, the willingness to make sacrifices, goodness, love of neighbor, hope for eternal life. It seems to me that this is important for the question of the salvific significance of world religions. These do not save, so to speak, as closed systems and through fidelity to the system, but they contribute to salvation insofar as they bring men "to ask about God" or, as it is expressed in the Old Testament, "to seek his face," to seek "the kingdom of God and its righteousness."

Allow me finally to speak briefly about two other important concepts found in the encyclical. First, there is the reference to the circularity between theology and philosophy (*FR* 73). The encyclical understands this in the sense that theology must always take the Word of God as its starting point, but because this Word is truth, it remains in relationship to the human search for truth, to the connection of reason with truth, and therefore, it must remain in dialogue with philosophy.

Believers' search for truth takes place in a movement in which listening to the Word that has been spoken parallels the search of reason. Through this process, faith becomes more profound and more pure, and at the same time, human thought is enriched because of the new horizons open to it.

It seems to me that one could develop a bit further this notion of circularity. Philosophy, too, should not enclose itself in total particularity or simply in the results of its own reflections. As philosophy must be attentive to empirical discoveries, which occur in the various branches of knowledge, so, too, it should consider, as a source of knowledge for its enrichment, the holy tradition of religions and, above all, the message of the Bible.

In fact, all great philosophies have received illumination and direction from religious tradition. We need only think of the philosophies of Greece and India or those that have developed within Christianity, or even those recent philosophies that, although they are convinced of the autonomy of reason and see it as the highest measure of human thought, at the same time remain indebted to the great impulse the biblical faith has given to philosophy along the way. Kant, Fichte, Hegel, and Schelling would be unthinkable without the preceding substructure of faith, and Marx, with his radical reinterpretation of the horizon of hope, was influenced by what he had absorbed from the religious tradition. When philosophy completely extinguishes this dialogue with the thinking of faith, it ends up, as Jaspers once formulated it, in an "empty seriousness."

In the end, philosophy that is forced to renounce the question of truth—that is, to relinquish its very nature for a philosophy that no longer asks about who we are, why we exist, whether God and eternal life exist—has, as philosophy, abdicated.

I would like to mention a second thought connected with these considerations. The encyclical speaks explicitly of the contribution that faith has made to philosophy and of the tasks undertaken by philosophy with this contribution. It mentions first some fundamental elements of knowledge, some concepts that cannot be overlooked in philosophical thought: the idea of a personal God and, with it, in general the concept of the "person," which was formulated for the first time in the encounter between faith and philosophy (*FR* 76).

In this context, the encyclical refers to the concept of man as the image of God—that is, to the relational anthropology of the Bible, which understands man as a being in relation. From this—from the relational being of man—God, whose image is portrayed within, can be seen (FR 80).

The notion of sin and guilt is presented as another fundamental anthropological concept; further on, the idea of the equality and freedom of man, as well as the idea of a philosophy of history, is included. Then the pope formulates three postulates of faith in philosophy: it must recover its sapient dimension as a search for the ultimate and all-encompassing meaning of life (FR 81); it should attest to the human capacity to know the truth (FR 82); and third, following from these, there is a need for a philosophy of genuinely metaphysical range. This means that human thought cannot stop at the level of appearance but must reach beyond appearance to being itself; it must go from "phenomenon to foundation" (FR 83).

In today's context, the impossibility of passing beyond what is apparent—that is, of passing beyond phenomena—has indeed become a kind of dogma. But isn't the human person then cut off from his innermost self, if he stops simply at appearances? Doesn't one then begin to lead a life that is simply appearance? It is at this crucial point of contemporary thought that we touch on the heart of the gospel message. For the Gospel of St. John, the Christian faith decision is precisely this: that one not yield to appearances or raise appearances to the level of the highest reality, but rather that, beyond appearances, one seek and direct oneself to the glory of God, the radiant splendor of truth. Today, the dictatorship of appearances can be clearly seen on two planes: on the level of political activity, where, in many cases, what really counts is what "appears" about facts, what is said, what is written, what is presented, more than the facts themselves. Widespread opinion assumes a greater importance than what, in fact, really happened. Something similar occurs on the theological level, where, in approaching the biblical message, the so-called modern worldview (in the thought of Bultmann, for example) becomes the single measure for judgment, which decides about what can or cannot be, though in fact this worldview, if correctly represented, does not even attempt to decide on questions of being or ultimate reality, or final possibility, but rather seeks to understand the laws that govern the things that are apparent to us, and nothing more.

In this connection, the Holy Father emphasizes the limits of the concept of "experience, which today, in keeping with the dominant limitation to what is apparent, is often elevated even in theology to the level of the ultimate standard." As the encyclical explains, "The word of God refers constantly to things which transcend human experience" (FR 83).

It can do so because human beings are not limited to the world of appearances or to subjective experience. Indeed, the reduction to experience traps the human person in the subjective. Revelation is more than experience, and only thus does it give us an experience of God and help us bring our own experiences together, order them rightly, and through positive and critical discernment, understand and communicate them. I am convinced that, in our current philosophical and theological debate, precisely this section of the encyclical must be given further thought and investigation; it could well become a valuable source of enrichment for cultural research in our time.

I would like to close by referring to a comment on the encyclical that appeared in *Die Zeit,* a German weekly newspaper that is not usually very favorable to the church. The commentator, Jan Ross, grasped the essence of the pope's message very well when he noted that the dethroning of theology and metaphysics had made human thought "not only more free, but also more narrow"; indeed, he was not afraid to speak of a "*Verdummung durch Unglauben,*" a dumbing-down through unbelief.

He writes: "As reason has turned away from the ultimate questions, it has become indifferent and tiresome, it has become incompetent to address the life questions of good and evil, of death and immortality." The voice of the pope has "inspired many persons and entire peoples, it has sounded harsh and trenchant to the ear of many and even aroused hatred, but if it falls silent, this would be a moment of dreadful silence."

In fact, if we no longer speak about God and man, about sin and grace, about death and eternal life, then all that remains is sound and fury, a useless attempt to cover up the silencing of what is authentically human. With the fearless frankness of faith, the pope has pitted himself against the danger of this silence and in doing so, he has rendered a service not only to the church but to humanity, as well. For this we should be grateful to him.

Crises of Law

I wish to express my profound and heartfelt gratitude to the Faculty of Juris-prudence of LUMSA [Libera Università Maria SS. Assunta] for the great honor of conferring on me a Doctorate Honoris Causa. Church and law, faith and law, are united by a profound bond and related in a variety of ways. Suffice it to recall that the fundamental part of the Old Testament Canon is under the title *Torah* (law). Israel's liberation from Egypt did not end with the Exodus—it only began. It became full reality only when Israel received a juridical ordering from God, which regulated the relation with God, with the community of the people, and with each individual in the community, as well as the relation with foreigners: common law is a condition of human liberty. As a result, the Old Testament ideal of the pious person was the *zaddik*—the just, the man who lives justly and acts justly according to the order of the law given by God. In the New Testament, in fact, the word *zaddik* was replaced by the term *pistos:* the essential attitude of the Christian is faith, which renders him "just." But how did the importance of law fade? Was the juridical ordering of the environment turned away from the sacred and allowed to become simply profane? This problem has been intensely debated, especially since the sixteenth-century Reformation. It is for this reason that the concept of "law" (Torah) appears in Pauline writing with problematic accents and later, in Luther, is thought to be diametrically opposed to the gospel. The development of law in modern times has been profoundly characterized by these contradictory positions.

This is not the place for extensive development of the problem. Nevertheless, I would like to speak briefly about two current risks to law, which, between them, have a theological component and, therefore, refer not only to jurists but also to theologians. The "end of metaphysics," which in broad sectors of modern philosophy is imposed as an irreversible fact, has led to juridical positivism, which today especially has taken on the form of a theory of consensus: if reason is no longer able to find the way to metaphysics as the source of law, the state can only refer to the common convictions of its citizens' values, convictions that are reflected in the democratic consensus. Truth does not create consensus, and consensus does not create truth as much as it does a common ordering. The majority determines what must be regarded as true and just. In other words, law is exposed to the whim of the majority and depends on awareness of the values of the society at any given moment, which, in turn, is determined by a multiplicity of factors. This is manifested concretely by the progressive disappearance of the fundamentals of law inspired by the Christian tradition. Matrimony and family are less and less the accepted form of the statutory community and are replaced by multiple, even fleeting, problematic forms of living together. The relation between man and woman becomes conflictive, as does the relation between generations. The Christian order of time is dissolved.

Sunday disappears and is increasingly replaced by changing forms of free time. The sense of the sacred no longer has any meaning for law; respect for God and for that which is sacred to others is now regarded with difficulty as a juridical value; it is displaced by the allegedly more important value of limitless liberty in speech and judgment. Even human life is something that can be disposed of: abortion and euthanasia are no longer excluded from juridical ordering. Manipulation of human life is manifested in the areas of embryo experimentation and transplants, in which man arrogates to himself the ability not only to dispose of life and death, but also of his being and development. Thus, the point has recently been reached of going so far as to claim the programmed selection and breeding for the continuous development of the human species, and the essential difference between man and animal is up for debate. Because, in modern states, metaphysics and Natural Law are devalued, there is an ongoing transformation of law, the ulterior steps of which cannot yet be foreseen; the very concept of law is losing its precise definition.

There is also a second threat to law, which today seems less imminent than it was ten years ago but can re-emerge at any moment and find a link with the theory of consensus. I am referring to the dissolution of law through the spirit of utopia, which assumed a systematic and practical form in Marxist thought. The point of departure was the conviction that the present world is evil—a world of oppression and lack of liberty, which must be replaced by a better way of planning and working. In this case, the ultimate source of law becomes the idea of the new society, which is moral, of juridical importance, and useful to the advent of the future world. Based on this criterion, terrorism was articulated as a totally moral plan: killings and violence seemed like moral actions because they were at the service of the great revolution, the destruction of the present evil world, and the great ideal of the new society. Even here, we find the end of metaphysics, whose place is taken in this case not by the consensus of contemporaries but by the ideal of the future world.

There is even a crypto-theological origin for this negation of law. Because of this, it can be understood why vast currents of theology—especially the various forms of liberation theology—were subject to these temptations. It is not possible for me to present these connections here because of their extent. I shall content myself with pointing out that a mistaken Pauline idea has rapidly given way to radical and even anarchic interpretations of Christianity. Not to speak of the Gnostic movements, in which these tendencies were initially developed, which together with the "no" to God the Creator included also a "no" to metaphysics, a law of creatures, and Natural Law. We will not take time to analyze the social unrest and agitation of the sixteenth century, which resulted in the radical currents of the Reformation that gave life to revolutionary and utopian movements. Instead, I shall focus on a phenomenon that appears innocuous: an interpretation of Christianity that from the scientific point of view seems altogether respectable, which was developed in the last century by the great Evangelical jurist Rudolph Sohm. Sohm proposes the thesis that Christianity as gospel, as a break with the law, originally would not have been able and would not have wanted to include laws, but that the church was born initially as a "spiritual anarchy," which later, no doubt because of external needs of ecclesial existence already manifest at the end of the first century, was replaced by sacramental law. Instead of this law based, so to speak, on Christ's flesh, on the body of Christ, and of a sacramental nature, in medieval times it became the right not of Christ's body but of the corporation of Christians—in fact, it became the ecclesial law with which we are familiar. But for Sohm, the real model remained spiritual anarchy: in reality, in the ideal condition of the church, there is no need for law. In our century what has become fashionable, based on these positions, is the confrontation between the church of law and the church of love, law as the opposite of love. A similar contrast can, of course, emerge in the concrete application of law, but to raise this to a principle distorts the essence of law, as well as the essence of love. These concessions are ultimately uprooted from reality and fail to arrive at the spirit of utopia, but seem as if they do, and are amply diffused in our society. The fact that since the 1950s, "law and order" has become an insult—even worse, "law and order" is regarded as fascist—stems from these conceptions. Moreover, to turn law into irony was a precept of National Socialism (I am not sufficiently familiar with the situation in regard to Italian Fascism). In the so-called years of struggle, law was consciously castigated and opposed to so-called healthy popular feeling. The Führer was declared the only source of law, and as a result, absolute power replaced law. The denigration of law is never in any way at the service of liberty but is always an instrument of dictatorship. To eliminate law is to despise man; where there is no law, there is no liberty.

At this point an answer can be given to the basic question I have been addressing in these reflections, but perhaps only in summary form. What can faith and theology do in this situation for the defense of law? I would like to attempt an answer to this question, in a summary and certainly very insufficient way, by proposing the following two theses:

1. The elaboration and structure of law is not immediately a theological problem but a problem of "*recta ratio,*" right reason. Beyond opinions and currents of thought, this right reason must try to discern what is just—the essence of law—in keeping with the internal need of human beings everywhere to distinguish the good from that which is destructive to man. It is the duty of the church and faith to contribute to the sanity of "ratio" and, through the proper education of man, to preserve his capacity to see and perceive. Whether this right is to be called natural right or something else is a secondary problem. But wherever this interior demand of the human being, which is directed to law or needs that go beyond changing currents, can no longer be perceived, thus marking the "end of metaphysics," the human being is undermined in his dignity and his essence.

2. The church must make an examination of conscience on the destructive forces of law, which have their origin in unilateral interpretations of faith and have formed the history of this century. Its message goes beyond simple reason and leads to new dimensions of liberty and communion. But faith in the Creator and his Creation is inseparably joined to faith in the Redeemer and the Redemption. Redemption does not dissolve Creation and its order but, on the contrary, restores the possibility of perceiving the voice of the Creator in his Creation and, consequently, of better understanding the foundations of law. Metaphysics and faith, nature and grace, law and gospel are not opposed but intimately connected. Christian love, according to the Sermon on the Mount, can never be the foundation of statute law. It goes well beyond this, and can only be realized, at least in an embryonic way, in faith. But this does not go against Creation and its law; rather, it is based on it. Where there is no law, even love loses its vital context. Christian faith respects the nature of the state itself, especially the state of a pluralist society, but it also feels responsibility to ensure that the fundamentals of law continue to remain visible and the state is not deprived of direction and left at the mercy of changing currents. Since, in this sense, even with all the distinctions between reason and faith, between statutory law—necessarily drawn up with the help of reason—and the vital structure of the church, they are nevertheless in a reciprocal relation and are responsible for each other, this honorary doctorate is for me at once an occasion of gratitude and a call to develop my own work even further.

The Problem of
Threats to Human Life

THE BIBLICAL FOUNDATIONS

To deal adequately with the problem of threats to life and find the most effective way to defend human life against these threats, we must first of all determine the essential components, positive and negative, of the contemporary anthropological discussion.

The essential point of departure is and remains the biblical vision of man, formulated in an exemplary way in the accounts of Creation. The Bible defines the human being in his essence (which precedes all history and is never lost in history) with two distinctive features:

Man is created in the image and likeness of God (Gn 1:26). The second account of Creation expresses the same idea, saying that man, taken from the dust of the earth, carries in himself the divine breath of life. Man is characterized by an immediacy with God that is proper to his being; man is *capax Dei,* and because he lives under the personal protection of God, he is "sacred": "If anyone sheds the blood of man, by man shall his blood be shed, for in the image of God has man been made" (Gn 9:6). This is an apodictic statement of divine right that does not permit exceptions: human life is untouchable because it is divine property.

All human beings are one because they come from a single father, Adam, and a single mother, Eve, "the mother of all the living" (Gn 3:20). This oneness of the human race, which implies equality and the same basic rights for all, must be solemnly repeated and inculcated again after the Flood. To affirm again the common origin of all men, the ninth chapter of Genesis fully describes the origin of all humanity from Noah: "These three were the sons of Noah, and from them the whole earth was peopled" (Gn 9:19).

Both aspects, the divine dignity of the human race and the oneness of its origin and destiny, are definitively sealed in the figure of the second Adam,

Christ: the Son of God died for all, to unite everyone in the definitive salvation of divine filiation. And so the common dignity of all men appears with total clarity: "There is neither Jew nor Greek, there is neither slave nor free person, there is not male and female; for you are as one in Christ Jesus" (Gal 3:28).

This biblical message, identical from the first page to the last, is the bedrock of human dignity and human rights; it is the great inheritance of the authentic humanism entrusted to the church, whose duty it is to incarnate this message in every culture and in every constitutional and social system.

THE DIALECTICS OF THE MODERN AGE

If we look briefly at the modern age, we face a dialectic that continues even today. On the one hand, the modern age boasts of having discovered the idea of human rights inherent in every human being and antecedent to any positive law, and of having proclaimed these rights in solemn declarations. On the other hand, these rights, thus acknowledged in theory, have never been so profoundly and radically denied on the practical level. The roots of this contradiction are to be sought at the height of the modern age: in the Enlightenment theories of human knowledge and the vision of human freedom connected with them, and in the theories of the social contract and their idea of society.

The fundamental dogma of the Enlightenment is that man must overcome the prejudices inherited from tradition; he must have the boldness to free himself from every authority in order to think on his own using nothing but his own reason. From this point on, the search for truth is no longer conceived of as a community effort, in which human beings joined in space and time help each other discover what is difficult to discover on one's own. Reason, free from any bond, from any relation with what is other, is turned back on itself. It winds up being thought of as a closed, independent tribunal. Truth is no longer an objective datum, apparent to each and every one, even through others. It gradually becomes something merely external, which each one grasps from his own point of view, without ever knowing to what extent his viewpoint corresponds to the object in itself or with what others perceive.

The truth about the good becomes similarly unattainable. The idea of the good in itself is put outside of man's grasp. The only reference point for each person is what he conceives on his own as good. Consequently, freedom is no longer seen positively as a striving for the good, which reason uncovers with help from the community and tradition, but is defined rather as an emancipation from all conditions that prevent each one from following his own reason. It is termed "freedom of indifference."

As long as at least an implicit reference to Christian values is made to orient the individual reason toward the common good, freedom will impose limits on itself in the service of a social order and a liberty guaranteed to all.

Thus, the great theories about liberty and democratic institutions, for example Montesquieu's, always presuppose the recognition of a law already guaranteed by God, and of universal values that these institutions, by limiting individual liberties, conspire to have respected by those who permit them to be practiced in this way. The great declarations on human rights were pronounced in this framework.

The theories of the social contract were founded on the idea of a law antecedent to individual wills that was to be respected by them. From the moment at the end of the seventeenth century when religions showed themselves to be unable to guarantee peace, being, rather, a cause of war, theories of the "social contract" were elaborated (cf. Hobbes): what would bring harmony among men was a law recognized by reason and commanding respect by an enlightened prince who incarnates the general will.

Here where the common reference to values and ultimately to God is lost, society appears merely as an ensemble of individuals placed side by side, and the contract that ties them together is necessarily perceived as an accord among those who have the power to impose their will on others.

To illustrate one aspect of this dialectic between theoretical affirmation of human rights and their practical denial, I would like to refer to the Weimar Constitution of the first German republic of August 11, 1919. This constitution does, indeed, speak of basic rights, but puts them in a context of relativism and indifferentism regarding values, which the legislators considered to be a necessary consequence of tolerance and therefore obligatory. But this absolutizing of tolerance to the point of total relativism also relativized basic rights in such a way that the Nazi regime saw no reason to remove these articles, the foundation of which was too weak and ambiguous to offer indisputable protection from the destruction of human rights.

Thus, by a dialectic within modernity, one passes from an affirmation of the rights of freedom, detached from any objective reference to a common truth, to the destruction of the very foundations of this freedom. The "enlightened despot" of the social-contract theorists became the tyrannical state, in fact totalitarian, which disposes of the life of its weakest members, from the unborn baby to the elderly in the name of a public usefulness that is really only the interest of a few.

This is precisely the striking characteristic of the current position on respect for life: it is no longer a question of purely individual morality but one of social morality, since states and even international organizations became guarantors of abortion and euthanasia, passed laws that authorize them, and provide the wherewithal to put them into practice.

THE WAR ON LIFE TODAY

Though today we can observe a mobilizing of forces for the defense of human life in the various "pro-life" movements, a mobilization that is encouraging and gives cause for hope, we must nevertheless frankly realize that till now the opposite movement has been stronger: the spread of legislation and practices that willfully destroy human life, above all the life of the weakest: unborn babies. Today we are the witnesses of a true war of the mighty against the weak, a war that looks to the elimination of the disabled, of those who are a nuisance, and even of those who are poor and "useless" in all the moments of their existence. With the complicity of states, colossal means have been used against people at the dawn of their life, when their life has been rendered vulnerable by accident or illness, or when they are near death.

A violent attack is made on developing life through abortion (with the result that there are 30 to 40 million abortions a year worldwide), and to facilitate abortion, millions have been invested to develop abortifacient pills (RU-486). Millions more have been budgeted for making contraception less harmful to women, with the result that most chemical contraceptives on sale now act primarily against implantation, that is, as abortifacients, without women knowing it. Who will be able to calculate the number of victims from this massacre?

Surplus embryos, the inevitable product of in vitro fertilization, are frozen and eliminated, unless they join their little aborted brothers and sisters who are to be turned into guinea pigs for experimentation or into raw materials for curing illnesses such as Parkinson's disease and diabetes. In vitro fertilization itself frequently becomes the occasion for "selective" abortions (for example, choice of sex), when there are undesired multiple pregnancies.

Prenatal diagnosis is almost routinely used by women "at risk" to eliminate systematically all fetuses that could be more or less malformed or diseased. All of those who have the good fortune to be carried to term by their mother but have the misfortune of being born disabled run the serious risk of being eliminated immediately after birth or being deprived of nourishment and the most elementary care.

Those whom illness or accident cause to fall into an "irreversible" coma are put to death to answer the demand for organ transplants or they may even be used for medical experiments ("warm cadavers"). Finally, when the prognosis is terminal, many are tempted to hasten its arrival by euthanasia.

REASONS FOR THE OPPOSITION TO LIFE: THE LOGIC OF DEATH

But why is there this victory of legislation and antihuman practice precisely at a time when the idea of human rights seemed to have gained universal and unconditional recognition? Why do even Christians, even persons of great moral formation, think that the norms regarding human life could and should be a compromise necessary to political life? Why do they fail to see the insuperable limit of any legislation worthy of the name: the point at which "right" becomes injustice and crime?

At the first stage of our reflection, I think I can point to two reasons, behind which others are probably hiding. One reason is reflected in the opinion of those who hold that there must be a separation between personal ethical convictions and the political sphere in which laws are formulated. Here, the only value to be respected would be the complete freedom of choice of each individual, depending on his own private opinions.

In a world in which moral convictions lack a common reference to the truth, such convictions have the value of mere opinion. It would be an expression of intolerance to seek to impose a conviction on others through legislation, thus limiting their freedom. Social life, which cannot be established on any common objective referent, is seen as the result of a compromise of interests, with a view to guaranteeing the maximum freedom for each. In reality, however, wherever the decisive criterion for recognizing rights is the majority opinion, wherever the right to express one's own freedom prevails over the right of a voiceless minority, there might has become the criterion of right.

It is even more obvious and extremely serious when, in the name of freedom for those who have power and voice, the fundamental right to life is denied to those who cannot make themselves heard. In reality, in order to exist, political community must recognize a minimum of objectively established rights not granted by social conventions but antecedent to any political system of law. The same *Universal Declaration of Human Rights* signed by almost all the countries of the world in 1948, after the terrible experience of the Second World War, expresses even in its title the awareness that human rights (the most basic of which is the right to life) belong to man *by nature*, that the state *recognizes* them but does not confer them, and that they belong to all human beings inasmuch as they are human beings and not because of secondary characteristics that others would have the right to determine arbitrarily.

One understands, then, how a state that arrogates to itself the prerogative of defining which human beings are or are not the subject of rights and which consequently grants to some the power to violate others' fundamental right to life contradicts the democratic ideal to which it continues to appeal and undermines the very foundations on which it is built. By allowing the rights of the weakest to be violated, the state also allows the law of force to prevail over the force of law. One sees, then, that the idea of an absolute tolerance of freedom of choice for some destroys the very foundation of a just life for men. The separation of politics from any natural content of right, which is the inalienable patrimony of everyone's moral conscience, deprives social life of its ethical substance and leaves it defenseless before the will of the strongest.

Someone may ask us, however, When does the person, the subject of basic rights that must be absolutely respected, begin to exist? If we are dealing not with a social concession but rather a recognition, the criteria for this determination must be objective, as well. Now, as *Donum vitae* (I:1) has confirmed, modern genetics shows that "from the time that the ovum is fertilized, a new life is begun which is neither that of the father nor of the mother; it is rather the life of a new human being with his own growth." Science has shown "that from the first instant, the program is fixed as to what this living being will be: a man, this individual-man with his characteristic aspects already well determined. Right from fertilization is begun the adventure of a human life, and each of its great capacities requires time to develop, and to be in a position to act."[1] The recent discoveries of human biology recognize that "in the zygote resulting from fertilization the biological identity of a new human individual is already constituted." Certainly no experimental datum can be sufficient in itself to bring us to the recognition of a spiritual soul; nevertheless, the conclusions of science regarding the human embryo provide a valuable indication for discerning by the use of reason a personal presence at the moment of the first appearance of a human life: how could a human individual not be a human person? Regarding this question, if the magisterium has not expressed itself in a binding way by a philosophical affirmation, it has taught consistently that from the first moment of its existence as the product of human generation, the embryo must be guaranteed the unconditional respect that is morally due to a human being in his spiritual and bodily totality. "The human being is to be respected and treated as a person from the moment of conception; and therefore, from that same moment his rights as a person must be recognized, among which in the first place is the inviolable right of every innocent human being to life."

A second reason for the prevalent mentality opposed to life, I think, is the very concept of morality that is widespread today. Often, a merely formal idea of conscience is joined to an individualistic view of freedom, understood as the absolute right to self-determination on the basis of one's own convictions. This view is no longer rooted in the classical conception of the moral conscience, which involves (according to Vatican II) a law that man does not give himself, but which he must obey (cf. *Gaudium et Spes,* no. 16). In this conception, common to the entire Christian tradition, conscience is the capacity to be open to the call of truth, which is objective, universal, the same for all who can and must seek it. It is not isolation but communion: *cum scire* ("to know together with") in the truth concerning the good, which accompanies human beings in the intimacy of their spiritual nature. It is in this relationship with common and objective truth that continuing formation should occur. For the Christians, this naturally entails a *sentire cum Ecclesia* ("to think with the Church"), and so, an intrinsic reference to the authentic magisterium of the church.

On the other hand, in the new conception, clearly Kantian in origin, conscience is detached from its constitutive relationship with a content of moral truth, and is reduced to a mere formal condition of morality. Its suggestion, "do good and avoid evil," would have no necessary and universal reference to the truth concerning the good, but would be linked only with the goodness of the subjective intention. Concrete actions would depend for their moral qualification on the self-understanding of the individual, which is always culturally and circumstantially determined. In this conception, conscience is nothing but subjectivity elevated to the ultimate criterion of action. The fundamental Christian idea that nothing can be opposed to conscience no longer has the original and inalienable meaning that truth can only be imposed in virtue of itself, that is, in personal inferiority. Instead we have the divinization of subjectivity, the infallible oracle of conscience, never to be doubted by anyone or anything.

THE ANTHROPOLOGICAL DIMENSIONS OF THE CHALLENGE

It is necessary to investigate the roots of this opposition to life more deeply. On a second level, reflecting a more personalist approach, we find an anthropological dimension where we should pause briefly.

It should be noted here that Western culture increasingly affirms a new dualism where some of its characteristic traits converge: individualism, materialism, utilitarianism, and the hedonist ideology of self-fulfillment. In fact, the body is no longer perceived naturally by the subject as the concrete form of his relations with God, other persons, and the world, that is, as that datum in which, in the midst of a universe being built, a conversation in course, a history rich in meaning, one can participate positively only by accepting its rules and language. Rather, the body appears to be a tool to be utilized for one's well-being, worked out and implemented by technical reason, which figures out how to draw the greatest profit from it.

Respect for body as given (datum) vs. Use of body as tool

In this way even sexuality becomes depersonalized and exploited. Sexuality becomes merely as an occasion for pleasure and no longer as an act of self-giving or the expression of a love in which another is accepted completely as he or she is, and which opens itself to the richness of life it bears, that is, a baby who will be the fruit of that love. The two meanings of the sexual act, unitive and procreative, become separated. Union is impoverished, while fruitfulness is reduced to the sphere of a rational calculation: "A child? certainly. But when and how I want one."

It is clear that this dualism between technology and the body viewed as an object permits man to flee from the mystery of being. In reality, birth and death, the appearance and passing of another, the arrival and dissolution of the ego, all direct the subject immediately to the question of his own meaning and his own existence. And perhaps to escape this anguishing question, he seeks to guarantee for himself the most complete dominion possible over these two key moments in life; he seeks to put them under his own control. It is an illusion to think that man is in complete possession of himself, that he enjoys absolute freedom, that he can be manufactured according to a plan that leaves nothing uncertain, nothing to chance, nothing in mystery.

A world that makes such an absolute option for efficiency, a world that so approves of utilitarian logic, a world that for the most part thinks of freedom as an absolute right of the individual and conscience as a totally solitary, subjectivist court of appeal necessarily impoverishes human relations to the point of considering them finally as relations of power and of not allowing the weakest human beings to have the place that is their due. From this point of view, utilitarian ideology heads in the direction of *machismo*, and *feminism* becomes the legitimate reaction against the exploitation of woman.

However, so-called *feminism* is frequently based on the same utilitarian presuppositions as *machismo* and, far from liberating woman, contributes, rather, to her enslavement.

When, in line with the dualism just described, woman denies her own body, considering it simply as an object to be used for acquiring happiness through self-achievement, she also denies her own femininity, a properly feminine gift of self and acceptance of another person, of which motherhood is the most typical sign and the most concrete realization.

When woman opts for free love and claims the right to abortion, she helps to reinforce a notion of human relations according to which the dignity of each one depends, in the eyes of another, on how much he is able to give. In all of this, woman takes a position against her own femininity and against the values of which she is the bearer: acceptance of life, availability to the weakest, unconditional devotion to the needy. An authentic feminism, working for the advancement of woman in her integral truth and for the liberation of all women, would also work for the advancement of the whole human person and for the liberation of all human beings. This feminism would, in fact, struggle for the recognition of the human person in the dignity that is due to him or her from the sole fact of existence, of being willed and created by God, and not for his or her usefulness, power, beauty, intelligence, wealth, or health. It would strive to advance an anthropology that values the essence of the person as made for the gift of self and the acceptance of the other, of which the body, male or female, is the sign and instrument.

It is precisely by developing an anthropology that presents man in his personal and relational wholeness that we can respond to the widespread argument that the best way to fight abortion would be to promote contraception. Each of us has already heard this rebuke leveled against the church: "It is absurd that you want to prevent both contraception and abortion. Blocking access to the former means making the latter inevitable." Such a claim, which at first glance seems totally plausible, is, however, contradicted by experience: the fact is that typically an increase in the rate of contraception is paralleled by an increase in the rate of abortion. It must be noted, in fact, that contraception and abortion both have their roots in that depersonalized and utilitarian view of sexuality and procreation that we have just described, which, in turn, is based on a truncated notion of man and his freedom.

It is not a matter of assuming a stewardship that is responsible and worthy of one's own fertility as the result of a generous plan that is always open to the possible acceptance of new, unforeseen life, but rather of ensuring complete control over procreation, rejecting even the idea of an unplanned child. Understood in these terms, contraception necessarily leads to abortion as a "backup solution." One cannot strengthen the contraceptive mentality without strengthening at the same time the ideology that supports it, and therefore, without implicitly encouraging abortion. On the contrary, if one develops the idea that man only discovers himself fully in the generous gift of himself and in the unconditional acceptance of the other, simply because the latter exists, then abortion will increasingly appear as an absurd crime.

An individualistic type of anthropology, as we have seen, leads one to consider objective truth as inaccessible, freedom as arbitrary, conscience as a tribunal closed in on itself. Such an anthropology leads woman not only to hatred of men but also to hatred of herself and of her own femininity, and above all, of her own motherhood.

More generally, such an anthropology leads human beings to hatred of themselves. Man despises himself; he is no longer in accord with God, who found his human creation to be "something very good" (Gn 1:31). On the contrary, man today sees himself as the destroyer of the world, an unhappy product of evolution. In reality, man, who no longer has access to the infinite, to God, is a contradictory being, a failed product. Thus, we see the logic of sin: by wanting to be like God, man seeks absolute independence. To be self-sufficient, he must become independent; he must be emancipated even from love, which is always a free grace and not something that can be produced or made. However, by making himself independent of love, man separates himself from the true richness of his being and becomes empty. Opposition to his own being is inevitable. "It is not good to be a human being"—the logic of death belongs to the logic of sin. The road to abortion, euthanasia, and the exploitation of the weakest lies open.

To sum up everything, then, we can say: the ultimate root of hatred of human life, of attacks on human life, is the loss of God. Where God disappears, the absolute dignity of human life disappears, as well. In light of the revelation concerning the creation of man in the image and likeness of God, the intangible sacredness of the human person has appeared. Only this divine dimension guarantees the full dignity of the human person. Therefore, a purely vitalist argument we often see used (e.g., in the sense intended by A. Schweitzer) can be a first step, but it remains insufficient and never reaches the intended goal. In the struggle for life, talking about God is indispensable. Only in this way does the value of the weak, the disabled, the nonproductive, the incurably ill become apparent; only in this way can we relearn and rediscover, too, the value of suffering: the greatest lesson on human dignity always remains the cross of Christ, our salvation has its origin not in what the Son of God did but in his suffering, and whoever does not know how to suffer does not know how to live. *compassion*

POSSIBLE RESPONSES TO THE CHALLENGE OF OUR TIME

What should be done in this situation to respond to the challenge just described?

For my part, I would like to confine myself to the possibilities associated with the magisterium. Magisterial statements on this problem have not been wanting in recent years. The Holy Father tirelessly insists on the defense of life as a fundamental duty of every Christian; many bishops speak of it with great competence and force. In the past few years, the Congregation for the Doctrine of the Faith has published several important documents on moral themes related to respect for human life. In 1974, the congregation issued a *Declaration on Procured Abortion* in 1980; with the instruction *Jura et Bona*, it published a statement on the problems of euthanasia and care for the terminally ill; in 1987, the instruction *Donum Vitae* confronted, in the context of dealing with medically assisted procreation, the problem of respect for human embryos, of the so-called surplus products of in vitro fertilization, their freezing and destruction, as well as selective abortion following multiple implantations.

In spite of these position statements, in spite of numerous pontifical addresses on some of these problems or on their particular aspects, the field remains wide open for a global restatement on the doctrinal level, which would go to the deepest roots of the problem and denounce the most aberrant consequences of the "death mentality."

One could think, then, of a possible document on the defense of human life, which, in my opinion, should have two original characteristics in respect to the preceding documents. First of all, it should not only develop a treatment of individual morality, but should also give consideration to social and political morality. To be specific, the threats to human life could be confronted from five points of view: doctrinal, cultural, legislative, political, and finally, practice.

From the specifically *doctrinal point of view,* the magisterium today could propose a solemn affirmation of the principle that "the direct killing of an innocent human being is always a source of grave sin." Without being a formal dogmatic pronouncement, this affirmation would nevertheless have the weight of a dogmatic pronouncement. Its key elements—"direct killing," "innocent human being," "a source of grave sin"—can be defined with precision. This affirmation lacks neither biblical foundations nor a basis in tradition.

Such a strictly doctrinal position, taken with a high degree of authority, could have the greatest importance at a time of widespread doctrinal confusion. However, that is not enough. The reasons for our faith—its human evidence—must be apparent in the context of our time. Hence, it is necessary to develop the church's teaching by following other points of view.

The *cultural point of view* would allow for a denunciation of the anti-life ideology, which is based on materialism and justified by utilitarianism.

The *legislative point of view* could present an outline of the different types of legislation that are being planned in regard to abortion, the embryo trade, euthanasia, and so on. This would make it possible to highlight the presuppositions of these laws, to show that they are intrinsically immoral, and to clarify the proper function of civil law in relation to moral law.

The *political point of view* would be one of the most important elements. It would be a matter of showing that laws are always the implementation of a social plan, and that the implicit intention in antilife laws is totalitarian within society and imperialistic on the part of the developed countries of the West toward Third World countries. The former use any means to contain the latter on the pretext of demographic politics.

From the *practical point of view,* finally, we could commit ourselves to making people aware of the wickedness involved in using certain abortifacient or contraceptive-abortifacient means, of the evil implicit in belonging to or promoting so-called right to death with dignity associations or in distributing pamphlets that explain how to commit suicide.

In this context, one could also speak of the role of the mass media, of parties and parliaments, of doctors and health-care personnel, always mentioning the positive and negative aspects: denouncing complicity while encouraging, praising, and motivating activities that favor life.

And so we arrive at the second original feature of a possible new document: although there should be room for denunciation, this would not be the main feature. Above all, it would involve a joyous restatement of the immense value of each and every human being, however poor, weak, or suffering he or she may be. The statement would show how this value is seen in the eyes of philosophers, but above all, in the eyes of God, as Revelation teaches us.

It would involve recalling with wonder the marvels of the Creator toward his Creation, the marvels of the Redeemer toward those he came to meet and save. It would show how receptivity to the Spirit entails in itself a generous availability to other people and, thus, receptivity toward every human life from the first moment of its existence until the time of its death.

In short, against all ideologies and politics of death, it is a matter of recalling all that is essential in the Christian Good News: beyond all suffering, Christ has cleared the way to thanksgiving for life, in both its human and divine aspects.

More important than any document will be a coherent and committed proclamation of the gospel of life by all preachers in the world, to rebuild the clarity and joy of the faith and offer believers the reasons for our hope (1 Pt 3:15), which can also convince nonbelievers.

PART EIGHT

GOD IS LOVE

Deus Caritas Est
(God Is Love)

Encyclical Letter of the Supreme Pontiff Benedict XVI to the Bishops, Priests and Deacons, Men and Women Religious, and All the Lay Faithful

DECEMBER 25, 2005

INTRODUCTION

1. "God is love, and he who abides in love abides in God, and God abides in him" (1 Jn 4:16). These words from the First Letter of John express with remarkable clarity the heart of the Christian faith: the Christian image of God and the resulting image of mankind and its destiny. In the same verse, St. John also offers a kind of summary of the Christian life: "We have come to know and to believe in the love God has for us."

We have come to believe in God's love: in these words the Christian can express the fundamental decision of his life. Being Christian is not the result of an ethical choice or a lofty idea but the encounter with an event, a Person, which gives life a new horizon and a decisive direction. St. John's Gospel describes that event in these words: "God so loved the world that he gave his only Son, that whoever believes in him should ... have eternal life" (3:16). In acknowledging the centrality of love, Christian faith has retained the core of Israel's faith, while at the same time giving it new depth and breadth. The pious Jew prayed daily the words of the Book of Deuteronomy, which expressed the heart of his existence: "Hear, O Israel: the LORD our God is one LORD, and you shall love the LORD your God with all your heart, and with all your soul and with all your might" (6:4–5). Jesus united into a single precept this commandment of love for God and the commandment of love for neighbor found in the Book of Leviticus: "You shall love your neighbor as yourself" (19:18; cf. Mk 12:29–31). Since God has first loved us (cf. 1 Jn 4:10), love is now no longer a mere "command"; it is the response to the gift of love with which God draws near to us.

In a world where the name of God is sometimes associated with vengeance or even a duty of hatred and violence, this message is both timely and significant. For this reason, I wish in my first encyclical to speak of the love that God lavishes upon us and that we, in turn, must share with others. That, in essence, is what the two main parts of this letter are about, and they are profoundly interconnected. The first part is more speculative, since I wanted here—at the beginning of my pontificate—to clarify some essential facts concerning the love that God mysteriously and gratuitously offers to man, together with the intrinsic link between that love and the reality of human love. The second part is more concrete, since it treats the ecclesial exercise of the commandment of love of neighbor. The argument has vast implications, but a lengthy treatment would go beyond the scope of the present encyclical. I wish to emphasize some basic elements, so as to call forth in the world renewed energy and commitment in the human response to God's love.

PART I: THE UNITY OF LOVE IN CREATION AND IN SALVATION HISTORY

A Problem of Language

2. God's love for us is fundamental to our lives, and it raises important questions about who God is and who we are. In considering this, we immediately find ourselves hampered by a problem of language. Today, the term *love* has become one of the most frequently used and misused of words, a word to which we attach quite different meanings. Even though this encyclical will deal primarily with the understanding and practice of love in sacred scripture and in the church's tradition, we cannot simply prescind from the meaning of the word in different cultures and in present-day usage.

Let us first of all bring to mind the vast semantic range of the word *love:* we speak of love of country, love of one's profession, love between friends, love of work, love between parents and children, love between family members, love of neighbor, and love of God. Amid this multiplicity of meanings, however, one in particular stands out: love between man and woman, where body and soul are inseparably joined and human beings glimpse an apparently irresistible promise of happiness. This would seem to be the very epitome of love; all other kinds of love immediately fade in comparison. So we need to ask: are all these forms of love basically one, so that love, in its many and varied manifestations, is ultimately a single reality, or are we merely using the same word to designate totally different realities?

"Eros" and "Agape"—Difference and Unity

3. That love between man and woman that is neither planned nor willed but somehow imposes itself upon human beings was called *eros* by the ancient Greeks. Let us note straightaway that the Greek Old Testament uses the word *eros* only twice, while the New Testament does not use it at all: of the three Greek words for love, *eros, philia* (the love experienced in friendship), and *agape,* New Testament writers prefer the last, which occurs rather infrequently in Greek usage. As for the term *philia,* the love in friendship, it is used with added depth of meaning in St. John's Gospel to express the relationship between Jesus and his disciples. The tendency to avoid the word *eros,* together with the new vision of love expressed through *agape,* clearly points to something new and distinct about the Christian understanding of love. In the critique of Christianity that began with the Enlightenment and grew progressively more radical, this new element was seen as thoroughly negative. According to Friedrich Nietzsche, Christianity had poisoned *eros,* which, for its part, while not completely succumbing, gradually degenerated into vice.[1] Here the German philosopher was expressing a widely held perception: doesn't the church, with all her commandments and prohibitions, turn to bitterness the most precious thing in life? Doesn't she blow the whistle just when the joy that is the Creator's gift offers us a happiness that is itself a certain foretaste of the divine?

4. But is this the case? Did Christianity really destroy *eros?* Let us take a look at the pre-Christian world. The Greeks—not unlike other cultures—considered *eros* principally as a kind of intoxication, the overpowering of reason by a "divine madness" that tears man away from his finite existence and enables him, in the very process of being overwhelmed by divine power, to experience supreme happiness. All other powers in heaven and on earth thus appear secondary: "*Omnia vincit amor,*" says Virgil in the *Bucolics*—love conquers all—and he adds: "*et nos cedamus amori,*" let us, too, yield to love.[2] In the religions, this attitude found expression in fertility cults, part of which was the "sacred" prostitution that flourished in many temples. *Eros* was thus celebrated as divine power, as fellowship with the divine.

The Old Testament firmly opposed this form of religion, which represents a powerful temptation against monotheistic faith, combating it as a perversion of religiosity. But it in no way rejected *eros* as such; rather, it declared war on a warped and destructive form of it, because this counterfeit divinization of *eros* actually strips it of its dignity and dehumanizes it. Indeed, the prostitutes in the temple, who had to bestow this divine intoxication, were treated not as human beings and persons but simply used as a means of arousing "divine madness": far from being goddesses, they were human persons being exploited. An intoxicated and undisciplined *eros*, then, is not an ascent in "ecstasy" toward the divine, but a fall, a degradation of man. Evidently, *eros* needs to be disciplined and purified if it is to provide not just fleeting pleasure but a certain foretaste of the pinnacle of our existence, of that beatitude for which our whole being yearns.

5. Two things emerge clearly from this rapid overview of the concept of *eros* past and present. First, there is a certain relationship between love and the divine: love promises infinity, eternity—a reality far greater and totally other than our everyday existence. Yet we have also seen that the way to attain this goal is not simply by submitting to instinct. Purification and growth in maturity are called for; and these also pass through the path of renunciation. Far from rejecting or "poisoning" *eros*, they heal it and restore its true grandeur.

This is first and foremost because man is a being made up of body and soul. Man is truly himself when his body and soul are intimately united; the challenge of *eros* can be said to be truly overcome when this unification is achieved. Should he aspire to be pure spirit and to reject the flesh as pertaining to his animal nature alone, then spirit and body would both lose their dignity. Should he deny the spirit and consider matter, the body, to be the only reality, he would likewise lose his greatness. The epicure Gassendi used to offer Descartes the humorous greeting "O Soul!" And Descartes would reply: "O Flesh!"[3] Yet it is neither the spirit alone nor the body alone that loves: it is man, the person, a unified creature composed of body and soul, who loves. Only when both dimensions are truly united does man attain his full stature. Only thus is love—*eros*—able to mature and attain its authentic grandeur.

Nowadays Christianity of the past is often criticized as having been opposed to the body, and it is quite true that tendencies of this sort have always existed. Yet the contemporary exaltation of the body is deceptive. *Eros,* reduced to pure "sex," has become a commodity, a mere "thing" to be bought and sold, or rather, man himself has become a commodity. This is hardly man's great "yes" to the body. On the contrary, he now considers his body and his sexuality as the purely material part of himself, to be used and exploited at will. He sees it not as an arena for the exercise of his freedom, but rather as a mere object that he attempts, as he pleases, to make both enjoyable and harmless. Here we are actually dealing with a debasement of the human body: no longer is it integrated into our overall existential freedom; no longer is it a vital expression of our whole being; now it is relegated more or less to the purely biological sphere. The apparent exaltation of the body can quickly turn into a hatred of bodiliness. Christian faith has always considered man a unity in duality, a reality in which spirit and matter mix, where each is brought to a new nobility. True, *eros* tends to rise "in ecstasy" toward the divine, to lead us beyond ourselves; yet for this very reason it calls for a path of ascent, renunciation, purification, and healing.

6. Concretely, what does this path of ascent and purification entail? How might love be experienced so that it can fully realize its human and divine promise? We can find a first, important indication in the Song of Songs, an Old Testament book well known to the mystics. According to the interpretation generally held today, the poems contained in this book were originally love songs, perhaps intended for a Jewish wedding feast and meant to exalt conjugal love. In this context it is highly instructive to note that in the course of the book, two different Hebrew words are used to indicate "love." First there is the word *dodim,* a plural form suggesting a love that is still insecure, indeterminate, and searching. This is then replaced by the word *ahabà,* which the Greek version of the Old Testament translates with the similar-sounding *agape,* which, as we have seen, is the typical expression for the biblical notion of love. By contrast with an indeterminate, "searching" love, this word expresses the experience of a love which involves a real discovery of the other, moving beyond the selfish character that prevailed earlier. Love now becomes concern and care for the other. No longer is it self-seeking, a sinking in the intoxication of happiness; instead it seeks the good of the beloved: it becomes renunciation and it is ready, even willing, for sacrifice.

It is part of love's growth toward higher levels and inward purification that it now seeks to become definitive, and it does so in a twofold sense: both in the sense of exclusivity (this particular person alone) and in the sense of being "forever." Love embraces the whole of existence in every dimension, including the dimension of time. It could hardly be otherwise, since its promise looks toward its definitive goal: love looks to the eternal. Love is indeed "ecstasy," not in the sense of a moment of intoxication but rather as a journey, an ongoing exodus from the closed, inward-looking self toward liberation through self-giving, and thus toward authentic self-discovery and indeed the discovery of God: "Whoever seeks to gain his life will lose it, but whoever loses his life will preserve it" (Lk 17:33), as Jesus says throughout the Gospels (cf. Mt 10:39, 16:25, Mk 8:35, Lk 9:24, Jn 12:25). In these words, Jesus portrays his own path, which leads through the cross to the Resurrection: the path of the grain of wheat that falls to the ground and dies, and in this way bears much fruit.

Starting from the depths of his own sacrifice and of the love that reaches fulfillment therein, he also portrays in these words the essence of love and, indeed, of human life itself.

7. By their own inner logic, these initial, somewhat philosophical reflections on the essence of love have now brought us to the threshold of biblical faith. We began by asking whether the different, even opposed, meanings of the word *love* point to some profound underlying unity, or whether, on the contrary, they must remain unconnected, one alongside the other. More significantly, though, we questioned whether the message of love proclaimed to us by the Bible and the church's tradition has some points of contact with the common human experience of love, or whether it is opposed to that experience. This, in turn, led us to consider two fundamental words: *eros*, as a term to indicate "worldly" love, and *agape*, referring to love grounded in and shaped by faith. The two notions are often contrasted as "ascending" love and "descending" love. There are other, similar classifications, such as the distinction between possessive love and oblative love (*amor concupiscentiae, amor benevolentiae*), to which is sometimes also added love that seeks its own advantage.

In philosophical and theological debate, these distinctions have often been radicalized to the point of clear antithesis: descending, oblative love (*agape*) would be typically Christian, while ascending, possessive, or covetous love (*eros*) would be typical of nonChristian—particularly, Greek—culture. Were this antithesis to be taken to extremes, the essence of Christianity would be detached from the vital relations fundamental to human existence and would become a world apart, admirable perhaps but decisively cut off from the complex fabric of human life. Yet *eros* and *agape*—ascending love and descending love—can never be completely separated. The more the two, in their different aspects, find a proper unity in the one reality of love, the more the true nature of love in general is realized. Even if *eros* is at first mainly covetous and ascending, a fascination with the great promise of happiness in drawing near to the other, it becomes less and less concerned with itself, increasingly seeks the happiness of the other, is concerned more and more with the beloved, bestows itself and wants to "be there for" the other. The element of *agape* thus enters into this love, for otherwise *eros* is impoverished and even loses its own nature. On the other hand, man cannot live by oblative, descending love alone. He cannot always give; he must also receive. Anyone who wishes to give love must also receive love as a gift. Certainly, as the Lord tells us, one can become a source from which rivers of living water flow (cf. Jn 7:37–38). Yet to become such a source, one must constantly drink anew from the original source, which is Jesus Christ, from whose pierced heart flows the love of God (cf. Jn 19:34).

In the account of Jacob's ladder, the fathers of the church saw this insepa-rable connection between ascending and descending love, between *eros* that seeks God and *agape* that passes on the gift received, symbolized in various ways. In that biblical passage, we read how the patriarch Jacob saw in a dream, above the stone that was his pillow, a ladder reaching up to heaven, on which the angels of God were ascending and descending (cf. Gn 28:12, Jn 1:51). A particularly striking interpretation of this vision is presented by Pope Gregory the Great in his *Pastoral Rule*. He tells us that the good pastor must be rooted in contemplation. Only in this way will he be able to take upon himself the needs of others and make them his own: "*Per pietatis viscera in se infirmitatem caeterorum transferat.*"[4] St. Gregory speaks in this context of St. Paul, who was borne aloft to the most exalted mysteries of God, and hence, having descended once more, he was able to become all things to all men (cf. 2 Cor 12:2–4, 1 Cor 9:22). He also points to the example of Moses, who entered the tabernacle time and again, remaining in dialogue with God, so that when he emerged he could be at the service of his people. "Within [the tent] he is borne aloft through contemplation, while without he is completely engaged in helping those who suffer: *intus in contemplationem rapitur, foris infirmantium negotiis urgetur.*"[5]

8. We have thus come to an initial, albeit still somewhat generic, response to the two questions raised earlier. Fundamentally, "love" is a single reality, but with different dimensions; at different times, one or the other dimension may emerge more clearly. Yet when the two dimensions are totally cut off from one another, the result is a caricature, or at least an impoverished form of love. And we have also seen, synthetically, that biblical faith does not set up a paral-lel universe or one opposed to that primordial human phenomenon that is love, but rather accepts the whole man; it intervenes in his search for love in order to purify it and reveal new dimensions of it. This newness of biblical faith is shown chiefly in two elements, which deserve to be highlighted: the image of God and the image of man.

The Newness of Biblical Faith

9. First, the world of the Bible presents us with a new image of God. In sur-rounding cultures, the image of God and of the gods ultimately remained unclear and contradictory. In the development of biblical faith, however, the content of the prayer fundamental to Israel, the *Shema,* became increasingly clear and unequivocal: "Hear, O Israel, the LORD our God is one LORD" (Dt 6:4). There is only one God, the Creator of heaven and earth, who is thus the God of all. Two facts are significant about this statement: all other gods are

not God, and the universe in which we live has its source in God and was created by him. Certainly, the notion of creation is found elsewhere, yet only here does it become absolutely clear that it is not one god among many, but the one true God himself who is the source of all that exists; the whole world comes into existence by the power of his creative Word. Consequently, his Creation is dear to him, for it was willed by him and "made" by him. The second important element now emerges: this God loves man. The divine power that Aristotle at the height of Greek philosophy sought to grasp through reflection is, indeed, for every being an object of desire and of love—and as the object of love this divinity moves the world[6]—but in itself it lacks nothing and does not love: it is solely the object of love. The one God in whom Israel believes, however, loves with a personal love. His love, moreover, is an elective love: among all the nations he chooses Israel and loves her—but he does so precisely with a view to healing the whole human race. God loves, and his love may certainly be called *eros*, yet it is also totally *agape*.[7]

The prophets, particularly Hosea and Ezekiel, described God's passion for his people using boldly erotic images. God's relationship with Israel is described using the metaphors of betrothal and marriage; idolatry is thus adultery and prostitution. Here we find a specific reference—as we have seen—to the fertility cults and their abuse of *eros*, but also a description of the relationship of fidelity between Israel and her God. The history of the love relationship between God and Israel consists, at the deepest level, in the fact that he gives her the Torah, thereby opening Israel's eyes to man's true nature and showing her the path leading to true humanism. It consists in the fact that man, through a life of fidelity to the one God, comes to experience himself as loved by God, and discovers joy in truth and righteousness—a joy in God that becomes his essential happiness: "Whom do I have in heaven but you? And there is nothing upon earth that I desire besides you.... [F]or me it is good to be near God" (Ps 73 [72]:25, 73 [72]:28).

10. We have seen that God's *eros* for man is also totally *agape*. This is not only because it is bestowed in a completely gratuitous manner, without any previous merit, but also because it is love that forgives. Hosea above all shows us that this *agape* dimension of God's love for man goes far beyond gratuitousness. Israel has committed "adultery" and has broken the covenant; God should judge and repudiate her. It is precisely at this point that God is revealed to be God and not man: "How can I give you up, O Ephraim! How can I hand you over, O Israel!... My heart recoils within me, my compassion grows warm and tender. I will not execute my fierce anger, I will not again destroy Ephraim; for I am God and not man, the Holy One in your midst" (Hos 11:8–9). God's passionate love for his people—for humanity—is at the same time a forgiving

love. It is so great that it turns God against himself, his love against his justice. Here Christians can see a dim prefiguring of the mystery of the cross: so great is God's love for man that by becoming man he follows man even into death, and so reconciles justice and love.

The philosophical dimension to be noted in this biblical vision, as well as its importance from the standpoint of the history of religions, lies in the fact that, on the one hand, we find ourselves before a strictly metaphysical image of God: God is the absolute and ultimate source of all being; but this universal principle of creation—the Logos, primordial reason—is at the same time a lover with all the passion of a true love. *Eros* is thus supremely ennobled, yet at the same time it is so purified as to become one with *agape*. We can thus see how the reception of the Song of Songs in the Canon of sacred scripture was soon explained by the idea that these love songs ultimately describe God's relation to man and man's relation to God. Thus the Song of Songs became, both in Christian and Jewish literature, a source of mystical knowledge and experience, an expression of the essence of biblical faith: that man can indeed enter into union with God—his primordial aspiration. But this union is no mere fusion, a sinking in the nameless ocean of the divine; it is a unity that creates love, a unity in which both God and man remain themselves and yet become fully one. As St. Paul says: "He who is united to the Lord becomes one spirit with him" (1 Cor 6:17).

11. The first novelty of biblical faith consists, as we have seen, in its image of God. The second, essentially connected to this, the image of man. The biblical account of Creation speaks of the solitude of Adam, the first man, and God's decision to give him a helper. Of all other creatures, not one is capable of being the helper that man needs, even though he has assigned a name to all the wild beasts and birds and thus made them fully a part of his life. So God forms woman from the rib of man. Now Adam finds the helper that he needed: "This at last is bone of my bones and flesh of my flesh" (Gn 2:23). Here one might detect hints of ideas that are also found, for example, in the myth mentioned by Plato, according to which man was originally spherical, because he was complete in himself and self-sufficient. But as punishment for pride, he was split in two by Zeus, so that now he longs for his other half, striving with all his being to possess it and thus regain his integrity.[8] While the biblical narrative does not speak of punishment, the idea is certainly present that man is somehow incomplete, driven by nature to seek in another the part that can make him whole, the idea that only in communion with the opposite sex can he become "complete." The biblical account thus concludes with a prophecy about Adam: "Therefore a man leaves his father and his mother and cleaves to his wife and they become one flesh" (Gn 2:24).

Two aspects of this are important. First, *eros* is somehow rooted in man's very nature; Adam is a seeker who "abandons his mother and father" in order to find woman; only together do the two represent complete humanity and become "one flesh." The second aspect is equally important. From the standpoint of Creation, *eros* directs man toward marriage, to a bond that is unique and definitive; thus, and only thus, does it fulfill its deepest purpose. Corresponding to the image of a monotheistic God is monogamous marriage. Marriage based on exclusive and definitive love becomes the icon of the relationship between God and his people. God's way of loving becomes the measure of human love. This close connection between *eros* and marriage in the Bible has practically no equivalent in extrabiblical literature.

Jesus Christ—The Incarnate Love of God

12. Though up to now we have been speaking mainly of the Old Testament, nevertheless the profound intermixing of the two testaments as the one scripture of the Christian faith has already become evident. The real novelty of the New Testament lies not so much in new ideas as in the figure of Christ himself, who gives flesh and blood to those concepts in an unprecedented realism. In the Old Testament, the novelty of the Bible consisted not merely in abstract notions but in God's unpredictable and, in some sense, unprecedented activity. This divine activity now takes dramatic form when, in Jesus Christ, it is God himself who goes in search of the "stray sheep," a suffering and lost humanity. When Jesus speaks in his parables of the shepherd who goes after the lost sheep, of the woman who looks for the lost coin, of the father who goes to meet and embrace his prodigal son, these are no mere words: they are an explanation of his very being and activity. His death on the cross is the culmination of that turning of God against himself in which he gives himself in order to raise man up and save him. This is love in its most radical form. By contemplating the pierced side of Christ (cf. Jn 19:37), we can understand the starting point of this encyclical letter: "God is love" (1 Jn 4:8). It is there that this truth can be contemplated. It is from there that our definition of love must begin. In this contemplation the Christian discovers the path along which his life and love must move.

13. Jesus gave this act of oblation an enduring presence through his institution of the Eucharist at the Last Supper. He anticipated his death and Resurrection by giving his disciples, in the bread and wine, his very self, his body and blood, as the new manna (cf. Jn 6:31–33). The ancient world had dimly perceived that man's real food—what truly nourishes him as man—is ultimately the Logos, eternal wisdom: this same Logos now truly becomes food

for us—as love. The Eucharist draws us into Jesus's act of self-oblation. More than just statically receiving the incarnate Logos, we enter into the very dynamic of his self-giving. The imagery of marriage between God and Israel is now realized in a way previously inconceivable: it had meant standing in God's presence, but now it becomes union with God through sharing in Jesus's gift of self, sharing in his body and blood. The sacramental "mysticism" grounded in God's condescension toward us operates at a radically different level and lifts us to far greater heights than anything that any human mystical elevation could ever accomplish.

14. Here we need to consider yet another aspect: this sacramental "mysticism" is social in character, for in sacramental communion I become one with the Lord, like all the other communicants. As St. Paul says, "Because there is one bread, we who are many are one body, for we all partake of the one bread" (1 Cor 10:17). Union with Christ is also union with all those to whom he gives himself. I cannot possess Christ just for myself; I can belong to him only in union with all those who have become, or who will become, his own. Communion draws me out of myself toward him, and thus also toward unity with all Christians. We become "one body," completely joined in a single existence. Love of God and love of neighbor are now truly united: God incarnate draws us all to himself. We can thus understand how *agape* also became a term for the Eucharist: there God's own *agape* comes to us bodily, in order to continue his work in us and through us. Only by keeping in mind this Christological and sacramental basis can we correctly understand Jesus's teaching on love. The transition he makes from the law and the prophets to the twofold commandment to love God and neighbor, and his grounding of the whole life of faith on this central precept, is not simply a matter of morality—something that could exist apart from and alongside faith in Christ and its sacramental re-actualization. Faith, worship, and *ethos* are interwoven as a single reality that takes shape in our encounter with God's *agape*. Here the usual contraposition between worship and ethics simply falls apart. "Worship" itself, eucharistic communion, includes the reality both of being loved and of loving others in turn. A Eucharist that does not pass over into the concrete practice of love is intrinsically fragmented. Conversely, as we shall consider in greater detail below, the "commandment" of love is only possible because it is more than a requirement. Love can be "commanded" because it has first been given.

15. This principle is the starting point for understanding the great parables of Jesus. The rich man (cf. Lk 16:19–31) begs from his place of torment that his brothers be informed about what happens to those who ignore the poor man in need. Jesus takes up this cry for help as a warning to help us return to the right path. The parable of the Good Samaritan (cf. Lk 10:25–37) offers

two particularly important clarifications. Until that time, the concept of "neighbor" was understood as referring essentially to one's countrymen and to foreigners who had settled in the land of Israel—in other words, to the closely knit community of a single country or people. This limit is now abolished. Anyone who needs me and whom I can help is my neighbor. The concept of neighbor is now universalized, yet it remains concrete. Despite being extended to all mankind, it is not reduced to a generic, abstract, undemanding expression of love, but calls for my own practical commitment here and now. The church has the duty to interpret ever anew this relationship between near and far with regard to the actual daily life of her members. Lastly, we should especially mention the great parable of the Last Judgment (cf. Mt 25:31–46), in which love becomes the criterion for the definitive decision about a human life's worth or lack thereof. Jesus identifies himself with those in need, with the hungry, the thirsty, the stranger, the naked, the sick, and those in prison. "As you did it to one of the least of these my brethren, you did it to me" (Mt 25:40). Love of God and love of neighbor have become one: in the least of the brethren we find Jesus himself, and in Jesus we find God.

Love of God and Love of Neighbor

16. Having reflected on the nature of love and its meaning in biblical faith, we are left with two questions concerning our own attitude: can we love God without seeing him? And can love be commanded? These questions raise a double objection to the double commandment of love. No one has ever seen God, so how could we love him? Moreover, love cannot be commanded; it is ultimately a feeling that is either there or not, and it cannot be produced by the will. Scripture seems to reinforce the first objection when it states: "If anyone says, 'I love God,' and hates his brother, he is a liar; for he who does not love his brother whom he has seen, cannot love God whom he has not seen" (1 Jn 4:20). But this text hardly excludes the love of God as something impossible. On the contrary, the whole context of the passage quoted from the First Letter of John shows that such love is explicitly demanded. The unbreakable bond between love of God and love of neighbor is emphasized. One is so closely connected to the other that to say that we love God becomes a lie if we are closed to our neighbor or hate him altogether. St. John's words should be interpreted to mean that love of neighbor is a path that leads to the encounter with God, and that closing our eyes to our neighbor also blinds us to God.

17. True, no one has ever seen God as he is. And yet God is not totally invisible to us; he does not remain completely inaccessible. God loved us first, says the Letter of John quoted above (cf. 4:10), and this love of God has appeared

in our midst. He has become visible inasmuch as he "has sent his only Son into the world, so that we might live through him" (1 Jn 4:9). God has made himself visible: in Jesus we are able to see the Father (cf. Jn 14:9). Indeed, God is visible in a number of ways. In the love story recounted by the Bible, he comes toward us and seeks to win our hearts, all the way to the Last Supper, to the piercing of his heart on the cross, to his appearances after the Resurrection, and to the great deeds by which, through the activity of the apostles, he guided the nascent church along its path. Nor has the Lord been absent from subsequent church history: he encounters us ever anew, in the men and women who reflect his presence in his Word, in the sacraments, and especially in the Eucharist. In the church's liturgy, in her prayer, in the living community of believers, we experience the love of God, we perceive his presence, and we thus learn to recognize that presence in our daily lives. He loved us first and he continues to do so; we, too, then, can respond with love. God does not demand of us a feeling that we ourselves are incapable of producing. He loves us, he makes us see and experience his love, and since he has "loved us first," love can also blossom as a response within us.

In the gradual unfolding of this encounter, it is clearly revealed that love is not merely a sentiment. Sentiments come and go. A sentiment can be a marvelous first spark, but it is not the fullness of love. Earlier we spoke of the process of purification and maturation by which *eros* comes fully into its own, becomes love in the full meaning of the word. It is characteristic of mature love that it calls into play all man's potential; it engages the whole man, so to speak. Contact with the visible manifestations of God's love can awaken within us a feeling of joy born of the experience of being loved. But this encounter also engages our will and our intellect. Acknowledgment of the living God is one path toward love, and the "yes" of our will to his will unites our intellect, will, and sentiments in the all-embracing act of love. But this process is always open-ended; love is never "finished" and complete; throughout life, it changes and matures, and thus remains faithful to itself. *Idem velle atque idem nolle*[9]—to want the same thing and to reject the same thing—was recognized by antiquity as the authentic content of love: the one becomes similar to the other, and this leads to a community of will and thought. The love story between God and man means that this communion of will increases in a communion of thought and sentiment, and thus our will and God's will increasingly coincide: God's will is no longer for me an alien will, something imposed on me from without by the commandments; rather, it is now my own will, based on the realization that God is, in fact, more deeply present to me than I am to myself.[10] Then self-abandonment to God increases and God becomes our joy (cf. Ps 73 [72]:23–28).

18. Love of neighbor is thus shown to be possible in the way proclaimed by the Bible, by Jesus. It consists in the very fact that, in God and with God, I love even the person whom I do not like or even know. This can only take place on the basis of an intimate encounter with God, an encounter that has become a communion of will, even affecting my feelings. Then I learn to look on this other person not simply with my eyes and my feelings, but from the perspective of Jesus Christ. His friend is my friend. Going beyond exterior appearances, I perceive in others an interior desire for a sign of love, of concern. This I can offer them not only through the organizations intended for such purposes, accepting it perhaps as a political necessity; seeing with the eyes of Christ, I can give to others much more than their outward necessities—I can give them the look of love they crave. Here we see the necessary interplay between love of God and love of neighbor of which the First Letter of John speaks with such insistence. If I have no contact whatsoever with God in my life, then I see in the other nothing more than the other, and I am incapable of seeing in him the image of God. And if in my life I fail completely to heed others, solely out of a desire to be "devout" and to perform my "religious duties," then my relationship with God will also grow arid. It will become merely "proper," and loveless. Only my readiness to encounter my neighbor and to show him love makes me sensitive to God, as well. Only if I serve my neighbor can my eyes be opened to what God does for me and how much he loves me. The saints—consider the example of Blessed Teresa of Calcutta—constantly renewed their capacity for love of neighbor from their encounter with the eucharistic Lord, and conversely this encounter acquired its realism and depth in their service to others. Love of God and love of neighbor are thus inseparable; they form a single commandment. But both live from the love of God who has loved us first. No longer is it a question, then, of a "commandment" imposed from without and calling for the impossible, but rather of a freely bestowed experience of love from within, a love that by its very nature must then be shared with others. Love grows through love. Love is "divine" because it comes from God and unites us to God; through this unifying process, it makes us a "we" that transcends our divisions and makes us one, until in the end God is "all in all" (1 Cor 15:28).

PART II: CARITAS: THE PRACTICE OF LOVE BY THE CHURCH AS A "COMMUNITY OF LOVE"

The Church's Charitable Activity As a Manifestation of Trinitarian Love

19. "If you see charity, you see the Trinity," wrote St. Augustine.[11] In the foregoing reflections, we have been able to focus our attention on the Pierced One

(cf. Jn 19:37, Zech 12:10), recognizing the plan of the Father who, moved by love (cf. Jn 3:16), sent his only begotten Son into the world to redeem man. By dying on the cross—as St. John tells us—Jesus "gave up his Spirit" (Jn 19:30), anticipating the gift of the Holy Spirit that he would make after his Resurrection (cf. Jn 20:22). This was to fulfill the promise of "rivers of living water" that would flow out of the hearts of believers, through the outpouring of the Spirit (cf. Jn 7:38–39). The Spirit, in fact, is that interior power that harmonizes their hearts with Christ's heart and moves them to love their brethren as Christ loved them, when he bent down to wash the feet of the disciples (cf. Jn 13:1–13), and, above all, when he gave his life for us (cf. Jn 13:1, 15:13).

The Spirit is also the energy that transforms the heart of the ecclesial community, so that it becomes a witness before the world to the love of the Father, who wishes to make humanity a single family in his Son. The entire activity of the church is the expression of a love that seeks the integral good of man: it seeks his evangelization through Word and sacrament, an undertaking that is often heroic in the way it is acted out in history, and it seeks to promote man in the various arenas of life and human activity. Love is, therefore, the service that the church carries out in order to attend constantly to man's sufferings and needs, including material needs. And this is the aspect, this *service of charity*, on which I want to focus in the second part of the encyclical.

Charity As a Responsibility of the Church

20. Love of neighbor, grounded in the love of God, is first and foremost a responsibility for each individual member of the faithful, but it is also a responsibility for the entire ecclesial community at every level: from the local community to the particular church and to the church universal in its entirety. As a community, the church must practice love. Love thus needs to be organized if it is to be an ordered service to the community. The awareness of this responsibility has had a constitutive relevance in the church from the beginning: "All who believed were together and had all things in common; and they sold their possessions and goods and distributed them to all, as any had need" (Acts 2:44–45). In these words, St. Luke provides a definition of the church, whose constitutive elements include fidelity to the "teaching of the apostles," "communion" (*koinonia*), "the breaking of the bread," and "prayer" (cf. Acts 2:42). The element of "communion" (*koinonia*) is not initially defined but appears concretely in the verses quoted above; it means believers hold all things in common and among them there is no longer any distinction between rich and poor (cf. also Acts 4:32–37). As the church grew, this radical form of material communion could not be preserved, but its essential core remained:

within the community of believers there can never be room for a poverty that denies anyone what is needed for a dignified life.

21. A decisive step in the difficult search to put this fundamental ecclesial principle into practice is illustrated in the choice of the seven, which marked the origin of the diaconal office (cf. Acts 6:3–6). In the early church, in fact, in the daily distribution to widows, a disparity had arisen between Hebrew speakers and Greek speakers. The apostles, who had been entrusted primarily with "prayer" (the Eucharist and the liturgy) and the "ministry of the word," felt overburdened by "serving tables," so they decided to reserve the principal duty to themselves and to designate for the other task, also necessary in the church, a group of seven persons. Nor was this group to carry out a purely mechanical work of distribution; they were to be men "full of the Spirit and of wisdom" (cf. Acts 6:1–6). In other words, the social service they were meant to provide was absolutely concrete yet also a spiritual service; theirs was a truly spiritual office that carried out an essential responsibility of the church— namely, a well-ordered love of neighbor. With the formation of this group of seven, *diaconia*—the ministry of charity exercised in a communitarian, or- derly way—became part of the fundamental structure of the church.

22. As the years went by and the church spread farther afield, the exercise of charity became established as one of her essential activities, along with the administration of the sacraments and the proclamation of the Word; love for widows and orphans, prisoners, and sick and needy of every kind is as essential to her as the ministry of the sacraments and preaching of the gospel. The church cannot neglect the service of charity any more than she can neglect the sacraments and the Word. A few references will suffice to demonstrate this. Justin Martyr (d. ca. 155), in speaking of the Christians' celebration of Sunday, also mentions their charitable activity, linked with the Eucharist. Those who are able make offerings in accordance with their means, each as he or she wishes; the bishop in turn makes use of these to support orphans, widows, the sick, and those who for other reasons find themselves in need, such as prison- ers and foreigners.[12] The great Christian writer Tertullian (d. after 220) relates that the pagans were struck by the Christians' concern for the needy of every sort.[13] And when Ignatius of Antioch (d. ca. 117) described the church of Rome as "presiding in charity [*agape*],"[14] we may assume that with this definition was also intended in some sense to express her concrete charitable activity.

23. Here it might be helpful to allude to the earliest legal structures associ- ated with the service of charity in the church. Toward the middle of the fourth century, we see the development in Egypt of the *diaconia*: the institution within each monastery responsible for works of relief, that is to say, for the service of charity. By the sixth century, this institution had evolved into a corporation

with full juridical standing, which the civil authorities entrusted with part of the grain for public distribution. In Egypt not only each monastery but each individual diocese eventually had its own *diaconia;* this institution then developed in both East and West. Pope Gregory the Great (d. 604) mentions the *diaconia* of Naples, while in Rome the *diaconiae* are documented from the seventh and eighth centuries. But charitable activity on behalf of the poor and suffering was naturally an essential part of the church of Rome from the very beginning, based on the principles of Christian life given in the Acts of the Apostles. It found vivid expression in the case of the deacon Lawrence (d. 258). The dramatic description of Lawrence's martyrdom was known to St. Ambrose (d. 397), and it provides an authentic picture of the saint. As the one responsible for the care of the poor in Rome, Lawrence had been given a period of time after the capture of the pope and of Lawrence's fellow deacons, to collect the treasures of the church and hand them over to the civil authorities. He distributed to the poor whatever funds were available and then presented to the authorities the poor themselves as the real treasure of the church.[15] Whatever historical reliability one attributes to these details, Lawrence has always remained present in the church's memory as a great exponent of ecclesial charity.

24. A mention of the emperor Julian the Apostate (d. 363) can also show how essential the early church considered the organized practice of charity. As a child of six years, Julian witnessed the assassination of his father, brother, and other family members by the guards of the imperial palace; rightly or wrongly, he blamed this brutal act on the emperor Constantius, who passed himself off as an outstanding Christian. The Christian faith was thus definitively discredited in his eyes. Upon becoming emperor, Julian decided to restore paganism, the ancient Roman religion, while reforming it in the hope of making it the driving force behind the empire. In this project he was amply inspired by Christianity. He established a hierarchy of metropolitans and priests who were to foster love of God and neighbor. In one of his letters,[16] he wrote that the sole aspect of Christianity that had impressed him was the church's charitable activity. He thus considered it essential for his new pagan religion that, alongside the system of church's charity, an equivalent pagan activity be established. According to him, this was the reason for the popularity of the "Galileans." They needed to be imitated and outdone. In this way, then, the emperor confirmed that charity was a decisive feature of the Christian community, the church.

25. Thus far, two essential facts have emerged from our reflections:

(a) The church's deepest nature is expressed in her threefold responsibility: of proclaiming the Word of God (*kerygma-martyria*), celebrating the sacraments (*leitourgia*), and exercising the ministry of charity (*diakonia*). These duties presuppose each other and are inseparable. For the church, charity is not a welfare activity that could equally well be left to others, but is a part of her nature, an indispensable expression of her very being.[17]

(b) The church is God's family in the world. In this family no one ought to go without the necessities of life. Yet at the same time *caritas-agape* extends beyond the frontiers of the church. The parable of the Good Samaritan remains as a standard imposing universal love for the needy whom we encounter "by chance" (cf. Lk 10:31), whoever they may be. Without in any way detracting from the commandment of universal love, the church also has a specific responsibility: within the ecclesial family no member should suffer from being in need. The teaching of the Letter to the Galatians is emphatic: "So then, as we have opportunity, let us do good to all, and especially to those who are of the household of faith" (6:10).

Justice and Charity

26. Since the nineteenth century, an objection has been raised to the church's charitable activity, subsequently developed with particular insistence by Marxism: the poor, it is claimed, need not charity but justice. Works of charity—almsgiving—are, in effect, a way for the rich to shirk their obligation to work for justice, a means of soothing their consciences while preserving their own status and robbing the poor of their rights. Instead of contributing through individual works of charity to maintaining the status quo, we need to build a just social order in which all receive their share of the world's goods and no one has to depend on charity. There is admittedly some truth to this argument, but also much that is mistaken. It is true that the pursuit of justice must be a fundamental norm of the state and that the aim of a just social order is to guarantee to each person, according to the principle of subsidiarity, his share of the community's goods. This has always been emphasized by Christian teaching on the state and by the church's social doctrine. Historically, the issue of the just ordering of the collectivity had acquired a new dimension with the industrialization of society in the nineteenth century. The rise of modern industry caused the old social structures to collapse, while the growth of a class of salaried workers provoked radical changes in the fabric of society. The relationship between capital and labor now became the decisive issue—an issue that was previously unknown in that form. Capital and the means of production were a new source of power that, concentrated in the hands of a few, led to the suppression of the rights of the working classes, provoking them to rebel.

27. It must be admitted that the church's leadership was slow to realize that the just structuring of society needed to be approached in a new way. There were some pioneers, such as Bishop Ketteler of Mainz (d. 1877), and concrete needs were met by a growing number of groups, associations, leagues, federations, and in particular, by the new religious orders founded in the nineteenth century to combat poverty and disease and to provide better education. In 1891, the papal magisterium intervened with the encyclical *Rerum Novarum* of Leo XIII. This was followed in 1931 by Pius XI's encyclical *Quadragesimo Anno*. In 1961 Blessed John XXIII published the encyclical *Mater et Magistra*, and Paul VI, in the encyclical *Populorum Progressio* (1967) and in the apostolic letter *Octogesima Adveniens* (1971), insistently addressed the social problem, which had meanwhile become especially acute in Latin America. My great predecessor, John Paul II, left us a trilogy of social encyclicals: *Laborem Exercens* (1981), *Sollicitudo Rei Socialis* (1987), and finally, *Centesimus Annus* (1991). Faced with new situations and issues, Catholic social teaching thus gradually developed, and has now found a comprehensive presentation in the *Compendium of the Social Doctrine of the Church* published in 2004 by the pontifical council Iustitia et Pax. Marxism had seen world revolution and its preliminaries as the panacea for social problems: revolution and subsequent collectivization of the means of production, so it was claimed, would immediately change things for the better. This illusion has vanished. In today's complex situation, not least because of the growth of a globalized economy, the church's social doctrine has become a set of fundamental guidelines offering approaches that are valid even beyond the confines of the church: in the face of ongoing development, these guidelines need to be addressed in the context of dialogue with all those seriously concerned for humanity and for the world in which we live.

28. In order to define more accurately the relationship between the necessary commitment to justice and the ministry of charity, two fundamental situations need to be considered:

(*a*) The just ordering of society and the state is a central responsibility of politics. As Augustine once said, a state that is not governed according to justice would be just a bunch of thieves: "*Remota itaque iustitia quid sunt regna nisi magna latrocinia?*"[18] The distinction between what belongs to Caesar and what belongs to God is fundamental to Christianity (cf. Mt 22:21)—in other words, the distinction between church and state, or, as the Second Vatican Council puts it, the autonomy of the temporal sphere.[19] The state may not impose religion, yet it must guarantee religious freedom and harmony between the followers of different religions. For her part, the church, as the social expression of Christian faith, has a proper independence and is structured, on the basis of her faith, as a community that the state must recognize. The two spheres are distinct, yet always interrelated.

Justice is both the aim and the intrinsic criterion of all politics. Politics is more than a mere mechanism for defining the rules of public life: its origin and its goal are found in justice, which, by its very nature, has to do with ethics. The state must inevitably face the question of how justice can be achieved here and now. But this presupposes an even more radical question: what is justice? The problem is one of practical reason; but if reason is to be exercised properly, it must undergo constant purification, since it can never be completely free of the danger of a certain ethical blindness caused by the dazzling effect of power and special interests.

Here politics and faith meet. Faith, by its specific nature, is an encounter with the living God—an encounter opening up new horizons extending beyond the sphere of reason. But it is also a purifying force for reason itself. From God's standpoint, faith liberates reason from its blind spots and therefore helps it to be ever more fully itself. Faith enables reason to do its work more effectively and to see its proper object more clearly. This is where Catholic social doctrine has its place: it has no intention of giving the church power over the state. Even less is it an attempt to impose on those who do not share the faith ways of thinking and modes of conduct proper to faith. Its aim is simply to help purify reason and to contribute, here and now, to the acknowledgment and attainment of what is just.

The church's social teaching argues on the basis of reason and natural law—namely, on the basis of what is in accord with the nature of every human being. It recognizes that it is not the church's responsibility to make this teaching prevail in political life. Rather, the church wishes to help form consciences in political life and to stimulate greater insight into the authentic requirements of justice, as well as greater readiness to act accordingly, even when this might involve conflict with one's personal interest. Building a just social and civil order, in which each person receives his or her due, is an essential task that every generation must take up anew. As a political task, this cannot be the church's immediate responsibility. Yet, since it is also a most important human responsibility, the church is duty-bound to offer, through the purification of reason and ethical formation, her own specific contribution toward understanding the requirements of justice and achieving them politically.

The church cannot and must not take upon herself the political battle to bring about the most just society possible. She cannot and must not replace the state. Yet at the same time she cannot and must not remain on the sidelines in the fight for justice. She has to play her part through rational argument and reawaken the spiritual energy without which justice, which always demands sacrifice, cannot prevail and prosper. A just society must be the achievement of politics, not the church. Yet the promotion of justice through efforts to bring about openness of mind and will to the demands of the common good concerns the church deeply.

(b) Love—*caritas*—will always prove necessary, even in the most just society. There is no ordering of the state so just that it can eliminate the need for a service of love. Whoever wants to eliminate love is preparing to eliminate man as such. There will always be suffering that cries out for consolation and help. There will always be loneliness. There will always be situations of material need where help in the form of concrete love of neighbor is indispensable.[20] The state that would provide everything, absorbing everything into itself, would ultimately become a mere bureaucracy incapable of guaranteeing the very thing the suffering person—every person—needs: namely, loving personal concern. We do not need a state that regulates and controls everything, but a state that, in accordance with the principle of subsidiarity, generously acknowledges and supports initiatives arising from the different social forces and combines spontaneity with closeness to those in need. The church is one of those living forces: she is alive with the love enkindled by the Spirit of Christ. This love offers people not simply material help but refreshment and care for their souls, which often is even more necessary than material support. In the end, the claim that just social structures would make works of charity superfluous masks a materialist conception of man: the mistaken notion that man can live "by bread alone" (Mt 4:4, cf. Dt 8:3), a conviction that demeans man and ultimately disregards all that is specifically human.

29. We can now determine more precisely, in the life of the church, the relationship between commitment to the just ordering of the state and society on the one hand, and organized charitable activity on the other. We have seen that the formation of just structures is not directly the duty of the church, but belongs to the world of politics, the sphere of the autonomous use of reason. The church has an indirect duty here, in that she is called to contribute to the purification of reason and to the reawakening of those moral forces without which just structures are neither established nor prove effective in the long run.

The duty to work for a just ordering of society is proper to the lay faithful. As citizens of the state, they are called to take part in public life in a personal capacity. Thus they cannot relinquish their participation "in the many different economic, social, legislative, administrative and cultural areas, which are intended to promote organically and institutionally the *common good*."[21] The mission of the lay faithful is, therefore, to configure social life correctly, respecting its legitimate autonomy and cooperating with other citizens according to their respective competences and fulfilling their own responsibility.[22] Even if specific expressions of ecclesial charity can never be confused with the activity of the state, it still remains true that charity must animate the entire lives of the lay faithful and, therefore also, their political activity, lived as "social charity."[23]

The church's charitable organizations, on the other hand, constitute an *opus proprium,* a task agreeable to her, in which she does not cooperate collaterally but acts as a subject with direct responsibility, doing what corresponds to her nature. The church can never be exempted from practicing charity as an organized activity of believers, and there will never be a situation where the charity of each individual Christian is unnecessary, because, in addition to justice, man needs and will always need love.

The Multiple Structures of Charitable Service in the Social Context of the Present Day

30. Before attempting to define the specific profile of the church's activities in the service of man, I wish to consider the overall situation of the struggle for justice and love in the world today.

(*a*) Today mass communication has made our planet smaller, rapidly narrowing the distance between different peoples and cultures. This "togetherness" at times gives rise to misunderstandings and tensions, yet our ability to know almost instantly about the needs of others challenges us to share their situation and their difficulties. Despite the great advances made in science and technology, each day we see how much suffering there is in the world on account of different kinds of poverty, both material and spiritual. Our times call for a new readiness to assist our neighbors in need. The Second Vatican Council had made this point clearly: "Now that, through better means of communication, distances between peoples have been almost eliminated, charitable activity can and should embrace all people and all needs."[24]

On the other hand—and here we see one of the challenging yet also positive sides of the process of globalization—we now have at our disposal numerous means for offering humanitarian assistance to our brothers and sisters in need, not least modern systems of distributing food and clothing and of providing housing and care. Concern for our neighbor transcends the confines of national communities and has increasingly broadened its horizon to the whole world. The Second Vatican Council rightly observed that "among the signs of our times, one particularly worthy of note is a growing, inescapable sense of solidarity between all peoples."[25] State agencies and humanitarian associations work to promote this, the former mainly through subsidies and tax relief, the latter by making available considerable resources. The solidarity shown by civil society thus significantly surpasses that shown by individuals.

(b) This situation has led to the birth and the growth of many forms of cooperation between state and church agencies, which have borne fruit. Church agencies, with their transparent operation and their faithfulness to the duty of witnessing to love, are able to give a Christian quality to the civil agencies, too, favoring a mutual coordination that can only redound to the effectiveness of charitable service.[26] Numerous organizations for charitable or philanthropic purposes have also been established, and these are committed to achieving adequate humanitarian solutions to the social and political problems of the day. Significantly, our time has also seen the growth and spread of different kinds of volunteer work, which assume responsibility for providing a variety of services.[27] I wish here to offer a special word of gratitude and appreciation to all those who take part in these activities in whatever way. For young people, this widespread involvement constitutes a school of life that offers them a formation in solidarity and readiness to offer others not simply material aid, but their very selves. The anticulture of death, which finds expression, for example, in drug use, is thus countered by an unselfish love that shows itself to be a culture of life by the very willingness to "lose itself" (cf. Lk 17:33 et passim) for others.

In the Catholic Church, and also in the other churches and ecclesial communities, new forms of charitable activity have arisen, while other, older ones have taken on new life and energy. In these new forms, it is often possible to establish a fruitful link between evangelization and works of charity. Here I would clearly reaffirm what my great predecessor, John Paul II, wrote in his encyclical Sollicitudo Rei Socialis[28] when he asserted the readiness of the Catholic Church to cooperate with the charitable agencies of these churches and communities, since we all have the same fundamental motivation and look toward the same goal: a true humanism, which acknowledges that man is made in the image of God, and wants to help him to live in a way consonant with that dignity. His encyclical Ut Unum Sint emphasized that the building of a better world requires Christians to speak with a united voice in working to inculcate "respect for the rights and needs of everyone, especially the poor, the lowly and the defenceless."[29] Here I would like to express my satisfaction that this appeal has found a wide resonance in numerous initiatives throughout the world.

The Distinctiveness of the Church's Charitable Activity

31. The diversified organizations engaged in meeting various human needs has increased ultimately because the command of love of neighbor is inscribed by

the Creator in man's very nature. It is also a result of the presence of Christianity in the world, since Christianity constantly revives and acts out this imperative, so often profoundly obscured in the course of time. The reform of paganism attempted by the emperor Julian the Apostate is only an initial example of this effect; here we see how the power of Christianity spread well beyond the frontiers of the Christian faith. For this reason, it is important that the church's charitable activity maintains all of its splendor and does not become just another form of social assistance. So what are the essential elements of Christian and ecclesial charity?

(a) Following the example given in the parable of the Good Samaritan, Christian charity is, first of all, the simple response to immediate needs and specific situations: feeding the hungry, clothing the naked, caring for and healing the sick, visiting those in prison, and so on. The church's charitable organizations, beginning with those of *caritas* (at diocesan, national, and international levels), ought to do everything in their power to provide the resources and, above all, the personnel needed for this work. Individuals who care for those in need must first be professionally competent: they should be properly trained in what to do and how to do it, and committed to continuing care. Yet, while professional competence is a primary, fundamental requirement, it is not of itself sufficient. We are dealing with human beings, and human beings always need something more than technically proper care. They need humanity. They need heartfelt concern. Those who work for the church's charitable organizations must be distinguished by the fact that they do not merely meet the needs of the moment, but they dedicate themselves to others with heartfelt concern, enabling them to experience the richness of their humanity. Consequently, in addition to their necessary professional training, these charity workers need a "formation of the heart": they need to be led to that encounter with God in Christ that awakens their love and opens their spirits to others. As a result, love of neighbor will be for them no longer a commandment imposed, so to speak, from without, but a consequence deriving from their faith, a faith that becomes active through love (cf. Gal 5:6).

(b) Christian charitable activity must be independent of parties and ideologies. It is not a means of changing the world ideologically, and it is not at the service of worldly stratagems; rather, it is a way of making present here and now the love that man always needs. The modern age, particularly from the nineteenth century on, has been dominated by various versions of a philosophy of progress whose most radical form is Marxism. Part of Marxist strategy is the theory of impoverishment: in a situation of unjust power, it is claimed, anyone who engages in charitable initiatives is actually serving that unjust system, making it appear, at least to some extent, tolerable. This, in turn, slows down a potential revolution and thus blocks the struggle for a better world. Seen in this way, charity is rejected and attacked as a means of preserving the status quo. What we have here, though, is really an inhuman philosophy. People of the present are sacrificed to the *Moloch* of the future—a future whose effective realization is at best doubtful. One does not make the world more human by refusing to act humanely here and now. We contribute to a better world only by personally doing good now, with full commitment and wherever we have the opportunity, independently of partisan strategies and programs. The Christian's program—the program of the Good Samaritan, the program of Jesus—is "a heart that sees." This heart sees where love is needed and acts accordingly. Obviously, when charitable activity is carried out by the church as a communitarian initiative, the spontaneity of individuals must be combined with planning, foresight, and cooperation with other similar institutions.

(*c*) Charity, furthermore, cannot be used as a means of engaging in what is nowadays considered proselytism. Love is free; it is not practiced as a way of achieving other ends.[30] But this does not mean that charitable activity must somehow leave God and Christ aside, for it is always concerned with the whole man. Often the deepest cause of suffering is the absence of God. Those who practice charity in the church's name will never seek to impose the church's faith upon others. They realize that a pure and generous love is the best witness to the God in whom we believe and by whom we are driven to love. A Christian knows when it is time to speak of God and when it is better to say nothing and to let love alone speak. He knows that God is love (cf. 1 Jn 4:8) and that God's presence is felt at the very moment when all we do is to love. He knows—to return to the questions raised earlier—that disdain for love is disdain for God and man alike; it is an attempt to do without God. Consequently, the best defense of God and man consists precisely in love. It is the responsibility of the church's charitable organizations to reinforce this awareness in their members, so that by their activity—as well as their words, their silence, their example—they may be credible witnesses to Christ.

Those Responsible for the Church's Charitable Activity

32. Finally, we must turn our attention once again to those who are responsible for carrying out the church's charitable activity. As our preceding reflections

have made clear, the true subject of the various Catholic organizations that carry out a ministry of charity is the church herself—at all levels, from the parishes, through the particular churches, to the universal church. For this reason it was most opportune that my venerable predecessor Paul VI established the pontifical council *Cor Unum* as the agency of the Holy See responsible for orienting and coordinating the organizations and charitable activities promoted by the Catholic Church. In conformity with the episcopal structure of the church, the bishops, as successors of the apostles, are charged with the primary responsibility for carrying out in the particular churches the program set forth in the Acts of the Apostles (cf. 2:42–44): today as in the past, the church as God's family must be a place where help is given and received, and at the same time, a place where people are prepared to serve those outside her confines who are in need of help. In the rite of episcopal ordination, prior to the act of consecration itself, the candidate must respond to several questions, which express the essential elements of his office and recall the duties of his future ministry. He promises expressly to be, in the Lord's name, welcoming and merciful to the poor and to all those in need of consolation and assistance.[31] The *Code of Canon Law,* in the canons on the ministry of the bishop, does not expressly mention charity as a specific sector of episcopal activity, but speaks in general terms of the bishop's responsibility for coordinating the different works of the apostolate with due regard for their proper character.[32] Recently, however, the *Directory for the Pastoral Ministry of Bishops* explored more specifically the duty of charity as a responsibility incumbent upon the whole church and upon each bishop in his diocese,[33] and it emphasized that the exercise of charity is an action of the church as such, and that, like the ministry of Word and sacrament, it, too, has been an essential part of her mission from the very beginning.[34]

33. With regard to the personnel who carry out the church's charitable activity on the practical level, the essential has already been said: they must not be inspired by ideologies aimed at improving the world, but should rather be guided by the faith that works through love (cf. Gal 5:6). Consequently, more than anything, they must be persons moved by Christ's love, persons whose hearts Christ has conquered with his love, awakening within them a love of neighbor. The criterion inspiring their activity should be St. Paul's statement in the Second Letter to the Corinthians: "The love of Christ urges us on" (5:14). The consciousness that, in Christ, God has given himself for us, even unto death, must inspire us to live no longer for ourselves but for him and, with him, for others. Whoever loves Christ loves the church and desires the church to be increasingly the image and instrument of the love that flows from Christ. The personnel of every Catholic charitable organization want to

work with the church and, therefore, with the bishop, so that the love of God can spread throughout the world. By their sharing in the church's practice of love, they wish to be witnesses of God and of Christ, and they wish for this very reason freely to do good to all.

34. Interior openness to the Catholic dimension of the church cannot fail to dispose charity workers to work in harmony with other organizations in serving various forms of need, but in a way that respects what is distinctive about the service Christ requested of his disciples. St. Paul, in his hymn to charity (cf. 1 Cor 13), teaches us that it is always more than activity alone: "If I give away all I have, and if I deliver my body to be burned, but do not have love, I gain nothing" (v. 3). This hymn must be the Magna Carta of all ecclesial service; it sums up all the reflections on love I have offered throughout this encyclical letter. Practical activity will always be insufficient, unless it visibly expresses a love for man, a love nourished by an encounter with Christ. My deep personal sharing in the needs and sufferings of others becomes a sharing of my very self with them: if my gift is not to prove a source of humiliation, I must give to others not only what is my own but my very self; I must be personally present in my gift.

35. This proper way of serving others also leads to humility. The one who serves does not consider himself superior to the one served, however miserable his situation at the moment. Christ took the lowest place in the world—the cross—and by this radical humility he redeemed us and constantly comes to our aid. Those who are in a position to help others will realize that in doing so they themselves receive help; being able to help others is no merit or achievement of their own. This duty is a grace. The more we do for others, the more we understand and can appropriate the words of Christ: "We are useless servants" (Lk 17:10). We recognize that we are not acting on the basis of any superiority or greater personal efficiency, but because the Lord has graciously enabled us to do so. There are times when the burden of need and our own limitations might tempt us to become discouraged. But precisely then we are helped by the knowledge that, in the end, we are only instruments in the Lord's hands; and this knowledge frees us from the presumption of thinking that we alone are personally responsible for building a better world. In all humility we will do what we can, and in all humility we will entrust the rest to the Lord. It is God who governs the world, not we. We offer him our service only to the extent that we can, and for as long as he grants us the strength. To do all we can with what strength we have, however, is the task that keeps the good servant of Jesus Christ always at work: "The love of Christ urges us on" (2 Cor 5:14).

36. When we consider the immensity of others' needs, we can be driven toward an ideology that would aim at doing what God's governance of the world apparently cannot: fully resolving every problem. Or we can be tempted to give in to inertia, since it would seem that in any event nothing can be accomplished. At such times, a living relationship with Christ is decisive if we are to keep on the right path without falling into an arrogant contempt for man, which is not only unconstructive but actually destructive, surrendering to a resignation that would prevent us from being guided by love in the service of others. Prayer, as a means of drawing ever new strength from Christ, is concretely and urgently needed. People who pray are not wasting their time, even though the situation appears desperate and seems to call for action alone. Piety does not undermine the struggle to eliminate the poverty of our neighbors, however extreme. In the example of Blessed Teresa of Calcutta we have a clear illustration of the fact that time devoted to God in prayer not only does not detract from effective and loving service to our neighbor, but is, in fact, the inexhaustible source of that service. In her letter for Lent 1996, Blessed Teresa wrote to her lay co-workers: "We need this deep connection with God in our daily life. How can we obtain it? By prayer."

37. It is time to reaffirm the importance of prayer in the face of the activism and the growing secularism of many Christians engaged in charitable work. Clearly, the Christian who prays does not claim to be able to change God's plans or correct what he has foreseen. Rather, he seeks an encounter with the Father of Jesus Christ, asking God to be present with the consolation of the Spirit to him and his work. A personal relationship with God and an abandonment to his will can prevent man from being demeaned and save him from falling prey to the teaching of fanaticism and terrorism. An authentically religious attitude prevents man from presuming to judge God, accusing him of allowing poverty and failing to have compassion for his creatures. When people claim to build a case against God in defense of man, on whom can they depend when human activity proves powerless?

38. Certainly Job could complain before God about the presence of incomprehensible and apparently unjustified suffering in the world. In his pain he cried out: "Oh, that I knew where I might find him, that I might come even to his seat!... I would learn what he would answer me, and understand what he would say to me. Would he contend with me in the greatness of his power?... Therefore I am terrified at his presence; when I consider, I am in dread of him. God has made my heart faint; the Almighty has terrified me" (23:3, 23:5–6, 23:15–16). Often we cannot understand why God refrains from

intervening. Yet he does not prevent us from crying out, like Jesus on the cross: "My God, my God, why have you forsaken me?" (Mt 27:46). We should continue asking this question in prayerful dialogue to his face: "Lord, holy and true, how long will it be?" (Rv 6:10). It is St. Augustine who gives us faith's answer to our sufferings: "*Si comprehendis, non est Deus*"—"If you understand him, he is not God."[35] Our protest is not meant to challenge God, or to suggest that error, weakness, or indifference can be found in him. For the believer, it is impossible to imagine that God is powerless or that "perhaps he is asleep" (cf. 1 Kgs 18:27). Instead, our crying out is, as it was for Jesus on the cross, the deepest and most radical way of affirming our faith in his sovereign power. Even in their bewilderment and failure to understand the world around them, Christians continue to believe in the "goodness and loving kindness of God" (Ti 3:4). Immersed like everyone else in the dramatic complexity of historical events, they remain unshakably certain that God is our Father and loves us, even when his silence remains incomprehensible.

39. Faith, hope, and charity go together. Hope is practiced through the virtue of patience, which continues to do good even in the face of apparent failure, and through the virtue of humility, which accepts God's mystery and trusts him even in times of darkness. Faith tells us that God has given his Son for our sakes and gives us the victorious certainty that it is really true: God is love! It thus transforms our impatience and our doubts into the sure hope that God holds the world in his hands and that, as the dramatic imagery of the end of the Book of Revelation points out, in spite of all darkness, he ultimately triumphs in glory. Faith, which sees the love of God revealed in the pierced heart of Jesus on the cross, gives rise to love. Love is the light—and in the end, the only light—that can always illuminate a world grown dim and give us the courage needed to keep living and working. Love is possible, and we are able to practice it because we are created in the image of God. To experience love and, in this way, to cause the light of God to enter into the world—this is the invitation I would like to extend with the present encyclical.

Conclusion

40. Finally, let us consider the saints, who exercised charity in an exemplary way. Our thoughts turn especially to Martin of Tours (d. 397), the soldier who became a monk and a bishop: he is almost like an icon, illustrating the irreplaceable value of the individual testimony to charity. At the gates of Amiens,

Martin gave half his cloak to a poor man: Jesus himself, that night, appeared to him in a dream wearing that cloak, confirming the permanent validity of the gospel saying: "I was naked and you clothed me ... as you did it to one of the least of these my brethren, you did it to me" (Mt 25:36, 25:40).[36] Yet in the history of the church, how many other testimonies to charity could be quoted! In particular, the entire monastic movement, from its origins with St. Anthony the Abbot (d. 356), expresses an immense service of charity toward neighbors. In his encounter "face to face" with the God who is Love, the monk senses the impelling need to transform his whole life into service to his neighbor, in addition to service to God. This explains the great emphasis on hospitality, refuge, and care of the infirm in the vicinity of the monasteries. It also explains the immense initiatives of human welfare and Christian formation, aimed above all at the very poor, who became the object of care first for the monastic and mendicant orders, and later for the male and female religious institutes all through the history of the church. Saints such as Francis of Assisi, Ignatius of Loyola, John of God, Camillus of Lellis, Vincent de Paul, Louise de Marillac, Giuseppe B. Cottolengo, John Bosco, Luigi Orione, Teresa of Calcutta, to name but a few—stand out as lasting models of social charity for all people of good will. The saints are the true bearers of light within history, for they are men and women of faith, hope, and love.

41. Outstanding among the saints is Mary, Mother of the Lord and mirror of all holiness. In the Gospel of Luke we find her engaged in a service of charity to her cousin Elizabeth, with whom she remained for "about three months" (1:56) to assist her in the final phase of her pregnancy. "*Magnificat anima mea Dominum,*" she says on the occasion of that visit, "My soul magnifies the Lord" (Lk 1:46). With these words she expresses her whole program of life: not setting herself at the center, but leaving space for God, who is encountered both in prayer and in service to the neighbor—only then does goodness enter the world. Mary's greatness consists in the fact that she wants to magnify God, not herself. She is lowly: her only desire is to be the handmaid of the Lord (cf. Lk 1:38, 1:48). She knows that she will only contribute to the salvation of the world if, rather than carrying out her own projects, she places herself completely at the disposal of God's initiatives. Mary is a woman of hope: only because she believes in God's promises and awaits the salvation of Israel can the angel visit her and call her to the decisive service of these promises. Mary is a woman of faith: "Blessed are you who believed," Elizabeth says to her (cf. Lk 1:45). The *Magnificat*—a portrait, so to speak, of her soul—is entirely woven from threads of holy scripture, threads drawn from the Word of God. Here we see how completely at home Mary is with

the Word of God, with what ease she moves in and out of it. She speaks and thinks with the Word of God; the Word of God becomes her word, and her word issues from the Word of God. Here we see that her thoughts are attuned to the thoughts of God; her will is one with the will of God. Since Mary is completely imbued with the Word of God, she is able to become the Mother of the Word Incarnate. Finally, Mary is a woman who loves. How could it be otherwise? As a believer who in faith thinks with God's thoughts and wills with God's will, she cannot fail to be a woman who loves. We sense this in her quiet gestures, as recounted by the infancy narratives in the Gospel. We see it in the delicacy with which she recognizes the need of the spouses at Cana and makes it known to Jesus. We see it in the humility with which she recedes into the background during Jesus's public life, knowing that the Son must establish a new family and that the Mother's hour will come only with the cross, which will be Jesus's true hour (cf. Jn 2:4, 13:1). When the disciples flee, Mary remains beneath the cross (cf. Jn 19:25–27); later, at the hour of Pentecost, they will gather around her as they wait for the Holy Spirit (cf. Acts 1:14).

42. The lives of the saints are not limited to their earthly biographies, but also include their being and working in God after death. In the saints, one thing becomes clear: those who draw near to God do not withdraw from men, but rather become truly close to them. In no one do we see this more clearly than in Mary. The words addressed by the crucified Lord to his disciple—to John and through him to all disciples of Jesus: "Behold, your mother!" (Jn 19:27)—are fulfilled anew in every generation. Mary has truly become the Mother of all believers. Men and women of every time and place have re-course to her motherly kindness and her virginal purity and grace, in all their needs and aspirations, their joys and sorrows, their moments of loneliness, and their common endeavors. They constantly experience the gift of her goodness and the unfailing love she pours out from the depths of her heart. The testimonials of gratitude, offered to her from every continent and culture, are a recognition of that pure love, which is not self-seeking but simply be-nevolent. At the same time, the devotion of the faithful shows an infallible in-tuition of how such love is possible: it becomes so as a result of the most intimate union with God, through which the soul is totally pervaded by him—a condition that enables those who have drunk from the fountain of God's love to become, in their turn, a fountain from which "flow rivers of living water" (Jn 7:38). Mary, Virgin and Mother, shows us what love is and whence it draws its origin and its constantly renewed power. To her we entrust the church and her mission in the service of love:

Holy Mary, Mother of God,
you have given the world its true light,
Jesus, your Son—the Son of God.
You abandoned yourself completely
to God's call
and thus became a wellspring
of the goodness which flows forth from him.
Show us Jesus. Lead us to him.
Teach us to know and love him,
so that we, too, can become
capable of true love
and be fountains of living water
in the midst of a thirsting world.

GIVEN IN ROME, AT SAINT PETER'S,
ON DECEMBER 25, THE SOLEMNITY OF
THE NATIVITY OF THE LORD, IN THE YEAR 2005,
THE FIRST OF MY PONTIFICATE.

BENEDICTUS PP. XVI

Notes

INTRODUCTION

1. Ratzinger himself has noted that his point of departure is first of all the Word: "That we believe the word of God, that we try really to get to know it and understand it, and then, as I said, to think it together with the great masters of the faith. This gives my theology a somewhat biblical character and also bears the stamp of the Fathers, especially Augustine" (*Salt of the Earth*, p. 66).

2. Cf. Joseph Ratzinger, *Von Sinn des Christlichen* (Munich 1965, reprinted 2005), pp. 21–22.

3. It is difficult to give an overview of Ratzinger's publications because of the vast scope of his subject matter, the fragmentary nature of most of his writings, and the sheer volume of publications: some 86 books, 471 articles and prefaces, and 32 contributions to various encyclopedias and dictionaries. For the most up-to-date bibliography, see Joseph Cardinal Ratzinger, *Pilgrim Fellowship of Faith: The Church as Communion*, a collection of articles assembled by his former doctoral and postdoctoral students on the occasion of his seventy-fifth birthday and edited by Stephan Otto Horn and Vinzenz Pfnür (San Francisco: Ignatius Press, 2005), pp. 299–379.

4. The following first appeared as part of "The Mind of Benedict XVI" in the *Claremont Review of Books* (Fall 2005) and is reproduced here with the permission of the editors.

5. Joseph Cardinal Ratzinger, *Truth and Tolerance: Christian Belief and World Religions*, trans. Henry Taylor (San Francisco 2004).

6. Cardinal Ratzinger's contribution is reprinted in *Values in a Time of Upheaval*, ch. 2.

7. "I have never tried to create a system of my own, an individual theology. What is specific, if you want to call it that, is that I simply want to think in communion with the faith of the Church, and that means above all to think in communion with the great thinkers of the faith. The aim is not an isolated theology that I draw out of myself but one that opens as widely as possible into the common intellectual pathway of the faith" (*Salt of the Earth*, p. 66).

8. See "A Question of Fairness," *Homiletic & Pastoral Review* 102/1 (2001), pp. 53–54.

9. Joseph Ratzinger, *Die sakramentale Begründung christlicher Existenz* (Meitingen-Freising 1970). This is the text of a four-hour lecture he delivered at the Salzburg Hochschulwoche in 1965. It is primarily concerned with finding a new approach to the reality of the sacraments and their central significance in a world that has lost touch with the sacramental dimension of Christian living. The second pamphlet reproduced a lecture given at the Catholic Theology Faculty of the University of Eichstätt

on January 23, 1978, entitled *Zum Begriff des Sakramentes* [Eichstätt Hochschulreden, p. 15] (Munich 1979).

10. A number of seminarians came later to see me to tell me that, though they had been through the rites of initiation as children, they only understood them for the first time after hearing my lectures.

11. *Salt of the Earth*, p. 79.

12. See his comments on the two ways of interpreting the council: the hermeneutics of rupture and discontinuity—which only accepted as authentic what was "new" and so rejected traditional elements found in the documents as compromises needed to introduce the "new," and therefore not binding—and the hermeneutics of reform, which interpreted the council within the larger picture of tradition in its entirety (Address to the Roman Curia, December 22, 2005). The hermeneutics of discontinuity produced "the spirit of Vatican II."

13. *Salt of the Earth*, p. 61.

14. For Ratzinger's evaluation of the significance of his study of Bonaventure, see *Salt of the Earth*, pp. 61–63.

15. See esp. Eric Voegelin, *The New Science of Politics: An Introduction* (Chicago: University of Chicago Press, 1952), ch. 4, esp. pp. 111–27. I had often noted that Ratzinger's theology of politics echoed central themes common to Voegelin but did not suspect any direct influence, despite the occasional reference to Voegelin in Ratzinger's published oeuvre (e.g., *Die Einheit der Nationen: Eine Vision der Kirchenväter* [Salzburg-Munich 1971, rpt. 2005], p. 25; *Der Gott Jesu Christi: Betrachtungen über den Dreieinigen Gott* [Munich 1976], p. 36). Recently, a colleague in Maynooth, Thomas Norris, gave me a copy of a letter from Ratzinger, written when he was archbishop of Munich, to Eric Voegelin, thanking him for a book with a personal dedication that he had received along with an invitation to a celebration to mark Voegelin's eightieth birthday. "It was as a great surprise as it was a joy for me to receive your philosophical meditation, which you kindly sent to me with a personal dedication, in which you intend to awaken such a necessary and such a very fragile consciousness of the imperfect in opposition to the magic of the Utopian. Even since your small book, *Science, Politics and Gnosticism*, came into my hands in 1959, your thinking has fascinated and stimulated me, even though I was unfortunately unable to study it with the thoroughness I would have wished."

16. "The historico-critical method is a marvelous instrument for reading historical sources and interpreting texts" (*Truth and Tolerance*, p. 133). His basic criticism is that underlying much historico-critical study of scripture are philosophical assumptions of a positivistic nature that are inimical to the very content of scripture. Since they are generally not subject to any criticism, they can lead exegetes to conclusions that are unacceptable. Although these findings may be presented as objective or scientific, they generally reflect more the unquestioned assumptions of the exegete (pp. 133–36). See also his comments in *Milestones, Memoirs*, p. 127.

17. See his "Biblical Interpretation in Crisis: On the Question of the Foundations and Approaches of Exegesis Today. Erasmus Lecture 1988" in *This World: A Journal of Religion and Public Life* 22 (Summer 1988) 1–19; for an extended version of this text, see Joseph Ratzinger (ed.), *Schriftauslegung im Widerstreit, Quaestiones Disputatae* 117 (Freiburg-Basel-Vienna: Herder, 1989), pp. 7–44.

18. According to Rahner, all religions embody salvific values that, in principle, enable those adherents to become recipients of grace. All, therefore, who receive divine grace can be described as anonymous Christians, since all grace comes through the one mediator, Jesus Christ (1 Tim 2:5). What is *implicitly* true for redeemed humanity has, Rahner claims, become *explicit* in Christianity.

19. These include Martin Trimpe on the theology of the Petrine ministry of the Bishop of Rome, according to the sixteenth-century England of Cardinal Reginald Pole, and Stephan Otto Horn on Pope Leo the Great and the Council of Chalcedon. Father Bartholomé Adoukonou's thesis on a Christian hermeneutic of Dahomian Voodoo influenced Ratzinger's theology of religions and their relationship to the paschal mystery, while he draws on Frederick Hartl's postdoctoral thesis on Ernst Block and Franz von Baader in his analysis of neo-Marxism. And there are many others.

20. See, e.g., his address to the prestigious Westphalian Academy of Sciences (*Westfälische Akademie der Wissenschaften, Geisteswissen-schaften Vorträge* G279, Opladen, 1986). This is a detailed analysis of a foundational text of liberation theology, Gutierriez's *Theology of Liberation,* and probably functioned as preparation for the two *Instructions on Liberation Theology* issued by the CDF in 1984 and 1986. Similarly, his publications on the relationship between Christianity and Judaism, such as *Many Religions—One Covenant* (San Francisco: Ignatius, 1999), were probably part of his study of the question in preparation for the impressive document issued under his chairmanship by the Pontifical Biblical Commission, *The Jewish People and Their Sacred Scripture in the Christian Bible* (2002). See also his address to an historic meeting of rabbis and church leaders in Jerusalem, 1994 (cf. *Inside the Vatican,* May 2005, pp. 42–44). For his preparatory work on *Dominus Iesus,* see below.

21. "Man Between Reproduction and Creation: Theological Questions on the Origins of Human Life," *Communio* 16 (1989), pp. 197–211. This is an extraordinary article on contemporary developments in biotechnology, outlining the philosophical and theological background in European cultural history (going back as far as the Kabbalah) that is at the root of these revolutionary developments. The article was originally an address given at the University of Bologna, April 30, 1988, and seems to have been part of his reflections on or in preparation for *Donum vitae* (*Instruction on Respect for Human Life in Its Origin and on the Dignity of Procreation,* February 22, 1987).

22. *Truth and Tolerance,* p. 63.

23. *Turning Point for Europe,* pp. 28–29. There Ratzinger takes up and develops the insights of C. S. Lewis, *The Abolition of Man* (Oxford 1943).

24. *Turning Point for Europe,* p. 37; *Principles of Catholic Morality,* pp. 43–66. In stressing what is common to the wisdom traditions of mankind, Ratzinger may have left himself open to the criticism that he fails to give sufficient attention to what is specifically Christian—that newness which is our life in Christ; cf. Servais Pinckaers OP, *The Sources of Christian Ethics,* translated from the third edition by Sr. Mary Thomas Noble OP (Edinburgh 1995).

25. Originally published in Italian in 1985. The English translation by Salvator Attanasio and Graham Harrison was published by Ignatius Press, San Francisco, in the same year.

26. Originally appeared in German in 1996. The English translation by Adrian Walker was published by Ignatius Press in 1997.

27. Published in German in 2000 and translated by Henry Taylor Benedict (San Francisco 2002).

28. First appeared in Italian in 1997; English translation by Erasmo Leiva-Merikakis in 1998.

29. I coined the term *theology of politics* to contrast with *political theology*, a concept that he rejects. This includes any theology, such as that of J. B. Metz or the classical forms of liberation theology, that involves the instrumentalization of the church or of the faith for political purposes or the attribution of sacral or salvific significance to politics. Moreover, Ratzinger used the related term *theology of political life* to describe Augustine's understanding of politics, which he forged in his intense debate in the *City of God* with the "political theology" that characterized the sacral nature of the Roman Empire; cf. Joseph Ratzinger, *Die Einheit der Nationen: Eine Vision der Kirchenväter* (Salzburg-Munich 1971, rpt. 2005), p. 80.

30. The English translation is reprinted in *Crisis of Conscience*, ed. J. M. Haas (New York 1996). See also my forthcoming book, *Pope Benedict XVI: The Conscience of Our Age: A Theological Portrait* (San Francisco 2007).

31. The numbers refer to the paragraph, as is customary in Vatican documents, not to the page.

32. See esp. pp. 232–34.

CHAPTER 11: CHRIST THE LIBERATOR

1. Cf. the convincing remarks of P. Evdokimov, *L'Art de l'icone: Théologie de la beauté* (Paris 1970), pp. 265–75.

2. PG 43:440–64; cf. Evdokimov, 270. On the textual history of the homily, cf. Clavis Patrum Graecorum II (1974), no. 3768; cf. also J. Quasten, *Patrology* 3 (Utrecht 1960): 395.

3. Eph 5:14; Ps.—Epiphanius (see note 2 above).

4. A. Grillmeier cites this dictum of a Syrian Monophysite in *TheolPhil* 55 (1980): 589. The original reference is in A. de Halleux, *Philoxene de Mabbog* (Louvain 1963).

CHAPTER 12: AT THE ROOT OF THE CRISIS

1. An interview with Joseph Cardinal Ratzinger by journalist Vittorio Messori (1985).

CHAPTER 15: THE LOCAL CHURCH AND THE UNIVERSAL CHURCH

1. *Theology of the New Testament*, 3d ed. (Tübingen 1958), p. 96.

CHAPTER 16: THE CANON OF CRITICISM

1. From *The Salt of the Earth*.

CHAPTER 17: THE BASIS OF CHRISTIAN BROTHERHOOD: FAITH

1. See G. Schrenk's article on *pater* (father) in TWNT, V, pp. 951f.

2. See the texts quoted in Schrenk, p. 954.

3. *Diss.*, I, pp. 19, 9; Schrenk, pp. 955, 28.

4. J. Pedersen, *Israel: Its Life and Culture*, I–II (London 1946).

5. See, for example, O. Cullmann, *The Christology of the New Testament* (London 1959), pp. 275–305. Concerning the disputed interpretation of Mark 14:61, see the controversy between Blinzler and Stauffer in *Hochland* 49 (1956–57): 563–68.

6. According to Quell, 984f., *Abba* is, in fact, an expression that a child would use, almost like "daddy." In any case it expresses the reality of the new child-father relationship.

7. Schrenk, pp. 957ff.

8. De dom. or., 8, CSEL, III, 1 (Hartel), 271f.; see Ratzinger, *Volk und Haus Gottes,* p. 99.

9. Ratzinger, *Volk und Haus Gottes,* p. 99.

10. A. von Harnack, *What Is Christianity?* (London 1958), pp. 95ff.

11. Schrenk, p. 952f.

12. Schrenk, p. 952f.

13. Schrenk, p. 952f. See also Schmid, *Matthaus,* p. 126.

14. D. von Hildebrand, *Die Umgestaltung in Christus* (Einsiedeln 1950), pp. 326–38.

15. The axiom *"assumpsit naturam,"* *Sermones de tempore,* VI, 2, p. 57, in Meister Eckhart, *Lateinische Werke,* vol. 4, ed. Benz-Decker-Koch (Stuttgart 1956), p. 56f. The quoted text from the forty-seventh German sermon, pp. 158, 1–3, can be found on p. 57, n. 1, and a large number of parallel texts. For the whole, see also Ratzinger, *Volk und Haus Gottes,* 234ff. (esp. p. 235).

CHAPTER 19: ON THE THEOLOGICAL BASIS OF PRAYER AND LITURGY

1. Published as N. Lobkowicz and A. Hertz, *Am Eüde aller Religion? Ein Streitgespräch* (Zurich 1976).

2. Lobkowicz and Hertz, p. 21.

3. Lobkowicz and Hertz, p. 21.

4. Lobkowicz and Hertz, p. 21.

5. Lobkowicz and Hertz, p. 26.

6. Lobkowicz and Hertz, p. 27. The following is characteristic: "Not only has God many names; there is also a wealth of possibilities of communication with him. Perhaps this is something we have yet to learn if we are to realize that, in spite of the decline of the traditional religions, we are nearer to God than we think."

7. Lobkowicz and Hertz, p. 34.

8. Lobkowicz and Hertz, p. 17. It must be mentioned here that, at the conclusion of the debate, Hertz seems to make large concessions to Lobkowicz, most noticeably when he says: "I do believe that this God whom Jesus proclaimed, who bears good will to all men, can be our partner in prayer when we speak to him of our joys, sorrows and anxieties. This is no mythical God but the God who reveals himself in Jesus Christ." However, this does not square with the overall impression he gives, where the received Christian faith is completely absorbed into the general history of religion, causing Lobkowicz rightly to comment on Hertz's initial explanations: "In the same breath you speak of the Christian faith in God, the Greek oracles and the Etruscan divination practice of inspecting entrails" (p. 61). Even in the conciliatory conclusion, however, the personal God disappears into the mist—and never in the discussion had he achieved the status of a God who acts—when Hertz says: "Is it not enough to believe that in and through Jesus Christ the 'Kingdom of God' has come to us and that we men are called to collaborate in bringing about this kingdom of peace and love? God wills the salvation of all men, and in his kindness he will bring to a happy conclusion the good he has begun in us" (p. 84). In plain language this means that it is up to us to work for a better future; God is allotted a modest place in it insofar as he will eventually take a hand, too.

9. G. Hasenhüttå, *Einführung in die Gotteslehre* (Darmstadt 1980), pp. 242f. For a systematic presentation of the underlying rationale, cf. G. Hasenhuttå, *Kritische Dogmatik* (Graz 1979). A central axiom of the *Gotteslehre:* "God is a predicate of man, says something about man in the area of relational communication" (p. 132). For a detailed analysis of Hasenhüttå's position, cf. F. Courth, "Nur ein anderer Weg der Dogmatik? Zu G. Hasenhüttås kritischer Dogmatik" in *TThZ* 89 (1980): pp. 293–317. Cf. also the reviews of P. Hunermann, in *Theol. Revue* 76 (1980): pp. 212–25 (with a response from Hasenhüttå, 409f.): W. Beinert in *Theol. prakt. Quartalschr.* 128 (1980): 304; W. Loser, in *Theol. Phil.* 55 (1980): pp. 616f.

10. Thus it is one of Hertz's false alternatives (*Am Eüde aller Religion?* 26f.), in which he gives the impression that one must either maintain an unbridgeable gulf between transcendence and immanence or consign both of them to a philosophy of "transcendence." In fact, as we can see clearly in the case of Jaspers, "transcendence" thus becomes totally inaccessible, whereas an understanding of God that includes creation and revelation involves the reciprocal relationship and union of immanence and transcendence.

11. In connection with these remarks on the ancient world's notion of God, cf. my own *Volk und Haus Gottes in Augustins Lehre von der Kirche* (Munich 1954); also in brief my *Introduction to Christianity* (London 1969, New York 1979), pp. 94–104.

12. J. Monod, *Zufall und Notwendigkeit: Philosophische Fragen der modernen Biologie* (Munich 1971). In its consistent thought, this book seems to me to be one of the most important works contributing to a deeper dialogue between science and theology. It carefully presents the current state of scientific knowledge and conscientiously uncovers the philosophical presuppositions and, in doing so, gets beyond the usual blurring of issues. Cf. the foolish and wrongheaded approach of A. Dumas and O. H. Pesch on "creation," in J. Feiner and L. Vischer, *Neues Glaubensbuch* (Freiburg 1973), pp. 430–39. Here they say that concepts like selection and mutation are "intellectually more honest than that of creation" (p. 433). "Creation is thus an unreal concept" (p. 435). "Creation refers to man's vocation"(p. 435). Corresponding to this reinterpretation of the concept of creation, the teaching on faith lacks any element of belief in creation; the pages referred to come from the chapter "History and Cosmos," included in the area of ethics (part 4, "Faith and the World"). From a historical point of view, this elimination of faith in creation is Gnostic, strictly speaking; cf. J. Ratzinger, *Konsequenzen des Schöpfungsglaubens* (Salzburg 1980). Cf. also the thorough treatment of the doctrine of creation in J. Auer, *Die Welt—Gottes Schöpfung* (Regensburg 1975).

13. For a presentation of the problem (albeit not very convincing when it comes to a solution), cf. M. Maas, *Unveränderlichkeit Gottes* (Paderborn 1974). There are important clues to a new approach in H. U. von Balthasar, *Theologie der Geschichte* (Einsiedeln 1959); von Balthasar, *Das Ganze im Fragment* (Einsiedeln 1963); valuable remarks on a correct understanding of eternity in E. Brunner, *Dogmatik I* (Zurich 1953), pp. 282–88. Cf. the book referred to in note 16 below.

14. Cf. the section in this book "On the Theological Basis of Church Music," note 29.

15. As Hasenhüttå expressly says, cf. the passages mentioned by Courth, "Nur ein anderer Weg der Dogmatik?" pp. 299f.

16. In a publication of this kind I need not give an exhaustive list of available literature on the philosophy and theology of prayer. As an example there is the penetrating book by H. Schaller, *Das Bittgebet: Eine theologische Skizze* (Einsiedeln 1979).

17. Cf. H. U. von Balthasar, *Theologie der Geschichte*, pp. 31–39.
18. J. Pieper, *Zustimmung zur Welt: Eine Theorie des Festes* (Munich 1963).
19. Thus we can oppose Harnack's well-known verdict in *Das Wesen des Christentums* that "the Father alone, not the Son, belongs to the gospel which Jesus preached." Harnack is blind to the indirect Christology of Jesus's words, deeds, and prayers.
20. Cf. on identity and identification, J. Ratzinger and K. Lehmann, *Mitder Kirche leben* (Freiburg 1977).
21. Cf. the sections "On the Theological Basis of Church Music" and "On the Structure of the Liturgical Celebration" in the volume.
22. Cf. J. Ratzinger, *Dogma and Verkündigung* (Munich 1973), pp. 119–32: H.Schaller, *Das Bittgebet*, pp. 167–90.

CHAPTER 20: THE REGENSBURG TRADITION AND THE REFORM OF THE LITURGY

1. On these frescoes, see H. Stampfer and H. Walder, *Die Krypten von Marienberg im Vinschgau* (Bozen 1982).
2. An important book on the *vita angelica* is J. Leclercq, *Wissenschaft und Gottverlangen* (Düsseldorf 1963), p. 70; see also Stampfer and Walder, *Die Krypten von Marienberg im Vinschgau*, p. 20.
3. Harold Schutzeichel, *Wohin soll ich mich wenden? Zur Situation der Kirchenmusik im deutschen Sprachraum: Stdz*, 209 (1991): 363/74.
4. Original Italian text in AAS 36 (1904): 329/39; English translation in R. F. Hayburn, *Papal Legislation on Sacred Music* (Collegeville 1979), pp. 223/31.
5. In the introduction to the *motu proprio* (Hayburn, *Papal Legislation on Sacred Music*, p. 224) and section II/3 (p. 225), we find explicit mention of the active participation of the faithful as a fundamental liturgical principle. G. Romanato, *Pio X: La Vita di Papa Sarto* (Milano 1992), pp. 179ff., 213–14, 247–48, 330, describes the prehistory of the *motu proprio* in Pope Pius's life. He had conducted the student choir in the seminary at Padua and made notes on that task in a notebook that he still carried with him as patriarch of Venice. As bishop of Mantua, during his reorganization of the seminary, he devoted a great deal of time and energy to the *schola di music* (music class). There he also made the acquaintance of Father Lorenzo Perosi, who remained closely associated with Sarto. From his years of study in Regensburg, Perosi had received important influences, which remained a powerful factor during his long career as a church musician. The connection with Perosi continued when Sarto was promoted to the see of Venice, where in 1895 he published a pastoral letter based on a memorandum he had sent in 1893 to the Congregation of Rites—a document that anticipated almost verbatim the *motu proprio* of 1903. Text in Hayburn, pp. 205–31.
6. Romanato, *Pio X*, 247, also refers to the judgment of church historian Roger Aubert, who described Pius X as the greatest reformer of intramural church life since the council of Trent.
7. H. Schützeichel, *Wohin soll ich mich wenden? Zur Situation der Kirchenmusik im deutschen Sprachraum: StdZ* 209 (1991): 363–74.
8. *Catechism of the Catholic Church*, p. 1069.
9. *Catechism of the Catholic Church*, p. 1069.
10. *Catechism of the Catholic Church*, p. 1097.
11. See *Sacrosanctum Concilium*, p. 8, as well as the note that follows.

12. *Catechism of the Catholic Church,* 1090; *Sacrosanctum Concilium* 8. The *Catechism* also notes the fact that the same idea is expressed in the last paragraph of *Lumen gentium,* para. 50.

13. Ph. Harnoncourt, *Gesang und Musik im Gottesdienst,* in H. Schützeichel (ed.), *Die Messe: Ein Kirchenmusikalisches Handbuch* (Düsseldorf 1991), pp. 9–25, here 13.

14. Harnoncourt, *Gesang und Musik im Gottesdienst,* p. 17.

15. Schützeichel, *Die Messe,* p. 366: "*Im Prinzip kann jede Musik innerhalb des Gottesdienstes verwendet werden, von der Gregorianik bis zum Jazz. Natürlich gibt es Musik, die für den Gottedienst geeigneter und wenig geeignet ist. Entscheidend ist die Qualität.*" [In principle, any music can be used within the church service, from Gregorian chant to jazz. Of course some music is more suitable and some less for the church service. The quality is crucial.]

16. Harnoncourt, *Gesang und Musik im Gottesdienst,* p. 24.

17. *De dominica oratione* 4, CSEL III 1 (ed. Hartel), pp. 268f.

18. Ph. Harnoncourt, *Gesang und Musik im Gottesdienst,* p. 17.

19. On this, see the thorough work of W. Menke, *Stellvertretung: Schlüsselbegriff christlichen Lebens und theologische Crundkategorie* (Einsiedeln-Freiburg 1991).

20. Harnoncourt, *Gesang und Musik im Gottesdienst,* p. 21.

21. E. J. Lengeling, *Die neue Ordnung der Eucharistiefeier* (Regensburg 1971), p. 234; see also B. Jeggle-Merz and H. Schützeichel, *Eucharistiefeier,* in H. Schützeichel (ed.), *Die Messe,* pp. 90–151, here pp. 109f.

22. See K. Onasch, *Kunst und Liturgie der Ostkirche* (Wien-Köln-Graz 1984), p. 329.

23. This is J. A. Jungmann, *Missarum sollemnia II* (Freiburg 1952), pp. 168ff.

24. Jungmann, *Missarum sollemnia,* p. 174.

25. Jungmann, *Missarum sollemnia,* pp. 175–76.

26. Jungmann, *Missarum sollemnia,* p. 172. English ed., p. 384.

27. See K. Onasch, *Kunst und Liturgie der Ostkirche,* p. 329; Jungmann, *Missarum sollemnia,* 166. Already in Clement (Cor. 34), we find the connection of Jeremiah 6 with Daniel 7–10, which is presupposed in the shape of the liturgical *Sanctus.* It is exactly the same vision we found in the frescoes of Mount St. Mary: "Let us consider the vast multitude of His angels, and see how they stand in readiness." On the dating of First Clement, see Th. J. Herron, *The Dating of the First Epistle of Clement to the Corinthians* (Rome 1988), who attempts to show that First Clement dates from around 70 AD and not, as is customarily held, around 96 AD.

28. Jungmann, *Missarum sollemnia,* pp. 170f, notes 41 and 42.

29. Jungmann, *Missarum sollemnia,* p. 171, note 42; see R. Pesch, *Das Markusevangelium II* (Freiburg 1977), p. 184.

30. See Jungmann, *Missarum sollemnia,* p. 165. In this connection, it is interesting to note that in the 1903 *motu proprio* of St. Pius X, the pontiff insists that only the prescribed liturgical texts may be sung at Holy Mass, with one exception: "According to the custom of the Roman Church, to sing a motet in honor of the Blessed Sacrament after the *Benedictus* at High Mass."

31. Jungmann, *Missarum sollemnia,* pp. 413–22.

CHAPTER 22: SACRED PLACES

1. The word *orientation* comes from *oriens,* "the East." *Orientation* thus means "east-ing," turning toward the east.

CHAPTER 24: ON THE MEANING OF FAITH

1. *Catechism of the Catholic Church*, p. 166.
2. *Catechism of the Catholic Church*, p. 151.
3. *Catechism of the Catholic Church*, p. 152.
4. *Catechism of the Catholic Church*, p. 167.
5. Cf. *Catechism of the Catholic Church*, p. 192.
6. "Wär nicht das Auge sonnenhaft, die Sonne könnt 'es nicht er-kennen."
7. "God alone suffices." –Tr.
8. Dante, *Paradiso*, 33:145.

CHAPTER 26: RELATIVISM: THE CENTRAL PROBLEM FOR FAITH TODAY

1. An overview of the most significant authors of the pluralist theology of religion can be found in P. Schmidt-Leukel, "Des Pluralistische Modell in der Theologie der Religionen: Ein Literaturbericht," in *Theologische Rewe*, 89 (1993): pp. 353–70. Cf. M. von Bruck and J. Werbick, *Der einzige Weg zum Heil—Die Herausforderung des christlichen Absolutheitsanspruchs durch pluralistische Religions theologian* (*Quaestiones Disputatae*, 143, Freiburg: Herder, 1993); K. H. Menke, *Die Einzighei Jesu Christi im Horizont der Sinnfrage* (Freiburg 1995), esp. pp. 75–176. Menke offers an excellent introduction to the thinking of two significant representatives of this theology, John Hick and Paul F. Knitter. The following reflections are based mainly on this author. The discussion of the problem in the second part of Menke's book contains many important and relevant elements, but other questions remain open. An interesting systematic attempt to cope with the problem of religions from the Christological point of view is given by B. Stubenrauch, *Dialogisches Dogma: Der christliche Auftrag zur interreligiosen Begegnung* (QD 158, Freiburg 1995). The question will also be treated by a document of the International Theological Commission, in preparation.
2. Cf. the very interesting editorial, "II cristianesimo e le altre religione," in *Civilta Cattolica* 1 (Jan. 20, 1996): 107–120. The editorial examines most of all the thinking of Hick, Knitter, and Raimondo Panikkar.
3. Cf. for example John Hick, *An Interpretation of Religion: Human Responses to Transcendent* (London 1989); Menke, *Die Einzighei Jesu Christi*, p. 90.
4. Cf. E. Frauwallner, *Geschichte der indischen Philosophie*, 2 vols. (Salzburg 1953 and 1956); S. N. Dasgupta, *History of Indian Philosophy*, 5 vols. (Cambridge 1922–1955); K. B. Ramakrishna Rao, *Ontology of Advaita with Special Reference to Maya* (Mulki 1964).
5. An author belonging clearly to this trend is F. Wilfred, *Beyond Settled Foundations: The Journey of Indian Theology* (Madras 1993); "Some Tentative Reflections on the Language of Christian Uniqueness: An Indian Perspective," in the Pontifical council for Interreligious Dialogue's *Pro Dialogo*, Bulletin, 85–86 (1994/1), pp. 40–57.
6. John Hick, *Evil and the God of Love* (Norfolk 1975), pp. 240f.; *An Interpretation of Religion*, pp. 236–40; cf. Menke, pp. 81f.
7. The main work of Paul Knitter, *No Other Name! A Critical Survey of Christian Attitudes Toward the World Religions* (New York 1985), has been translated in many languages. Cf. Menke, *Die Einzighei Jesu Christi*, pp. 94–110. A refined critical statement is offered also by A. Kolping in his recension in *Theologische Revue*, 87 (1991): pp. 234–40.
8. Cf. Menke, *Die Einzighei Jesu Christi*, p. 95.
9. Cf. Menke, *Die Einzighei Jesu Christi*, p. 109.

10. Both Knitter and Hick base their refusal of the Absolute in history on Kant; cf. Menke, *Die Einzighei Jesu Christi,* pp. 78, 108.

11. The concept of New Age or of the Time of the Waterman was introduced in the middle of the century by Raul Le Cour (1937) and Alice Bailey, who, in messages received in 1945, spoke about a new order and a new religion of the world. Between 1960 and 1970, the Esalen Institute was established in California. Today Marilyn Ferguson is the best-known representative of New Age. Michael Fuss, "New Age: *Supermarket alternativer Spiritualitat,*" *Communio,* 20 (1991): 148–57, defines *New Age* as the result of a mixture of Jewish and Christian elements with the process of secularization, along with Gnosticism and elements of Oriental religions. The pastoral letter, translated in many languages, of Cardinal G. Danneels, "*Le Christ ou le Verseau*" (1990), offers a useful orientation for this problem. Cf. also Menke, *Die Einzighei Jesu Christi,* pp. 31–36; J. LeBar (ed.), *Cults, Sects and the New Age* (Huntington, Ind., 1989).

12. "*Das Subjekt, das sich alles unterwerfen wollte, will sich nun in 'das Ganze 'aufbeben.*" Menke, *Die Einzighei Jesu Christi,* p. 33.

13. Two different expressions of New Age can be distinguished more and more clearly: the Gnostic-religious form, which searches for the transcendental and transpersonal being and the true self, and the ecological-monistic expression, which worships matter and Mother Earth and is coupled with feminism in the form of ecofeminism.

14. See questions in Menke, *Die Einzighei Jesu Christi,* pp. 90 and 97.

15. Cf. note 10 supra.

16. Kant, *Religion Within the Limits of Reason Alone,* B 302.

17. This can be seen clearly in the confrontation between A. Schlatter and A. von Harnack at the end of the last century, presented carefully by W. Neuer and Adolf Schlatter, *Ein Leben fur Theologie und Kirche* (Stuttgart 1996), pp. 301ff. I have tried to show my own view of the problem in the *questio disputata* edited by myself: *Schriftauslegung im Widerstreit* (Freiburg 1989), pp. 15–44. Cf. also the collection of I. de la Poiterie, G. Guardini, J. Ratzinger, G. Colombo, and E. Bianchi, *L'esegesi cristiana oggi* (Piemme 1991).

18. Michael Waldstein, "The Foundations of Bultmann's Work," *Communio* (Spring 1987), pp. 115–34.

19. Cf. for example the collection edited by C. E. Braaten and R. W. Jensson: *Reclaiming the Bible for the Church* (Cambridge, Mass., 1995), especially the article of B. S. Childs, "On Reclaiming the Bible for Christian Theology," pp. 1–17.

20. Even though in the thinking of H. J. Verweyen, *Gottes letztes Wort* (Dusseldorf 1991), many important and valid elements can be found, to me its essential philosophical error consists in attempting to offer a rational foundation for the faith that is independent of the faith, an attempt that cannot convince in its pure abstract rationality.

   The thinking of Verweyen is also mentioned by Menke, *Die Einzighei Jesu Christi,* pp. 111–76. To me the position of J. Pieper, *Schriften zum Philosophiebegriff* (Hamburg 1995), has a better foundation and is more convincing from the historical and objective point of view.

CHAPTER 27: BIBLICAL INTERPRETATION IN CRISIS

1. With refreshing directness and yet impressive literary ability, C. S. Lewis describes this situation in his *Fern-seed and Elephants and Other Essays on Christianity,* ed. W. Hooper (London 1975). German title: *Was der Laie blökt, Christliche Diagnosen* (Einsiedeln 1977), esp. pp. 11–35. For reflections on the problem based upon a broad

knowledge of the subject, see also E. Kästner, *Die Stundentrommel vom heiligen Berg Athos* (Inselverlag 1956). Significant also for an analysis of the situation is J. Guitton, *Silence sur l'essentiel* (Paris 1986), pp. 47–58. W. Kümmel's *Das Neue Testament: Geschichte der Erforschung seiner Probleme* (Freiburg 1958) is also suitable for a review of the history of historical-critical exegesis.

2. On the evangelical side, P. Tillich's *Systematische Theologie* (Stuttgart 1956, rpt. 1966) can serve as an example. The author's index for all three volumes claims—this is not an approximation—but a scant two pages. On the Catholic side, Rahner in his later years came to consider theology, as in *Grundkurs des Glaubens* (Freiburg 1976), as quite independent from exegesis (cf., for example, p. 25).

3. Cf. J Guitton, *Silence sur l'essentiel*, pp. 56ff.; R. Guardini, *Das Christusbild der paulinischen und johanneischen Schriften* (Wurzburg 1961), p. 15.

4. Kästner (*Die Stundentrommel*, 121) puts it this way; he thereby made use of the thought of L. Kolakowski, *Die Gegenwärtigkeit des Mythos* (Munich, 1973), pp. 95f.

5. This is evidenced especially by a look at the works of P. Ricoeur, e.g., *Hermeneutik und Strukturalismus* 1 (1973); *Hermeneutik und Psychoanalyse* (1974). P. Stuhlmacher offers a useful perspective and orientation for the present state of the question with his *Vom Verstehen des Neuen Testaments: Eine Hermenuetik* (Göttingen 1986). Important attempts can moreover be found in I. de la Potterie's preface to P. Toinet, *Pour une théologie de l'exégèse* (Paris 1983); R. Laurentin, *Comment réconcilier l'exégèse et la foi* (Paris 1984); P. Grech, *Ermeneutica e Teologia biblica* (Rome 1986); P. Grelot, *Evangiles et histoire* (Paris 1985). Tübingen's *Die Theologische Quartalschrift* dedicated an entire issue (1970, pp. 1–71) to the discussion of this question in the context of a debate over the contribution of J. Blank, *Exegese als theologische Basiswissenschaft* (pp. 2–23). Unfortunately, this contribution is not productive, for it appears to trace the problems arising from exegesis ultimately back to a dogmatism that has not yet arrived at the heights of historical thought.

6. Characteristic of this are the new forms of materialist and feminist interpretation of the scriptures. Cf., for example, K. Füssel, "Materialistische Lektüre der Bibel," in *Theologische Berichte*, vol. 13: *Methoden der Evangelien-Exegese* (Einsiedeln,1985), pp. 123–63.

7. Cf. W. Heisenberg, *Das Naturbild der heutigen Physik* (Hamburg 1955), esp. pp. 15–23.

8. I am referring here to P. Stuhlmacher (*Vom Verstehen*). He gives his own response to the problems in a "Hermeneutik des Einverständnisses mit den biblischen Texten," pp. 222–56.

9. Bo Reicke, ed., *Theologische Dissertationen*, vol. 16 (Basel 1981).

10. Cf. R. Blank, "Analysis," p. 72. On the other side is E. Kästner (*Die Stundentrommel*, p. 120), who speaks about *"Aberglauben ... es sei alles und jedes aus seinen Entstehungen zu verstehen. ..."*

11. Cf. R. Blank, "Analysis," p. 97.

12. R. Blank, "Analysis," p. 154.

13. Cf. R. Blank, "Analysis," pp. 89–183. Characteristic of the practical and general acceptance of this standard—to cite only one example—is the uncritical way in which L. Oberlinner takes it for granted that the "reflection [is] doubtlessly earlier [in contradistinction to Paul], exemplified in the ecclesiology and eschatology" that he finds in the Synoptic Gospels and which he proposes as a criterion for dating (review of J. Carmignac, *La naissance des Evangiles Synoptiques* [Paris 1984], in *Theologische Revue* 83 [1987]: 194). What is the criterion according to which one reflection is to be

designated as more and another as less developed? Presumably it still depends upon the perspective of the observer. And even if the standard proves correct, who can show that there follows from it an "earlier" corresponding to a "later"?

14. R. Blank, "Analysis," pp. 11–46.

15. R. Blank, "Analysis," p. 98.

16. M. Dibelius, "Die Unbedingtheit des Evangeliums und die Bedingtheit der Ethik," *Christliche Welt*, 40 (1926): cols. 1103–1120, esp. 1107 and 1109; *Geschichtliche und übergeschichtliche Religion im Christentum* (Göttingen 1925); cf., in addition, R. Blank, "Analysis," pp. 66–71.

17. Cf. R. Bultmann, *Urchristentum* (Zürich 1954), esp. p. 101ff.; cf. R. Blank, "Analysis," pp. 172ff.

18. Cf. R. Blank, "Analysis," pp. 111, 175.

19. Cf. W. Klatt and Hermann Gunkel, *Zu seiner Theologie der Religionsgeschichte und zur Entstehung der formgeschichtlichen Methode* (1969).

20. Cf. the questions raised in the debate over demythologization. The most significant contributions to this discussion are assembled in the five volumes edited by H. W. Bartsch, *Kerygma und Mythos* (Hamburg 1948–1955).

21. Brilliant analyses in this regard may be found in Peter Berger, *A Rumor of Angels: Modern Society and the Rediscovery of the Supernatural* (Garden City, NY, 1969). Just one citation here: "The present, however, remains strangely immune from relativization. In other words, the New Testament writers are seen as afflicted with a false consciousness rooted in their time, but the contemporary analyst takes the consciousness of his time as an unmixed intellectual blessing. The electricity and radio users are placed intellectually above the Apostle Paul" (p. 41). For the question concerning the worldview, there are important considerations in H. Gese, *Zur biblischen Theologie* (Munich 1977), pp. 202–22.

22. Cf. R. Blank, "Analysis," p. 137: "Die Ungeschichtlichkeit der Wundergeschichten war für ihn [= Bultmann] keine Frage." On the Kantian philosophical background and a critique of it, cf. J. Zoharer, *Der Glaube an die Freiheit und der historische Jesus, Eine Untersuchung der Philosophie Karl Jaspers 'unter christologischem Aspekt* (Frankfurt 1986).

23. Gregory of Nyssa, *Contra Eunomium* 10, ed. W. Jaeger, pp. 227, 26 (*Patrologia Graeca*, 45, 828 C); cf. also hom. 11, in cant, *Patrologia Graeca* 44, 1013. C. E. Kästner expresses it in much the same way in *Die Stundentrömmel*, p. 117: "*Jeder fühlt es: Wissenschaft and Forschungsergebnis sinkt dahin im Vergleiche zu dem, was in Unwissen jene Holzbildhauer ersannen. Der Gewinn ist erschlichen und dürftig. Das Organ, mut dem jene suchten, ist das edlere von beiden gewesen: ein Auge, während historisches Forschen nur ein Greiforgan ist. Begreifen will es, das sagt es ja selbst.*"

24. So states H. U. von Balthasar in his introduction to *Gregor v. Nyssa: Der versiegelte Quell: Auslegung des Hohen Liedes* (Einsiedeln 1984), p. 17.

25. R. Guardini, *Das Christusbild der paulinischen und johanneischen Schriften* (Würzburg 1961), p. 14. The reflections on methodology that Guardini develops in this work (pp. 7–15) should be counted, in my opinion, among the most significant thus far advanced regarding the problem of method in the interpretation of scripture. Guardini had already dealt explicitly with this problem in the early period of his career, with his article "Heilige Schrift und Glaubenswissenschaft," *Die Schildgenossen*, 8 (1928): pp. 24–57. M. Theobald takes a critical position with regard to Guardini's exegetical

theory and practice in "Die Autonomie der historischen Kritik—usdruck des Unglaubens oder theologische Notwendigkeit? Zur Schriftauslegung R. Guardinis," in *Auslegungen des Glaubens: Zur Hermeneutik christlicher Existenz*, ed. L. Honnefelder and M. LutzBachmann (Berlin 1987), pp. 21–45.

26. Gregor of Nyssa, hom. 10 in cant. *Patrologia Graeca*, 44, 980 B-C, in the edition of W. Jaeger, ed. H. Langerbeck (Leiden 1960), 6:295, 5:296, 3. German translation by H. U. von Balthasar (see note 24 supra), p. 78.

27. Cf. Guardini, *Das Christusbild*, p. 11.

28. Cf. also J. Bergmann, H. Lutzmann, W. H. Schmidt, *däbär*, in *Theol. Wörterbuch zum Alten Testament*, 2, ed. G. J. Botterweck and H. Ringgren (1977), pp. 89–133; O. Proksch, *legö*, in *Theologisches Wörterbuch zum Neuen Testament*, 4, esp. pp. 91–97. On the unity of word and event in Thomas, cf. M. Arias-Reyero, *Thomas von Aquin als Exeget* (Einsiedeln 1971), pp. 102, 246f., *et passim*.

29. For a correct understanding of teleology, see R. Spaemann and R. Löw, *Die Frage Wazu? Geschichte und Wiederentdeckung des Teleologischen Denkens* (Munich and Zurich 1981).

30. "*Officium est enim boni interpretis non considerare verba sed sensum.*" In Matthaeum 27, no. 2321, ed. R. Cai (Turin, Rome 1951), p. 358; cf. Arias, *Thomas von Aquin*, p. 161.

31. H. Schlier, "Was heisst? Auslegung der Heiligen Schrift?" in *Besinnung auf das Neue Testament: Exegetische Aufsätze und Vortaräge*, 2 (Freiburg 1964), pp. 35–62, here p. 62; cf. J. Gnilka, "Die biblische Exegese im Lichte des Dekretes über die göttliche Offenbarung," *Münchnere Theologische Zeitschrift*, 36 (1985): p. 14.

32. Gnilka, "Die biblische Exegese," 14.

CHAPTER 28: SIN AND SALVATION

1. For stimulating thoughts that contributed to this homily, I am grateful to J. Pieper, *Über den Begriff der Sünde* (Munich 1977).

2. *Gravity and Grace*, trans. E. Craufurd (London 1952), p. 64; Pieper, *Begriff*, p. 69. Pieper calls attention to some words of Goethe in *Dichtung und Wahrheit*, 2.8, where he says that we cannot see a mistake until we are free of it.

3. On the religious-historical background of the serpent, see esp. J. Scharbert, *Genesis I–II* (Würzburg 1983), p. 55; and C. Westermann, *Genesis* 1 (Neukirchen 1974), pp. 323–28 (which is exhaustive, if not in every respect convincing). G. Von Rad, *Genesis: A Commentary*, trans. J. H. Marks (Philadelphia 1972), does not go much further in his interpretation of the meaning of the serpent, but at eighty-nine he observes very well that the kernel of the temptation was the possibility of an extension of human existence beyond the limits set for it by God at creation.

4. On this interpretation, cf. esp. von Rad, pp. 87–90. There are related comments in J. Auer, *Die Welt—Gottes Schöpfung* (Regensburg 1975), pp. 527–28.

5. The following considerations are based on the careful reflections on the concept of sin developed in Pieper, *Begriff*, pp. 27–47.

6. For both these examples, cf. Pieper, *Begriff*, pp. 38, 41.

7. On the variations of the tradition of the Fall and their different biblical forms, as well as their non-Israelite background, there is some information in A. Weiser, *Das Buch Hiob* (Göttingen 1964), pp. 113–14.

CHAPTER 29: MEDITATION ON THE PRIESTHOOD

1. For the interpretation of these two texts, I have availed myself especially of H. Schurmann, *Das Lukasevangelium* I (Freiburg 1969); C. M. Martini, *II Vangelo secondo Giovanni nell 'esperienza degli Esercizi Spirituali* (Rome 1980); J. Hauck, in ThWNT III.
2. St Jerome, *In Psalmum 141 ad neophytos*, C Chr LXXVIII 544.
3. H. J. Kraus, *Psalmen* I (Neukirchen 1960).
4. E. Ionesco, *Antidotes* (Paris 1977).
5. P. Handke, Uber die Dörfer (Frankfurt 1981). P. Handke is a young Austrian poet well known in Germany.
6. *Libro de vida*, pp. 22, 15.

CHAPTER 30: THE PLACE OF MARIOLOGY IN THE BIBLE

1. Cf., for example, H. Küng, *Christ sein* (Munich 1974), p. 452: "Thus one should allow more freedom to poetic statements in the Catholic tradition ... and especially to forms of personal or national piety." On another page, Küng says: "It is conspicuous that Mary plays ... no role at all in the early Christian witnesses" (p. 448). Küng's exceptionally coarse reassumption of the old liberal hypothesis about the Øeotokos is on the same lines. He speaks of "Cyril of Alexandria's magnificently designed manipulation of the council of Ephesus and his (!) definition of the Mother of God before the arrival at the council of the other party from Antioch" (p. 450). "Especially in the East, the fifth century arrived at the definition of Mary ... as 'Mother of God': a new, postbiblical title, securely attested for the first time in the previous century, yet now, after Cyril's action, received enthusiastically by the people in the city of the old 'Great Mother' (originally the virgin goddess Artemis, Diana)" (p. 450).
2. Cf. esp. F. M. Braun, *La mère des fidèles* (Tournai 1954); K. Wennemer, "Die heilsgeschichtliche Stellung Marias in johanneischer Sicht," in *Die Heilsgeschichtliche Stellvertretung der Menschheit durch Maria*, ed. C. Feckes (Paderborn 1954), pp. 42–78.
3. A penetrating discussion of this position is to be found in the small but important book of Louis Bouyer, *Mystère et ministères de la femme* (Paris 1976); in German: *Frau und Kirche* (Einsiedeln 1977); in English: *Woman in the Church* (San Francisco 1979).
4. Louis Bouyer, *Frau und Kirche*, pp. 17f., beautifully shows, nevertheless, that in the Old Testament an important cultic and religious position belongs to woman.
5. There is more detail given in my contribution, "*Zur Theologie der Ehe*," in *Theologie der Ehe*, ed. Greeven et al. (Regensburg-Göttingen 1969), pp. 81–115.
6. Especially instructive in this respect is the study of Indian religion, even if the great ideal of Bhakti (Love) in the context of the figure of Krishna is presented in the symbol not of married love but of adultery and free love; cf. J. Neuner, "Das Christus-Mysterium und die indische Lehre von den Avataras," in *Das Konzil von Chalkedon* III, ed. A. Grillmeier and H. Bacht (Würzburg 1954), pp. 785–824, esp. 801, note 34. The development goes much further in Shaktism; interesting texts and interpretations on this question can be found in P. Hacker, *Prahlada: Werden und Wandlungen einer Idealgestalt* II (Wiesbaden 1960), esp. pp. 220ff.
7. Cf. the articles by Kapelrud and Ringgren in *Theologisches Worterbuch zum Alten Testament* II, ed. Botterweck and Ringgren, pp. 794–89 and pp. 874–98.
8. Parallel to this is the reversal of values in men, where the younger seems finally to be preferred to the elder; cf. my article "Fraternité," in *Dictionnaire de spiritualité ...* V, pp. 1141–67.

9. Cf. Louis Bouyer, *Frau und Kirche*, pp. 14f.

10. Cf. V. Hamp, "Bund," in *Lexikon fur Theologie und Kirche* II, pp. 770–4; N. Lohfink, "Bund," *Bibellexikon*, ed. H. Haag, 2d ed. (Einsiedeln, 1968), pp. 267–73.

11. Cf. H. Gross, "Das Hohelied der Liebe Gottes: Zur Theologie von Hosea II," *Mysterium der Gnade* (Festschrift J. Auer), eds. H. Rossmann and J. Ratzinger (Regensburg 1975), pp. 83–91.

12. Cf. Louis Bouyer, *Frau und Kirche*, pp. 34ff.; Henri de Lubac, *Der geistige Sinn der Schrift* (Einsiedeln 1956), p. 103.

13. Gerhard von Rad, *Weisheit in Israel* (Neukirchen-Vluyn 1970), esp. pp. 189–228.

14. Hans Urs von Balthasar persuasively points to personalization as constitutive of the New Testament's figure of the covenant in "Umkehr im Neuen Testament," *Internationale katholische Zeitschrift*, 3 (1974), pp. 481–91; the church's personal concreteness in Mary is a fundamental concern of his thought; cf. most recently *Der antirömische Affekt* (Freiburg 1974), pp. 153–87.

15. Cf. the profound theology of the *sacrum commercium* in the late work of E. Przywara. There he first gave to his *analogia entis* doctrine its full theological form (theology of the cross), which has unfortunately been hardly noticed. See esp. *Alter und Neuer Bund* (Vienna 1956).

CHAPTER 32: THE MINISTRY AND LIFE OF PRIESTS

1. Lecture given on October 24, 1995, during the International Symposium organized by the Vatican Congregation for the Clergy on the occasion of the thirtieth anniversary of the promulgation of *Presbyterorum Ordinis*.

2. This idea of mutual relationship has been developed in my little book *Evangelium-Katechese-Katechismus* (Munich 1995), pp. 35–43.

3. F. Genn, *Trinität und Amt nach Augustinus* (Einsiedeln 1986), p. 181.

4. F. Genn, *Trinität und Amt nach Augustinus*, p. 183.

5. Cf. Robert Aron, *Jesus of Nazareth: The Hidden Years* (London 1962), pp. 170–71; J. Neusner, *A Rabbi Talks with Jesus* (New York 1993), p. 30.

6. Cf. Genn, *Trinität und Amt nach Augustinus*, pp. 101–23; on the general use of the expression *Servus Dei* at the time of St. Augustine, see Peter Brown, *Augustine of Hippo* (Oxford 1967), pp. 132–37.

7. Genn, *Trinität und Amt nach Augustinus*, pp. 34, 63ff.; on the ancient concept of character (corresponding to the Greek *stigma, sphragis*), cf. H. Schlier, *Die Brief an die Galater* (Göttingen 1962), p. 284, for additional bibliography.

8. Sermo 293, pp. 1–3 (*Patrologia Latina* [ed. Migne], vol. 38, pp. 1327ff.)

9. Genn, *Trinität und Amt nach Augustinus*, pp. 139ff.

10. *Acta Ecclesiae Mediolanensis* (Milan 1599), pp. 1177ff.; Reading of the Liturgy of the Hours for November 4.

11. L. Grygiel, *La "Dieci" di Don Didimo Mantiero* (ed. San Paolo 1995), p. 54.

12. Cf. Neusner, *A Rabbi Talks with Jesus*, e.g. pp. 114ff.

13. Genn, *Trinität und Amt nach Augustinus*, pp. 117ff.

CHAPTER 34: EUROPE'S CRISIS OF CULTURE

1. *The Rule of St. Benedict*, chap. 72.

CHAPTER 35: TRUTH AND FREEDOM

1. K. Marx and F. Engels, *Werke,* 39 vols. (Berlin 1961–71), 3:33.
2. I cite Szizypiorski from the manuscript provided during the University Weeks.
3. On the whole of what follows, cf. e.g., E. Lohse, *Martin Luther* (Munchen 1981), pp. 60f., 86ff.
4. Cf. D. Wyss, "Zur Psychologie und Psychopathologie der Verblendung: J. J. Rousseau und M. Robespierre, die Begrunder des Sozialismus," in *Jahres-und Tagungsbericht der Gorres-Gesellschaft* (1992), pp. 33–45; R. Spaemann, *Rousseau-Burger ohne Vaterland: Von der Polis zur Natur* (Munchen 1980).
5. Cf. P. Koster, *Der sterbende Gott, Nietzsches Entwurf ubermenschlicher GroB* (Meisenheim 1972); R. Low, *Nietzsche Sophist und Erzieher* (Weinheim 1984)
6. Cf. T. Steinbuchel, *Die philosophische Grundlegung der christlichen Sittenlehre* I, 1 (Dusseldorf 1947), pp. 118–32.
7. Cf. J. Pieper, "Kreaturlichkeit und menschliche Natur: Anmerkungen zum philosophischen Ansatz von J P Sartre," in *Uber die Schwierigkeit, heute zu glauben* (Munchen 1974), pp. 304–21.
8. [*Right* renders the German *Recht.* Although the term *Recht* can mean "right" in the sense of "human rights," it may also be used to mean "law," with the more or less explicit connotation of "just order," "order embodying what is right." It is in this latter sense that Ratzinger takes *Recht* both here and in the following discussion; *Recht* has been translated in this context either as *right* or (less frequently) as *just order* or a variant thereof. —Tr.]
9. H. Jonas, *Das Prinzip Verantwortung* (Frankfurt a.M. 1979).
10. J. Fest, *Die schwierige Freiheit* (Berlin 1993), esp. pp. 47–81. Fest sums up his observations on Küng's "planetary ethos": "The farther the agreements—which cannot be reached without concessions—are pushed, the more elastic and consequently the more impotent the ethical norms become, to the point that the project finally amounts to a mere corroboration of that unbinding morality which is not the goal, but the problem" (p. 80).
11. See the penetrating remarks on this point in J. Pieper, *Schriften zum Philosophiebegriff* III, ed. B. Wald (Hamburg 1995), pp. 300–23, as well as pp. 15–70, esp. pp. 59ff.
12. Cf. *Gaudium et Spes,* n. 78: "*Numquam pax pro semper acquisita est*" (Peace is never acquired once and for all).
13. Cf. J. Fest, *Die schwierige Freiheit,* p. 79: "None of the appeals addressed to man is able to say how he can live without a beyond, without fear of the last day and yet time after time act against his own interests and desires." Cf. also L. Kolakowski, *Falls es keinen Gott gibt* (Munchen 1982).
14. Cf. J. Pieper, *Schriften zum Philosophiebegriff,* III.

CHAPTER 36: THE CHURCH'S TEACHING

1. Thus, H. Küng, *On Being a Christian* (London 1977), p. 542: "The distinguishing feature even of the Old Testament ethos did not consist in the individual precepts or prohibitions, but in the Yahweh faith.... The directives of the 'second tablet ' ... have numerous analogies in the Near East.... These fundamental minimal requirements then are not specifically Israelite.... All that is specifically Israelite is the fact that these requirements are subordinated to the authority of Yahweh, the God of the Covenant." In reply to this we must ask: Did Israel's idea of God, then, arise without any borrowing, without any parallels in its environment? Is it not the case that, in the East as elsewhere, ethical and

legal demands are associated with the authority of the people's particular deity? Similar questions raise their heads when we find Küng speaking of the New Testament thus: "The ethical requirements of the New Testament ... did not fall from heaven either in content or in form" (p. 543). Does he imply that the rest of the New Testament *did* fall from heaven? Clearly, there can be no argument along these lines.

2. This question is carefully discussed—though in pursuing quite a different course—in B. Schüller, "Die Bedeutung des natürlichen Sittengesetzes für den Christen," in G. Teichtweier and W. Dreier, *Herausforderung und Kritik der Moraltheologie* (Würzburg 1971), pp. 105–30. The following quotation can be regarded as a summary of the synthesis he attempts: "In view of the fact that all ethical demands are in principle accessible to rational insight, the ethical message of the New Testament must be seen as a communication of ethical insight in a Socratic manner" (p. 118). Here everything depends on how one interprets his "in principle accessible to rational insight" and what is meant by "Socratic." I cannot shake off the impression that Schüller is using the concept of reason all too blithely, as if it were unproblematic. See, e.g., p. 111: "Romans 1 suggests that man is aware of himself as a moral being. This being so, reason can appreciate the validity of the commandment to love God and one's neighbor." This basic position is certainly fundamental; yet what is gravely lacking is the realistic context of experience by which Paul explicates and qualifies it.

3. Cf. H. Cazelles, "Dekalog," in H. Haag, *Bibel-Lexikon* (Benziger 1968), pp. 319–23 (lit.); G. von Rad, *Old Testament Theology* I (London 1975), pp. 190ff.

4. G. von Rad, *Old Testament Theology* I, p. 192.

5. Cf. esp. E. Peterson, "Christianus," in his *Frühkirche, Judentum und Gnosis* (Freiburg 1959), pp. 64–87. I have received valuable pointers on this issue from the thesis submitted to the University of Regensburg in 1974 by K. Bommes, *Das Verständnis des Martyriums bei Ignatius von Antiochien*.

6. Peterson, "Christianus," p. 80.

7. *Magn.*, 5:1f.

8. *Magn.*, 10:1

9. Peterson, pp. 77ff.

10. *Magn.*, 10:1.

11. *Apol* III 5 (C Chr I 92); *Ad Nat* I 3, 8f. (C Chr I 14): "*Christianum vero nomen ... de unctione interpretatur. Etiam cum corrupte a vobis Chrestiani pronuntiamur ... sic quoque de suavitate vel bonitate modulatum est.*" Cf. Peterson, p. 85.

12. Thus, doctrine and life are mutually interdependent in the Christian baptismal catechesis as in the baptismal rite, where the structure of affirmation and rejection combines the profession of faith with a moral confession (and vow). Not only is this unity basic to the whole patristic tradition from Justin (e.g., *Apol* I 61, 1: *hósoi an ... pisteúōsin alēthē tauta ... kai bioun houtōs dúnasthai húpischnōntai*) to Basil (*De Spiritu Sancto*, pp. 15, 35f. pp. 32, 130f., where the whole interpretation of the central baptismal action is dependent on it); it applies to the New Testament itself, where the moral exhortation in the letters clearly points to baptismal catechesis and baptismal obligations. So the preaching of John the Baptist could be read as a Christian prebaptismal catechesis; cf. the interpretation of Luke 3:1–20 in H. Schümann, *Das Lukasevangelium I* (Freiburg 1969), pp. 148–87.

13. I have deliberately avoided becoming involved with the specialists' debate in current moral theology concerning "deontological" or merely "teleological" ethical norms. For

a perceptive and thorough treatment, cf. B. Schüller, "Neuere Beiträge zum Thema 'Begründung sittlicher Normen,'" in J. Pfammatter and F. Furger, *Theologische Berichte* IV (Einsiedeln 1974), pp. 109–81. As far as the establishment of concepts and a methodically worked-out system are concerned, any answer must be sought within the technical debate and cannot be prejudged on the basis of the preconceptual nature of the biblical facts. In spite of this necessary methodological limitation, there *are* pointers that, as far as I can see, have not been sufficiently taken account of up to now. In this context, the "short formulas" produced by the "teleological norm" approach are clearly inadequate—e.g., "Intrinsically evil and thus absolutely to be avoided is every action which objectively—according to right reason—fails to do justice to concrete human reality" (J. Fuchs, "Der Absolutheits-charakter sittlicher Handlungsnormen," in *Testimonium Veritatis* (Frankfurt 1971), pp. 211–40. We would have to ask what is meant by "concrete human reality" and "right reason"; in propositions such as these, the expressions are only formal and ultimately say nothing, even if, like Schüller (p. 173), one attempts to fill them with definite content in the sense of Kant's categorical imperative. Even if the problems of establishing concepts and systemizing are left open, we still need to ask whether, in the light of the clear and constant elements that manifest themselves in the course of the biblical history of faith and are fixed in baptismal catechesis, there is not an indispensable bedrock of "deontological" norms. As I have already indicated in note 2, I feel that the real problem here lies in the abstract neutrality of the concept of reason operating without people being aware of it; further discussion would need to address itself particularly to this issue.

14. H. Schlier, *Besinnung auf das Neue Testament* (Freiburg 1964), pp. 340–57.
15. Schlier, *Besinnung auf das Neue Testament,* pp. 341–44.
16. Schlier, *Besinnung auf das Neue Testament,* pp. 344–52. Paul here is just as much aware of the "teleological" aspect (the coming judgment and reward/punishment) as of the "deontological" aspect (e.g., his argument from the implications of being a member of the body of Christ).
17. Schlier, *Besinnung auf das Neue Testament,* pp. 352ff., esp. p. 355.
18. Schlier, *Besinnung auf das Neue Testament,* p. 343: "The pupils of the apostles and the other Christians all exhort on the basis of the apostolic exhortation; they take it as a normative tradition and apply it to their particular situation." I regard this as a fundamental statement with respect to the permanent substantive basis of Christian ethics and its nature as a whole; i.e., the development of the apostolic exhortation as a normative tradition in the face of particular situations.
19. In this connection, cf. F. Mussner, "Die Una Sanctanach Apg 2:42," in *Praesentia salutis* (Dusseldorf 1967), pp. 212–22.
20. Cf. L. Bouyer, *L'Eglise de Dieu: Corps du Christ et temple de l'Esprit* (Paris 1970), pp. 401–47; Y. Congar, *Ministères et communion ecclésiale* (Paris 1971), pp. 51–94.

CHAPTER 37: CULTURE AND TRUTH: SOME REFLECTIONS ON THE ENCYCLICAL LETTER *FIDES ET RATIO*

1. C. S. Lewis, *The Screwtape Letters,* pp. 107–8.

CHAPTER 39: THE PROBLEM OF THREATS TO HUMAN LIFE

1. *Donum vitae* (The Gift of Life), 1987. Part I. Pope Paul VI.

CHAPTER 40: *DEUS CARITAS EST* (GOD IS LOVE)

1. Cf. *Jenseits von Gut und Böse*, IV, p. 168.
2. Virgil, *Bucolics*, X, p. 69.
3. Cf. R. Descartes, *Œuvres*, ed. V. Cousin, vol. 12 (Paris 1824), pp. 95ff.
4. II, 5: SCh 381, p. 196.
5. II, 5: SCh 381, p. 198.
6. Cf. *Metaphysics*, XII, p. 7.
7. Cf. Ps.-Dionysius the Areopagite, who in his treatise *The Divine Names*, IV, pp. 12–14: PG 3, 709–713 calls God both *eros* and *agape*.
8. Plato, *Symposium*, XIV–XV, pp. 189c–192d.
9. Sallust, *De coniuratione Catilinae*, XX, p. 4.
10. Cf. St. Augustine, *Confessions*, III, 6, 11: CCL 27, 32.
11. *De Trinitate*, VIII, 8, 12: CCL 50, 287.
12. Cf. *I Apologia*, 67: PG 6, 429.
13. Cf. *Apologeticum*, 39, 7: PL 1, 468.
14. *Ep. ad Rom.*, *Inscr*: PG 5, 801.
15. Cf. St. Ambrose, *De officiis ministrorum*, II, 28, 140: PL 16, 141.
16. Cf. *Ep.* 83: J. Bidez, *L'Empereur Julien: Œuvres complètes* (Paris 1960), v. I, 2ᵃ, p. 145.
17. Cf. Congregation for Bishops, Directory for the Pastoral Ministry of Bishops, *Apostolorum Successores* (22 February 2004), p. 194 (Vatican City 2004), p. 213.
18. *De Civitate Dei*, IV, 4: CCL 47, 102.
19. Cf. Pastoral Constitution on the Church in the Modern World, *Gaudium et Spes*, p. 36.
20. Cf. Congregation for Bishops, Directory for the Pastoral Ministry of Bishops, *Apostolorum Successores* (22 February 2004), p. 197 (Vatican City 2004), p. 217.
21. John Paul II, Post-Synodal Apostolic Exhortation, *Christifideles Laici* (30 December 1988), 42: AAS 81 (1989), p. 472.
22. Cf. Congregation for the Doctrine of the Faith, *Doctrinal Note on Some Questions Regarding the Participation of Catholics in Political Life* (24 November 2002), 1: *L'Osservatore Romano*, English edition, 22 January 2003, p. 5.
23. *Catechism of the Catholic Church*, 1939.
24. Decree on the Apostolate of the Laity, *Apostolicam Actuositatem*, p. 8.
25. Decree on the Apostolate of the Laity, *Apostolicam Actuositatem*, p. 14.
26. Cf. Congregation for Bishops, Directory for the Pastoral Ministry of Bishops, *Apostolorum Successores* (22 February 2004), p. 195 (Vatican City 2004), pp. 214–16.
27. Cf. John Paul II, Post-Synodal Apostolic Exhortation, *Christifideles Laici* (30 December 1988), 41: AAS 81 (1989), pp. 470–72.
28. Cf. No. 32: AAS 80 (1988), p. 556.
29. No. 43: AAS 87 (1995), p. 946.
30. Cf. Congregation for Bishops, Directory for the Pastoral Ministry of Bishops, *Apostolorum Successores* (22 February 2004), p. 196 (Vatican City 2004), p. 216.
31. Cf. Pontificale Romanum, *De ordinatione episcopi*, p. 43.
32. Cf. can. 394; *Code of Canons of the Eastern Churches*, can. 203.
33. Cf. nos. 193–98: pp. 212–19.
34. Cf. 194: pp. 213–14.
35. *Sermo* 52, 16: PL 38, 360.
36. Cf. Sulpicius Severus, *Vita Sancti Martini*, 3, 1–3: SCh 133, 256–58.

Bibliography

SELECTED PRE-PAPAL WRITINGS IN ENGLISH OF JOSEPH CARDINAL RATZINGER

Ratzinger, Joseph Cardinal. *Behold the Pierced One*. San Francisco: Ignatius Press, 1987.

_____. *Called to Communion*. San Francisco: Ignatius Press, 1996.

_____ , with William May and Albert Vanhove. *The Catholic Priest as Moral Teacher*. San Francisco: Ignatius Press, 1990.

_____. *Christianity and the Crisis of Cultures*. San Francisco: Ignatius Press, 2005.

_____. *Church, Ecumenism, Politics: New Essays in Ecclesiology*. New York: Crossroad Publishing Co., 1988.

_____. *Co-Workers of the Truth*. San Francisco: Ignatius Press, 1992.

_____. *Dogma and Preaching*. Chicago: Franciscan Herald Press, 1985.

_____. *Eschatology, Death, and Eternal Life*. Washington, D.C.: Catholic University of America Press, 1988.

_____. *The Feast of Faith: Essays in the Theology of Worship*. San Francisco: Ignatius Press, 1986.

_____. *God and the World*. San Francisco: Ignatius Press, 2002.

_____. *God Is Near Us: The Eucharist, the Heart of Life*. San Francisco: Ignatius Press, 2003.

_____. *The God of Jesus Christ: Reflections on the Trinitarian God*. Chicago: Franciscan Herald Press, 1979.

_____. *Gospel, Catechesis, Catechism: Sidelights on the Catechism of the Catholic Church*. San Francisco: Ignatius Press, 1997.

_____. *In the Beginning ... A Catholic Understanding of the Story of Creation and the Fall*. Grand Rapids, MI: Wm. B. Eerdmans, 2005.

_____. *Introduction to Christianity*. New York: Seabury Press, 1969; rev. eds., San Francisco: Ignatius Press, 1990, 1994.

_____. *Journey Towards Easter*. New York: Crossroad Publishing Co., 1987.

_____, ed. by Robert Moynihan. *Let God's Light Shine Forth.* New York: Doubleday, 2005.

_____. *Many Religions—One Covenant: Israel, the Church, and the World.* San Francisco: Ignatius Press, 1999.

_____ and Hans Urs von Balthasar. *Mary: The Church at the Source.* San Francisco: Ignatius Press.

_____. *Mary: God's Yes to Man.* San Francisco: Ignatius Press, 1988.

_____. *Meaning of Christian Brotherhood.* San Francisco: Ignatius Press, 1993.

_____. *Milestones.* San Francisco: Ignatius Press, 1998.

_____. *Ministers of Your Joy: Scriptural Meditation of Priestly Spirituality.* Cincinnati, OH: Servant Publications, 1989.

_____. *The Nature and Mission of Theology: Approaches to Understanding Its Role in the Light of Present Controversy.* Trans. by Adrian Walker. San Francisco: Ignatius Press, 1995.

_____. *A New Song for the Lord: Faith in Christ and Liturgy Today.* New York: Crossroad Publishing Co., 1997.

_____. *The Open Circle: The Meaning of Christian Brotherhood.* New York: Sheed & Ward, 1966.

_____. *Principles of Catholic Theology: Building Stones for a Fundamental Theology.* San Francisco: Ignatius Press, 1987.

_____. *Principles of Christian Morality.* San Francisco: Ignatius Press, 1986.

_____. *The Ratzinger Report.* San Francisco: Ignatius Press, 1985.

_____. *The Salt of the Earth: The Church at the End of the Millennium.* San Francisco: Ignatius Press, 1997.

_____. *Seeking God's Faith.* Chicago: Franciscan Herald Press, 1982.

_____. *The Spirit of the Liturgy.* San Francisco: Ignatius Press, 2000.

_____. *Theological Highlights of Vatican II.* Mahwah, NJ: Paulist Press, 1966.

_____. *Theology of History in St. Bonaventure.* Chicago: Franciscan Herald Press, 1989.

_____. *To Look on Christ: Exercises in Faith, Hope, and Love.* New York: Crossroad Publishing Co., 1991.

_____. *Truth and Tolerance.* San Francisco: Ignatius Press, 2004.

_____. *Values in a Time of Upheaval: How to Survive the Upheavals of the Future.* San Francisco: Ignatius Press, 2006.

_____. *What It Means to Be a Christian.* San Francisco: Ignatius Press, 2006.

_____ with Marcello Pera. *Without Roots: The West, Relativism, Christianity, Islam.* San Francisco: Ignatius Press, 2005.

SELECTED PAPAL WRITINGS OF BENEDICT XVI

Pope Benedict XVI. *God Is Love (Deus Caritas Est)*. First encyclical of Pope Benedict XVI.

_____. *God's Revolution: World Youth Day and Other Cologne Talks*. San Francisco: Ignatius Press, 2006.

_____ et al. *Handing on the Faith in an Age of Disbelief*. San Francisco: Ignatius Press, 2006.

_____. *Images of Hope: Reflections on Major Feasts*. San Francisco: Ignatius Press, 2006.

SOME BOOKS ABOUT POPE BENEDICT XVI

Allen, John, Jr. *Pope Benedict XVI: A Biography of Joseph Ratzinger*. New York: Continuum International Publishing Group, 2000, 2005.

_____. *The Rise of Benedict XVI*. New York: Doubleday, 2005.

Bardazzi, Marco. *In the Vineyard of the Lord: The Life, Faith and Teachings of Joseph Ratzinger, Pope Benedict XVI*. New York: Rizzoli, 2005.

Fischer, Heinz-Joachim. *Pope Benedict XVI: A Personal Portrait*. New York: Crossroad, 2005.

Gibson, David. *The Rule of Benedict*. San Francisco: HarperSanFrancisco, 2006.

Horn, Stephan Otto, and Vinzenz Pfnür, eds. *Pilgrim Fellowship of Faith: The Church as Communion*. San Francisco: Ignatius Press, 2005. Contains an extensive bibliography of Benedict's writings.

Nichols, Aidan, O.P. *The Thought of Benedict XVI. An Introduction to the Theology of Joseph Ratzinger*. New York: Burns & Oates. A Continuum Imprint. 2005.

Rose, Michael S. *Benedict XVI: The Man Who Was Ratzinger*. Texas: Spence Publishing Co.: 2006.

Seewald, Peter. *Pope Benedict XVI: Servant of the Truth*. San Francisco: Ignatius Press, 2006.

Twomey, D. Vincent, SVD. *Pope Benedict XVI: The Conscience of Our Age: A Theological Portrait*. San Francisco: Ignatius Press, forthcoming, 2007.

SELECTED INTERNET WEB SITES

http://www.popebenedictxvifanclub.com/benedict_online.html
www.ratzingerreport.com/homilies
www.zenit.org

Index

Acknowledgments

For permission to reprint some of the selections found in *The Essential Pope Benedict XVI*, the Editors wish to thank and acknowledge those sources listed below. To permit readers of this book to identify any of these selections, the boldface numbers following each alphabetized source refer to the chapter numbers in our table of contents

America **15.** "The Local Church and the Universal Church," reprinted from *America*, Nov. 19, 2001, with permission of America Press, Inc. © 2001. All rights reserved.

Communio: International Catholic Review **35.** "Truth and Freedom," translated by Adrian Walker; originally published in *Communio* 23, no. 1 (Spring 1996).

Crisis **10.** "Guardini on Christ in Our Century," translated by John M. Haas, *Crisis*, June 1996. © 1995–1996 Crisis Magazine.

Crossroad Publishing Company 29. "Meditation on the Priesthood," reprinted from *Journey Towards Easter: Retreat Given in the Vatican in the Presence of Pope John Paul II*, 1987, pp. 143–159; English ed.: St. Paul Publications, Middlegreen, Slough SL3 6BT, England. English translation copyright © St. Paul Publications, 1987.

Eerdmans 28. "Sin and Salvation," reprinted from *In the Beginning: A Catholic Understanding of the Story of Creation and the Fall*, Grand Rapids, Mich.: William B. Eerdmans Publishing Co., pp. 59–77. © 1995 by Wm. B. Eerdmans Publishing Co.

Ignatius Press 1., 11., 12., 16., 19., 21., 22., 23., 24., 25., 30., 32., 36.

1. "Yesterday, Today, and Tomorrow" reprinted from *Introduction to Christianity*, *Communio* 31 (Fall 2004). © 2004 by *Communio: International Catholic Review*. English translation originally published in Joseph Ratzinger, *Introduction to Christianity*, 2nd ed. (San Francisco: Ignatius Press, 2004). Reprinted by permission. All rights reserved.

11. "Christ the Liberator: An Easter Homily," reprinted from *Behold the Pierced One: An Approach to a Spiritual Christology*. Ignatius Press, 1986, pp. 123–28.

12. "At the Root of the Crisis: The Idea of Church," reprinted from *The Ratzinger Report: An Exclusive Interview on the State of the Church.* Ignatius Press, 1985, pp. 45–53.

16. "The Canon of Criticism," reprinted from *The Salt of the Earth: Christianity and the Catholic Church at the End of the Millennium,* pp. 181–213. © 1997 Ignatius Press.

19. "On the Theological Basis of Prayer and Liturgy," reprinted from *The Feast of Faith: Approaches to a Theology of the Liturgy.* © 1986 Ignatius Press, 1986, pp. 11–32.

21. "Music and Liturgy. How Does Music Express the Word of God, the Vision of God?" reprinted from *The Spirit of the Liturgy.* San Francisco: Ignatius Press, 2000.

22. "Sacred Places—The Significance of the Church Building," reprinted from *The Spirit of the Liturgy,* pp.62–73. © 2000 Ignatius Press, San Francisco.

23. "Beginning of the Council and Transfer to Münster," reprinted from *Milestones: Memoirs 1927–1977,* pp. 120–31. © Ignatius Press, San Francisco.

24. "On the Meaning of Faith," *Gospel, Catechesis, Catechism: Sidelights on the Catechism of the Catholic Church,* pp. 23–34. © 1997 Ignatius Press, San Francisco.

25. "Liberation Theology," reprinted from *The Ratzinger Report.* San Francisco: Ignatius Press, 1985.

30. "The Place of Mariology in the Bible," from *Daughter Zion: Meditations on the Church's Marian Belief,* pp. 9–29. © 1983 Ignatius Press, San Francisco.

32. "The Ministry and Life of Priests," reprinted from the August–September 1997 issue of *Homiletic & Pastoral Review.* © 2005 Ignatius Press—Homiletic & Pastoral Review.

36. "The Church's Teaching: Authority—Faith—Morals," reprinted from Heinz Schürmann, Joseph Cardinal Ratzinger, and Hans Urs von Balthasar, *Principles of Christian Morality,* pp. 47–73. © 1986 Ignatius Press, San Francisco.

Libreria Editrice Vaticana (LEV) 3., 4., 5., 6., 8., 9., 13., 14., 26., 27., 31., 33., 34., 39., 40.

(*Note:* some of the following citations note an original source of publication, but LEV controls all reproduction rights.)

3. *Adoremus Bulletin* "Homily at the Mass for the Election of the Roman Pontiff," St. Peter's Basilica, April 18, 2005. Copyright © Libreria Editrice Vaticana.

4. "First Homily of His Holiness Benedict XVI at the End of the Eucharistic Concelebration with the Cardinal Electors in the Sistine Chapel at the Mass for the Election of the Roman Pontiff," St. Peter's Basilica, April 18, 2005. Copyright © Catholic News Agency.

5. "Homily of His Holiness Benedict XVI at the Mass for the Inauguration of the Pontificate of Pope Benedict XVI. St. Peter's Square," Sunday, 24 April 2005. Copyright © Libreria Editrice Vaticana.

7. Address of Cardinal Joseph Ratzinger to Pope John Paul II at a Concert Offered by the Mitteldeutscher Rundfunk Orchestra on the Twenty-fifth Anniversary of His Pontificate, October 7, 2003. Copyright © Libreria Editrice Vaticana.

Congregation of the Doctrine of the Faith 8., 9., 27.

8. "The Assisi Day of Prayer. The Splendor of the Peace of Francis."

9. "The Feeling of Things, the Contemplation of Beauty." Message of His Eminence Cardinal Joseph Ratzinger to the Communion and Liberation (CL) meeting at Rimini, August 24–30, 2002.

27. "Biblical Interpretation in Crisis: On the Question of the Foundations and Approaches of Exegesis Today," a lecture delivered on January 27, 1988, at Saint Peter's Church in New York City.

Eternal Word Television Network 26.

"Relativism: The Central Problem for Faith Today," address during the meeting of the Congregation for the Doctrine of the Faith with the presidents of the Doctrinal Commissions of the Bishops' Conferences of Latin America, Guadalajara, Mexico, May 1996.

***L'Osservatore Romano* 13., 14., 31., 33., 39.**

13. "Eucharist, Communion and Solidarity," lecture given at the Eucharistic Congress of the Archdiocese of Benevento, Italy, June 2, 2002. © L'Osservatore Romano.

14. "Ecclesiology of the Constitution on the Church," Vatican II, *Lumen Gentium*. © L'Osservatore Romano.

31. "The Nature of the Priesthood," speech given at the opening of the VIII Ordinary Assembly of the Synod of Bishops on priestly formation, October 1, 1990. A translation of the Cardinal's twenty-two-page Latin speech entitled "On the Nature of the Priesthood." © L'Osservatore Romano.

33. "The Sacrament of Reconciliation." Presentation by Cardinal Joseph Ratzinger. Apostolic Letter in the form of a *Motu Proprio Misericordia Dei*, published on May 2, 2002. © L'Osservatore Romano.

39. "The Problem of Threats to Human Life," from the April 8, 1991, issue of *L'Osservatore Romano*.

40. *Deus Caritas est.* © Copyright 2005, Libreria Editrice Vaticana.

***Romana* 6.** "Message on the 25th Anniversary of the Pontificate of Pope John Paul II from the College of Cardinals," October 18, 2003, reprinted from *Romana: Bulletin of the Prelature of the Holy Cross and Opus Dei*.

ZENIT 2., 34., 38.

2. Cardinal Ratzinger's Homily at John Paul II's Funeral Mass in St. Peter's Square, Vatican City, ZE05040802, "He Roused Us from a Lethargic Faith." Original text in Italian; translation issued by Holy See. © Innovative Media, Inc.

34. "Europe's Crisis of Culture." ZE05072927. A translation by ZENIT of a lecture given in Italian by Cardinal Joseph Ratzinger, now Pope Benedict XIV, in the convent of Saint Scholastica in Subiaco, Italy, the day before Pope John Paul II died. This lecture took place April 1, when he received the St. Benedict Award for the promotion of life and the family in Europe.

38. "Crises in Law," ZE99111520. © Innovative Media, Inc.

Oriens **18.** "Theology of the Liturgy," a lecture by His Eminence Joseph Cardinal Ratzinger, Prefect of the Congregation for the Doctrine of the Faith, delivered during the Journées liturgiques de Fontgombault, 22–24 July 2001, reprinted from *Oriens,* Summer 2002, Vol. 7, No. 2.

The Patrician **37.** "Culture and Truth: Some Reflections on the Encyclical Letter *Fides et Ratio,*" a lecture reprinted in *The Patrician,* Winter 1999.

Sacred Music **20.** "In the Presence of the Angels I Will Sing Your Praise," reprinted from *Sacred Music* (the publication of Church Music Association of America), Spring 1995.

Sheed and Ward 17. "The Basis of Christian Brotherhood: Faith," reprinted from *The Meaning of Christian Brotherhood,* pp. 45–55. First English edition © 1966, Sheed and Ward, New York.